CIVIL PROCEDURE

Second Edition

Cavendish
Publishing
Limited

London • Sydney • Portland, Oregon

CIVIL PROCEDURE

Second Edition

Paula Loughlin
LLB, LLM, Solicitor

and

Stephen Gerlis
District Judge, Recorder

Cavendish
Publishing
Limited

London • Sydney • Portland, Oregon

Second edition first published in Great Britain 2004 by
Cavendish Publishing Limited, The Glass House,
Wharton Street, London WC1X 9PX, United Kingdom
Telephone: + 44 (0)20 7278 8000   Facsimile: + 44 (0)20 7278 8080
Email: info@cavendishpublishing.com
Website: www.cavendishpublishing.com

Published in the United States by Cavendish Publishing
c/o International Specialized Book Services,
5824 NE Hassalo Street, Portland,
Oregon 97213-3644, USA

Published in Australia by Cavendish Publishing (Australia) Pty Ltd
45 Beach Street, Coogee, NSW 2034, Australia
Telephone: + 61 (2)9664 0909   Facsimile: + 61 (2)9664 5420
Email: info@cavendishpublishing.com.au
Website: www.cavendishpublishing.com.au

© Loughlin, Paula, Gerlis, Stephen   2004
First edition   2001
Second edition   2004

British Library Cataloguing in Publication Data
Loughlin, Paula
Civil procedure – 2nd ed
1 Civil procedure – England 2 Civil procedure – Wales
I Title II Gerlis, SM (Stephen M)
347.4'2

Library of Congress Cataloguing in Publication Data
Data available

ISBN 1-85941-775-2

1 3 5 7 9 10 8 6 4 2

Printed and bound in Great Britain

FOREWORD

The modern Civil Procedure Rules (CPR) pioneered by Lord Woolf are proving to be one of the real success stories in the history of English law. It was not written in the stars that this would be so. One of their early critics, Professor Michael Zander, predicted that passive resistance by the legal profession could and probably would wreck them. A combination of judicial enforcement and voluntary culture change within the profession has proved him wrong. But old habits die hard, and courts and practitioners still have things to learn and problems to work out under the new dispensation. English justice, while now speedier and generally simpler, can still be unacceptably expensive.

These changes, however, did not take place in isolation. They formed part of the most important tectonic shift in our legal system since the reforms of the 1870s. It is a shift which fundamentally reformed the legal aid system, with implications for access to justice, changes in the structure of the legal profession, and – arching over all of these – the Human Rights Act 1998 which, by bringing the effect of Article 6 of the European Convention on Human Rights into our law, placed on every court a duty to ensure proper access and a fair hearing for everyone.

The tension between this fundamental obligation and the need for speed and simplicity runs through the CPR. It is what makes a book like this so necessary for anyone who is brought either by their work or by misfortune (for nobody in their right mind willingly goes to law) into a legal system which hopes it has finally exorcised the ghost of Jarndyce. But the combination of rules, practice directions, protocols and residual sources of procedural law is already creating an editorial maze, as a glance at the standard volumes will show. The way this book is organised and presented is therefore especially welcome. Instead of simply tracking the rules numerically, it reallocates the disparate materials into subject headings, explaining each as it goes. Instead of a detailed map on which you have first to get your bearings, here is a user-friendly guidebook.

Like other guidebooks, it does not make maps unnecessary. Practitioners will always do well to consult both. The unexpected, as any lawyer will confirm, keeps happening, and occasional anomalies or omissions are bound to be revealed from time to time in the CPR. This second edition notes and assimilates the appellate decisions which have sandpapered some of the rough edges of the new system and sought to body out the Woolf principles in practice. In a developing field such as civil procedure, the task of updating a practice book is akin to running up the down escalator; but provided practitioners check for very recent developments, they will find that this work continues to be a clear, readable and practical guide to the tricky terrain of litigation.

Stephen Sedley
The Rt Hon Lord Justice Sedley
Royal Courts of Justice
London

PREFACE

In this second edition, I have attempted not just to update *Civil Procedure*, but to substantially rewrite the whole of the text. In so doing my aim has been to fully review and expand upon each area, identified by its chapter title, and to incorporate all developments to the relevant parts of the Civil Procedure Rules 1998 (CPR) since the first edition was published. As a result, not surprisingly, *Civil Procedure* has 'grown' to a considerable extent.

Whilst I undertook the main task of rewriting and updating *Civil Procedure*, Stephen Gerlis contributed to the second edition as well as identifying a number of important new guideline cases.

Since 2001, when the first edition of *Civil Procedure* was published, there have been a substantial number of cases dealing with issues raised by the CPR. These include the Court of Appeal's landmark ruling in *Hollins v Russell* [2003] EWCA Civ 718, clarifying much of the law on the enforceability of conditional fee agreements (CFAs) and deciding that in most cases a CFA should be disclosed to an opponent on detailed assessment.

There have in fact been significant cases on almost all areas of civil procedure including those relating to costs, the deemed date of service of proceedings and applications to extend the time allowed for service of the claim form, as well as a number of cases clarifying the operation and effect of Part 36 payments and offers to settle, to identify but a few. In writing this second edition I have attempted to summarise and analyse the most significant cases, the majority of which have emanated from the Court of Appeal, but also from the House of Lords, including *Three Rivers DC v Governor & Co of the Bank of England* [2001] UKHL 16 with its important ruling on summary judgment. This increased coverage of significant cases also accounts for the book's expanded girth.

Within the context of the CPR, there have been important new provisions such as the introduction of a General Pre-action Protocol applying to all types of claims not covered by an approved protocol, and new procedures for making applications to the Court of Appeal and High Court to re-open a final determination of an appeal.

The Human Rights Act 1998 continues to play an important role in influencing and shaping decisions on potentially the whole of civil procedure. This is in accordance with the court's duty not to act in a manner inconsistent with the European Convention on Human Rights and to construe legislation in a way which is compatible with those rights, as can be seen in decisions such as *Goode v Martin* [2001] EWCA Civ 1899, although arguably less so in the controversial decision of *Jones v University of Warwick* [2003] 1 WLR 954.

The second edition was being written during the time when the Government announced 'overnight' that the Lord Chancellor's Department and the Office of the Lord Chancellor were to be abolished and replaced with the Department for Constitutional Affairs. Readers will note that there are references to these momentous changes throughout the second edition but should be aware that the new address for the Department's website is www.dca.gov.uk, whilst the CPR can be found at www.dca.gov.uk/civil/procrules_fin/index.htm.

We would again like to thank everyone at Cavendish Publishing for their hard work, help and encouragement, but special thanks must go to Sanjeevi Perera in particular. Paula thanks Edward for supporting her decision to rewrite the whole text, as well as for his patience and understanding (and not least that of Fran and

Noah), as the task extended throughout one of the hottest summers on record. Stephen assures me that he couldn't have contributed effectively without the support of his wife, Ann Conlon JP.

We attempt to state the rules as of September 2003. Readers will be able to obtain regular (quarterly) updates online at www.cavendishpublishing.com/civprocedure, summarising new developments in all areas covered by *Civil Procedure*; a service designed to keep readers abreast of the inevitable updates to the CPR as well as informed of significant new cases, statutes and statutory instruments.

Paula Loughlin
and Stephen Gerlis
January 2004

CONTENTS

TABLE OF CASES

TABLE OF STATUTES

TABLE OF STATUTORY INSTRUMENTS

TABLE OF INTERNATIONAL INSTRUMENTS

CHAPTER 1

INTRODUCTION

THE WOOLF REFORMS

In 1994, Lord Woolf, then Master of the Rolls, was assigned the task of fundamentally reforming the civil procedure system to resolve its perennial problems, that is, being too expensive, too slow and too complex. The concern was not with judicial decisions at trial, but with the 'processes leading to the decisions made by the courts', that is, civil procedure – the subject matter of this book.

The findings and recommendations for reform following this review were published in two reports under the heading *Access to Justice*, consisting of the Interim Report (IR), published in June 1995, and the Final Report (FR), published in July 1996, along with a set of draft civil procedure rules. Copies of both reports are available from the Department for Constitutional Affairs website at www.dca.gov.uk/civil/interfr.htm and www.dca.gov.uk/civil/final/index.htm.

In his reports, Lord Woolf recommended fundamental changes to the whole basis of our civil litigation system and his recommendations were substantially adopted. The resulting reforms are very much identified with the main author of them, reference being made to the Woolf Report, the Woolf reforms, and to a litigation climate which is 'Woolfian' or 'post-Woolf'.

As a result of the implementation of the Woolf reforms, the former civil procedure rules which applied separately to the High Court and county courts were abolished and replaced by a single set of rules, the Civil Procedure Rules 1998 (CPR), applying to both courts. The CPR contain the substance and detail of most of the civil procedure system and are the main means through which the Woolf reforms have been put into effect.

FUNDAMENTAL REFORM

The background to the commissioning of the Report was apparently a concern felt throughout the common law world that civil litigation was too expensive, too slow and too complex, resulting in inadequate access to justice and an inefficient and ineffective system. Lord Woolf recognised the crucial importance of civil procedure and the Interim Report starts with a commitment to the principle of access to justice as the constitutional right of citizens to enforce civil rights and obligations (IR, Chapter 1).

Before publishing his findings, Lord Woolf conducted a wide consultation programme and held public seminars in order to canvass opinion from a broad spectrum of the population. He perceived a widespread dissatisfaction with the existing system and a belief that its defects were impeding access to justice. He found that even lawyers specialising in litigation 'accepted that the situation [could not] continue' as it did under the old civil procedure system (IR, Chapter 3, para 17).

Prior to the publication of *Access to Justice* there had been 60 reports on aspects of civil procedure and the organisation of the courts. Yet, despite this, the civil litigation system was felt to be in crisis. Lord Woolf believed that the failure of previous attempts to reform the system was not due to the inadequacy of the previous reforms, but because they were only partially (and not completely) implemented (IR, Chapter 3, para 1). He put forward his reform programme as a 'whole', and argued that unless it was implemented as a whole it would not achieve the results it was designed to produce (IR, Chapter 4, para 29). In the event, Lord Woolf's proposed reforms, which recommended fundamental changes to the civil litigation system, were accepted and implemented with only minor exceptions and adjustments. Moreover, some of his proposals that were not implemented immediately are being implemented in stages (for example, pre-trial fixed costs for fast track cases, recommended in the FR, Chapter 4, are yet to be introduced for low value road traffic accident cases, whereas pre-proceedings fixed costs in such cases are now in existence).

THE PROBLEMS AND THEIR CAUSES

In his Reports, Lord Woolf set out the problems with the existing civil litigation system, the causes of those problems and his proposed solutions. However, he started by analysing how a civil litigation system *should* operate.

The ideal system

Lord Woolf provided a list of the basic principles that a civil justice system should meet in order to ensure access to justice. He stated that the system should:

(a) be just in the results it delivers;

(b) be fair in the way it treats litigants;

(c) offer procedures and costs proportionate to the nature of the issues involved;

(d) deal with cases with reasonable speed;

(e) be understandable to those who use it;

(f) be responsive to the needs of those who use it;

(g) provide as much certainty as the nature of particular cases allows; and

(h) be effective, adequately resourced and organised so as to give effect to the above principles (IR, Chapter 1, para 3; FR, Section I, para 1).

He did not believe that the former civil litigation system was fulfilling these basic principles.

The problems

The adversarial system

Lord Woolf concluded that the unrestrained adversarial culture of the former civil justice system was largely to blame for the fact that the system did not conform with the basic principles he believed were necessary to ensure access to justice (IR, Chapter 4, para 1).

Under the operation of the old civil procedure rules, the adversarial system left responsibility for the conduct of proceedings with the parties to the case. The judge acted solely in the role of umpire, adjudicating on the issues selected by the parties when they chose to present them to the court.

Lord Woolf believed that where only the parties are in control of the pace and conduct of litigation, 'the litigation process is too often seen as a battlefield where no rules apply. In this environment, questions of expense, delay, compromise and fairness may have only low priority. The consequence is that expense is often excessive, disproportionate and unpredictable; and delay is frequently unreasonable' (IR, Chapter 3, para 4). Examples cited of the resulting evils were the failure to establish the real issues in dispute in the case, excessive and inefficient disclosure of documents, and the exertion of partisan pressure on experts (IR, Chapter 3, paras 8–11).

It was also felt that the timetables and other requirements in the previous rules were flouted on a vast scale and complied with only when convenient to the interests of one of the parties (IR, Chapter 3, para 6).

The expense of litigation

Lord Woolf believed that for 'individual litigants the unaffordable cost of litigation constitutes a denial of access to justice' (IR, Chapter 3, para 13). Lord Woolf took into account the cost not only in financial terms, but also in terms of time and diversion from normal activities. He felt that the problem of expense included the problem of uncertainty as to the amount that would be incurred in legal costs, and this in turn was caused by the uncontrolled nature of the litigation process.

He also raised the issue of disproportionate costs, particularly in smaller cases where 'the costs of litigation, for one side alone, frequently equal or exceed the value of what is at issue' (IR, Chapter 3, para 18).

Lord Woolf ultimately believed that under the system existing at the time he wrote his Report, 'there can be no effective control of costs because there is no effective control of the work' (IR, Chapter 3, para 24).

Delay

Lord Woolf was scathing in his criticism of the legal profession in the context of delay. He said that delay was 'of more benefit to legal advisers than to parties' as it allowed 'litigators to carry excessive caseloads in which the minimum possible action occurs over the maximum possible timescale' (IR, Chapter 3, para 31). He also believed that most delays were caused by the legal profession, arising from 'failure to progress a case efficiently, wasting time on peripheral issues or procedural skirmishing to wear down an opponent or excuse failure to get on with the case'. He also blamed excessive discovery and the use of sought-after experts as a cause of delays (IR, Chapter 3, para 36).

Lord Woolf believed that the practice of reaching a settlement at a very late stage in proceedings was endemic throughout the system, but involved the parties in substantial additional costs (IR, Chapter 3, para 38).

He also lamented the fact that there was no certainty as to the time that a hearing would take, with parties' time estimates bearing insufficient relation to reality. He believed this was due to the fact that there was no plan or programme for the hearing, nor any attempt to concentrate on key issues and key evidence (IR, Chapter 3, paras 42–43).

Complexity

Lord Woolf believed that the complexity involved in bringing civil proceedings was caused by:

(a) the state of the rules of court;

(b) the existence of different procedures and jurisdictions for the High Court and county courts, as well as for the different divisions of the High Court;

(c) the variety of ways of initiating proceedings;

(d) multiplicity of practice directions; and

(e) obscure and uncertain substantive law (IR, Chapter 3, para 44).

According to Lord Woolf, in the light of the fact that legal advice and assistance were increasingly unavailable to litigants, due to their excessive cost and due to the limited availability of legal aid, more litigants were being forced to act in person. However, owing to its complexity, most litigants in person could not understand the procedure and so they and the courts had problems when they were involved (IR, Chapter 3, paras 45–47).

THE SOLUTIONS

Judicial case management

If an unrestrained adversarial culture was the main reason why the civil litigation system failed to provide access to justice, then judicial case management was primarily the answer to this problem. Lord Woolf did not advocate the abolition of the adversarial system in favour of an inquisitorial system; what he proposed was to keep the adversarial system, but give a more interventionist management role to the court in order to control what he described as the excesses of the adversarial system (IR, Chapter 5, para 15).

Lord Woolf believed that there was now 'no alternative to a fundamental shift in the responsibility for the management of civil litigation from litigants and their legal advisers to the courts' (IR, Chapter 4, para 2), and that this would require a radical change of culture for all those involved in the civil justice system (IR, Chapter 4, para 4).

Judicial case management would mean not only that the court could control the progress of proceedings, but also that the court could determine how much of the court's resources should be allotted to the resolution of a particular case, and that all of this would be achieved primarily through the allocation of cases to a case management track with case management by the courts thereafter (IR, Chapter 4, para 8).

Lord Woolf believed that judicial case management would 'facilitate and encourage earlier settlement through earlier identification and determination of issues and tighter timetables' (IR, Chapter 4, para 12).

The overriding objective

An important and distinctive innovation of the new rules was the introduction of the overriding objective, this being to enable the court to deal with cases justly. The CPR are not meant to be definitive of civil procedure and, instead, the court is given a discretion in the application and interpretation of the rules to a particular case in accordance with the overriding objective (FR, Chapter 20, para 20). This is meant to facilitate the operation of the rules in order to do justice in a particular case and in order to prevent a complex procedural system growing up around the rules based on a plethora of case law precedent.

Sanctions

Judicial case management would be enforced by the use of sanctions, intended to deter breaches of the rules rather than to impose punishment. A range of sanctions would be introduced, tailored to fit the seriousness of a party's breach. Lord Woolf's proposal under the new rules was for sanctions to have effect unless the party in breach of the rules applied for relief, rather than following the previous practice of obliging the other party to apply for an order that the offending party comply with the rules and be punished for breach (FR, Chapter 6, para 3).

Proportionality

Proportionality is a key concept to the present civil litigation system. In Lord Woolf's view, it involves the recognition that '[t]he achievement of the right result needs to be balanced against the expenditure of the time and money needed to achieve that result' (IR, Chapter 4, para 6). It also means that the amount and importance of what is at stake will govern how much time and cost should be allotted to the resolution of a dispute both in terms of recoverable legal costs and the use of court time, resources and procedures.

If proceedings are commenced, they should be subject to a predetermined timetable from which it will be difficult to depart. The courts should consider the needs not only of the litigants before them at any given time, but also those of the other litigants in the court system. Moreover, through judicial case management, disclosure and evidence should be limited to that which is just and appropriate for the disposal of a dispute (IR, Chapter 4, para 7).

In Lord Woolf's view, the principle of proportionality of cost dictates that the scope of expert evidence must be limited (FR, Chapter 13, para 15). A key method to limit expert evidence was through the use of a single expert, jointly instructed by the parties but neutral of both and with an overriding duty to the court (IR, Chapter 23).

A single procedural code

In order to address the complexity of the present rules of procedure, Lord Woolf proposed a single set of rules applying to the High Court and county courts. The rules would be more simply drafted in plain English, and special rules for specific types of litigation would be reduced to a minimum (FR, Section I, para 9).

The overall aim was for the rules to be understandable to those who used them, which would include litigants in person. In furtherance of this, Lord Woolf also recommended that terminology and expressions that were meaningless or confusing to non-lawyers would not be used in the new rules. Examples of replacements for such terminology are:

- 'claimant' for 'plaintiff';
- 'statement of case' for 'pleading';
- 'disclosure' for 'discovery';
- 'remedy' for 'relief'; and
- 'a claim' for the various terms for methods of starting an action, such as writ, summons and originating application (oddly, one or two archaic names remain, including 'a writ of *fieri facias*').

Lord Woolf also believed that a change of terminology, and one which in particular shunned legal jargon, would help to underpin a change of attitude and culture within the legal profession itself (FR, Chapter 20, para 14). In order to further the simplification of the litigation process, all proceedings would be commenced in the same way, by claim form (FR, Section I, para 9).

Avoiding litigation

Lord Woolf declared that one of the working objectives for the new system of civil litigation would be for the parties to settle their disputes before resorting to the courts, whenever it was reasonable for them to do so. There would therefore be an emphasis on pre-commencement resolution of disputes and, if proceedings became necessary, an onus on the parties to work to achieve a settlement at as early a stage as possible. Also, where an alternative method of resolving disputes otherwise than through court proceedings exists, this should be used before court proceedings are resorted to (IR, Chapter 4, para 7).

Lord Woolf reported that in recent years, both here and abroad, there had been a growth in Alternative Dispute Resolution (ADR). ADR is a generic name for various dispute-resolving mechanisms that are alternative to litigation in the court; it includes arbitration, ombudsmen schemes, conciliation and mediation. Lord Woolf extolled the virtues of ADR, claiming that it saved scarce judicial and other resources, was usually quicker and cheaper, and often achieved a more mutually satisfying outcome for the parties than litigation (IR, Chapter 18, paras 1, 2).

Accordingly, part of judicial case management is to include the diversion of cases to ADR where it is likely to be beneficial (IR, Chapter 5, para 17). Although Lord Woolf proposed an active encouragement of the use of ADR, he stressed that he did not propose that it should be compulsory (IR, Chapter 18, para 3). However, he did propose that the court should take into account an unreasonable refusal to resort to ADR as a relevant factor in deciding issues as to costs (FR, Section I, para 18). Lord Woolf also proposed new procedures designed to encourage settlement and the early resolution of disputes. These include claimants' offers to settle (IR, Chapter 4, para 27; FR, Chapter 11), defendants' applications for summary judgment (IR, Chapter 4, para 28 and Chapter 6, paras 17–21), and the obligation on legal representatives to provide costs information to their clients and to their opponents at various stages of the proceedings (IR, Chapter 4, para 7).

Change of culture

In order to give full effect to the reforms, Lord Woolf believed it was necessary not only to reform the rules and procedures, but also to bring about a fundamental change in the culture of civil litigation. In place of the traditional adversarial approach to litigation, there would be an expectation of openness and co-operation between the parties from the outset, and a principle that litigation would be a last resort for the resolution of a dispute. This new culture would be supported by the introduction of pre-action protocols setting standards for reasonable pre-action behaviour, which parties would be expected to follow and which would include voluntary pre-action exchange of information and the identification of the issues in dispute at the earliest stage (FR, Section I, para 9).

THE CPR IN PRACTICE

The CPR were introduced in April 1999 to bring into effect the substance of Lord Woolf's proposed reforms of the civil justice system. However, it is a matter of some debate whether the CPR have achieved Lord Woolf's intended objectives.

The Lord Chancellor's Department (since 12 June 2003, the Department for Constitutional Affairs) attempted to monitor the effects of the civil justice reforms through the use of questionnaires, surveys, research programmes and pilot schemes. The results so far have been published in two papers, *Emerging Findings*, published in March 2001 (www.dca.gov.uk/civil/emerge/emerge.htm), and *Further Findings*, published in August 2002 (www.dca.gov.uk/civil/reform/ffreform.htm).

The initial results reported in *Emerging Findings* were confirmed in *Further Findings*. Both papers reported an overall view that the reforms were working well and had succeeded in bringing about a change of culture. There was found to be substantial support for a number of new innovations brought in by the CPR, namely, pre-action protocols, claimant Part 36 offers to settle, single joint experts and case management conferences, all of which were said to work well.

Statistics showed there to be a drop in the number of claims issued since the introduction of the CPR and, after a substantial rise in the first year following the introduction of the CPR, a levelling-off in the use of ADR. Although the time between issue and hearing for cases that go to trial was found to have fallen as a result of judicial case management, it was found to have risen for cases allocated to the small claims track. This was felt to be because of an increase in the number of higher value cases within the small claims track. Following the introduction of new rules relating to appeals, there was also found to be a sharp fall in the number of appeals against case management decisions.

However, there is no evidence that one of the key objectives of Lord Woolf's reforms is being achieved, namely, making litigation less expensive and the costs more proportionate to the value and complexity of the claim. Indeed, the only evidence there is suggests that the cost of litigating has increased. There is also criticism that reforms such as the introduction of pre-action protocols have led to the 'front-loading' of costs. Anecdotal evidence suggests that requirements such as preparation for and attendance at pre-trial reviews and case management conferences increase rather than reduce costs. Likewise the requirement, at various stages of proceedings, to prepare and serve costs estimates.

Further, the appointment of a single joint expert is said to increase the amount of expert evidence obtained by parties, who instruct their own expert, in addition to the single joint expert, to advise separately on the evidence of the single joint expert and, if necessary, challenge it. There is also felt to be uncertainty and unpredictability in the processes of summary and detailed assessment of costs. Efforts are being made to simplify the assessment of costs with the introduction of pre-issue fixed fees in low value road traffic accident cases following an initiative of the Civil Justice Council. However, there is fierce resistance to the introduction of fixed fees for other types of litigation and for post-issue costs. Indeed, excessive costs, and difficulties in assessing costs, are felt to be the biggest problems within the system, and such that they could endanger the success of the CPR. There is also no obvious solution to such problems.

Accompanying such difficulties, the fundamental changes to the funding of litigation through Conditional Fee Agreements, which allow the success fee and/or insurance premium to be recoverable from an unsuccessful opponent, have led to much satellite litigation in an attempt to avoid this additional costs burden.

The Department for Constitutional Affairs (created on 12 June 2003) is continuing to evaluate the reforms and plans to issue a further paper in 2004 publishing its findings into research on case management, the Court of Appeal and litigants in person.

CHAPTER 2

SOURCES OF CIVIL PROCEDURE: STRUCTURE AND JURISDICTION OF THE CIVIL COURTS

SOURCES OF CIVIL PROCEDURE

The Civil Procedure Rules 1998

The main source of civil procedural law is contained in the Civil Procedure Rules 1998 (CPR), which came into force on 26 April 1999 (SI 1998/3132). The rules are a single procedural code applying to both the High Court and county courts, and replace the Rules of the Supreme Court (RSC) and the County Court Rules (CCR). The statutory basis of the CPR is the Civil Procedure Act 1997 (CPA). The CPR are a form of delegated legislation and are drafted by the Civil Procedure Rule Committee which replaced the Supreme Court Rule Committee and the County Court Rule Committee.

The main body of the CPR consists of rules and practice directions. The rules are divided into parts dealing with different aspects of procedure, and most parts are accompanied by a practice direction (PD). The practice directions are subordinate to the rules (Sched 1, para 6 to the CPA) and were described by May LJ as 'at best a weak aid to the interpretation of the rules themselves' (*Godwin v Swindon BC* [2001] EWCA Civ 1478 at [11]). However, in any event, no rule should be read without considering its relevant practice direction and vice versa.

The schedules to the CPR

Although the CPR abolished the former RSC and CCR, some of these former rules were immediately brought back into force in the form of schedules to the CPR. The remaining RSC are contained in Sched 1 and the remaining CCR in Sched 2. The old rules still cover such matters as committal proceedings and a number of other aspects of procedure that have not yet been drafted into the form of the new rules. However, some aspects of the retained RSC and CCR have been brought into line with the CPR, so, for instance, if an application must be made under any of the RSC or CCR in the schedules, in many cases it must be made in accordance with Part 23 of the CPR.

Pre-action protocols

The CPR also contain a number of pre-action protocols which set standards for reasonable pre-action behaviour. There are currently six approved pre-action protocols. When a protocol is approved it is set out in the schedule of the practice direction to the protocols, which is the mechanism to bring them within the ambit of the CPR. A party cannot be compelled to comply with a protocol, but if proceedings are started the court can take failure to comply into account when exercising case management powers, imposing sanctions or making orders for costs (rr 3.1(4); 3.9(1)(e); 44.3(5)(a)).

The Glossary

There is also a short Glossary, defining some of the terms referred to in the rules, which is meant for assistance only, particularly for litigants in person, and is not meant to provide a meaning to any term which it otherwise would not have (r 2.2(1)). Words appearing in the CPR which are included in the Glossary are followed by '(GL)' (r 2.2(2)). Also, unlike terms which are defined within the main body of the rules, the terms in the Glossary are not meant to affect the way the rules operate (see *Access to Justice*, Final Report, Chapter 20, para 16, www.dca.gov.uk/civil/final/index.htm).

The overriding objective of the CPR

The CPR describe themselves as 'a new procedural code with the overriding objective of enabling the court to deal with cases justly' (r 1.1(1)). The court must seek to give effect to this overriding objective when exercising any power under the rules or interpreting any rule (r 1.2). In the Final Report (FR) Lord Woolf said: 'As part of a comprehensive package of reforms ... modernised and improved rules have a major part to play' (see FR, Chapter 20, para 29). The rules are meant to cover the main principles of the matter dealt with whilst the practice directions supply the detail.

The intention was to move away from the old civil procedure system where the rules had become dense and convoluted, covering every eventuality and bound by case law precedent, to a system of procedural rules drafted in plain English which give the court a wide discretion to make decisions in order to deal justly with a particular case in accordance with the overriding objective. As Lord Woolf expressed it: 'Every word in the rules should have a purpose, but every word cannot sensibly be given a minutely exact meaning. Civil procedure involves more judgment and knowledge than the rules can directly express' (FR, Chapter 20, para 10).

There is well-established authority that when interpreting a new code of law, the proper course, in the first instance, is to examine the language of the new rules and ask what its natural meaning is, uninfluenced by any considerations derived from the previous state of the law: see Lord Herschell's judgment in the House of Lords' decision of *Bank of England v Vagliano Bros* [1891] AC 107; [1891–94] All ER Rep 93, at 113 E–I, where the proper interpretation of the code of law relating to negotiable instruments, the Bills of Exchange Act 1882, was considered. It is certainly the expressed opinion of the Court of Appeal that cases decided under the previous system are not binding under the new rules (see the judgment of Lord Woolf MR in *Biguzzi v Rank Leisure plc* [1999] 1 WLR 1926; [1999] 4 All ER 934; and *Walsh v Misseldine* [2000] All ER (D) 261). In *Shikari v Malik* (1999) *The Times*, 20 May, a case dealing with an application commenced under the old rules to strike out a case for want of prosecution, the Court of Appeal said that litigants whose actions had commenced before the new rules came into force cannot rely on what had been tolerated in the past being tolerated in the future. However, the principle may not be absolute – in *Deg-Deutsche Investitions und Entwicklungsgesellschaft GmbH v Koshy & Others* [2000] TLR 1, *per* Rimer J, it was considered that *Re Elgindata (No 2)* [1992] 1 WLR 1207 might be referred to for general principles as to costs. Lord Herschell, in *Bank of England v Vagliano Bros*, acknowledged that where a provision was unclear resort might be had to the previous state of the law in order to aid in the construction of the provisions of a new code ([1891–94] All ER Rep 93 at 113H).

However, the purpose of the overriding objective is to enable judges to exercise their discretion to deal with a case justly without necessarily being bound by decisions in other cases under the new rules. In *Hamblin v Field* (2000) *The Times*, 26 April, Chadwick LJ said 'it is of little assistance to this court to have cited to it decisions on the application of the overriding objective to particular circumstances in other cases'. Similarly, in *Purdy v Cambran* [1999] CPLR 843, May LJ endorsed Lord Woolf's opinion that 'reference to authorities under the former rules is generally no longer relevant', holding that instead 'it is necessary to concentrate on the intrinsic justice of a particular case in the light of the overriding objective'. However, he did acknowledge that the underlying thought processes of previous decisions should not be completely thrown overboard.

In reality, there have already been a number of guideline cases decided by the Court of Appeal on the interpretation of the rules and, significantly, when sitting in such appeals, Lord Woolf often took the opportunity to provide general guidance on the operation of the rules (see, for example, *Ford v GKR Construction* [2000] 1 All ER 802).

Statute law

The CPA is the statutory basis for the CPR, which are made by statutory instrument under the Act (s 3 of the CPA). Updates and amendments to the CPR are made by statutory instrument, the 31st update to the rules being made by the Civil Procedure (Amendment) Rules 2003 (SI 1998/3132).

The Human Rights Act 1998 (HRA), which came into force on 2 October 2000, has an important effect on procedural law. The HRA incorporates the Convention rights set out in the European Convention on Human Rights (ECHR) into English domestic law (s 1 of the HRA). Article 6 of the Convention, the right to a fair trial, has obvious relevance to procedural matters. Further, when the court is exercising a discretion, such as that under the overriding objective of the CPR, it should, as a public authority, do so in a Convention-compatible way (s 6(1) of the HRA).

Other main statutory sources of procedural law are the Supreme Court Act 1981 and the County Courts Act 1984, governing the constitution and powers of the Supreme Court and county courts respectively. There are a number of other important statutes including the Access to Justice Act 1999, governing such matters as reforms to funding and appeals, and the Civil Evidence Act 1995, which reformed the law about the admissibility of hearsay evidence in civil proceedings.

There is also a variety of statutory instruments such as the High Court and County Courts Jurisdiction Orders, which deal with the jurisdiction of the courts, and the Supreme Court and the County Court Fees Orders, which set out the current fees payable in the Supreme Court and county courts.

The court's inherent jurisdiction

The High Court retains a general jurisdiction to govern its own procedures (s 19 of the Supreme Court Act 1981). This is referred to as the court's inherent jurisdiction and is understood to be expressly retained by CPR r 3.1, which refers to 'any other enactment or any powers [the court] may otherwise have'. The court's inherent jurisdiction should be distinguished from the court's discretion exercisable under the rules in accordance with the overriding objective. The court will invoke its inherent jurisdiction when there is no rule governing a particular situation but its intervention is called for to avoid injustice. For example, in *Secretary of State for Trade and Industry v Staton* [2001] 1 BCLC 84, the court was of the opinion that under its inherent jurisdiction it could decline to proceed with a trial which it could no longer conduct fairly because of delay caused by the court. In that case there was a 10-week delay to proceedings caused by the court's failure to list a hearing. However, the court held that in giving effect to the overriding objective it would not be just or proportionate to strike out the claimant's proceedings because of delay which was not the fault of the claimant but of the court.

Under the former rules a county court was held to have the same inherent jurisdiction to regulate its own procedures in *Langley v North West Water Authority* [1991] 1 WLR 697. This also would appear to be expressly retained by r 3.1, as the CPR apply both to the High Court and to county courts.

Proceedings to which the CPR apply

The CPR apply to all proceedings in the county courts, the High Court and the Civil Division of the Court of Appeal, apart from some important exceptions such as family and insolvency proceedings (although there is a practice direction relating to insolvency proceedings (PD – Insolvency proceedings)). Following a practice direction issued by the President of the Family Division on 24 October 2000, costs directions under the CPR now apply to family proceedings and Family Division proceedings, although Part 36 (offers to settle and payments into court) does not. It is still not possible to enter into an enforceable conditional fee agreement in family proceedings (s 58A of the Courts and Legal Services Act 1990). Further, the principles of the overriding objective and proportionality now apply to ancillary relief proceedings. The following types of proceedings are also not covered by the CPR: non-contentious or common form probate proceedings; proceedings in the High Court when acting as a Prize Court; proceedings before the judge within the meaning of Part VII of the Mental Health Act 1983; and adoption proceedings (r 2.1(2)).

THE CIVIL COURTS

The civil litigation system is administered through the civil courts, consisting of the Supreme Court and the county courts.

The Supreme Court

The Supreme Court consists of the High Court, the Court of Appeal and the Crown Court. When the Department for Constitutional Affairs was created on 12 June 2003 the Lord Chancellor ceased to be President of the Supreme Court (s 1 of the Supreme Court Act 1981 (SCA)).

In the Supreme Court, civil cases are heard only in the High Court, with appeals being heard in the Civil Division of the Court of Appeal. The High Court consists of the Queen's Bench Division (QBD), Chancery Division and Family Division (s 5 of the SCA). The Queen's Bench Division deals with contract and tort matters and includes the Commercial Court and the Admiralty Court. The Chancery Division deals with equity and trusts matters, contentious probate, tax, partnerships and bankruptcy, and includes the Companies Court and the Patents Court. The Family Division deals with dissolution of marriages, matrimonial proceedings and proceedings relating to children (Sched 1 to the SCA).

In London, the High Court sits at the Royal Courts of Justice. In other areas of the country, the High Court sits at district registries. The High Court judiciary consists of the Vice Chancellor (Head of the Chancery Division), the Lord Chief Justice (Head of the QBD), the Vice-President of the QBD, the President of the Family Division, the Senior Presiding Judge, High Court (or *puisne*) judges, and Masters and district judges (s 4 of the SCA).

The county courts

The county court is held for a geographical district (s 1 of the County Courts Act 1984 (CCA)), but for the most part the place for *issue* of proceedings is not dependent on a geographical connection. The county courts deal with the majority of civil litigation. Circuit judges, recorders, district judges and deputy district judges preside over the business of the county courts.

JURISDICTION OF THE HIGH COURT AND COUNTY COURTS

The High Court and county courts have concurrent jurisdiction over most actions and, as a general rule, proceedings in which both the county courts and High Court have jurisdiction may be commenced in either court. However, there are some important exceptions to this rule, as detailed below.

Jurisdiction of the High Court

The High Court has almost unlimited jurisdiction over most matters (s 19 of the SCA). However, the intention is to reserve the High Court for only the most valuable, complex and important cases.

Unless the value of a monetary (non-personal injury) claim is more than £15,000, it cannot be commenced in the High Court (High Court and County Courts Jurisdiction Order 1991 (SI 1991/724), para 4A). In order to start such proceedings in the High Court, a party must state on the claim form that the value of the claim is worth more than £15,000 (PD 7, para 3.6). For personal injury claims, except clinical negligence claims, the value of the claim must be more than £50,000 (High Court and County Courts Jurisdiction Order 1991, para 5), and this must also be stated on the claim form before proceedings can be commenced in the High Court (PD 7, para 3.6). The financial value of a claim is calculated in accordance with r 16.3(6) (High Court and County Courts Jurisdiction Order 1991, para 9).

Also, if a claim with an estimated value of less than £50,000 is issued in the Royal Courts of Justice, unless it is required by a statutory enactment to be tried in the High Court, it falls within a specialist list, or is a type of claim suitable for trial in the Royal Courts of Justice, it will be transferred to a county court (PD 29, para 2.2). The type of claims suitable for trial in the Royal Courts of Justice include professional negligence claims, Fatal Accidents Act 1976 claims, fraud or undue influence claims (PD 29, para 2.6).

Apart from these provisions, a claim should be started in the High Court only if by reason of its financial value and the amount in dispute, and/or the complexity of the facts, legal issues, remedies or procedures involved, and/or the public importance of the outcome, the claimant believes that the claim ought to be dealt with by a High Court judge (PD 7, para 2.4).

Jurisdiction of Masters and district judges in the High Court

Most of the case management of cases in the High Court is dealt with by judges known as Masters in the Royal Courts of Justice and as district judges in the district registries. As a general principle, a Master or district judge can exercise any function of the court except where an enactment, rule or practice direction provides otherwise (r 2.4). Practice Direction 2B specifies those matters over which Masters and district judges have no jurisdiction and where a judge must make the order instead. This includes the power to:

(a) make search orders, freezing orders, an ancillary order under r 25.1(g), or an order authorising a person to enter land to recover, inspect or sample property;

(b) make an order for an injunction, except where the terms are agreed by the parties, where it is in connection with a charging order or appointment of a receiver by way of equitable execution or in proceedings under CPR Sched 1 RSC Ord 77, r 16 (order restraining person from receiving sum due from the Crown). Also, a Master or district judge may make an order varying or discharging an injunction or undertaking if the parties consent to the variation or discharge;

(c) try a multi-track case unless all the parties consent, or where the case is treated as allocated to the multi-track because it is proceeding under Part 8 (PD 2B, paras 2.1, 2.4, 4.1).

However, these restrictions on jurisdiction do not prevent Masters or district judges from:

(a) hearing applications for summary judgment or, if the parties consent, the determination of a preliminary issue;

(b) assessing damages due to a party under a judgment without limit as to the amount (PD 2B, paras 4.1, 4.2).

Jurisdiction of the county courts

The county courts have general jurisdiction to hear and determine any claim founded on contract or tort whatever its financial value, complexity or importance (s 15(1) of the CCA). However, there are certain contract/tort claims over which the county courts have no jurisdiction, the most important of which being most claims for libel or slander (s 15(2) of the CCA).

The county courts have unlimited jurisdiction to hear claims for the recovery of land (s 21 of the CCA).

The county courts have jurisdiction in equity and contentious probate proceedings where the estate, fund or assets involved do not exceed £30,000 (ss 23 and 32 of the CCA and the County Courts Jurisdiction Order 1981 (SI 1981/1123)). However, the county court will have jurisdiction to hear equity claims exceeding this amount if the parties agree that it should have jurisdiction, except in respect of proceedings under the Variation of Trusts Act 1958 (s 24 of the CCA).

Although, as a general principle, the county courts have the same jurisdiction as the High Court to award remedies and relief, including interim injunctions, this is apart from the remedies or relief of judicial review, freezing injunctions or search orders, which must be obtained in the High Court (s 38 of the CCA, County Court Remedies Regulations 1991 (SI 1991/1222)).

Jurisdiction of district judges in the county court

All district judges in the county court outside of London are also appointed district judges of the High Court so that they can sit in the district registry. The trial jurisdiction of district judges includes:

(a) trials of cases allocated to the small claims and fast track or, with exceptions, certain proceedings which are treated as allocated to the multi-track under r 8.9(c) and Table 2 of PD 8B (PD 2B, para 11.1 should be consulted for the exceptions);

(b) proceedings for the recovery of land;

(c) the assessment of damages or other sum due to a party under a judgment without any financial limit;

(d) any other case with the consent of all the parties and the permission of the designated civil judge (PD 2B, para 11.1).

The district judge has jurisdiction to grant an injunction where:

(a) the injunction is to be made in proceedings where a district judge otherwise has jurisdiction (see above);

(b) the injunction is sought in a money claim which has not yet been allocated to a track, where the amount claimed does not exceed the fast track financial limit;

(c) in the circumstances where a High Court Master or district judge has jurisdiction to grant an injunction (see above) (PD 2B, paras 8.1, 8.2).

Court manager and 'proper officer'; devolution to administrative staff

The court manager is responsible for the administrative running of the county court, and any complaints about the administration should be made to him or her and not to the judge who has no jurisdiction concerning such matters.

Rule 2.5 provides that, where the rules permit it, an act of a 'formal or administrative' character can be carried out by a court officer, defined by r 2.3 as 'a member of the court staff'. Thus, for example, a member of staff can deal with a request for a default judgment. As a rough guide it can be taken that a court officer will not be permitted to carry out any act that requires a judicial decision. However, in some cases the rules go beyond allowing officers of the court to perform acts of a formal or administrative nature, in particular with regard to the enforcement of judgments.

TRANSFER OF PROCEEDINGS

Consequences of commencing proceedings in the wrong court

If proceedings are brought in the High Court that should have been started in a county court, the High Court must either transfer the proceedings to a county court or strike them out (s 40(1) of the CCA 1984). The High Court can strike out the proceedings only if it is satisfied that the person bringing them knew that they should have been brought in a county court instead (s 40(1)(b) of the CCA). Even if the High Court is so satisfied, the decision to strike out is discretionary and in most cases it will not be appropriate to exercise it (*Restick v Crickmore* [1994] 2 All ER 112). In *Restick* the court gave some examples of when it may be appropriate for the High Court to exercise its discretion to strike out under s 40(1)(b) – for instance, where the claim should plainly have been started in a county court and the failure to do so was not due to a *bona fide* mistake but done as an attempt to harass a defendant or deliberately run up unnecessary costs – but provided in all cases that it is a proportionate response, bearing in mind the right to a fair trial preserved by Art 6(1) of the ECHR.

Similarly, if proceedings are brought in a county court which should have been brought in the High Court, the county court must either transfer the proceedings to the High Court or, where it is satisfied that the person bringing them knew they should have been brought in the High Court, strike them out (s 42(1) of the CCA 1984).

In all cases the established policy of the courts is not to strike out a claim merely because of some mistake of procedure (*Restick v Crickmore*, above). This established policy has survived the introduction of the CPR. See, for instance, *Hannigan v Hannigan* [2000] All ER (D) 693, where it was held that striking out a claim for an 'arid technicality' would be contrary to the overriding objective. However, under the CPR the court is more likely to impose sanctions on parties for failing to comply with the requirements of the rules.

Sanction for commencing proceedings in the High Court

If a claimant commences proceedings in the High Court that should have been commenced in the county court, the court has a discretion to penalise the claimant by reducing the costs he would otherwise have been awarded by a maximum of 25% (s 51(8) and (9) of the SCA).

Transfer of proceedings between the High Court and county courts

The High Court and county courts have general jurisdiction, subject to specific jurisdictional rules, to transfer proceedings to the other court either of their own motion or on the application of a party (ss 40(2), (3) and 42(2), (3) of the CCA). The High Court has general jurisdiction to order the transfer of any proceedings from the county court to the High Court (s 41 of the CCA).

When deciding whether to transfer proceedings between the High Court and a county court, between county courts, or between the Royal Courts of Justice and district registries, the court must have regard to the matters referred to in r 30.3(2) (r 30.3(1)). However, this does not apply to the automatic transfer provisions, whereby proceedings are automatically transferred to the defendant's home court when a defendant who is an individual files a defence to a claim for a specified amount. The court will also transfer cases allocated to the multi-track to a Civil Trial Centre for case management (for details, see Chapter 16, 'Judicial Case Management: Allocation').

Transfer between county courts

A county court may order the proceedings before it, or any part of them, such as a counterclaim or application, be transferred to another county court if it considers it justified having regard to the matters referred to in r 30.3(2), or if proceedings for the detailed assessment of costs or for the enforcement of a judgment or order could be more conveniently or fairly taken in that other county court (r 30.2(1)). The words 'conveniently or fairly' are not defined and mirror those used in the former CCR Ord 16, r 1(a). The court does, however, have full discretion to transfer with which an appellate court will not interfere, provided the discretion is used judicially (*Birch v County Motor and Engineering Co Ltd* [1958] 3 All ER 175, CA) and the criteria in r 30.3 are borne in mind as well as the overriding objective. In county court cases, assessment may be remitted to the Supreme Court Costs Office (SCCO) without the case being transferred (r 47.4), usually where the amount of costs involved exceeds a certain amount, decided upon by the SCCO from time to time.

If proceedings have been started in a county court which is not the correct county court according to the CPR, a judge may order that the proceedings:

(a) be transferred to the county court in which they ought to have been started;

(b) continue in the county court in which they have been started; or

(c) be struck out (r 30.2(2)).

However, in accordance with the overriding objective, the court will not usually strike out proceedings for a mistake in procedure (*Hannighan v Hannighan* [2000] All ER (D) 693).

Nevertheless, where proceedings must be started in a particular county court in accordance with an enactment other than the CPR, r 30.2 does not give the court the power to transfer the proceedings to a county court which is not the court in which they should have been started, or to order them to continue in the wrong court (r 30.2(7)).

A transfer to another county court can be made by the court of its own motion or on the application of a party, which must be made to the county court where the claim is proceeding (r 30.2(3)).

Transfer between the Royal Courts of Justice and a district registry

The High Court may, having regard to the matters referred to in r 30.3(2), order proceedings in the Royal Courts of Justice, or any part of them, such as a counterclaim, to be transferred to a district registry, or those in a district registry to be transferred to the Royal Courts of Justice or another district registry (r 30.2(4)). The transfer may be made by the court of its own motion or on the application of a party, which must be made to the district registry where the claim is proceeding (r 30.2(6)).

Transfers between district registries

In the case of proceedings for the detailed assessment of costs, a district registry may order that the proceedings be transferred to another district registry if satisfied that they could be more conveniently or fairly heard in that other registry (r 30.2(5)). The transfer may be made by the court of its own motion, or on the application of a party to the district registry where the proceedings are currently being heard (r 30.2(6)).

Transfers between divisions and to and from a specialist list

The High Court may order proceedings in any Division of the High Court to be transferred to another Division. Also, the court may order proceedings to be transferred to or from a specialist list. If a party wishes to transfer proceedings to or from a specialist list, an application must be made to a judge dealing with claims in that list (r 30.5).

Matters in r 30.3(2) to which the court should have regard when transferring proceedings

The matters to which the court should have regard when transferring proceedings between the High Court and a county court, or between county courts, or between the Royal Court of Justice and the district registries, include such matters as:

(a) the financial value of the claim, or the amount in dispute (if different);

(b) the convenience or fairness of hearings being held in another court;

(c) the availability of a judge specialising in the type of claim in question;

(d) the complexity of the facts, legal issues, remedies or procedures;

(e) the public importance of the claim;

(f) the facilities available at the court where the claim is being dealt with, in particular with regard to any disabilities of a party or witness; and

(g) where there is a real prospect that the making of a declaration of incompatibility under s 4 of the Human Rights Act 1998 may arise (r 30.3(2)).

In *Pepin v Taylor* [2002] EWCA Civ 1522, the Court of Appeal said that there are strong reasons for fixing a venue for the proceedings at a place convenient for the defendant, as the defendant 'does not choose to be sued'. The fact that the defendant may counterclaim does not detract considerably from that principle. However, where the only party giving evidence is the claimant, for example, in personal injury cases where only quantum of damages is in dispute, there may be an argument that the claimant's court is the most convenient. In *Fradkina v Network Housing Association* [2002] EWCA Civ 1715, the Court of Appeal ordered proceedings to be transferred away from a county court where the claimant had been 'poorly served by the court' and where 'the court had not adequately dealt with consolidated cases in the past'. Such a situation should be regarded as rare.

The court may disregard any amount admitted when making its decision (cf r 26.8(2)). As to transfer between High Court and county court, note the financial limits set out in the High Court and County Courts Jurisdiction Order 1991, as amended, and the provisions of PD 29, para 2.

Transfer of place of hearing

Under r 30.6, the court has power to specify the place where hearings are to be held, and may do so without ordering the proceedings themselves to be transferred. This enables a hearing to take place in another court without the proceedings actually being transferred, to accommodate the convenience of the parties and to ensure efficiency of trial listing.

In particular, fast track cases from several courts are likely to be listed together and, especially in London, to be subject to some last-minute re-arranging of venue to ensure that a judge is available to hear a case on the date fixed.

The court will want to take into account the answers to the question in the allocation questionnaires which invites the parties to suggest which court would be most convenient for them, but is not bound by such answers.

Setting aside an order of transfer

A party may apply to set aside an order transferring the proceedings if the transfer was made following an application made without notice by another party, or by the court of its own motion (r 23.10; PD 30, para 6.1). The application to set aside the transfer should be made to the court that made the order transferring the proceedings, and should be made in accordance with Part 23 (PD 30, paras 6.1, 6.2).

Appeal against an order of transfer

Where an order transferring the proceedings was made following an application on notice, a party who objects to the order may appeal the order. If the order transferring proceedings was made by a district judge, and both the transferring and the receiving courts are county courts, the appeal should be made in the receiving court (PD 30, para 5.1). However, if it is more convenient for the parties, the receiving court may remit the appeal to the transferring court to be dealt with there (PD 30, para 5.2).

SPECIALIST PROCEEDINGS

When the CPR first came into force certain types of proceedings were identified as specialist proceedings under Part 49. Although the CPR apply to these specialist proceedings, they do so only in so far as they are not inconsistent with separate practice directions for each type of specialist proceedings (r 49(1)). The only remaining specialist proceedings identified in Part 49 are proceedings under the Companies Act 1985 and the Companies Act 1989 (r 49(2)).

Those proceedings which were formerly specialist proceedings are now governed by separate parts of the CPR: admiralty proceedings (Part 61); arbitration proceedings (Part 62); Commercial Court proceedings (Part 58); mercantile courts proceedings (Part 59); patents and other intellectual property claims (Part 63); technology and construction court claims (Part 60); and contentious probate proceedings (Part 57).

Prior to the introduction of the CPR, such specialist proceedings were conducted in accordance with a separately developed procedure that was felt to be efficient and effective and suited to the nature of the specialist proceedings, and which was accordingly retained. Therefore, although the CPR purport to provide a unified system of procedure for all types of civil proceedings, in fact many variations and differences remain depending on the nature of the claim litigated. Various guides are produced by committees of the specialist courts, such as the *Admiralty and Commercial Court Guide*, which gives further guidance about bringing proceedings of this type. Although chancery proceedings are not treated as specialist proceedings under the CPR, there is a guide published to proceedings in the Chancery Division that provides additional information not already contained in the CPR relating to procedure for claims brought in this division of the High Court. A similar guide has also been produced for the Queen's Bench Division, known as the *Queen's Bench Guide*.

COMPUTATION OF TIME UNDER THE CPR

Clear days

Where a period of time for doing any act is specified as a number of days by the rules, practice directions, or by a judgment or an order of the court, it is computed as *clear days*. Clear days mean that in computing the number of days, the day on which the period begins is excluded and, if the end of the period is defined by reference to an event, such as a hearing, the day on which the event occurs is excluded (r 2.8(1), (2) and (3)). For example, if the court orders an applicant to serve notice of the application on another party at least three days before the hearing, and the hearing is listed for Friday, 20 October, the last day for service is Monday, 16 October.

Accordingly, if the end of the period of time is not defined by reference to an event, for example, if a rule specifies that a statement of case must be served within 14 days of service of the claim form, and the claim form is served on 2 October, then the last day of the period is included and therefore the last day for service of the particulars of claim is 16 October.

Periods of time of five days or less

If the specified period is five days or less, if the period of time includes a Saturday, Sunday, Bank Holiday, Christmas Day or Good Friday, that day does not count (r 2.8(4)). For example, where an application is listed for Monday, 20 October, and notice of the application must be served at least three days before the hearing, the last date for service is Tuesday, 14 October.

Court office

If a rule, practice direction, judgment or order specifies a period of time for doing any act at the court office, if that period of time ends on a day when the court office is closed, that act shall be in time if done on the next day on which the court office is open (r 2.8(5)). Practice Direction 2, paras 2 and 3 set out the days and times when the court offices of the Supreme Court and county courts are closed.

Meaning of month

Where a judgment, order, direction or other document refers to a 'month' it means a calendar month (r 2.10).

Dates for compliance

Rule 2.9 provides that where the court gives a judgment, an order or a direction which imposes a time limit for doing any act, the last date for compliance must, whenever practicable, be expressed as a calendar date and include the time of day by which the act must be done. Thus the courts, when imposing a time limit, will now whenever possible refrain from any formula such as 'within 21 days' and instead say 'by no later than 4 pm on Friday, 27 October 2003' (or as the case may be).

Time limits varied by the parties

Rule 2.11 states that as a general rule, unless the rules, a practice direction or the court direct otherwise, the time specified for a person to do any act may be varied by the written agreement of the parties. However, there are quite widespread restrictions in the CPR on agreeing to a different time period to that specified.

If a rule, practice direction or court order requires a party to do something within a specified time, and also specifies the consequences of failure to comply, the time for doing the act may not be extended by agreement of the parties (r 3.8(3)).

Also, for cases allocated to the fast track or multi-track, the parties cannot agree to vary certain key dates. In the fast track, these key dates are the date for the return of a pre-trial checklist, the trial or the trial period. In the multi-track, the key dates are the same as for the fast track, but also include the date of a case management conference or a pre-trial review. If a party wishes to vary these dates, an application must be made to the court (rr 28.4 and 29.5).

The parties can agree to extend the period of time within which a defence is served, but only for a maximum period of a further 28 days. If such an agreement is reached, the defendant must notify the court of it in writing (r 15.5).

COURT FORMS

Court forms are specified for use by the parties in proceedings. Where a form is specified in a practice direction, that particular form must be used (r 4(1)). As an example, PD 7, para 3.1 specifies that Form N1 or N208 must be used to start proceedings.

Although a form may be varied if this is required by the circumstances of a particular case, such variations cannot leave out any information or guidance intended for the recipient (r 4(2) and (3)). Also, if a form is sent by the court or by one party for use by another, it must be sent without any variation except that which is required for the circumstances of the particular case (r 4(4)). A party does not have to use the actual versions printed by The Stationery Office (formerly HMSO) and in fact can fill in interactive forms downloaded from the court service website, or those provided by commercial publishers on computer disks. If a form has the Royal Arms at the head of the first page, this must be replicated on the form used by the party (r 4(5)).

Practice direction 4 lists all the forms to be used in civil proceedings since the introduction of the CPR. It is divided into three tables:

- Table 1 lists forms required by the main body of the CPR.
- Table 2 lists the High Court forms previously in use under the old rules and still retained for certain matters.
- Table 3 lists the former county court forms which are still required for certain matters (see PD 4).

The practice direction also refers to the fact that other forms may be authorised for use in specialist proceedings by the practice directions relevant to the specialist proceedings in question (PD 4, para 2.1).

Filing of documents at court

The rules indicate when documents must be filed at court and the time for doing so. Filing a document at court means simply delivering it to the court (r 2.3(1)). This can be achieved by a number of methods, the most common being by post, but it can also be delivered by hand or by fax.

'Delivery to the court' involves a unilateral, not a transactional, act as it is delivery to a place not a person, so no reciprocal act of acceptance is required. Therefore, if a document must be filed by a certain date it will be sufficiently filed if posted through the court's letter-box after the court office has closed (*Van Aken v Camden LBC* [2002] EWCA Civ 1724). In *Van Aken* the claimant wished to appeal against the defendant's decision that it had discharged its statutory duty to provide her with suitable accommodation as a homeless person. On the last day for filing the appeal the claimant's solicitors posted the appeal documents through the court's letter-box after the court office had closed. The Court of Appeal held that the claimant had complied with the time limits for filing the appeal documents at the court by delivering them to the court on the last day for doing so, even though the court staff would not process the documents until the next day when the court office opened again.

Filing by facsimile

In relation to documents delivered at court by means of fax, the document is not filed until it is delivered by the court's fax machine; the time of transmission from the party's fax machine is not taken into account (PD 5, para 5.3(3)). If the document is delivered by fax after 4 pm, it will be treated as filed on the next day the court office is open (PD 5, para 5.3(6)). Where a party serves a document by fax he must not send a 'hard' copy by post or document exchange as well (PD 5, para 5.3(2)). A fax can be used to file such documents as statements of case, but should not be used to send letters or documents of a routine or non-urgent nature to court (PD 5, para 5.3(8)).

As a general rule a fax should not be used, except in an unavoidable emergency, to deliver the following:

(a) a document which attracts a court fee;

(b) a Part 36 payment notice;

(c) a document relating to a hearing less than two hours ahead; or

(d) trial bundles or skeleton arguments (PD 5, para 5.3(9)).

In the case of a document which attracts a court fee or a Part 36 payment notice, the fax should explain the nature of the emergency and include an undertaking that the fee or money has been dispatched that day by post, or will be paid at the court office counter the following business day (PD 5, para 5.3(10)).

The date of filing will be recorded on the document by the court office (PD 5, para 5.3(4)). On filing, particulars such as the date of delivery at the court and the title of the proceedings will be entered in the court records (PD 5, para 5.2).

Filing by email

A pilot scheme has been introduced, operating from 2 December 2002 to 31 January 2004, allowing parties to claims in Walsall County Court and Preston County Court and district registry to communicate with the court and file specified documents at court by email (PD 5B, paras 1.1, 1.2).

In summary, parties to proceedings in the participating courts may file specified documents at court and send general correspondence and inquiries to the court by email. The documents specified include a notice of acting by a solicitor, an acknowledgment of service and a defence (see the full list of documents at PD 5B, para 2.2). However, it should be noted that the specified documents do not include the claim form, or any other document on which a fee is payable on filing, except an application notice for which special provisions apply (PD 5B, paras 2.1, 7.1). The practice direction contains detailed information as to requirements for the format and contents of the email (PD 5B, paras 3.1–3.5).

Where a party files a document by email, he must not send a hard copy in addition (PD 5B, para 4.1). The document is not filed until the email is received by the court, and if it is received after 4 pm it will be treated as filed on the next day the court office is open (PD 5B, paras 4.2, 4.4).

If a document must be verified by a statement of truth, the requirement is satisfied for documents filed by email by that person typing his name underneath the statement of truth. However, the statement of truth must still be signed in manuscript in any hard copies of the document served on other parties (PD 5B, para 5.2).

If a party files a document by email he must still comply with any rule or practice direction requiring the document to be served on any other person (PD 5B, para 2.3).

Court documents sealed on issue

When the court issues the claim form it will place the court seal on it (r 2.6(1)(a)). The seal is placed on a document either by hand, or by printing a facsimile of the seal on the document, whether electronically or otherwise (r 2.6(2)).

The court will place the seal on any other document it is required to under any rule or practice direction when it issues the document (r 2.6(1)(b)).

CHAPTER 3

LIMITATION PERIODS

INTRODUCTION

If a person has grounds to bring proceedings against another person, they have a limited period of time within which to do so, which varies according to the nature of the cause of action out of which the right to bring proceedings arises. The time limits for bringing proceedings are entirely statutory and most are contained in the Limitation Act (LA) 1980.

Although the periods of time are relatively long, a balance is struck between a person's right to sue another to establish a right, to recover a loss or for harm caused and the right not to be perpetually exposed to the risk of litigation. It is also true that after long periods of time evidence to rebut a claim may no longer be available to a defendant, and so it is felt to be in the public interest that a person with a good cause of action should be compelled to pursue it within a reasonable period (see *dicta* of Lord Millett in *Cave v Robinson Jarvis & Rolf (A Firm)* [2002] UKHL 18 at [6]).

If proceedings are brought outside of these periods they will not be a nullity, it being incumbent on the defendant to plead a defence based on expiry of the limitation period for that cause of action (see *Dismore v Milton* [1938] 3 All ER 762, CA). The defendant is required to give details in his defence showing that the limitation period has expired (PD 16, para 13.1). Thus, the court cannot strike out proceedings because it appears to the court that the limitation period has expired, if the point is not taken by the defendant. However, there is nothing to stop the court pointing out the apparent expiry to the parties. Where a limitation period has expired, the proceedings are often referred to as 'statute-barred' in reference to the fact that the defendant will have a complete defence under the LA 1980.

For some types of proceedings, such as certain personal injury claims, the court has a discretion to disapply the limitation period and allow the claim to continue (see pp 35–36 below, 'Discretion to disapply limitation period'). On the other hand, for other types of claim such as proceedings to recover unregistered land, or a claim based on defective products brought under the Consumer Protection Act 1987, the cause of action will be extinguished and not just statute-barred, following the expiry of the limitation period (see p 30 below, 'Claims to recover land', and pp 37–38 below, 'Defective products').

Time when proceedings are brought

Proceedings are brought when the court issues a claim form at the request of the claimant (r 7.2(1)). However, if the claim form is received at the court office on a date earlier than that on which it was issued, the claim is brought on that earlier date for the purposes of the LA 1980 (PD 7, para 5.1).

TIME LIMITS

The LA 1980 is divided into two parts. Part I gives the 'ordinary' time limits for claims (often referred to as the primary limitation period), that is, a basic limitation period within which proceedings should be commenced. Part II deals with the circumstances in which the ordinary time limits can be extended or excluded for certain causes of action.

CONTRACT AND TORT

Contract

The time limit for bringing a claim based on simple contract is six years from the date on which the cause of action accrued (s 5 of the LA 1980).

Simple contracts

A simple contract is a contract that is not a contract of record or a contract under seal, for example, a contract for the provision of goods or services.

Contracts under seal

In the case of a contract under seal (for example, a deed) or other speciality, the time limit for bringing a claim is 12 years from the date on which the cause of action accrued (s 8 of the LA 1980).

Tort

The time limit for bringing a claim based in tort is six years from the date on which the cause of action accrued (s 2 of the LA 1980). However, certain claims based on tort have different limitation periods, for example, personal injury claims based on negligence, nuisance or breach of duty.

Latent damage

A separate limitation period applies to negligence claims, except for personal injury claims, where the damage caused by the negligence is latent. In such cases, the limitation period runs either six years from the date on which the cause of action accrued, or three years from the date when the claimant had the right to bring a claim and knowledge of certain facts if those are discovered later (s 14A(4) and (5) of the LA 1980).

Knowledge under s 14A is defined in a similar way to that under s 14 in respect of personal injury and death claims, covering such matters as knowledge of the identity of the defendant, that the damage was caused by the defendant's negligence, and that the damage was sufficiently serious to justify instituting proceedings against the defendant.

Negligence claims based on latent damage which fall under the above provisions are subject to a long-stop period of 15 years from the date of the negligent act or omission which is alleged to have caused the damage (s 14B of the LA 1980).

Section 14A does not apply where the claim is based solely on contract (*Société Commerciale de Réassurance v ERAS (International) Ltd* [1992] 2 All ER 82). However, where there is concurrent liability in contract and tort, for instance, in cases of professional negligence, the claimant can frame his case in tort in order to take advantage of the latent damage provisions (*Henderson v Merrett Syndicates Ltd* [1994] 3 WLR 761, HL).

Also, a subsequent owner of property is entitled to rely on the alternative limitation period of three years from the date of knowledge if the property is disposed of before the damage is discovered by the original owner. The three years run from the date when the subsequent owner acquires an interest in the property (s 3(1) of the Latent Damage Act 1976). However, the primary limitation period of six years and the 15-year long-stop period run from the date when the damage occurred.

Date when cause of action accrues

In a claim based on contract, the cause of action accrues from the date of breach of the contract, even if damage is not suffered until a later date (*Gibbs v Gibbs* (1881) 8 QBD 296).

For the type of tort that is established only if damage occurs, such as in negligence claims, the cause of action accrues from the date of damage (*Pirelli General Cable Works Ltd v Oscar Faber and Partners (A Firm)* [1983] 1 All ER 65, HL). For the cause of action to accrue, therefore, there must be some actual damage caused by the negligent act which is recoverable at law and not too remote (see *Forster v Outred and Co* [1982] 1 WLR 86; *Nykredit Mortgage Bank plc v Edward Erdman Group Ltd (No 2)* [1997] 1 WLR 1627). However, the cause of action will accrue and time starts running as soon as some damage has occurred, even if separate loss subsequently occurs which is much more serious than the original damage (*Knapp v Ecclesiastical Insurance Group plc* [1998] PNLR 172).

In *Knapp*, the claimants had a fire at their home on 16 October 1990. They were insured with the first defendants and had renewed their policy on 12 April 1990 through brokers, the second defendants, who the claimants alleged knew all material facts and completed the proposal form on their behalf. The first defendants avoided the policy on the grounds of non-disclosure of material facts. On 16 October 1996, the claimants issued a claim against both defendants. The Court of Appeal held that the claim against the second defendants, the brokers, was issued outside the limitation period because the cause of action against them accrued on 12 April 1990 when the claimants suffered loss due to the second defendant's negligence, as the policy renewed on that date was voidable for non-disclosure. The court held this to be the case even though more serious loss arising from that negligence arose only when the claimants subsequently suffered a fire at their home.

This principle was reinforced in the Court of Appeal decision of *Malik Khan v RM Falvey* [2002] EWCA Civ 400, where the claimant brought a claim for professional negligence against his former solicitor for allowing claims he was pursuing to be struck out for want of prosecution. The limitation period for the claims which had been struck out had clearly expired, but the issue was whether the claimant was entitled to recover damages from his former solicitor for the loss of opportunity to pursue those claims, or whether that claim was also statute-barred. The answer to this all depended on when the cause of action against the former solicitor arose, and this in turn depended on when actual damage first occurred. The Court of Appeal held that damage occurred when there was a serious risk that the original claim could be dismissed for want of prosecution, as this would diminish the value of the claimant's original claim and the cause of action would therefore run from that date rather than the later date when the claim was actually struck out. As the risk of dismissal for want of prosecution was found to have occurred more than six years before the claimant began his claim against his former solicitor, his claim was held to be statute-barred. The decision in *Khan* was followed by the Court of Appeal in *Anthony Arthur Hatton v Messrs Chafes (A Firm)* [2003] EWCA Civ 341.

Where negligence results in an allegedly unfavourable contract, the six-year limitation period will start to run at the date of the contract if it can be shown that the claimant has suffered relevant and measurable damage at that date. This rule was confirmed in *McCarroll v Statham Gill Davis (A Firm)* (2002) LTL, 28 November, QBD, in which it was alleged that a recording contract negotiated on behalf of the group 'Oasis' created a conflict of interest because it was more favourable to the Gallagher brothers than to the other members of the band.

If the tort is actionable without proof of damage, such as in the case of intentional trespass, the cause of action accrues on the date the tort was committed (*Granger v George* (1826) 5 B & C 149).

Equitable remedies

The time limits under the LA 1980 do not apply to any claim for specific performance of a contract, an injunction or any other equitable relief, except in so far as the court may apply any time limit by analogy (s 36(1) of the LA 1980). Instead, the court applies equitable principles such as laches and acquiescence when deciding whether to refuse to grant such remedies, and the Act does not interfere with the court's equitable jurisdiction to do so (s 36(2) of the LA 1980).

OTHER CAUSES OF ACTION

Special time limit for claims in respect of certain loans

In the case of a contract of loan which does not provide for the repayment of the debt on or before a fixed or determinable date, and which does not make repayment conditional on a demand for repayment, the cause of action to recover the debt will run from the date on which a written demand for repayment is made, and not from the date the contract of loan was made (s 6(1), (2) and (3) of the LA 1980). This provision is meant to cover the making of loans between family and friends, although it is not limited to such circumstances.

Acknowledgment or part payment of debts

In the case of a claim to recover a debt or other liquidated pecuniary claim, if the person liable to repay it makes any payment in respect of it, or makes an acknowledgment of the claim in writing and signed by him, the cause of action to recover the money will be treated as running from the date of the acknowledgment or part payment and not before (ss 29 and 30 of the LA 1980).

Although the limitation period may be repeatedly extended by further acknowledgments or payments, once the limitation period has expired it will not be revived by any subsequent acknowledgment or payment (s 29(7) of the LA 1980).

Sums recoverable by statute

If a sum of money is recovered by virtue of any statute, it shall not be recoverable after the expiration of six years from the date on which the cause of action accrued (s 9 of the LA 1980).

Conversion

A claim for conversion, being a claim in tort, must be brought within six years from the date the cause of action accrued (s 2 of the LA 1980). The owner's title in the converted goods is extinguished if the goods are not recovered within the time limit for bringing a claim (s 3(2) of the LA 1980). If goods are converted and, before the owner recovers possession, a further act of conversion takes place, the limitation period of six years runs from the date of the original conversion (s 3(1) of the LA 1980).

Theft

If goods are stolen rather than converted, the limitation periods under ss 2 and 3 of the LA 1980 do not apply and there is no limitation on the period within which the owner of the goods can bring a claim to recover the goods from the thief. If goods are stolen and then disposed of to someone who is not a purchaser in good faith, the owner can bring a claim against the thief and/or the person to whom the goods are disposed without limitation as to time. If goods are stolen and then sold to someone who purchases them in good faith, the owner will not be able to bring a claim against the purchaser after the expiry of six years following the purchase, although the right to bring a claim against the thief will continue without limitation as to time. However, if goods are converted and then subsequently stolen by another person, the owner will not be able to bring a claim against either the person who converted the goods or the thief after the expiry of six years following the conversion (s 4 of the LA 1980).

Defamation or malicious falsehood

A claim for libel, slander or malicious falsehood must be brought within one year from the date on which the cause of action accrued (s 4A of the LA 1980).

The court has a discretion, if it appears equitable to do so, to allow such a claim to proceed notwithstanding the expiry of the one-year limitation period (s 32A of the LA 1980). See *Oyston v Blaker* [1996] 2 All ER 106 for an example of the exercise of this discretion.

Claim for a contribution

Under s 1 of the Civil Liability (Contribution) Act 1978, any person liable in respect of any damage suffered by another person may recover a contribution from any other person liable in respect of the same damage (whether jointly liable or otherwise). A claim for a contribution must be brought within two years of the date on which the right accrues (s 10(1) of the LA 1980). In the case of proceedings that result in judgment, the right to claim a contribution accrues from the date of the judgment (s 10(3) of the LA 1980). In the case of an agreement to provide compensation, without judgment being obtained, the right to claim a contribution accrues from the date the agreement is made (s 10(4) of the LA 1980).

Claims to recover land

Under the current law a claim to recover land, whether registered or unregistered, must be brought within 12 years from the date the cause of action accrued (s 15 of the LA 1980). Therefore, if an owner allows a squatter to be in possession of land for at least 12 years, he will lose his right to recover the property from the squatter, who will have acquired title to the land by means of adverse possession (see *Pye v Graham* [2002] UKHL 30, which provides an authoritative definition of the meaning of adverse possession). In the case of unregistered land, at the expiration of the limitation period the owner's title will be extinguished (s 17 of the LA 1980). In the case of registered land, at the expiration of the limitation period the title is not extinguished but the registered proprietor is deemed to hold the land thereafter on trust for the squatter (s 75(1) of the Land Registration Act 1925). The squatter can then apply to be registered as proprietor of that estate.

The current position changed on the coming into force of ss 96–98 of and Sched 6 to the Land Registration Act 2002 on 13 October 2003. The purpose of those provisions is to make it more difficult for a squatter to obtain title, at least in relation to registered land. They will not affect the position regarding unregistered land. In summary, a new mechanism will apply enabling a squatter to apply to be registered as proprietor after 10 years of adverse possession. However, the registered proprietor (and other interested persons) will be notified by the Land Registry of the squatter's application and effectively have a two-year period within which to oppose the squatter's application for title and bring proceedings to recover possession of the property, if necessary. If the registered proprietor fails to take possession proceedings within that two-year period and the squatter remains in adverse possession, he will be entitled to apply once again to be registered and this time will succeed, whether or not the registered proprietor objects.

Claims to recover sums due under a mortgage or charge

There is a 12-year limitation period for the recovery of any *principal* sum of money due under a mortgage or other charge on property, or to recover the proceeds of the sale of land, for example, under a trust for sale (s 20(1) of the LA 1980).

In *Bristol & West v Bartlett* [2002] EWCA Civ 1181, the Court of Appeal confirmed that when a mortgagee has repossessed and exercised his power of sale, if he issues any proceedings to recover any shortfall from the security, the claim arises from the mortgage document by which the mortgage was created and is therefore governed by the 12-year limitation period specified in s 20 rather than the six-year period provided by s 5 for simple contract claims (see p 26 above, 'Contract').

However, a six-year limitation period is specified for the recovery of any *interest* due under a mortgage or charge (s 20(5) of the LA 1980), and the Court of Appeal confirmed in the *Bartlett* case that this six-year period applies to such claims, and not the 12-year period under s 8, even though the mortgage is likely to be contained within a deed or other speciality.

Claims to recover rent

A claim to recover arrears of rent, or damages in respect of arrears of rent, must be brought within six years from the date on which the arrears became due (s 19 of the LA 1980).

Claims to redeem a mortgage

The mortgagor's legal or equitable right to redeem the mortgage is barred if the mortgagee remains in possession of the mortgaged land for 12 years or more without giving any written acknowledgment of the title of the mortgagor or of his equity of redemption and without receiving any payment on account of principal or interest made by or on behalf of the mortgagor (s 16 of the LA 1980). In the case of unregistered land, after the limitation period has expired the mortgagor's title will be extinguished (s 17 of the LA 1980); in the case of registered land, the mortgagor will hold the land on trust for the mortgagee (s 75(1) of the Land Registration Act 1925).

Claims in respect of trust property

A claim by a beneficiary to recover trust property or in respect of any breach of trust must be brought within six years from the date on which the cause of action accrued (s 21(3) of the LA 1980).

However, no period of limitation under the Act will apply where the claim by the beneficiary under the trust is in respect of any fraud or fraudulent breach of trust to which the trustee was a party or was privy to, or where the trustee has converted trust property to his own use (s 21(1) of the LA 1980).

Claims to enforce a judgment

A claim to enforce a judgment must be brought within six years from the date on which the judgment became enforceable (s 24(1) of the LA 1980).

It should be noted that in *Lowsley v Forbes (t/a Le Design Services)* [1998] 3 All ER 897, HL, it was held that the word 'action' (now 'claim') does not include processes of execution, which are procedural matters. However, leave is often required to issue such processes of execution where more than six years have elapsed since the judgment was obtained.

Under Civil Procedure Rules (CPR Sched 1) RSC Ord 46, r 2, and CPR Sched 2 CCR Ord 26, r 5, it is necessary to obtain the court's permission to issue a warrant of execution where more than six years have elapsed between obtaining judgment and attempting to enforce it. Indeed, in *Patel v Singh* [2002] All ER (D) 227, CA, it was held that the judgment creditor must show that there are extraordinary circumstances to justify the granting of permission to issue a warrant where more than six years have elapsed. In that case the claimant applied for a writ of execution seven and a half years after default judgment. Permission was refused as there were no exceptional circumstances justifying the delay.

However, although procedural steps to execute a judgment may be taken more than six years after the judgment was obtained, arrears of interest accruing in respect of any judgment debt are not recoverable more than six years after the date on which the interest became due (s 24(2) of the LA 1980).

For the purposes of enforcing an order for costs, the limitation period under s 24 of the LA 1980 begins to run only from the date that the costs have been certified (on assessment) and not from the date when the order for costs is made, because at that date the amount of costs had not yet been ascertained and there would therefore be no sum of which to enforce payment (*Times Newspapers v Chohan* [2001] 1 WLR 1859).

PERSONAL INJURY AND DEATH CLAIMS

Personal injury claims

A claim brought for damages which consist of or include damages in respect of personal injuries to the claimant or any other person, whether the claim is based on negligence, nuisance or breach of duty, must be brought within three years from either:

(a) the date on which the cause of action accrued; or

(b) the date of knowledge (if later) of the person injured (s 11(1), (3) and (4) of the LA 1980).

Time limits if person suffering personal injuries dies

If a person suffering personal injuries caused by another person's negligence, nuisance or breach of duty dies from those injuries, two independent causes of action potentially will arise. One is the injured person's own cause of action for his personal injuries, which may be brought following his death on behalf of his estate under the Law Reform (Miscellaneous Provisions) Act 1934. The other is an entirely separate cause of action which can be brought by the deceased's dependants for financial loss caused by the death under the Fatal Accidents Act 1976.

Claim on behalf of the estate

If the person injured dies before the time limit for bringing a personal injury claim expires, the time limit within which a claim must be brought on behalf of his estate under s 1 of the Law Reform (Miscellaneous Provisions) Act 1934 is three years from either:

(a) the date of death; or

(b) the date of the personal representative's knowledge,

whichever is later (s 11(5) of the LA 1980).

Claim by dependants

For a claim to be brought by the dependants it is necessary that the circumstances of the death are such that the deceased himself could have brought a claim against the person responsible had he not died.

The time limit within which a claim must be brought by the dependants under s 1 of the Fatal Accidents Act 1976 is three years from either:

(a) the date of death; or

(b) the date of knowledge of the dependant,

whichever is later (s 12(2) of the LA 1980).

Where there are two or more dependants, the time limit under s 12(2) of the LA 1980 is applied separately for each person, such that the court will direct that any dependant for whom the claim would be outside the time limit shall be excluded from bringing a claim (s 13 of the LA 1980).

Breach of duty

The words 'breach of duty' refer to a breach of a duty not to cause personal injury to a person, rather than breach of an obligation not to infringe another person's legal rights (*Stubbings v Webb* [1993] 1 All ER 322). Therefore, damages for personal injuries arising from claims for trespass to the person, false imprisonment, malicious prosecution or defamation of character would be claims for tort under s 2 of the LA 1980 and subject to a six-year limitation period from the date of accrual of the cause of action, rather than claims under s 11 and subject to a three-year limitation period from the date of accrual of the cause of action or the date of knowledge if that is later. This also means that there is no discretion to disapply the limitation period in the case of personal injury claims based on intentional harm.

Date of knowledge

The date of knowledge is defined in s 14 of the LA 1980 as the date on which the injured person had knowledge of all of the following facts:

(a) that the injury was significant; and

(b) that the injury was attributable, in whole or in part, to the action or omission of the proposed defendant which is alleged to constitute the negligence, nuisance or breach of duty;

(c) the identity of the defendant; and

(d) if it is alleged that the act or omission was that of a person other than the defendant, the identity of that person and the additional facts supporting the bringing of a claim against the defendant.

However, knowledge that the act or omission in question amounted as a matter of law to negligence, nuisance or breach of duty is irrelevant (s 14 of the LA 1980).

Knowledge

A person's 'knowledge' is not entirely subjective, as it includes knowledge a person would reasonably have been expected to acquire from facts observable or ascertainable by him, or from facts ascertainable with the help of medical or other appropriate expert advice that it is reasonable for him to seek (s 14(3) of the LA 1980).

In the case of *Rowbottom v Royal Masonic Hospital* [2002] EWCA Civ 87, the claimant suffered an infection following an operation, which resulted in him having his left leg amputated. The issue was the date of the claimant's knowledge that failure to administer antibiotics was the cause of his injury. The Court of Appeal found that the claimant had knowledge of that omission only when his expert confirmed in a second medical report that since the claimant's medical records showed no sign of antibiotics being administered the likelihood was that none were administered. The claimant was not fixed with knowledge at an earlier date, when his expert had advised in his first report that failure to administer antibiotics was a possible cause but had gone on to say that he had no knowledge of whether or not antibiotics had been administered.

The court described this as a 'borderline case', because the absence of any mention of antibiotics in the medical record would normally have been sufficient to support an inference that none had been given and it would not be necessary to seek expert medical opinion in order to be in a position to make such an inference. However, in the circumstances of this case, in particular the fact that the claimant mistakenly believed that antibiotics had been administered to him after his operation, the claimant's knowledge would not be fixed until the date he received the expert's second report.

However, s 14(3) goes on to provide that a person will not be fixed with knowledge of a fact ascertainable only with the help of expert advice so long as he has taken all reasonable steps to obtain and, where appropriate, act on that advice. Therefore, in the case of *Ali v Courtaulds Textiles Ltd* (1999) *The Times*, 28 May, where the claimant sought a medical opinion as to whether his deafness was noise-induced or age-induced, it was held that the claimant would not be fixed with the knowledge that his deafness was noise-induced at the time that he was aware of his deafness, as the issue as to the cause of his deafness was ascertainable only by means of expert advice, which it was not only reasonable but essential for him to obtain.

Significant injury

A significant injury is defined as one that a person would reasonably consider to be sufficiently serious to justify him instituting proceedings for damages against a defendant who did not dispute liability and was able to satisfy a judgment (s 14(2) of the LA 1980).

Injury caused by defendant

It is enough that the person knows that the injuries complained of were caused by the act or omission of the proposed defendant; it is not necessary to know that they were caused by the *fault or negligence* of the defendant (*Dobbie v Medway HA* [1994] 1 WLR 235). In *Dobbie*, the claimant had her breast removed on the assumption that a lump was cancerous, when further investigation would have revealed that the lump was benign. The personal injury claimed was the removal of the claimant's breast and the psychological and physical harm that that caused. The claimant was aware of the injury shortly after the operation and reasonably considered it to be significant. She also knew that this personal injury was a direct result of an act or omission by the defendant health authority. The Court of Appeal therefore held that under s 14 of the LA 1980, time started to run from the time that she became aware of all of these matters and not from the later time when she became aware that the health authority's act in carrying out the operation was allegedly negligent or blameworthy.

Restoring a company to facilitate a personal injury claim

The court has power under s 651 of the Companies Act 1985 to restore a dissolved company to enable a claimant to bring a personal injury claim against the company, for example, in order to take advantage of any insurance it may have had at the relevant time. The effect of a restoration is as though the dissolution never happened, so the normal limitation period applies. However, the court also has power under s 651 to make a declaration that the period between dissolution and restoration be disregarded for limitation purposes. In *Smith v White Knight Laundry* [2001] EWCA Civ 660, the Court of Appeal laid down guidelines for the making of such a declaration:

(a) Such a direction should normally be made only if:
- notice has been served on all parties who may be expected to oppose it – including the company's insurers;
- the court is satisfied that it has all the evidence that the parties would wish to adduce on an application under s 33 of the LA 1980 (disapplying the normal three-year period); and
- such an application would be bound to succeed.

(b) If these conditions are not met the applicant should seek relief under s 33 of the LA 1980.

Discretion to disapply limitation period

For personal injury and death claims under ss 11 and 12 of the LA 1980, the court has a wide discretion to disapply the limitation period so that a claim can be brought even though the limitation period has expired if it appears equitable to the court to allow the claim to proceed (s 33(1) of the LA 1980). The court balances the prejudice that would be suffered by the claimant if it decided to hold that the limitation period should apply against the prejudice that would be suffered by the defendant if the court decided to disapply the limitation period (s 33(1) of the LA 1980).

Although the claim on behalf of the estate or a dependant's claim will be statute-barred if the injured person's claim was statute-barred at the time of his death, the court has a discretion to disapply the limitation period under s 33 of the LA 1980 for the benefit of the estate or the dependants (ss 12(3) and 33 of the LA 1980).

It is only in those personal injury or death claims arising from negligence, nuisance or breach of duty where the court has a discretion to disapply the limitation period; the court has no discretion to disapply the limitation period for other types of personal injury claims, such as those arising from intentional trespass to the person (*Stubbings v Webb* [1993] 1 All ER 322).

In *Stubbings v Webb*, the applicant had suffered sexual abuse whilst a child and wished to bring a claim against her abusers for the psychological problems she suffered as a consequence of the abuse. It was accepted that although the applicant had always remembered that she had been abused, she did not realise that she had suffered sufficiently serious injury to justify bringing a claim until she was in her 30s and through therapy came to understand the causal link between the assaults and her mental health problems. However, the House of Lords held that the words 'breach of duty' in s 11(1) of the LA 1980 did not include actions based on intentionally inflicted injuries such as rape and indecent assault. Instead, such actions of intentional trespass were subject to the six-year limitation period provided for in s 2, which the court had no power to disapply. In the applicant's case, because she was a child at the time of the assaults, the limitation period was extended for six years from the date of her 18th birthday, but, as she did not start proceedings until she was in her 30s, her claim was therefore out of time.

It is important that personal injury lawyers do not overlook the three-year limitation period, which may expire while negotiations are in progress. The defendant will be estopped from raising a limitation defence only if he has made an unequivocal and unambiguous promise that he does not intend to enforce his strict legal rights. Thus, in the case of *Seechurn v Ace Insurance SA NV* [2002] EWCA Civ 67, a mere invitation to the claimant to provide further medical evidence (made while the limitation period was still running) was held not sufficient to create an estoppel. As stated by Ward LJ (at [58]): 'To assert that the door to compromising the claim was still open was not impliedly to promise that a limitation point would not be taken if the negotiations failed and the proceedings started out of time.'

Matters the court will take into account when deciding whether to disapply the limitation period

The court will take all the circumstances into account when deciding whether to disapply the limitation period, and in particular it will take into account the matters specified in s 33(3) of the LA 1980. These include:

(a) the length of and reasons for the claimant's delay in bringing proceedings;

(b) the effect the delay is likely to have on the evidence;

(c) the conduct of the defendant since the cause of action arose in co-operating with any requests from the claimant to provide information or access for inspection of property;

(d) the duration of any disability (that is, a child or a person with a mental disorder) of the claimant since the cause of action arose;

(e) whether the claimant acted reasonably and promptly once he was aware that he had a good cause of action against the defendant; and

(f) the steps (if any) the claimant took to obtain medical, legal or other expert advice, and the nature of any such advice he received.

When considering the relative prejudice to the parties, the court can take into account in deciding not to disapply the limitation period the fact that the claimant has a good cause of action against his legal advisers for failing to commence proceedings in time. However, although the existence of such a remedy is a highly relevant factor, this has to be offset by the fact that such a person would be prejudiced to some degree by having to bring a fresh claim in negligence against his solicitor, as his advisers will be aware of all the difficulties and weaknesses with his personal injury claim (*Thompson v Brown Construction (Ebbw Vale) Ltd and Others* [1981] 2 All ER 296, HL).

Second claim brought after the limitation period has expired

If a claimant brings a personal injury or death claim which for any reason is struck out or discontinued and the limitation period expires, the court will not exercise its discretion under s 33 of the LA 1980 to disapply the limitation period in order to allow the second claim to go ahead (*Walkley v Precision Forgings Ltd* [1979] 2 All ER 548, HL), apart from where there are exceptional circumstances (*White v Glass* (1989) *The Times*, 18 February, CA). The rationale for this rule is that the claimant was not prejudiced by the limitation period because he was able to bring his first claim within time; rather, he was prejudiced by his own, or his legal adviser's, delay in prosecuting his claim.

Defective products

The Consumer Protection Act 1987 introduced strict liability (that is, liability without proof of negligence) for damage caused by defective products in order to implement the EU Directive on liability for defective products (Directive 85/374/EC). A special limitation period applies to claims brought under the Consumer Protection Act (s 11A of the LA 1980). In the case of claims for personal injury, or death or damage to property (other than to the defective product itself), the same limitation period of three years applies as under s 11 and s 12 of the Act (s 11A(4) and (5) of the LA 1980).

Section 11A(3) of the LA 1980 provides that there shall be a long-stop period of 10 years from the date that the product was supplied to the consumer within which to bring a claim under the Consumer Protection Act 1987. A long-stop period applies as the preamble to the Directive recognises that it would not be reasonable to make a producer liable for defects in products for an unlimited period of time, because products age, higher safety standards develop, and the state of science and technology progresses over the course of time.

Further, s 11A(3) of the LA 1980 provides that the cause of action shall be extinguished, rather than simply becoming 'statute-barred', once this 10-year period has expired. This long-stop period is absolute, and once it has expired it overrides the court's power to disapply the limitation period for personal injury and death claims under s 33 of the LA 1980, the extension of the limitation period under s 28 of the LA 1980 in cases of disability, and the postponement of the limitation period under s 32 of the LA 1980 where there has been deliberate concealment of facts.

However, the long-stop period does not override the court's power to substitute a defendant after the expiry of the limitation period (*SmithKline Beecham plc v Horne-Roberts* [2001] EWCA Civ 2006). In that case the claimant, who was vaccinated against measles, mumps and rubella (MMR), alleged that due to defects in the vaccine he had become autistic. At the time MMR vaccines were manufactured by three pharmaceutical companies, including SmithKline Beecham. The claimant's solicitors correctly identified the batch number of the vaccine as No 108A41A, but mistakenly attributed it to Merck, one of the other two pharmaceutical companies manufacturing the vaccine, and therefore commenced proceedings against the wrong defendant. However, the claimant's solicitors were notified of their mistake, and that SmithKline Beecham were the manufacturers of the claimant's vaccine, only after the limitation period under s 11A(3) had expired. The claimant applied under r 19.5 to substitute SmithKline Beecham as the defendant to its proceedings.

Rule 19.5 is governed by s 35(6) of the LA 1980, which allows, where it is necessary, for a new party to be substituted for a party whose name was given by mistake, after the expiry of the limitation period. The Court of Appeal held that the claimant was entitled to rely on that provision and amend the name of the defendant to Smithkline Beecham, because although the claimant wrongly named the manufacturer as Merck, his intention was always to sue the person meeting a particular description specific to his case, namely, the manufacturer of vaccine batch No 108A41A.

TIME LIMITS FOR CHILDREN AND PATIENTS

If the person to whom the cause of action accrues is under a disability, that is, is a child (a person under 18) or a patient (a person who, by reason of a mental disorder within the meaning of the Mental Health Act 1983, is incapable of managing and administering his own affairs), the limitation period runs from the date when the child dies or comes of age, or the patient dies or recovers from his mental disorder, even if the ordinary limitation period for that cause of action has already expired (s 28 of the LA 1980). Therefore if a six-year-old child is injured in an accident caused by the negligence of the defendant, the limitation period is extended by three years from the date the child reaches the age of 18.

Section 28 of the LA 1980 applies only where the person is under a disability at the time the cause of action accrues. It would not apply if after the limitation period had started to run, a person became under a disability.

The extended limitation period is subject to a long-stop period of 30 years for a claim to recover land or money charged on land, from the date on which the cause of action accrued (s 28(4) of the LA 1980).

Also, for claims under the Consumer Protection Act 1987, this extension of limitation periods for children and patients will not override the long-stop period of 10 years prescribed by s 11A(3) of the LA 1980, which runs from the time the defective product was supplied (s 28(7) of the LA 1980). Nor will it override the long-stop period of 15 years in the case of latent damage in negligence claims, prescribed by s 14B (s 28A) of the LA 1980.

EXTENSION OF THE LIMITATION PERIOD IN CASES OF FRAUD, CONCEALMENT OR MISTAKE

In the case of a cause of action where:

(a) the claim is based upon the fraud of the defendant (s 32(1)(a) of the LA 1980);

(b) any fact relevant to the claimant's cause of action has been deliberately concealed from the claimant by the defendant (s 32(1)(b) of the LA 1980); or

(c) the claim is for relief from the consequences of a mistake (s 32(1)(c) of the LA 1980),

the limitation period shall not begin to run until the claimant has discovered the fraud, concealment or mistake, or could with reasonable diligence have discovered it (see *Peco Arts Inc v Hazlitt Gallery Ltd* [1983] 1 WLR 1315 for a definition of reasonable diligence). Lord Millett stated in *Cave v Robinson Jarvis & Rolf (A Firm)* [2002] UKHL 18 at [7]: 'In common justice a [claimant] ought not to find that his action is statute-barred before he has had a reasonable opportunity to bring it.'

An analysis of s 32(1)(b) of the LA 1980 requires the court to establish first what facts are relevant to a claimant's cause of action and then whether any one of them has been deliberately concealed from the claimant by the defendant. In such a case, the claimant must have been ignorant of the relevant facts during the period preceding the alleged concealment; if he knew of them, no subsequent act of the defendant can have amounted to 'concealment' (*Ezekiel v Lehrer* [2002] EWCA Civ 16, CA).

In *Sheldon v RHM Outhwaite Ltd* [1995] 2 All ER 558, the House of Lords held, by a majority ruling, that where there was deliberate concealment by the defendant of facts relevant to the claimant's cause of action, s 32(1)(b) of the LA 1980 would postpone the running of time regardless of whether the concealment took place at the same time as the accrual of the cause of action or at a later date. In reaching this decision the House of Lords overturned the decision of the Court of Appeal, but in doing so it recognised that its decision was not without difficulty as the words of s 32(1) of the LA 1980, 'the limitation period shall not begin to run', would not seem to apply to the situation where the limitation period had already started running prior to the act of deliberate concealment by the defendant (at 565g–h, *per* Lord Keith).

Deliberate concealment of facts/deliberate breach of duty

Deliberate commission of a breach of duty in circumstances where it is unlikely to be discovered for some time amounts to deliberate concealment of the facts involved in that breach of duty (s 32(2) of the LA 1980). The long-stop period of 15 years prescribed for latent damages claims in negligence does not apply where there has been deliberate concealment of facts by the defendant relevant to the claimant's cause of action. Instead, the claimant will have six years to commence proceedings from the time he discovers the concealment, or from the time he could with reasonable diligence have discovered it (s 32(5) of the LA 1980).

In *Cave v Robinson Jarvis & Rolf (A Firm)*, the House of Lords clarified the circumstances in which s 32(2) of the LA 1980 will apply. In that case, the claimant, Mr Cave, wished to bring an action in professional negligence against the dependants, his solicitors, Robinson Jarvis & Rolf, arising out of a transaction completed in March 1989. The claimant alleged that the defendants had negligently failed to ensure that he obtained a proprietary interest in mooring rights that would be binding on successors in title. In February 1994, when the company that granted him the rights went into receivership, the claimant was informed by the receivers that his rights were no longer exercisable. The claimant did not contact the defendants until November 1995. He subsequently contacted the defendants on a number of occasions in 1996 but received no answer to his letters; he then consulted other solicitors who issued proceedings against the defendants on 16 January 1998.

The primary limitation period for the negligence action expired in March 1995, as the claimant suffered loss in March 1989 by the defendants' negligent failure to ensure that the mooring rights were proprietary rather than contractual in nature. However, the claimant alleged that the negligent drafting of the agreement fell within s 32(2) of the LA 1980 because, it being an intentional act, it was a breach of duty which in the circumstances was unlikely to be discovered by the claimant for some time. The claimant therefore argued that he had begun his claim within the six-year limitation period for negligence actions because time did not begin to run until he discovered, or could with reasonable diligence have discovered, the breach, which in this case was not until February 1994.

The House of Lords held that in order to show deliberate concealment of facts under s 32(1)(b) of the LA 1980, the claimant must show that some fact relevant to his right of action has been concealed from him either by a positive act of concealment, or by a withholding of relevant information, but in either case with the *intention* of concealing the fact in question. This is the case notwithstanding that proving an omission, rather than a positive act, is often very difficult to do.

Accordingly, in this case the claimant was unable to establish that the mere failure to answer his letters constituted deliberate concealment of facts. The House of Lords recognised that s 32(2) of the LA 1980 was enacted to cover cases where proof of active concealment should not be required. However, their Lordships stressed that such cases were limited in two respects: first, the defendant must have been guilty of a *deliberate* commission of a breach of duty; and, secondly, the circumstances must make it unlikely that the breach of duty will be discovered for some time. The classic example is deliberately putting in bad foundations to a house (see the judgment of Lord Denning MR in *King v Victor Parsons & Co* [1973] 1 WLR 29, 33–34). In these circumstances the defendants would not therefore be deprived of a limitation defence because they had simply been negligent and, being unaware of their error or failure to take proper care, had nothing to disclose to the claimant.

In reaching this decision the House of Lords held that *Liverpool Roman Catholic Archdiocese Trustees Inc v Goldberg* [2001] 1 All ER 182 was wrongly decided, and that in so far as *Brocklesby v Armitage & Guest* [2002] 1 WLR 598 held that a defendant's actions could be brought within s 32(2) of the LA 1980 even where he is ignorant of the error and his own inadvertent breach of duty, that too was wrongly decided.

NEW CLAIMS IN EXISTING PROCEEDINGS

A new claim in existing proceedings is a claim by way of set off or counterclaim and any claim involving the addition of a new cause of action, or the addition or substitution of a new party (s 35(2) of the LA 1980; rr 17.4, 19.5).

Section 35 of the LA 1980 specifies that any new claim made in the course of any proceedings shall be deemed to be a separate claim and commenced, in the case of a new claim made in or by way of third party proceedings, on the date when those proceedings are commenced, and in any other case on the same date as the original proceedings.

New cause of action

Apart from the court's power to disapply the limitation period in personal injury claims, after the expiry of the limitation period the court may allow an amendment to add a new cause of action only if the new cause of action arises out of the same facts or substantially the same facts as the original claim (s 35(5) of the LA 1980; r 17.4(2)).

Under s 35(5) of the LA 1980, the prohibition is against making an amendment that adds a new *cause of action* after the limitation period has expired. An accepted definition of a cause of action is that provided by Brett J in *Cooke v Gill* (1873) 8 CP 107:

> … every fact which is material to be proved to entitle the [claimant] to succeed – every fact which the defendant would have a right to traverse.

The definition of 'cause of action' refers to the essential facts which need to be proved; non-essential facts must be left out of account. Therefore, in the case of *Savings and Investment Bank Ltd v Fincken* [2001] EWCA Civ 1639, the Court of Appeal held that the claimant was entitled to amend its statement of case, after the limitation period had expired, to plead negligent misrepresentation in the alternative to fraudulent misrepresentation, as the essential facts pleaded in the amended statement of case did not materially differ from the essential facts pleaded in the original statement of case.

It also seems clear that the addition of a claim for a new remedy will not constitute the addition of a new cause of action. An example given to illustrate why this would not constitute a new cause of action is where a claim is brought for not very serious personal injuries and then the claimant subsequently develops epilepsy arising out of the injuries which the claimant received in the accident. The fact that a serious illness arising out of the same facts is pleaded by amendment can clearly be seen not to constitute a new cause of action.

New party

In the same way that the court can allow an amendment to a cause of action outside of the limitation period if it arises out of the same facts as the existing claim, so the court can, in addition, add or substitute a party outside of the period (r 17.4(3); r 19.5). The court may add or substitute a party only where the relevant limitation period had not expired when the proceedings were commenced and the addition or substitution is necessary (r 19.5(2)). Rule 19.5(3) provides that the addition or substitution is 'necessary' only where it is required:

(a) to substitute the correct party for one incorrectly named (cf r 17.4(3) below);

(b) to enable the claim to be properly pursued where the claim cannot be pursued by or against the original party; or

(c) to continue a claim against a deceased or bankrupted party's representative.

Rule 17.4(3) (in comparison with r 19.5) allows the court to amend the name of a party where the *correct* party has been joined in proceedings but a mistake has been made with their name. In *Gregson v Channel Four Television* (2002) *The Times*, 11 August, CA, the claimant issued proceedings against the defendants for libel, but he made a mistake in their name on the claim form. As it was accepted as a genuine mistake, an amendment was allowed under r 17.4(3), even though the matter was now outside the limitation period. The court held that r 19.5 did not apply as no new party was being substituted.

FOREIGN LIMITATION PERIODS

In general terms, where in any proceedings, in accordance with rules of private international law, the law of any other country is to be taken into account in the determination of any matter, the law of that other country relating to limitation shall apply in respect of that matter for the purposes of the proceedings (s 1(1) of the Foreign Limitation Periods Act 1984).

LIMITATION PERIODS AND HUMAN RIGHTS

There have been a number of cases where claimants have argued that limitation periods infringe their access to justice under Art 6 of the European Convention on Human Rights which is incorporated into the Human Rights Act 1998 (HRA).

Article 6 was used to challenge the limitation period which prevented the applicant bringing proceedings in the case of *Stubbings v United Kingdom* (1996) 23 EHRR 213 (for the facts of this case see p 36 above: *Stubbings v Webb* [1993] 1 All ER 322). In that case, whilst the applicant accepted the validity of limitation periods in general, she asserted that the inflexible six-year period applied in her case could not be said to pursue a legitimate aim and was not proportionate. In response, the Government denied that the very essence of the applicant's right of access to court was impaired, because she had six years from her 18th birthday in which to commence proceedings. Also, the six-year limitation period pursued a legitimate aim, namely, to provide finality and legal certainty, and to prevent stale claims from coming to court. The European Court decided that the limitation period applied to the applicant's cause of action was not contrary to Art 6: the six-year time limit was not unduly short, it was proportionate to the aims sought to be achieved, and Contracting States are entitled to exercise a discretion to impose differential limitation periods for different causes of action.

In *Goode v Martin* [2001] EWCA Civ 1899, the Court of Appeal interpreted s 35 of the LA 1980 in a way which was compatible with Art 6 in order to allow a claimant to pursue her claim most effectively. In that case, the claimant suffered a near fatal head injury on the defendant's yacht. The nature of the injury was such that she had no recollection of how it happened and had therefore to depend solely on the evidence of other witnesses, who were friends of the defendant and reluctant to assist her. After the limitation period for the claimant's action expired the defendant served an amended defence, which for the first time pleaded his version of events which had previously been unknown to the claimant.

The claimant applied for permission to amend her statement of case to rely, in the alternative, on the facts as pleaded by the defendant on the grounds that she could establish that the defendant was negligent even if his own version of events was accepted. The Court of Appeal accepted that strictly speaking the facts on which the claimant was now seeking to rely did not fall within the provisions of s 35 of the LA 1980, which allow an amendment to add a new claim after the limitation period has expired only if the new claim arises out of the same facts or substantially the same facts as the original claim (see p 41 above 'New cause of action'). However, in seeking to read the 1980 Act in a way which was compatible with the Convention rights set out in Sched 1 to the HRA (s 3(1) of the HRA) so as not to violate the claimant's Art 6 rights, and in giving effect to the overriding objective to deal with cases justly, the court held that the amendment should be allowed. The Court of Appeal did not consider that the provisions of s 35 of the LA 1980 had any legitimate aim when applied to the facts of this case, and whether the defendant put forward his version of events before or after the expiry of the limitation period ought to make no difference to the claimant's ability to adopt it as part of her case.

Goode v Martin was applied in *Hemmingway v Roddam* (2003) LTL, 18 September.

PROPOSALS FOR REFORM

The Law Commission has recommended fundamental reform of the law on limitation periods, having concluded that it is needlessly complex, outdated and, in some respects, unfair (see Law Commission Report No 270, *Limitation of Actions*, available at www.lawcom.gov.uk). The law on limitation was also criticised for lacking coherence due to its development in an ad hoc way over a long period of time.

In finding that 'simplification is both necessary and achievable' the Law Commission has (in summary) proposed the following reforms:

- There should be a 'core regime' (applying as far as possible to all claims) consisting of an initial limitation period of three years that would run from when the claimant knows, or ought reasonably to know, that he has a cause of action.

- There would be a long-stop limitation period of 10 years, or in personal injury claims of 30 years, running from the date of the act or omission which gives rise to the claim.

- The claimant's disability would extend the initial limitation period, whilst deliberate concealment would extend the long-stop. The court would not have a discretion to disapply the limitation period.

The Law Commission reforms are now contained within a draft Bill that is currently awaiting parliamentary time to be placed before Parliament.

CHAPTER 4

FUNDING LITIGATION

INTRODUCTION

Lord Woolf was of the opinion that 'The problem of cost is the most serious problem besetting our litigation system' (Interim Report (IR), Chapter 25, para 1). He believed that 'the unaffordable cost of litigation constitutes a denial of access to justice' (IR, Chapter 3, para 13). In his exploration for the reasons for the excessive cost of litigating, Lord Woolf criticised traditional charging methods used by lawyers (by the hour for solicitors, and by the day for barristers) as having an inflationary effect on costs (as the more that is done, the more the lawyer is paid) and he urged the adoption of charging on a fixed fee basis instead whenever possible (IR, Chapter 25, para 8).

Many aspects of the Civil Procedure Rules (CPR) are intended to reduce the cost of litigating. This includes measures to reform the system in order to make it more efficient, such as the introduction of judicial case management, but measures have also been introduced in order to limit the recoverability of costs. For instance, the requirement to provide costs estimates at various stages of proceedings, the rule about fixed trial costs for cases heard on the fast track and, more generally, through the introduction of the concept of proportionality in the assessment of costs. Despite Lord Woolf's criticisms and the introduction of the new measures, lawyers continue to charge on the traditional basis, it being very unusual for them to offer their services, in a matter involving litigation, on a fixed fee basis.

The Lord Chancellor's Department (LCD) (now the Department for Constitutional Affairs) also criticised the cost of litigation and the charging practices of lawyers, stating that the current system 'does not encourage legal representatives – who are paid the same, win, lose or draw – to weed out weak cases'. The LCD was of the opinion that conditional fee agreements (CFAs) were better than traditional methods of charging because they 'ensure that the risks of litigation are shared with the lawyer and the client: clients do not pay their lawyers' fees unless they win; and lawyers, when they win, receive a level of fees that recognises the risks they have taken' (see *Access to Justice with Conditional Fees*, Consultation Paper, March 1998, www.dca.gov.uk/consult/leg-aid/laconfr.htm).

As part of its reform of the civil litigation system, the Government was determined to limit and control the legal aid budget and produced various statistics showing that while spending under legal aid increased year on year, the number of cases brought and people helped under the scheme constantly decreased. The then Lord Chancellor, Lord Irvine, believed that making CFAs (backed by legal expenses insurance) more widely available, while on the one hand providing some justification for abolishing legal aid for negligence-based personal injury claims, and effectively for most other civil proceedings, on the other hand also furthered his aim of increasing access to justice (see *Access to Justice with Conditional Fees* above).

It was against this background that on 1 April 2000, two fundamental reforms were introduced which had a profound effect on the way civil litigation is funded. On that date the Civil Legal Aid System, administered by the Legal Aid Board, was replaced by the Community Legal Service (CLS), administered by the Legal Services Commission. Under the CLS, public funding is now no longer available for negligence-based personal injury claims or for most other civil claims, apart from social welfare type cases. Also, for those entering into a CFA from that date, the success fee and any legal expenses insurance premium are now recoverable from the unsuccessful opponent along with the usual costs of the proceedings.

By making CFAs more attractive in this way, the expectation was that they would allow any client, regardless of means, to bring or defend proceedings. However, in practice the recoverability of success fees and insurance premiums has been fiercely resisted, mainly by defendant insurance bodies liable to pay compensation and costs for personal injury claims. This has generated an enormous amount of 'satellite litigation', which was described by Brooke LJ in *Hollins v Russell* [2003] EWCA Civ 718 as 'trench warfare ... waged between claimants' solicitors and solicitors acting for liability insurers before district judges and circuit judges up and down the country' (para [42]). The resulting uncertainty has undermined the availability of this form of funding to litigants and brought into question the whole future of the funding of litigation. The Court of Appeal has attempted to dampen down the appetite for satellite litigation with its important guideline decision in *Hollins v Russell*, and legislative changes to the indemnity principle in relation to CFAs are also expected to make this form of funding simpler and remove the opportunity for challenges to its validity based on breach of the indemnity principle (see p 47 below, 'Conditional fee agreements and the indemnity principle').

THE INDEMNITY PRINCIPLE

The general rule is that an unsuccessful party to litigation will be ordered to pay the costs of the successful party (r 44.3(2)). The costs that an opponent will be ordered to pay are no more than an indemnity to the person entitled to them – that is, the amount which the successful party has to pay his solicitor and no more – they are not ordered as a punishment on the party who pays them, or as a bonus to the party who receives them (*Gundry v Sainsbury* [1910] 1 KB 99). Section 60(3) of the Solicitors Act 1974 puts the indemnity principle into statutory form in respect of contentious business agreements entered into between client and solicitor.

In the light of this so called indemnity principle, it is therefore important to establish the basis on which a client is obliged to pay his solicitor's costs, not least because if a client is not obliged to pay his solicitor's costs he cannot recover any costs from his opponent. It was said by the costs judge, Master Rogers, in *Sarwar v Alam* (2003) LTL, 23 March, that the true test of whether there is a breach of the indemnity principle is whether 'there is unequivocal evidence that in no circumstances will the client be liable for the costs involved'. However, so long as the client is under a legal obligation to pay his solicitor's costs the indemnity principle will be satisfied and the client can recover his costs from his opponent (if so entitled), even if the solicitor never expected to enforce that liability (*R v Miller & Glennie* [1983] 1 WLR 1056). It should be noted, however, that a client is unlikely to recover from his opponent all of the costs that he is legally obliged to pay his solicitor due to the basis on which costs liabilities between the parties are assessed (see Chapter 34, 'Costs of Proceedings').

CFAs and the indemnity principle

CFAs which comply with the Conditional Fee Agreements Regulations 2000 (SI 2000/692) (CFAR 2000) are enforceable even though the essence of such an agreement is that the client will not have to pay his solicitor any costs if his case is unsuccessful (s 58(3)(c) of the Courts and Legal Services Act (CLSA) 1990. However, now that the success fee and after the event insurance premium are potentially recoverable from the unsuccessful opponent along with the other costs of the proceedings, the paying party frequently seeks to challenge the validity of the CFA on the grounds that it does not comply with CFAR 2000. This is because it is argued that if the CFA is unenforceable against the client then no costs are payable by the party ordered to pay costs due to the operation of the indemnity principle.

Abolition of the indemnity principle for certain types of CFA

Regulations that came into force on 2 June 2003 (Access to Justice Act 1999 (Commencement No 10) Order 2003 (SI 2003/1241); Conditional Fee Agreements (Miscellaneous Amendments) Regulations 2003 (SI 2003/1240); Civil Procedure (Amendment No 2) Rules 2003 (SI 2003/1242)) abrogate the indemnity principle in respect of certain types of CFAs entered into after that date. Such agreements can now validly provide, without breaching the indemnity principle, that the client is liable to pay his legal representative's costs only if, and to the extent that, he recovers damages and costs in the proceedings, and the costs of such an agreement will be recoverable costs for the purposes of CPR Parts 44–48 (r 43.2(3), (4)). As a CFA in this form will be simpler and more transparent than standard CFAs it has been dubbed 'CFA lite'. The Regulations will make the agreements simpler and more transparent for clients, and will allow solicitors to guarantee that clients will receive all the damages awarded.

However, so long as a client is properly advised, the parties will remain free to agree that if damages are paid but, for whatever reason, costs are irrecoverable, the legal representative's costs can be taken from those damages. If money is taken from damages in those exceptional circumstances the Law Society recommends that no more than 25% of any damages should be deducted in payment of those costs. This is in line with previous guidance issued by the Law Society before the success fee could be recovered from the losing opponent (see p 62 below, 'Limits on the success fee'.

The indemnity principle and disclosure

There is a presumption that a client is personally liable for his solicitor's costs (*R v Miller & Glennie* [1983] 1 WLR 1056; *Bailey v IBC Vehicles Ltd* [1998] 3 All ER 570). Also, the solicitor's signature on the bill of costs under the rules is effectively the certificate by an officer of the court that the receiving party's solicitors are not seeking to recover more than they have agreed to charge their client. Unless there is evidence to the contrary, the court should assume that the indemnity principle has not been offended (*Bailey v IBC Vehicles Ltd*). However, this presumption does not apply to the solicitor's signature on a bill of costs where a CFA is in place (see p 49 below, 'Disclosure of the Conditional Fee Agreement').

Therefore, it will not be enough for a paying party to put the receiving party to proof as to his entitlement to costs, as the receiving party would be entitled to rely on the presumption in his favour. The paying party would need to raise a genuine issue as to whether the receiving party is liable for his solicitor's costs before the receiving party will be called upon to adduce evidence to show that he is entitled to them (*Hazlett v Sefton Metropolitan BC* (2001) 1 Costs LR 89).

If a party applies for detailed assessment, although he must file all relevant documents with the court, there is no automatic disclosure of these documents to the paying party. However, if a genuine issue is raised as to whether the receiving party is liable for his solicitor's costs, and the receiving party wishes to rely on a document to establish this, the court has a discretion to ask the receiving party to elect whether to disclose the document to the paying party or rely on other evidence instead (PD 47, para 40.14).

In *Dickinson (t/a John Dickinson Equipment Finance) v Rushmer (t/a FJ Associates)* (2002) LTL, 14 January, the claimant successfully recovered damages and interest from the defendant of about £25,000. The defendant unsuccessfully appealed and the costs awarded to the claimant were assessed in the region of £88,000. The defendant raised as a preliminary issue in the costs proceedings whether the costs claimed by the claimant breached the indemnity principle, on the grounds that the claimant, being of limited means, could not have assumed a personal liability to pay the costs claimed and/or that there was evidence that the costs were being paid by a third party. In response to the defendant's challenges the claimant produced to the costs judge a copy of his solicitor's client care letter and other documents to establish that there was a lawful retainer between the claimant and his solicitor. The judge found himself satisfied that there had been no breach of the indemnity principle, but refused to order that the documents produced to him be disclosed to the defendant. The appeal court held that although a solicitor's bills of costs to his client are privileged documents, calculations showing what a client has paid and a client care letter (in so far as it only contains the terms on which the solicitor is to act for the client) are not. The court found that the costs judge's procedure was unfair in refusing to order that the claimant disclose the calculations of what was paid and the client care letter.

The court found that where there was a disputed issue of fact, namely, whether the indemnity principle had been satisfied, if the claimant chose to prove that disputed issue by reference to certain documents, basic principles of fairness would dictate that the claimant must disclose those documents to the defendant. Rimer J said:

> A claim by one party to recover costs from another may well in practice prove to be just as important, perhaps even more so, to one or other or both sides as the resolution of the substantive issues in the action. This case provides a good example of that. The claimant was seeking on the detailed assessment to recover a sum of costs from the defendant which vastly exceeded the damages and interest he had recovered in the action, and his claim to do so was obviously of great importance to both parties. The defendant was entitled to a fair trial of the claim, just as he was entitled to a fair trial of the issues in the action.

Further, in *South Coast Shipping Co Ltd v Havant BC* [2002] 3 All ER 779, the court held that where a possible breach of the indemnity principle arises on a detailed assessment, and the receiving party wishes to disclose to the costs judge documents for which he claims legal professional privilege, the interests of fairness require that if the documents are of sufficient importance the receiving party should be put to his election either of waiving privilege, or of adducing secondary evidence about the contents of the documents. This is in accordance with PD 47, para 40.14 and does not infringe the Convention rights of the receiving party.

Disclosure of the CFA

In *Hollins v Russell*, the Court of Appeal decided six cases (*Dunn v Ward, Worth v McKenna, Pratt v Bull, Tichband v Hurdman, Sharratt v London Central Bus Co Ltd*, and the *Accident Group* test cases) which dealt with important points of principle where challenges have been made to the validity of the CFA. So important was the decision of the Court of Appeal in these conjoined appeals that interested representative bodies intervened to make representations. The interveners were the Association of Personal Injury Lawyers (APIL), the Motor Accident Solicitors' Society (MASS), the Forum of Insurance Lawyers (FOIL) and the Law Society.

One of the issues dealt with was whether the paying party (usually defendant liability insurers) was entitled to see the receiving party's CFA during the assessment proceedings. It was recognised in *Hollins* that resistance to demands to see CFAs was leading to a significant amount of litigation. The Court of Appeal distinguished *Bailey v IBC Vehicles Ltd* (see pp 47–49 above, 'The indemnity principle and disclosure') in respect of CFAs. The solicitor's certificate on the bill of costs was not sufficient where a CFA was involved. The court held that the combination of the indemnity principle and a significant increase in the paying party's liabilities results in there ordinarily being a sufficient ground, in cases involving a CFA, for the paying party to require the court to exercise its discretion under PD 47, para 40.14 to put the receiving party to his election to produce the CFA to the paying party or rely on other evidence to prove his entitlement to the costs claimed under the CFA. The court hoped, as it was now clear from their judgment that this was to be the general practice, that receiving parties would disclose the CFA 'without more ado' (at [82]). However, the court held that disclosure of the attendance notes prepared by the receiving party's solicitors, showing compliance with reg 4 of the CFAR 2000, should not be required unless the paying party raised a genuine issue as to whether there had been compliance with reg 4 (see pp 57–59 below, 'Duties of the legal representative before the CFA is made').

Maintenance and champerty

Maintenance is said to occur if a person supports litigation in which he has no legitimate concern without just cause or excuse. Champerty is said to occur when the person maintaining the litigation stipulates for a share of the proceeds of the claim. Lord Mustill said in the case of *Giles v Thompson* [1994] 1 AC 142 at 164, that whether an agreement is champertous depends on whether 'there has been wanton and officious intermeddling with the disputes of others, in which the meddler has no interest whatsoever and where the assistance he renders to one or the other party is without justification or excuse'.

Maintenance and champerty were formerly both crimes and torts. Now under ss 13(1) and 14(1) of the Criminal Law Act 1967, maintenance and champerty can result in such contracts being held unenforceable on the grounds of public policy. The public policy interest is the proper administration of justice with particular regard to the interests of the defendant.

In some circumstances the law expressly prohibits agreements that could be classed as champertous. For example, r 8 of the Solicitors' Practice Rules 1990 expressly prohibits solicitors from entering into contingency agreements (which provide for the legal representative's costs to be taken as a share or percentage of the damages) in contentious proceedings. Where there is no express prohibition, according to Lord Phillips in *R (Factortame) v Secretary of State for Transport* [2002] EWCA Civ 932, the facts of a particular situation must be considered to decide whether the agreement in question 'might tempt the allegedly champertous maintainer for his personal gain, to inflame the damages, to suppress evidence, to suborn witnesses or otherwise to undermine the ends of justice'.

The issue is not whether the agreement in question has caused the corruption of public justice; it is whether it has the *tendency* to corrupt public justice. In applying that principle the Court of Appeal in *Factortame* did not find an agreement champertous which provided for a firm of accountants to be paid in fees 8% 'of the final settlement received'. This was because the accountants did not perform the role of expert witnesses; other experts were retained for that purpose who were entirely independent, and the accountants' work consisted largely of important back-up services for the two independent experts. However, it is likely to be contrary to public policy for an expert witness to give evidence on a contingency fee basis. An expert witness owes an overriding duty to the court, and it would give the expert a significant financial interest in the outcome of the case which would undermine his independence were he to give evidence on a contingency fee basis (see judgment of Lord Phillips in *Factortame*).

The issues of maintenance and champerty were considered in detail by the Court of Appeal and House of Lords in *Giles v Thompson* [1993] 3 All ER 321, CA; [1994] 1 AC 142, HL. This case involved a number of conjoined appeals about whether claimants could recover as damages the cost of hiring cars to replace those put out of commission by a defendant's negligence. The claimants entered into credit agreements with the hire companies in respect of the hire charges until the claimants recovered damages and, in some cases, gave the hire companies the right to pursue actions against the defendants in the claimant's name to recover those damages. It was argued by the defendants, amongst other things, that the hire company's right to payment of the hire charges was conditional upon the success of the action, and that the agreements were therefore unenforceable on the grounds of maintenance and champerty. In holding that the agreements were not champertous the court took into account the fact that the hire contracts did not give the hire companies any legal interests in the proceeds of the litigation and that the hirers were under a residual liability to pay the hire charges. Also in respect of those agreements, where the hire company had the right to appoint its own solicitor to pursue an action for damages in the hirer's name, where there was any conflict between the hire company and the claimant the wishes of the claimant were likely to prevail.

Giles v Thompson was applied in *Crittenden v Bayliss* [2002] EWCA Civ 50. In that case the parties had been involved in a number of joint business ventures. It was agreed between the parties that the claimant would give the defendant assistance in the conduct of litigation, referred to as the 'Lloyds litigation', and in return the claimant would receive a share of the proceeds of the litigation on a 50:50 basis – the same basis as their other joint ventures. The defendant subsequently sought to argue that the agreement was champertous. In holding that the agreement was not champertous, the Court of Appeal was of the opinion that the claimant was not meddling in a matter that was none of his business. The outcome of the litigation, if the defendant was unsuccessful, could be extremely damaging to the defendant's financial position. The claimant had an interest in that because the defendant's continuing financial prosperity was an important element in the claimant's future in the joint ventures. The court was also not persuaded by the argument that the agreement should be unenforceable on public policy grounds because the claimant carried out work which would have been carried out by a solicitor and so should be subject to the same prohibition as applied to a solicitor in terms of entering into a contingency agreement (see above). The court found that the claimant's work in the claim was subject to the control of a solicitor instructed by the defendant, so the interest that the rule of champerty exists to protect, that of the opposite party, was protected by the judgment of the solicitor who was actually conducting the claim. However, the court said that had the claimant been assisting the defendant as a *McKenzie* friend (a person who does not act for but provides assistance to a party during the conduct of proceedings) instead, it would have been very likely that such an agreement would be contrary to public policy if conducted on a contingency fee basis.

TRADITIONAL METHODS OF FUNDING LITIGATION

In respect of civil litigation, a privately paying client (as opposed to a publicly funded client) usually enters into a contract with his solicitor to provide legal services. This is known as 'a retainer'. The retainer can be oral or written, express or implied. Solicitors are subject to the Solicitors' Practice Rules 1990 (as amended by the Solicitors' Practice (Costs Information and Client Care) Amendment Rules 1999), r 15 of which imposes obligations on solicitors to provide information about costs and other matters to clients. If solicitors properly comply with the obligations imposed by r 15 of the 1990 Rules, this will mean in most cases that a written agreement is entered into with the client.

In respect of proceedings in a county court, s 74(3) of the Solicitors Act (SA) 1974 limits the amount a solicitor can recover from his client in costs to that which could have been allowed for those costs between the parties, unless the solicitor and client have entered into a written agreement which expressly permits payment to the solicitor of an amount of costs greater than that which the client could have recovered from another party to the proceedings (r 48.8(1A)). The existence of this provision should be an incentive for solicitors to enter into written agreements with their clients.

Contentious and non-contentious business

A distinction is made between contentious and non-contentious business. Contentious business is defined by s 87(1) of the SA 1974 as:

... business done whether as a solicitor or advocate in or for the purposes of
proceedings begun before a court or before an arbitrator appointed under the
Arbitration Act 1950 other than non-contentious probate business.

An example of contentious business is proceedings started in the county courts or
the Supreme Court, including appeal proceedings. Non-contentious business is 'any
business done as a solicitor which is not contentious business' (s 87(1) of the SA 1974)
and includes proceedings before all tribunals, except for the Lands Tribunal and the
Employment Appeals Tribunal.

The difference between contentious and non-contentious business has a number
of important consequences. A solicitor is expressly forbidden from entering into a
contingency agreement in respect of contentious business, but is free to do so in
respect of non-contentious business, where a commission or percentage-based fee is
common for conveyancing and probate work (r 8 of the Solicitors' Practice Rules 1990;
s 57 of the SA 1974). Also, there are important differences in the methods a client can
use to challenge the amount a solicitor charges under a contentious and a non-
contentious business agreement (see below 'Assessment of solicitor and client costs').

If proceedings are never started, the work done before proceedings are
commenced will be non-contentious. However, when proceedings are started, all
work carried out prior to proceedings being started automatically becomes
contentious (*Re Simpkin Marshall Ltd* [1959] Ch 229).

Assessment of solicitor and client costs

Although a client will be liable to pay his solicitor under the terms of their
agreement, for both contentious and non-contentious business, the client is entitled,
in certain circumstances, to apply for his solicitor's bill to be assessed by the court
(s 70 of the SA 1974; r 48.8).

Gross sum and detailed itemised bills

Contentious business

It is a solicitor's bill of costs that is subject to assessment by the court. For
contentious business (except where a contentious business agreement is in place) a
solicitor's bill may, at the option of the solicitor, be either a bill containing detailed
items or a gross sum bill (s 64 of the SA 1974). However, if a client is sent a gross sum
bill he is entitled to request his solicitor to send him a detailed itemised bill instead,
so long as he makes such a request within three months from the date the bill was
delivered to him, or before he is served with a claim form seeking payment of the
bill, whichever is earlier (s 64(2) of the SA 1974). In these circumstances, if the
detailed itemised bill is higher than the gross sum bill, the solicitor is entitled to
claim that higher amount.

Non-contentious business

For non-contentious business a solicitor may also, at his option, send either a bill
containing detailed items or a gross sum bill. However, a client does not have the

right to require a solicitor to deliver a detailed itemised bill instead of a gross sum bill, although he does have the right to seek a Remuneration Certificate from the Law Society (see Solicitors' (Non-Contentious Business) Remuneration Order 1994 (SI 1994/2616)) as well as having the bill assessed by the court. If a Remuneration Certificate is sought, the Law Society will consider the client's file and will issue a certificate stating what sum in their opinion would be fair and reasonable for the work done.

Final and interim bills

For both contentious and non-contentious business a solicitor can, at the outset of the retainer, require the client to make payments on account of costs and disbursements.

Further, for contentious business, a solicitor is entitled to send a client an interim bill requesting payment on account of a final bill that is to be delivered at a later date. A solicitor is entitled to terminate a retainer if a client fails to pay an interim bill on account within a reasonable time (s 65(2) of the SA 1974).

Contentious business agreements

Section 59(1) of the SA 1974 regulates the making of a contentious business agreement. The section provides as follows:

> ... a solicitor may make an agreement in writing with his client as to his remuneration ... providing that he is remunerated by gross sum or by reference to an hourly rate, or by a salary, or otherwise ...

A contentious business agreement must be in writing and signed by the client. It must also show all the terms of the agreement (*Chamberlain v Boodle & King* [1982] 3 All ER 188). The reason why a solicitor may wish to enter into a contentious business agreement is because the client cannot apply for assessment of costs under the agreement, except where the agreement provides for hourly rates. However, the client can apply to the court for the agreement to be examined, and if it is found to be unfair or unreasonable it can be set aside. Also, if the agreement relates to hourly rates, although the agreed hourly rate will not be open to challenge, the court may consider the number of hours worked and whether they were excessive. A solicitor cannot bring a debt claim for unpaid costs arising from the contentious business agreement and must apply to the court where the contentious work was carried out for it to determine whether the agreement is fair and reasonable and enforce it or set it aside, as appropriate (s 61 of the SA 1974).

Non-contentious business agreement

By definition, a non-contentious business agreement will not relate to litigation. However, for the purposes of comparison with a contentious business agreement its main features are briefly summarised here.

Under s 57 of the SA 1974, a solicitor and client can enter into a non-contentious business agreement so long as such an agreement is in writing, signed by the client, provides for remuneration by a gross sum, or by reference to an hourly rate, or by a commission or percentage, or by a salary or otherwise and stipulates whether the remuneration includes all or any disbursements in respect of searches, plans, travelling, stamps, fees and other matters.

As with contentious business agreements, a client has restricted rights to apply for assessment of the non-contentious business agreement. However, if the solicitor seeks to rely on the agreement, the client can apply to the court for the agreement to be set aside on the grounds that it is unfair and unreasonable. Also, if the agreement relates to hourly rates, although the agreed hourly rate will not be open to challenge, the court may consider the number of hours worked and whether they were excessive. Further, unlike a contentious business agreement, a solicitor can bring simple debt recovery proceedings to recover unpaid sums under the agreement (s 57 of the SA 1974).

CONDITIONAL FEE AGREEMENTS

Background

It is possible to enter into an enforceable CFA for all types of civil litigation, except family proceedings. CFAs are not permissible in criminal proceedings apart from those under s 82 of the Environmental Protection Act 1990 (ss 58(1) and 58A(1) of the CLSA 1990).

Historically, CFAs were held to be contrary to public policy on the basis that it was undesirable for legal representatives to have an interest in the outcome of the cases they were conducting. This long-standing policy was changed by s 58 of the CLSA 1990, which was the framework legislation paving the way for the introduction of CFAs. They were initially introduced only for certain types of case to be specified by regulations made by the Lord Chancellor. In 1995, the Conditional Fee Agreements Order 1995 (SI 1995/1674) provided that CFAs were permissible for personal injury, insolvency and cases before the European Commission of Human Rights and the European Court of Human Rights. In July 1998, the Conditional Fee Agreements Order 1998 (SI 1998/1860) extended CFAs to all civil non-family proceedings. It is anticipated that they will eventually be extended to those aspects of family cases concerned with the division of matrimonial property (see proposals contained in the Government's White Paper, *Modernising Justice*, 2 December 1998, www.dca.gov.uk/consult/access/mjwpcon.htm).

Although CFAs are lawful, they should be distinguished from contingency fee agreements, which are not lawful for contentious matters. Contingency fee agreements allow the legal representative to take a proportion of the damages recovered by the client if the case is successful. It is thought to be undesirable, and therefore against public policy, for a legal representative to have a direct interest not only in the outcome of litigation, but also in the amount of damages recovered by a client (see pp 49–51 above, 'Maintenance and champerty').

Definition of 'conditional fee agreement'

A CFA (commonly known as a 'no win, no fee' agreement) is defined as 'an agreement with a person providing advocacy or litigation services which provides for his fees and expenses, or any part of them, to be payable only in specified circumstances' (s 58(2)(a) of the CLSA 1990; PD 43, para 2.2).

The 'specified circumstances' will be defined in the written agreement constituting the CFA. For instance, in the Law Society Model CFA for use in personal injury cases, the specified circumstances are if the party 'wins' their claim. This is further defined as meaning if the party's 'claim for damages is finally decided in [their] favour, whether by a court decision or an agreement to pay [their] damages' (see condition 3 of the Law Society Conditions of their Model CFA agreement for personal injury cases).

The success fee

Most CFAs also provide for payment of a success fee to the legal representative in addition to his usual fees, the rationale being to 'reward' the legal representative for taking the risk of losing the case and recovering no fees and so having done the work for nothing. The elements of the legal representative's fees which do not form part of the success fee are known as the base costs (PD 43, para 2.2).

However, a CFA does not need to provide for a success fee in order to fall within the definition. An agreement that provides for the legal representative to be paid usual costs if the case is won, but no or lower costs if the case is lost, is a form of CFA. This latter type of CFA has come to be known as a 'Thai Trading Agreement' after the name of the case where such an agreement was held to be lawful and not contrary to public policy (Thai Trading Co v Taylor [1998] 3 All ER 65). In that case, it was recognised that such agreements are often entered into by solicitors on an informal basis with their clients, the agreement consisting of no more than an expectation that fees will be paid only if the case is successful. However, the Thai Trading decision was subsequently disapproved in Awwad v Geraghty and Co (A Firm) [2000] 1 All ER 608, where it was held that acting for a client under a CFA not sanctioned by statute is against public policy. Under the new provisions, in order to be enforceable, such an agreement will have to comply with the onerous formal requirements specified for CFAs under the CLSA 1990 and accompanying regulations. However, such agreements entered into before the new legislation came into force are potentially unenforceable.

LEGAL EXPENSES INSURANCE

Although a litigant entering into a CFA will not have to pay any fees to his lawyer if his case is unsuccessful, owing to the 'indemnity costs' system, whereby the loser is usually ordered to pay the winner's costs, an unsuccessful litigant with a CFA is at risk of being ordered to pay the opponent's costs. Therefore, in order for CFAs to be a viable option for litigants they are usually supported by a legal expenses insurance policy to insure against the risk of having to pay the opponent's costs if the case is lost. This type of legal expenses insurance is known as 'after the event' insurance (AEI), as compared to 'before the event' legal expenses insurance policies (BEI), frequently attached to car and home insurance, which provide legal expenses insurance cover before any claim has arisen.

There are now also AEI policies that allow a litigant to recover his own lawyer's costs as well as the opponent's where the litigant has not taken out a CFA with his own lawyer. As might be expected, such policies, which cover the risk of paying one's own as well as the opponent's costs, are much more expensive than those AEI policies which are limited to paying the opponent's costs.

NEW FUNDING ARRANGEMENTS

There is now a presumption that where the court makes an order for the losing party to pay the winning party's costs, the costs payable include the success fee and any insurance premium unless the court orders otherwise (s 58A(6) of the CLSA 1990; PD 43, para 2.1; PD 44, para 9.1). If a CFA includes one or both of these so called additional liabilities (success fee or insurance premium), it will fall within the definition of a funding arrangement (r 43.2(1)(k), (o)).

Before this new legislation came into force on 1 April 2000, a successful litigant taking on a CFA expected to pay the cost of any insurance premium and the success fee out of the damages he recovered. The Government hopes that this change will not only make CFAs more attractive to parties seeking compensation, as the compensation is no longer eroded by payment of the success fee and insurance premium, but also that defendants and litigants seeking non-monetary remedies will be more likely to use CFAs knowing that, if they are successful, they can recover the insurance premium and success fee from their opponent. The justification for the new rule is that the losing party, having caused the need for litigation, should pay all the winner's costs, including the success fee and any insurance premium (see para 2.14, *Access to Justice with Conditional Fees*, Consultation Paper, March 1998, www.dca.gov.uk/consult/leg-aid/confrefr.htm).

In order to be enforceable, CFAs must currently comply with regulations prescribed by the Lord Chancellor (which office has now been replaced by the Secretary of State for Constitutional Affairs) (s 58(3)(c) of the CLSA 1990). Those regulations are now the CFAR 2000, made under ss 58 and 119 of the CLSA 1990 (which revoked the earlier 1995 Regulations). Rules and practice directions under the CPR cover the procedure for recovering the success fee and insurance premium from an unsuccessful opponent.

Consequences of failure to comply with CFAR

In *Hollins v Russell*, the Court of Appeal had to consider whether a CFA would be enforceable if it did not comply in every particular with the requirements of s 58(3) of the CLSA 1990 or CFAR 2000. The court accepted that a CFA was a contentious business agreement to which s 60(3) of the SA 1974 applied. Accordingly, if the CFA is unenforceable against the client then the amounts provided for in the agreement are not payable by the client at all and, due to the indemnity principle, they cannot be recovered from the other side.

In construing s 58(3) of the CLSA 1990, the court held that the key question is whether the regulations made under that section have been *sufficiently* complied with. The legislation aimed to balance a number of competing objectives: increasing access to justice; protecting the client; acknowledging the legitimate interests of the other party to the litigation; and furthering the administration of justice. In *Hollins v Russell*, Brook LJ said (at [224]):

The court should be watchful when it considers allegations that there have been breaches of the Regulations. The parliamentary purpose is to enhance access to justice, not to impede it, and to create better ways of delivering litigation services, not worse ones. These purposes will be thwarted if those who render good service to their clients under CFAs are at risk of going unremunerated at the culmination of the bitter trench warfare which has been such an unhappy feature of the recent litigation scene.

When considering whether failures to comply with the regulations make a CFA unenforceable, costs judges must ask themselves whether the particular failure, either on its own or in conjunction with any other failure, had a materially adverse effect either upon the protection afforded to the client, or upon the proper administration of justice. If the answer is 'no' the failure is immaterial and the conditions have been satisfied. In general, a CFA will not be held to be unenforceable for immaterial breaches of the regulations under the principle that the law does not concern itself with little things. However, if the costs judge considers that the client would have just cause for complaint because some requirement introduced for his protection was not satisfied, or that the CFA otherwise offends public policy (because, for instance, it relates to proceedings which cannot be the subject of an enforceable CFA), then the CFA will be unenforceable and the indemnity principle will operate in favour of the paying party.

The court held in the *Tichband v Hurdman* appeal (see *Hollins v Russell*) that the regulations were obviously met where the failure consisted of not inserting the percentage uplift in the clause of the CFA where it should have been inserted, because the percentage uplift was clearly stated in the risk assessment part of the CFA.

Recovering the insurance premium and disbursements if the CFA is held to be unenforceable

If a CFA is held to be unenforceable, either for failure to comply with CFAR 2000 or for any other reason, the receiving party will still be able to recover after the event insurance premiums (AEI) and the costs of paid disbursements (*Hollins v Russell*). The client's liability to pay the insurance premium arises from the contract of insurance, not from the contract with his legal representative. It will therefore be recoverable whether or not the CFA is enforceable. Also, where a client has paid for disbursements, either personally or by taking out a loan to do so, the amounts paid are recoverable by the client as costs even if the CFA is unenforceable. This is because the costs claim is that of the client, not of the solicitor. Accordingly, if the client has actually paid a debt to a third party, properly incurred in the conduct of litigation, there would be no reason why this should not be recoverable from the paying party, so long as it is reasonable and proportionate.

ENTERING INTO A CONDITIONAL FEE AGREEMENT

Duties of the legal representative before the CFA is made

A CFA is a rather complex contract, and CFAR 2000 impose obligations on the legal representative to inform the client about certain matters and explain the effect of a

CFA to the client before he enters into it. The legal representative is required to give any explanation in plain English, in order to ensure that the client fully understands the type of agreement he is entering into.

A solicitor is entitled to delegate these duties to someone who is to perform them on his behalf even if that person is not a qualified solicitor or a legal executive (*Hollins v Russell*). In the TAG test cases (see judgment in *Hollins v Russell*), the CFA was challenged on the grounds that solicitors, who were panel members of the Accident Advice Bureau Ltd, delegated the duty to explain the effect of the CFA to the claims handling company, who sent employees, who were not legally qualified, to the client's home to carry out the task. The court held that a solicitor is entitled to delegate the performance of his CFAR 2000, reg 4, duties to a claims handling company, but the solicitor will remain professionally responsible for the performance of the person who actually carries out the duties. Therefore, it will remain a question of fact whether the person carrying out the duties has complied with the requirements of the regulations.

Information that must be given orally

The legal representative must inform the client orally before the CFA is made (whether or not this information is also given in writing):

(a) about the circumstances in which the client may be liable to pay the costs of the legal representative under the agreement (for example, if the client's case is successful, but also, for instance, if the client terminates the agreement before the conclusion of the case);

(b) about the circumstances in which the client may seek, and the procedure for seeking, assessment of the legal representative's fees and expenses;

(c) as to whether the legal representative considers that the client's possible liability for costs in respect of the proceedings is already covered by an existing contract of insurance (for example, before the event insurance as contained in some household contents insurance policies or car insurance policies); but, if none is in existence;

(d) whether some other method of financing those costs is available to the client (for example, after the event legal expenses insurance (reg 4(2)(a)–(d) of the CFAR 2000).

Information that must be given both orally and in writing

The following information must be given both orally and in writing to the client before the CFA is entered into:

(a) an explanation to the client of the effect of the CFA (reg 4(3) of the CFAR 2000); and

(b) if the legal representative recommends a particular after the event insurance policy to cover payment of costs for which the client may become liable, information as to why he recommends such a policy and a statement as to whether he has an interest in doing so (reg 4(2)(e) of the CFAR 2000).

Moreover, there is also a general requirement to provide as much further explanation, advice or information to the client about the CFA as the client reasonably demands (reg 4(1)(b) of the CFAR 2000).

However, these obligations do not apply when a CFA is entered into between a solicitor and a barrister (reg 4(6) of the CFAR 2000). Nor does such an agreement between legal representatives need to be in writing (reg 5(2) of the CFAR 2000).

In the *Pratt v Bull* appeal (see *Hollins v Russell*), the claimant was an 80-year-old claimant who was severely injured by the defendant's car when she was using a pedestrian crossing. The following month, when she had recovered enough to give instructions, a solicitor visited her in hospital and a standard CFA was entered into. When the claimant sought to recover her costs the defendants demanded not only a copy of the CFA, but also the attendance notes and documents to show that the claimant had been given all the oral and written information required by reg 4 of the CFAR 2000. In particular, the defendants expressed concern that other methods of funding might not have been properly explored. The Court of Appeal held that this was a classic case in which there was no good reason to think that the regulations had not been satisfied. The court recognised that there were limits to what can reasonably be expected of the interchange between solicitor and client in such circumstances. It found it ridiculous to expect a solicitor dealing with a seriously ill old woman in hospital to delay making a CFA while her home insurance policy was found and checked. It was sufficient to satisfy s 58 of the CLSA 1990 that the solicitor had discussed it with her and formed a view on the funding options.

In the *Dunn v Ward* appeal (see *Hollins v Russell*), the solicitor failed to inform the client that he had no interest in recommending a particular AEI contract. The Court of Appeal held that the purpose of reg 4(2)(e) of the CFAR 2000 was to ensure that the client knew whether the legal representative had an interest in a particular product he recommended. It would be of no consequence to the client if he had no such interest. The *raison d'être* of the CFA regime was to increase and facilitate access to justice, and it could not be right to declare a CFA unenforceable merely because it did not mention some fact that was wholly immaterial.

Due to an administrative error, the solicitor in *Dunn v Ward* also failed to explain the effect of the CFA in writing to the client before she entered into it. The solicitor merely sent the client the CFA, which was based on the Law Society's July 2000 Model CFA and included the conditions attached to that agreement. The court took into account the fact that the Law Society Model agreement and conditions won a 'Plain English' award for their clarity of wording when accepting that the client would have been able to read the effect of the CFA which was expressed in clear terms. The court upheld the costs judge's decision that this clear explanation of the effect of the CFA did not contravene the requirements of reg 4(5) of the CFAR 2000 even though it was contained in a document forming part of the CFA. Although the court saw no reason in principle why the CFA should not contain an explanation of its own terms and effect, it was of the opinion that it would be better to have a free-standing document containing the required explanation.

The contents of a CFA

The CFAR 2000 specify particular requirements that the contract containing the CFA must fulfil in order to make it enforceable. The regulations distinguish between CFAs where a success fee is payable and those where one is not. For all CFAs, there are general requirements that must be fulfilled. There are then additional requirements that must also be fulfilled for CFAs providing for a success fee.

General requirements for all CFAs

The CFA must:

- be in writing and signed by both the client and the legal representative (s 27(3)(a) of the Access to Justice Act 1999; reg 5(1) of the CFAR 2000);
- specify the particular proceedings (or parts) to which it relates (reg 2(1)(a) of the CFAR 2000). Therefore, the CFA should contain sufficient information to identify the proceedings, such as the type of claim involved, the relevant date of the incident or cause of action, and the identity of the defendant;
- specify whether the CFA includes any appeal, counterclaim or proceedings to enforce any judgment or order obtained (reg 2(1)(a) of the CFAR 2000). If a client wishes to take further action, such as an appeal against a decision, then if such proceedings are not covered by the original CFA, the original agreement will have to be amended, or a separate agreement, which may be another CFA, will have to be entered into;
- specify the circumstances in which the legal representative's fees and expenses are payable (reg 2(1)(b) of the CFAR 2000);
- specify what payment is due if those circumstances only partly occur, irrespective of whether those circumstances occur, and on the termination of the agreement for whatever reason (reg 2(1)(c) of the CFAR 2000);
- specify the amounts which are payable in all the circumstances, or the methods used to calculate them (reg 2(1)(d) of the CFAR 2000);
- specify whether the amounts payable are limited by the damages which may be recovered on behalf of the client (reg 2(1)(d) of the CFAR 2000). Before it became possible to recover the success fee and insurance premium from the losing opponent, the Law Society recommended that in no case should the success fee exceed 25% of the damages recovered by the client. Now that these sums are recoverable from the unsuccessful opponent, the Law Society no longer makes this recommendation of voluntary restraint;
- contain a statement that the duties of the legal representative under reg 4 to inform the client about various matters before the CFA is entered into have been complied with (reg 2(2) of the CFAR 2000).

CFAs providing for success fees

A CFA with a success fee will specify a percentage, the 'percentage increase' or 'percentage uplift', by which the amount of the legal representative's fee can be increased in the event of success. The success fee is designed to reflect the degree of risk the legal representative has taken in entering into the agreement, so the weaker and less likely to succeed the case, the higher the percentage success fee, and vice versa.

It is permissible to include a success fee in all CFAs allowed under the CLSA 1990, apart from proceedings under s 82 of the Environmental Protection Act 1990 (reg 3 of the Conditional Fee Agreements Order 2000 (SI 2000/823) (CFAO 2000)). These are criminal proceedings which allow a person afflicted by a statutory nuisance to seek an order for the nuisance to be remedied. A common use of this provision is by a tenant against a landlord who has failed to maintain the rented accommodation in a habitable condition. Although it is permissible to enter into a CFA for this type of claim, it is the only type of claim (of those permitted) for which a success fee is prohibited.

Additional formalities for CFAs providing for success fees

Where the CFA includes a success fee, the CFA must:

- briefly specify the reasons for setting the percentage increase at the level stated in the agreement (reg 3(1)(a) of the CFAR 2000). There must, therefore, be a written record of the reasons for setting the success fee at the chosen percentage increase at the time the agreement was entered into. This provision anticipates any challenge to the level of the success fee at a later date and can be seen as a protection for the legal representative, as he has a contemporaneous record of the relevant factors that affected his judgment as to the level of risk, which he can use to distinguish factors discoverable only with hindsight;

- specify how much of the percentage increase, if any, relates to the cost to the legal representative of the postponement of the payment of his fees and expenses (reg 3(1)(b) of the CFAR 2000). When fixing the level of the success fee, some legal representatives take into account the effect CFAs have on their cash flow, due to the fact that payment of fees is made only at the conclusion of the case. This element of the success fee, the cost to the legal representative caused by postponement of payment of his fees, is not recoverable from the losing opponent (r 44.3B(1)(a)). However, there is no requirement to include such an element in the calculation of the success fee.

CFAs which provide for success fees and which relate to court proceedings must also include the following terms:

- that if the percentage increase becomes payable as a result of proceedings, and the fees subject to the increase are assessed, the client or the legal representative is permitted to disclose the reasons for setting the success fee at the rate specified in the CFA if required to do so by the court (reg 3(2)(a) of the CFAR 2000);

- if the success fee is assessed and any amount of the percentage increase is disallowed on assessment on the ground that the level at which the increase was set was unreasonable in view of facts which were or should have been known to the legal representative at the time it was set, the amount ceases to be payable under the agreement unless the court is satisfied that it should remain payable (reg 3(2)(b) of the CFAR 2000);

- if the fees are not assessed but the legal representative agrees with the paying party to accept a lower percentage increase than that specified in the CFA, the amount of the percentage increase specified in the CFA shall be reduced accordingly unless the court is satisfied that the full amount should remain payable (reg 3(2)(c) of the CFAR 2000).

The court will therefore have the power in any assessment proceedings to disallow any amount in respect of the percentage increase on the grounds that the level was unreasonable in the light of facts which were known or should have been known to the legal representative at the time the success fee was set. This means that the success fee can be extinguished or reduced. Regulation 3(2)(b) of the CFAR 2000 provides that in these circumstances, this amount ceases to be payable under the agreement, unless the court orders otherwise. The same result will follow if the fees are not assessed but simply agreed, and part of the agreement is for a reduction in the percentage of the success fee.

This ensures that if the losing opponent does not have to pay the success fee, or the full amount of the success fee set under the agreement, the client will not be left to pay it instead unless the legal representative can persuade the court that it would be reasonable for the client to pay it. Such provisions will obviously deter legal representatives from setting an unduly high success fee.

Amendment of a CFA

A CFA will often not extend to the bringing of an appeal against the decision at trial. In those circumstances, if the client loses his case at first instance and wishes to appeal, and the legal representative is prepared to act for the client under a CFA, then either a new CFA to cover those proceedings will have to be entered into or the original agreement will have to be amended. If the original agreement is amended, the amendments must be in writing and must comply with the formalities specified for the original agreement under regs 2, 3 and 5 of the CFAR 2000 (reg 6(a) of the CFAR 2000). Also, the requirement under reg 4 of the CFAR 2000 to provide specified oral and written information to the client before a CFA is entered into must be complied with in so far as the information is relevant to the amendments (reg 6 of the CFAR 2000).

A CFA in the form of the Law Society's Model CFA will include the costs aspects of a claim, including costs-only proceedings (*Halloran v Delaney* [2002] EWCA Civ 1258).

Limits on the success fee

The maximum percentage increase allowed for a success fee has been fixed at 100% (reg 4 of the CFAO 2000). When the success fee was payable by the winning client out of damages recovered, the Law Society recommended that solicitors voluntarily limit the uplift to an amount which did not exceed 25% of the damages recovered. Now that the success fee is recoverable from the opponent, this recommendation has been dropped.

Law Society model agreement for personal injury cases

The Law Society produces a Model CFA for personal injury cases, as well as guidance on compliance with the regulations. The Law Society intends to produce a model agreement for use in other types of case as CFAs become more common in other areas.

DISCLOSURE OF FUNDING ARRANGEMENTS

Disclosure of the funding arrangement

In accordance with the general principle that a party should be informed about the full extent of any potential liability he may have to meet if he is unsuccessful in bringing or defending a claim, a party who has entered into a funding arrangement must disclose this to his opponent at various stages of the proceedings. A failure to give the necessary disclosure will result in the additional liability being irrecoverable.

Pre-commencement disclosure

Paragraph 4A.1 of the Practice Direction Protocols provides in general terms that where a party enters into a funding arrangement within the meaning of r 43.2(1)(k), he should inform other potential parties to the claim that he has done so. This rule applies to all proceedings whether or not subject to a pre-action protocol (PD Protocols, para 4A.2). Although the Practice Direction is not precise as to the stage at which notification should be given, it does provide a cross-reference to r 44.3B(1)(c), which sets out the consequences of a failure to provide the proper notification once proceedings have begun (namely, that any additional liability will not be recoverable from the opponent). Therefore, to be on the safe side, a party should inform any other potential party as soon as the funding agreement is entered into.

Disclosure on commencement of proceedings

Where a party has entered into a funding arrangement before proceedings are started, if proceedings are started he is required to file at court and serve on the other parties a notice containing information about the arrangement as specified in Form N251 and which is signed by the party or his legal representative (PD 44, paras 19, 20).

On issuing a claim form, the claimant must also file the notice at court at the same time as the claim form. If the court is to effect service of the claim form, and sufficient copies of the notice have been filed, the court will also serve the notice along with the claim form. Otherwise, the claimant must serve the notice on the other parties himself (PD 44, para 19.2(1)).

A defendant who has entered into a funding arrangement before filing any documents at court files the notice when he files his first document at court. The first document a defendant files at court is likely to be an acknowledgment of service or a defence. Again, if the court is to effect service of the defendant's documents, and sufficient copies of the notice have been provided, the court will also serve the notice at the same time (PD 44, para 19.2(3)).

In all other circumstances, for instance, if the funding arrangement is entered into after the claimant starts proceedings or after the defendant files his first document at court, a party must file and serve notice of the funding arrangement within seven days of entering into it (PD 44, para 19.2(4)).

Contents of the notice

The information that must be provided in the notice as set out in Form N251 is:

- whether the party has entered into a CFA providing for a success fee;
- if so, the date of the agreement and the claim or claims to which it relates;
- whether the party has taken out an insurance policy to insure against liability for costs;
- if so, the name of the insurer, the date of the policy and the claim or claims to which it relates.

If both a CFA providing for a success fee and an insurance policy have been entered into, one notice can contain all the relevant information (PD 44, para 19.4(5)).

It should be noted that, at this stage, the requirements are to disclose the fact that a CFA providing for a success fee and/or an insurance policy have been entered into as well as other formalities, but not the amount of the percentage increase or cost of the insurance (rr 44.3A and 44.15; PD 44, para 19.1). A requirement to disclose the level of the percentage increase or the amount of the insurance premium would cause serious disadvantage to a party with a funding arrangement, as it would allow the opponent to assess how the other party viewed the strength of their case, as obviously the higher the percentage increase the lower the perceived chance of success.

Notice of change of information

There is a duty on a party to give notice of any change if the information about the funding arrangement he previously provided is no longer accurate (r 44.15(2); PD 44, para 19.3). For instance, if one insurance policy is cancelled and another entered into.

Failure to disclose the funding arrangement

A failure to disclose the required details of the funding arrangement at the time or times specified will result in the sanction that any additional liability over any period in which there was a failure to provide the information will be irrecoverable (r 44.3B(1)(c)).

However, a party who is in default would be able to apply under the provisions of rr 3.8 and 3.9 (which have general application) for relief from that sanction. It is likely that if the failure to disclose is a pure oversight and is quickly remedied, a party will be unlikely to lose the benefit of the success fee in those circumstances. Such an application is made under Part 23 and supported by evidence (PD 44, para 10).

RECOVERING THE ADDITIONAL LIABILITY

The general principle is that if an order for costs is made against an opponent, this will include payment of the additional liability (PD 43, para 2.1; PD 44, para 9.1).

However, this is subject to the court's general discretion to order otherwise (r 44.3). Also, a party will not recover the additional liability for any period in the proceedings during which he failed to comply with the disclosure requirements referred to above (r 44.3B(1)(c)). Further, a party will not recover the success fee if he fails, when required, to disclose in any assessment proceedings the reasons for setting the percentage increase of the success fee at the level specified in the CFA (r 44.3B(1)(d)). It should also be noted that a party cannot recover the additional liability on any costs incurred before the funding arrangement was entered into (PD 48, para 57.9(3)).

Although in most cases the parties will agree costs, including the level of the success fee and insurance premium, if no agreement can be reached a party can ask for these additional liabilities to be assessed by the court at the end of the proceedings (r 44.3A).

The court will not assess the additional liability until the conclusion of the proceedings to which the funding arrangement relates (r 44.3A(1)). The court can either:

(a) make a summary assessment of all costs, including any additional liability;

(b) make an order for detailed assessment of the additional liability but make a summary assessment of the other costs; or

(c) make an order for detailed assessment of all costs (r 44.3A(2)).

It should be noted that the court cannot make a detailed assessment of the base costs and a summary assessment of the additional liability.

Challenging the success fee

On commencing detailed assessment proceedings a party claiming a success fee must serve on the opponent a statement of the reasons for setting the percentage increase at the level stated in the agreement which should have been given in accordance with reg 3 of the CFAR 2000 (PD 47, para 32).

When deciding whether the percentage increase is reasonable, the court may take the following factors into account:

(a) the chances of success of the case as they reasonably appeared to the legal representative at the time when the CFA was entered into;

(b) the legal representative's liability for disbursements;

(c) what other methods of financing the costs were available to the party who entered into a CFA (PD 44, para 11.8).

The court will have regard to the facts and circumstances as they reasonably appeared to the legal representative when the funding arrangement was entered into, or at the time of any variation, that is, without the benefit of hindsight (PD 44, para 11.7). However, the court is expressly restrained from applying principles of proportionality to reduce the amount of the percentage increase. Accordingly, PD 44, para 11.9 states that the court cannot reduce a percentage increase simply on the ground that when added to base costs which are reasonable and proportionate, the total appears disproportionate.

Chances of success

In *Halloran v Delaney*, the Court of Appeal held that for simple road traffic accident cases (RTAs), entered into on or after 1 August 2001, which settle without the need to commence proceedings, the claimant's solicitor's success fee should be limited to 5%, unless the court is persuaded that a higher uplift is appropriate in the particular circumstances of the case. The court stated that it was time to reappraise the permissible level of the success fee in simple RTAs since the Court of Appeal gave judgment in *Callery v Gray (No 1)* [2001] EWCA Civ 117 and *Callery v Gray (No 2)* [2001] EWCA Civ 1246. In *Callery v Gray* [2002] UKHL 28, the House of Lords approved the Court of Appeal's decision that *for modest and straightforward personal injury claims resulting from traffic accidents*, where a CFA had been entered into from the outset, 20% was the maximum success fee that could reasonably be agreed. This figure was arrived at working from the premise that 90% of such cases would be successful. It was also held in that case that the Court of Appeal was the appropriate forum to monitor and control the developing practice in the area of the recoverability of success fees and insurance premiums.

It should be noted that these maximum figures for success fees are expressly limited to modest and straightforward RTAs, and it was accepted that even for those cases a higher percentage success fee might be justified where the circumstances of an individual case warranted it.

The court is also able to allow different percentage increases for different items of costs, or for different periods during which costs were incurred (PD 44, para 11.8(2)). For instance, in *Callery v Gray* [2002] UKHL 28 and *Halloran v Delaney*, the concept of a two-stage success fee was approved under which the success fee is fixed at a high level, say 100% at the outset, but it is agreed that it will be reduced to a much lower level, say 5%, if the claim settles at an early stage.

A 100% success fee was held to be justified in *Sarwar v Alam* (2003) LTL, 23 March where the case was held to be finely balanced and the solicitors assumed a substantial risk in entering into a CFA.

Costs of costs-only proceedings

Where a litigant enters into a CFA that includes a success fee in respect of a claim which settles before proceedings are issued, a success fee is potentially recoverable on costs incurred in any 'costs-only proceedings' (*Halloran v Delaney*). If parties settle a dispute before proceedings are started and reach agreement on all issues, including which party is to pay costs, but the parties cannot agree the amount of costs, either party may start costs-only proceedings to decide the amount of those costs (r 44.12A).

In *Halloran v Delaney*, the Court of Appeal held that on its proper construction, the claimant's CFA (which was in the form of the Law Society's Model CFA) embraced the costs-only proceedings and the court was satisfied that the costs aspects formed an integral part of the underlying claim.

Challenging the amount of an insurance premium

On commencing detailed assessment proceedings, a party claiming to recover an AEI premium must serve on his opponent a copy of the insurance certificate showing which party's costs are covered, whether his own and/or his opponent's, the maximum extent of the cover and the amount of the premium (PD 47, para 32.5(2)).

The factors that the court must take into account when deciding whether the amount of an insurance premium is reasonable include:

- where the insurance cover is not purchased in support of a CFA (such as 'own costs' insurance, see below), how its cost compares with the equivalent cost of funding the case with a CFA providing for a success fee and supported by insurance;

- the availability of any pre-existing insurance cover;

- the level and extent of the cover provided;

- whether any part of the premium would be rebated in the event of early settlement;

- the amount of any commission payable to the receiving party, or his legal representatives or other agents (PD 44, para 11.10).

The last three factors could be said to be an assessment of the 'value for money' aspect of the insurance premium. It could be argued that a seemingly expensive premium is in fact justified if it pays out on a higher level of legal costs.

Where the level of an insurance premium is fixed as a percentage of damages such an agreement will not be champertous (*Pirie v Ayling* (2003) LTL, 5 March. This was said to be because there is no danger that the insurer will be tempted for his own personal gain to inflame the damages, to suppress evidence, or even to suborn witnesses. Further, the insurance company makes its profits from the insurance not from the litigation; it does not divide the spoils but relies upon the fruits of the litigation as a source from which the insured can satisfy her liability for the premium in return for the provision of a genuine service, namely, the AEI which is external to the litigation (at para 9, *per* Chief Master Hurst, Senior Costs Judge).

'Own costs' insurance

It is possible to purchase after the event legal expenses insurance as a 'stand alone' policy that is not in support of a CFA. Such an insurance product insures against the risk of paying your own legal representative's costs as well as those of your opponent, so if the case is unsuccessful, the insurance premium covers both sets of costs. Under such an arrangement, as the party's legal representative will be paid his costs whether the party's case is successful or not, the costs payable to the party's legal representative would be ordinary base costs and would not include any element of a success fee. As such a policy covers the risk of paying both sides' costs, as compared with a CFA legal expenses insurance policy which will only cover the risk of paying the opponent's costs, the premium is usually considerably higher than that for those policies which support CFAs.

The Court of Appeal held in *Callery v Gray (No 1)* that a reasonable insurance premium paid to insure against the failure to recover one's own costs was also recoverable against the unsuccessful opponent as it fell within the definition of a 'costs liability in the proceedings' under s 29 of the Access to Justice Act 1999.

The availability of pre-existing insurance cover

When assessing whether it is reasonable for a litigant to recover an AEI premium from an opponent, the court must take into account whether BEI cover was available instead (PD 44, para 11.10). If BEI was available but was not used there is a risk that any AEI will not be recoverable. The BEI premium itself, which is usually a very small element added onto household or motor car insurance, is treated as an expense incurred in the past which is not therefore recoverable.

Sarwar v Alam [2001] EWCA Civ 1401 involved a straightforward and modest claim for personal injuries in a RTA, brought by a passenger against the driver of the car in which he was travelling. The passenger's claim for compensation was funded by a CFA and he took out AEI to cover the risk of liability for costs. After the claim had settled it became apparent that the driver's motor insurance policy contained a provision for legal expenses insurance which would have covered the claimant passenger's claim against the insured driver. The Court of Appeal held that in this case the claimant would have been entitled to refuse to use the BEI cover available to him on the grounds that it was not appropriate cover in the circumstances. This was because the cover available would have obliged him to entrust the care of his claim to the insurers acting for the driver against whom he was claiming, who were to have full conduct and control of his claim, and where he was denied the opportunity of instructing a solicitor of his choice except in the unlikely event that legal proceedings were started.

In Sarwar v Alam, the Court of Appeal laid down some guidance, which was not to be seen as a strict code, as to the level of inquiry legal advisers should embark upon when investigating whether a client may have the benefit of BEI. The legal adviser should invite a client to bring along to the first interview any relevant motor insurance policy, any household insurance policy and any stand alone BEI policy belonging to any spouse/partner living in the same household. However, the court stressed that the legal adviser is 'not obliged to embark on a treasure hunt seeking to see the insurance policies of every member of the client's family in case by chance they contain relevant BEI cover which the client might use' (Lord Phillips MR at [46]). The court also recognised that the time involved in making such inquiries should be proportionate and restricted to what is reasonable in the light of the alternative availability of AEI at a modest premium.

The amount of the insurance premium

In Callery v Gray (No 2) [2001] EWCA Civ 1246, the Court of Appeal had also to rule on whether the amount of the insurance premium (£350) was reasonable. The court appointed Master O'Hare, costs judge, as assessor, to submit a report to the court in order to assist it in reaching its decision as to the reasonableness of the insurance premium. In the light of his report the Court of Appeal held that the cost of the premium was reasonable; it was not disproportionate to the risk covered and was suitable to the claimant's needs. However, the court stressed that its decision should not be taken as laying down a general principle that a premium of £350 is reasonable, even in cases of the same type, that is, simple RTAs. The court held that when more information and experience about the AEI market became available there would be a sounder basis on which guidelines cases, setting benchmark figures, could be decided.

However, *In the Matter of Claims Direct Test Cases* [2003] EWCA Civ 136, the Court of Appeal said that the court should consider what was being provided for in return for a 'premium', as it was only that element which was insurance against liability for costs that would be a recoverable premium under s 29 of the Access to Justice Act 1999 and not something in additional to that, for instance, in that case, a claims handling fee. The court therefore approved the costs judge's assessment that the sum of £621.13 was recoverable as a premium under the Act out of the sum of £1,312.50 claimed. However, the court did indicate that if work done by a claims manager represented a disbursement for work which a solicitor would otherwise have performed himself, the cost of that work would be properly recoverable as part of the solicitor's bill but not as an insurance premium.

An insurance premium fixed at 20% of damages awarded or agreed whatever they may be was held to be 'inherently flawed' by Chief Master Hurst, Senior Costs Judge in *Pirie v Ayling*. Chief Master Hurst considered that if the case had settled for £1,300 the premium would have been £260, a figure which in his experience was lower than that charged in many straightforward low value claims. On the other hand, if the case had settled for £130,000 the premium would have been £26,000, which was more than two and a half times the level of the indemnity. In his opinion a premium of 20% of damages, whatever they may be, is likely to be unreasonable in all simple road accident cases in which the compensation payable exceeds about £2,000. He allowed a figure of £350 instead (paras 14–16).

It was held in the costs litigation arising from the decision in *Sarwar v Alam* (2003) LTL, 23 March that in the circumstances of that case a premium of £62,500 was reasonable even though the claimant had been prepared to settle for damages of £2,250. The claimant had difficulties obtaining suitable insurance cover for an appeal to the Court of Appeal, the case having failed before the district judge and the circuit judge. Master Rogers therefore found it was a risky case that called for a tailor-made insurance premium rather than a standard premium. The claimant's advisers had tried to obtain an alternative quotation at a lower rate but were unsuccessful. Master Rogers took into account the fact that the law was in a state of flux and insurers were understandably reluctant to commit themselves to a large potential liability.

Challenging the stage at which a CFA/AEI was entered into

There have been a number of challenges to the recoverability of a success fee and/or AEI in the circumstances where a claimant has entered into a CFA and/or AEI at an early stage, for instance, at the first appointment with his solicitor, rather than at a later stage when the defendant's response to the claim was known and the claimant could therefore more accurately assess the risk of failure. However, in *Callery v Gray* [2002] UKHL 28, the House of Lords again upheld the Court of Appeal's decision that a success fee and AEI would be recoverable even where the CFA and AEI had been entered into at an early stage before the defendant had been notified of the claim.

In *Ashworth v Peterborough United Football Club Ltd* (2002) LTL, 4 July, Supreme Court Costs Office, the court held that an AEI policy with a premium of some £46,000 taken out at a late stage was the premium recoverable from the defendant. The reasons given were:

(a) the evidence showed that the policy would probably not have been available at the outset of the proceedings, and accordingly the claimant was entitled to take out the policy at a later date when the proceedings were well advanced;

(b) a party challenging the amount of a premium must show that it was not proportionate to the matters in issue under r 44.4(2), and the defendants had failed to do this in the instant case;

(c) it would not have been reasonable to have expected the claimant to seek cover from other insurers – this would have contravened r 1.1(2)(c);

(d) the claimant's solicitors had given the defendants' solicitors as much information as they were obliged to give.

Recovering the percentage increase from the client

If, on assessing costs, the court disallows or reduces the percentage increase payable under the CFA, the general rule is that the disallowed or reduced percentage increase ceases to be payable under the agreement. This means effectively that the client will not be liable to pay it. However, the legal representative can apply to the court for an order that his client continue to be liable for the percentage increase, and the court can make such an order if it considers it a suitable order to make (PD 44, para 20).

Client challenging the level of the success fee

A client who has entered into a CFA can apply for the assessment of either the base costs, or the percentage increase of the success fee or both (PD 48, para 54.5(1)).

A client who applies to the court for the percentage increase under the CFA to be reduced must set out in his application notice:

(a) the reasons why the percentage increase should be reduced; and

(b) what the percentage increase should be.

When deciding whether the percentage increase is reasonable, the court will have regard to all the relevant factors as they appeared to the solicitor or counsel when the CFA was entered into (PD 48, para 54.5(2)):

(a) the risk that the circumstances in which the fees or expenses would be payable might not occur;

(b) the disadvantages relating to the absence of payment on account;

(c) whether the amount which might be payable under the CFA is limited to a certain proportion of any damages recovered by the client;

(d) whether there is a CFA between the solicitor and counsel;

(e) the solicitor's liability for any disbursements.

TRANSITIONAL PROVISIONS

A CFA entered into before 1 April 2000 does not fall within the definition of a funding arrangement. The practical effect of this is that any success fee or legal expenses insurance attached to the CFA will not be recoverable from the losing opponent. This restriction cannot be avoided simply by ending the original agreement and entering into a new one after 1 April 2000.

In the circumstances where a party entered into a funding arrangement and started proceedings after 1 April 2000 but before 3 July 2000 (when the new Costs PDs came into effect), the party had 28 days to comply with the requirements of the new rules and PDs in order for the additional liability to be recoverable (r 39 of the Civil Procedure (Amendment No 3) Rules 2000 (SI 2000/1317)).

MEMBERSHIP ORGANISATIONS

Certain membership organisations, such as trade unions, fund litigation on behalf of their members from their own resources. The nature and size of the organisation is such that they self-insure rather than take out insurance against potential costs liabilities arising from the litigation. Under s 30 of the Access to Justice Act 1999 and provisions of the Access to Justice (Membership Organisations) Regulations 2000 (SI 2000/693), such membership organisations can now also recover, as part of an order for costs, a sum that reflects the provision the organisation has made against the risk of having to meet the liabilities of the member whose case it has underwritten. The membership organisations that qualify, the formalities that must be complied with and the method by which the sum is calculated are set out in the Access to Justice (Membership Organisations) Regulations 2000.

THE COMMUNITY LEGAL SERVICE

Introduction

The CLS was launched on 3 April 2000. It is administered by the Legal Services Commission, which is a non-departmental public body. The CLS is funded from moneys out of the CLS Fund.

The CLS replaces the civil and family legal aid system. The attitude of the Government to the former legal aid system may be summed up by this quote from Lord Irvine in a statement he made to the House of Lords on the publication of a Consultation Paper, *Access to Justice with Conditional Fees*, on 4 March 1998 (www.dca.gov.uk):

> At present the legal aid system is failing us all. It is failing the many millions of people on modest incomes who do not qualify for legal aid and who simply cannot contemplate going to law because of the potential legal costs if they lose. It is failing people on legal aid, because the Government cannot direct money to those who need it most and to those cases where there is a public interest in seeing justice done. Finally, it is failing the taxpayer who year on year is being asked to pay more and more, and yet can rarely get help from legal aid when it is actually needed.

The CLS is supposed to be more than a replacement for the previous legal aid system. It is intended to bring together and co-ordinate all the sources of information and advice so that a person with a legal problem can find the best and most appropriate source of help. In this sense, it provides a 'directory' service which is available to everyone, the idea being that a person looking for legal advice and assistance can find out which is the best body or person to approach for help or information. The *Community Legal Service Directory* provides details of all the approved sources of help and information, and copies are available in places such as libraries and solicitors' firms (who are part of the scheme) and on the dedicated website www.justask.org.uk and telephone line 0845 608 1122. The Government believes that it will, therefore, improve access to legal and advice services (see *The Community Legal Service Performance Indicators for Community Legal Service Partnerships*, Consultation Paper, April 2000, available on www.dca.gov.uk/consult/general/030400fr.htm).

However, although anyone can access the *Community Legal Service Directory* to identify a source of help for their problem, this does not mean that everyone will qualify for State funding to bring legal proceedings. Although the availability of legal aid was, in practice, very limited (as, in order to qualify, a case not only had to satisfy a merits test, but the individual concerned also had to satisfy a means test set at a very low level), funding for a case under the CLS will be even more limited. Unlike the Legal Aid Fund, the CLS Fund has a limited amount of resources to spend on legal services. Also, whereas legal aid was available for most types of civil case (there were some exceptions, such as defamation), funding from the CLS depends not only on whether the person seeking the help meets the merits test (just as stringent as under legal aid), but also on whether the case falls into one of the limited categories of types of case funded by the scheme.

The main change to the scope of cases qualifying for State funding is that personal injury claims arising from negligence (except clinical negligence cases) are expressly excluded from funding under the CLS, along with conveyancing, boundary disputes, partnership, company and business issues, will making, defamation or malicious falsehood, and trust law (Sched 2, para 1 to the Access to Justice Act 1999). Also, all other civil money claims (apart from family cases) are effectively excluded on the basis that they can be funded instead via a CFA. On the other hand, 'social welfare' cases have been prioritised for help: these are said to include family, benefits, debt, employment, rent and mortgage arrears, immigration and nationality issues. However, it should be borne in mind that personal injury and death claims that are not based on negligence, for example, cases of trespass to the person, are not excluded from CLS funding.

It should be noted that one effect of litigants obtaining public funding is that costs can only very rarely be awarded against them or the Fund, and certainly not without an assessment of their means (see Chapter 34, 'Costs of Proceedings'). Those embarking on litigation against, or facing litigation by, assisted persons will have to bear in mind that not only might there be difficulties in enforcing judgment against a person of limited means, but they also have little or no chance of recovering costs. This does also bring into question r 1.1(2)(a), which requires the court, as part of the overriding objective, to ensure that the parties are on an equal footing.

Community Legal Service partnerships

CLS partnerships are an important part of the CLS. The partnership consists of those bodies and organisations that fund legal and advice services (the principal funders being the Legal Services Commission and local authorities, but also local and national charities) and those CLS approved individuals and bodies who supply the legal services (such as legal representatives and advice centres).

The CLS partnerships are to have responsibility for assessing the requirements for legal services in their area and ensure that a service is in place to meet previously identified priority needs for that area. CLS partnerships are designed to respond to local differences on the basis that different areas and communities will have different needs for legal and advice services. Funding at a set level will then be made available by the Department for Constitutional Affairs to meet those needs which have been identified. In this way, it is hoped that public funding for legal services will be controlled by limiting it to identified priority needs in an area at a previously set level which cannot be exceeded. When the CLS was launched, partnerships had not been established over all areas of England and Wales, although the plan is that they will eventually exist to cover every area of the jurisdiction.

The Community Legal Service Quality Mark

Organisations and individuals providing services under the CLS can qualify for the CLS Quality Mark. This will be awarded to legal service providers that achieve the specified minimum standards of the CLS. Once qualified, they can display and advertise their body with the CLS Quality Mark logo. This Quality Mark is based on the Legal Aid Franchise Quality Assurance Standard that was introduced under the former legal aid system. Firms of solicitors who previously qualified for a legal aid franchise automatically acquired the Community Legal Service Quality Mark when the CLS was launched.

However, in recognition that the CLS is not just about the provision of legal advice from legal representatives, the CLS Quality Mark is awarded for three different levels of service:

* information;
* general help; and
* specialist help.

Information

Those organisations displaying the CLS Quality Mark for Information simply provide access to information about the provision of legal services in an area, but in order to qualify for the Quality Mark, are likely to be able to supply information such as leaflets and other reference material, access to the CLS Directory of Services and/or access to the CLS website. Places such as libraries are likely to deal at this level of the service.

General help

At this level, basic advice is provided in the form of information about rights and responsibilities and some services such as helping to fill in forms, writing letters and negotiating on behalf of the inquirer. This type of help is typically provided by organisations such as Citizens Advice Bureaux, who offer advice and assistance for problems through volunteers who are trained, but not usually legally qualified.

Specialist help

At this level, help is provided for complex legal problems or where legal representation is required. Organisations offering this level of service will be solicitors' firms and law centres. Solicitors' firms who are approved providers of the CLS who have been awarded a contract by the Legal Services Commission and have achieved the CLS Quality Mark will be able to take on certain types of cases with funding from the CLS Fund.

Scope of the Community Legal Service Fund

In order to secure funding from the Community Legal Service Fund, the application must fulfil certain requirements. Funding is available for legal services in relation to the areas of law set out in s 4(2) of the Access to Justice Act 1999. In very general terms, funding will be available for social welfare type cases, such as housing and benefit claims. Funding is available only for individuals and not, therefore, for firms, companies or other corporate bodies (s 4 of the Access to Justice Act 1999).

Excluded services

Under Sched 2 to the Access to Justice Act 1999, certain areas of law are expressly excluded from funding (apart from the provision of general information about the law, legal system and availability of legal services). These are:

(a) personal injury and death claims (apart from clinical negligence claims) and damage to property claims *caused by negligence*. These claims are excluded on the grounds that most of them can be funded by a CFA (it should be noted, however, that personal injury and death claims not based on negligence, for example, trespass to the person, are not excluded from CLS funding);

(b) conveyancing, boundary disputes, the making of wills, matters of trust law, defamation or malicious falsehood, matters of company or partnership law, and other matters arising out of the carrying on of a business. These claims are excluded on the grounds that they are not considered to have sufficient priority to justify public funding.

Exceptions to the exclusions

In some circumstances, cases in areas of law normally falling within the excluded category can receive funding from the CLS. These include cases which can be shown to have a wider public interest, proceedings against public authorities alleging serious wrongdoing, such as abuse of power or breach of human rights, and personal injury cases with very high investigative costs (s 6(8) of the Access to Justice Act 1999).

FURTHER REFORM

Abolition of the indemnity principle

The introduction of provisions to allow the success fee and insurance premiums to be recoverable from an unsuccessful opponent, along with the other costs of the proceedings, has resulted in much satellite litigation in which such unsuccessful opponents resist having to pay this additional liability. It is argued that the application of the indemnity principle makes CFAs and AEI policies which are technically defective for failure to comply with the CFAR 2000 unenforceable against a client, and therefore unenforceable against the opponent (see p 47 above). However, the indemnity principle has been abolished in respect of certain types of CFAs which provide that the client is liable to pay his legal representative's costs only if, and to the extent that, he recovers damages and costs in the proceedings (Conditional Fee Agreements (Miscellaneous Amendments) Regulations 2003; Civil Procedure (Amendment No 2) Rules 2003).

However, in recognition of the difficulties caused by such challenges, and in furtherance of Government policy to make it easier and more affordable to use CFAs and AEI, the Government has proposed the complete abolition of the indemnity principle to the assessment of costs (see Government's conclusions following consultation on the *Collective Conditional Fees*, Consultation Paper, September 2000, www.dca.gov.uk/consult/collconfees0600). The need for reform was felt particularly in the case of collective conditional fee agreements, where there is a more fundamental challenge to their validity in terms of the indemnity principle because a third party (often a union) rather than the client will be liable for the costs.

The statutory provision in the form of s 31 of the Access to Justice Act is already drafted, which will pave the way for the indemnity principle to be abolished. Section 31, which amends s 51 of the Supreme Court Act 1981, provides that the amount recoverable by way of costs may not be limited to 'what would have been payable by [the client] to [his lawyers] if he had not been awarded costs'. However, this provision is not yet in force and rules of procedure are still awaited from the Civil Procedure Rules Committee to give effect to it. Once this provision is in force and the necessary rules are in place, it will allow a party to receive reasonable and proportionate costs from his opponent (if so entitled) irrespective of the terms of the agreement in cases where an additional liability is claimed.

CHAPTER 5

PRE-ACTION PROTOCOLS

INTRODUCTION

In *Access to Justice*, Lord Woolf said: 'My approach to civil justice is that disputes should, wherever possible, be resolved without litigation.' (See *Access to Justice*, Final Report (FR), Chapter 10, para 2 (www.dca.gov.uk/civil/final/index.htm.) This statement was made in the context of his proposals for pre-action protocols, and it could be argued that pre-action protocols epitomise, more than any other aspect of the Civil Procedure Rules (CPR), Lord Woolf's approach to reforming the civil justice system, since the main purpose of a pre-action protocol is to facilitate the settlement of a dispute without litigation. Along with this, Lord Woolf emphasised that the quality and timing of a settlement are also important, not just the fact that a settlement has been made (see FR, Chapter 10, para 3).

Pre-action protocols are designed to enable the parties to be well informed about the other side's case in order to reach a mutually satisfying settlement, or to make meaningful offers to settle. The protocols expect identification of the issues and voluntary disclosure of relevant documents before litigation is begun in order to encourage the early resolution of a dispute. In Lord Woolf's opinion, it is most inappropriate to settle a dispute at the door of a court as, by that stage, maximum cost and delay will have been incurred (see FR, Chapter 10, para 3).

Lord Woolf was also dissatisfied by the knowledge that many disputes settle because the claimant is tired of waiting and does not have the energy or resources to pursue the claim further; often, this is as a result of deliberate delaying and wearing down tactics adopted by the opponent (see FR, Chapter 10, para 3). The hope is that pre-action protocols, which encourage parties to behave in a reasonable and less adversarial way, even before proceedings have started, will help to curtail such tactics and save costs.

The obligation to behave reasonably in notifying and responding to a claim prior to the issue of proceedings, in exchanging information and documents, in agreeing the selection and/or instruction of a mutually acceptable expert and in co-operating with a view to resolving the dispute without the need for litigation, extends to all disputes whether or not they are covered by an approved pre-action protocol. A general framework for reasonable pre-action behaviour is set out in the practice direction to the Protocols and applies to all cases not covered by an approved protocol (PD Protocols, paras 4.1–4.10).

Critics of the reforms complain that things such as pre-action protocols result in the 'front-loading' of litigation, making many disputes more expensive and time-consuming rather than less. They argue that if a dispute settles, time and costs spent preparing a case to a standard as if it were ready for trial will be wasted. Lord Woolf's response to such criticism was to say that bringing work forward on a case will enable some cases to settle earlier. He felt that if that does not happen, early defining of issues and disclosure of documents will increase the likelihood of a settlement being reached; and if that does not happen, such early work will enable the case to proceed more quickly and smoothly if litigation is started (see FR, Chapter 10, para 6; para 16).

A clear message from the CPR is that litigation is an act of last resort, and parties should be able to demonstrate from their pre-action conduct that they made a concerted effort to settle the dispute before issuing proceedings. Moreover, if litigation is started, the parties should approach it with a view to settlement at the earliest opportunity.

The status of protocols

The pre-action protocols were described by Lord Woolf as 'codes of sensible practice which parties are expected to follow' (see FR, Chapter 10, para 6). Approved pre-action protocols are set out in the schedule to the Practice Direction, which is the mechanism to bring them within the ambit of the CPR.

Although para 2.2 of the Practice Direction to the Protocols states that 'the court will expect all parties to have complied in substance with the terms of an approved protocol', a party cannot be compelled to comply. If proceedings are never commenced, a defaulting party will not be punished for failing to comply with a protocol.

Although the protocols cannot be enforced, if proceedings are started the court has substantial powers to penalise a party for failing to comply with a pre-action protocol. Accordingly, throughout the CPR reference is made to the court's powers to take compliance with the protocols into account when exercising case management powers, imposing sanctions or making orders for costs. The court can also impose sanctions for failure to comply. The sanctions include indemnity costs and penalty interest (PD Protocols, para 2.3; see pp 96–99 below, 'Sanctions for failure to follow the protocols').

The protocols and limitation periods

The pre-action protocols do not alter the statutory limitation periods. Therefore, if the limitation period for a claim is close to expiry, the claimant should issue proceedings even if he has not complied with a relevant protocol.

Each protocol sets out steps the parties should take if, due to the imminent expiry of the limitation period, proceedings are issued before complying with the relevant protocol. For claims which are covered by the general procedure in the Practice Direction to the Protocols (because they are not covered by a specific protocol) the parties are encouraged to agree to apply to the court for a stay of the proceedings while they follow the Practice Direction (PD Protocols, para 3.5).

THE PRE-ACTION PROTOCOLS

The Glossary to the CPR describes pre-action protocols as 'statements of understanding between legal practitioners and others about pre-action practice and which are approved by a relevant practice direction'.

Protocols are drafted by interested groups such as specialist practitioner associations and relevant industry bodies, who are taken to have experience and expertise in identifying good and bad practice in litigating disputes in their specialist areas. In *Carlson v Townsend* [2001] EWCA Civ 511, a case about disclosure of medical reports under the Pre-action Protocol for Personal Injury Claims, Brooke LJ said of protocols (at [31]): 'They are guides to good litigation and pre-litigation practice, drafted and agreed by those who know all about the difference between good and bad practice.'

Pre-action protocols set out the steps and the timescale that parties should follow when notifying and responding to a potential claim. The intention is that proceedings, if necessary, should not be issued until the parties have fully complied with the requirements of the protocol.

It was never Lord Woolf's intention that there be a pre-action protocol for every type of dispute. Instead, he believed that they should cover specific types of dispute such as personal injury, clinical negligence ('clinical negligence' is the phrase for what would formerly have been known as medical negligence disputes; the phrase was felt to be more accurate and understandable, as it covers not just medical negligence disputes, but also disputes involving dentists and nurses, etc) and housing (see FR, Chapter 10, paras 6–8). There are now pre-action protocols applying to the following types of claim:

- personal injury;
- clinical negligence;
- construction and engineering disputes;
- defamation;
- professional negligence; and
- judicial review.

(See PD Protocols, para 5.1.)

General pre-action protocol

The Lord Chancellor's Department (LCD), now the Department for Constitutional Affairs, put out for consultation a proposal that a general pre-action protocol be published which would apply to all disputes not covered by an approved protocol (see LCD Consultation Paper, *General Pre-action Protocol*, October 2001, www.dca.gov.uk/consult/preaction.htm).

In the light of the responses to that proposal the LCD decided not to proceed with a general pre-action protocol (see *Responses to the Consultation Paper, General Pre-action Protocol*, July 2002, www.dca.gov.uk/consult/preaction/preactionresp.htm). It was felt that such a protocol would be too general and likely to lead to confusion and unnecessary delay. However, whilst abandoning the proposal to introduce a General Pre-action Protocol on the grounds that it was 'too ambitious', the LCD emphasised its commitment to exploring ways to build on the existing provisions within the CPR which require reasonable pre-action behaviour and underline the court's powers to impose sanctions for conduct which falls short of this. It was in the light of these conclusions that the 30th update to the CPR amended the Practice Direction to the Protocols to provide a general framework for reasonable pre-action behaviour, which applies to all cases not covered by an approved protocol.

Draft protocols

There are also a number of draft pre-action protocols, prepared by various interested bodies, which may become approved. In practice, the parties to disputes covered by a draft protocol often agree to voluntarily comply with it. However, until such time as further protocols are approved, where the claim is not covered by an approved protocol and the parties do not agree to comply with a relevant draft protocol, the parties should follow the general procedures set out in the Practice Direction to the Protocols.

The objectives of the protocols

The objectives of the pre-action protocols are broken down into three main elements, the first objective being:

• To encourage the exchange of early and full information about the prospective legal claim (PD Protocols, para 1.4(1)).

The intention is to enable each side to be fully informed of the other's case and in the process (it is hoped) to screen out those claims or defences that are weak or frivolous.

The second objective can be seen as a natural progression from the first objective, because, having seen the measure of the opponent's case, the second objective is:

• To enable parties to avoid litigation by agreeing a settlement of the claim before the commencement of proceedings (PD Protocols, para 1.4(2)).

It is hoped that each side is now in a position to make a meaningful offer in settlement which has more prospect of being acceptable in the light of the mutual awareness of the strengths and weaknesses of each other's cases brought about by the operation of the first objective. However, it is expected that even where settlement is not reached, and the second objective is not fulfilled, the process of compliance with the protocol will result in the third objective being realised, which is:

• To support the efficient management of proceedings where litigation cannot be avoided (PD Protocols, para 1.4).

It is hoped that this 'front-loading' of the litigation is not in vain, as the very process of obliging parties to identify and narrow the issues between them through compliance with a protocol, if it does not result in settlement, will at least enable the case to run more smoothly through the case management system once proceedings are issued.

PRE-ACTION BEHAVIOUR IN CASES NOT COVERED BY A PRE-ACTION PROTOCOL

In accordance with the overriding objective, the parties to all disputes will be expected to act reasonably in exchanging relevant information and documents, and in generally trying to avoid the necessity for the start of proceedings, whether a case is covered by a pre-action protocol or not (PD Protocols, para 4.1).

The Practice Direction to the Protocols identifies what a reasonable pre-action procedure should include for those cases not covered by an approved protocol.

Notification of the claim

The claimant should send a letter of claim containing sufficient detail to enable the recipient to investigate the claim; enclosing copies of essential documents relied on by the claimant; asking for a prompt acknowledgment of the letter and a full response within a reasonable stated period (standard being one month); indicating whether court proceedings will be issued if a full response is not received within the stated period; if applicable, requesting essential documents; and, if applicable, stating whether the claimant wishes to use a form of Alternative Dispute Resolution (ADR) to resolve the matter (PD Protocols, para 4.3(a)–(f)).

The claimant should also draw attention to the court's powers to impose sanctions for failure to comply with the Practice Direction and enclose a copy of the Practice Direction if the recipient is likely to be unrepresented (PD Protocols, para 4.3(g)).

Response to the claim

In return, the defendant should acknowledge receipt of the claimant's letter within 21 days of receipt, indicating when the defendant will give a full written response. If the defendant specifies a longer period than that stipulated by the claimant he should give reasons why a longer period is necessary (PD Protocols, para 4.4).

The defendant's response should, as appropriate, accept the claim in whole or in part and make proposals for settlement, or deny the claim (PD Protocols, para 4.5).

If the claim is not accepted the defendant's response should give detailed reasons why it is not accepted; enclose copies of essential documents relied on by the defendant; enclose copies of documents asked for by the claimant, or explain why they are not enclosed; identify and ask for copies of essential documents in the claimant's possession; and state whether the defendant is prepared to use a form of ADR to resolve the dispute (PD Protocols, para 4.6).

Further steps

If the dispute is not resolved the parties should promptly engage in appropriate negotiations with a view to settling the dispute and avoiding litigation (PD Protocols, para 4.7).

The Practice Direction encourages the parties to engage an agreed expert if expert evidence is necessary to resolve the dispute (para 4.9). However, it also goes on to warn that the parties will need permission from the court to rely on expert evidence in any subsequent proceedings and that such permission may not always be given, and that consequently the cost of engaging an expert is not always recoverable (para 4.10).

INFORMATION ABOUT FUNDING ARRANGEMENTS

Funding arrangements include conditional fee agreements, which provide for a success fee and after the event legal expenses insurance. Success fees and after the event insurance premiums fall within the definition of an additional liability and are potentially recoverable from an unsuccessful opponent under an order for costs so long as notification of the funding agreement has been given to the opponent in accordance with the relevant rules and practice directions. Under para 4A of the Protocols Practice Direction, the notification requirements include an obligation, even before proceedings are commenced, to inform an opponent that such an arrangement has been entered into. There is no prescribed form for providing the notification, so the likely method will be by means of a letter.

It should be noted that this obligation applies whether the type of claim involved is covered by a pre-action protocol or not (PD Protocols, paras 4A1 and 4A2). The time within which the notification must be given is not specified, but it is likely that the same consequences will apply as where proceedings have been started and notification has not been given, namely, that a party will not be able to recover any additional liability for any period in which he failed to provide information about the funding arrangement (r 44.3B(1)(c)).

PRE-ACTION PROTOCOL FOR PERSONAL INJURY CLAIMS

This was the first pre-action protocol to be drafted. The most prominent feature of this Protocol is its promotion of the *joint selection* of a mutually acceptable expert by both parties before proceedings are commenced.

The notes of guidance to the Protocol state that it is intended to apply to all claims that include a claim for personal injury (except industrial disease claims) and to the entirety of those claims, not just the personal injury element of them (Protocol, para 2.2). So, for instance, if there is a claim for personal injury and property damage then the Protocol will apply to the whole claim even if the personal injury claim forms only a small element of the whole.

The Protocol is primarily intended for road traffic, tripping and slipping, and accident at work cases that include an element of personal injury with a value of less than £15,000 and are likely to be allocated to the fast track (Protocol, para 2.3). The expressed reasoning for this is that, owing to the short timetable of 30 weeks between the start of proceedings and trial on the fast track, in order realistically to comply with the timetable and ensure that the case is ready for trial, the parties will need to have exchanged relevant information and narrowed the issues between them before proceedings are started (Protocol, para 2.3).

However, the notes of guidance go on to stipulate that the 'spirit, if not the letter of the Protocol, should still be followed for multi-track type claims'. In such claims, in accordance with reasonable pre-action behaviour, the court will expect to see detailed letters before action, voluntary exchange of information and documents, and joint selection of experts (Protocol, para 2.4).

Notification of the claim

Early notification

The notes of guidance to the Protocol refer to the fact that in some cases, the claimant's legal representative may wish initially to notify the defendant of the likelihood of a claim being brought against him without sending a detailed letter of claim. This may be the case if the claimant is not yet in a position to send a detailed letter of claim but wishes to give the defendant early notification of a potential claim. Examples given are where, for instance, the defendant is unlikely to have any, or only limited, knowledge of the incident giving rise to the claim, or if the claimant is incurring significant expense as a result of the accident which he expects to claim from the defendant. The Protocol states that such early notification will not activate the timetable for responding (Protocol, para 2.6).

The letter of claim

As soon as sufficient information is available to substantiate a realistic claim, a claimant should send two copies of a letter of claim to the defendant, one for passing on to his insurers. The Protocol states that this should be done before issues of quantum are addressed in detail (Protocol, para 3.1). Therefore, a letter of claim should be sent as soon as a potential claim is identified, even though the extent of the loss suffered is not yet fully quantified or quantifiable.

The Protocol sets out, at Annex A, a standard format of a letter of claim that should be used, or amended to suit a particular case. The letter of claim should contain a clear summary of the facts on which the claim is based, an indication of the nature of the injuries suffered and any financial loss incurred (Protocol, para 3.2). At this stage, 'sufficient information should be given in order to enable the defendant's insurer/solicitor to commence investigations and at least put a broad valuation on the "risk"' (Protocol, para 3.5).

In road traffic accident claims, the letter of claim should provide the name and address of the hospital where treatment has been obtained and the claimant's hospital reference number (Protocol, para 3.2). The claimant's National Insurance number and date of birth need to be supplied only once the defendant has responded to the letter of claim and confirmed the identity of the insurer (Protocol, para 3.4).

It is recognised in the notes of guidance to the Protocol that the defendant may have no personal financial interest in the outcome of the dispute because he is insured. In those circumstances, court-imposed sanctions will be ineffective against the defendant. For these reasons the draft letter of claim emphasises the importance of the defendant passing the letter of claim on to his insurers and warns the defendant that his insurance cover may be affected if he fails to do so. The notes of guidance also state that in those circumstances where the defendant has delayed passing the letter of claim on to his insurers, the insurers would be justified in asking the claimant for more time to respond to the letter of claim (Protocol, para 2.7).

The defendant's response

The Protocol allows the defendant a two-stage response to the claimant's claim. The initial response can be simply an acknowledgment of the claim, which indicates to the claimant that the matter is being investigated and that the claimant should hold off from issuing proceedings. The defendant then has a period of time to investigate, after which a full letter of response should follow.

The defendant should reply within 21 calendar days of the date of posting of the letter of claim, identifying the insurer (if any). The Protocol states that if there is no reply within that time limit, either from the defendant or from the insurer, the claimant will be entitled to issue proceedings (Protocol, para 3.6).

The defendant (or his insurer) has a maximum of three months from the date of acknowledgment of the claimant's letter of claim to investigate the claim. The defendant or his insurers should reply within that three-month time limit stating whether liability is denied and giving reasons for any denial (Protocol, para 3.7). Where liability is admitted, it will be presumed that the defendant is bound by this admission for all claims with a total value of up to £15,000 (Protocol, para 3.9).

Status of letter of claim/response

The letter of claim and letter of response are not intended to have the same status as a statement of case (Protocol, para 2.9). Moreover, it is recognised that matters may come to light as a result of investigation after the letter of claim has been sent, or after the defendant has responded, and at para 2.9 the notes of guidance state that:

> These circumstances could mean that the 'pleaded' case of one or both parties is presented slightly differently than in the letter of claim and response. It would not be consistent with the spirit of the Protocol for a party to 'take a point' on this in the proceedings, provided that there was no obvious intention by the party who changed their position to mislead the other party.

Disclosure of documents

The Protocol encourages voluntary early disclosure of relevant documents that would be likely to be the subject of an order for disclosure either through an application for pre-action disclosure, or by disclosure in the course of proceedings (Protocol, para 3.10). To this end, Annex B to the Protocol contains standard disclosure lists identifying types of document that are likely to be material to the types of dispute specifically covered by the Protocol. So, there are standard disclosure lists for road traffic accident, tripping and slipping, and workplace claims. The idea is that when the defendant receives a letter of claim in respect of one of these types of dispute, he should consult the list and voluntarily disclose, with the letter of reply, any documents he may have which are identified on the list. The lists are not intended to be exhaustive, so the defendant should also disclose any other relevant 'disclosable' documents even if they are not on the list (Protocol, para 3.10).

Where the claimant's investigation of the claim is well advanced, the notes of guidance state that the claimant's letter of claim could indicate which classes of document are considered relevant for early disclosure by the defendant (Protocol, para 3.11). Where the defendant alleges contributory negligence of the claimant, he should give reasons for this and disclose any documents from the list relevant to this issue, and the claimant should respond to these allegations before proceedings are issued (Protocol, para 3.12).

Although Lord Woolf recommended that disclosure be enforced through practice directions, in fact that recommendation was not followed, and disclosure under the Protocol is entirely voluntary. However, if a party refuses to disclose relevant documents without good reason, the other party may be able to make use of the provisions on pre-action disclosure under s 33 of the Supreme Court Act 1981 and s 53 of the County Courts Act 1984 to enforce compliance with their request. It should always be remembered also that any unreasonable conduct and failure to follow an appropriate protocol can be taken into account by the court and makes a party vulnerable to sanctions if proceedings are commenced.

Selection of mutually acceptable expert

The provisions in the Protocol about the selection of a mutually acceptable expert should be distinguished from the instruction of a single joint expert. In the former case, although the selection of the expert has been agreed, only one party instructs the expert; in the latter case both the selection *and the instruction* of the expert is done jointly by the parties.

Under the Protocol the idea is that rather than both parties instructing their own expert, the parties agree the selection of a mutually acceptable expert who is then instructed by one party. When the report is obtained by the instructing party it is disclosed to the other side, who then asks questions of the expert or agrees the report but does not obtain his own report (Protocol, para 2.11). Although the Protocol envisages that the instructing party will disclose the expert's report it does not require it. Therefore, failure to disclose the report will not be a breach of the Protocol, although instructing an expert without first giving the other party an opportunity to object to the instruction of that expert is (see *Carlson v Townsend* [2001] EWCA Civ 511).

In order to make such a provision fully effective, the mutually acceptable expert needs to be instructed before either party instructs their own expert. If a party goes ahead and instructs their own expert, before trying to agree the selection of a mutually acceptable expert with the other side, they run the risk that once proceedings have started the court will order the appointment of a single joint expert and that party will be unable to recover the costs of their own expert.

The Protocol sets out steps a party should follow in order to agree to the instruction of a mutually acceptable expert (Protocol, paras 3.14–3.21). Annex C to the Protocol contains a draft letter of instruction to a medical expert. The notes of guidance also refer to the fact that some solicitors obtain medical reports through medical agencies rather than from a specific doctor or hospital. In those circumstances, the Protocol states that if the defendant so requests, the agency should be asked to provide the names of the doctors whom they are considering instructing (Protocol, para 2.12).

Mechanism for selecting an expert

The expert evidence provisions of the Protocol apply to both parties, not just the claimant. Therefore, the instruction of a mutually acceptable expert could come through the initiative of the defendant rather than the claimant. However, in practice it will usually be the claimant who instructs an expert to provide a medical report, because it is a requirement in personal injury claims for the claimant to attach a medical report about his personal injuries to his particulars of claim (PD 16, paras 4.1–4.3).

The Protocol refers to the party proposing and eventually instructing the expert as the 'first party', and to the party asked to agree to the proposal and instruction of the expert as the 'second party'. Paragraph 3.14 of the Protocol provides that:

> Before any party instructs an expert he should give the other party a list of the name(s) of one or more experts in the relevant speciality whom he considers are suitable to instruct.

Where it is a medical expert, the Protocol states that the claimant's solicitor will obtain access to the claimant's medical records (Protocol, para 3.15).

The second party will then have 14 days in which to object to one or more of the named experts. The first party should then instruct a mutually acceptable expert (Protocol, para 3.16). If the second party objects to all the listed experts, the parties may then instruct experts of their own choice. However, such a course of conduct runs the risk of the court finding that one or both parties behaved unreasonably in not agreeing an expert (Protocol, para 3.17).

Once an agreed expert has been nominated, the second party is not entitled to rely upon his own expert evidence within that speciality unless the first party agrees, the court so directs, or the first party's expert report has been amended and the first party is not prepared to disclose the original report (Protocol, para 3.18).

Either party can send written questions on the report via the first party's solicitors. The expert should send the answers to the questions separately and directly to each party (Protocol, para 3.19).

The instructing first party usually pays the fee for the agreed expert's report. However, if a party asks questions of the expert, the party asking the questions usually meets the cost of the expert replying to the questions (Protocol, para 3.20).

The Protocol also provides that if the defendant admits liability in whole or in part, before proceedings are issued, any agreed medical report should be disclosed to the defendant. The claimant should postpone issuing proceedings for 21 days from disclosure of the report to see if a settlement can be reached (Protocol, para 3.21).

Privilege and the mutually selected expert

If a party instructs an expert whose selection has been agreed with the other party and obtains a report, that report will remain privileged and the other party will not be entitled to see the report unless the instructing party agrees (*Carlson v Townsend*).

In *Carlson v Townsend*, the claimant gave the defendant a list of three names of consultant orthopaedic surgeons. The defendant objected to one of the three so the claimant instructed one of the remaining two. However, having obtained the report, the claimant then declined to disclose it, and instead instructed another expert who was not one of those originally named. The claimant served a copy of his preferred expert's report on the defendant, who then applied for an order that the claimant be compelled to disclose a copy of the report obtained from the mutually selected expert. The Court of Appeal held that the claimant was not obliged to disclose the report.

While finding that the Protocol contemplates the voluntary disclosure of the mutually selected expert's report, the court accepted that it did not compel disclosure, and in any event the Protocol would not override the substantive law of privilege which would prevent the defendant from being entitled to see the contents of the report if the claimant objected. The court distinguished the practice of selecting a mutually acceptable expert from the court's power to direct that evidence be given by a single joint expert (r 35.7). A single joint expert is instructed by both parties, who have an equal liability for his fees and an equal right to see his report.

Settling and stocktaking

The parties and their legal representatives are encouraged by the Protocol, para 2.13 to enter into discussions and/or negotiations prior to starting proceedings. The Protocol does not specify when or how this might be done, but parties should bear in mind that the courts increasingly take the view that *litigation should be a last resort*, and that claims should not be issued prematurely when a settlement is in reasonable prospect.

Where settlement is not achieved, it is suggested by para 2.14 of the Protocol that the parties might wish to carry out a stocktake of the issues in dispute, and the evidence that the court is likely to need to decide those issues, *before proceedings are started*. Where the defendant is insured and the pre-action steps have been conducted by the insurer, the insurer would normally be expected to nominate solicitors to act in the proceedings, and the claimant's solicitor is recommended to invite the insurer to nominate solicitors to act in the proceedings and do so 7–14 days before the intended issue date (Protocol, para 2.14).

PRE-ACTION PROTOCOL FOR THE RESOLUTION OF CLINICAL DISPUTES

The general aims of the Clinical Disputes Protocol are to maintain/restore the patient/healthcare provider relationship and to resolve as many disputes as possible without litigation (Protocol, para 2.1).

The Protocol was the initiative of the Clinical Disputes Forum, a multi-disciplinary body that was formed in 1997 as a result of Lord Woolf's reports on access to justice. One of the aims of the Forum was to find less adversarial and more cost-effective ways of resolving disputes about healthcare and medical treatment.

It is recognised that the number of complaints and claims against healthcare providers is growing as patients become more prepared to question their treatment and more aware of their rights. There was felt to be a risk that patient/healthcare provider relationships would be damaged, disputes unnecessarily prolonged, the resources for treating patients reduced, additional work created and the morale of healthcare providers lowered if there was a climate of mistrust and lack of openness in the handling of complaints and claims. It was therefore felt to be in the interests of both patients and healthcare providers that complaints and claims should be resolved as quickly, efficiently and professionally as possible, and that this should be done in a climate of openness, trust and co-operation (Protocol, para 1).

Health records

The Protocol sets out standard forms for patients to use to obtain copies of their clinical records (Protocol, Annex B). The copy records should be provided within 40 days of the request and at a charge not exceeding those permissible under the Access to Health Records Act 1990 (Protocol, para 3.9). If the healthcare provider fails to provide the clinical records within 40 days (without good reason) the patient can apply for an order for pre-action disclosure (Protocol, para 3.12).

Letter of claim

If, on receipt and analysis of the clinical records, the patient is advised that there are grounds for a claim, he should send a letter of claim to the healthcare provider as soon as is practicable (Protocol, para 3.15). The Protocol includes a recommended letter of claim in Annex C1, which the patient should use (Protocol, para 3.14).

The letter of claim should contain:

(a) a clear summary of the facts;

(b) the main allegations of negligence;

(c) details of the patient's injuries;

(d) the claimant's financial losses in outline; and

(e) in more complex cases, a chronology of events.

There should be reference to any relevant documents, plus copies if they are not already in the defendant's possession. It is also advised that the letter contains an offer to settle, if relevant (Protocol, paras 3.16–3.20).

Letter of response

The healthcare provider should acknowledge receipt of the letter of claim within 14 days of receipt and should identify who will be dealing with the matter (Protocol, para 3.24).

Within three months of the letter of claim the healthcare provider should provide a reasoned answer, following the template for a letter of response in Annex C2 of the Protocol (Protocol, para 3.23). The letter of response should:

(a) indicate whether the claim, or part of the claim, is admitted;

(b) if the claim is denied, include specific comments on the allegations of negligence;

(c) if the patient's facts are disputed, provide the healthcare provider's version of events;

(d) provide copies of any documents relied upon; and

(e) give a response to any offer to settle made by the patient (Protocol, paras 3.25–3.26).

Experts

The Protocol states that 'It is recognised that in clinical negligence disputes, the parties and their advisers will require flexibility in their approach to expert evidence' (Protocol, para 4.2). Expert opinions may be needed on breach of duty and causation; on the patient's condition and prognosis; and to assist in valuing the claim.

ADR and the Protocol

While reminding the parties that the courts increasingly expect parties to try to settle their differences by agreement before issuing proceedings, the Protocol does not give detailed guidance on how the parties should go about doing so. It does identify various forms of resolving disputes without litigation, such as discussion and negotiation, the NHS Complaints Procedure, mediation, arbitration, determination by an expert, and early neutral evaluation by a medical or legal expert (Protocol, paras 5.2–5.3).

PRE-ACTION PROTOCOL FOR CONSTRUCTION AND ENGINEERING DISPUTES

The Construction and Engineering Protocol applies to all construction and engineering disputes, including professional negligence claims against architects, engineers and quantity surveyors (Protocol, para 1.1). However, the Protocol will not apply to disputes that include a claim for interim injunctive relief or summary judgment, or where the dispute has already been referred to arbitration or some other formal ADR procedure (Protocol, para 1.2).

A unique feature of this Protocol is that it requires the parties to hold at least one meeting but, unusually, does not recommend the disclosure of documents or the instruction of experts at the pre-action stage. The reason for this is that, because such disputes are often highly technical and document-heavy, it is thought to be counterproductive to the narrowing of the issues to compel parties to exchange such information at this stage. Instead, it is felt that requiring the parties to meet and identify the real issues between them is more likely to assist in the narrowing of the dispute, the saving of costs and the likelihood of settlement being reached.

Letter of claim

The claimant should send to each defendant a letter of claim which:

(a) contains the claimant's and each proposed defendant's full name and address;

(b) includes a clear summary of the facts on which the claim is based;

(c) sets out the basis of the claim, identifying the principal contractual terms and statutory provisions relied upon and details of the relief claimed.

If damages are claimed the claimant should provide a breakdown of how they have been quantified. The claimant should also notify the defendant of the names of any experts already instructed and the issues to which their evidence relates (Protocol, para 3).

The defendant's response

The defendant should acknowledge receipt of the letter of claim within 14 calendar days of its receipt and may provide the claimant with the name of his insurer, if any (Protocol, para 4.1).

Within 28 days of receipt of the letter of claim the defendant should send a letter of response to the claimant. The parties can agree to extend the period within which the defendant is to provide a response, up to a maximum of four months (Protocol, para 4.3.1).

The letter of response should indicate which facts set out in the letter of claim are agreed or not agreed and which claims are accepted or rejected. It should also contain details of any allegations of contributory negligence and details of any counterclaim the defendant proposes to make. The defendant should in turn notify the claimant of the names of any experts already instructed and the issues to which their evidence relates (Protocol, para 4.3.1).

Commencing proceedings

In the absence of a letter acknowledging receipt of the letter of claim within 14 days and in the absence of a letter of response within 28 days, or any extended period agreed by the parties, the claimant is entitled to start proceedings without further compliance with the Protocol (Protocol, paras 4.1 and 4.3.2).

Also, if the limitation period for the cause of action will expire before the Protocol can be complied with, the claimant can commence proceedings without complying with the Protocol. However, in those circumstances the claimant must, when issuing proceedings, apply to the court, on notice, for directions as to the timetable and form of procedure to be adopted. The court will then consider whether to order a stay of the whole or part of the proceedings so that the Protocol can be complied with (Protocol, para 6).

Challenging the court's jurisdiction

A party to a construction contract (as defined by the Housing Grants, Construction and Regeneration Act 1996) has the right to refer a dispute arising under the contract for adjudication (s 108 of the 1996 Act). If the defendant intends to take objection to all or part of the claimant's claim on the grounds that the court lacks jurisdiction, that the matter should be referred to arbitration, or that the claimant has named the wrong defendant, he should raise this objection with the claimant within 28 days of receipt of the letter of claim (Protocol, para 4.2.1).

If the defendant raises such an objection then he is not required to comply with the Protocol by sending a letter of response. However, if the defendant later withdraws his objection the Protocol will again apply to the dispute and it will be treated as if the letter of claim had been received on the date on which the defendant notified the claimant that the objection had been withdrawn (Protocol, paras 4.2.2, 4.2.3).

Pre-action meeting

As soon as possible after receipt of the letter of response the parties should normally meet (Protocol, para 5.1). The aim of the meeting is for the parties to agree the main issues in the case, to identify the root cause of disagreement in respect of each issue and to consider how the issues might be resolved without recourse to litigation and, if litigation is unavoidable, to agree what steps should be taken to ensure that it is conducted in accordance with the overriding objective of the CPR (Protocol, para 5.2).

The Protocol does not seek to prescribe in detail how the meeting (or more than one if necessary) is conducted, but it does set out a list of those it expects to attend the meeting. This includes the party, a legal representative (if one has been instructed), a representative of any insurer, and any other party on whose behalf the claim is made or defended (Protocol, para 5.3).

The parties should consider at the meeting whether some form of ADR would be more suitable than litigation to resolve the dispute (Protocol, para 5.4). However, if the parties cannot agree to ADR they should go on to identify a single joint expert (if expert evidence is required), agree the extent of disclosure of documents required, and agree the conduct of the litigation with a view to minimising cost and delay (Protocol, para 5.5).

Although the contents of the pre-action meeting are to be treated as 'without prejudice' the parties are entitled to disclose to the court whether a meeting took place or not; if so, who attended; whether any party refused to attend and why; and details of any agreements concluded at the meeting (Protocol, paras 5.6, 5.7).

PRE-ACTION PROTOCOL FOR DEFAMATION

The introduction to the Defamation Protocol recognises that when applying the Protocol the important features which distinguish defamation claims from other claims need to be borne in mind, namely, the uniquely short limitation period of one year and the fact that the claimant will, almost invariably, be seeking an immediate correction/apology as part of the process of restoring his reputation. Therefore, time will be very much 'of the essence' when applying and reviewing the application of this Protocol (Protocol, para 1.4).

In the light of the costly nature of this type of litigation the Protocol emphasises the need for the parties to act reasonably to keep costs proportionate to the nature and gravity of the case and the stage the complaint has reached.

Letter of claim

The claimant should send a letter of claim at the earliest reasonable opportunity (Protocol, para 3.1). The letter of claim should identify the words complained of and any factual inaccuracies or unsupportable comment, and include sufficient details to identify the publication or broadcast which contained them, with the date of publication, if known, and where possible should include a copy or transcript of the words complained of. The claimant should specify the nature of the remedies sought against the defendant and give details of any particular damage caused (Protocol, para 3.2).

Defendant's response

The defendant should provide a full response to the letter of claim as soon as reasonably possible. If the defendant believes he will be unable to respond within 14 days then he should inform the claimant of the date by which he intends to respond (Protocol, para 3.4).

The defendant's response should indicate whether and to what extent the claimant's case is accepted and any remedies the defendant is prepared to offer. The defendant should specify whether further information is needed to enable the claim to be dealt with and, if the claim is rejected, should explain why and give details of any facts the defendant is likely to rely on in his defence (Protocol, para 3.5).

ADR and the Protocol

The claimant and defendant have a positive obligation to provide evidence that ADR was considered to resolve the dispute. Although the Protocol does not provide a mechanism for the parties to decide which method of ADR to use to resolve their dispute, it does set out some of the available options. These include determination by an independent third party (such as an experienced defamation lawyer) jointly agreed by the parties, mediation, arbitration and other forms of ADR (Protocol, para 3.7).

PROFESSIONAL NEGLIGENCE PRE-ACTION PROTOCOL

The Professional Negligence Protocol applies to claims against professionals in negligence, or equivalent breach of contract (implied term to take reasonable skill and care) or breach of fiduciary duty claims. However, in order not to overlap with the pre-action protocols for construction and engineering disputes or clinical disputes, the Professional Negligence Protocol does not apply to claims against architects, engineers and quantity surveyors, or healthcare providers (Protocol, paras A1 and C2).

The aim of the Protocol is to establish a framework in which there is an early exchange of information to allow the claim to be fully investigated and, if possible, resolved without the need for litigation (Protocol, para A2).

The Protocol is accompanied by guidance notes, which provide guidance and explanation about the use of the Protocol. The guidance notes explain that the Protocol has been kept simple to promote ease of use, and remind the parties that the Woolf Reforms envisaged that the parties would act reasonably in the pre-action period. Accordingly, if within that period a problem arises which is not specifically addressed by the Protocol the parties should comply with the spirit of the Protocol by behaving reasonably (Protocol, para C1). As an example, the term 'professional' is not defined by the Protocol: if in any case there is a dispute as to whether someone is a professional, the Protocol suggests that it would not be reasonable for the parties to argue that point; rather, they should follow the Protocol, adapting it where appropriate (Protocol, para C2.3).

ADR and the Protocol

The Professional Negligence Protocol encourages the parties to consider using other forms of pre-action dispute resolution (such as internal complaints procedures) before embarking on the Protocol, but states that if those other procedures fail to resolve the dispute the Protocol should be followed before proceedings are started (Protocol, para A3).

Once the Protocol has been embarked upon the parties are still free to agree to seek mediation or some other form of ADR to settle the dispute (Protocol, para B6.1). Any party can at any stage refer the dispute to an ADR agency for mediation or some other form of ADR, and the other party must indicate whether they are prepared to participate and, if not, should give their reasons why ADR is not appropriate to resolve the dispute or not appropriate at that stage. The other party must respond in writing to the invitation to use ADR within 14 days, and the Protocol specifies that the letter can be disclosed to the court on the issue of costs (Protocol, para B6.3).

This approach is in keeping with recent case law on ADR (see *Dunnett v Railtrack plc* [2002] EWCA Civ 302; *Frank Cowl & Others v Plymouth CC* [2001] EWCA Civ 1935; *Hurst v Leeming* [2001] EWHC 1051). While stressing that no party can be compelled to mediate or use any other form of ADR (Protocol, para B6.4), the effect of the Protocol is to put a party at risk of costs penalties in any subsequent proceedings for unreasonably refusing to mediate.

Notification of the claim

Preliminary notice

The Protocol encourages the claimant to send a letter with a brief outline of the potential claim and a general indication of its financial value as soon as the claimant decides there is a reasonable chance he will bring a claim against the professional. The letter should ask the professional to inform his professional indemnity insurers of the potential claim immediately. The professional should then simply acknowledge receipt of the letter within 21 days of receiving it. There is no obligation on either party to take any further action at this stage (Protocol, para B1).

Letter of claim

Once the claimant decides there are grounds for a claim against the professional, he should write a detailed letter of claim to the professional. The Protocol sets out what the letter of claim should contain. This includes details of the allegations, a clear chronological summary of the facts on which the claim is based, an estimate of the financial loss suffered by the claimant and how it is calculated (Protocol, para B2.2).

The claimant should also confirm whether or not he has appointed an expert and, if so, provide details of his identity, discipline and date of appointment (Protocol, para B2.2(f)).

The claimant should enclose copies of key documents supporting the allegations and the financial loss, and should request that a copy of the letter of claim is forwarded to the professional's insurers, if any (Protocol, para B2.2(b), (e) and (g)).

Response to the claim

The professional should send a letter of acknowledgment within 21 days of receipt of the letter of claim (Protocol, para B3.1). The professional has three months from the date of the letter of acknowledgment to investigate the alleged claim (Protocol, para B4.1). However, the claimant should agree to any reasonable request for an extension of that period (Protocol, para B4.2).

As soon as the professional has completed his investigations he should send either a letter of response or a letter of settlement, or both (Protocol, para B5.1).

Letter of response

The letter of response should provide a reasoned answer to the claimant's allegations. It should state whether the claim is admitted in whole or in part, it should respond to the allegations, and it should provide details of the professional's version of events if different from the claimant's. The professional should also seek further information from the claimant if necessary and send the claimant copies of any documents he intends to rely upon (Protocol, para B5.2).

Status of the letter of claim/letter of response

As with the other protocols, the letter of claim and letter of response are not intended to have the status of a statement of case. However, if they differ materially from that party's statement of case in subsequent proceedings, the court may decide, in its discretion, to impose sanctions (Protocol, paras B2.3 and B5.3).

The Protocol proposes that the letter of claim and the letter of response should be open letters, rather than 'without prejudice' (Protocol, paras B2.2 and B5.2). This would therefore allow either party to rely on the letter of claim/response in any subsequent proceedings, and parties should obviously ensure that such letters are drafted with care.

Letter of settlement

If the professional intends to make proposals for settlement he should send a letter of settlement, which will normally be a 'without prejudice' letter setting out the proposals, or identifying any further information required before settlement proposals can be made. The professional should identify any issues that he believes are likely to remain in dispute in the letter of settlement, unless this information is contained within a letter of response (Protocol, para B5.4).

Experts

If the claimant has obtained expert evidence prior to sending the letter of claim the professional will also be entitled to obtain expert evidence before sending the letter of response/settlement (Protocol, para B7.1). The claimant should have confirmed whether he has appointed an expert when sending the letter of claim (Protocol, para B2.2(f)).

If the claimant has not appointed an expert prior to sending the letter of claim the parties are encouraged to appoint a single joint expert (Protocol, para B7.2). However, the Protocol goes on to provide that if agreement about a joint expert cannot be reached, the parties are free to appoint their own experts (Protocol, para B7.3).

Steps after the letter of response/settlement

If the letter of response denies the claim in its entirety and there is no letter of settlement, the claimant is entitled to commence proceedings (Protocol, para B5.5).

If this does not apply, the claimant and the professional should enter into a period of negotiations, which should aim to conclude within six months from the date of the *letter of acknowledgment* (*note*: not from the date of the letter of response) (Protocol, para B5.6).

If the claim is not settled within that six-month period the parties should agree within 14 days after the end of that period whether negotiations should continue and, if so, for how long, and they should seek to identify those issues which are agreed and those which are still in dispute (Protocol, para B5.7(a), (b)). However, if the parties cannot agree an extension of time it will be open to the claimant to commence proceedings (Protocol, para B5.7(c)).

The intention is that the claimant will not start proceedings against the professional until the Protocol has been complied with and either the professional's letter of response denies the claim in its entirety and there is no letter of settlement, or the period of negotiations ends but the claim has not been settled (Protocol, para B8.1). Before starting proceedings the claimant should give 14 days' written notice to the professional (Protocol, para B8.2).

For those cases where, due to the imminent expiry of the limitation period, the claimant has issued proceedings before complying with the Protocol, the parties are encouraged to agree to apply to the court for a stay of proceedings to enable the parties to work through the Protocol (Protocol, para C7).

PRE-ACTION PROTOCOL FOR JUDICIAL REVIEW

The Judicial Review Protocol must be considered and applied with the awareness that it does not displace the three-month time limit specified by r 54.5(1) for an application for judicial review which runs from the time the grounds to make the claim first arose.

The Protocol will not be appropriate for urgent cases, such as where the claimant seeks judicial review of a decision to remove him from the UK or the failure of a local housing authority to provide him with secure interim accommodation where the claimant is homeless.

The letter before claim

Before making a claim the claimant should send a letter to the defendant identifying the issues in dispute and seeking to establish whether litigation can be avoided

(Protocol, para 8). The Protocol contains a suggested format for the letter in Annex A, which the claimant should use (Protocol, para 9).

The suggested format for the letter before claim includes details of the decision, act or omission being challenged, with a summary of the facts and a request for any relevant information the claimant is seeking (Protocol, para 10, Annex A).

The letter of response

The defendant should normally respond to the claimant's letter within 14 days (Protocol, para 13). If the defendant is unable to reply within the proposed time limit he should send an interim reply and propose a reasonable extension (Protocol, para 14). The defendant should use the standard format for the letter of response at Annex B of the Protocol (Protocol, para 13).

If the defendant is conceding the claim in full, this should be stated in the letter of response in clear and unambiguous terms (Protocol, para 15). Otherwise the letter of response should state whether the claim is being conceded in part, or whether it is not conceded at all. The letter of response should (where appropriate) include a new decision identifying what aspects of the claim are being conceded and what are not; a timescale within which a new decision will be issued; a fuller explanation for the decision; address any points of dispute; enclose any relevant documents requested by the claimant; and confirm whether or not the defendant will oppose any application for an interim remedy (Protocol, para 16).

Use of the Protocol

As with the other protocols, the court will expect all parties to have complied with this Protocol and, if proceedings are issued, will take into account compliance or non-compliance when giving case management directions or making orders for costs (Protocol, para 7). However, in the case of an application for judicial review, the claimant will have to carefully consider whether it is appropriate to comply with the Protocol or whether urgent steps are needed, and the Protocol stresses the importance of making that decision with the benefit of legal advice (Protocol, para 4).

Even if compliance with the Protocol is not appropriate in emergency cases, it is good practice for the claimant to fax the defendant a draft of the claim form before issue and to notify the defendant when an interim mandatory order is being sought (Protocol, para 7).

SANCTIONS FOR FAILURE TO FOLLOW THE PROTOCOLS

Although a party cannot be compelled to comply with a pre-action protocol, non-compliance may be penalised in a variety of ways if proceedings are commenced.

Case management directions

Under the case management powers set out in Part 3 of the CPR, the court can take into account compliance or non-compliance with a pre-action protocol when giving directions for the management of proceedings (r 3.1(4)). So, the court may refuse to grant additional time for the doing of any act that should have been complied with under a pre-action protocol.

It should be noted that both parties are asked to indicate, when completing the allocation questionnaire, whether they have complied with a relevant pre-action protocol and, if not, why not. The court will therefore have this information to hand when ordering directions on the allocation of a case.

Ordering payment of sums into court

The power of the court, once proceedings are begun, to order a party to pay a sum of money into court, includes the circumstances where a party has refused, without good reason, to comply with a relevant pre-action protocol (r 3.1(5)).

Granting relief from sanctions

Further, when deciding whether to grant relief from a sanction, one of the matters to be taken into account by the court is the extent of compliance with any relevant pre-action protocol (r 3.9(1)(e)).

Costs orders

The court must also take into account the conduct of the parties when making an order for costs, and the conduct of the parties includes conduct before, as well as during, proceedings and, in particular, whether a party has followed any relevant pre-action protocol (r 44.3(5)(a)). Therefore, although the general rule is that the unsuccessful party will be ordered to pay the successful party's costs (r 44.3(2)), the successful party may be deprived of some or all of his costs, or ordered to pay costs to the unsuccessful party, if he has failed to comply with a pre-action protocol.

When deciding the amount of costs, the court must have regard to the conduct of all the parties, including conduct before as well as during the proceedings, and the efforts made, if any, before and during the proceedings to try to resolve the dispute (r 44.3(5)(a)).

Further, if a party applies for pre-action disclosure or disclosure against a third party, if the other party has not complied with a pre-action protocol (which encourages voluntary disclosure of relevant documents) the court may make a different order from the usual order for costs (which is that the court will award the person against whom the order is made his costs) and award costs against the non-disclosing party instead (r 48.1(3)(b)).

Sanctions under the Protocols Practice Direction

As well as the above powers, the court has the powers set out in the Practice Direction to the Protocols. The test as to whether these sanctions should be imposed is whether the defaulting party's conduct caused proceedings to be commenced or costs to be incurred which would otherwise not have been (PD Protocols, para 2.3). The court will aim to place the innocent party in no worse a position than if the protocol had been complied with (PD Protocols, para 2.4). Therefore, the court will impose the following sanctions only if non-compliance with a protocol has made a difference to the conduct or outcome of proceedings, something that in some circumstances may be very difficult to weigh up.

The following sanctions may be imposed:

(a) The court may order that the party at fault pay all or part of the other party's costs of the proceedings (PD Protocols, para 2.3(1)).

(b) If the above order is made, the court can order that those costs are paid on an indemnity basis (PD Protocols, para 2.3(2)).

(c) If the party at fault is a claimant who has been awarded damages, an order depriving that party of interest for a specified period or awarding interest at a lower rate than would otherwise have been awarded (PD Protocols, para 2.3(3)).

(d) If the party at fault is a defendant who has been ordered to pay damages to the claimant, an order that that party pay interest for a specified period at a higher rate, not exceeding 10% above base rate, than would otherwise be awarded (PD Protocols, para 2.3(4)).

The Practice Direction to the Protocols gives examples of how each party may have failed to comply with a protocol. So, for instance, a claimant may have failed to provide sufficient information to the defendant, or failed to follow the procedure for the instruction of a single joint expert (PD Protocols, para 3.1). On the other hand, a defendant may have failed to make a preliminary response to the letter of claim within the specified time of 21 days, or failed to make a full response within the specified time of three months or failed to disclose relevant disclosable documents (PD Protocols, para 3.2). However, from the wording of the Practice Direction, mere failure to follow the protocol itself will not be enough to invoke the court's powers to impose a penalty on the defaulting party; the court will still have to be satisfied that the failure caused proceedings to be commenced or costs incurred which would otherwise not have been.

An example of the court's use of its power to impose sanctions where a party was in clear breach of the Practice Direction to the Protocols is shown by the decision in *Paul Thomas Construction Ltd v Damian Hyland and Jackie Power* (2000) LTL, 5 December. In that case, although the Protocol for Engineering and Construction Disputes was not yet in place at the time the case was litigated, the parties were still obliged to comply with the general provisions set out in the Practice Direction to the Protocols to comply with the spirit of the protocols and to behave reasonably in dealing with the dispute. The judge found that the claimants' approach was exceedingly heavy-handed and unco-operative, and that it was wholly unnecessary for it to commence the litigation. The court found that the proper sanction to punish the claimants' behaviour was for the claimants to pay the defendants' costs of the claim on the indemnity basis.

Compliance with a protocol is therefore not mandatory, and in some circumstances a party may escape any penalty even if he does not comply. However, there is an expectation that the substance of a relevant protocol will be followed, and unless a party has a good reason for not doing so, a party who has not complied is likely to face a penalty subsequently if proceedings are commenced, either during the course of proceedings or at the end of proceedings when costs and other orders are made.

Transitional provisions

The court will not take into account compliance or non-compliance with any relevant pre-action protocol for claims started before the relevant protocol came into force (PD Protocols, para 5.2). For claims started after the date a relevant protocol came into force, the court will take compliance or non-compliance into account, except where the parties did not have sufficient time to comply with any requirements of the protocol between the publication date and the coming into force of the protocol (PD Protocols, para 5.4).

COSTS-ONLY PROCEEDINGS

Where the parties to a dispute have reached an agreement on all issues (confirmed in writing) without commencing proceedings, including who is to pay the costs, but have failed to agree on the amount of costs then either party can commence costs-only proceedings to have the costs assessed, without having to commence proceedings on the rest of the substantive claim (r 44.12A). This new procedure will obviously assist parties who have managed to settle a dispute without issuing proceedings following compliance with a pre-action protocol.

However, the procedure can be used only if a settlement confirmed in writing has been reached, which includes agreement as to which party is to pay the costs. In the absence of such agreement the other party can file an acknowledgment opposing the use of costs-only proceedings and the proceedings will be dismissed (r 44.12A).

PRE-HEARING FIXED FEES

For road traffic accident disputes occurring after 6 October 2003 which settle pre-issue for an agreed amount of damages not exceeding £10,000, only fixed costs are recoverable. The pre-issue scheme allows claimant solicitors to recover base costs of £800, plus 20% of any damages up to £5,000. They will receive 15% of any damages from £5,000 to £10,000. It includes a 12.5% success fee, certain disbursements such as medical reports and the insurance premiums but not counsel's fees unless the claimant is a child or patient (CPR Part 45, Section II).

These new provisions are a result of the deal, brokered by the Civil Justice Council, which ends the long-running feud between personal injury lawyers and the insurance industry on fixed fees for this type of case. There is no progress on proposals to extend fixed fees to claims after they have been issued. Insurers' organisations such as the Motor Accident Solicitors Society (MASS) have been campaigning for the introduction of fixed fees post-issue, but this is resisted by the Association of Personal Injury Lawyers (APIL).

CHAPTER 6

JUDICIAL CASE MANAGEMENT: THE OVERRIDING OBJECTIVE

INTRODUCTION

The essence of case management is that the court, rather than litigants or their legal advisers, exercises responsibility for the control of litigation. Although our system is still an adversarial one, case management gives the court an interventionist role. Case management covers such matters as identifying the issues in the case; summarily disposing of some issues and deciding in what order issues should be resolved; setting timetables for steps to be taken in the proceedings; controlling the amount of disclosure of documents necessary for a case; limiting the amount of expert and other evidence that should be heard; and setting timetables for the conduct of the trial.

Notwithstanding these specific aspects, the overall purpose of case management is to encourage settlement of disputes at the earliest opportunity and, if this is not achieved and a trial is necessary, for this to take place as soon as possible by means of a cost-effective hearing strictly limited to resolution of the true issues in dispute and strictly limited in duration (see *Access to Justice*, Interim Report, Chapter 5, www.dca.gov.uk/civil/interfr.htm).

THE OVERRIDING OBJECTIVE

The Civil Procedure Rules (CPR) are a procedural code with the overriding objective of enabling the court to deal with cases justly (r 1.1(1)). The court has a duty to give effect to the overriding objective when exercising any power under the CPR, or when interpreting any rule of the CPR (r 1.2).

As the CPR are a new code, case law authorities on matters of civil procedure decided before the rules came into force are no longer generally of any relevance to the application of the CPR (see the judgment of Lord Woolf in *Biguzzi v Rank Leisure plc* [1999] 1 WLR 1926; [1999] 4 All ER 934, and Lord Herschell's judgment in the House of Lords' decision of *Bank of England v Vagliano Bros* [1891] AC 107; [1891–94] All ER Rep 93 at 113E–I).

It was thought that the former civil procedure system had become too rigid, being bound by case precedent, and the CPR were designed to give the court more flexibility in dealing with individual cases. It was not therefore intended that case precedents as such would be part of the new system, and the case management judge should be free to decide what action is necessary for the case before him simply by applying the rules in the light of the overriding objective.

As May LJ said in *Purdy v Cambran* (1999) LTL, 17 December, when applying the CPR 'it is necessary to concentrate on the intrinsic justice of a particular case in the light of the overriding objective'. In *Purdy v Cambran*, the Court of Appeal upheld the decision of the lower court to strike out the claimant's claim for delay. The Court of Appeal was of the opinion that the lower court had correctly applied the overriding objective in reaching the decision that a fair trial was no longer possible because 10 years had passed since the accident occurred and the defendant's expert, who had examined the claimant, had died. In *Hamblin v Field* (2000) *The Times*, 26 April, the Court of Appeal said that excessive quoting of authorities was not of much assistance in applications to strike out in view of the wide discretion now given to the courts when dealing with such matters. Also in *UCB Corporate Services Ltd v Halifax (SW) Ltd* (1999) *The Times*, 23 December, the Court of Appeal confirmed that the exercise of the court's power to strike out a case was a matter for the judge in the exercise of his discretion in all the circumstances of a case. The court found that there was no reason to suppose that the judge was not aware of his power to make an order falling short of striking out, and it was clear that the judge regarded the flouting of the rules and court orders in that case as sufficiently serious to justify the striking out. The Court of Appeal could therefore see no ground on which it could interfere with the judge's discretion.

In *Biguzzi v Rank Leisure plc*, Lord Woolf said that where the issue was one of the exercise of a discretion under the CPR, the Court of Appeal would interfere only if it could be shown either that the judge had misdirected himself in law, or that his decision was plainly wrong. In that case the Court of Appeal fully supported the approach of the circuit judge when dealing with an application to strike out the claimant's case on the grounds of delay. In the circumstances of the case, although the circuit judge found that both sides had been guilty of delay, he was of the opinion that a fair trial was still possible and directed that the matter should proceed to be heard promptly. Lord Woolf further stated that the advantage of the CPR over the former rules was that the court's powers were much broader than they were, and in many cases there will be alternatives that enable a case to be dealt with justly without taking the draconian step of striking the case out.

Further, in *Powell v Pallisers of Hereford Ltd and Others* [2002] EWCA Civ 959, the Court of Appeal emphasised that the overriding objective imposes an obligation on the Court of Appeal to exercise a degree of self-discipline by respecting case management decisions made by judges in cases which they are to try. In *Powell*, at a case management conference, the judge refused to adjourn the trial date at the request of the defendant and ordered that Part 20 proceedings brought by the defendant must be tried separately because it was too late for them to be heard with the main claim. The Court of Appeal held that there was no basis for it to interfere with the judge's decision, which had been made properly in accordance with the overriding objective. Also, in *Nigel John Holmes v SGB Services plc* (2001) LTL, 19 February, the Court of Appeal said that, in seeking to give effect to the overriding objective when exercising a discretion, it is inappropriate to lay down any guidance as to the weight to be attached to the various factors which have to be considered.

However, despite the wide discretion given to the case management judge, there have been a number of guideline cases decided by the Court of Appeal on the interpretation of the rules and, significantly, when sitting in such appeals, Lord Woolf often took the opportunity to provide general guidance on the operation of the rules (see, eg, *Ford v GKR Construction* [2000] 1 All ER 802).

Limits to the overriding objective

The overriding objective does not give the court the power to interpret provisions in the CPR in a way contrary to their clear meaning. In *Vinos v Marks & Spencer plc*

[2001] 3 All ER 784, the Court of Appeal held that r 7.6(3) prescribes the only circumstances in which the court is able to extend the period for serving the claim form if the application is made after the period for service has expired. Although Mr Vinos's case was deserving, the Court of Appeal held that as the conditions in r 7.6(3) were not met, the overriding objective did not give the court a general discretion to grant an extension of time for service of the claim form.

Control over the court's exercise of the overriding objective

Although the overriding objective of the CPR gives the judge a wide discretion in exercising his case management powers, the Court of Appeal is prepared to overturn such case management decisions when they are clearly contrary to the interests of justice, including if they are a disproportionate response to a default by one or more of the parties.

In *Grundy v Naqvi* [2001] EWCA Civ 139, the Court of Appeal overturned a district judge's order that there be immediate judgment for the claimants in the light of the defendant's failure to comply with an unless order. The district judge had made an order against the defendant that unless she exchange witness statements by a specified date judgment would be entered against her. On receipt of the order the defendant made an application to the court seeking to amend her defence and applying for the unless order to be varied so as to require exchange of witness statements at a later date. At the hearing of the defendant's application the district judge refused to give the defendant permission to amend her defence and proceeded to enter immediate judgment for the claimant under the terms of the unless order. The Court of Appeal overturned the judge's decision to enter judgment for the claimant, on the grounds that such a draconian sanction was disproportionate to the defendant's default. Instead the court ordered that payment of a substantial sum into court, and the fixing of a new date by which witness statements were to be exchanged, would achieve justice in that case.

In *Law v St Margaret's Insurances Ltd* [2001] EWCA Civ 30, where defendants had made errors in procedure, the Court of Appeal, in overturning the district judge's order refusing to set judgment against the defendants aside, was of the view that the district judge had wrongly interpreted the overriding objective.

Also, where the judge has wrongly exercised his discretion under the rules the Court of Appeal will exercise the discretion afresh (for examples, see pp 113–16 below, 'Relief from sanctions').

The Human Rights Act and the overriding objective

Lord Woolf is of the opinion that so long as a judge, when making case management decisions, properly applies the overriding objective, there will be no risk that the decision can be challenged on grounds that it is contrary to the Human Rights Act 1998 (HRA). In *Daniels v Walker* [2000] 1 WLR 1382, an appeal against a case management decision, Lord Woolf said that arguments based on Art 6 of the European Convention on Human Rights (right to a fair trial) had nothing to add to the issues on appeal because the overriding objective made it clear that the obligation on the court is to deal with cases justly. This was supported by Gibson LJ in *Alliance & Leicester plc v Slayford* (2000) *The Times*, 19 December, where he said: 'Where the CPR, and in particular the overriding objective, cover the point which a litigant wishes to take, it adds nothing to try to dress up the point as one invoking a right under the Convention.'

In *Khalili v Christopher Bennett and Others* [2000] EMLR 996, CA, the Court of Appeal said that the parties' arguments under Art 6 did not 'add anything to the arguments under the Civil Procedure Rules'. The court held that a national court is entitled to prescribe timetables for steps to be taken in litigation within a limited period of time, so a claimant who has not complied with those steps normally cannot complain that he has been deprived of a fair trial under Art 6. Similarly, a defendant who has not suffered any prejudice because of delay cannot complain that he has been deprived of a fair hearing within a reasonable time under Art 6 because the test of a reasonable time under the Convention is usually whether the lapse of time has prejudiced the outcome of the case.

Further, in *Jones v University of Warwick* [2003] 1 WLR 954; [2003] 3 All ER 760, Lord Woolf equated the exercise of the overriding objective with the right to a fair trial under Art 6 and commented that since the coming into force of both the CPR and the HRA, the court, when exercising its discretion in accordance with the overriding objective, has a responsibility to consider not only the individual case it is dealing with, but also the effect of its decision upon litigation generally. In this case, an inquiry agent gained access to the claimant's home by pretending to be a market researcher – and then proceeded to take a secret film for use in litigation. The district judge had ruled the film inadmissible, but his decision was reversed on appeal. The Court of Appeal upheld the decision in favour of admissibility as it showed that the claimant's disability was not as great as claimed, the court favouring the interests of justice over improper tactics. However, the Court of Appeal considered that the conduct of the insurers, who had commissioned the film, was improper and unjustified, and therefore, subject to further argument, ordered the defendants to pay the costs of the admissibility proceedings.

Parties' obligations in respect of the overriding objective

The parties are also required to help the court to further the overriding objective (r 1.3). An obvious example of this would be an obligation on the parties to co-operate in providing information to the other party about their case and in actively seeking ways to settle the dispute.

However, the obligation seems to go further, in that in one case it was said to include an obligation to alert your opponent to the fact that he is using the wrong forms and procedure to pursue a case (*Hannigan v Hannigan* [2000] All ER (D) 693). In *Hannigan*, the claimant issued proceedings, shortly after the CPR had come into force, using the wrong form – an obsolete county court form rather than Form N208, a Part 8 claim form. There were also a number of other technical defects with the claim form and supporting evidence filed by the claimant. The defendant's application under r 3.4(2)(c) for the claimant's statement of case to be struck out for a failure to comply with the rules and practice directions was successful. In setting aside the order striking out the claimant's claim, the Court of Appeal referred to the fact that under r 1.3 the parties are required to help the court further the overriding objective, and it held that the administration of justice would have been better served if the defendant had simply pointed out to the claimant all the mistakes that had been made so that the claimant could quickly correct them and indemnify the parties for the expense unnecessarily incurred.

Further, it may no longer be appropriate for one party (usually the defendant) to sit back and allow the other party to do nothing when there are several steps that party could have taken to have a matter disposed of earlier (*Khalili v Christopher Bennett and Others*). In *Khalili*, the claimant, an art collector, started defamation proceedings in 1995 against newspapers for publishing articles suggesting that he knowingly received stolen antiques. The claimant was subsequently prosecuted by the French authorities in relation to the allegedly stolen antiques, but was eventually acquitted in April 1999. The defendant was aware that the claimant had decided not to pursue his libel action until the criminal proceedings were concluded, but the claimant did not apply for a stay of the proceedings. After his acquittal by the French authorities, the claimant gave the defendant notice of his intention to proceed with the libel proceedings and applied for directions. The defendant applied for the proceedings to be struck out under the court's inherent jurisdiction under r 3.4(2)(c) and on the grounds of inordinate and inexcusable delay. The judge at first instance held that there had been a disregard of the rules of court amounting to an abuse of process and struck out the claim. In finding that the defendant had suffered no prejudice by the delay, and that the claimant had good reason to await the outcome of the criminal proceedings before continuing with his action, the Court of Appeal held that the judge had erred in finding that there had been an abuse of process justifying the striking out of the claimant's case. Moreover, the court emphasised that both parties were required to help the court to further the overriding objective, and accordingly it may not have been appropriate for the defendant to allow the delay when it could have made its own application to have the matter disposed of earlier.

It is also considered that part of the obligation to help the court achieve the overriding objective (which includes taking into account the court's resources) involves informing the court office as soon as it is known that a hearing will not be effective, for example, if a claim has settled or if an application is withdrawn (*Tasyurdu v Immigration Appeal Tribunal* [2003] EWCA Civ 447).

Aspects of the overriding objective

Rule 1.1(2) contains a list of what dealing justly with cases includes. That is:

(a) ensuring that the parties are on an equal footing;

(b) saving expense;

(c) dealing with the case in ways which are proportionate:

- to the amount of money involved;
- to the importance of the case;
- to the complexity of the issues; and
- to the financial position of each party;

(d) ensuring that the case is dealt with expeditiously and fairly; and

(e) allotting to it an appropriate share of the court's resources, while taking into account the need to allot resources to other cases (r 1.1(2)).

Proportionality

A common theme is the concept of proportionality, which could indeed be said to be one of the cornerstones of the CPR. The message is that a party should not expend amounts of time, money and resources out of proportion to the value and importance of the matter in dispute. Whilst it is obviously for a party to decide how much time and money to devote to pursuing a case, if the costs are disproportionate they may not all be recovered from an unsuccessful opponent. Also, if court proceedings are started, the court will be able to exert case management control over the conduct of the proceedings and the amount of court resources devoted to resolving the dispute.

Note that the application of proportionality is both subjective (are the resources being spent on the particular case proportionate?) and objective (are the resources being spent on the case proportionate in relation to other cases that the court has to deal with?) Thus, the court may feel that it is not worth devoting a lot of court time and resources to a case where the value of the claim does not warrant it, for example, neighbour disputes over small strips of land.

However, a party's right of access to justice and to a fair trial, as enshrined in Art 6 of the European Convention on Human Rights, must ultimately temper the principle of proportionality. A small claim, if it has merits, should be allowed to proceed, even if the costs of proceeding may be more than the amount which will be recovered (as an example, see the Court of Appeal's decision in *Woodhouse v Consignia plc* [2002] EWCA Civ 275). On the other hand, Convention law recognises that national courts are entitled to regulate their domestic procedures, and this includes prescribing timetables and steps which the parties have to take within a limited period of time, and deciding how the court's resources are to be allocated between individual cases.

The financial position of the parties

When dealing with a case justly, in accordance with the overriding objective, the court must consider the position of each of the parties and ensure that they are on an equal footing (r 1.1(2)).

If one party has much greater financial resources than the other this can be compensated for, to some extent, by the orders made by the court. Therefore, in *Powell v Pallisers of Hereford Ltd and Others* [2002] EWCA Civ 959, the Court of Appeal supported the judge's decision at a case management conference to fix an early date for trial because of the claimant's financial difficulties in continuing to fund the litigation.

However, the overriding objective would not give the court the power to prevent a party instructing a legal representative of his choice (*Maltez v Lewis* (1999) *The Times*, 4 May), although the full cost of a party's chosen legal representative may not be recoverable from an opponent if the cost is disproportionate or unreasonable (see Chapter 34, 'Costs of Proceedings').

Litigants who have the benefit of public funding also enjoy a measure of protection against costs being awarded against them (see Chapter 4, 'Funding Litigation'). It would certainly appear to be arguable that they occupy an advantageous position compared to a privately funded litigant who has no such protection.

The court's resources

When making case management decisions, the court has to have regard not only to the interests of the individual litigants before it, but also to those of other litigants using the court system.

In *Swain v Hillman and Gay* [2001] 1 All ER 91, Lord Woolf stated that the appropriate use of the court's powers under Part 24 to order summary judgment against a party gave effect to the overriding objective by ensuring that only an appropriate share of the court's resources were allotted to a particular case. If a claimant's case is bound to fail, entering summary judgment against the claimant 'saves expense; it achieves expedition; it avoids the court's resources being used up on cases where this serves no purpose, and ... generally ... it is in the interests of justice' (for the facts of this case see Chapter 23, 'Summary Judgment').

Active case management

Specific case management functions are set out in the CPR for each procedural stage of a case, for example, allocation to one of the case management tracks (Part 26). Provisions throughout the CPR also deal with such matters as summary judgment (Part 24) and staying proceedings while the parties try to settle the case by Alternative Dispute Resolution or other means (r 26.4). However, apart from these specific case management functions, there is a general obligation on the court to further the overriding objective by actively managing cases. Rule 1.4 gives a general list of what active case management involves.

The list, which is not exhaustive, includes such matters as fixing timetables, controlling the progress of the case, ensuring that directions given are proportionate, and giving directions to ensure that the trial proceeds quickly and efficiently (r 1.4(2)(g), (h), (l)). This can encompass directions about disclosure, witness statements, the use of expert evidence and the fixing of a trial timetable. The court also has an obligation to encourage the parties to co-operate with each other and to help the parties to settle their case (r 1.4(2)(a), (f)). Other aspects of active case management include taking steps to identify the issues in the case at an early stage, deciding the order in which those issues are resolved, and disposing summarily of issues where appropriate (r 1.4(2)(b), (c), (d)).

Encouraging the use of ADR

An important aspect of active case management is the obligation to encourage and facilitate the parties in the use of ADR procedures where there is a prospect of resolving a dispute by a satisfactory alternative to the court process (r 1.4(e)). Although the use of ADR is not compulsory, a party is at risk of adverse costs orders if it unreasonably refuses to use ADR (*Malkins Nominees Ltd v Société Financière Mirelis SA and Others* [2002] EWHC 1221, where the successful party was awarded only 85% of costs partly because of an unreasonable refusal to resolve the matter by ADR), particularly if its use is recommended by the court (*Dunnett v Railtrack plc* [2002] EWCA Civ 302). As the parties have a duty to assist the court to further the overriding objective (r 1.3), this will include their taking an active part in seeking to resolve their dispute by means of ADR if appropriate. Therefore, in *Malkins Nominees Ltd*, it was held that where one party had made a genuine offer to resolve the matter by ADR, it was incumbent on the other party to return, at an appropriate time, to take up that suggestion.

In *Dunnett v Railtrack*, Ms Dunnett brought proceedings against Railtrack for negligence when her horses strayed onto a railway line and were killed. Although she lost at first instance, she intended to appeal in order to rely on a stronger cause of action under the Railway Clauses Consolidation Act 1845, which she had not relied upon in the court below. In granting Ms Dunnett permission to appeal, the court strongly suggested that the parties attempt to resolve the matter by mediation or arbitration. Railtrack, no doubt aware of the difficulty Ms Dunnett would face in seeking to rely on a fresh cause of action at the appeal stage, refused to contemplate any form of ADR with Ms Dunnett. Even though the Court of Appeal dismissed Ms Dunnett's appeal it refused to order that she pay Railtrack's costs, because the court felt the appeal hearing could have been avoided if Railtrack had agreed to resolve the matter by means of mediation or arbitration, particularly as use of ADR had been strongly recommended by the judge below.

In *Frank Cowl and Others v Plymouth CC* [2001] EWCA Civ 1935, which involved an application for judicial review of a council's decision to close a residential care home for the elderly, Lord Woolf criticised the claimants for failing to take up an offer from the council to settle their dispute through a statutory complaints panel. Lord Woolf said, 'Today sufficient should be known about ADR to make the failure to adopt it, in particular when public money is involved, indefensible'. He felt it was of 'paramount importance' to avoid litigation whenever possible, even in disputes between public authorities and the members of the public for whom they are responsible.

ADR will not be appropriate in every case and, if it is not, a party will not be punished for refusing to agree to it, as long as he has compelling reasons for refusing to do so (*Hurst v Leeming* [2001] EWHC 1051; *Gold v Mincoff Science and Gold (A Firm)* (2002) LTL, 19 July, CA; *Société Internationale de Télécommunications Aéronautiques SC v Wyatt Co (UK) Ltd and Others (Maxwell Batley) (A Firm), Pt 20 Defendant* [2002] EWHC 2401, Ch D). In the *Hurst* case, Mr Hurst, a solicitor, brought proceedings in professional negligence against Mr Leeming, a barrister, who had acted for him in proceedings that were unsuccessful. Mr Hurst's claim against Mr Leeming was struck out, but Mr Hurst argued that Mr Leeming should not be entitled to his costs because he had refused Mr Hurst's invitation to mediate the dispute. Mr Leeming gave five reasons why he refused to mediate with Mr Hurst, only one of which was accepted by the court as a justifiable reason not to mediate. The first reason was that he had already incurred heavy costs in meeting the allegations, the second was the seriousness of the allegations of professional negligence made against him, the third that he believed there was no substance in Mr Hurst's case against him, and the fourth that Mr Leeming had already supplied a full and detailed refutation of Mr Hurst's case. None of these reasons was treated by the court as justifying a refusal to mediate. However, Mr Leeming's fifth reason – that when objectively viewed, given the character and attitude of Mr Hurst, mediation had no realistic prospect of success – was accepted as a sufficient reason in this case. The court felt that Mr Hurst had shown himself to be incapable of making a balanced evaluation of the facts, that he was obsessed with the notion that an injustice had been perpetrated on him, and that his object in proposing mediation was to obtain a substantial payment from Mr Leeming when in fact there was no merit in his claim.

GENERAL POWERS OF CASE MANAGEMENT

Part 3 of the CPR contains a list of general powers of judicial case management. These powers, as with all the court's powers under the rules, must be exercised in accordance with the overriding objective (r 1.2). This general list is expressly stated to be in addition to any powers given to the court by any other rule, practice direction or enactment, or any other powers the court may have (r 3.1(1)). It should therefore be recognised that, although wide-ranging, these powers are not the extent of the court's judicial case management powers, and r 3.1 expressly preserves the court's inherent jurisdiction to protect its process from abuse (see the discussion of the court's inherent jurisdiction in Chapter 2). Also, the court's powers are such that, where it makes an order, it can also vary or revoke the order it has made (r 3.1(7)).

On the other hand, it should also be recognised that the court's general powers cannot be applied to vary the operation of a rule, practice direction or court order if the particular rule, practice direction or court order is expressed not to be subject to such variation (r 3.1(2)). For instance, r 7.6(3) prescribes the only circumstances in which the court is able to extend the period for serving the claim form if the application is made after the period for service has expired. It was held in *Vinos v Marks & Spencer plc* that the discretionary power in the rules to extend time periods under r 3.1(2)(a) did not apply to r 7.6(3) because r 7.6(3) specifically forbids extensions of time unless the circumstances in that rule are satisfied.

Rules as to time

The court has the power to extend or shorten the time for compliance with any rule, practice direction or court order (r 3.1(2)(a)). There is a difference between an application for an extension of time made prospectively, that is, one made before the expiry of the relevant time limit, and an application made after the relevant time has expired for doing something required by a rule, practice direction or court order. In *Robert v Momentum Services Ltd* [2003] EWCA Civ 299, the Court of Appeal considered that applications for an extension of time made prospectively are usually simple and straightforward affairs which require swift decisions with brief, clear reasons. Rule 3.1(2)(a) does not contain a checklist like r 3.9 and the Court of Appeal held that for such applications the discretion should be exercised by simply having regard to the overriding objective.

Although a party is more likely to be successful in seeking extra time for compliance if the application is made before the original time for compliance has expired, the court also has the power to grant extra time even if the application is made *after* the time for compliance has expired (r 3.1(2)(a)). However, where the time limit has expired the application may well be in the nature of an application for relief from a sanction imposed for failure to comply with a rule, practice direction or court order. In those circumstances it would be appropriate for the court to take into account the matters in r 3.9 when exercising its discretion.

In *Law Debenture Trust Corp (Channel Islands) Ltd v Lexington Insurance Company and Others* (2002) LTL, 11 November, the Court of Appeal held that the case management judge had exercised too rigid an approach to a deadline within which the parties were entitled to make amendments to their statements of case. The court found that the judge erred in principle in failing to consider what prejudice the other parties would suffer if the defendants were allowed to amend their defence after the deadline imposed by the court for doing so. In the circumstances the court found that the judge was wrong to refuse permission to make the amendment where the amended defence was arguable and the other parties would not suffer any prejudice by reason of the lateness of the amendments which could be compensated for in costs.

The court will have no power to extend time for compliance if the rule, practice direction or court order provides otherwise (for an example, see *Vinos v Marks & Spencer plc* above).

The parties also have the power to agree to vary time limits by written agreement in respect of certain steps in the proceedings (r 2.11).

The circumstances in which a party may wish to apply to shorten time for compliance are, for instance, if he is required to serve a document on a party within at least a minimum time period before a hearing, but he has failed to do so. Although the CPR were drafted on the premise that parties should carry out procedural steps within the time specified by the rules or the court, this rule ensures that the court has the power to grant a party an indulgence if justice requires.

Attendance at and form of hearing

The court has a general power to order a party or its legal representative to attend court (r 3.1(2)(c)). For instance, the court may require attendance at an allocation hearing in order to assist the court to decide to which track to allocate a case. This is particularly true of case management conferences, where the person attending must be familiar with the case and able to deal with all issues which may arise (r 29.3(2) and PD 29, para 5.2(2)), in default of which a wasted costs order may be made if an adjournment is necessitated (PD 29, para 5.2(3) and see *Baron v Lovell* (1999) *The Times*, 14 September, CA).

The court can decide to receive evidence or hold a hearing by means of a video link or the telephone (r 3.1(2)(d)). This power is being used more and more regularly as it is recognised to be more cost-effective for parties and the court to hold hearings by such means rather than require parties to attend oral hearings at court. The form of general application (Form N244) contains provision for the applicant to request a telephone conference, and many judges' chambers are provided with suitable equipment for the purpose.

Adjournment of proceedings

The court has a general power to adjourn or bring forward a hearing (r 3.1(2)(b)). The court should exercise its powers in accordance with the overriding objective, taking into account the position of both parties, the resources of the court and the interests of other litigants. Where an application has been made for proceedings to be adjourned, the court has to take a number of factors into account in deciding whether or not to grant the application. Those factors include:

(a) the importance of the proceedings and their likely adverse consequences to the other party seeking the adjournment;

(b) the risk of the party being prejudiced in the conduct of the proceedings if the application is refused;

(c) the risk of prejudice or other disadvantage to the other party if the adjournment is granted; and

(d) the extent to which the party applying for the adjournment has been responsible for creating the difficulty which led to the application (*Great Future International Ltd v Sealand Housing Corp* [2001] All ER (D) 56).

In *Fox v Graham Group plc* (2001) *The Times*, 3 August, the court refused to grant an adjournment requested by a litigant in person who said he was too ill to attend the hearing, on the grounds that the application was bound to fail. In reaching its decision the court found that it would be wholly unfair to the interests of the respondent, who would suffer delay and costs if the hearing were adjourned, whilst it would cause no prejudice to the applicant because 'to adjourn it would simply be putting off the evil day'. The court also took into account that an adjournment would waste public money and delay the hearing of cases of other litigants. However, the court said that generally, where a litigant in person was seeking to adjourn for the first time on the grounds that he was ill, the court should be very slow to proceed in his absence unless it was minded to find in his favour.

Managing the issues in a case

Part of the general powers of case management enable the court to direct the order in which issues are heard and whether parts of the case should be heard separately or at a different time. Therefore, the court can:

- direct that part of any proceedings (for example, a counterclaim) is dealt with as separate proceedings (r 3.1(2)(e));

- stay the whole or part of any proceedings or judgment either generally, or until a specified date or event (r 3.1(2)(f));

- consolidate proceedings (r 3.1(2)(g));

- try two or more claims on the same occasion (r 3.1(2)(h));

- direct a separate trial of any issue (r 3.1(2)(i));

- decide the order in which issues are to be tried (r 3.1(2)(j)).

Active case management also requires the court to exercise decisions as to which are the real issues in dispute between the parties despite how a party has presented his case. Therefore, the court has the power to:

- exclude an issue from consideration (r 3.1(2)(k));

- dismiss or give judgment on a claim after a decision on a preliminary issue (r 3.1(2)(l)).

Trial of a preliminary issue

Under r 3.1(2)(i), under its general case management powers, the court can direct a separate trial of any issue. In appropriate cases, the court can therefore direct that there be a trial of a preliminary issue on the grounds that the determination of that issue may determine the whole case, or at least some aspect of it.

However, it is quite rare for a case to contain a single issue which can be separately identified and disposed of without considering the surrounding facts, which may well be strongly contested. The use of this procedure has therefore been described in the past as a 'treacherous shortcut' which can lead to 'delay, anxiety and expense' (*per* Lord Scarman, *Tilling v Whiteman* [1980] AC 1). In *Steele v Steele* (2001) *The Times*, 5 June, the judge refused to hear a trial of a preliminary issue even though it had been proposed by the court below. The judge was of the opinion that in the circumstances a trial of a preliminary issue would not achieve a speedy and inexpensive resolution of some or all of the issues in the case. He held that even if the issue of whether the limitation period had expired was determined as a preliminary issue, the same facts and underlying cause of action would still need to be determined at trial in respect of another part of the claimant's case which was not affected by the issue as to whether there was a limitation period defence. The court must therefore be satisfied that a substantial saving in time and costs will be achieved before ordering the trial of a preliminary issue.

Further powers

As a reflection of the fact that the court is not limited in its role of managing cases in order to achieve a just result, there is also provision in the list of general powers for the court to take any other step, or make any other order for the purpose of managing the case and furthering the overriding objective (r 3.1(2)(m)).

COURT MAKING ORDERS OF ITS OWN INITIATIVE

A major innovation of the CPR was to boost the power of the court to make orders of its own initiative instead of only being able to exercise powers on the application of a party. Rule 3.3(1) provides, therefore, that the court can exercise its powers either on an application, or of its own initiative, unless expressly restricted from doing so by a rule or some other enactment.

When making an order of its own initiative, the court can either:

(a) notify any party likely to be affected by the order that it is proposing to make the order and give that party an opportunity to make representations *before* the order is made (r 3.3(2)(a)). If the court decides to hear representations before making the order, it must notify the affected parties of the specified time and the manner by which their representations must be made (r 3.3(2)(b)). The court does not have to hold a hearing to decide whether to make the order and can order written representation to be made instead. Where a hearing is to be held, the court must give any affected party at least three days' notice of the hearing (r 3.3(3)(b)); or

(b) make the order without hearing the parties or giving them an opportunity to make representations (r 3.3(4)). If the court makes an order of its own initiative without hearing the parties or giving them an opportunity to make representations, a party affected by the order has the right to apply to have it set aside, varied or stayed, and the court order must inform the party of his right to do so (r 3.3(5)). The application challenging the order must be made within the time period specified by the court in the order or, if none is specified, not more

than seven days after the date on which the order was served on the party
(r 3.3(6)). Ideally it should be made to the judge who made the original order, if
at all possible.

SANCTIONS

A major change under the CPR was the introduction of the rule that a sanction
specified by a rule would have effect unless a party obtained relief from the sanction
(r 3.8). Under the previous system, if a party failed to comply with a rule, practice
direction or court order, the other party would have to apply to the court for any
sanction to be imposed. Lord Woolf was of the opinion that this practice was one of
the causes of delay under the old system, was a disincentive to compliance with the
rules and allowed a party to act oppressively towards his opponent. He also believed
that in order for the new system of case management to work, there must be an
effective system of sanctions in operation designed to prevent and deter breaches of
the rules rather than to punish (see *Access to Justice*, Final Report (FR), Chapter 6,
www.dca.gov.uk/civil/final/index.htm)).

Sanctions applying automatically

Rule 3.8 states that where a party has failed to comply with a rule, practice direction
or court order, any sanction for failure to comply imposed by the rule, practice
direction or court order has effect unless the party in default applies for and obtains
relief from the sanction. If the court makes an order which specifies the consequences
of failure to comply it is known as an 'unless order', because it is phrased in terms
'unless the [claimant] files an allocation questionnaire by 4.00 pm on [date] the
claimant's claim will be struck out' or otherwise as the case may be.

If a rule, practice direction or court order requires a party to do something within
a specified time and specifies the consequences of failure to comply, the time for
doing it may not be extended simply by agreement between the parties (r 3.8(3)).
Accordingly, even if the innocent party does not object to the defaulting party
obtaining relief from the sanction, the defaulting party is nevertheless obliged to
seek relief from the sanction (*RC Residuals Ltd (Formerly Regent Chemicals Ltd) v Linton
Fuel Oils Ltd and Others* [2002] 1 WLR 2782).

Where the sanction is the payment of costs, the party in default can obtain relief
only by appealing against the order for costs (r 3.8(2)).

Relief from sanctions

In accordance with the general scheme of the CPR, the court has a wide discretion,
when applying the overriding objective, to decide whether to grant relief to a party
from any sanction imposed for failure to comply with a rule, practice direction or
court order.

Rule 3.9 states that when hearing any application for relief from a sanction
imposed for failure to comply with any rule, practice direction or court order, the
court will consider all the circumstances of the case. However, the rule also goes on
to provide a list of the matters that will be considered by the court when exercising

its discretion to grant relief, and it has been held that the court should consider each matter in this list systematically (*Bansal v Cheema* (2001) LTL, 13 September; *Woodhouse v Consignia plc* [2002] EWCA Civ 275). This list is broadly based on the test set out in the case of *Rastin v British Steel* [1994] 1 WLR 732, a decision made before the CPR came into effect but endorsed and adopted by Lord Woolf in his drafting of the rules (see FR, Chapter 6, para 14). This is an example of where the CPR sets out in a codified form the various matters that the court will take into account when deciding how to exercise its discretion so as to avoid the need, which existed under the former rules, for litigants to be familiar with judge-made case law. As Brooke LJ said, 'One of the great demerits of the former procedural regimes was that simple rules got barnacled with case law' (see *Woodhouse v Consignia plc* at [32]).

The following matters will be included among the circumstances the court will consider:

- the interests of the administration of justice;
- whether the application for relief was made promptly;
- whether the failure to comply was intentional;
- whether there is a good explanation for the failure;
- the extent to which the party in default has complied with other rules, practice directions, court orders and any relevant pre-action protocol;
- whether the failure to comply was caused by the party or his legal representative;
- whether the trial date or the likely trial date can still be met if relief is granted;
- the effect which the failure to comply had on each party; and
- the effect which the granting of relief would have on each party (r 3.9(1)(a)–(i)).

Matters to be taken into account when deciding whether to grant relief from a sanction

In *Woodhouse v Consignia plc* [2002] EWCA Civ 275, the Court of Appeal gave judgment in two appeals dealing with the same issues of general importance under the CPR. Mr Woodhouse began proceedings in April 1998 against his employers for damages for providing an unsatisfactory reference, which he alleged contained false information and failed to give a fair and accurate view of his employment history. Mr Woodhouse committed suicide 17 days later. Although the defendants had filed a defence, nothing further happened in the action for more than two years. In June 2000, Mrs Woodhouse made an application for an order removing the automatic stay that was imposed on the action when the CPR came into force (PD 51, para 19; see Chapter 41, 'Transitional Arrangements') and for an order that she be substituted for her husband as claimant. The only evidence Mrs Woodhouse placed before the court in support of her application to remove the stay was to the effect that her husband's untimely death had caused her immense grief and distress but she now felt able to continue with the claim. The district judge refused to remove the stay due to the inordinate delay.

The automatic stay imposed by PD 51, para 19 is treated as a sanction imposed for failure to comply with a rule, practice direction or court order, within the meaning of r 3.9 (*Audergon v La Baguette Ltd* [2002] EWCA Civ 10).

When granting Mrs Woodhouse relief from the sanction and removing the stay, the Court of Appeal found that the district judge was wrong to concentrate only on the length of delay; instead, he should have considered each of the matters listed in r 3.9 in so far as they were relevant to the case. The court exercised its discretion afresh and found that items (a), (b), (d), (f), (h) and (i) of r 3.9(1) were relevant to the case. In considering these items the court found that in this case they were neutral, or favoured the claimant being entitled to have access to the court to progress her case.

When considering the appeal in *Woodhouse*, the Court of Appeal recognised that the circumstances in which the court may be asked to grant relief from a sanction are infinitely varied, and that was why r 3.9 instructs the court to consider all the circumstances of the particular case, including the nine listed items. Further, the purpose of the rule was to encourage structured decision-making by requiring a judge to go through the exercise of considering all the items on the list when determining how, on balance, he should exercise the court's discretion.

The court made it clear that provided that judges made their decisions within the general framework of r 3.9 and in accordance with the overriding objective, it is very unlikely that an appeal court will interfere with their decisions and it is unlikely that their decisions will fall foul of Art 6 of the European Convention on Human Rights.

In *Bansal v Cheema* (2001) LTL, 13 September, the district judge refused to grant an extension of time for exchange of witness statements when the claimant failed to comply with an order for exchange by a particular date. The district judge then proceeded to strike out the claim on the basis that it must fail if the claimant could not adduce any evidence at the trial. The Court of Appeal overturned this decision on the grounds that the judge did not systematically take into account the list of matters he had to take into account under r 3.9, and that as a result a substantial injustice was done in that case. In particular, the court found that under r 3.9(1)(i) the judge did not take into account the effect which the granting of relief would have on each party. The effect of the refusal would have a catastrophic effect on the claimant whose claim would be struck out, while the defendant would have the unsolicited windfall that a substantial claim against him would be dismissed. As the district judge had not properly exercised his discretion, the Court of Appeal exercised its discretion afresh and allowed the claimant to rely on witness statement evidence that it had now served.

In *RC Residuals Ltd (formerly Regent Chemicals Ltd) v Linton Fuel Oils Ltd and Others* [2002] 1 WLR 2782, an order was made for the claimant to serve its expert reports by 4.00 pm on 12 April 2002; failing such service it would be debarred from calling that expert. The claimant failed by a matter of minutes to serve the reports and was therefore obliged to seek relief from the sanction. The judge at first instance refused to grant relief from the sanction on the grounds of the failure to comply with the order and because the claimant had previously failed to comply with orders in the case. The judge also took into account the fact that if it became known that the court would readily grant relief from unless orders, they would be unlikely to serve the purposes sought to be achieved by the rules so far as the administration of justice is concerned.

The Court of Appeal held that although the judge was entitled to take these matters into account when deciding whether to grant relief from the sanction, he had erred by failing to carry out the balancing exercise required by going through the list in r 3.9(1) and seeing whether there were factors that pointed in the other direction.

The court therefore exercised the discretion afresh and found that when it came to balancing the consequences of the making of the order against all the other matters in the case, the balance tilted very firmly in favour of allowing the expert to give evidence on behalf of the claimant. The court arrived at this conclusion after taking into account the fact that the claimant would be deprived of the chance of pursuing a very substantial part of its claim; it had tried to comply with the order; the failure was not a substantial one; it had no consequences for the defendant; and it had no effect upon the matter proceeding to trial on the date indicated.

In *Jones v Williams* (2002) LTL, 27 May, where a judge had to consider whether to grant relief from a sanction on the day of a trial, the Court of Appeal held that it was not incumbent upon him to go through the list in r 3.9(1) pedantically and say, item by item, what his view was. This was because a number of the tests set out on the list are much better suited to a consideration of a case management decision made weeks or months before the date of the trial. However, the judge did have to give considerable weight to the one item on the list which was of crucial relevance to such a decision made on the day of the trial, namely, item (i) – the effect the granting of relief would have on each party. In that case the defendant had failed to serve witness statements in accordance with an agreed timetable. The judge failed to grant relief from the resulting sanction, with the consequence that the defendant was unable to give evidence in a case where everything turned on whether the judge preferred the evidence of the claimant or that of the defendant as to oral transactions. The judge had failed to consider that the granting of relief would not have had a deleterious effect on the claimant, because he already had had a copy of the witness statement before the trial. However, the effect on the defendant was disastrous. If the judge had no evidence about the oral transaction from the defendant then the effect of that was inevitably to decide the case in favour of the claimant. The Court of Appeal therefore held that by failing to take this consideration into account the judge had wrongly exercised his discretion in refusing to grant relief from that sanction, and his decision would be overturned and the case remitted for retrial.

Also in *Whittaker v Soper* [2001] EWCA Civ 1462, in deciding that it was not a proportionate sanction to strike out a defendant's defence on the day of the trial, the Court of Appeal held that striking out a claim or defence was the ultimate sanction which should only be used proportionately and should be viewed against the backdrop of the other powers and sanctions available to the court to deal with a breach of a rule, practice direction or court order.

Leave to appeal out of time – application of r 3.9

In *Sayers v Clarke-Walker* [2002] EWCA Civ 645, the Court of Appeal held that in a case of any complexity, it was appropriate for a court to have regard to the checklist in r 3.9 when it was considering an application for an extension of time for appealing. The reason is that if the applicant needs an extension of time for appealing he will not have complied with r 52.4(2) and if the court is unwilling to grant him relief from his failure to comply, through the extension of time he is seeking, the consequence will be that the order of the lower court will stand and he cannot appeal it. Although the court acknowledged that this may not be a sanction expressly 'imposed' by the rule, the consequence will be exactly the same as if it had been, and the court thought it 'far better for courts to follow the check-list contained in CPR 3.9 on this occasion, too, than for judges to make their own check-lists for cases where sanctions are implied and not expressly imposed' (at [21]).

In *Sayers v Clarke-Walker*, relevant considerations under the checklist were that the application for an extension of time, although not made promptly, was made very soon after the defendant received notice of the decision (r 3.9(1)(b)). Also, the failure to comply was not intentional (r 3.9(1)(c)). Further, the explanation for the failure, namely, that the defendant's solicitors had misinterpreted the time limits under Part 52, although not categorised as good, was understandable in the early days of the CPR (r 3.9(1)(d)). The court also took into account that the defendant had a bad record of non-compliance with court orders (r 3.9(1)(e)). The court also felt that the failure to comply had caused distress to the claimant, because he was unsure whether the defendant intended to appeal, and the defendant had not made any payment on account of the claimant's costs. However, after taking all these matters into consideration the court found that this was a case where the court ought, in the exercise of its discretion, to grant the extension of time sought by the defendant. Although a number of the items pointed in the claimant's favour, the court felt it would be a disproportionate response to deny the defendant the opportunity to persuade the court that it should be permitted to appeal.

Deliberate failure to comply with a rule, practice direction or court order

It is important to note that if a party intentionally fails to comply with a rule, practice direction or court order, or if the party in default has previously failed to comply with any rule, practice direction, court order or relevant pre-action protocol, the court will take these matters into account when exercising its discretion whether to grant relief from a sanction (*Woodhouse v Consignia plc* [2002] EWCA Civ 275). Thus the more frequent the defaults, the less likely that relief from sanctions will be granted.

Applying for relief from a sanction

The application for relief should be made under Part 23 and must be supported by evidence (r 3.9(2)). The Court of Appeal warned in *Woodhouse v Consignia plc* that parties applying for relief from a sanction should ensure that they provide sufficient evidence to justify their application, as otherwise they may be refused relief.

It is likely that the court will order summary assessment and immediate payment (that is, within 14 days) of the costs of the application by the party in default.

ORDERING SUMS TO BE PAID INTO COURT

Power to impose conditions on orders

The court has the power to make an order subject to conditions, including the payment of a sum of money into court (r 3.1(3)(a)). The court also has the power to specify the consequences of failure to comply with an order or any condition (r 3.1(3)(b)). Such an order is known as an 'unless order' because it is phrased in terms *'unless* the [claimant] file an allocation questionnaire by 4.00 pm on [date] the claimant's claim will be struck out' or otherwise as the case may be.

Payment into court on failure to comply with a rule, practice direction or court order

If a party without good reason fails to comply with a rule, practice direction or applicable pre-action protocol, the court may order that party to pay a sum of money into court as punishment (r 3.1(5)).

The circumstances in which the court is likely to order a payment into court are where, for example, a party has a history of repeated breach of timetables or court orders, or if there is something in the conduct of the party that gives rise to a suspicion that they may not be *bona fide* and the court thinks that the other side should have some financial security or protection. Where a party is simply late in complying with the court timetable, and the other side is not prejudiced by that delay, it is not appropriate for the court to punish that type of default by means of a payment into court; instead the penalty in such circumstances is for the party in default to seek relief from any sanction imposed (see the judgment of Buckley J in *Mealey Horgan plc v Horgan & Hill Samuel Bank Ltd* (1999) *The Times,* 6 July (cited with approval in *Olatawura v Abiloye* [2002] EWCA Civ 998)).

It was recognised by the Court of Appeal in *Olatawura v Abiloye* [2002] EWCA Civ 998 that provisions such as r 3.1(5), PD 24, para 4 (payment into court as condition for continuing to bring or defend a claim) were tantamount to orders for security for costs outside the provisions of Part 25 (Section II). However, it was accepted that under the CPR the court had an altogether wider discretion than under the former rules to ensure that justice can be done in a particular case, including making such orders. In that case the Court of Appeal upheld the district judge's reasons for ordering the claimant to pay the sum of £5,000 into court as security for costs. Those reasons were that the claimant's claim had only limited prospects of success; the claimant had been conducting the case in a wholly unreasonable way and was set to continue doing so; and the claimant was not permanently resident in the jurisdiction, making enforcement of any adverse costs order more difficult. It should be noted that before considering whether to make the order the district judge had also taken into account that the making of the order would not prevent the claimant from continuing to litigate his claim. The court described this finding as essentially a pre-condition to making any such order (at [27]).

When deciding whether to exercise the power to order a party to pay a sum of money into court, the court must have regard to the amount in dispute and the costs which the parties have incurred or may incur (r 3.1(6)).

The court is likely to be proportionate when deciding on the amount a party must pay into court and should ensure that the imposition of this penalty does not make it impossible for a party to continue with the litigation (*Chapple v Williams* (1999) LTL, 8 December). However, a party cannot complain that the amount ordered is difficult for him to pay, and a party is likely to have to be prepared to provide full and frank disclosure of his financial circumstances in order to avoid or reduce the amount ordered to be paid into court (*Training in Compliance Ltd (t/a Matthew Read) v Dewse (t/a Data Research Co)* (2000) LTL, 2 October, CA). Where a party is ordered to pay a sum of money into court, the money shall be security for any sum payable by that party to any other party in the proceedings. However, a defendant can instead elect to treat any ordered payment in as a Part 36 payment (r 3.1(6A)).

ERRORS OF PROCEDURE

If a party makes an error in procedure – for instance, fails to use the correct prescribed form – the error does not invalidate any step taken in the proceedings, unless the court so orders and the court has a general power to remedy the error (r 3.10).

In *Hannigan v Hannigan* [2000] All ER (D) 693, the Court of Appeal exercised its power under r 3.10 to correct errors in procedure where the errors were merely technical in nature and had not caused any disadvantage to the defendant. The claimant's solicitor had started proceedings in the wrong form and made a number of other technical errors. The defendant applied for an order that the claimant's claim should be struck out under r 3.4(2)(c) on the grounds of the claimant's failure to comply with the rules and practice directions. The lower court was extremely critical of the failure to comply with the rules and struck out the claimant's claim. The Court of Appeal overturned this decision on the grounds that it was a disproportionate response to the procedural errors made by the claimant, particularly when the claimant's statement of case and supporting evidence provided the defendant with all the information it needed to know the nature of the claimant's claim.

The Court of Appeal said that although this was strictly speaking an application for the court to exercise its discretion under r 3.10, it was appropriate for the judge to take into account each of the factors listed in r 3.9 in so far as they were relevant, as well as any other relevant matters. In that case the court found that the only matters that could be taken into account in the defendant's favour were the sheer number of technical defects made by the claimant with no good reason. As against this the scales were 'tipped overwhelmingly in [the claimant's] favour by the interests of the administration of justice and the fact that to strike out her claim in these circumstances [would be] a totally disproportionate response to the errors that were made'.

Although the Court of Appeal did not condone 'sloppy and inefficient practices', and there were a number of sanctions which could be imposed for such practices in appropriate circumstances, it was not the intention of the CPR to strike out proceedings for 'arid technicalities' and the 'old turf wars between solicitors over technicalities were being superseded by a new climate in which the emphasis was the achievement of justice at a cost which was not disproportionate to the matters involved in the dispute' (*per* Brooke LJ).

In *Law v St Margaret's Insurances Ltd* [2001] EWCA Civ 30, solicitors acting for the defendant made a number of procedural errors when applying to set aside judgment in default, in a case where the defendant had a good defence on the merits. The court dismissed the application on the grounds that it was defective. In the Court of Appeal, Brown LJ held that the procedural errors committed by the defendant's solicitors could not justify shutting out for all time a substantive and sound defence to the claim. The court exercised its discretion under r 3.10 to remedy the defects and set the judgment aside so that there could be a proper hearing on the merits of the claimant's claim.

However, r 3.10 does not give the court the power to do what a rule specifically forbids. Therefore, as r 7.6(3) sets out the only circumstances in which the court can extend the period for serving the claim form after the period for service has expired, r 3.10 does not give the court a general power to extend the period of time if the conditions in r 7.6(3) are not satisfied (*Vinos v Marks & Spencer plc* [2001] 3 All ER 784).

SANCTIONS FOR NON-PAYMENT OF CERTAIN FEES

It was recognised that with the introduction of case management, judicial and court staff would have a greater burden imposed upon them in carrying out their new functions and that parties might be asked to contribute to the additional costs resulting from the reforms. Since the introduction of the CPR, it is no coincidence that there has also been a dramatic rise in the level of court fees in bringing a civil claim, as well as the introduction of new fees at various stages in the proceedings, most noticeably at allocation and listing.

Allocation and listing fees

A fee is payable by the claimant when the allocation questionnaire and pre-trial checklist are filed, unless the claimant successfully applies for exemption from or remission of payment of the fee. However, even in those cases where the court has dispensed with the need for an allocation or pre-trial checklist, or one is not required under the rules, the fee will still be payable. In those circumstances, the fee will be payable either within 14 days of the date the notice of allocation to track has been sent to the parties by the court, or where there is automatic allocation or no allocation to a track, within 28 days of the filing of the defence, or if there is more than one defendant, the last defence, or within 28 days of expiry of the time for filing all defences if sooner (see Supreme Court Fees Order 1999 (SI 1999/687) and the County Court Fees Order 1999 (SI 1999/689), as amended).

An allocation fee will not be payable when the only claim is to recover a sum of money which does not exceed £1,000 (see County Court Fees Order 1999, as amended). Also, no listing fee is payable for a case allocated to the small claims track, as pre-trial checklists are not normally used.

In the usual course of events, the court serving the allocation or pre-trial checklist on the claimant will also remind the claimant of the fee that is due on filing of that document. If the claimant does not pay the relevant fee at the time that it is due, or apply for exemption from or remission of payment, the court will, in the first instance, serve a notice on the claimant requiring payment of the fee (r 3.7(2)). The court will also give a deadline by which the fee must be received (r 3.7(3)).

Sanction for non-payment

If the claimant does not pay the fee, or make an application for exemption from or remission of the fee, by the date specified in the court notice, the claim will be struck out and the claimant will be liable for the defendant's costs of the claim unless the court orders otherwise (r 3.7(4)).

If the claimant has made an application for exemption from or remission of payment of the allocation or listing fee, but the application is refused, the court will serve a notice on the claimant requiring payment of the relevant fee by a specified date (r 3.7(5)). Again, if the fee is not paid by the specified date, the claim will be struck out and the claimant will be liable for the defendant's costs of the claim unless the court orders otherwise (r 3.7(6)).

A claimant whose claim has been struck out will be able to apply to have his claim reinstated under the court's general powers to grant relief from sanctions under r 3.9. If the court grants relief and reinstates the claim, this will be conditional on the claimant paying the relevant fee, or filing evidence of exemption from payment or remission of the fee within two days of the date of the order granting such relief (r 3.7(7)).

If a claim is struck out for failure to pay the relevant fee, the court will notify the defendant that this has occurred (PD 3B, para 1).

In a case where an interim injunction has been obtained, the interim injunction will cease to have effect 14 days after the date the claim is struck out under r 3.7 (r 25.11 and PD 3B, para 2). However, if the claimant applies to reinstate the claim before the interim injunction ceases to have effect, the injunction will continue until the hearing of the application, unless the court orders otherwise (r 25.11(2) and PD 3B, para 2).

CHAPTER 7

PARTIES TO AND TITLE OF PROCEEDINGS

INTRODUCTION

The issue of whom a party may sue in respect of a cause of action is a question of substantive law. However, having decided upon the person or body to sue, rules of procedure govern how that person or body must be identified in the title of the proceedings.

TITLE OF PROCEEDINGS

The claim form and every other statement of case must be headed with the title of the proceedings. Practice Direction 7 includes provisions as to the title of the proceedings. In respect of the claim form, the notes for guidance on completing the claim form should also be taken into account. The title should state:

- the number of the proceedings;
- the court or division in which they are proceeding;
- the full name of each party and his status in the proceedings (that is, claimant/defendant);
- where there is more than one claimant (and/or more than one defendant), the parties should be numbered and described as follows, as the case may be:

  (1) AB
  (2) CD   Claimants
      and
  (1) EF
  (2) GH   Defendants

(PD 7, paras 4.1–4.2.)

The number of the proceedings

Obviously, when completing the claim form for filing and issue at court, the claimant will not be in a position to know the number of the proceedings, so at this stage the relevant part of the claim form and any statement of case is left blank. Once proceedings are issued, the court will give the proceedings a number and send a notice of issue to the claimant on which the number of the proceedings will be entered. The court will also enter the number onto the claim form, a copy of which will be served on the defendant.

The heading of statements of case

Despite the reforms brought about by the CPR to the content of statements of case (formerly known as pleadings), and the absence of detailed rules as to how the heading of statements of case must be presented, a conventional heading is usually adopted by legal representatives which is the same as was formerly used under the old rules. The convention is for the court or division in which the matter is proceeding to appear in the top left hand corner of the document in capital letters. The number of the proceedings appears on the same line, but at the right hand side of the document. On the next line appears the word 'between' and the names of the parties appear beneath this, in the centre, separated by the word 'and', while the party's status appears alongside at the far right hand side and underlined. The type of statement of case is presented in capital letters beneath the title and enclosed in tramlines. An example is given at Figure 7.1 below.

Figure 7.1: Heading of statements of case

IN THE CHELTENHAM COUNTY COURT   Claim no: CH123456

Between

John Doe   <u>Claimant</u>

– and –

Richard Roe   <u>Defendant</u>

PARTICULARS OF CLAIM

PARTIES TO PROCEEDINGS

Different rules apply to such matters as how a party is described in proceedings and how he is served with documents, depending on the capacity of that party. The various capacities in which a party can be sued are set out below.

Individuals

The notes for the claimant on completing a claim form (attached to the claim form) provide that when a party is suing or being sued as an individual, the title of the party must be provided, such as Mr, Mrs, Miss, Ms, etc. The claimant must also provide all known forenames and the surname of the defendant, along with a residential address in England and Wales, including the postcode and telephone number.

For other statements of case, such as particulars of claim, it is conventional just to give the details of the full name (excluding the title) of the person who is suing and being sued (as in the example at Figure 7.1 above). However, in accordance with PD 16, paras 2.2 and 3.8, and the accompanying notes to the claim form, the claimant must also provide, among other things, his address for service on the statement of case, as well as on the claim form, if the former is a separate document.

Children and patients

Where the party suing or being sued is a child, the child's full name should be given but the following words should appear in brackets after the name: '(a child by [Mr] AB [his father] and litigation friend).' Where the child is conducting proceedings on his own behalf, the words '(a child)' should appear after the child's name (PD 21, para 1.5).

Where the party suing or being sued is a patient, the patient's full name should be given but the following words should appear in brackets after the name: '(by [Mr] AB [his] litigation friend)' (PD 21, para 1.3).

Trading names

If the person suing is the sole proprietor of a business, his full name should be given followed by the words 'trading as' and the trading name. If such a person is the person being sued, the claimant can either sue him in his own name with the words 'trading as' and the trading name given, or sue him simply in his trading name, followed by the words in brackets 'a trading name' (CPR Sched 1 RSC Ord 81, r 9; CPR Sched 2 CCR Ord 5, r 10).

If the person is sued in his trading name alone, he is treated as if he is a partner and the name in which he carries on business is the name of his firm (RSC Ord 81, r 9; CCR Ord 5, r 10). Whether such a person is sued as an individual or in his trading name is significant, because if he is sued in his trading name, the rules on the automatic transfer of proceedings on the filing of a defence by an individual would appear not to apply to that defendant (r 26.2).

Deceased's estate

Where the estate of a deceased person is suing or being sued, the full name of the deceased's personal representative (either executor or administrator) should be given, followed by the words, 'as the representative of x (deceased)'.

Where a grant of probate or administration has been made, any claim against the defendant's estate must be brought against the defendant's personal representatives (r 19.8(2)(a)). Where a grant of probate or administration has not been made, proceedings may be commenced against a defendant's estate even if no personal representatives have been appointed; but in order to proceed with the claim, the claimant must apply to the court for an order appointing a person to represent the estate as a real defendant, having legal personality and being capable of identification (r 19.8(2)(b); *Piggott v Aulton (deceased)* [2003] EWCA Civ 24).

Change of party by reason of death or bankruptcy

Where a party to a claim dies or becomes bankrupt but the cause of action survives (generally all causes of action except defamation), the proceedings are not a nullity because of the death or bankruptcy (s 1(1) of the Law Reform (Miscellaneous Provisions) Act 1934). An order should be sought for the substitution of the appropriate representative party (rr 19.4 and 19.8).

In the case of the death of a party, if the action continues but the party has no personal representative, the court may order the claim to proceed in the absence of a person representing the estate of the deceased or that a person be appointed to represent the estate of the deceased (r 19.8).

Clubs/unincorporated associations

If a club or other unincorporated association is suing or being sued, the full name of one or more members of the committee or trustees of the club or other unincorporated association should be given followed by the words 'suing/sued on behalf of' and the name of the club or other unincorporated association.

Partners

Although a partnership does not have separate legal identity, two or more persons carrying on business as a partnership may sue or be sued in the name of the firm (CPR Sched 1 RSC Ord 81, r 1; CPR Sched 2 CCR Ord 5, r 9). The firm's name should be given followed by the words, 'a firm'. The individuals who make up the firm can sue or be sued individually instead. The claimant should also provide an address for service of the firm on the claim form, which should be either a partner's residential address, or the principal or last known place of business of the firm.

Where partners sue or are sued in the name of the firm, the other party to the proceedings can demand, by making a request in writing, that the partners deliver and file at court a statement of the names and places of residence of all the persons who were partners in the firm when the cause of action arose. If the partners fail voluntarily to comply with such a request, the other party can apply to the court for an order that the partners must furnish such a statement verified on oath and direct that if they fail to do so the proceedings will be stayed (if the partners are claimants) or they will be debarred from defending the claim (if the partners are defendants). Where the names and places of residence of the partners have been so provided the proceedings will continue in the name of the firm (CPR Sched 1 RSC Ord 81, r 2; CPR Sched 2 CCR Ord 5, r 9).

Corporations

A company is a separate legal entity and can sue or be sued as such. In the case of a company registered in England and Wales, the full name of the company should be given including the words 'Limited' or 'plc'. In the case of a corporation other than a company, the full name of the corporation should be given. In the case of an oversea company as defined by s 744 of the Companies Act 1985, the full name of the company should be given.

The claimant should also provide an address for service of the corporation on the claim form. In the case of a company registered in England and Wales, it should be either the company's registered office or any place of business which has a real, or the most, connection with the claim. In the case of a corporation other than a company, it should be either its principal office or any other place where the corporation carries on activities and which has a real connection with the claim. In the case of an oversea company, it should be the address registered under s 691 of the Act, or the address of the place of business having a real, or the most, connection with the claim.

Derivative claims

If a derivative claim is brought by minority shareholders that a company or other incorporated body or trade union is entitled to a remedy, the company, other incorporated body or trade union must be made a defendant to the claim.

After the claim form has been issued the claimant must apply to the court, with evidence supporting the allegations made, for permission to continue the claim. The claim form, application notice and written evidence in support of the application must be served on the defendant within the period within which the claim form must be served, and in any event, at least 14 days before the court is to deal with the application (r 19.9(1)–(5)).

If the court gives the claimant permission to continue the claim, the defendant must file a defence 14 days after the permission was given, or within such other time as the court may order (r 19.9(6)).

Representative parties

If there is more than one person who has the same interest in a claim, the claim may be begun, or the court may order that the claim be continued, by or against one or more of the persons who have the same interest, as representatives of any other persons who have that interest. Unless the court orders otherwise, any judgment or order given in such a claim is binding on all persons represented in the claim, but may only be enforced against a person who is not a party to the claim with the permission of the court (r 19.6).

It is more efficient to sue or be sued in a representative capacity where there are numerous people all having the same interest. An example is the case of *Moon v Atherton* [1972] 2 QB 43, where one of 11 tenants in a block of flats brought an action on behalf of herself and the tenants against their landlord for failing to carry out repairs. The full name of the representative or representatives should be given followed by the words 'on behalf of himself/herself/themselves' and then the description of the group represented.

It has been held that there is a sufficient commercial interaction between counterfeiters to treat them all as a group (*EMI Records v Kudhail* [1985] FSR 36). In that case, the claimant sought injunctive relief against Mr Kudhail and other unnamed persons in respect of alleged infringements of its copyright and for passing off. Although Mr Kudhail's identity was known, the claimant did not know the identity of the other parties engaged in distributing counterfeit recordings. However, the court was prepared to make an order against Mr Kudhail on his own behalf and as representing all other persons engaged in the counterfeiting. It concluded that the common link afforded by that activity and the common interest in wishing to remain anonymous were sufficient to justify the order.

Proceedings against an unnamed defendant

There is no requirement under the CPR that a defendant *must* be named, merely a direction that he should be. Therefore, where the identity of a defendant is not known, a defendant can be described otherwise than by name; this is often known as a 'John Doe' order (*Bloomsbury Publishing Group Ltd and JK Rowling v News Group Newspapers Ltd and Others* [2003] EWHC 1087; [2003] EWHC 1205). In the *JK Rowling* case, copies of the fifth book in the Harry Potter series were taken away from the printers without authority and offered to the press at varying prices. The person offering the unauthorised copies to the press did not divulge his name, so, when applying for an injunction against him, the claimant referred to the defendant by description, that is, as 'the person or persons who have offered the publishers of *The Sun*, the *Daily Mail* and the *Daily Mirror* newspapers a copy of the book *Harry Potter and the Order of the Phoenix* by JK Rowling'. The court was of the opinion that in a suitable case, if someone can be identified clearly enough, the court should do what it can to allow injunctive relief, even if it is not possible to identify the defendant by name. The description used must be sufficiently certain as to identify both those who are included and those who are not. The Vice Chancellor was of the opinion that not to allow such a claim to proceed would show an undue reliance on form over substance, which would be inconsistent with the overriding objective ([2003] EWHC 1205 at [19]).

A 'John Doe' order should be distinguished from the procedure under r 8.2A whereby a person seeking a direction or order from the court – typically a trustee or an executor who intends to bring or defend a claim seeking a direction from the court authorising him to do so – makes an application without naming any defendants in the proceedings. Such an application is known as a 'Beddoe' application (see Chapter 15, 'Part 8 Claims', for details). A 'Beddoe' application is made to the court by the trustee or executor in circumstances where there is no defendant to the proceedings, as distinguished from a 'John Doe' order in which there is a defendant to the proceedings but his identity is not known.

GROUP LITIGATION

Where there is a number of either claimants or defendants whose claims or defences give rise to common or related issues of law or fact, but who do not have the same interest in a claim, such as in the case of product liability relating to a particular drug, or large-scale transport accidents, a Group Litigation Order (GLO) may be made so that all the different cases can be managed together (r 19.11). This type of order will be appropriate where there is a substantial number of such claimants or defendants, as, for example, in the litigation relating to the MMR vaccine: *Paul Sayers and Others v SmithKline Beecham plc and Others* [2003] EWHC 104. A GLO is an efficient and cost-effective way to establish issues relating to liability, for example, whether the MMR vaccine can cause autism, which will be binding on all the cases within the GLO. However, if liability is established it will be for the individual litigants to prove they suffered harm as a result and to quantify their individual losses.

Application for a GLO

A solicitor considering applying for a GLO should consult the Law Society's Multi-Party Actions Information Service in order to obtain information about other cases giving rise to the proposed GLO issues. Practice Direction 19B encourages the claimants' solicitors to form a Solicitors' Group and to appoint one of their number to take the lead in applying for the GLO and in litigating the GLO issues (PD 19B, para 2.2).

If a GLO is appropriate, an application should be made in accordance with Part 23, supported by written evidence summarising the nature of the litigation; the number and nature of claims already issued; the number of parties likely to be involved; the GLO issues likely to arise in the litigation; and whether there are any matters that distinguish smaller groups of claims within the wider group (PD 19B, para 3.2).

GLO

If a GLO is made, it must: contain directions about the establishment of a register of all the claims managed as a group under the GLO; specify the GLO issues which will identify the claims to be managed as a group under the GLO; and specify the management court which will manage the claims on the group register (r 19.11).

Directions are also likely to be made for the publicising of the GLO by supplying copies to the Law Society and the Senior Master of the Queen's Bench Division of the Royal Courts of Justice (PD 19B, para 11). The Law Society will publish it in the *Law Society's Gazette*. For an example see the notice in the *Law Society's Gazette* publicising the GLO made on 27 November 2002 in respect of individuals who were subjected to sexual, physical and emotional abuse in a number of children's homes in South Wales. Notice was given to solicitors who had clients wishing to join the litigation to register their claim no later than 26 May 2003, after which the permission of the court would be required ((2003) 100/14 Gazette 37).

Effect of the GLO

The effect of the GLO is that a judgment or order relating to a GLO issue made in a claim which is on the group register will be binding on the parties to all other claims on the group register at the time the judgment or order is made, unless the court orders otherwise (r 19.12(1)(a)). However, a party can seek permission to appeal the judgment or order if it adversely affects him (r 19.12(2)).

Also, if the court makes an order for disclosure of any document relating to the GLO issues by a party to a claim on the group register, the document will be disclosed to all parties to claims on the group register (r 19.12(4)).

Case management of the GLO

The management court may give case management directions at the time the GLO is made or subsequently, and the directions will generally be binding on all claims on the group register (PD 19B, para 12.1).

Directions may include such matters as appointing a lead solicitor for the claimant or defendants; specifying the details to be included in a statement of case in order to meet the criteria for entry of the claim on the group register; specifying a cut-off date for entry of a case onto the group register; ordering that one or more claims on the group register proceed as test claims (r 19.13; PD 19B, paras 12, 13).

A direction may also be made that the GLO claimants serve 'Group Particulars of Claim' which set out the various claims of all the claimants on the group register at the time the particulars are filed. Such particulars of claim will usually contain general allegations relating to all claims and a schedule containing entries relating to each individual claim, specifying which of the general allegations are relied on and any specific facts relevant to the claimant (PD 19B, para 14).

Costs of a GLO

Under r 48.6A(5), where there has been an application or hearing involving GLO issues and an issue relevant only to individual claims, the court should direct what proportion of the costs are common costs of the GLO and what proportion relates to individual costs.

If the court does not make such an order under r 48.6A(5), it will fall to the costs judge to do so at or before the commencement of the detailed assessment of those costs (PD 19B, para 16.2).

CHAPTER 8

ISSUING A CLAIM

INTRODUCTION

One of the fundamental principles of the civil justice reforms was that there should be a single means of starting proceedings. Lord Woolf argued that the complexity of the old rules of court was an obstacle to access to justice, citing as a prime example of that complexity the multiplicity of forms that could be used to commence an action. In his view, the rules on starting proceedings needed simplification and should be the same for both the High Court and county courts (see *Access to Justice*, Final Report, Chapter 12, paras 1–3, www.dca.gov.uk/civil/final/index.htm).

The former rules offered a number of different forms to choose from to start proceedings. Thus, when commencing proceedings in the High Court, a choice had to be made between a writ, an originating summons, an originating motion or a petition, depending on the type of action. In the county courts the choice was a summons, an originating application, a petition and notice of appeal. There were further variations within those categories; for instance, there were three types of form of originating summons and several different forms of summons.

The Civil Procedure Rules (CPR) provide for one basic form to be used in both the High Court and the county courts: the claim form – the term 'summons' for an originating process has now gone. Although, superficially, this makes the process of starting a claim simpler (one form fits all), the claim form is modified to take account of differences in the nature of certain types of proceedings. Therefore, although there is a 'standard' claim form that is used for most claims, this is modified for specialised proceedings.

So, for example, in claims about the construction of a document, where there is no dispute of fact, it would not be appropriate to use a standard claim form followed by particulars of claim and a defence. Instead, the claim form contains the question of construction the court is asked to decide, along with a witness statement from the claimant containing any evidence in support. Thus, although called a claim form, a claim form for the type of claim where the claimant seeks the court's decision on a question that is unlikely to involve a substantial dispute of fact is in a different form and follows a different procedure, known as the alternative procedure for claims (Part 8). It is used for those types of claim formerly commenced by originating summons. Also, for specialist proceedings, such as commercial and admiralty claims, practice directions specify practice forms that must be used to start those proceedings. New forms and procedures were introduced on 15 October 2001 for possession and landlord and tenant claims (Parts 55 and 56).

Thus, although the reforms profess to simplify the rules on starting a claim and introduce only one form by which to do so, the reality is different. On the surface, there is now only one form to start a claim, but scratch the surface and the complexities demanded by the peculiarities of proceedings reappear. In theory, a single claim form seems desirable, but in real life variations are necessary to smooth the procedural path for claims of a different nature or specialism. Indeed, paradoxically, the fact that substantially different forms come under the single name of a claim form could be said to make starting a claim more confusing rather than less.

Issuing proceedings

Proceedings are started when the court issues a claim form at the request of the claimant (r 7.2(1)). On issue, the court will stamp the claim form with the court seal. The claim form is issued on the date entered on the form by the court (r 7.2(2)). The claimant can either post (send via DX) or deliver the claim form to the court office for issuing.

The date of issue is important because, once issued, proceedings must be served within a limited period of time (or extra time must be requested to serve them). Further, in some cases, the date a claim was brought can be significant as far as limitation periods are concerned (see Chapter 3, 'Limitation Periods'). Practice Direction 7 provides that where the claim form was received in the court office on a date earlier than that on which it was issued by the court, the claim is *brought* on that earlier date for the purposes of the Limitation Act 1980 and any other relevant statute (PD 7, para 5.1). The date on which the claim form was received by the court will be recorded by a date stamp either on the claim form held on the court file, or on the letter that accompanied the claim form when it was received by the court (PD 7, para 5.2). In a homelessness appeal case it was held that if a document must be filed by a certain date it will be sufficiently filed if posted through the court's letter-box even after the court office has closed (*Van Aken v Camden LBC* [2002] EWCA Civ 1724). However, filing a document at court means simply delivering it to the court (r 2.3(1)) and it is arguable, therefore, whether the decision in *Van Aken* applies to the issue of proceedings, which occurs when the claim form is *received* in the court office. 'Receiving' a document indicates a reciprocal act of acceptance, which would not seem to occur if the court office is closed at the time the document is delivered.

Practice Direction 7 anticipates that in proceedings issued very close to the time that the limitation period for bringing that claim is about to expire, establishing that the claim was brought before the limitation period expired may be crucial in deciding whether the claim can proceed. The practice direction therefore warns parties to recognise the importance of establishing the date the claim form was received by the court and make arrangements themselves to record that date (PD 7, para 5.4).

Rule 2.8(5) may be of relevance here in particular cases, because it provides that when a rule, practice direction, judgment or court order specifies a period of time for doing any act at the court office, and that period of time ends on a day when the office is closed, the act shall be in time if done on the next day on which the court office is open. Therefore, if the last day for bringing a claim falls on a Sunday, the party will still be in time under the Limitation Act 1980 if the claim form is received the following Monday, or the next day when the court office reopens.

Which court?

Although procedure has been unified for the High Court and the county courts, the courts still retain their distinct existence and, for certain types of claim, separate jurisdiction. The CPR reinforce the trend that was started with the High Court and County Courts Jurisdiction Order 1991 (SI 1991/724), namely, reserving the High Court for specialist proceedings and those which are more valuable, serious and complex.

Restrictions on issuing proceedings in the High Court

There are restrictions on issuing proceedings in the High Court. Unless the monetary value of a claim is more than £15,000, or an enactment specifies that the claim may be commenced in the High Court, or the case needs to be in one of the specialist High Court lists, the claim should not be started in the High Court (r 16.3(5)). Proceedings that include a claim for damages in respect of personal injuries must not be started in the High Court unless the value of the claim is £50,000 or more (PD 7, para 2.2; High Court and County Courts Jurisdiction Order 1991, Art 5). The threshold of £15,000 means that all claims in the High Court will be treated as multi-track cases.

For claims above those financial limits the claimant should start proceedings in the High Court only if by reason of:

(1) the financial value of the claim and the amount in dispute; and/or

(2) the complexity of the facts, legal issues, remedies or procedures involved, and/ or the importance of the outcome of the claim to the public in general;

(3) the claimant believes that the claim ought to be dealt with by a High Court Judge.

(PD 7, para 2.4.)

Further, in the case of claims issued in the Royal Courts of Justice, unless the estimated value of the claim is £50,000 or more, or it is the type of case that should be brought in the High Court and is suitable for trial in the Royal Courts of Justice, it is likely to be transferred to a county court (PD 29, para 2.2).

Chapter 12 ('Statements of Case') should be consulted for the requirements for statements of value on the claim form.

These rules restrict the issuing of proceedings in the High Court, but they are not rules of jurisdiction; so although, in some cases, a claim cannot be *started* in the High Court, this does not necessarily mean that it will not be *heard* in the High Court. Also, these rules do not limit the jurisdiction of the county courts, so there is no restriction on a claim that is valued over £15,000 being started in a county court. Further, the court has wide powers to transfer proceedings between the High Court and county courts (Part 30).

Court fees

The claimant is charged a court fee to issue proceedings. Litigants of modest means can apply to the court for an exemption or remission from the court fee, and those on State means-tested benefits are granted an automatic exemption (see the County Court Fees Order 1999 (SI 1999/689) and the Supreme Court Fees Order 1999 (SI 1999/687), as amended).

Since the introduction of the CPR, with their emphasis on avoiding litigation, the demand for civil litigation has fallen generally. Also, there has been a 76% decrease in the amount of litigation in the High Court due to the restrictions introduced for commencing proceedings in the High Court. The fall in demand and rise in running costs led to a review of court fees and proposals for increases (see the Consultation Paper, *Fee Changes*, published in September 2002 by the Court Service, available on www.courtservice.gov.uk/docs/fee_consultation.pdf).

The County Court Fees (Amendment) Order 2003 (SI 2003/648) and the Supreme Court Fees (Amendment) Order 2003 (SI 2003/646) introduced new schedules of fees as from 1 April 2003. The increases in fees are the first since April 2000, and the new schedules reflect comments made in the consultation process, as well as the principles followed for the setting of civil court fees, which the Lord Chancellor announced to Parliament in November 1998. The principles are designed to achieve a balance between recovering the cost of the service being provided and allowing access to justice.

A scale of fees has been set which rises according to the value of the claim. The new fees retain a common scale of fees payable on the issue of claims in both the High Court and county courts, but the new structure is loaded to generate more income from higher value claims, those above £15,000. This reflects the more complex and costly work required for High Court cases. This will not impact on the majority of civil court users – of total money claims issued in county courts or through the bulk-users' Claims Production Centre in 2001–02, 89% were not exceeding £5,000 in value (see Consultation Paper at www.courtservice.gov.uk/docs/fee_consultation.pdf).

The reasoning behind a sliding scale is the likelihood that higher value claims will be defended and the resulting hearings will last longer. The amount has been fixed to reflect the average cost of the service provided rather than the actual cost for a particular case. In consequence, since the introduction of the CPR, issue fees have been increased substantially.

It is Government policy to make the court system self-funding, and the message to litigants is that they should not expect the taxpayer to pay for, or subsidise, the court services they use. However, in order to protect access to justice, exemptions and remissions exist for litigants of modest means (see the Lord Chancellor's Consultation Paper, *Fee Levels and Charging Points*, November 1998, available on the Department for Constitutional Affairs website: www.dca.gov.uk/consult/civ-just/civilffr.htm). A self-funding court system is a completely novel concept in our legal system and provides evidence of the Government's desire to control the cost of the court system to the public purse. This policy has not, so far, been challenged under the Human Rights Act 1998 as a bar to access to the courts and, therefore, as a breach of Art 6 of the European Convention on Human Rights (right to a fair trial), although there remains the prospect that it will be. However, both the Master of the Rolls and the Lord Chief Justice have expressed their opposition to the idea of courts being self-financing ((2003) Legal Action 6).

THE CLAIM FORM

The vast majority of claims must be started using the prescribed claim form number N1 (PD 7, para 3.1). This is very similar in format to the old county court summons form. For those claims using the Part 8, alternative procedure for claims (for instance, claims about the construction of a document where there is no substantial dispute of fact), a different form, N208 is prescribed (PD 7, para 3.1). For those claims brought under the specialist jurisdictions a practice direction relating to that jurisdiction may specify a practice form that has been approved for those types of proceedings (PD 7, para 3.4).

Particulars of claim

Particulars of claim must be contained in, or served with, the claim form (r 7.4(1)(a)). Alternatively, particulars of claim can be served on the defendant within 14 days after service of the claim form (r 7.4(1)(b)). However, if the latter course is taken, the particulars of claim must be served on the defendant no later than the latest date for serving a claim form (r 7.4(2)). The claim form itself must be served within four months after the date of issue (r 7.5) (or six months where the claim form is to be served out of the jurisdiction (r 7.5(3))). Therefore, if service of the claim form is delayed until the end of that four-month period, the particulars of claim must also be served before the end of that four-month period, so the additional 14 days do not run after the end of the four-month period for issue. However, the court does have a discretion under r 3.10 to extend the time for service of particulars of claim after the expiry of the four-month period (see *Totty v Snowden* [2001] EWCA Civ 1415). As for the contents of the particulars of claim, see Chapter 12, 'Statements of Case'.

The possibility of serving a claim form giving a brief outline of the claim, followed by particulars of claim which supply the detail at a later date, effectively reproduces in the CPR the 'generally' versus 'specially' endorsed writ procedure formerly available under the old rules. The Civil Procedure Rules Committee gave lengthy consideration as to whether this distinction should be retained. The concern was that this procedure ran contrary to two fundamental principles of the civil justice reforms, namely (i) that there should be a unified procedure for claims, and (ii) that a claimant should be ready to proceed with a case when he starts a claim. It was also feared that it could be used as a delaying tactic. However, this procedure was allowed to continue for the reason that it enables claims to be commenced in emergency circumstances when there is not enough time to prepare the full claim form (see the Consultation Paper on the proposed new procedures for the specialist jurisdictions of the High Court at www.dca.gov.uk/consult/civ-just/accjus1.htm).

If the particulars of claim are not included in or have not been served with the claim form, the claim form must include a statement that particulars of claim will follow (r 16.2(2)).

If the particulars of claim are contained in or served with the claim form, a copy will be filed at the court on issue. If the claimant serves particulars of claim separately from the claim form he must, within seven days of service on the defendant, file a copy of the particulars together with a certificate of service (r 7.4(3)). The certificate of service must state that the particulars of claim have not been returned undelivered and specify the date of service. Which date to specify differs according to the method of service used, so, for instance, if postal service is used, the date of posting must be specified (r 6.10).

Statements of truth

The claim form must be verified by a statement of truth (r 22.1). If the particulars of claim are not included in the claim form, they must also contain a statement of truth (PD 7, para 7.1).

The Human Rights Act 1998

If a claimant is seeking a remedy under the Human Rights Act 1998, he must state that fact in his statement of case. The prescribed forms for starting a claim now include a box which the claimant must tick indicating whether or not his claim does or will include any issues under the Human Rights Act 1988. Further details of any such claim must be provided in the claimant's statement of case (PD 16, para 15.1).

Information on funding arrangements

If the claimant has entered into a funding arrangement (which includes conditional fee agreements which provide for a success fee and after the event legal expenses insurance), on issuing proceedings the claimant is required to file a copy of Form N251 at court along with his claim form (PD 44, Section 19.1–19.2). Form N251 requires the claimant to give specified details about the funding arrangement (see Chapter 4, 'Funding Litigation').

NOTICE OF ISSUE

When the claimant sends the claim form to the court for issue, the court will send a notice of issue, in one of three prescribed forms, to the claimant notifying the claimant that the claim has been issued. The notice, in Form N205A (notice of issue of claim for a specified amount of money), Form N205B (notice of issue of claim for an unspecified amount of money) or Form N205C (notice of issue of a non-money claim), will specify the date when the claim was issued and, if served by the court, the date when it was posted, and give the deemed date of service. The forms relating to money claims (N205A and N205B) also include a section for the claimant to complete and return to court to enter judgment if the defendant does not respond within the specified time.

FORMS FOR THE DEFENDANT

The 'Response Pack'

When particulars of claim are served on the defendant, whether with or on the claim form or separately, they must be accompanied by three forms:

- a form for defending the claim (and making a counterclaim);
- a form for admitting the claim; and
- a form for acknowledging service.

This is known as a 'Response Pack' (N9) (r 7.8(1)).

The defendant does not have to respond to proceedings at all until particulars of claim are served on him. However, service of the acknowledgment of service gives the defendant a further period in which to file his defence.

Part 8 claims

Where the claimant issues proceedings using the alternative procedure for claims under Part 8, the only form accompanying the claim form that must be served on the defendant is a form for acknowledging service (r 7.8(2)).

FIXED DATE CLAIMS

Rule 7.9 provides for a practice direction to set out the circumstances in which the court will give a fixed date for a hearing when it issues a claim. The practice direction supplementing this rule sets out this special procedure for Consumer Credit Act claims (PD 7B). This reproduces the procedure for such actions established under the old rules, which are an example of a specialised action that needs a modified procedure from that provided by the standard claim form procedure. Similarly, PD 7D provides that in cases brought by the Inland Revenue to recover taxes or National Insurance contributions, the court will fix a hearing on the filing of a defence rather than allocate to track.

The same rule also refers to a practice direction listing claims that will have their own specific claim form and modified procedure. There are already practice directions for specialised proceedings as defined under Part 49, which specify the content of the claim form for the claims to which they relate, but the rule also lays the foundation for further variations in the claim form for claims outside of these specialised proceedings that need a modified procedure.

PRODUCTION CENTRE FOR CLAIMS

A practice that was introduced under the old rules carries on under the CPR, namely, the existence of a Production Centre for claims (r 7.10). This was formerly known as the Summons Production Centre and is based at Northampton County Court. This is a court service for the bulk issue of claim forms. The Centre benefits from a computerised system that enables users to supply the necessary claim forms electronically.

It is only available for certain county court proceedings where the claim is for a specified sum of money of less than £100,000. A party must seek permission before issuing a claim through the Production Centre. Once permission is granted, the party will become a 'Centre user' (PD 7C). Such a service is used by large companies for collecting debts, often from defaulting consumers. Since large numbers of claim forms need to be processed, they are diverted to this special Centre rather than the usual court office and the claimant is given a favourable rate for the cost of processing each claim. Once a claim becomes defended, it will be transferred out of the Production Centre to an appropriate county court if the claimant indicates that he wishes to proceed with the matter (PD 7C, para 5.2(4)).

MONEY CLAIM ONLINE

A pilot scheme was introduced, known as Money Claim Online, and ran from 17 December 2001 to 31 January 2004, which enabled claimants to start certain types of county court claims electronically via the Court Service website (www.courtservice. gov.uk/mcol or www.moneyclaim.gov.uk) (PD 7E). Claims started using Money Claim Online are issued by Northampton County Court (PD 7E, para 1.4). Provision was made for the scheme to be extended after 31 January 2004 (r 7.12; PD 7E, para 1.1).

In order to use Money Claim Online the claim must be a Part 7 claim for a specified amount of money that is less than £100,000 (excluding interest and costs). The claimant must not be a child or patient, or be funded by the Legal Services Commission. The claim must be against a single defendant, but can be against two defendants if the claim is for a single amount against each of them. The defendant must not be the Crown, or a child or patient, and his address for service must be within England and Wales (PD 7E, para 4).

The claimant completes the claim form online and electronically pays the court issue fee (PD 7E, para 5.1). The defendant can file an acknowledgment of service, admission, defence or counterclaim either online, or by filing a written form at court in the usual way (PD 7E, para 6.1). Provision is made for the claimant to request judgment in default and for both parties to monitor the progress of the claim online (PD 7E, paras 13.1, 15.1).

VALIDITY OF THE CLAIM FORM

The rules provide that once a claim form has been issued, it *must* be served on the defendant (r 7.5(1)). This is in keeping with the general principles of the rules that once a party decides to start proceedings, he should pursue them with due diligence. In any event, as a general rule, the claim form must be served within four months after the date of issue (r 7.5(2)). The period of service is six months where the claim form is to be served out of the jurisdiction (r 7.5(3)).

Extension of time for serving a claim form

If a claimant is unable to serve a claim form within four months of the date of issue, he can apply for an order extending the period within which the claim form may be served (r 7.6(1)).

Period within which application for an extension should be made

In the first instance, the claimant should apply for an order extending the period within which the claim form may be served before the expiry of the initial four-month period of validity of the claim form (r 7.6(2)(a)). If an order is granted extending the time within which the claim form may be served, but the claimant requires a further period of time to serve the claim form, he should apply for a further extension of time before the expiry of the period granted by the original extension (r 7.6(2)(b)).

Applications for an extension outside the specified period

If the claimant does not apply for an extension of time, or further extension of time, within the time periods specified in r 7.6(2), the court may grant an extension of time for service of the claim form only if:

(a) the court has been unable to serve the claim form (r 7.6(3)(a)); or

(b) the claimant has taken all reasonable steps to serve the claim form but has been unable to do so (r 7.6(3)(b)); and

(c) in either case, the claimant has acted promptly in making the application for an extension of time (r 7.6(3)(c)).

Rule 7.6(3) prescribes the only circumstances in which the court is able to extend the period for serving the claim form if the application is made after the period for service has expired (*Vinos v Marks & Spencer plc* [2000] 3 All ER 784).

The words 'the court has been unable to serve' in r 7.6(3)(a) include all cases where the court has failed to serve, including where this is due to mere oversight on its part. It is not limited to those cases where the court has made an unsuccessful attempt to serve. The court therefore has the discretion in such circumstances to extend time for service, but each case will turn on its own facts. In some cases, although court neglect may have contributed to the failure to serve in time, the real cause may be the conduct of the claimant or his legal representative. In such cases the court may decide not to exercise its discretion to extend the time for service. For instance, where the cause of the court's failure to serve the claim form in time was that the claimant's legal representatives delayed sending the court written authority that the defendant's solicitors had authority to accept service of proceedings until a few days before the validity of the claim form expired, and did not impress upon the court the need for urgency of service, the Court of Appeal held that the court should not exercise its discretion to extend the time for service (*Cranfield v Bridgegrove Ltd* [2003] EWCA Civ 656).

In *Vinos* (above), the claimant suffered a personal injury whilst employed by the defendant. The claimant's and defendant's solicitors entered into co-operative negotiations and, without admitting liability, the defendant agreed to compensate the claimant in full and made an interim payment of £5,000. A week before the limitation period expired the claimant's solicitors issued proceedings, but did not immediately serve them on the defendant. Due to an oversight the claimant's solicitors did not serve the proceedings on the defendant until nine days after the expiry of the four-month period for service. At this stage the statutory limitation period had expired. It was held that the court had power to extend the time for serving the claim form after the period for its service had run out 'only if' the conditions stipulated in r 7.6(3) are fulfilled. The court found that none of the circumstances in r 7.6(3) applied: the court had not been unable to serve the claim form, it had not been asked to serve it; the claimant's solicitors had not taken all reasonable steps to serve the claim form but been unable to do so, they had simply made a mistake and failed to do so.

The claimant argued that the overriding objective, r 3.1(2)(a) (which gives the court a discretionary power to extend time periods) and the court's general powers in r 3.10 to remedy an error in procedure, gave the court a discretion to extend the time for serving the claim form. However, the court found that the discretionary power in the rules to extend time periods – r 3.1(2)(a) – did not apply to r 7.6(3) because of the introductory words to r 3.1(2)(a), where the power is expressed to apply '[e]xcept where the rules provide otherwise', and r 7.6(3) did provide otherwise. Also, the general words of r 3.10 did not extend to enable the court to do what r 7.6(3) specifically forbids. Further, the court held that: 'Interpretation to achieve the overriding objective does not enable the court to say that provisions which are quite plain mean what they do not mean, nor that the plain meaning should be ignored.'

The court also emphasised that one of the main aims of the CPR and the overriding objective is that civil litigation should be undertaken and pursued with proper expedition. Although the claimant's solicitor's error could be represented as small, the court was of the opinion that it was unsatisfactory to start proceedings at the last moment. The clear message is that if you leave issuing proceedings until the last minute and then fail to serve within the four-month time limit, and then do not satisfy the conditions in r 7.6(3), your claim will be lost; and if the limitation period has expired a new claim will be statute-barred.

Vinos was followed in *Kaur v CTP Coil* (2000) LTL, 10 July, CA, where the Court of Appeal applied the same reasoning to reject an argument that r 3.9 (relief from sanctions) could be used to enable the court to extend the time for service of a claim form in circumstances which did not fall within r 7.6(3). *Vinos* and *Kaur* were also followed in *Infantino v Maclean* [2001] 3 All ER 802 and *Nagusina Naviera v Allied Maritime Inc* (2002) LTL, 10 July.

However, r 7.6(3) does not apply to extensions of time to serve particulars of claim (*Totty v Snowden* [2001] EWCA Civ 1415). In *Totty*, the claim form had been served in time but the particulars of claim had not been served within the four-month period for service. The Court of Appeal held that particulars of claim are not an integral part of the claim form, and accordingly the claim form was not defective by virtue of the absence of service of the particulars of claim. There are no express terms in r 7.6 to show that it also applies to the particulars of claim. Where there are clear express words, the court cannot use the overriding objective to give effect to what it might otherwise consider to be the just way of dealing with the case; but where there are no express words, the court is bound to look at which interpretation better reflects the overriding objective. Accordingly, the court held that it did have a discretion under r 3.10 to extend time for the service of particulars of claim where the circumstances justified it.

Procedure for applying for an extension of time

In all circumstances, when an application for an extension of time for service of the claim form is made, it should be made in accordance with Part 23 and be supported by evidence (r 7.6(4)(a)).

The evidence should state: all the circumstances relied on; the date of issue of the claim; the expiry date of any order extending time for service; and a full explanation as to why the claim has not been served (PD 7, para 8.2).

As the defendant has not at this stage been served with the proceedings, the application can be made without notice (r 7.6(4)(b)). However, if the order is granted and the claim form is served, the defendant can apply to have service of the claim form set aside (r 23.10). If the claimant anticipates that the defendant will make such an application it may be more cost-effective, and in accordance with the overriding objective, to make the application for the extension of time for service *on notice* to the defendant, so that only one hearing will be necessary to decide all the relevant matters.

Issuing and serving a claim form when expiry of limitation period is imminent

It may be legitimate to issue and serve a claim form without a full particulars of claim where, for example, a limitation period is looming and the solicitors have only just been instructed by the claimant and there is no time for any appropriate pre-action protocol to be worked through. Such a course may be preferable to issuing the claim form and then applying to the court for extensions of time within which to serve the claim form, and was the course suggested by Lord Woolf in *Jones v Telford and Wrekin Council* (1999) *The Times*, 29 July, where the claimant was waiting for favourable medical reports and had applied for and been granted three extensions of time to serve proceedings. Lord Woolf favoured this course on the basis that a defendant should be notified of a claim as early as possible in order to take steps to defend it.

This is likely to be an increasing trend in the light of the various organisations that now encourage parties to make claims in respect of accidents. In that event, the court may be tempted to stay the proceedings to give the parties an opportunity to operate the pre-action protocol where there was not time before the issue of proceedings.

APPLICATION BY DEFENDANT FOR SERVICE OF THE CLAIM FORM

Rule 7.7 provides that where a claimant issues but does not serve a claim form on the defendant, the defendant can serve a notice on the claimant requiring him to serve the claim form or discontinue the claim. The defendant must give the claimant at least 14 days within which to serve or discontinue (r 7.7(2)). If the claimant fails to comply with the notice, the defendant can apply to the court, which can dismiss the claim or make any other order it thinks just (r 7.7(3)). So, rather than dismiss the claim, the court may decide to give the claimant another chance to comply and make an order in terms that, unless by a certain date the claim form is served, the claimant's claim will be struck out.

Rule 7.7 emphasises the premium the court puts upon the new culture to conduct litigation speedily, but also the intolerance that will be shown to the improper use of litigation, the desirability of notifying a defendant of a claim as soon as possible so that he can take appropriate steps to defend it, as well as the need to try to prepare all relevant information prior to the issue of proceedings, through the medium of pre-action protocols.

CHAPTER 9

RESPONDING TO A CLAIM

INTRODUCTION

Once a claimant has issued proceedings and they have been served on the other parties, those other parties must comply with the procedure for responding to those proceedings or risk judgment being entered against them in default.

There is a special procedure for responding to claims made under Part 8 of the Civil Procedure Rules (CPR), and different time limits apply to claims served outside of the jurisdiction. Also, different rules may apply to specialist proceedings. This chapter deals only with the procedure for responding to a claim started under Part 7 of the CPR and served within the jurisdiction.

RESPONSE TO PARTICULARS OF CLAIM

On issuing proceedings, the claimant has the option of either including particulars of claim within or attached to the claim form served on the defendant, or of serving particulars of claim separately within 14 days after service of the claim form on the defendant (r 7.4(1)).

If the defendant receives a claim form that states that particulars of claim are to follow, he need not respond to the claim form until particulars of claim have been served on him (r 9.1(2)). If the claimant shows no intention of serving particulars of claim, the defendant could apply for the claimant's claim to be struck out either on the grounds of failure to comply with a rule (being r 7.4(1)) under r 3.4(2)(c), or for abuse of process under r 3.4(2)(b). However, the defendant may understandably not wish to make such an application for fear of goading the claimant into making a cross-application for relief from such a sanction, unless the limitation period for the claimant's claim has also expired. The court, in the exercise of its case management powers, may strike out the claimant's claim in these circumstances in any event (rr 3.3, 3.4).

When particulars of claim are served on a defendant, they will be accompanied by a response pack (r 7.8). If the defendant does not accept the claim and pay the amount claimed (along with costs) within 14 days after service of the particulars of claim, he must return one of the relevant forms in the response pack, within that period of time, or risk judgment being entered by default (r 10.2). The forms in the response pack are an acknowledgment of service, an admission, or a defence (r 9.2). If the defendant admits only part of the claim, he should file both an admission form and a defence at court (r 9.2(b)).

If a claimant issues and serves a claim form and particulars of claim, and the defendant does not return an admission, or defence or counterclaim, but neither does the claimant apply for judgment in default or summary judgment, the claim will be stayed after six months have expired following the end of the period for filing a defence (r 15.11(1)). Any party may apply for this stay to be lifted (r 15.11(2)).

ACKNOWLEDGMENT OF SERVICE

A defendant has the opportunity to file an acknowledgment of service in order to give him more time to file a defence, or if he disputes that the court has jurisdiction to hear the claim. If the defendant files an acknowledgment of service, he then has a further 14 days after the time limit for acknowledgment has expired within which to file his defence. Filing an acknowledgment of service effectively gives the defendant 28 rather than 14 days after service of particulars of claim within which to file a defence.

Acknowledgment of service form

In order to acknowledge service, the defendant must file Form N9, the prescribed acknowledgment of service form, at court (PD 10, para 2). On receipt of this form the court will send Form N10 to the claimant notifying him, or his legal representative, that the defendant has acknowledged service (r 10.4).

The defendant must set out his name in full in the acknowledgment of service form. Where the claimant has incorrectly set out the defendant's name in the claim form, the defendant should set it out correctly in the acknowledgment of service form followed by the words 'described as' and the incorrect name used by the claimant in the claim form (PD 10, paras 5.1, 5.2). The court will then notify the claimant in Form N10 of the defendant's correct name as stated in the acknowledgment of service form.

The defendant must indicate on Form N9 whether he intends to defend all or part of the claim, or whether he intends to contest the court's jurisdiction.

Signing the acknowledgment of service form

Form N9 must be signed by the defendant, or by his legal representative on his behalf (PD 10, para 4.1).

If the defendant is a company or other corporation the acknowledgment of service may be signed by the legal representative or by a person holding a senior position in the company, such as a director or chief executive. The person signing on behalf of the company must state what position he holds in the company (PD 10, paras 4.2, 4.3).

If the defendant is a partnership, the acknowledgment of service may be signed by the legal representative or any of the partners, or by a person having control or management of the partnership business (PD 10, para 4.4). The person signing on behalf of the partnership must sign in his own name and not that of the partnership (CPR Sched 1 RSC Ord 81, r 4).

If the defendant is a child or a patient, the acknowledgment of service must be signed by his litigation friend or legal representative, unless the court orders otherwise (PD 10, para 4.5).

Address for service

When acknowledging service, the defendant must include his address for service within the jurisdiction (r 10.5). If the defendant has a legal representative acting on his behalf, he must give the legal representative's business address as the address for service (PD 10, para 3.2).

Multiple defendants

If there is more than one defendant, each defendant must file an acknowledgment of service form. However, if the same legal representative is acting for all the defendants, the legal representative may acknowledge service for all the defendants through one acknowledgment of service form (PD 10, para 5.3).

Amending or withdrawing acknowledgment of service

Once filed, an acknowledgment of service may be amended or withdrawn only with permission of the court. The application for permission to amend or withdraw must be made in accordance with Part 23 and supported by evidence (PD 10, paras 5.4, 5.5).

Time limits for filing an acknowledgment of service

If a defendant chooses to acknowledge service, he must do so by filing Form N9 at court within 14 days after service of particulars of claim on him. If particulars of claim are contained in or served with the claim form, he must acknowledge service within 14 days after service of the claim form. If particulars of claim are served separately from the claim form, the defendant must acknowledge service within 14 days after service of the particulars of claim (r 10.3).

ADMISSIONS

If a party makes a written admission as to the truth of the whole or part of another party's case, the other party may apply for judgment on that admission (r 14.3(1)). Whether judgment will be entered for the whole or part of a party's case depends on the extent of the admission that appears to the court to have been made (r 14.3(2)). The written admission does not have to be contained within a statement of case, but could be contained in a letter or other document (r 14.1(1) and (2)). Oral admissions may be relied upon as evidence to prove liability in a case, but cannot be relied upon to enter judgment without trial under the procedure set out in Part 14 (r 14.1(2)).

In some cases, a defendant will have no grounds to deny liability for a claim. In those circumstances, the cheapest option for a defendant is usually to accept liability before proceedings are issued and negotiate terms of settlement; or, if proceedings are issued, to admit liability and end the proceedings as soon as possible.

In many cases relating to the non-payment of a debt, a defendant has no defence to the claim but is unable or unwilling to pay. The claimant may have to use proceedings to enforce payment of the debt. In those circumstances, the defendant may admit liability but ask for time to pay.

ADMISSIONS IN MONEY CLAIMS

If a claimant brings a claim where the *only* remedy sought is the payment of money and the defendant makes an admission contained in one of the specified practice forms, whether as to the whole or part of the amount claimed, the claimant has the right to enter judgment against the defendant (apart from in some types of money claim where either party is a child or patient) (r 14.1(3) and (4)).

Time limits for making an admission

The defendant has 14 days after service of particulars of claim within which to return an admission (r 14.2(1)). However, the defendant will still be able to return an admission after this period of time as long as the claimant has not entered judgment in default and, if he does so, he will be treated as having complied with the time limits laid down in r 14.2(1) (r 14.2(3) and (4)). This rule is presumably subject to r 15.11 imposing an automatic stay on proceedings after six months' inactivity, so a defendant would also have to apply for the stay to be lifted in order to return an admission out of time in those circumstances. However, whether a party is required to obtain permission to admit a claim is unlikely to be an issue between the parties.

Amending or withdrawing an admission

If, having made an admission, a party wishes to amend the extent of the admission or withdraw it altogether, he must apply to the court for permission to do so (r 14.1(5)). The application should be made in accordance with Part 23. The court will balance the prejudice to each party when exercising its discretion whether to grant permission to withdraw an admission (*Sollitt v DJ Broady Ltd* (2000) LTL, 23 February). In *Sollitt v DJ Broady Ltd*, the claimant started a personal injury claim against the defendant. The defendant admitted liability but then applied to withdraw that admission on the grounds that a related company, which had no assets or insurance to meet the claim, was in fact liable instead. The Court of Appeal took into account that the defendant would suffer obvious prejudice if permission to withdraw the admission was not given. However, it found that the prejudice was almost entirely of the defendant's own making; it should have been aware that the claimant was suing the wrong defendant. Against this the court took into account 'the obvious injustice of denying a judgment to Mr Sollitt against a company which up to the door of the court had been admitting liability in principle', and therefore held that the defendant was not entitled to withdraw its admission.

When granting permission the court may make it subject to a condition, for instance, the payment of a sum of money into court (r 3.1(3)).

Defendant pays whole of specified money claim

If the claimant's only remedy is the payment of a specified sum of money and the defendant is prepared to pay the whole sum claimed (including interest and fixed costs as specified on the claim form), he should take or send the money to the claimant at the address given on the claim form within 14 days. If a defendant has no defence to the claim and accepts the amount owed, the advantage of paying the whole sum within 14 days is that the defendant can avoid a county court judgment being entered against him, with its attendant consequences in terms of its effect on his credit rating.

Defendant seeking time to pay

If the claimant's only remedy is the payment of a sum of money and the defendant admits liability, instead of paying the amount claimed immediately to the claimant, he can make a request for time to pay. The procedure varies according to the nature of the money claim and the extent of the admission.

If the defendant requests time to pay, he should complete either Form N9A (claim for a specified amount of money) or Form N9C (claim for an unspecified amount of money), which require the defendant to give information about his income and expenses and either to propose a date by which the sum admitted will be paid, or to propose a sum to be paid monthly (r 14.9(2)). The defendant should give as much detail about his means as requested either within Form N9A or Form N9C, or provide the same details in writing (PD 14, para 2.2). The defendant must also give brief reasons why the whole sum cannot be paid immediately.

ADMISSION OF WHOLE OF CLAIM FOR A SPECIFIED AMOUNT OF MONEY

If the claimant's only remedy is a specified amount of money and the defendant has admitted liability for the whole sum and not requested time to pay, the claimant can request that judgment be entered against the defendant by filing Form N205A and specifying either that payment be made immediately, or a date by which the whole sum is to be paid, or the times and rate of payment by instalments (r 14.4(4)). On receipt of Form N205A, the court will enter judgment for the claimant to be paid in the manner requested by the claimant (r 14.4(5) and (6)).

If the claimant's only remedy is a specified amount of money and the defendant admits liability for the whole sum but requests time to pay, the defendant should return the prescribed Form N9A to the claimant at the address on the claim form within 14 days of service of the claim form (rr 14.4, 14.9(2); PD 14, para 3.1).

If the defendant sends Form 9A to the claimant on which he has admitted liability and requested time to pay, the claimant should return Form N225 (along with Form N9A) to the court indicating whether he accepts the defendant's proposal as to payment or not.

If the claimant returns Form N225 indicating that he accepts the defendant's proposal as to payment, the court will enter judgment for the claimant with payment to be made at the time and rate specified in the defendant's proposal (r 14.9(4)–(6)).

If the claimant rejects the proposal, he should indicate on Form N225 how he wants the defendant to pay and the reasons for rejecting the defendant's proposals for payment. On receipt of Form N225, the court will enter judgment for the claimant, but with an order that the time and rate of payment will be decided by the court (r 14.10).

Claimant's entitlement to interest

Where a claimant is claiming a specified amount of money, if judgment is entered following the defendant's admission it will include an amount for interest up to the date of judgment so long as certain conditions are met. These are that the claimant must have given the requisite details about interest in his particulars of claim as required by r 16.4; the request for judgment includes a calculation of interest from the date of issue of the claim form to the date judgment is requested; and (if interest is claimed under s 35A of the Supreme Court Act 1981 or s 69 of the County Courts Act 1984) the rate claimed is no higher than that which was available under those provisions when the claim form was issued (r 14.14(1)).

If these conditions are not met, judgment will be for an amount of interest to be decided by the court (r 14.14(2)). On entering judgment, the court will give any directions it considers appropriate for deciding the amount of the interest; this can include allocating the case to a track (r 14.8).

ADMISSION OF PART OF CLAIM FOR A SPECIFIED AMOUNT OF MONEY

If the claimant's only remedy is a specified sum of money and the defendant admits liability for part of the sum claimed, he should complete Form N9A and file it at court within 14 days of service of the particulars of claim, indicating the amount for which he admits he is liable (PD 14, para 3.2). The defendant may also file a defence as to the rest of the claim (PD 14, para 3.3).

On receipt of the part admission, the court will serve Form N225A on the claimant. The claimant must file completed Form N225A at court and serve a copy on the defendant, within 14 days after it is served on him, indicating whether:

(a) he accepts the amount admitted in satisfaction of the claim (and the defendant's proposals for payment, if any);

(b) he does not accept the amount admitted by the defendant and wishes the proceedings to continue; or

(c) if the defendant has requested time to pay, he accepts the amount admitted in satisfaction of the claim but not the defendant's proposals as to payment (r 14.5(3) and (4)).

If the claimant accepts the defendant's part admission of liability in satisfaction of his claim, he can obtain judgment against the defendant by filing a request in Form N225A. If the defendant has not asked for time to pay, the claimant can indicate whether payment is to be made immediately, within a certain time, or specify the time and rate for payment by instalments (r 14.5(7)). Judgment will then be entered for the claimant for the amount admitted in the manner requested by the claimant and including an order for payment of fixed costs as stated on the claim form (r 14.5(9)).

If the claimant accepts the amount admitted in satisfaction of the claim, but not the defendant's proposals as to payment, the claimant should indicate on Form N225A how he wants the defendant to pay and the reasons for rejecting the defendant's proposals for payment. Judgment will be entered for the claimant, but the time and rate of payment will then be decided by the court (r 14.5(6)).

If the claimant does not accept the defendant's part admission of the claim and wishes proceedings to continue, they will be treated like any other defended claim and allocated in accordance with Part 26 (r 14.5(3)(b)).

If the claimant does not file the notice within 14 days after it is served on him, the claim will be stayed until he does serve the notice (r 14.5(5)).

ADMISSION OF WHOLE CLAIM FOR AN UNSPECIFIED AMOUNT OF MONEY

If the claimant's only remedy is an unspecified amount of money and the defendant admits liability for the claim by filing an admission in Form N9C, the court will serve a copy of Form N9C on the claimant, who can obtain judgment by filing Form N226.

On receipt of Form N226, the court will enter judgment for an amount to be decided by the court and costs (r 14.6). On entering judgment, the court will give any directions it considers appropriate for deciding the amount of the judgment; this can include allocating the case to a track (r 14.8).

If the claimant does not request judgment within 14 days after service of the admission on him, his claim will be stayed until he files the request for judgment (r 14.6(5)).

ADMISSION OF LIABILITY FOR AN UNSPECIFIED AMOUNT OF MONEY, WITH OFFER OF SUM IN SATISFACTION

If the claimant's only remedy is an unspecified amount of money and the defendant admits liability and offers a sum in satisfaction of the claim by filing an admission in Form N9C, the court will serve a copy of Form N9C on the claimant and the claimant will be required to indicate by returning Form N226 whether or not he accepts the amount in satisfaction of the claim (r 14.7(1)–(3)).

If the claimant accepts the defendant's offer in satisfaction of the claim, he can enter judgment against the defendant by filing a request in Form N226. If the defendant has not asked for time to pay, the claimant can indicate whether payment is to be made immediately, within a certain time, or specify the time and rate for payment by instalments (r 14.7(5) and (6)). Judgment will then be entered for the claimant for the amount admitted in the manner requested by the claimant and with an order for payment of fixed costs as stated on the claim form (r 14.7(7) and (8)).

If the claimant indicates on Form N226 that he does not accept the amount offered by the defendant in satisfaction of the claim, he may obtain judgment by filing a request on that form. The court will enter judgment for an amount to be decided by the court and costs (r 14.7(9) and (10)). On entering judgment, the court will give any directions it considers appropriate for deciding the amount of the judgment; this can include allocating the case to a track (r 14.8).

If the claimant accepts the amount admitted in satisfaction of the claim, but not the defendant's proposals as to payment, the claimant should indicate on Form N226 how he wants the defendant to pay and the reasons for rejecting the defendant's proposals for payment. Judgment will be entered for the claimant, but the time and rate of payment will then be decided by the court (r 14.7(9) and (10)).

If the claimant does not file Form N226 within 14 days after it has been served on him, the claim will be stayed until he files the notice (r 14.7(4)).

COURT DETERMINATION OF RATE OF PAYMENT

In those cases where the defendant has admitted liability for a money claim but has requested time to pay, and the claimant has indicated when returning the relevant practice form that he accepts the amount admitted by the defendant but does not accept the defendant's proposals as to the time and rate of payment, the court will fix the time and rate of payment (rr 14.9 and 14.10).

The time and rate of payment may be decided by either:

(a) a court officer; or

(b) a judge.

A court officer may determine the rate of payment where the only claim is for a specified amount of money and the amount outstanding (including costs) is not more than £50,000 (r 14.11(1); PD 14, para 5.2(2)). The court officer has no power to hold a hearing in order to determine this amount and will determine the time and rate of payment by considering the information provided by the claimant and defendant in writing (r 14.11(2)).

A judge can determine the amount either with or without a hearing (r 4.12(1)). If the judge decides to hold a hearing, he must give each party at least seven days' notice of the hearing (r 14.12(3)).

The proceedings will be transferred automatically to the defendant's home court if the following conditions are satisfied:

• the only claim is for a specified amount of money;

• the defendant is an individual;

• the claim has not been transferred to another defendant's home court, for example, under automatic transfer provisions when a defence is filed;

• the claim was not started in the defendant's home court; and

• the claim was not started in a specialist list.

When deciding on the time and rate of payment, the court will take into account the information provided by the defendant as to his means and the claimant's objections to the defendant's proposals set out in the relevant practice form (PD 14, para 5.1). If the defendant has shown by the completion of a statement of means that he would be financially unable to make anything other than a small instalment payment, and the claimant has been unable to present any evidence to contradict the defendant's statement of means, the court officer or judge is unlikely to order that a greater sum should be paid instead. This will be the case even if this means that it will take the defendant a number of years to repay the amount admitted.

Challenging court's determination of time and rate of payment

Where a court officer has determined the time and rate of payment, or a judge has made the determination without a hearing, either party may apply for the decision to be redetermined by a judge (r 14.13(1)).

If the determination was made by a court officer, the redetermination may be made by the judge without a hearing, unless the party applying for the redetermination requests a hearing (PD 14, para 5.4). However, if the determination was made by a judge, the redetermination must be made at a hearing unless the parties otherwise agree (PD 14, para 5.5).

The party wishing to apply for a redetermination must do so within 14 days of service on him of the original order as to the time and rate of payment (r 14.13(2)). The application must be made under Part 23.

If an application for a redetermination is made, in certain circumstances the proceedings will be transferred to the defendant's home court if the redetermination is to be by way of a hearing (r 14.13(3)).

Varying the rate of payment

If the defendant's circumstances change such that he can no longer afford to make payments at the rate determined or redetermined by the court, or if the claimant has evidence that the defendant's circumstances have changed and he can afford to make increased payments, either party can make an application under Part 23 to vary the time and rate of payment (PD 14, paras 6.1, 6.2).

DISPOSAL HEARINGS

If the claimant's claim is for an unspecified sum of money and judgment has been entered, following the defendant's admission of liability, for an amount of money and/or interest to be decided by the court plus costs, the court will give directions as to how that amount will be determined. This will include the circumstances where the court has entered judgment for an amount of interest to be decided by the court (r 14.8).

Where judgment is entered for an amount to be decided by the court following the defendant's admission, the case will not have been allocated to a case management track. The court will then need to decide what directions are necessary for the assessment of the amount claimed. If the financial value of the claim falls within the small claims track jurisdiction the court will allocate it to that track for the amount to be decided (PD 26, para 12.3(1)(b)). The hearing will be informal and subject to the 'no costs rule' (rr 27.8, 27.14).

However, where the financial value of the claim exceeds the jurisdiction of the small claims track, the court will order that the amount payable be decided at a disposal hearing, unless the amount payable appears to be genuinely disputed on substantial grounds, or the dispute is not suitable to be dealt with at a disposal hearing (PD 26, para 12.3(2)). A disposal hearing is defined as a hearing which will not normally last longer than 30 minutes and at which the court will not normally hear oral evidence (PD 26, para 12.4(1)). Therefore, a disposal hearing will be appropriate only where the amount of damages is not contested and/or the claim is straightforward.

If the court proceeds to deal with the matter at a disposal hearing, it will either decide the amount the claimant is entitled to on the judgment, or give directions for the matter to be decided and allocate the claim to a track. As oral evidence is usually not admitted, the evidence relied on at a disposal hearing should be in the form of a witness statement or statement of case and/or application notice if verified by a statement of truth (r 32.6). However, the court will not exercise its power to decide the amount there and then unless any written evidence the claimant is relying upon has been served on the defendant at least three days before the disposal hearing (PD 26, para 12.4(5)).

If the nature of the claim is such that the court is likely to use the disposal hearing in order to give directions for the assessment of the amount claimed, it is good practice for the parties to make proposals as to the directions that should be given and attempt to agree directions if possible. The court will then allocate to either the fast track or the multi-track, depending on the value of the claim.

Jurisdiction of Masters and district judges

The Masters and district judges have jurisdiction to determine the amount to be paid when judgment is entered following an admission, irrespective of the financial value of the claim and irrespective of whether the matter is dealt with at a disposal hearing or at a hearing following allocation to a track (PD 26, para 12.6).

Costs of the disposal hearing

The court has a discretion as to the costs of the disposal hearing. The court can also order a summary assessment of those costs. The usual order will be for the defendant to pay the claimant's costs of the disposal hearing, but the court can make other orders. However, if the claim has been allocated to the small claims track, the 'no costs rule' will apply. Similarly, if the case is allocated to the fast track, only fast track trial costs will be recoverable (PD 26, para 12.5).

DEFENCE

In order to defend all or part of a claim, a defendant must file a defence (r 15.2). A different procedure applies where the claimant starts a claim under Part 8 and in some cases relating to specialist proceedings, and this chapter is only concerned with the procedure where a claim not falling within the definition of specialist proceedings is started under Part 7.

The defence may deny liability for the claimant's claim, but it may also include a claim for a set off or counterclaim which can, in some cases, exceed the amount of the claimant's claim. If the defendant counterclaims against the claimant, the defence and counterclaim should be contained within the same document, with the counterclaim following on from the defence (PD 15, para 3.1).

The defendant can use either Form N9B (defence to a specified amount) or Form N9D (defence to an unspecified amount or non-money claim), contained in the response pack served on the defendant with the particulars of claim, for the purposes of a defence (PD 15, para 1.3).

The defendant's defence, like all other statements of case, should be verified by a statement of truth (r 22.1).

So long as the defendant files and serves a document which purports to be a defence within the requisite time limits, he will avoid judgment being entered against him in default (PD 12, para 1.1). However, if justified, the claimant can apply for the defence to be struck out under r 3.4 and for judgment to be entered, or for summary judgment under Part 24. The court can also strike out a defence of its own initiative (rr 3.3, 3.4).

Time limits for filing a defence

In most cases, a defendant must file a defence at court either:

(a) 14 days after service of the particulars of claim; or

(b) if the defendant files an acknowledgment of service, 28 days after service of the particulars of claim (r 15.4(1)).

These time limits do not apply if the claim form is served out of the jurisdiction, if the defendant makes an application disputing the court's jurisdiction, if the claimant applies for summary judgment before the defendant files a defence, and if the claim form is served on an agent of a principal who is overseas (r 15.4(2)).

Parties agreeing to extend time limit for service of the defence

The time limit can also be extended by up to 28 days if the claimant and defendant so agree. If such an agreement is made, the defendant must notify the court in writing (r 15.5).

Service of the defence

A copy of the defence must be served on every other party (r 15.6). This rule does not expressly state whether the defendant or the court will serve the defence on the other parties. In practice, the court will serve a copy of the defence on every other party to the proceedings if sufficient copies are supplied by the defendant and the defendant has not indicated that he will serve the defence.

Response to a defence

A claimant can file a reply to the defence if there are any matters raised by the defence which call for a reply. If the claimant wishes to file a reply, he must do so when he files his allocation questionnaire and he must serve a copy on all the other parties at the same time as he files it (r 15.8).

If the defendant has made a counterclaim against the claimant, this will be treated as a claim in its own right, and the claimant must file a defence to the claim or risk judgment being entered in default (r 12.3(2)). If the claimant serves a reply and defence to counterclaim, in most cases these should be contained in the same document, with the defence to counterclaim following on from the reply (PD 15, para 3.2). However, no party may file any further statement of case after a reply without the permission of the court (r 15.9).

Defendant's defence is that money claimed has been paid

It is sometimes the case that a defendant is served with proceedings claiming a specified amount of money and his defence is that he has paid the sum claimed to the claimant.

If the defendant states this in his defence, the court will send Form N236 to the claimant on which he must indicate whether he wishes the proceedings to continue (r 15.10(1)). The claimant must file at court his response in Form N236 and serve a copy on the defendant (r 15.10(2)).

If the claimant disputes that the defendant has paid the amount claimed, he should indicate in his response that he wishes the proceedings to continue. The court will then follow the procedure for allocation under Part 26.

If the claimant admits that the defendant has paid the amount claimed, he should then take steps to discontinue the proceedings. If a claimant discontinues, he will usually be liable to pay the defendant's costs of the claim (r 38.6).

If the claimant fails to respond to the court's notice within 28 days after service on him, his claim will be stayed (r 15.10(3)). Either party can apply for the stay to be lifted (r 15.10(4)). The defendant may apply to lift the stay if he is satisfied that he paid the sum claimed by the claimant before proceedings were started and he wishes the claimant to discontinue the claim and pay his costs incurred in responding to it.

CHAPTER 10

SERVICE OF DOCUMENTS

INTRODUCTION

The timing and method of service of a document can be of crucial importance in proceedings. For instance, the timing and method of service of a claim form will be very important when the limitation period for a claim is close to expiry. Similarly, where the court has ordered that a party must serve a document by a specified date or face the sanction that its claim or defence will be struck out, the timing and method of service employed will be crucial in determining whether that order has been complied with. It has long been the case, therefore, that our procedural rules have regulated the permissible methods of service of documents.

Although Lord Woolf recommended that there should be no restrictions on the methods by which documents could be served (so long as the serving party could satisfy the court that the method employed was likely to bring the document to the recipient's attention), in fact the Civil Procedure Rules (CPR) did not adopt such a *laissez-faire* approach and there is a limited number of prescribed methods of service of documents (although the court does have the power to sanction other methods not expressly provided for by the rules).

Under the CPR, the same rules of service apply to the claim form and all other documents. There are some additional rules for service of the claim form, but the main body of the rules on service is the same whichever document is being served. Even though there is now a number of ways to effect service of the claim form, including modern means of communication such as e-mail, the standard method is likely to be ordinary, pre-paid, first class post. The High Court and the county courts will effect service of documents such as the claim form, although a party can instead elect to effect service himself.

The rules on service of documents can be found in Part 6 and its accompanying practice directions. These rules apply to service of all documents unless any other enactment, a rule in another Part, or a practice direction makes different provision, or the court orders otherwise (r 6.1).

Who is to serve?

The general rule is that the court will serve a document that it has issued or prepared (r 6.3(1)). The new rules as to charging orders make no mention of who is to serve the interim charging order. Pursuant to r 6.3(1), the presumption must be that, in the absence of any other order, the court serves.

The court will always issue the claim form so, in general, the court will serve it. The party on whose behalf the document is to be served can notify the court that he wishes to serve it himself, but unless he does so the court will effect service (r 6.3(1)(b)). This unifies the position between the High Court and county courts, and will obviously assist litigants in person. It will also reduce the incidence of claims where proceedings are issued but not served because, unless the party notifies the court otherwise, the court will serve proceedings as a matter of course.

Although the general rule is that the court will effect service, this is a general rule that applies only to documents the court issues or prepares, and it will not apply if a rule or practice direction provides that a party must serve the document in question (r 6.3(1)(a) and (c)).

Where a party prepares a document that is to be served by the court, the party must file a copy for the court, and for each party to be served (r 6.3(3)).

Where the court effects service, the court decides which of the methods of service provided by the rules to employ (r 6.3(2)). However, that method will normally be first class post (PD 6, para 8.1). First class post is generally thought to be cheap and reliable. However, where the court attempts to serve the document and is unsuccessful, the court must send a notice of non-service to the party who requested service, stating which method of service was attempted (r 6.11).

It is expected that if the court is unable to effect service by first class post, it will notify the party requesting service and leave it to that party to attempt service rather than go on and use another permitted method. Moreover, when a party receives a notice of non-service from the court, he should take steps to effect service himself as the court is under no further duty to effect service (PD 6, para 8.2). The new rules do not permit personal service by the court bailiff, a method formerly available in the county court when postal service had failed (former County Court Rules Ord 7, r 10(4)).

METHODS OF SERVICE

For all documents (not just the claim form), the following are the available methods of service:

- personal service;
- first class post;
- leaving the document at an office, business or residential address;
- through a document exchange system;
- by fax or other means of electronic communication; or
- for a company, by any method permitted under Part 6 as well as by a method permitted by the Companies Act 1985 (r 6.2).

In addition, there are special rules about service of the claim form that include the provision of additional methods of service. These are:

- service of the claim form by a contractually agreed method (r 6.15); and
- service of the claim form on an agent of a principal who is overseas (r 6.16).

Personal service

Historically, personal service was the main method of service in the High Court until 1979. The rules were then changed to include service by post, which rapidly became the standard method. Under the old rules it was sufficient if the person to be served had the documents in his possession long enough to ascertain what they were, even if they were then handed back to the person effecting service (see *Nottingham Building Society v Peter Bennett and Co* (1997) *The Times*, 26 February). It is submitted that the same interpretation of the requirements of personal service will be adopted under the new rules, although it should be noted that such authorities on matters of civil procedure, decided before the CPR came into effect, are generally no longer of any relevance (see judgment of Lord Woolf MR in *Biguzzi v Rank Leisure plc* [1999] 1 WLR 1926; [1999] 4 All ER 934, CA).

Personal service may be favoured when there is not enough time to serve proceedings by any other means, for example, when a claim form is served on the last day of its validity and the limitation period for that particular cause of action is about to expire or has expired. Other reasons may include where the defendant is thought to be evading service.

Personal service on an individual involves leaving the document with that individual (r 6.4(3)). Personal service on a partnership, where partners are being sued in the name of the firm, involves leaving the document either with one of the partners, or with a person who, at the time of service, has control or management of the partnership business at its principal place of business (r 6.4(5)). Practice Direction 6 provides for a notice of service on a partner, which is to be in Form N218, to be given to the person who is served stating whether they are served as a partner, or as a person having control or management of the partnership business or both (PD 6, para 4.2).

Personal service on a company or other corporation involves leaving the document with a person holding a senior position within it (r 6.4(4)). A 'senior person' in a registered company or corporation is a director, treasurer, secretary, chief executive, manager or other officer of the company or corporation. In respect of a corporation that is not a registered company, in addition to the above, a 'senior person' also includes the mayor, chairman, president, town clerk or similar officer of the corporation (PD 6, para 6.2).

Personal service is allowed in all types of proceedings covered by the new rules. However, if a solicitor is authorised to accept service on behalf of a party and he has notified the person serving the document that he is so authorised, the document must be served on the solicitor rather than the party personally, unless personal service is required by an enactment, rule, practice direction or court order (r 6.4(2)).

Address for service

Unless proceedings fall under Section III of Part 6 (service out of the jurisdiction), a document must be served within the jurisdiction. It is to be noted that the CPR do not specify that the *person* to be served must be within the jurisdiction at the time of service, only that the *document* must be served within the jurisdiction. However, in *Chellaram v Chellaram* [2002] EWHC 632 at [47], the court held that it has always been, and remains, a fundamental rule of English procedure and jurisdiction that a defendant may be served with *originating process* (the claim form) within the jurisdiction only if he is present in the jurisdiction at the time of service or deemed service.

The CPR provide that a party must give an address for service within the jurisdiction (r 6.5(2)). Where a party who resides or carries on business within the jurisdiction does not give his solicitor's business address as his address for service, he must give his residence or place of business as his address for service (r 6.5(3)). However, where no solicitor is acting for the party to be served and the party has not given an address for service, the rules contain a table that specifies where the document to be served must be sent (r 6.5(6)).

In general terms, in the case of an individual, the document must be sent to the party's usual or last known residence. In the case of a proprietor of a business or a partnership, the document must be sent to the party's usual or last known place of residence or business. In the case of a company, the document must be sent to a principal office or place where the company carries on its business or activities and which has a real connection to the claim (see the table set out in r 6.5(6)).

Where no solicitor is acting for the party to be served, and the party has not given an address for service, then service under r 6.5(6) on the party at his usual or last known residence amounts to good service even if the person serving knows or believes that the person to be served is no longer living at his or her last known residence. The rule does not say that it is not good service if the person to be served does not in fact receive the document. The rule is intended to provide a clear and straightforward mechanism for effecting service where the two conditions precedent (no solicitor acting and no address for service given) are satisfied (*Cranfield v Bridgegrove Ltd and Linked Cases* [2003] EWCA Civ 656).

In the case of service of the claim form, if a defendant is acting through a solicitor, the claimant can serve the claim form on the defendant's solicitor only if the solicitor is authorised to accept service on the defendant's behalf (r 6.13(2)). Once the claimant has been notified in writing that the defendant's solicitor is authorised to accept service on the defendant's behalf, the claimant is obliged to serve the claim form upon that solicitor – service upon the defendant would be invalid (*Carmelita Nanglegan v The Royal Free Hampstead NHS Trust* [2001] EWCA Civ 127).

However, a solicitor does not generally have implied authority to accept service of a claim form on behalf of a client. If he does so without express authority he is in breach of his professional duty to his client. The mere fact that solicitors indicate that they are acting for a defendant after a claim has been intimated does not by itself imply that they have authority to accept service on his behalf (*Smith v Probyn and PGA European Tour Ltd* [2000] All ER (D) 250, CA). However, for any other document apart from the claim form, if a solicitor is acting for the party to be served, the address for service will automatically be the solicitor's business address (r 6.5(5)).

Where the claimant wishes the court to serve the claim form, it must include the defendant's address for service on the claim form (r 6.13(1)). What the defendant's address is for service should be determined in accordance with the above rules. It should be noted that where the defendant's solicitor has authority to accept service of proceedings, a claimant should include a copy of the defendant's solicitor's written authority when sending the claim form to the court for issue if he requires the court to effect service of the proceedings. If a party or his legal representative changes his address for service, he is under an obligation to give notice in writing of the change immediately to the court and to every other party (PD 6, para 7).

Service on children and patients

In the case of children and patients, there are special rules about on whom documents must be served (r 6.6). The person to be served with the claim form where the child is not also a patient is the child's parents or guardians, or, if none, the person with whom the child resides or in whose care the child is. Where the claim form would otherwise be served on a person who is a 'patient', service should be on the person (if any) authorised under Part VII of the Mental Health Act 1983 to conduct proceedings in the name of the patient, or the person with whom the patient resides or in whose care the patient is. With regard to any document other than the claim form, service will be on 'the litigation friend' (r 6.6).

First class post and leaving the document at the party's address

When the court effects service, although it can use any method of service specified by the rules, it will usually employ first class post (PD 6, para 8.1). The court will post the document to the address for service provided by the party in accordance with the rules set out above.

Alternatively, when the party effects service, it can post the document by first class post or simply leave the document at the relevant address. Unlike the old rules, there is no requirement that the document be inserted through a letter-box when it is left at the address for service. Although *prima facie* this would allow the use of any method to leave the document at the address, for example, under the door, or through a window, such methods would not necessarily be in the interests of the party serving the document. This is because in such circumstances, if there is any dispute about non-receipt, use of a more unconventional method of leaving the document at the address, which runs the risk of being overlooked by the party being served, may work against the party trying to prove service.

Document exchange

This method of service can be used only if either the address for service of the party to be served, or his legal representative's (if authorised to accept service) address for service includes a numbered box at a document exchange (DX), or one is set out on their writing paper. This is the only positive requirement imposed upon a party who wishes to utilise DX for service. In fact, if the address details include a DX number, in order to avoid service by DX, the party to be served must have indicated in writing that he is unwilling to accept service by DX (PD 6, para 2.1).

Service is effected by leaving the document addressed to the numbered box either at the DX of the party who is to be served, or at a DX which sends documents to that party's DX every business day (PD 6, para 2.2).

Service by electronic means

It is now possible to serve the claim form as well as other documents by electronic methods such as fax or email (r 6.2(1)(e)). Certain conditions must be fulfilled before these methods can be used, but there is no requirement that if such a method is used, it is followed up by a hard copy sent by post or DX. Instead it is left to the party who chooses to use this method to consider the wisdom of such a course. Practice Direction 6 does say, however, that if a hard copy is not sent and the document is proved not to have been received, the court may take account of the fact that a hard copy was not sent when considering any application arising out of that non-receipt (PD 6, para 3.4). Therefore, if a hard copy is not sent, it will be easier for the potential recipient to prove non-receipt.

Service by facsimile (fax)

In order to serve the claim form, or other document, by fax, the party who is to be served, or his legal representative, must previously have indicated in writing to the party serving that he is willing to accept service by fax and given the fax number to which the document is to be sent (PD 6, para 3.1).

Although there seems to be a positive requirement that the person to be served has agreed to be served by fax, and that is certainly true where a party is acting in person, it is, in fact, not entirely the case where the party is acting by a legal representative. This is because the mere fact that the legal representative has a fax number on his writing paper will be treated as sufficient written indication of acceptance of service by fax (PD 6, para 3.1(3)(b)). This is the reason why some firms of solicitors indicate on their writing paper, next to their fax number, that they do not accept service by fax. Formal rules for service do not apply to the making of Part 36 offers to settle, which can therefore be made by sending the document by fax to the offeree's solicitors even where the solicitors have indicated on their writing paper that they do not accept service by fax (*Charles v NTL Group Ltd* [2002] EWCA Civ 2004).

Also, if a fax number is set out on a statement of case or a response to a claim filed with the court (whether or not that party is legally represented), that too will be treated as sufficient written acceptance of service by fax (PD 6, para 3.1(3)(c)). If the party on whom the document is to be served is acting by a legal representative, the fax must be sent to the legal representative's business address (PD 6, para 3.1(2)).

Service by email and other electronic means

In order to use other electronic means for service, such as email, the party serving the document and the party on whom it is served must both be acting by a legal representative. The document must be served at the legal representative's business address, and the legal representative must have previously indicated, in writing, his willingness to accept service by this method and have provided his email address, or other electronic identification such as an ISDN or other telephonic link number (PD 6, para 3.3).

Service on a company

A company may be served by any method permitted under Part 6, as well as by methods set out in the Companies Act 1985, which in outline are:

- service by leaving a document at or posting it to an authorised place under s 725 of the Companies Act 1985;
- service on overseas companies under s 695 of the Companies Act 1985; and
- service of documents on companies incorporated outside the UK and Gibraltar and having a branch in Great Britain under s 694A of the Companies Act 1985.

An 'authorised place' is often held to be the registered office of the company. Although sending to the registered office is good service, as this is often situated away from company premises at the offices of accountants, solicitors, etc, it might be thought more prudent to effect service at the trading address of the company, where it might at least come to the more immediate attention of the company itself.

A claimant has the option of serving a claim form on a defendant company either by leaving it at, or sending it by post to, the company's registered office under s 725 of the Companies Act 1985, or by serving it in accordance with one of the methods permitted by the CPR. The two methods are true alternatives. There are differences between them. For instance, service under s 725 may be by second class post, whereas r 6(1) specifies service by first class post. Also, service under s 725 is deemed to have been effected at the time at which the letter would be delivered 'in the ordinary course of post unless the contrary is proved'. Rule 6.7, on the other hand, provides that where service is by first class post, the document is irrebuttably deemed to have been served on the second day after it was posted. Another difference is that service under s 725(1) must be by leaving the document at, or posting it to, the registered office, whereas r 6.2(1) provides for five permitted methods of service (*Cranfield v Bridgegrove Ltd* [2003] EWCA Civ 656).

Service by an alternative method

Where there is good reason to do so, the court can sanction service by a method not provided for by the rules as an alternative to the prescribed methods (r 6.8). Service by an alternative method is the new terminology for what was formerly known as 'substituted service'. Under the old rules, such an application was classically made when it was thought that a party was evading service and that, therefore, it would be difficult to effect service on him using standard methods of service. Also, an application was often made following road traffic accidents when the defendant was uninsured or untraceable and the claimant sought to serve proceedings on an insurer or the Motor Insurers' Bureau instead (*Gurtner v Circuit* [1968] 2 QB 587).

It has been held by the Court of Appeal that r 6.8 is prospective rather than retrospective in its operation (*Elmes v Hygrade Food* [2001] EWCA Civ 121). Therefore, where in *Elmes*, the claimant had wrongly served proceedings on the defendant's insurers rather than on the defendant, the court refused to apply r 6.8 after the event to cure the error already made in effecting service. The court held that it had no power either under r 6.8 or r 3.10 (general power to remedy errors in procedure) to deem the service on the defendant's insurers to be good service.

The application should be made only where the claimant has either tried other prescribed methods of service which have failed, or where the claimant has evidence that the prescribed methods are unlikely to be successful. The application should be made in accordance with Part 23 and be supported by evidence stating the reason why an order for an alternative method of service is sought and what steps have been taken to serve by other permitted means (r 6.8; PD 6, para 9.1). The application can be made without notice (r 6.8(2)).

Although not expressly required by the CPR, it is also likely that the court will expect the applicant to specify the alternative method of service that should be permitted and to explain why that method is likely to succeed in bringing the document to the party's attention. Examples of alternative methods are service at the address of a person with whom it is known the party to be served has contact, or by putting a notice in a newspaper.

An order permitting an alternative method of service will specify the method and will state the date when the document will be deemed served (r 6.8(3)).

Additional methods of service of the claim form

Service by a contractually agreed method

Often, contractual agreements contain a term specifying how, if it becomes necessary to start proceedings arising from the contract, those proceedings may be served. Under the CPR, if a claim form is issued containing a claim only in respect of that contract, service by the method specified in the contract will be valid (r 6.15). This is subject to the serving party seeking permission to serve proceedings out of the jurisdiction if such permission is necessary.

Service of claim form on agent of principal who is overseas

In certain circumstances, a party can make an application for a claim form to be served on the defendant's agent in the jurisdiction where the principal is overseas and cannot be served out of the jurisdiction. These circumstances are that the claimant entered into the contract with the defendant's agent within the jurisdiction, that the defendant's agent resides, carries on or has a place of business within the jurisdiction, and that at the time the application is made either the agent's authority has not been terminated, or he still has business relations with his principal. Also, at the time the contract was entered into and at the time of the application it must be the case that the principal was not residing or carrying on business within the jurisdiction (r 6.16; PD 6, para 9.2).

Service on members of HM Forces and US Air Force

Special rules exist for service of documents in civil proceedings on these parties (PD 6, para 5 and Annex).

Other rules about service

Part 6 contains the main body of rules about service of documents. However, specific rules about service may apply to specialised proceedings, and care should always be taken to ensure that the relevant rules are identified and followed. For instance, the rules on service of proceedings on the Crown are still contained in RSC Ord 77, r 4 (now CPR Sched 1 RSC Ord 77, r 4) and CCR Ord 42, r 7 (now CPR Sched 2 CCR Ord 42, r 7). Also, separate rules about service of the claim form apply to possession claims against squatters and are contained in r 55.6. The formal rules for service under Part 6 do not apply to the making of Part 36 offers to settle; accordingly, the offer is effected simply by being received by the offeree (see *Denise Charles v NTL Group Ltd* (2002) LTL, 13 December).

DEEMING SERVICE

If a document is personally served on a business day *before* 5 pm, service takes effect as soon as the document is left with the person to be served. A business day for these purposes is any day except Saturday, Sunday or a Bank Holiday (r 6.7(3)). However, if a document is personally served after 5 pm on a business day or on a day that is not treated as a business day, it will be treated as being served on the next business day (r 6.7(2)).

In all other cases, the table to r 6.7 sets out when a document that is served using other methods permitted by the rules is deemed to be served. This varies according to the method of service used. So, if a document is served by first class post, it will be deemed to be served the second day after it was posted, while a document will be deemed to be served the day after it was delivered to or left at a permitted address and the second day after it was left at the document exchange. If a document is transmitted by fax on a business day before 4 pm, it will be deemed to be served the same day, otherwise it will be deemed to be served on the next business day after the day it was transmitted. For any other electronic method, such as email, the document will be deemed to be served the second day after the day on which it was transmitted (r 6.7).

It should be noted that where not expressly excluded, Saturdays, Sundays and Bank Holidays are included in the calculation of the day of deemed service. Therefore, if a document is posted by first class post on Friday, it will be deemed to be served on Sunday, despite the fact that no post is delivered on that day (see *Anderton v Clwyd CC* [2002] EWCA Civ 933), a fact which was held to be 'legally irrelevant to the fiction of deemed service' by Mummery LJ (at [44]). This is the position despite the fact that r 2.8 (which excludes Saturdays, Sundays and Bank Holidays from calculations of periods of five days or less) is cross-referenced in brackets before the table of deemed dates at r 6.7.

When service is effected on a party's solicitor in accordance with the rules, the deemed date of service is also that set out in the table in r 6.7, and therefore depends on the method of service employed.

It has now been conclusively held by the Court of Appeal that the deemed day for service of documents laid down in the table to r 6.7 will be treated as the date of service, and that deemed date cannot be rebutted by evidence of the actual date when the document was received (see *Godwin v Swindon BC* [2001] EWCA Civ 1478, *Anderton v Clwyd CC* and *Wilkey v BBC* [2002] EWCA Civ 1561). Accordingly, if a defendant actually receives a claim form on the last day for service and on the last day before the expiry of the limitation period, but under the deeming provisions in r 6.7 service is deemed to occur after that day, the claim form will be treated as served on that later day and therefore as served out of time. Likewise, if a claimant posts a claim form by first class post to the defendant in accordance with the rules, the claim form will be deemed to be served on the second day after posting as specified in the table at r 6.7(1), even if the claim form is lost in the post and never reaches its intended destination.

As can be seen from the cases above, some confusion can arise as to service of proceedings. This has prompted the Civil Procedure Rule Committee to take another look at the 'deemed service' provisions of Parts 6 and 7 of the CPR with a view to amendments being made.

DISPENSING WITH SERVICE

The court has a general power to dispense with the requirement for service of a document 'if it is appropriate to do so' (r 6.9). An application under r 6.9 to dispense with service may be made without notice (r 6.9(2)).

A similar power existed under the old rules, and in many cases the power is exercised in uncontroversial circumstances, for instance, where a party has amended a statement of case with the consent of his opponent and the opponent is already in possession of a copy of the amended document, the court is likely to agree to a request to dispense with the formality of service of the amended document on the opponent.

However, the court is very unlikely to exercise its power to dispense with the requirement for service of a document in circumstances where it would in effect retrospectively be extending the time for service of the claim form (see *Wilkey v BBC* and *Anderton v Clwyd*). In *Wilkey v BBC*, the Court of Appeal held that where a claimant fails to effect service of the claim form within the permitted time limits, the circumstances in which the court can dispense with the need for service of the claim form are extremely limited. In that case the claimant issued a claim form two days before the expiry of the limitation period and then did not serve the claim form until the very last day of the four-month period allowed for service. However, the method of service employed by the claimant, leaving the claim form at the defendant's place of business, meant that service was not deemed to have occurred until the day after it was left at that address. Therefore, service was deemed to have occurred one day out of time.

Although the Court of Appeal went on to exercise its discretion to dispense with the need for service in this case, it made it clear that now that the rules for service under the CPR had bedded down and disputed interpretations had been clarified, future claimants would have very few, if any, acceptable excuses for failures to observe the rules for service of a claim form. Although recognising that a defendant in actual receipt of a claim form, but one which is deemed to be served after the last day for service and after the expiry of the limitation period, may not suffer any prejudice if the requirement for service is dispensed with, the court in *Wilkey v BBC* stressed that in the interests of certainty of the rules as to service, it would be very unlikely in the future to come to the assistance of the claimant by dispensing with the requirement for service of the claim form.

Also, where there are significant departures from the rules, rather than mere technicalities, the court will not exercise its exceptional jurisdiction (as identified in *Anderton v Clwyd*) to dispense with the need for service. Therefore, where the claimant's legal representative purported to serve a draft claim form, which was not stamped with the court seal and did not contain a statement of truth, on the defendant's insurers, who had no authority to accept service on the defendant's behalf, the Court of Appeal had no doubt that the case did not fall within the exceptional circumstances identified in *Anderton* and therefore refused to dispense with service under r 6.9 (*Cranfield v Bridgegrove Ltd and Linked Cases* [2003] EWCA Civ 656). In contrast, where a *copy* of the claim form (rather than the original) was sent to the right person at the right address for service, within the period of the validity of the claim form, the Court of Appeal would have decided (although the case was decided on other grounds) that in such unusual circumstances it would be right to dispense with service under r 6.9 (*Cranfield v Bridgegrove Ltd and Linked Cases*).

SERVICE OUTSIDE THE CPR

The CPR set out a number of permissible methods of service, but there is nothing in the rules that expressly prohibits the parties from agreeing between themselves on an ad hoc basis a mode of service not provided for by the rules. However, there is nothing in the rules that expressly allows them to do so either.

A case decided under the old rules, *Kenneth Allison Ltd (In Liquidation) v AE Limehouse and Co (A Firm)* [1991] 4 All ER 500, held that the party serving the document was entitled to rely on an ad hoc agreement, made between the parties at the time of service, as to the mode of service, even though it was not a method provided for by the rules. In that case, the plaintiffs issued proceedings for negligence against the defendants, a firm of chartered accountants. On the last day of validity of the writ (now claim form) and the last day before the expiry of the limitation period for the action, a process server attended at the defendants' offices where he told the senior partner's personal assistant that he wished to serve a writ. She consulted one of the partners and he authorised her to accept the writ. She then told the process server that she had been so authorised and received the writ from him. Such service did not constitute personal service on the partner because, for such service to be effective, the document had to be handed to or left in the possession of the party to be served.

It was argued by Lord Goff in that case that there was strong force in the argument that there should be mandatory methods of service so that those concerned at court offices, especially those who have to deal with applications for judgment in default, would know, by reference to rules of court, the precise date when proceedings were treated as having been served (p 513f–g). However, Lord Bridge of Harwich, who gave the leading judgment, also adopted the view that the rules should be the servants and not the masters of the court, and should not be construed so as to prevent the parties from acting reasonably when particular situations were met, in circumstances where there was no danger that the defendant would be unsure as to when service was effected (p 508f–g).

Under the CPR the message from the Court of Appeal is now clear: the court will not have much sympathy for a party who, through incompetence or delay, fails to effect service in accordance with the relevant rules (see *Wilkey v BBC*). It is submitted that if the point were to arise under the CPR, the *dictum* of Lord Goff would now be preferred to that of Lord Bridge (although authorities on matters of civil procedure decided before the CPR came into effect are generally no longer of any relevance; see the judgment of Lord Woolf MR in *Biguzzi v Rank Leisure plc* [1999] 1 WLR 1926; [1999] 4 All ER 934, CA). However, there may still be room for argument, perhaps supported by the principle of waiver, that if a similar situation were to arise under the CPR, the court, in applying the overriding objective to deal with cases justly, would be likely to treat service in such circumstances as valid.

CERTIFICATE OF SERVICE OF THE CLAIM FORM

When the court serves the claim form it will send the claimant a notice which will include the date when the claim form is deemed to be served in accordance with the above rules (r 6.14(1)). If the claimant elects to serve the claim form himself, he must file a certificate of service within seven days of service of the claim form (r 6.14(2)).

The certificate of service is in Form N215. Once filed, it will allow the court to act on the assumption that service has been effected successfully. The certificate of service must include a signed statement that the claim form has not been returned undelivered, and other details depending on which method of service was used. So, for postal service, the certificate must give the date of posting; for personal service, the date when it was personally served. The date of delivery to the document exchange or the date when the claim form was delivered to or left at the permitted place must be given if these methods were used. If service is effected by fax, the date and time of transmission must be given. For other electronic means, the date and time and means used must be given. Further, if the court permits an alternative method of service, the court will specify what information must be included in the certificate of service (r 6.10).

Failure to file a certificate of service of the claim form will preclude the claimant from entering judgment in default (r 6.14(2)(b)).

Such a certificate of service is always necessary if the claimant serves the claim form himself, but may also have to be filed in respect of other documents if required by a rule, practice direction or court order (r 6.10). One example of this is that if the claim form is served on the defendant without particulars of claim, the claimant must file a certificate of service within seven days of service of the particulars of claim (r 7.4(3)).

CHAPTER 11

SERVICE OUT OF THE JURISDICTION

INTRODUCTION

'Jurisdiction' is defined by r 2.3 as England and Wales and any part of the territorial waters of the UK next to England and Wales; therefore, service in any other place constitutes service out of the jurisdiction.

Where a defendant is resident outside the jurisdiction, consideration has to be given as to whether proceedings issued in the jurisdiction can be served upon him without permission, or whether the permission of the court is required. In broad terms, permission is not required where the court has jurisdiction to hear the claim under the Civil Jurisdiction and Judgments Act 1982 (CJJA) or where the court has been given jurisdiction to hear a claim by another enactment even though the defendant is not within the jurisdiction. In all other cases where the defendant is outside the jurisdiction the permission of the court is required.

The Civil Jurisdiction and Judgments Act 1982

The CJJA allows service of proceedings outside the jurisdiction without the permission of the court in a large number of civil cases where the Brussels (European Union, 'EU') and Lugano (European Free Trade Association, 'EFTA') Conventions apply. However, the Brussels Convention has been replaced to a large extent by Council Regulation 44/2001/EC (the Judgments Regulation), which came into force on 1 March 2002 and applies to civil proceedings between persons domiciled in Member States of the EU. In order to give effect to this the CJJA was amended by the Civil Jurisdiction and Judgments Order 2001 (SI 2001/3929). However, Denmark is not covered by the Judgments Regulation and is subject to the Brussels Convention instead.

The general rule is that a person must be sued in the State in which he is domiciled. However, a person domiciled in a EU or EFTA State may be sued in the court of another State as long as that is permitted by the Brussels or Lugano Conventions or the Judgments Regulation.

PERMISSION OF THE COURT NOT REQUIRED

There are broadly three situations where the permission of the court is not required to serve proceedings out of the jurisdiction. In respect of claims covered by the Brussels or Lugano Conventions, the permission of the court is not required to serve proceedings out of the jurisdiction where:

- the claim is one which the court has power to determine under the CJJA; and
- there are no other pending proceedings between the parties concerning the same claim either in the UK or any other Convention territory, that is, any country which is a signatory to the Brussels or Lugano Conventions; and

- the defendant is domiciled in the UK or in any Convention territory; and
- the relevant parts of the CJJA apply to the proceedings; or
- the defendant is a party to an agreement which confers jurisdiction under the CJJA (r 6.19(1)).

As stated above (see 'The Civil Jurisdiction and Judgments Act 1982'), the Brussels Convention has been replaced by the Judgments Regulation in respect of all EU Member States apart from Denmark.

The permission of the court is also not required to serve proceedings out of the jurisdiction:

- where the claim is one which the court has power to determine under the Judgments Regulation; and
- there are no other pending proceedings between the parties concerning the same claim either in the UK or any other Regulation State, that is all Member States of the EU apart from Denmark; and
- the defendant is domiciled in the UK or in any Regulation State; and
- the relevant part of the Judgments Regulation applies to the proceedings; or
- the defendant is a party to an agreement which confers jurisdiction under the Judgments Regulation (r 6.19(1A)).

As stated above (see 'The Civil Jurisdiction and Judgments Act 1982'), the Judgments Regulation applies to all EU Member States apart from Denmark.

Further, the permission of the court is not required to serve proceedings out of the jurisdiction where by any other enactment the court in this jurisdiction has power to determine the dispute even though the defendant to the claim is not within the jurisdiction or the facts giving rise to the claim did not occur within the jurisdiction (r 6.19(2)).

Jurisdiction for service out where the defendant is not domiciled in the UK

The Judgments Regulation and the Brussels Convention give jurisdiction for service of civil proceedings on a defendant who is not domiciled in the UK in a number of different types of situations. These include where the claim involves a contract that was to be performed in the UK. Also, where the claim is based on tort if the harmful event occurred in the UK.

Claims in respect of land or rights *in rem*

Where a claim is in respect of land or a right *in rem*, the Contracting State in which the property is located has exclusive jurisdiction to determine the claim regardless of the domicile of the parties (Art 22 of the Judgments Regulation; Art 16 of the Brussels Convention).

Position relating to co-defendants

Where a person who is domiciled in a Convention or Regulation State is one of a number of defendants to proceedings, and one of the defendants is domiciled in the

UK, any co-defendant may also be sued in the UK (Art 6 of the Judgments Regulation; Art 6 of the Brussels Convention).

Endorsement of claim form

The claim form must contain a statement of the basis on which the claimant is entitled to serve out of the jurisdiction without the permission of the court (r 6.19(3)). The usual form of words of the statement is:

> I state that the High Court of England and Wales has power under the Civil Jurisdiction and Judgments Act 1982 to hear this claim and that no proceedings are pending between the parties in Scotland, Northern Ireland or another Convention territory of any contracting State as defined by section 1(3) of the Act (PD 6B, para 1.1).

The usual form of words required by r 6.19(3) where the Judgments Regulation applies is:

> I state that the High Court of England and Wales has power under Council Regulation (EC) No 44/2001 of 22 December 2000 (on jurisdiction and recognition and enforcement of judgments in civil and commercial matters) to hear this claim and that no proceedings are pending between the parties in Scotland, Northern Ireland or any other Regulation State as defined by section 1(3) of the Civil Jurisdiction and Judgments Act 1982 (PD 6B, para 1.3A).

Different endorsements are specified for claims in respect of property located in the jurisdiction and where jurisdiction is conferred by any other enactment. Practice Direction 6B should be consulted for details.

PERMISSION OF THE COURT REQUIRED

Where the provisions of r 6.19 do not apply, the court's permission is required to serve proceedings out of the jurisdiction (r 6.20).

The court has a discretion to grant permission to serve the defendant in the following circumstances:

- if the claim is against someone domiciled within the jurisdiction, domicile being decided in accordance with ss 41 and 46 of the CJJA;
- where a claim is made for an injunction ordering the defendant to do or refrain from doing an act within the jurisdiction;
- where the claim is against someone on whom the claim form has been served and the claimant wishes to serve on another party;
- where a claim is made for an interim remedy as specified by s 25(1) of the CJJA;
- in respect of contracts, where the contract:
  - was made within the jurisdiction;
  - was made by or through an agent trading or residing within the jurisdiction;
  - is governed by English law; or
  - contains a provision that the courts here shall have jurisdiction to deal with any claim arising out of the contract.

In addition, permission will be required where the claim is in respect of a breach of contract committed within the jurisdiction, or for a declaration that no contract exists where, if it did exist, it would be a contract in respect of which the English courts would have jurisdiction;

- in respect of claims in tort, where damage was sustained within the jurisdiction or damage resulted from an act committed within the jurisdiction;
- where a claim is made to enforce any judgment or award of an arbitrator;
- where the claim wholly concerns property located within the jurisdiction;
- in respect of trusts, where the trust is one that ought to be executed according to English law and the person on whom the claim form is to be served is a trustee; concerning the administration of an estate of someone who died within the jurisdiction; rectification of a will; and various other trust proceedings;
- where a claim is made by the Inland Revenue other than against persons domiciled in the UK;
- where a claim is for costs against non-parties;
- in respect of admiralty claims, where the claim is in the nature of salvage and any part of the services took place within the jurisdiction; or to enforce a claim under s 153, 154 or 175 of the Merchant Shipping Act 1995;
- any other claims provided for by statute (r 6.20).

Similar endorsements on the claim form are also required in respect of service in other jurisdictions where permission is required (see PD 6B).

The application for permission

The application for permission must be supported by written evidence stating:

(a) the grounds on which the application is made and the relevant provisions of r 6.20;

(b) that the claimant believes that the claim has a reasonable chance of success; and

(c) the defendant's address, or the place where he is likely to be found if his address is not known (r 6.21(1)).

A complete set of documents must be provided for each party to be served out of the jurisdiction. These include a copy of the particulars of claim if not already included on the claim form, the claim form, the forms for responding to the claim and any translation that may be required by the courts (PD 6B, para 2.1).

Grounds on which permission will be granted

Permission will be dependent on the court here being satisfied that this jurisdiction is the proper place in which to bring the claim (r 6.21(2A)). The merits test for service out of the jurisdiction is not substantially different from that applied in considering an application to strike out a statement of claim or for summary judgment (*De Molestina and Others v Ponton and Others* [2002] 1 All ER (Comm) 587).

Where the application is for permission to serve a claim form in Scotland or Northern Ireland and the claim is one that could also be dealt with in those jurisdictions, the court will consider the question of cost and convenience (r 6.21(3)).

Validity of claim form for service out of the jurisdiction

Once issued, the claim form must be served within six months of the date of issue where the claim form is to be served out of the jurisdiction (r 7.5(3)). Therefore the claim form is valid for service for an additional two months compared to claim forms issued for service within the jurisdiction (see r 7.5(2)).

PROCEDURAL REQUIREMENTS

Time limits for responding to the claim

When permission is required to serve proceedings out of the jurisdiction, the court giving permission will specify the periods within which the respondent may answer the claim by filing an acknowledgment of service, admission or defence (r 6.21(4)). The relevant periods for responding to proceedings will depend on the country to which the notice is being sent. Practice Direction 6B, paras 7 and 10 should be consulted for the requisite number of days by reference to country.

Where permission is not required and the defendant is in Scotland, Northern Ireland or in the European territory of a Contracting State as defined by s 1(3) of the CJJA, the relevant period is 21 days from service of the particulars of claim, whether contained in the claim form or served later (r 6.22(2)). In the case of any other country which is a Contracting State, the relevant time period is 31 days (r 6.22(3)).

The relevant period for serving a defence where permission is not required is 21 days after service of the particulars of claim, or 35 days from service of the particulars of claim where the defendant has filed an acknowledgment of service where the defendant is in Scotland, Northern Ireland or in the European territory of a Contracting State as defined above (r 6.23(2)). In the case of any other country which is a Contracting State, the relevant time period is 31 days after service of the particulars of claim, or 45 days after service of the particulars of claim if the defendant files an acknowledgment of service (r 6.23(3)).

The rules provide for service to be effected by any method permitted by the law of the country in which it is to be served, or as is permitted by a Civil Procedure Convention or through foreign governments, judicial authorities and British consular authorities (r 6.24). There are also special provisions for service of the claim form on a State (r 6.27).

Service of documents other than the claim form

Where the court gives permission for a claim form to be served out of the jurisdiction and the claim form states that particulars of claim are to follow, permission is not required to serve the particulars of claim out of the jurisdiction (r 6.30(3)).

However, where permission of the court is required for service of a claim form out of the jurisdiction, it is also required to serve any notice of application out of the jurisdiction (r 6.30(2)). Similarly, where permission is not required to serve proceedings out of the jurisdiction, no permission is required to serve a notice of application out of the jurisdiction (r 6.30(2)).

The period for responding to an application notice will depend on the country to which the notice is being sent. Reference should be made to PD 6B, paras 8.1 and 10 as to the requisite number of days by reference to country.

Proof of service

Where the defendant does not turn up in response to a fixed date claim form, the claimant will not be able to proceed unless he is able to provide written evidence showing that the claim form has been properly served (r 6.31).

DISPUTING THE COURT'S JURISDICTION

Where a defendant is served with proceedings out of the jurisdiction and he disputes that the court has jurisdiction to try the claim, or believes that the court should not exercise its jurisdiction in the particular circumstances of the case, he should apply to the court for an order declaring that it has no such jurisdiction or that it should not exercise any jurisdiction which it may have (r 11(1)). However, before making such an application, the defendant must first file an acknowledgment of service (r 11(2)). The Civil Procedure Rules (CPR) specifically provide that filing an acknowledgment of service does not result in the defendant losing any right he may have to dispute the court's jurisdiction (r 11(3)).

Making an application to dispute the court's jurisdiction

The acknowledgment of service forms (N9 for claims under Part 7 and N210 for claims under Part 8) contain a box in which the defendant can indicate that he contests the court's jurisdiction. Having filed an acknowledgment of service indicating that he disputes the court's jurisdiction, the defendant should then apply to the court for an order declaring that it has no such jurisdiction or should not exercise any jurisdiction which it may have (r 11(1)).

The application, which should be made under Part 23, must be made within 14 days after the period of time for filing the acknowledgment of service and be supported by evidence (r 11(4)). If the defendant files an acknowledgment of service but does not make such an application with the time specified, he will be treated as having accepted that the court has jurisdiction to try the claim (r 11(5)). In such circumstances, if the defendant does in fact wish to contest the court's jurisdiction he should apply for an order for permission to do so out of time.

In the case of claims proceeding under Part 7, if the defendant makes an application to dispute the court's jurisdiction he does not need to file a defence to the claim before the application is heard (r 11(9)(a)). In the case of claims proceeding under Part 8, if the defendant makes an application to dispute the court's jurisdiction he does not need to file any other written evidence before the application is heard (r 11(9)(b)). This is for the obvious reason that if the court accepts the defendant's application and makes a declaration that the court does not have jurisdiction to hear the claim, a defence to the Part 7 claim or evidence in response to the Part 8 claim is unnecessary.

Orders the court may make

If the court makes an order declaring that the court has no jurisdiction to try the claim or will not exercise its jurisdiction, it may make further provision to dispose of the proceedings. This includes powers to make orders such as setting aside the claim form, setting aside service of the claim form, discharging any order made before the claim was commenced or before the claim form was served, or staying the proceedings (r 11.6).

If the court refuses to make a declaration that the court does not have jurisdiction or will not exercise jurisdiction, the defendant must then file a fresh acknowledgment of service in the proceedings within 14 days of the declaration, or such other period as the court may direct, as the original acknowledgment of service will no longer be effective (r 11(7)). On filing a fresh acknowledgment of service the defendant will be treated as having accepted that the court has jurisdiction to try the claim (r 11.8).

CHAPTER 12

STATEMENTS OF CASE

INTRODUCTION

The intention behind the Civil Procedure Rules (CPR) relating to statements of case is to replace the old technical form of pleading, often settled by counsel, with a plain English explanation of the position of each of the parties with regard to the claim. In order to signal the change in culture under the CPR the previous terminology, namely 'pleadings', has been replaced by 'statement of case'.

Under the former rules there was a substantial amount of case law governing the technicalities of pleading which Lord Woolf felt caused unnecessary costs, complications and delay to proceedings. Now, under the CPR a straightforward statement of the claimant's case must be put forward, to be met by a proper response from the defendant, bare denials not being acceptable.

In Lord Woolf's view the primary role of statements of case is succinctly to set out the facts relied on so that the court and the other party can ascertain what the dispute is about, and so that the court can make appropriate decisions about the management of the case (see *Access to Justice*, Interim Report (IR), Chapter 20, para 1, www.dca.gov.uk/civil/interfr.htm).

Statements of case

'Statement of case' is the term used for a pleading and includes:

- a claim form;
- particulars of claim where these are not included in a claim form;
- a defence;
- a Part 20 claim;
- a reply to defence; and
- any further information given in relation to them voluntarily or by court order (see definition in r 2.3(1)).

The provisions for statements of case are contained in Part 16 and its accompanying practice direction. Part 16 does not apply to the Part 8 alternative procedure (r 16.1). This is because Part 8 proceedings are for the type of claim that does not involve substantial disputes of fact, such as the construction of a trust deed or an application for a new business tenancy (see Part 56).

The function of statements of case

Statements of case primarily contain the facts on which a party's case is based. General guidance as to the function of statements of case was given by Lord Woolf in *McPhilemy v Times Newspapers Ltd* [1999] 3 All ER 775. In that case, Lord Woolf criticised the excessive particulars provided by the parties' statements of case, asserting instead that '[n]o more than a concise statement of [the] facts is required' (at 793b). Although he recognised that statements of case are 'critical to identify the issues and the extent of the dispute between the parties' (at 793a), he stated that the need for extensive statements of case should be reduced by the requirement to exchange witness statements and to identify and attach copies of documents which are relied on. He went on to say that he believed that 'excessive particulars can achieve directly the opposite result from that which is intended. They can obscure the issues rather than providing clarification' (at 793c).

Lord Woolf's view was endorsed in the case of *The Royal Brompton Hospital NHS Trust v Hammond and Others* (2001) 76 Con LR 148. In that case, Seymour J warned that the requirement for concise pleadings was not meant to convey the message that statements of case were no longer of importance in defining a party's case (which must be done accurately and with care), or that there would be a general licence to depart at will from a pleaded case.

THE CLAIM FORM

In order to start a claim under Part 7, the claimant must complete a claim form in Form N1 and file it at court (PD 7, para 3.1). Different forms are prescribed for claims commenced under Part 8 (Form N208), fixed date claims, claims issued by the Production Centre and for specialist proceedings.

A claimant should ensure that the correct claim form is identified and that it complies with the requirements of any relevant practice direction that may apply to the type of claim in question (for example, Part 55 for possession claims). The general rules about statements of case will apply to specialist proceedings only in so far as they are not inconsistent with the rules and practice directions for those specialist proceedings (r 16.2(1)(d); PD 16, para 1.2).

Nature of claim and remedy sought

The detail of a claimant's case is set out in his particulars of claim, but the claim form must contain a concise statement of the nature of the claim and specify the remedy which the claimant seeks (r 16.2(1)(a), (b)). For instance, a claimant's claim may be for damages for breach of contract, or for an injunction to restrain trespass. Form N1 includes a section headed 'Brief details of claim', into which the nature of the claim and remedy sought must be inserted.

Although a claimant should always complete the claim form carefully and clearly identify the remedy he seeks, it should be noted that the court is now expressly empowered to grant any remedy to which the claimant may be entitled whether or not the claimant has sought it (r 16.2(5)). This is a reflection of the greater flexibility given to the court under its case management powers to identify the real issues in dispute between the parties and to grant the relief to which a claimant is entitled. It is still common practice for claimants to include a statement that they seek such further or other relief as the court deems appropriate.

The claim form, like all other statements of case, should be verified by a statement of truth (r 22.1).

Claimant's address

The claimant must include his own address (where he resides or carries on business) in the claim form, even if his *address for service* is the business address of his solicitor (PD 16, para 2.2). A 'care of' or 'c/o' address will not be acceptable. Similarly, where the defendant is an individual, the claimant should, if he can, include the defendant's address (where he resides or carries on business) in the claim form, even if the defendant's solicitors have notified the claimant that they have authority to accept service of proceedings (PD 16, para 2.3).

Statement of value

Where the claimant is making a claim for money the claim form must contain a *statement of value* (r 16.2(1)(c)).

If the claimant is claiming a fixed amount he should specify the amount claimed (r 16.3(2)(a)). He should insert the figure claimed into the box marked 'amount claimed' on the claim form.

If the claimant is not claiming a specified amount he must state in the claim form that he expects to recover:

* not more than £5,000;
* more than £5,000 but not more than £15,000; or
* more than £15,000 (r 16.3(2)).

Alternatively, the claimant may state that he does not know how much he expects to recover. This is likely to be an unattractive option, as such a statement will almost inevitably lead to the court issuing the claim charging the maximum court fee!

It should be borne in mind by defendants that the statement of value in the claim form does not limit the power of the court to give judgment for the amount to which it finds the claimant is entitled (r 16.3(7)).

Claims for a specified/unspecified sum

There is a distinction between a claim for a specified sum and a claim for an unspecified sum. A claimant is entitled to put a figure on a claim for general damages and claim a specified amount rather than leave the court to quantify the damages. This will allow the claimant to enter judgment for a specified amount in default (if the defendant does not respond to the claim), rather than be limited to entering judgment for an amount to be decided by the court.

This change is of procedural significance only, as a claimant may recover only the amount to which he is entitled. Therefore, any sum specified by the claimant will be subject to challenge by the defendant and assessment by the court.

Calculating the value of the claim

When completing the *statement of value* and calculating how much he expects to recover, the claimant must disregard:

* interest;

- costs;
- the possibility that the court may make a finding of contributory negligence against him;
- the possibility that the defendant may make a counterclaim or claim a set off; or
- that the defendant may have to pay sums to the Secretary of State for Social Security under the recoupment provisions provided by s 6 of the Social Security (Recovery of Benefits) Act 1997 (r 16.3(6)).

Personal injury claims

In a personal injury claim the claimant must also state in the claim form whether the amount which he expects to recover as general damages for pain, suffering and loss of amenity is more or not more than £1,000 (r 16.3(3)). This is relevant on allocation of the claim to track should it become defended. If the pain, suffering and loss of amenity element of the claim exceeds £1,000, the claim will not be allocated to the small claims track even if the total value of the claim is less than £5,000 (r 26.6).

Claims by tenants for repair of residential premises

Similarly, in a claim that includes a claim by a tenant of residential premises against his landlord, where the tenant is seeking an order that the landlord carry out repairs or other work to the premises, the claimant must state whether the amount of damages he expects to recover for this part of the claim, or any other claim for damages, exceeds or does not exceed £1,000 (r 16.3(4)). Again, if the value of the repairs or other damages claim is expected to exceed £1,000, it will not be allocated to the small claims track should it become defended (r 26.6).

Issuing claims in the High Court

Where the claim form is issued in the High Court, the claimant must either state that he expects to recover more than £15,000, or £50,000 or more if the claim is for personal injuries, or else he must show, by naming it, an enactment which provides that the claim may be commenced only in the High Court, or otherwise he must state that the claim is one of those on the specialist jurisdiction lists (r 16.3(5)).

Service of particulars of claim

Particulars of claim should, if practicable, be contained in the claim form (PD 16, para 3.1), in the section indicated on the claim form. Alternatively, the particulars of claim can be contained in a separate document served with the claim form (PD 16, para 3.2(1)). Where a legal representative is instructed it is usual for the particulars of claim to be contained in a separate document, unless the claim can be stated shortly and simply (for example, an unpaid invoice).

The claimant does not have to serve particulars of claim with the claim form, but if he decides not to do so he must indicate on the claim form that particulars of claim are to follow (r 16.2(2)). The claimant should serve the particulars of claim within 14 days after service of the claim form (r 7.4(1)(b)), but in any event no later than the latest time for serving a claim form (r 7.4(2)).

If the particulars of claim are contained in a separate document they must contain the name of the court, the claim number, the title of the proceedings and the claimant's address for service (PD 16, para 3.8). They should also be verified by a separate statement of truth (PD 16, para 3.4).

CONTENTS OF PARTICULARS OF CLAIM

Facts of the claim

It is a general requirement that all particulars of claim include a concise statement of the facts on which the claimant relies. Lord Woolf wanted to ensure that this basic function of statements of case, to state succinctly the facts relied on, was clearly restated in the CPR (see IR, Chapter 20, para 4).

In drafting particulars of claim the claimant should break down each element of the cause of action relied upon, and then identify and set out the particular facts of his case that establish each element of the cause of action.

There are certain facts that must be specifically pleaded. These include allegations in respect of the defendant's state of mind or serious allegations of misconduct, such as allegations of fraud, the fact of any illegality, details of any misrepresentation, details of breaches of trust, notice or knowledge of a fact, details of unsoundness of mind or undue influence and details of wilful default (PD 16, para 8.2). If a claimant wishes to rely on any such matters he must clearly plead them.

For certain types of claim, additional details are specified in PD 16.

Points of law

Apart from pleading the facts on which his claim is based, the claimant can also plead a point of law (PD 16, para 13.3(1)). Although a claimant is not obliged to plead a point of law, it would, it is submitted, be good practice to do so, if it would assist in identifying the real issues in dispute between the parties and give the defendant early notice of the legal basis of the claimant's claim.

Identity of witnesses

A claimant can also include in his particulars of claim the name of any witness he intends to rely upon to support his claim (PD 16, para 13.3(2)). A claimant may wish to include such details to indicate the strength of his claim.

Mitigation of loss

A claimant must also set out any facts relating to mitigation of loss or damage where he wishes to rely on them in support of his claim (PD 16, para 8.2). In most cases, it will be the defendant who is asserting that the claimant has failed to mitigate his loss, and the claimant does not have a duty to prove that he has mitigated his loss if this is not put in issue by the defendant.

Evidence of previous convictions

In some cases conduct that has given rise to criminal proceedings will also give rise to civil proceedings against the same defendant by the victim of the crime. For instance, in road traffic accident claims, the driver of a vehicle that caused the claimant personal injuries may have already been convicted of careless driving.

The fact of such a conviction will often be enough to prove that the defendant was negligent in causing the claimant's injuries, and under s 11 of the Civil Evidence Act 1968 the claimant is entitled to rely on the conviction to prove that the defendant committed the offence, where it is relevant to the claimant's claim. The effect of s 11 is to reverse the burden of proof, so that it will be for the defendant to prove that he did not commit the offence.

A claimant who wishes to rely on a conviction for a criminal offence must give details in the particulars of claim of the conviction and its date, the court or court-martial which made the conviction and the issue in the claim to which it relates (PD 16, para 8.1).

Finding or adjudication of adultery or paternity

Section 12 of the Civil Evidence Act 1968 allows a claimant to rely on previous findings or adjudications of adultery or paternity against a defendant as evidence in civil proceedings, where such a finding is relevant to any issue in the case as to whether the defendant committed the adultery or is the father of a child.

A claimant who wishes to rely on such a finding or adjudication must give details in the particulars of claim of the finding or adjudication and its date, the court which made the finding or adjudication and the issue in the claim to which it relates (PD 16, para 8.1).

Interest

If a claimant wishes to recover interest, he must claim it and provide relevant details in his particulars of claim (r 16.4(1)(b)). It is important to note that if a claim for interest is not made, none will be recoverable. The details required vary according to the basis on which interest is claimed (court, statutory or contractual interest) and whether the claim is for a specified or an unspecified sum.

Interest on a specified sum

If the claim is for a specified amount of money, the claim for interest must include:

- the percentage rate of interest claimed;
- the date from which interest is claimed and the date to which it is calculated, which must not be later than the date of issue of the claim form;

- the total amount of interest claimed at the date of issue; and
- the daily rate at which interest accrues thereafter (r 16.4(2)(b)).

In the case of a claim for a specified amount of money, if the claimant has provided the requisite details regarding any claim for interest, if judgment is entered in default it will include the amount claimed for interest.

Contractual interest

Interest may be recoverable as of right at a specified rate and from a specified time under the terms of a contract. In order to claim contractual interest, the claimant must state in his particulars of claim that he is claiming under the terms of a contract (r 16.4(2)(a)(i)). The claimant should identify the term in the contract that provides for interest, when it applies and what rate of interest was agreed.

Where there is an express term in a contract entitling a party to interest, this will potentially form a claim in its own right, even if the debt or damages on which the interest accrues are paid before proceedings are commenced. However, in the absence of a contractual or statutory entitlement there is no general right at common law to interest for late payment of a debt after it becomes contractually due (*President of India v La Pintada Compañía Navigación SA* [1984] 2 All ER 773). Therefore, in such a case, if the debt is paid prior to the commencement of proceedings there will be no separate right to claim interest.

Statutory interest

Various statutes give a right to claim interest on unpaid sums. Under the Solicitors' (Non-Contentious Business) Remuneration Order 1994 (SI 1994/2616), solicitors are entitled to charge their clients interest one month after the delivery of a bill of costs in a non-contentious matter, provided certain information was provided to the client. The rate of interest will be 8% unless another rate was agreed with the client.

Under the Bills of Exchange Act 1882, a claimant is entitled to claim interest on a dishonoured cheque.

The Late Payment of Commercial Debts (Interest) Act 1998

The Late Payment of Commercial Debts (Interest) Act 1998 (LPCD Act) was introduced to meet the Government's obligations under an EU directive regarding the protection of businesses (see Directive 2000/35/EC on combatting late payment in commercial transactions). Statistics show that many businesses, particularly small businesses, fail because of cash flow problems.

If the LPCD Act 1998 applies, by s 1 a term is implied into the contract that the debt carries interest at the rate of 8% above the official dealing rate of the Bank of England (base rate). The official dealing rate to be used is that in force on 30 June (for interest which starts to run between 1 July and 31 December) or 31 December (for interest which starts to run between 1 January and 30 June) in the relevant year (Late Payment of Commercial Debts (Rate of Interest) (No 3) Order 2002 (SI 2002/1675)). The official dealing rate can be found on the Bank of England website (www.bankofengland.co.uk).

As a term is implied into the contract, interest can be claimed in its own right even if proceedings are not issued or the debt is paid before proceedings are issued (so long as payment is not made and accepted in full and final settlement).

The LPCD Act 1998 applies only to contracts for the supply of goods or services where both parties are acting in the course of a business (s 2 of the LPCD Act 1998). If the agreement already includes an express contractual term as to interest for late payment, it is unlikely that the supplier will be able to claim interest under the 1998 Act unless the right to interest under the contract does not provide a *substantial remedy* for the late payment (s 8 of the LPCD Act 1998).

The LPCD Act 1998 was introduced in three stages. It first applied to contracts entered into on or after 1 November 1998 but before 1 November 2000, where a small business supplier (one employing 50 or fewer full-time employees) is entitled to claim the interest from a large business purchaser (one employing more than 50 full-time employees) or a public authority. The next stage came into effect for contracts entered into on or after 1 November 2000 but before 7 August 2002, where a small business supplier is entitled to claim the interest from both a large business/public authority purchaser and another small business purchaser. The final stage came into effect for contracts entered into on or after 7 August 2002, where all business/public authority suppliers (large and small) can claim the interest from another business purchaser whether large/public authority or small.

Interest under the LPCD Act 1998 starts to run on the day after the agreed date for payment of the debt. If no date is agreed interest will run either 30 days after the supplier has performed his part of the contract (for example, delivered goods), or 30 days after the day when the purchaser was notified of the amount of the debt, if that is later (s 4 of the LPCD Act 1998).

For contracts entered into after 7 August 2002, the creditor can also claim an additional fixed sum, as well as interest. If the debt is for less than £1,000 the fixed sum is £40; for a debt of £1,000 or more but less than £10,000, £70; and for a debt of £10,000 or more, £100 (s 5A of the LPCD Act 1998). This additional fixed sum is in compensation for the administrative costs of pursuing payment from the debtor and is part of the term implied into the contract, so it can also be claimed even if proceedings are not issued or the debt is paid before proceedings are issued (s 5A(3) of the LPCD Act 1998).

Normally, county court judgments under £5,000 do not carry interest, but if the debt falls under the LPCD Act 1998 judgment interest will accrue at the County Court Judgment rate (currently 8%) whatever the amount of the judgment debt (County Courts (Interest on Judgment Debts) (Amendment) Order 1998 (SI 1998/2400)).

Court's discretion to award interest

If a contract does not specify that interest is recoverable following breach, or where the claim is not based on a contract, the claimant may seek interest under s 35A of the Supreme Court Act 1981 (SCA) for High Court claims or s 69 of the County Courts Act 1984 (CCA) for county court claims. Whether such statutory interest is recoverable is in the court's discretion, although it is almost invariably awarded. The current rate of interest is 8%.

Part payment of a debt or damages

If a defendant pays part of the debt or damages claimed after proceedings have been issued, the claimant can claim interest on the sum partly paid, up to the date of payment, and interest on the balance of the claim up to the date of judgment (s 35A(1) of the SCA; s 69(1) of the CCA).

Payment of whole of debt prior to judgment

In the case of a debt (but not damages), if the defendant pays the whole sum owed after issue of proceedings but before judgment, the claimant can still claim interest on the sum claimed between the date when the cause of action arose and the date of payment (s 35A(3) of the SCA; s 69(3) of the CCA).

Payment of debt or damages prior to issue of proceedings

The court has no power to award interest under the SCA or CCA where sums owed are paid prior to the commencement of proceedings (*IM Properties plc v Cape & Dalgleish* [1998] 3 All ER 203).

Interest in personal injury claims

In the case of personal injury or death claims, the court should award interest if the damages exceed £200 unless the court is satisfied that there would be satisfactory reasons not to do so (s 35A(2) of the SCA; s 69(2) of the CCA).

Aggravated and exemplary damages

If the claimant is seeking aggravated or exemplary damages, he must state this in his particulars of claim and give his grounds for claiming them (r 16.4(1)(c)).

Contract claims

Where a claimant brings a claim based on a written agreement, a copy of the contract, or documents constituting the agreement, should be attached to, or served with, the particulars of claim. The claimant should also bring the original documents to the hearing (PD 16, para 7.3(1)). Note that this provision would also apply to a residential possession claim (Part 55), where a copy of the tenancy agreement, mortgage deed etc, together with any appropriate notices, should be attached to the particulars of claim. This practice tends to be honoured more in the breach than in observance.

If the contract incorporates general conditions of sale, these too should be attached to or served with the particulars of claim (PD 16, para 7.3(2)). However, if the contract documents are bulky, it will be enough for the claimant to attach and serve only the parts relevant to the claim (PD 16, para 7.3(2)).

Where the claim is based upon an oral agreement, the particulars of claim should specify the words used and state by whom, to whom, when and where they were spoken (PD 16, para 7.4).

Where the claim is based upon an agreement by conduct, the particulars of claim must specify the conduct relied on and state by whom, when and where the acts constituting the conduct were done (PD 16, para 7.5).

Supporting documents

A claimant is entitled to attach to his claim form or particulars of claim a copy of any document he considers necessary to support his claim (PD 16, para 13.3(3)). This may include a copy of an expert's report on which he intends to rely.

PARTICULAR TYPES OF PROCEEDINGS

Personal injury claims

In a personal injury claim, the particulars of claim must include the claimant's date of birth and brief details of the personal injuries (PD 16, para 4.1).

Medical evidence

Where the claimant is relying on the evidence of a medical practitioner, the claimant must attach to or serve with his particulars of claim a report from a medical practitioner about the personal injuries that he alleges in his claim (PD 16, para 4.3). In a case decided under the former rules, *Knight v Sage Group plc* (1999) LTL, 28 April, a litigant in person who served only a preliminary report prepared by her GP with her particulars of claim was held to have satisfied the requirement to serve a medical report that substantiated her injuries for the initial stage of the proceedings. The claimant was given a further period of time within which to serve a further medical report substantiating her injuries.

It is submitted that under the CPR the court is likely to be much less sympathetic to a claimant who fails to serve a medical report with his particulars of claim where one is needed to prove the nature and/or cause of his personal injuries. This is particularly so given the existence of the pre-action protocol for personal injury claims, and such conduct is likely to be excused only where the limitation period is imminently due to expire. Indeed, in *Jones v Telford and Wrekin Council* (1999) *The Times*, 29 July, the claimant had not yet obtained favourable medical reports but, because the limitation period was close to expiry, had issued, but not served, the claim form and then applied for and was granted three extensions of time to serve proceedings. Lord Woolf indicated in that case that it might be acceptable to issue and serve a claim form without full particulars of claim (or a medical report) where the limitation period was about to expire, solicitors had only just been instructed and there was no time to work through the protocol. He said that such a course was preferable to issuing the claim form and then applying to the court for extensions of time within which to serve it, because a defendant should be notified of a claim as early as possible in order to take steps to defend it.

Where the claimant has attached a medical report to his particulars of claim, the defendant should state in his defence whether he agrees, disputes, or neither agrees nor disputes but has no knowledge of the matters contained in the medical report. If the defendant disputes the report he must give his reasons for doing so, and if he has obtained his own medical report on which he intends to rely he should attach it to his defence (PD 16, para 12.1).

Special damages

The claimant must attach to his particulars of claim a schedule of details of any past and future expenses and losses which he claims (PD 16, para 4.2).

The defendant should attach a counter-schedule to his defence stating with which items in the claimant's schedule he agrees, disputes, or neither agrees nor disputes but has no knowledge of. The defendant should also supply alternative figures where he is in a position to do so (PD 16, para 12.2).

Provisional damages

In a personal injury claim a claimant may seek provisional damages. Provisional damages are an award of damages to an injured person based on the assumption that he will not develop an identified disease or suffer a deterioration in a condition, but with the right to claim further damages in the future if he does so (see Chapter 26, 'Provisional Damages').

The claimant must state in his particulars of claim that he is seeking an award of provisional damages under either s 32A of the SCA or s 51 of the CCA. He must also state that there is a chance that at some future time he will develop some serious disease or suffer some serious deterioration in his physical or mental condition, and specify the disease or type of deterioration in respect of which an application may be made at a future date (r 16.4(1)(d); PD 16, para 4.4).

Fatal accident claims

If a person suffering personal injuries caused by another's negligence, nuisance or breach of duty dies from those injuries, two independent causes of action potentially arise. One is the injured person's own cause of action for his personal injuries, which may be brought following his death on behalf of his estate under the Law Reform (Miscellaneous Provisions) Act 1934. The other is an entirely separate cause of action, which can be brought by the deceased's dependants for financial loss cause by the death under the Fatal Accidents Act 1976.

In a fatal accident claim, the claimant must state in his particulars of claim that the claim is brought under the Fatal Accidents Act 1976; identify the dependants on whose behalf the claim is made; give the date of birth of each dependant; and give details of the nature of the dependency claim (PD 16, para 5.1). Fatal accident claims may include a claim for damages for bereavement (PD 16, para 5.2).

Hire-purchase claims

For claims against an individual under a hire-purchase agreement, the claimant must include prescribed information in the particulars of claim as specified in PD 16, paras 6.1 and 6.2.

Claims in respect of land

Where the claimant brings a claim for an injunction or declaration in respect of or relating to any land or the possession, occupation, use or enjoyment of any land, the particulars of claim must state whether or not the injunction or declaration relates to residential premises and identify the land, by reference to a plan where necessary (PD 16, para 7.1).

Where a claimant landlord/mortgage/licensor is seeking to recover possession of land from a tenant/trespasser, the particulars of claim must contain specified information (see r 55.4 and PD 55, para 2.1). Also, the particulars of claim must be filed and served with the claim form (r 55.4).

THE DEFENCE

In order to dispute all or part of the claim the defendant must file a defence (r 15.2). The defendant will receive a *response pack* with the particulars of claim (r 7.8(1)). The *response pack* includes two types of defence form, Form N9B, where the claimant is claiming a specified amount of money, and Form N9D, where the claimant is claiming an unspecified amount of money or making a non-money claim. The defendant can either insert details of his defence into the space provided in the appropriate court form, or attach a separate document containing his defence.

Defendant's address

If the defendant is an individual his defence must include correct details of his address, where he resides or carries on business, in the box provided in the defence form, if the claimant has not already provided those details, or has provided incorrect details, in the claim form (PD 16, para 10.4). The defendant must provide details of his address even if his *address for service* is not where he resides or carries on business, for example, his address for service is his solicitor's business address (PD 16, para 10.5). A 'care of' or 'c/o' address will not be acceptable.

Responding to the particulars of claim

The defendant should address every allegation made in the particulars of claim with either an admission, or a denial or a non-admission. If the defendant fails to deal with an allegation, apart from in limited circumstances, he will be taken to admit it (r 16.5(5)).

Admissions

The defendant must state which of those facts in the particulars of claim are admitted (r 16.5(1)(c)). There are usually a number of non-contentious facts pleaded in a particulars of claim which a defendant can safely admit. For instance, in a dispute involving a claim for damages for breach of contract, the fact that the contract was entered into may not be disputed, even if the allegation that it was breached is. There may also be some facts which the defendant cannot deny and which he should therefore admit, even if such admissions will go to establish the claimant's case.

Denials

Prior to the introduction of the CPR, a defence could simply consist of bare denials of allegations in the particulars of claim. Under the CPR the defendant has a positive burden to set out the basis and details of any denials. Therefore, if the defendant denies an allegation he must state his reasons for doing so (r 16.5(2)(a)). If he intends to put forward his own version of events he must set it out in his defence (r 16.5(2)(b)).

Non-admissions

There are some allegations which the defendant will not be in a position either to admit or deny, because he has no direct knowledge of them, but he may wish to put the burden on the claimant to prove. For instance, a claimant may allege that he suffered depression as a consequence of the defendant's actions, but the defendant may have no knowledge as to whether this is true or not. In those circumstances the defendant can plead a 'non-admission', that is, state that he is unable to admit or deny the allegation but that he requires the claimant to prove it (r 16.5(1)(b)).

A defendant who does not directly deal with an allegation but who has set out the nature of his case in relation to the issue to which that allegation is relevant, is taken to require that allegation to be proved (r 16.5(3)).

Where a claim includes a claim for money, the defendant is automatically taken to require the claimant to prove the *amount* claimed, unless he expressly admits it (r 16.5(4)).

Disputing the statement of value

If the defendant disputes the claimant's *statement of value*, he should give reasons for this in his defence and, if he is able to do so, give his own statement of value of the claim (r 16.5(6)).

Defence of set off

The defendant's defence may be that the amount claimed by the claimant is set off by sums owed by the claimant to the defendant. If the defendant's claim to money from the claimant amounts to a legal, equitable or statutory set off then it may constitute a defence to the whole or part of the claimant's claim. The defendant will therefore be entitled to plead such a set off as a defence to the claimant's claim, whether or not the defendant also makes a Part 20 claim against the claimant for the amount claimed in the set off (r 16.6).

If the claimant and defendant owe each other mutual debts then the defendant can in defence set off the amount owed by the claimant to him against the amount he owes to the claimant.

Where a supplier brings a claim against a consumer for the price of the goods or services supplied, a consumer can set up any breach of the implied statutory warranties in diminution or extinction of the price (s 53 of the Sale of Goods Act 1979).

An *equitable set off* can arise where there is such an interconnection between the claim and cross-claim as to make it inequitable to enforce the one without the other, so that an unliquidated counterclaim can be set off against a liquidated debt (*Hanak v Green* [1958] 2 QB 9). It arises where the cross-claim is one 'flowing out of and inseparably connected with the dealings and transactions which also give rise to the claim' (in *Bank of Boston Connecticut v European Grain & Shipping Co Ltd* [1989] 1 AC 1056, *per* Lord Brandon).

There is a wide range of circumstances in which an equitable set off may arise. It was confirmed in *Bim Chemi AB v Blackburn Chemicals* [2001] 2 Lloyd's Rep 93 that it is not necessary that the cross-claim should arise out of the same contract; all that is required is that it should flow from the dealings and transactions which gave rise to the subject of the claim. In the case of *Railtrack plc v Marconi* [2002] EWHC 1546, an equitable set off was said to arise where there was a joint venture between the parties and the respective agreements were interdependent. However, in that particular case the court questioned the merits of the cross-claim and ordered the defendants to pay a substantial sum into court as a condition of defending the claim.

A defendant can also plead the set off as a counterclaim to which the provisions of Part 20 would apply and for which a court fee would be payable. If, therefore, the defendant is alleging a true set off and it is for the same amount, or for less than the claimant is claiming, under r 16.6 the defendant can avoid issuing a Part 20 claim against the claimant, and paying the accompanying issue fee, by simply pleading the set off as a defence.

Cheque rule

It should be noted that if the defendant pays by cheque which is then dishonoured, the claimant will be entitled to judgment and the defendant will be unable to raise a set off defence to avoid payment (*Nova (Jersey) Knit Ltd v Kammgarn Spinnerei GmbH* [1977] 1 WLR 713). The reason for this so called 'cheque rule' is to maintain the confidence of the business community in the system of payment by cheque. The court therefore treats payment by cheque as if payment had been made by cash.

In *Esso Petroleum Co v Milton* [1997] 2 All ER 593, the Court of Appeal (Thorpe LJ dissenting) held that it was a natural evolution of the *Nova (Jersey) Knit* principle for payment made by direct debit to be treated in the same way as payment by cheque.

There are a limited number of defences to the cheque rule, which are: denial of the validity of the cheque; that the cheque was obtained by fraud; the cheque relates to an illegal contract, for example, gambling; or total failure of consideration, or partial failure giving rise to a liquidated sum (see *Nova (Jersey) Knit*).

Limitation defence

If the defendant's defence is that the limitation period for the claimant's cause of action has expired, and that the claimant's claim is therefore statute-barred, the defendant must expressly plead this in his defence (PD 16, para 13.1). There is therefore a positive onus on the defendant to plead such a defence, and if he fails to do so the claimant will be entitled to pursue his claim even if it is statute-barred (*Dismore v Milton* [1938] 3 All ER 762, CA).

Defence of tender before claim

Where the claimant claims payment of a debt, the defendant may allege that he tendered the amount owing before the issue of proceedings, and therefore it was unnecessary for the claimant to commence proceedings and the claimant should thus not be entitled to recover the costs of those proceedings from the defendant. In such cases the real issue in dispute between the parties is as to the amount of the sum owed.

In order to rely on a defence of tender before claim the defendant must, when filing his defence: pay the sum tendered into court; file a notice of payment into court; and file a certificate of service confirming service of his defence and the notice of payment in on the claimant. He must also serve a copy of the notice of payment into court on the claimant (see r 37.3; PD 37, para 2.1).

In *JM Greening & EJ Greening (t/a Automania) v Raymond Williams* (1999) *The Times*, 10 December, a case decided under the former rules, the Court of Appeal held that in addition to the payment in of the amount pleaded, the defendant must also serve a notice on the plaintiff of the payment in. If the defendant fails to serve the requisite notice on the plaintiff, he will not be entitled to rely on the defence of tender before claim. Although this case was decided under the former rules, and is not therefore binding on the court applying the CPR, it is submitted that the same approach will be taken under the CPR given the mandatory requirement for the serve of a notice of payment in on the claimant.

Other matters

The defendant can include in his defence details of a point of law, the name of any witness on whose evidence he intends to rely, and attach copies of any documents on which he intends to rely, in the same way as the claimant (PD 16, para 13.3).

REPLY

A claimant is entitled to file a reply to the defendant's defence, but this is optional. The claimant is not entitled to raise new claims in the reply, its purpose being to address issues raised by the defence. It is not necessary to file a reply because a claimant is taken not to admit any of the matters raised in the defence (r 16.7(1)). However, a claimant may wish to file a reply where the defendant raises matters not dealt with by the particulars of claim that the claimant wishes to address.

A claimant may file a reply that addresses only part but not all of the defence, and if he does so it will be taken that the claimant requires the defendant to prove the other matters contained in the defence (r 16.7(2)).

If the claimant does wish to file a reply in response to the defence, he should do so when he files his allocation questionnaire and serve a copy on every other party at the same time (r 15.8). There are to be no further 'statements of case' after a reply without the permission of the court (r 15.9). Lord Woolf was of the view that if a case 'genuinely required unravelling to this extent the proper approach would be for the court to hold a case management conference to establish the issues' (IR, Chapter 20, para 29).

STATEMENT OF TRUTH

All statements of case should be verified by a statement of truth. This is a statement that the party putting forward a document believes it to be true. It is usually signed by a party, litigation friend or legal representative (r 22.1(6)). Practice Direction 22, para 3.11 sets out who should sign the statement in the case of managing agents, trusts, companies, insurers, the Motor Insurers' Bureau, and in-house legal advisers.

If there is no signed statement of truth then the party cannot rely on the document as evidence of any of the matters set out in it, and/or a statement of case not so verified may be struck out (PD 22, para 4). The costs consequences for failing to verify a statement of case are set out at PD 22, para 4.3, and will usually mean that the costs will have to be paid by the party who failed to verify in any event and forthwith. The effect of having the signed statement of truth is to turn the statement of case into evidence that can be used to support an application such as for summary judgment.

The form of statement is (PD 22, para 2):

I believe [or, as the case may be, 'the claimant believes'] that the facts in this [name of document being verified] are true.

A false statement amounts to a contempt (r 32.14), so practitioners are advised that only those with direct knowledge of the facts should actually sign the statement of truth, although the form of the statement of truth does allow the signatory to say that 'the claimant believes' it to be true. Practitioners cannot sign a witness statement other than their own. Where a party is legally represented, and the legal representative signs the statement of truth, it will be assumed that he did explain to the client beforehand the possible consequences if the statement turns out not to be true (PD 22, para 3.8). Note that the cost of using an affidavit instead of a statement verified under Part 22 can be recovered only if the rule or practice direction requires an affidavit (r 32.15(2)). The net result of this is that affidavits are now much less likely to be used.

The purpose of the requirement that a statement of case must be verified by a statement of truth was considered in *Clarke v Marlborough Fine Art (London) Ltd* [2002] 1 WLR 1731. It was stated in that case that the purpose of verification by a statement of truth was to eliminate claims in which a party had no honest belief. However, although a party is required to certify that the facts alleged in the statement of case are true, he is not required to vouch for the legal consequences that he attaches to those facts, which is a matter for argument and for the decision of the court.

NOTICE OF FUNDING ARRANGEMENT

If a party has entered into a *funding arrangement* (conditional fee agreement providing for a success fee, or after the event legal expenses insurance), he must file at court and serve on the other parties a notice in Form N251 (PD 44, paras 19.1–19.2). Form N251 should be filed and served with the claim form, acknowledgment of service or defence, as the case may be, if a party is to ensure that he will be entitled to recover the additional liability from his opponent (see Chapter 4, 'Funding Litigation', for more details).

FURTHER INFORMATION

A party may require clarification of another party's case, or further information about it in order to prepare his own case or to understand the case he has to meet. A party can seek such clarification or further information about the other party's case even if the matter in question is not referred to in a statement of case (r 18.1). Part 18 therefore applies to both clarification of a party's pleaded case and further information about the other party's case, which is not confined to further information arising from matters pleaded in the statement of case.

This Part gives the court a broad discretion to order a party to provide further clarification and information about his case. However, the court is unlikely to support an unnecessarily excessive or burdensome request for further information which will not assist in clarifying the issues in dispute. In addition, careful consideration should be given to the efficacy of making a request before disclosure and the exchange of witness statements, as this may be considered premature (see *Hall v Selvaco* (1996) *The Times*, 27 March, CA, but note that this is a decision decided under the former rules).

A party making a request is known as the 'first party' and the party responding is known as the 'second party'.

The Request for further information

The party seeking clarification or further information should first seek to obtain it from the other party voluntarily. This should be done by means of service of a *Request* for clarification or information, stating a date, being a reasonable time to respond, by which the response to the Request should be served (PD 18, para 1.1).

All Requests should be concise and strictly confined to what is reasonably necessary and proportionate for that party to prepare his own case or understand the case he has to meet (PD 18, para 1.2).

If the Request and its reply are likely to be brief, the Request can be in the form of a letter, but otherwise it should be contained in a separate document (PD 18, para 1.4). If the Request is in the form of a letter, the letter should deal only with the Request, and it should state that it contains a Request made under Part 18 (PD 18, para 1.5). Where the Request is in a separate document, this may be prepared in such a way that the response can be given on the same document. This should be done by putting the numbered paragraphs of the Request on the left hand side of the page, so that the paragraphs of the response may be inserted on the right hand side of the page (PD 18, para 1.6(2)).

A Request, whether made by letter or in a separate document, must comply with the following requirements:

(a) it must be headed with the name of the court and the title and number of the claim;

(b) it must state in its heading that it is a Request made under Part 18, identify the first party and the second party and state the date when it is made;

(c) it must set out each request in a separate numbered paragraph;

(d) it must identify any document, relevant paragraph or words to which the Request relates; and

(e) it must state a date by which the first party expects a response (PD 18, para 1.6).

Responding to the Request

A response to a Request must be in writing, dated and signed by the second party or his legal representative (PD 18, para 2.1).

If the Request is contained in a letter, the response can also be by means of a letter, or in a separate document. If in a letter, it should identify itself as a response to the Request, and the letter should not deal with any other matter (PD 18, para 2.2).

If the Request is in a separate document, but not one which is divided into halves so that the response can be inserted into the document (see above), the response must comply with the following requirements:

(a) it must be headed with the name of the court and the title and number of the claim;

(b) it must state in its heading that it is a response to the Request;

(c) it must repeat the text of each separate paragraph of the Request and set out under each paragraph the response to it; and

(d) it must refer to and have attached to it a copy of any document not already in the possession of the first party which forms part of the response (PD 18, para 2.3).

The response to the Request, even if supplied voluntarily, will become a part of the second party's statement of case (r 2.3(1)). As it is a statement of case it will also need to be verified by a statement of truth (r 22.1). Also, the second party must, when he serves his response on the first party, serve on every other party and file with the court a copy of the Request and of his response (PD 18, para 2.4).

If the second party objects to complying with the Request, or is unable to do so at all or in the time specified, or if he considers that a response could be made only at disproportionate expense, he must notify the first party, with reasons, within the time specified for the response (PD 18, paras 4.1, 4.2).

Orders for further information

If the second party fails to provide a response to a Request voluntarily, the first party can apply to the court for an order that he provide the further information or clarification sought (r 18.1). The application is made in accordance with Part 23, and the application notice should specify the terms of the order and the matters in respect of which clarification or further information is sought. The first party should state whether a Request has been made and if not, why not, or alternatively explain what response was received to his Request, if any (PD 18, paras 5.2, 5.3).

If 14 days have elapsed since the service of the Request on the second party, and the time specified for a response has also elapsed, the first party can apply to the court, without notice to the second party, and the court may deal with the application without a hearing (PD 18, para 5.5). Otherwise the first party must apply to the court on notice to the second party (PD 18, para 5.6).

If the court makes an order for further information, the second party must file his response and serve it on the other parties within the time specified by the court (r 18.1(3)).

AMENDMENTS TO STATEMENTS OF CASE

A subsequent statement of case must not contradict or be inconsistent with an earlier one; for example, a reply to a defence must not bring in a new claim. Where new matters have come to light, the appropriate course may be to seek the court's permission to amend the statement of case (PD 16, para 9.2).

Amendments without permission

The previous, rather lax, system in the county court of allowing amendments without leave up to a return day has been tightened up. A statement of case which has not yet been served may always be amended, and no permission is required (r 17.1(1)).

However, if a statement of case is amended where permission is not required, the court can subsequently disallow the amendment (r 17.2(1)). If a party served with a statement of case which has been amended without the court's permission, wishes to apply for an order that the amendment be disallowed, he should do so within 14 days of service of the amended statement of case on him (r 17.2(2)).

A party is most likely to apply for such an order for the same reasons as he would oppose amendments to a statement of case where permission was required.

Amendments by consent or with permission

Once a statement of case has been served, it may be amended only if all the other parties to the proceedings provide their written consent, or the court gives permission for it to be amended (r 17.1(2)).

Consent of the parties

In most cases the best course for a party wishing to amend his statement of case is for him to seek the consent of all the other parties to the proceedings for him to do so (r 17.1(2)(a)). If the other parties to the proceedings are prepared to consent, the party wishing to make the amendment should draft a consent order to be signed by all the other parties, expressing their agreement to the amendment, and file this at court. The party filing the consent order will be required to pay a court fee of £30 (Supreme Court Fees (Amendment No 2) Order 2003 (SI 2003/717); County Court Fees (Amendment No 2) Order 2003 (SI 2003/718)).

Application for permission to amend

If the other parties will not, or are not asked to, consent to the amendment, the party wishing to amend must make an application to the court for permission to do so (r 17.1(2)(b)).

The party should file at court an application notice (in accordance with Part 23) and a copy of the statement of case with the proposed amendments (PD 17, para 1.2), along with the appropriate court fee, which will be £30 if the application is without notice or £60 if it is made on notice (Supreme Court Fees (Amendment No 2) Order 2003; County Court Fees (Amendment No 2) Order 2003).

The application can be dealt with either at a hearing, or without a hearing if the parties agree to it being so dealt with or the court thinks it would be appropriate to do so (PD 17, para 1.1).

When will amendments be allowed?

In general terms, but subject to the circumstances of the case, a party should consent to an amendment if he will suffer no prejudice as a result, or if the court is likely to give permission for the amendment to be made. For instance, if a claimant obtains new evidence that shows a further breach of contract not previously pleaded, the defendant should usually consent to such an amendment, particularly if the claimant could not have known of the further breach when the claim was originally made.

In the case of most applications for amendments to a statement of case the court has a discretion whether or not to grant permission for the amendment. The court must exercise its discretion in accordance with the overriding objective, and whether an amendment will be allowed at all depends on the circumstances of the case. However, different considerations apply where the limitation period for bringing a cause of action has expired (r 17.4).

In *Cobbold v Greenwich LBC* (2001) LTL, 24 May, the Court of Appeal held that the judge erred in law in the exercise of his discretion in refusing to allow the defendant to amend its defence. The court found that the judge had failed to take relevant matters into account. These included the fact that the claimant had known the facts of the defendant's amended case for a substantial period of time and that the reason why the amendment was made at a late stage was because the court office had not notified the defendant of the hearing date. When giving permission to the defendant to make the amendments, Gibson LJ said, 'There is always prejudice where a party is not allowed to put forward his real case, provided that that is properly arguable'. He was also of the opinion that:

> ... amendments in general ought to be allowed so that the real dispute between the parties can be adjudicated upon provided that any prejudice to the other party or parties caused by the amendment can be compensated for in costs, and the public interest in the efficient administration of justice is not significantly harmed.

Amending to plead inconsistent/alternative facts

A party will not be permitted to amend to add facts which are *inconsistent* with his original claim, as he will be unable to verify the amendment with a statement of truth that he believes the facts in the amended statement of case are true if they are inconsistent with the facts in the original claim (*Clarke v Marlborough Fine Art (London) Ltd*).

In *Clarke v Marlborough Fine Art (London) Ltd*, a claim was brought by the executor of the will of the artist, Francis Bacon, against the gallery, Marlborough, which had dealt with his paintings from 1968 until his death in 1992. The claimant wished to amend the particulars of claim to introduce a claim for actual undue influence in addition to the existing claim for breach of fiduciary duty and presumed undue influence already pleaded.

The claim for breach of fiduciary duty and presumed undue influence relied on the alleged fact that Francis Bacon maintained trust and confidence in Marlborough and relied upon them to give him a fair deal for his art work. However, the claim for actual undue influence relied on the alleged fact that during the same period of time Francis Bacon was blackmailed by Marlborough into remaining with them by a threat to expose his tax fraud and to deprive him of access to funds in his Swiss account if he took his work to another gallery which had offered him more advantageous terms.

The court found that as it was essential to the plea of blackmail that Francis Bacon knew that the terms offered by the other gallery were more advantageous than those offered by Marlborough, it was not possible for him at the same time to maintain the belief, necessary for his claim for breach of fiduciary duty and presumed undue influence, that Marlborough was giving him a fair deal. The court therefore refused to allow the particulars of claim to be amended to introduce an additional claim that was inconsistent with the original claim. However, the court was prepared to allow the claimant to amend the particulars of claim to plead the claim of actual undue influence in the *alternative* to the claim for breach of fiduciary duty and presumed undue influence. The court was of the opinion that if an alternative set of facts is clearly pleaded as an alternative then the claimant is not necessarily stating that he believes both sets of facts are true. Unless the alternative version of facts is unsupported by any evidence, and is therefore pure speculation or invention, then the claimant would be entitled to verify the alternative version of facts with a statement of truth.

It should be noted that this claim was decided at first instance and the judge expressly stated that he had reached his decision with hesitation and called for proper and clear guidance from the Civil Procedure Rule Committee on when a party would be entitled to plead alternative claims.

Stage of proceedings

In theory an amendment may be allowed at any stage of the proceedings up to, and even after, judgment has been delivered, but before it is sealed or perfected. However, an application made after judgment has been given is subject to a more stringent test than an application made prior to judgment being given (*Stewart v Engel & Hayward* [2000] 1 WLR 2268). In *Stewart v Engel & Hayward*, the claimant was granted permission by the trial judge to amend her statement of case to add a new claim after judgment had been delivered dismissing her claim but before the judgment was sealed. However, the Court of Appeal overturned the judge's decision to allow the amendment in that case.

The court held that in the circumstances of this case, the matter could not be looked at simply as a question of exercising a discretion to grant leave to amend. The judge had already pronounced judgment in favour of the defendants. Further, the judge had specifically inquired of the claimant's counsel during the defendants' application for summary judgment, and when judgment was pronounced, whether the amendment had been considered and whether it was going to be applied for, and was told that it had been considered and would not be applied for. The Court of Appeal held that a party seeking to reopen full and final judgment must be able to demonstrate that it is an exceptional case or that there are strong reasons for doing so, but in this case the claimant did not begin to do so. Examples of circumstances or strong reasons for reopening a judgment are a plain mistake on the part of the court; a failure of the parties to draw to the court's attention a fact or point of law that was plainly relevant; discovery of new facts subsequent to the judgment being given; or where a party is taken by surprise by a particular application in which the court ruled against him and he did not have a fair opportunity to consider (*Re Blenheim Leisure (Restaurants) Ltd (No 3)* (1999) *The Times*, 9 November).

In *Maguire v Molin* [2002] EWCA Civ 1083, the claimant started proceedings for personal injuries she suffered due to carbon monoxide poisoning caused by a defective heater in a flat rented from the defendant. The damages claimed were originally limited to £15,000 and the claim was allocated to the fast track. After liability was determined in favour of the claimant, the claimant made an application to amend her statement of case to include an additional claim for loss of earnings, which the claimant's solicitors had negligently failed to include when the claim was originally pleaded. The proposed amendments increased the value of the claimant's claim to approximately £80,000. The Court of Appeal upheld the trial judge's decision to refuse the claimant permission to amend her statement of case to include the additional claim for damages so that her claim was heard only in respect of the original statement of case. The court found that the defendant would be prejudiced by the amendment, because he might have deployed more resources in his defence if he had known from the outset that he was facing a claim for approximately £80,000 that would have been heard on the multi-track. Also, the court was of the opinion that if the amendment had been allowed, given the substantial increase in value, the district judge hearing the trial would have had no alternative but to re-allocate the claim to the multi-track and order a rehearing before a circuit judge. A decision to re-allocate at a very late stage would have caused considerable disruption to the progress of the litigation. The court held that the defendant should not be prejudiced by such an amendment when the need for the amendment arose from the claimant's solicitors' failure to make a proper appraisal of the true value of the claim in due time. In the circumstances the district judge was held to have been entitled to exercise his discretion to refuse to abort the trial at such a late stage and to keep the case in the fast track instead.

Amendments to add a new claim after the limitation period has expired

If the limitation period has expired and a party wishes to amend his statement of case to add or substitute a new claim, the court will be able to allow the amendment only if the new claim arises out of the same facts or substantially the same facts as a claim for which that party has already claimed a remedy in the proceedings (r 17.4(2)). This is a rule of substantive law under s 35 of the Limitation Act 1980. In

Abbey National plc v John Perry and Co and Others [2001] EWCA Civ 1630, the Court of Appeal affirmed the judge's decision that the proposed amendment did not add a new cause of action because the amendment, to insert a reference to an implied rather than a constructive trust, was not, in the circumstances, a matter of substance. The court also found that the new allegations were amplifications of the original pleading rather than new facts.

Rule 17.4(2) must be given effect to in a way which is compatible with the Convention rights incorporated into the Human Rights Act 1998. Accordingly, in *Goode v Martin* [2001] EWCA Civ 1899, the court interpreted r 17.4(2) consistently with the claimant's Art 6 right to a fair trial, so as to allow a claimant to amend her statement of case after the limitation period for her cause of action had expired to rely on facts not previously pleaded by her. The defendant had served an amended defence that for the first time pleaded his version of events which had previously been unknown to the claimant. The claimant wished to rely on the facts pleaded by the defendant in his defence, on the grounds that she could establish that the defendant was negligent even if his own version of events were accepted. The court held that r 17.4(2) should be read as if it included the words 'facts as are already in issue', which would therefore allow the claimant to amend her statement of case to rely on the facts alleged by the defendant in his amended defence. The principle in *Goode v Martin* was applied in *Hemmingway v Roddam* (2003) LTL, 18 September.

Amendments to correct the name of a party after the limitation period has expired

Where a party has made a mistake as to the name of a party, the court may allow an amendment to correct that mistake, but only where the mistake was genuine and was not one which would cause reasonable doubt as to the identity of the party in question (r 17.4(3)). Rule 17.4(3) therefore covers cases where the claimant misnames the defendant.

In *Gregson v Channel Four Television Corp* [2000] All ER (D) 956, the claimant had issued a claim for libel against *Channel Four Television Co Ltd*, a wholly-owned subsidiary of *Channel Four Television Corp*, when in fact the latter company had broadcast the offending programme. The defendants conceded that this was a mistake as to name that was genuine and not one which would cause reasonable doubt as to the identity of the party in question. The court therefore held that this was sufficient to enable the discretion under r 17.4(3) to be exercised so as to allow the claimant to amend to correct that mistake after the limitation period had expired.

Amendments to add, remove or substitute a party after the limitation period has expired

If a statement of case has been served, an application to amend it by removing, adding or substituting a party must be made in accordance with r 19.5.

In contrast to r 17.4, where the defendant is misnamed, r 19.5 applies to the more fundamental mistake of naming the wrong party as defendant, which can be cured only if a new party is substituted (see Chapter 14, 'Adding or Substituting a Party').

Amendments to the capacity of claimant after the limitation period has expired

The court may allow a party to amend in order to alter the capacity in which he claims if the new capacity is one that the party had when the proceedings started, or which he has since acquired (r 17.4(4)).

Amending the statement of case

Although the amended statement of case does not always need to show the original text that has been amended (PD 17, para 2.2), the usual practice is to leave the original text in the amended statement of case but strike it through in coloured ink.

Also, where the court thinks it desirable for the original text and the amendments to be shown, it will make an order either that the replacement text be inserted or underlined in colour and the deleted text struck through in colour, or that the amendments be shown by a numerical code in a monochrome computer-generated document (PD 17, para 2.2).

If the amendments are shown in colour the first amendment will be shown in red. If the statement of case is amended more than once, further amendments are made using different colours in the following order: green; violet; and yellow (PD 17, para 2.4).

If the substance of the statement of case is changed by reason of the amendment, the statement of case should be re-verified by a statement of truth (PD 17, para 1.4).

The order to amend

If permission to amend is granted, the party should file the amended statement of case at court within 14 days of the date of the order (PD 17, para 1.3).

A copy of the order and the amended statement of case should be served on every party to the proceedings, unless the court orders otherwise (PD 17, para 1.5). The court may give directions about service, for instance, as to the time limits within which the amended statement of case must be served (r 17.3(1)). Often, service of the amended statement of case is dispensed with where all the parties are already in receipt of a copy.

On granting permission to amend, the court also usually makes an order granting the other parties permission to amend their statements of case, if necessary, in order to respond to the amendment, and gives a time limit within which they must file and serve their amended statement of case (r 17.3(1)). For instance, if a new claim is added, the defendant will need to respond with an admission, a denial or a non-admission and provide any other details as specified in Part 16.

Under PD 17, para 2.1, the amended statement of case and the court copy must be endorsed with a statement in one of two forms. If permission was required, the endorsement should be as follows:

Amended [describe statement of case] by Order of [Master ...] [District
Judge ...] dated ...

If the court's permission was not required, the endorsement should be as follows:

Amended [describe statement of case] under CPR [r 17.1(1) or (2)(a)] dated ...

The endorsement is usually inserted by the court office at which the amended statement of case is filed.

Costs of the amendment

In most cases where an amendment is applied for, the party applying will be responsible for the costs of and occasioned by the amendment. If a party seeks the other party's consent to the amendment, consent is usually given on condition that the party wishing to make the amendment agrees to pay the costs caused by the amendment. In most cases such costs will not be substantial in any event.

However, the circumstances in which the amendment arises should be considered, as it may be more appropriate for an order for 'costs in the case' to be made if, for instance, the need for the amendment arises as a result of the discovery of new loss or damage caused by the other party's breach which was not known about at the time of the original claim.

CHAPTER 13

PART 20 CLAIMS

INTRODUCTION

Any claim other than a claim by a claimant against a defendant is a Part 20 claim (r 20.2(1)). Part 20 claims include counterclaims made by a defendant against a claimant (or other party); claims for contributions and indemnities between co-defendants; and claims by a defendant against a non-party. The common use of the title 'Part 20' for these different types of claim has caused confusion and, in practice, legal representatives often refer to the former terminology – counterclaim, contribution or indemnity, and third party proceedings – in order to distinguish the type of Part 20 proceedings in question.

Scope of Part 20 claims

Part 20 claims fall into four categories:

- counterclaims against claimant(s);
- counterclaims against claimant(s) and a non-party;
- claims for contribution or indemnity made between defendants to the claim;
- any other claim made by a defendant against a non-party (r 20.2(1)).

Any person who becomes a defendant to a Part 20 claim may himself bring a similar claim against another (whether or not already a party), and this too will be a Part 20 claim.

Court fees on filing of Part 20 claim

Where the Part 20 claim is a counterclaim, the court fee payable on filing the counterclaim at court is the same as if the counterclaim was a claim made in separate proceedings (Supreme Court Fees Order 1999 (SI 1999/687), r 1.4; County Court Fees Order 1999 (SI 1999/689), r 1.5).

However, where the Part 20 claim is a claim against a party or parties not named in the original proceedings, the court fee payable is £30 (Supreme Court Fees Order 1999, para 1.3; County Court Fees Order 1999, r 1.4).

CPR applying to Part 20 claims

The Civil Procedure Rules (CPR) apply generally to Part 20 claims as if they were claims (r 20.3(1); PD 20, para 3). However, by r 20.3(2), the following rules do not apply to Part 20 claims:

(a) rr 7.5 and 7.6 (time within which a claim form must be served);

(b) r 16.3(5) (statement of value where claim to be issued in the High Court); and

(c) Part 26 (case management – preliminary stage);

and by r 20.3(3) and (4) the following rules do not apply except where the Part 20 claim is a counterclaim:

(a) Part 12 (default judgment); and

(b) Part 14 (admissions), except r 14.1(1) and (2) (which provide that a party may admit in writing the truth of another party's case) and r 14.3 (admission by notice in writing – application for judgment).

Title to Part 20 proceedings

Practice Direction 20 sets out the requirements for the title to Part 20 proceedings. Accordingly, when filing a Part 20 claim the title should contain:

(a) the full name of each party; and

(b) his status in the proceedings (for example, claimant, defendant, Part 20 claimant, Part 20 defendant), for example:

AB claimant

CD defendant/Part 20 claimant

EF Part 20 defendant

(PD 20, para 7.1.)

Where a defendant makes a counterclaim not only against the claimant but also against a non-party the title should show this as follows:

AB claimant/Part 20 defendant

CD defendant/Part 20 claimant

and

XY Part 20 defendant

(PD 20, para 7.2.)

Where there is more than one Part 20 claim, the parties to the first Part 20 claim should be described as 'Part 20 claimant (1st claim)' and 'Part 20 defendant (1st claim)'; the parties to the second Part 20 claim should be described as 'Part 20 claimant (2nd claim)' and 'Part 20 defendant (2nd claim)', and so on. For example:

AB	claimant and Part 20 defendant (2nd claim)
CD	defendant and Part 20 claimant (1st claim)
EF	Part 20 defendant (1st claim) and Part 20 claimant (2nd claim)
GH	Part 20 defendant (2nd claim)

(PD 20, para 7.3.)

Where the full name of a party is lengthy it must appear in the title, but thereafter in the statement of case it may be identified by an abbreviation such as initials or a recognised shortened name (PD 20, para 7.4).

In recognition of the confusion that can occur in identifying the parties to Part 20 proceedings, PD 20 provides that where a party to the proceedings has more than one status, for example, claimant and Part 20 defendant (2nd claim) or Part 20 defendant (1st claim) and Part 20 claimant (2nd claim), the combined status must appear in the title but thereafter it may be convenient to refer to the party by name, for example, Mr Smith, or, if the name is lengthy, by initials or a shortened name (PD 20, para 7.5).

COUNTERCLAIMS

A defendant to a claim may bring a counterclaim against the claimant in respect of the same subject matter of the claim or in respect of any other matter, whether related to the claimant's claim or not.

Circumstances where permission required to make a counterclaim

A defendant may make a counterclaim against a claimant without the court's permission if he files it with his defence (r 20.4(2)(a)). If a defendant wishes to make a counterclaim against the claimant at any other time after filing his defence he must seek the court's permission to do so (r 20.4(2)(b)).

However, the court's permission is required if the defendant wishes to make a counterclaim against a person other than the claimant (r 20.5(1)).

A party to a Part 8 claim may not make a counterclaim, or any other Part 20 claim, without first obtaining the court's permission (r 8.7).

In *Sterling Credit Ltd v Rahman* [2001] 1 WLR 496, the Court of Appeal gave the defendant permission to make a counterclaim against the claimant even though the claimant had already obtained a possession order against the defendant. The defendant had entered into a loan agreement secured by a legal charge on his property. As a result of arrears a possession order was obtained against the defendant. However, the defendant still made monthly instalments and was in occupation of the property. The defendant applied to set aside the possession order and for permission to file a counterclaim alleging that the loan agreement was an extortionate credit bargain under s 139 of the Consumer Credit Act (CCA) 1974.

The Court of Appeal held that the claim was not at an end. The claimant continued to accept monthly payments and the defendant continued to occupy the property. Although judgment for possession had been obtained it had not been satisfied, and it could not be satisfied without a further application to the court for a warrant of execution. Such an application would fall within the definition of proceedings to enforce the security relating to the credit bargain within the meaning of s 139(1)(b) of the CCA 1974. In the circumstances, including the connection between the subject matter of the claim and counterclaim and the ability of the court to deal with the case expeditiously and fairly within the same proceedings, the defendant was given permission to make the counterclaim.

Form of counterclaim and the reply

The response pack sent out by the court with the claim form to a defendant includes a section for the making of a counterclaim against the claimant. Ironically, a response pack, indicating the need to serve and file a defence to the counterclaim, is not provided for the recipient of a Part 20 counterclaim, which may cause problems when it comes to filing a defence and thereby avoiding judgment in default.

However, where a defence and counterclaim are filed by the defendant, the practice in many courts is to specify in the court order notifying the claimant that a defence has been filed the date by which the claimant must file a defence to the counterclaim. The date for the claimant to file a defence to counterclaim is usually the same date as that by which the claimant must file a completed allocation questionnaire at court.

The defendant makes a counterclaim by filing particulars of the counterclaim at court (r 20.4(1)). A counterclaim is a statement of case and, therefore, subject to the requirements of Part 16 (see Chapter 12, 'Statements of Case').

The defendant can make a counterclaim against the claimant in respect of any cause of action whether or not it is connected to the claimant's claim against him. However, if the counterclaim is in respect of a totally unrelated matter, the court is likely to order that it be dealt with separately and not as part of the claimant's claim.

Where a defendant to a claim serves a counterclaim, the defence and counterclaim should normally form one document with the counterclaim following on from the defence (PD 20, para 6.1).

Where a claimant serves a reply and a defence to counterclaim, the reply and the defence to counterclaim should normally form one document with the defence to counterclaim following on from the reply (PD 20, para 6.2).

As a Part 20 claim is a statement of case it must be verified by a statement of truth (r 22.1; PD 20, para 4.1). The form of the statement of truth should be as follows: '[I believe] [the [Part 20 claimant] believes] that the facts stated in this statement of case are true.' (PD 20, para 4.2.)

Counterclaims against non-party

Permission is always required to bring a new party into existing proceedings, and accordingly a defendant must apply for permission to make a counterclaim against a party other than the claimant (r 20.5(1)).

If the court grants permission, it will also give directions as to the management of the case (r 20.5(3)).

The application must be made under Part 23 and can be made without notice. However, if the court grants permission following an application without notice, the joined party can apply for the order to be set aside (r 23.10).

CLAIMS FOR A CONTRIBUTION OR INDEMNITY FROM A CO-DEFENDANT

A defendant who has filed an acknowledgment of service or a defence may make a Part 20 claim for a contribution or indemnity against a co-defendant to the claim (r 20.6(1)).

The claim is made by filing a notice containing a statement of the nature and grounds of the claim for a contribution or indemnity and serving it on the defendant to the Part 20 claim (r 20.6(1)).

A defendant may make a claim for a contribution or indemnity against a co-defendant without the court's permission if he files and serves a notice with his defence (r 20.6(2)(a)(i)).

If the defendant's claim for a contribution or indemnity is against a defendant added to the claim at a later stage, he may make that claim without permission if he files and serves a notice within 28 days after that defendant files his defence (r 20.6(2)(a)(ii)). At any other time the defendant must seek the court's permission to file a notice seeking a contribution or indemnity against a co-defendant (r 20.6(2)(b)).

A claim for contribution arises only if there is liability in respect of 'the same damage'. Under s 1(1) of the Civil Liability (Contribution) Act 1978, the words 'the same damage' are to be given their ordinary and natural meaning, and therefore are not to be interpreted as meaning substantially or materially similar damage. In *Royal Brompton Hospital NHS Trust v Hammond and Others* [2002] UKHL 14; [2002] 2 All ER 801, the employer had claims against the contractor in a building contract for delay and against the architect for negligent design and construction. The damage flowing from these claims was not the same; accordingly the judge struck out a Part 20 claim by the contractor for contribution from the architect. The House of Lords ruled that the strike out was correct.

OTHER PART 20 CLAIMS

A Part 20 claim other than a counterclaim or a claim for a contribution or indemnity against a co-defendant may be brought by a defendant against any person who is not already a party to the proceedings for a contribution, or indemnity or some other remedy (r 20.7). Such claims were formerly known as 'third party claims'.

This type of Part 20 claim is made when the court issues a Part 20 claim form (r 20.7(2)). It may be made without permission if it is issued before or at the same time as the defendant files his defence (r 20.7(3)(a)). If a defendant wishes to make such a Part 20 claim at any other time he must seek the court's permission to do so (r 20.7(3)(b)).

PROCEDURAL REQUIREMENTS FOR PART 20 CLAIMS

Filing and service of Part 20 claims made without the court's permission

A counterclaim is made by filing particulars of the counterclaim at court (r 20.4(1)). The counterclaim must be served on every other party at the same time as the defence (r 20.8(1)(a)).

A defence to the counterclaim must be filed within 14 days of service of the counterclaim (rr 15.4, 20.3). Under r 20.4(3) an acknowledgment of service may not be filed in relation to a counterclaim, which is anomalous because it may be used for every other form of Part 20 claim, thereby giving the defendant to the Part 20 claim an additional 14 days in which to file a defence. A counterclaimant may therefore be in the position of having to file his allocation questionnaire before he knows how the claimant (defendant to counterclaim) pleads to the counterclaim. Indeed the court often directs the claimant to file a defence to counterclaim no later than the date specified for filing the allocation questionnaire.

A defendant who wishes to make a Part 20 claim for a contribution or indemnity from a co-defendant without the court's permission must file and serve a notice of such a Part 20 claim when he files and serves his defence (r 20.6(2)(i)). However, if his Part 20 claim is against a co-defendant who was added to the claim later, his notice of the Part 20 claim may be served within 28 days after that defendant files his defence (r 20.6(2)(ii)).

In the case of a Part 20 claim other than a counterclaim or a claim for a contribution of indemnity from a co-defendant, the Part 20 claim form must be served on the person against whom it is made within 14 days after the date on which the party making the Part 20 claim files his defence if it is to be made without the court's permission (r 20.8(1)(b)).

Where a Part 20 claim form is served on a person who is not already a party (which includes where a counterclaim is served on a person other than the claimant) it must be accompanied by:

(a) a form for defending the claim;

(b) a form for admitting the claim;

(c) a form for acknowledging service; and

(d) a copy of:

- every statement of case which has already been served in the proceedings; and

- such other documents as the court may direct (r 20.12).

Application for permission to make a Part 20 claim

Where a Part 20 claim is a counterclaim against a person other than the claimant, or any other type of Part 20 claim not made within the timescale specified by Part 20, a party wishing to make such a Part 20 claim must apply to the court for permission to do so (rr 20.4(2)(b), 20.5(1), 20.6(2)(b), 20.7(3)(b)).

An application for permission to make a Part 20 claim should be made in accordance with Part 23 and must be supported by evidence stating:

(a) the stage which the action has reached;

(b) the nature of the claim to be made by the Part 20 claimant or details of the question or issue which needs to be decided;

(c) a summary of the facts on which the Part 20 claim is based; and

(d) the name and address of the proposed Part 20 defendant (PD 20, para 2.1).

Where delay has been a factor contributing to the need to apply for permission to make a Part 20 claim, an explanation of the delay should be given in evidence (PD 20, para 2.2).

Where possible, when making the application the applicant should provide a timetable of the action to date (PD 20, para 2.3).

An application for permission to counterclaim against a person other than the claimant, and an application to join a third party under r 20.7, may be made without notice (rr 20.5(2), 20.7(5)).

Permission to make a Part 20 claim involves an application supported by elaborate evidence, and accordingly it is obviously strongly advisable to serve all Part 20 claims with the defence if at all possible, although it should be remembered that permission is always required where the defendant wishes to counterclaim against a person other than the claimant. The application is likely to be dismissed if not supported by the mandatory supporting evidence required by PD 20, para 2.

When considering the application for permission to make a Part 20 claim the court will take into account the matters set out at r 20.9(2) (see below, 'Decision as to whether Part 20 claim should be heard with the main claim').

Where the court gives permission to make a Part 20 claim, it will at the same time give directions as to the service of the Part 20 claim (r 20.8(3)).

Decision as to whether Part 20 claim should be heard with the main claim

Although in some circumstances a party can make a Part 20 claim without permission, the court retains the power to decide subsequently to dismiss the Part 20 claim or to require it to be dealt with separately from the claim by the claimant against the defendant (rr 3.1(2)(e), (j), 20.9(1)). In particular, the addition by the defendant of a counterclaim against a person other than the claimant, or the joining in of a third party to the proceedings, is likely to increase the cost and complexity of the proceedings and may cause the hearing of the claimant's claim to be delayed. The claimant may therefore be motivated to apply to the court for the Part 20 claim to be heard separately from the main claim.

Whenever the court is considering whether to give permission for a Part 20 claim to be made, or to dismiss it or require it to be dealt with separately, it may have regard to the matters set out in r 20.9(2). Those are:

(a) the connection between the Part 20 claim and the claim made by the claimant against the defendant;

(b) whether the Part 20 claimant is seeking substantially the same remedy which some other party is claiming from him; and

(c) whether the Part 20 claimant wants the court to decide any question connected with the subject matter of the proceedings:

- not only between existing parties but also between existing parties and a person not already a party; or

- against an existing party not only in a capacity in which he is already a party but also in some further capacity.

The court has a wide discretion to make a decision in order to ensure that the proceedings are dealt with justly in accordance with the overriding objective. For an example of a decision where the court exercised its discretion to give a defendant permission to make a counterclaim, see *Sterling Credit Ltd v Rahman*, considered above at p 203, 'Circumstances where permission required to make a counterclaim'.

Case management under Part 20

If a defence to a Part 20 claim is filed, the case will be referred to the procedural judge for him to consider giving management directions (r 20.13(1)). Note that under r 20.3(2)(c), Part 26 (Allocation) does not apply to Part 20 claims. However, the judge must ensure that, so far as practicable, the Part 20 claim and the main claim are managed together (r 20.13(2)).

Where a Part 20 defendant files a defence other than to a counterclaim, the court will arrange a hearing to consider case management of the Part 20 claim (PD 20, para 5.1). The court will give notice of the hearing to each party likely to be affected by any order made at the hearing (PD 20, para 5.2).

At the case management hearing the court may:

(a) treat the hearing as a summary judgment hearing;

(b) order that the Part 20 proceedings be dismissed;

(c) give directions about the way any claim, question or issue set out in or arising from the Part 20 claim should be dealt with;

(d) give directions as to the part, if any, the Part 20 defendant will take at the trial of the claim;

(e) give directions about the extent to which the Part 20 defendant is to be bound by any judgment or decision to be made in the claim (PD 20, para 5.3).

Default judgment in Part 20 claims

Judgment in default under Part 12 applies to a Part 20 claim only if it is a counterclaim (r 20.3(3)). Also, the same provisions apply to counterclaims as to any other application for summary judgment, including the provision that if the counterclaim is for money, or delivery of goods where the defendant (to the counterclaim) is given the alternative of paying the value of the goods, judgment can be entered administratively (see Chapter 22, 'Judgment in Default').

There is no provision for any form of default judgment or other consequence for failure to file a defence in the case of a claim by a defendant for a contribution or indemnity against a co-defendant under r 20.6 (r 20.11(1)(a)(ii)).

In the case of any other Part 20 claim (except a counterclaim, or a claim for a contribution or indemnity from a co-defendant), if the party against whom a Part 20 claim is made fails to file an acknowledgment of service or defence the following consequences apply:

(a) the defendant is deemed to admit the Part 20 claim;

(b) the defendant is bound by any judgment in the main proceedings so far as it is relevant to the Part 20 claim (r 20.11(2)(a)).

Further, if the claimant obtains default judgment against the Part 20 claimant, where the Part 20 defendant has not filed an acknowledgment of service or a defence, the Part 20 claimant may obtain judgment in respect of the Part 20 claim by filing a request in the relevant practice form (r 20.11(2)(b)). However, the Part 20 claimant will be able to enter such judgment only with the court's permission if he has not satisfied the default judgment obtained against him by the claimant, or if he wishes to obtain judgment against the Part 20 defendant for any other remedy apart from a contribution or an indemnity (r 20.11(3)). The court also has the power to set aside or vary such judgment entered against the Part 20 defendant (r 20.11(5)).

CHAPTER 14

ADDING OR SUBSTITUTING A PARTY

INTRODUCTION

There are no limits to the number of claimants or defendants who may be joined as parties to a claim (r 19.1). It may become apparent, after proceedings have been issued, that another party should be added to the proceedings, or that a party should be substituted for an existing party or that an existing party should be removed from the proceedings.

Part 19 and its accompanying practice directions govern the procedure that should be followed. In general terms the court has a wide discretion, which it will exercise in accordance with the overriding objective, to add, substitute or remove a party from proceedings, but the court has a much more limited power to add or substitute new parties after the limitation period for the relevant cause of action has expired.

ADDITION, SUBSTITUTION AND REMOVAL OF PARTIES BEFORE THE END OF A RELEVANT LIMITATION PERIOD

Parties may be added, substituted or removed in existing proceedings either on the court's own initiative, in the exercise of its case management functions, or on the application of an existing party or of a party who wishes to become a party (PD 19, para 1.1). In broad terms the test is whether it is *desirable* for the party to be added, substituted or removed in order to resolve the matters in dispute in the proceedings between the correct parties. This gives the court a wide discretion to make an appropriate decision suitable to the circumstances of the case.

Addition of parties

A party may be added as a new party to existing proceedings if it is desirable to add the new party so that the court can resolve all the matters in dispute in the proceedings, or there is an issue involving the new party and an existing party which is connected to the matters in dispute in the proceedings, and it is desirable to add the new party so that the court can resolve that issue (r 19.2(2)).

For instance, in the case of *World Wide Fund for Nature v World Wrestling Federation v THQ/Jakks Pacific* [2002] EWHC 2580, THQ/Jakks Pacific was added as a third party and made an application in existing proceedings between the World Wide Fund for Nature and the Wrestling Federation. THQ/Jakks Pacific applied for a declaration that it was not in breach of an injunction obtained by the World Wide Fund for Nature against the World Wrestling Federation by producing video games that were embedded with the 'WWF' logo. When the court at first instance refused to grant the declaration and THQ/Jakks Pacific appealed, the World Wrestling Federation was allowed to join in the appeal proceedings as an intervener as the outcome directly affected its liability to THQ/Jakks Pacific with whom it had a licence agreement (*World Wide Fund for Nature v World Wrestling Federation v THQ/Jakks Pacific* [2003] EWCA Civ 401).

In *Earl of Portsmouth v Hamilton v Al Fayed* (2000) *The Times*, 13 October, the Earl of Portsmouth, who had contributed £100,000 to Neil Hamilton's 'fighting fund' for his unsuccessful defamation action against Mohammed Al Fayed, applied to be joined as a party to Mr Hamilton's application for permission to appeal against the judgment. The Earl of Portsmouth submitted that as he was a funder of Mr Hamilton's unsuccessful action, Mr Al Fayed might seek an order against him under s 51 of the Supreme Court Act 1981 that, as a non-party, he was liable to pay the costs of the action. He therefore had an interest in the outcome of any appeal. However, the Court of Appeal held that that risk was taken by anyone who chose to fund someone else's litigation and did not entitle the funder of the litigation to be joined as a party to the substantive hearing, otherwise anyone could buy the right to take part in litigation by funding it (see Chapter 34, 'Costs of Proceedings', for the decision as to whether Mr Hamilton's funders were liable to pay Mr Al Fayed's costs under s 51 of the 1981 Act).

Joint entitlement to a remedy

Where a claimant claims a remedy to which some other person is jointly entitled with him, the other person jointly entitled must be made a party to the proceedings, unless the court orders otherwise (r 19.3(1)). This will apply, for instance, where more than one person enters into a contract and wishes to sue the other parties to the contract for a remedy under the contract.

If any person jointly entitled to a remedy does not agree to be joined as a claimant, he must be made a defendant unless the court orders otherwise (r 19.3(2)).

Under r 19.3(3), this rule does not apply in probate proceedings where, for instance, parties jointly entitled under a will bring proceedings to contest the entitlement of the other party.

Substitution of parties

A new party may be substituted for an existing one if the existing party's interest or liability has passed to the new party and it is desirable to substitute the new party so that the court can resolve the matters in dispute in the proceedings (r 19.2(4)).

Indeed, if the existing party's interest or liability has passed to a new party, an application should be made to substitute the new party, as otherwise the proceedings may not be effective by or against the existing party (PD 19, para 5.1).

Removal of parties

The court may order that any party cease to be a party if it is not desirable for that person to be a party to the proceedings (r 19.2(3)).

PROCEDURE TO ADD, SUBSTITUTE OR REMOVE A PARTY

Adding, substituting or removing a party before service of the claim form

A claimant can add, substitute or remove a party without the permission of the court as long as the claim form has not been served (r 19.4(1)).

Adding, substituting or removing a party after service of the claim form

Once the claim form has been served, a party must obtain the court's permission to add, substitute or remove a party (r 19.4(1)). The application for permission may be made by an existing party, or by a person who wishes to become a party (r 19.4(2)).

Adding or substituting a party as claimant

A party cannot be added to proceedings as claimant without his written consent. Therefore, when applying to add or substitute a party as claimant, the signed, written consent of the proposed claimant must be filed at court with the application (r 19.4(4)). Until the signed, written consent of the proposed new claimant has been filed at court, any order to add or substitute a party as claimant will not take effect (PD 19, para 2.2).

The party applying to add or substitute a new party as claimant must file at court the application notice, the proposed amended claim form and particulars of claim, and the signed written consent of the proposed new claimant (PD 19, para 2.1).

If the court makes an order adding or substituting a new claimant it will usually direct that a copy of the statements of case and any documents referred to in any statement of case must be served on the new claimant. The party who made the application will also usually be ordered to file an amended claim form and particulars of claim with the court within 14 days (PD 19, para 2.3).

Adding or substituting a party as defendant

A new defendant does not become a party to the proceedings until the amended defence has been served on him (*Ketteman v Hansel Properties Ltd* [1987] AC 189, HL, as referred to in PD 19, para 3.3).

Where the court makes an order adding or substituting a party as a defendant it will usually order the claimant to serve the amended claim form and particulars of claim, the response pack and any documents referred to in any statement on the new defendant and any other defendants to the proceedings (PD 19, para 3.2).

The claimant will also usually be ordered to file an amended claim form and particulars of claim with the court within 14 days (PD 19, para 3.2).

Adding a party after judgment

On the true construction of Part 19, the relevant question is whether, after judgment has been given, the proceedings are still continuing, namely, whether they are 'existing'. *Prima facie*, the court has the power, in a proper case, to add a party for the purposes of execution. However, the court will not allow a party to amend a cause of action once judgment has been passed by adding fresh parties, since that amounts to an abuse of process (*Kooltrade Ltd v XTS Ltd and Others* [2001] ECDR 11; [2001] FSR 13, Ch D (Pat Ct)).

The application to add or substitute a party

An application to add or substitute a party must be made in accordance with Part 23. The application notice in Form N244 should be filed at court and served on the proposed new party and all the other parties to the proceedings (PD 19, para 1.4). However, where an existing party's interest or liability has passed to a new party, an application to substitute the new party can be made without notice to the other parties (r 19.4(3)).

In all cases the application should be supported by evidence setting out the proposed new party's interest in or connection with the claim (r 19.4(3); PD 19, para 1.3). Where the interest or liability of an existing party has passed to some other party the supporting evidence should show what stage the proceedings have reached and what change has occurred to cause the transfer of interest or liability to the new party (PD 19, para 5.2).

If all the existing parties and the proposed new party agree to the addition or substitution of the party, the application may be dealt with without a hearing (PD 19, para 1.2).

In *Borealis AB v Stargas Ltd and M/V 'Berge Sisar'* [2002] EWCA Civ 757, a party made an application, a few months before the date fixed for trial, to join another party to the claim. One of the other existing parties to the proceedings objected because it meant that the trial date would be adjourned. The Court of Appeal upheld the judge's decision to refuse the application. The court stressed that the question of joinder was a case management decision that was peculiarly in the judge's discretion and, in accordance with general principles, it would be slow to interfere with that exercise of discretion.

The court found in this case that there had been no adequate explanation as to why it took the party a year, after it became aware of the need to join another party, for it to make the application. The court held that against the background of an increasingly imminent trial date, the importance in such circumstances of a proper and frank explanation of the reason for the delay should not be underestimated. The danger is that if the delay is for tactical reasons, such reasons should not justify disrupting the trial. It was of the opinion that, whether as a matter of fairness, proportionality, or overall justice, the court is not able to take a safe decision on such questions without a proper explanation.

The court accepted that a party may have a delicate line to tread between privilege and candour, but felt that if a party asks for a special dispensation to be shown, for example the joinder of a new party to long-existing proceedings, close to the trial date, then the party must carefully consider how candid it can be with the court. Although a party is fully entitled to rest on its privilege, if it does the court is not assisted with an explanation. The Court of Appeal therefore held that it was not proportionate, fair or just to increase the costs of the claim and put off the imminent trial for an uncertain period of one or two years, or even more, in order to allow the applicant to join another party to the proceedings.

Order giving permission to add or substitute a party

The order giving permission to add or substitute a party will be drawn up and served by the court on every other party to the proceedings and any other person affected by the order, unless the party making the application wishes to serve it or the court orders otherwise (r 19.4(5); PD 19, para 1.5).

Order removing a party from proceedings

Where the court makes an order removing a party from the proceedings, the claimant must file at court an amended claim form and particulars of claim. A copy of the order removing the party must be served on every party to the proceedings and any other person affected by the order (PD 19, para 4).

Costs of application to add, substitute or remove a party

The court will usually order that the party applying for an order to add, substitute or remove a party must pay the costs incurred, including the costs of the other parties to the proceedings incurred as a result of the order. However, costs are in the discretion of the court and a different order may be made if, for instance, the need for the amendment to add, substitute or remove a party arose through no fault of the party requesting the amendment.

Joining the Crown to a human rights claim

The court may not make a declaration of incompatibility in accordance with s 4 of the Human Rights Act (HRA) 1998 unless 21 days' notice, or such other period of notice as the court directs, has been given to the Crown (r 19.4A(1)). Where notice has been given to the Crown, a minister, or other person permitted by the HRA 1998, will be joined as a party on giving notice to the court (r 19.4A(2)).

The formal notice required by both r 19.4A and the HRA 1998 should always be given by the court, because the court is in the best position to assess whether there is a likelihood of a declaration of incompatibility being made. The party intending to raise the issue of compatibility should, nevertheless, give informal notice of its intention to do so to both the court and the Crown at the earliest possible opportunity, so as to give as much notice as possible. Both notices to the Crown should be given to the person named in the list published under s 17 of the Crown Proceedings Act 1947 (see PD 19, para 6.6 and the guidance given in *Poplar Housing and Regeneration Community Association Ltd v Donoghue* [2001] EWCA Civ 595; [2002] QB 48, CA).

Supply of documents to new parties

Where a party is added or substituted as a party, he can insist that the party joining him to the proceedings supply him, without charge, and within 48 hours of his written request, with a copy of all orders made in the proceedings along with all statements of case, written evidence and any documents appended to statements of case which relate to any issues between the joining party and the party joined (PD 5, para 3.1).

If a party joined is not supplied with those documents within 48 hours of his written request, he can apply to the court under Civil Procedure Rules (CPR) Part 23 for an order that they be supplied (PD 5, para 3.2).

Special provisions about adding or substituting parties after the end of the relevant limitation period

When a party applies to add or substitute a party after the end of a relevant limitation period different considerations apply because the application is governed by the substantive law relating to limitation periods as contained in the Limitation Act 1980 and the Foreign Limitation Periods Act 1984.

Under s 35(6) of the Limitation Act 1980, after the limitation period has expired the test is no longer whether it is *desirable* to add or substitute a party but whether it is *necessary* to add or substitute a party. Further, the circumstances when it will be *necessary* to add or substitute a party are clearly defined and very limited.

Accordingly, after the limitation period has expired the court may add or substitute a party only if the limitation period was current when the proceedings were started and the addition or substitution is necessary (r 19.5(2)). The addition or substitution will be necessary in only three circumstances, namely, where the court is satisfied that:

(a) the new party is to be substituted for a party who was named in the claim form in mistake for the new party;

(b) the claim cannot properly be carried on by or against the original party unless the new party is added or substituted as claimant or defendant; or

(c) the original party has died or had a bankruptcy order made against him and his interest or liability has passed to the new party (r 19.5(3)).

The court maintains a discretion whether to add or substitute a party even if the provisions of r 19.5 are satisfied, and will exercise its discretion in accordance with the overriding objective taking into account the circumstances of the particular case.

Party named in the claim form by mistake

In *SmithKline Beecham plc v Horne-Roberts* [2001] EWCA Civ 2006, the court considered the nature of the 'mistake' which empowers the court under r 19.5, if it sees fit, to allow the substitution of a new party after the limitation period has expired.

In that case the claimant, who was vaccinated against measles, mumps and rubella (MMR), alleged that due to defects in the vaccine he had become autistic. At the time, MMR vaccines were manufactured by three pharmaceutical companies, including SmithKline Beecham. The claimant's solicitors correctly identified the batch number of the vaccine as No 108A41A, but mistakenly attributed it to Merck, one of the other two pharmaceutical companies manufacturing the vaccine, and therefore commenced proceedings against the wrong defendant. However, the claimant's solicitors were notified of their mistake, and that SmithKline Beecham were the manufacturers of the claimant's vaccine, only after the limitation period under s 11A(3) of the Limitation Act 1980 had expired. The claimant applied under r 19.5(3)(a) to substitute SmithKline Beecham as the defendant to its proceedings.

The Court of Appeal held that the claimant was entitled to rely on r 19.5 and amend the name of the defendant to SmithKline Beecham, because although the claimant wrongly named the manufacturer as Merck, his intention was always to sue the person meeting a particular description specific to his case, namely, the manufacturer of vaccine batch No 108A41A.

In order to identify whether r 19.5(3)(a) was satisfied, the Court of Appeal endorsed the test formulated by Stocker LJ in *The 'Sardinia Sulcis' and 'Al Tawwab'* [1991] 1 Lloyd's Rep 201, namely: 'can the intending claimant or defendant be identified by reference to a description which is specific to the particular case, eg, landlord, employers, shipowners, manufacturers of a particular vaccine?' (Although that case was decided under the former rules it is, it is submitted, still applicable because the former rule, equivalent to r 19.5, like the current rule, was designed to give effect to the provisions of s 35(6) of the Limitation Act 1980.)

It should be noted that the court has a discretion whether to exercise its power under r 19.5(3) even if the requirements of the rule are satisfied. In an appropriate case the court may refuse to exercise its discretion, where, for instance, the court is asked to substitute a new defendant unconnected with the original defendant and unaware of the claim until after the expiry of the limitation period.

Relationship between r 17.4 and r 19.5

Rule 19.5 applies where the application is to substitute a new party for a party who was mistakenly named in the claim form, whereas r 17.4(3) (amendments to statements of case after the end of a relevant limitation period) applies where the intended party was named in the claim form but there was a genuine mistake as to the name of the party and no one was misled. There is no significant conflict between the two rules (*International Distillers & Vintners Ltd (t/a Percy Fox & Co) v JF Hillebrand (UK) Ltd and Others* (2000) *The Times*, 25 January, QBD).

Rule 19.5 covers a more fundamental matter, where a new party is to be substituted (as in the case of *SmithKline Beecham plc v Horne-Roberts*, above), rather than the correction of a mistake as to a party's name. An example of the latter occurred in *David Gregson v Channel Four Television Corp* (2000) *The Times*, 11 August, CA. In that case the claimant issued a claim for libel against Channel Four Television Co Ltd, a wholly-owned subsidiary of Channel Four Television Corp, when in fact the latter company had broadcast the offending programme. The defendants conceded that this was a mistake as to name which was genuine and not one which would cause reasonable doubt as to the identity of the party in question. The court therefore exercised its discretion under r 17(4) to allow the claimant to amend the claim form to correct that mistake after the limitation period had expired.

Party's interest/liability passed to a new party

Where a party has taken over the interest or liability of another party, an application can be made to substitute it as the new party even after the limitation period has

expired, as long as the original claim was commenced within the limitation period
(r 19.5(3)(b); see *Industrie Chimiche Italia Centrale v Alexander GT Savlins and Sons
Maritime Co (The Choko Star)* [1996] 1 All ER 114, a case decided under similar
provisions of the former rules).

Death or bankruptcy

Where a party dies and his interest or liability passes to his estate, or a person is
made bankrupt and his interest or liability passes to the trustee in bankruptcy, the
party's estate or trustee in bankruptcy can be substituted as parties to the
proceedings even after the limitation period has expired (r 19.5(3)(c)).

Adding or substituting parties after the end of the limitation period in personal injury and fatal accident claims

The court also has a wide discretion in personal injury and fatal accident claims to
disapply ss 11 and 12 of the Limitation Act 1980 so as to allow the claimant to bring a
claim against a defendant even though the limitation period has expired, if it
appears equitable to the court to allow the claim to proceed (s 33 of the Limitation
Act 1980; r 19.5(4)).

Joining parties in claim for wrongful interference with goods

A claimant in a claim for wrongful interference with goods must, in the particulars of
claim, state the name and address of every person who, to his knowledge, has or
claims an interest in the goods and who is not a party to the claim (r 19.5A(1)). This
provision reduces the likelihood of there having to be more than one set of
proceedings.

Under r 19.5A(2), a defendant to a claim for wrongful interference with goods
may apply for a direction that another person be made a party to the claim to
establish whether the other person:

(a) has a better right to the goods than the claimant; or

(b) has a claim which might render the defendant doubly liable under s 7 of the
Torts (Interference with Goods) Act 1977.

Where the person referred to in r 19.5A(2) fails to attend the hearing of the
application, or to comply with any directions, the court may order that he is
deprived of any claim against the defendant in respect of the goods (r 19.5A(3)).

The application notice must be served on all parties and on the person referred to
in r 19.5A(2).

CHAPTER 15

PART 8 CLAIMS

INTRODUCTION

Although Lord Woolf recommended the introduction of a single method to start proceedings, the same procedure is not suitable for all claims. The procedure for bringing a claim under Part 7 is suitable for proceedings that are primarily concerned with disputed issues of fact. However, not all claims involve disputes of fact. The facts may be agreed and the dispute may be about the application of a point of law to those agreed facts or the construction of a document, such as a will or trust deed. Alternatively, the parties may need to apply to the court for approval of a settlement, such as for a child or patient, or to approve the exercise of a power vested in the party, for instance as a trustee, for which there may be no opponent, or to determine the terms of a new business tenancy. These types of claim would previously have been brought by originating summons in the High Court and originating application in the county court.

For those type of proceedings, the procedure followed when a Part 7 claim form is issued, geared as it is to identifying the factual issues in dispute and preparing for a hearing to decide the disputed issues of fact, would not be appropriate. Therefore, in order to provide an appropriate procedure for other types of claim, the Civil Procedure Rules (CPR) provide an 'alternative procedure for claims' under Part 8.

PART 8 CLAIMS

The Part 8 procedure should be used either where a claimant seeks the court's decision on a question which is unlikely to involve a substantial dispute of fact, or where the Part 8 procedure is specified for a particular type of proceedings (r 8.1(2), (6); PD 8, paras 1.1, 1.2).

This general rule is subject to any express prohibition in any rule or practice direction from using the Part 8 procedure for a particular type of claim. Further, the Part 8 procedure may be modified for particular types of claim, and any such modified procedure must be complied with (r 8.1(4), (6); PD 8, para 1.3). The Part 8 procedure is, for instance, specified for landlord and tenant claims under Part 56, but subject to modifications to accommodate those specialist proceedings.

Proceedings specifying the use of a Part 8 claim

Practice Direction 8 gives examples of when the procedure may be used:

(a) a claim by or against a child or patient which has been settled before the commencement of proceedings and the sole purpose of the claim is to obtain the approval of the court to the settlement;

(b) a claim for provisional damages which has been settled before the commencement of proceedings and the sole purpose of the claim is to obtain a consent judgment;

(c) provided there is unlikely to be a substantial dispute of fact, a claim for a summary order for possession against named or unnamed defendants occupying land or premises without the licence or consent of the person claiming possession (proceedings against squatters) (PD 8, para 1.4).

Practice Direction 8B sets out a list of all those proceedings where the Part 8 procedure *must* be used, modified if so specified, in accordance with a rule or practice direction relating to particular types of proceedings. It is divided into two sections, A and B. Section A applies to:

• all claims listed in Table 1 to the practice direction;

• claims where an Act provides that an application or claim is to be brought by originating summons; and

• claims or applications that before 26 April 1999 (the date of the coming into force of the CPR) would have been brought by originating summons, but provided that no other method of bringing the claim after 26 April 1999 is prescribed in a rule or practice direction (PD 8B, Section A1).

The matters listed in Table 1 are all *High Court* matters that were formerly governed by the Rules of the Supreme Court (now contained in Sched 1 to the CPR), and include some proceedings by and against the Crown and interpleader proceedings. The list of proceedings specified in Table 1 has steadily reduced as specific rules under the CPR have been formulated for particular types of proceedings (for example, possession matters which are now covered by Part 55).

Section B applies to:

• all claims listed in Table 2 to the practice direction;

• in the county court, claims for:

  ○ damages for harassment under s 3 of the Protection from Harassment Act 1997;

  ○ claims that before 26 April 1999 would have been brought in the High Court by originating motion, in the county court, by originating application or by petition, provided that no other procedure is prescribed in an Act, rule or practice direction.

The matters listed in Table 2 include applications and appeals to the High Court under various Acts, such as proceedings under s 85(7) of the Fair Trading Act 1973 and the Financial Services and Markets Act 2000, which were formerly governed by the Rules of the Supreme Court ('RSC', now contained in Sched 1 to the CPR). Table 2 also includes applications to the county court under various Acts, such as an application for an injunction under the Housing Act 1996, formerly governed by the County Court Rules ('CCR', now contained in Sched 2 to the CPR).

For those Part 8 claims identified in Table 2, the general Part 8 procedure is followed subject to some modifications. Where a numbered claim form is listed against the particular claim referred to in Table 2, that claim form must be used; if none is specified the Part 8 claim form must be used (PD 8B, para B.8).

When the court issues the claim form it will fix a date for the hearing and notify the parties accordingly (PD 8B, para B.9). The claim form must be served not less than 21 days before the hearing date (PD 8B, para B.10). The defendant is not required to file an acknowledgment of service (PD 8B, para B.12).

CPR Sched 2 CCR Ord 6 makes special provision for the contents and service of the particulars of claim in hire-purchase claims as well as special provisions relating to the venue for bringing proceedings and for periods of notice for hearings. Practice Direction 8B, paras B.2 and B.3 make it clear that the claimant must comply with any special provisions relating to particular types of proceedings but, subject to that, comply with the general provisions of the practice direction.

Failure to follow Part 8 procedure

In the case of *Hannigan v Hannigan* [2000] All ER (D) 693, the claimant used the wrong form to commence a Part 8 claim and made a number of other procedural errors, and the defendant applied to have the claim struck out on those grounds. The claimant had fully set out the nature of her claim against the defendant and, although the court did not condone sloppy practices, such as failing to follow the correct procedure, it held that it would not be in accordance with the overriding objective to strike out the whole proceedings for a mere procedural failure.

However, although in most cases substance will be more important than form when deciding whether proceedings should be struck out, the court did warn that there were plenty of other sanctions that the court would use to punish failures to comply with the rules. It should also be borne in mind that at the time the claimant started proceedings the CPR had been in force for only six weeks, and a court is likely to look much less favourably on a party's failure to follow the correct procedure now that the CPR have been in force for a number of years.

Part 20 claims

A party to a Part 8 claim may not make a Part 20 claim (counterclaims and other additional claims) without first obtaining the court's permission (r 8.7).

Differences between Part 7 and Part 8 claims

The main differences between the general procedure under Part 7 and the Part 8 procedure are that under Part 8:

- the claimant must file and serve any evidence on which he wishes to rely with the claim form;
- the defendant must file and serve any evidence on which he wishes to rely when he files and serves his acknowledgment of service;
- the acknowledgment is served by the defendant;
- a defence is not required;
- default judgment is not available;
- the claim is treated as allocated to the multi-track;
- the claimant must file and serve any evidence in reply within 14 days of service of the defendant's evidence (subject to agreement for an extension of time);
- the court may require or permit any party or witness to attend to give oral evidence or to be cross-examined.

A defendant may object to the use of the Part 8 procedure and the court has power, whether of its own motion or otherwise, to order that the procedure should cease to apply.

CONTENTS OF THE PART 8 CLAIM FORM

The Part 8 claim form should be in Form N208 and under r 8.2 *must* state:

(a) that Part 8 applies to the proceedings; and

(b) either the question which the claimant wants the court to decide, or the remedy which the claimant is seeking, with the legal basis for it.

Also, the Part 8 claim form *must* state such of the following as are applicable:

(a) any enactment under which the claim is being made;

(b) any representative capacity the claimant is claiming under;

(c) any representative capacity the defendant is being sued under (r 8.2; PD 8, para 2.2).

The Part 8 claim form must also comply with the requirements of any practice direction under which the claim is brought and which permits or requires the use of the Part 8 procedure (PD 8, para 2.2).

The Part 8 claim form must be verified by a statement of truth (r 22.1).

ISSUE OF A PART 8 CLAIM FORM

Part 8 proceedings are started when the Part 8 claim form is issued by the court. The same rules on issue and service of a claim form under Part 7 apply to a Part 8 claim form (PD 8, para 2.1). Therefore, the Part 8 claim form must be served on the defendant (if any) within four months of its being issued, or within six months if it is served out of the jurisdiction (r 7.5).

Additional information about a funding arrangement

If a party has entered into a funding arrangement, such as a conditional fee agreement which provides for a success fee, or after the event legal expenses insurance, he is required to give his opponent certain information about the funding arrangement. On issuing the Part 8 claim form, the claimant must file at court and serve on the other parties a notice containing information about the arrangement as specified in Form N251 (PD 44, paras 19.1–19.2). If the defendant has entered into a funding arrangement, he must file the notice in Form N251 when he files his acknowledgment of service.

In all other circumstances, for instance, if the funding arrangement is entered into after the claimant starts proceedings or after the defendant files his acknowledgment of service at court, a party must file and serve notice of the funding arrangement within seven days of entering into it (PD 44, Section 19.2(4)).

RESPONDING TO A PART 8 CLAIM FORM

Time and method for responding

If a defendant is served with a Part 8 claim form, he must file and serve an acknowledgment of service on every other party, not more than 14 days after service of the Part 8 claim form on him (r 8.3(1)). The acknowledgment of service should be in Form N210, but an informal document, such as a letter, will also be acceptable (PD 8, para 3.2). It should be noted that the defendant does not file or serve a defence to the Part 8 claim (r 8.9(a); PD 8, para 3.1).

Different time periods for acknowledging service apply where the claim form is served out of the jurisdiction and where it is served on an agent of a principal who is overseas (r 8.3(3)(a)).

Contents of the acknowledgment of service form

The defendant must indicate in the acknowledgment of service form whether he contests the claim (r 8.3(2)(a)). Also, if he seeks a different remedy to that set out in the claim form, he must state what that remedy is (r 8.3(2)(b)).

The acknowledgment of service form must be signed by the defendant or his legal representative and include the defendant's address for service (rr 8.3(3)(b) and 10.5).

Consequences of failure to respond to Part 8 claim form

If a defendant fails to file an acknowledgment of service to the Part 8 claim form within the time period specified, although the defendant may attend the subsequent hearing of the claim, he may not take part in it unless the court gives permission for him to do so (r 8.4). It should be noted that the claimant will not be able to enter judgment in default on the defendant's failure to file an acknowledgment of service.

Default judgment or judgment on an admission not applicable to Part 8 claims

Judgment in default under Part 12 is not available for proceedings commenced under Part 8 (r 8.1(5); PD 8, para 3.5). Nor can the claimant obtain judgment by request on an admission (r 8.9(b)).

DIRECTIONS IN PART 8 PROCEEDINGS

The court may give directions immediately a Part 8 claim form is issued, either on the application of a party or of its own initiative. This may include fixing a hearing date where there is no dispute, such as claims for the approval of child or patient settlements, or in claims where there is a dispute but a date for a hearing could be conveniently given, such as claims for mortgage possession or the appointment of a trustee (PD 8, para 4.1).

Where the court does not fix a hearing date when the Part 8 claim form is issued, it will give directions for the disposal of the claim as soon as practicable after the defendant has acknowledged service, or if the defendant fails to acknowledge service, after the time period for doing so has expired (PD 8, para 4.2).

Certain applications under Part 8 may not require a hearing, being dealt with on paper instead, such as a consent application under s 38 of the Landlord and Tenant Act 1954 (PD 8, para 4.3). However, in more complicated cases, the court may convene a directions hearing before giving directions (PD 8, para 4.4).

Allocation to a track

All Part 8 claims shall be treated as allocated to the multi-track, so the court does not have to apply Part 26 and decide to which track to allocate a claim (r 8.9(c)).

FILING AND SERVICE OF EVIDENCE

The claimant *must* file, and serve copies on every other party, any written evidence on which he intends to rely, at the same time as filing and serving the claim form (r 8.5(1) and (2)).

The defendant *must* file, and serve copies on every other party, any written evidence on which he intends to rely, when he files and serves his acknowledgment of service (r 8.5(3) and (4)).

If the defendant relies on written evidence, the claimant may, within 14 days of service of the evidence on him, file and serve on every other party further written evidence in reply (r 8.5(5) and (6)).

If a party fails to file and serve copies of the written evidence in accordance with the rules, he may not rely on it at the hearing unless the court gives permission (r 8.6(1)). However, the parties can agree in writing to grant each other extra time to file evidence: in the case of a defendant, up to a maximum of 14 days after he files his acknowledgment of service, so long as the written agreement to this effect is filed at court by the defendant at the same time as the acknowledgment of service; in the case of a claimant, the parties can agree in writing to extend the time for the claimant to file evidence in reply to the defendant's evidence up to a maximum of 28 days after the defendant serves his evidence on the claimant (PD 8, para 5.6).

If the other party will not agree, a party may apply to the court under Part 23 for an extension of time to serve and file evidence, or for permission to serve and file additional evidence (PD 8, para 5.5). If a party needs extra time to serve evidence, he should apply for it before the original time limit fixed by the rules expires, as the court is more likely to grant the extra time at that stage than if the application is made only after that time.

If it is deemed necessary for a party to give oral evidence at the hearing, the court will give directions requiring the attendance at the hearing of the witness who has given written evidence so that he is available for cross-examination (r 8.6(2) and (3)).

Written evidence will normally be in the form of a witness statement or affidavit (PD 8, para 5.2). The claimant may rely on the matters set out in his claim form as evidence if the claim form is verified by a statement of truth (r 8.5(7)).

ISSUE OF PART 8 CLAIM FORM WITHOUT NAMING DEFENDANTS

There are some circumstances when the court may give permission for a claim form to be issued under Part 8 without naming a defendant. An example is where a trustee wishes to bring or defend proceedings on behalf of a trust and seeks the court approval to do so in order to protect his position on costs. Such an application will be made to court without naming a defendant and is known as a *'Beddoe'* application after the case of *Re Beddoe, Downes v Cottam* [1893] 1 Ch 547, CA. The nature of a *'Beddoe'* application is such that if the trustee or executor is granted authority to bring proceedings, the order ensures that the trustee or executor is entitled, win or lose, to his costs out of the estate, before the facts have been fully explored or the relevant law argued. When deciding whether to make the order the court will take into account that it is the duty of trustees and executors to protect the estate, and that they are entitled to be indemnified out of the estate for all the costs incurred in bringing or defending proceedings on behalf of the estate.

A *'Beddoe'* application should be distinguished from a 'John Doe' application, which is made where there is a defendant to proceedings but his identity is unknown (see Chapter 7, 'Parties to and Title of Proceedings').

An application for permission should be made by application notice, under Part 23, before the claim form is issued. The application need not be served on any other person and must be accompanied by a copy of the claim form the applicant proposes to issue. If the court gives permission, it will give directions for the future management of the claim (r 8.2A).

INAPPROPRIATE USE OF PART 8 PROCEDURE

If a claimant issues a Part 8 claim form and a court officer believes that the Part 8 procedure is inappropriate for the claimant's claim, he may refer the matter to the judge for the judge to consider the point (PD 8, para 1.5). If the judge decides that the Part 8 procedure is inappropriate for the claim, he may order that the claim continue as if the claimant had not used the Part 8 procedure (r 8.1(3)). The court will then allocate the claim to a track and give appropriate directions for the further conduct of the matter (PD 8, para 1.6).

If the defendant does not believe that the Part 8 procedure is appropriate, because there is a substantial dispute of fact and its use is not required or permitted by any rule or practice direction, he must state his reasons in writing for this belief when he files his acknowledgment of service. If the statement setting out the reasons includes matters of evidence, it should be verified by a statement of truth (r 8.8(1); PD 8, para 3.6).

When the court receives the defendant's acknowledgment of service and any written evidence, it will give directions as to the future management of the case (r 8.8(2)).

CHAPTER 16

JUDICIAL CASE MANAGEMENT: ALLOCATION

INTRODUCTION

Part 26 deals with case management for what is described as the 'preliminary stage'. The preliminary stage involves such matters as automatic transfer and allocation to a track. The next stage of case management will begin if a case proceeds to be allocated to a track. If this stage is reached, the nature and extent of the case management carried out by the court will depend on the track to which the case is allocated.

AUTOMATIC TRANSFER

A claimant is free to start proceedings in a court located in any part of the jurisdiction of England and Wales. However, under r 26.2, if the defendant files a defence, the proceedings will be automatically transferred to the defendant's home court if the following circumstances all apply:

- the claim is for a specified amount of money;
- the claim was commenced in a court which is not the defendant's home court;
- the claim has not been transferred to another defendant's home court under r 13.4 or r 14.12;
- the defendant is an individual; and
- the claim was not commenced in a specialist list.

Note that for there to be automatic transfer, the defendant must be an 'individual'. While this clearly excludes companies and multiple partnerships, what is not so clear is whether a defendant who uses a trade name, for example, 'James Smith trading as Smith and Co', should also be treated as an 'individual' for these purposes.

Where the claim was issued out of the Production Centre at Northampton and the defendant files a defence, the court will serve a notice requiring the Centre User to notify the court within 28 days whether he wishes the claim to proceed. If the defendant is an individual and the circumstances in r 26.2 apply, the proceedings will not be automatically transferred unless the claimant notifies the court that he wants the case to continue (PD 7C, paras 1.3 and 5.2).

Where proceedings are started using money claim online, if the defendant is an individual and the circumstances in r 26.2 apply, the proceedings will be automatically transferred to the defendant's home court (PD 7E, para 14.1).

The defendant's home court

Depending on whether the case is proceeding in the High Court or a county court, the defendant's home court is defined as either the county court for the district in which the defendant resides or carries on business, or the district registry for the district in which the defendant resides or carries on business or, if there is no district registry, the Royal Courts of Justice (r 2.3). It should be noted that the reference is to the home court of the defendant personally and does not include the defendant's solicitor's home court – that provision was removed (2 October 2000) as the solicitor's address was often some distance from that of the client.

Where there are two or more defendants to a claim who have different home courts, the proceedings will be transferred to the home court of the defendant who files a defence first, as long as the above circumstances also apply (r 26.2(5)).

If a defendant files a defence to a claim on the basis that the money claimed has been paid, or if the defendant admits part of a claim for a specified amount of money, the claimant will be asked to notify the court whether he wishes to proceed with the claim (see rr 14.5 and 15.10). If the claimant notifies the court that he does wish to proceed, and the above circumstances apply, the proceedings will be transferred to the defendant's home court on receipt of the claimant's notification (r 26.2(4)).

ALLOCATION

If a claim is defended, the court will allocate the claim to one of the three case management tracks. It is expressly provided that in exercising its powers of case management to allocate a case to a track, the court will expect to do so as far as possible in co-operation with the parties in order to deal with cases justly in accordance with the overriding objective (PD 26, para 4.1).

The three case management tracks are the small claims track, the fast track and the multi-track. Which track a case should be allocated to will depend on a number of factors, such as the amount claimed, the length of any trial, the complexity of the case and the type of remedy sought. The level of case management involved for each track increases, with the least being applied to cases allocated to the small claims track and the most to those cases on the multi-track.

THE ALLOCATION QUESTIONNAIRE

In order to assist the court in its decision regarding to which track a claim should be allocated, both parties must return an allocation questionnaire. Form N150 is the prescribed form for the allocation questionnaire (PD 26, para 2.1(1)).

Timing for court service of allocation questionnaire

The court will serve an allocation questionnaire on each party when a defence is filed (r 26.3(1)).

Where there are two or more defendants and at least one of them files a defence, the court will serve the allocation questionnaire either when all the defendants have filed a defence, or when the period for the filing of the last defence has expired, whichever is the sooner (r 26.3(2)).

When a defence is filed and the circumstances are such that proceedings will be automatically transferred to the defendant's home court, the court in which proceedings were commenced will serve an allocation questionnaire before the proceedings are transferred (r 26.3(3)). However, if the defendant admits part of the claimant's claim, or the defendant's defence is that money claimed has been paid, and the circumstances are such that the proceedings will *not* be transferred to the defendant's home court, an allocation questionnaire will not be served until the claimant notifies the court whether he wishes to proceed with the claim (r 26.3(4)). Nevertheless, if a part admission is made, or the defence is that money claimed has been paid, but the circumstances are such that proceedings *will* be automatically transferred to the defendant's home court, it would seem that r 26.3(3) will apply, and the court will serve an allocation questionnaire on the parties *before* transferring the proceedings and *before* the claimant has notified the court that he wishes to proceed with the claim.

If a defence is filed, the claimant can apply to the court for the allocation questionnaire to be served earlier than it would be under the above rules (r 26.3(5)).

Contents of the allocation questionnaire

The allocation questionnaire is designed to provide the court with enough information about the case so that it can decide which track to allocate it to and which case management directions to order, without requiring the parties to provide further information or hold a hearing to decide. The expectation is that the information provided by the parties in their statements of case and the allocation questionnaires will be sufficient for most cases (PD 26, para 4.2(1)).

The allocation questionnaire consists of eight sections (A–H) designed to provide the court with enough information to allocate the claim to a track. The information that a party must provide is as follows:

- whether a party would like a stay of proceedings in order to attempt to settle the case by Alternative Dispute Resolution (ADR) or other means;

- which track the party considers is most suitable for the case. The court will take the views of the parties into account, but ultimately this decision is for the court to make. If a party believes that the case should be allocated to a track which is not the normal track for a case, he should give reasons for his belief, for example, if a case within the financial limits of the small claims track arises out of a complex matter such that it would not be suitable to be heard on the small claims track;

- whether the party has complied with any applicable pre-action protocol and, if not, why not, and if no pre-action protocol applies to the claim, whether the party has exchanged information and documents in order to assist in settling the claim;

- whether the party intends to make any applications, for example, for summary judgment or permission to join another party. If the party indicates that he is likely to make such an application, the court is unlikely to allocate the case until the application is heard;

- the identity of the party's witnesses of fact and the facts of which they will give evidence. If a party intends to rely on a number of witnesses to a number of different issues this may indicate that any trial would be likely to last longer than one day, making the case unsuitable for the small claims or fast track;

- whether a party would like permission to use expert evidence at trial and, if so, whether that should be oral or written evidence: if oral, the reason why such evidence is necessary and whether the party considers the case suitable for a single joint expert;
- a figure for the amount of the claim in dispute;
- whether the party would like the case heard at a court in a particular location. A party may, for instance, request that the case is heard at a local court if that would be convenient for his witnesses;
- an estimate of the length of the trial and trial dates to avoid;
- an estimate of costs incurred to date and to be incurred;
- confirmation as to whether suggested directions are attached to the allocation questionnaire and an indication as to whether they are agreed;
- other information, which may assist the court to manage the claim.

Co-operation in completing the allocation questionnaire

In keeping with the obligation of the parties to help the court further the overriding objective, there is an onus on the parties to consult one another and co-operate in completing their allocation questionnaires and provide the court with the necessary information so that it can decide to which track to allocate a case and which case management directions are necessary. In this way, the parties should try to agree the case management directions which they will invite the court to make (PD 26, para 2.3(1) and (2)). However, being involved in consultation with the other party about case management directions would not justify delay in filing the allocation questionnaire (PD 26, para 2.3(3)).

Note that the parties are not obliged by any rule or practice direction to serve the allocation questionnaires on each other, but the court will serve a copy of the other party's allocation questionnaire, along with any additional information, on each party when it serves notice of allocation (r 26.9).

Additional information

If the allocation questionnaire does not provide the court with enough information to allocate a claim to a track, the court will order a party to provide further information about his case within 14 days of the order (r 26.5(3); PD 26, para 4.2(2)). The court will serve the order seeking further information in Form N156. Such further information may also be sought if the court is deciding whether it is necessary to hold an allocation hearing before allocating proceedings to a track (r 26.5(3)).

A party can also provide the court with additional information outside of that which must be provided in the allocation questionnaire if he believes it may affect the court's decision about allocation to a track or case management (PD 26, para 2.2(1)). Examples of additional information that would help the court are given in PD 26. These are listed as:

- a party's intention to apply for summary judgment or some other order that may dispose of the case or reduce the amount in dispute or the number of issues remaining to be decided;

- a party's intention to issue a Part 20 claim or to add another party;
- the steps the parties have taken in the preparation of evidence (in particular, expert evidence), the steps they intend to take and whether those steps are to be taken in co-operation with any other party;
- the directions the party believes will be appropriate to be given for the management of the case;
- any particular facts that may affect the timetable the court will set; and
- any facts which may make it desirable for the court to fix an allocation hearing or a hearing at which case management directions will be given (PD 26, para 2.2(3)(a)–(f)).

If a party believes that there is additional information that should be provided to the court, he should either get the agreement of the other party that the information is correct and should be put before the court, or at least deliver a copy of the additional information to the other party. Unless this is done and confirmed in the document containing the additional information, as a general rule the court will not take the information into account (PD 26, para 2.2(2)).

Allocation hearings

If it is necessary to do so, the court will order an allocation hearing of its own initiative before allocating a claim to a track (r 26.5(4); PD 26, para 6.1). The circumstances in which the court is likely to hold an allocation hearing are if, for example, one of the parties has failed to file an allocation questionnaire or failed to provide further information after being ordered to do so by the court, or if the parties have requested the case be allocated to different tracks and it is not clear which track is the most appropriate.

If the court decides to hold an allocation hearing, it will serve notice of the hearing in Form N153 at least seven days before the hearing is to take place. Form N153 will give a brief explanation of the reason for ordering the hearing (PD 26, para 6.2).

With the advent of active judicial case management and the duty of the parties to assist the court in dealing justly with cases in accordance with the overriding objective, the legal representative attending any allocation hearing ought to be the person responsible for the case. If this is not possible, the person attending must in any event be familiar with the case and be able to provide the court with the information it is likely to need in order to decide to which track to allocate the case and which case management directions to make. The person attending must also have sufficient authority to deal with any issues that are likely to arise (PD 26, para 6.5).

If the court orders an allocation hearing because a party has failed to file an allocation questionnaire or failed to provide extra information which the court has ordered, the court is likely to order the party in default to pay the costs on the indemnity basis of any other party who has attended the hearing, summarily assess those costs and order them to be paid forthwith or within a stated period. The court is also likely to order that if the party in default does not pay those costs within the time stated, his statement of case will be struck out. If the party in default does not attend the hearing or carry out the necessary steps, the court is likely to order that unless those steps are carried out within the time specified, his statement of claim will be struck out (PD 26, para 6.6). These are specified as the usual sanctions for failure to comply with the allocation procedure, but the court has the power to order otherwise (PD 26, para 6.6(1)).

Applications made before allocation

In some cases, a court hearing will take place before the claim is allocated to a track, for instance, where a party makes an application for an interim injunction or summary judgment. In those circumstances, the court can treat the hearing as an allocation hearing, allocate the case to a track and give case management directions (PD 26, para 2.4(1)). The court does not have to notify the parties that it proposes to treat the hearing as an allocation hearing (PD 26, para 6.3). Alternatively, if the application is made before the parties have filed allocation questionnaires, the court can fix a date for allocation questionnaires to be filed and give other directions (PD 26, para 2.4(2)).

A party who intends to make the type of application which may result in the early termination of a case, such as an application to strike out a statement of case or part of a statement of case, or an application for summary judgment, should make the application before or when filing his allocation questionnaire (PD 26, para 5.3(1)). If a party makes an application for such an order before the case has been allocated to a track, the court will not normally allocate the case before the hearing of the application (PD 26, para 5.3(2)).

If a party indicates in his allocation questionnaire that he intends to make the type of application referred to above which may result in the early termination of a case, but he has not yet made the application, the judge will usually direct that an allocation hearing is listed (PD 26, para 5.3(3)), the intention being that the application is heard at the allocation hearing, so long as the application has been issued and served giving the other party the requisite notice (PD 26, para 5.3(4)).

Where the court proposes to make such an order of its own initiative, it will not allocate the claim to a track, but instead will either:

(a) fix a hearing, giving the parties at least 14 days' notice of the date of the hearing and of the issues which it is proposed that the court will decide; or

(b) make an order directing a party to take the steps described in the order within a stated time and specifying the consequence of not taking those steps, for example, an order for a party to file a properly formulated statement of case within a specified time, otherwise the claim or defence will be struck out (PD 26, para 5.4).

Where the court decides, at a hearing in which a party is applying for the early termination of a case, or if the court has ordered such a hearing of its own initiative, that the claim should continue, it will either treat the hearing as an allocation hearing, or allocate the claim and give case management directions or give other appropriate directions (PD 26, para 5.5).

Filing the allocation questionnaire

The court serving the allocation questionnaire will specify a date by which the completed allocation questionnaire must be filed. The court will serve Form N152 on the parties, which contains a notice that a defence or counterclaim has been filed and which specifies a date by which, and the court to which, completed allocation questionnaires must be filed. This date must be at least 14 days after the date when the allocation questionnaire is deemed to be served on the party in question (r 26.3(6)).

The date specified by the court for filing the completed allocation questionnaires may not be varied by agreement of the parties (r 26.3(6A)).

Unless he obtains an exemption or a remission, the claimant must pay a court fee of £80 when filing the allocation questionnaire. The fee does not apply where the amount claimed is £1,000 or less. If the case is proceeding on a counterclaim alone, the fee is payable by the defendant. The fee is still payable even if the court dispenses with the need for allocation questionnaires (Supreme Court Fees Order 1999 (SI 1999/687), Sched 1, para 2.1; County Court Fees Order 1999 (SI 1999/689), Sched 1, para 2.1).

If the claimant does not pay the fee, the court may send out a notice in Form N173 requiring payment within a specified time and warning the claimant that if he does not pay, his claim will be struck out and he will be liable for the costs of the defendant (r 3.7).

Failure to file an allocation questionnaire

If no party files an allocation questionnaire within the time specified by the court, the file will be referred to the judge for directions (PD 26, para 2.5(1)(a)). Under r 26.5(5), the judge can make any order he considers appropriate, but the usual order he will make in those circumstances is for the claim and any counterclaim to be struck out unless an allocation questionnaire is filed within three days from service of that order (PD 26, para 2.5(1)(b)).

Where one party files an allocation questionnaire but another party does not, the court may allocate the claim to a track if it considers it has enough information to do so, or list an allocation hearing and order all parties or any party to attend (PD 26, para 2.5(2)). It is likely that if it is necessary for the court to hold an allocation hearing in these circumstances, it will order the party in default to pay the costs of the hearing.

Costs estimate

For claims outside the limits of the small claims track the parties must give an estimate in the allocation questionnaire of costs incurred to date and an estimate of their overall costs. Further, in *substantial* cases, a costs estimate in the form provided in Part 43 must be filed at court and served on all other parties when the allocation questionnaire is filed (PD 43, para 6). The solicitor acting for a party must also deliver a copy of the costs estimate to his client no later than the time when he files it at court. There is no definition of a *substantial* case.

The costs estimate should be substantially in the form of Precedent H in the Schedule of Costs Precedents annexed to the Practice Direction (PD 43, para 6) and in substantial cases a legal representative should not simply provide total figures for current and estimated costs in the spaces indicated in the allocation questionnaire.

The costs estimate should give an itemised breakdown showing separately the amounts for profit costs, disbursements and VAT incurred and to be incurred which the party expects to recover from the other party if successful. Only base costs need be shown, and not the amounts of any additional liability if a funding arrangement has been entered into (PD 26, para 2.1(2)(c)). The court may have regard to the estimates when dealing with any final order for costs (PD 43, para 6), so care should be taken not to overestimate or underestimate.

Stay to allow for settlement

In accordance with the overriding objective, part of the court's case management function involves encouraging the parties to use ADR if appropriate, and helping the parties to settle the case (r 1.4(2)(e) and (f)). The allocation questionnaire contains a section asking the parties whether they would like the proceedings to be stayed in order to give them an opportunity to settle the case by ADR or other means (r 26.4(1)).

Length of stay

If all the parties request a stay, or if the court considers of its own initiative that such a stay would be appropriate, the court will order that the proceedings be stayed, in the first instance, for one month to give time for a settlement to be reached (r 26.4(2)).

The court has the power to extend the stay for a further period, or until a specified date (r 26.4(3)). It is likely to do this if, for instance, the parties ask for extra time to reach a settlement. The procedure to apply to extend the stay is contained in PD 26, para 3.1. This provides that one of the parties, or his solicitor, should send a letter to the court confirming that all the parties have agreed to apply for an extension of the stay and explaining what steps are being taken to settle the dispute, and identifying any mediator or expert assisting to bring about a settlement. The court will generally extend the stay for a maximum period of four weeks unless the parties give good reasons to justify a longer period of time. There is no limit on the number of extensions of time the court may grant.

There is provision for a party to apply for the stay to be lifted (PD 26, para 3.3). This may be appropriate if a party believes that there is no prospect of a settlement being reached and resolution of the dispute is simply being delayed whilst proceedings are stayed.

If the claimant alone requests a stay, the court may be disposed to grant it. However, if the defendant alone requests a stay, the court may be more circumspect, especially if it is thought that the request is merely a delaying tactic.

Notification of settlement

If a settlement is reached during the period of the stay, the claimant must notify the court accordingly (r 26.4(4)).

If the whole of the proceedings are settled during a stay and a party takes one of the following steps:

(a) applies to the court for a consent order to give effect to the settlement; or

(b) applies for approval of a settlement where one of the parties is under a disability; or

(c) gives notice of acceptance of money paid into court in satisfaction of the claim, or applies for money in court to be paid out,

it will be treated as an application for the stay to be lifted (PD 26, para 3.4).

If the claimant does not notify the court that a settlement has been reached, once the period of the stay has expired the court will give case management directions for the next stage of the case (r 26.5(2)). Rule 26.5 provides that if the court has stayed proceedings under r 26.4, it will allocate the claim to a track at the end of the period of the stay (r 26.5(2)). However, it would appear that the court will allocate the claim to a track only if that is appropriate, and before doing so the court may require a party to provide further information or decide to hold an allocation hearing (PD 26, para 3.2). Many courts have now adopted the practice of sending out 'unless' orders in the absence of any feedback after the expiry of the period of stay, with striking out of the claim and defence in default of any further response.

ALLOCATION TO A TRACK

In most cases, once every defendant to a claim has filed an allocation questionnaire, or when the period for filing the allocation questionnaire has expired (whichever is sooner), the court will allocate the claim to one of the three tracks (r 26.5(1)).

A case will not be allocated at this stage if:

(a) proceedings have been stayed under r 26.4 (r 26.5(1)); or

(b) the court has dispensed with the need for allocation questionnaires (r 26.5(1)); or

(c) the court has ordered the party under r 26.5(3) to provide further information about his case; or

(d) the court has ordered an allocation hearing under r 26.5(4).

SCOPE OF EACH TRACK

Financial value of the claim

The scope of each track is primarily limited by the financial value of the claim. It is for the court to assess the financial value of a claim (PD 26, para 7.3(1)). In most cases, the court will simply accept the claimant's valuation of the claim as set out in his statement of case. However, if the court believes that the amount the claimant is seeking exceeds what he may reasonably expect to recover, it may order the claimant to provide further information to justify the amount claimed (r 26.5(3); PD 26, para 7.3(2)).

The financial value of a claim, for the purposes of considering which track it should be allocated to, does *not* include:

(a) any amount not in dispute;

(b) any claim for interest;

(c) costs; and

(d) any contributory negligence (r 26.8(2)).

Any amount not in dispute

General guidance is given in PD 26 as to how the court will decide whether an amount is in dispute between the parties. The general principles the court will take into account are stated as follows:

- any amount for which the defendant does not admit liability is in dispute;
- any sum in respect of an *item* forming part of the claim for which judgment has been entered (for example, summary judgment) is not in dispute;
- any specific sum claimed as a *distinct item* and which the defendant admits he is liable to pay is not in dispute;
- any sum offered by the defendant which has been accepted by the claimant in satisfaction of any *item* which forms a *distinct* part of the claim is not in dispute (PD 26, para 7.4).

Therefore, if before allocation the value of a claim is above the small claims limit, but the defendant makes an admission that reduces the amount in dispute to a figure below £5,000, the normal claim for the track will be the small claims track (PD 26, para 7.4). However, the claimant can apply, before allocation, for judgment with costs on the amount of the claim that has been admitted (r 14.3; PD 44, para 15.1(2)).

THE SMALL CLAIMS TRACK

Financial value

The small claims is the normal track for any claim that has a financial value of not more than £5,000 (r 26.6(3)).

Special rules for personal injury claims and repairing orders

The financial value of a claim is calculated in a different way for personal injury claims and those claims where a tenant of residential premises is seeking an order for repair against his landlord. This was introduced to avoid a tenant being refused public funding for the case, where appropriate, on the basis that the case was merely on the small claims track, bearing in mind the principle of equality between the parties as contained in the overriding objective.

A personal injury claim will be allocated to the small claims track only where the damages claimed for pain, suffering and loss of amenity are less than £1,000 *and* the financial value of the claim is not more than £5,000 (rr 26.6(1)(a) and 26.6(2)). Therefore, if the damages claimed for pain, suffering and loss of amenity exceed £1,000, the claim will not be allocated to the small claims track even if the financial element of the claim is less than £5,000.

Order for repair of residential premises

Where a tenant brings a claim in which he seeks an order requiring the landlord to carry out repairs or other works to the premises, the claim will be allocated to the small claims track only if the costs of the repairs or other work to the premises are estimated not to exceed £1,000 *and* the financial value of any other claim for damages does not exceed £1,000 (r 26.6(1)(b)). Again, both conditions must be met in order for such a case to be allocated to the small claims track.

Features of the small claims track

The small claims track is meant for straightforward claims that do not require substantial preparation and are suitable for a relatively informal hearing. The small claims track procedure is intended to be accessible to litigants in person (ie, those not acting through or represented by solicitors or counsel). In accordance with the principle of proportionality, as the value of the claims is not more than £5,000, it is intended that claims allocated to the small claims track will not incur substantial legal costs, and the 'no costs' rule is a deterrent to parties obtaining legal representation to bring their claim.

Practice Direction 26, para 8.1(1)(c) lists the types of case suitable for the small claims track as consumer disputes, accident claims, disputes about the ownership of goods, and most disputes between a landlord and tenant other than those for possession. It is also specifically provided that a case involving a disputed allegation of dishonesty will not be suitable for allocation to the small claims track (PD 26, para 8.1(1)(d)).

If both parties consent, a claim that is normally outside the small claims track limit can be allocated to that track. However, the court does not have to allocate such a claim to the small claims track if it is not satisfied that it is suitable for hearing on that track (PD 26, para 8.1(2)).

THE FAST TRACK

Financial value

The fast track is the normal track for any claim that has a financial value of more than £5,000 but not more than £15,000 (r 26.6(4)). However, this general rule is subject to further requirements, namely, that the fast track will be the normal track for claims with a financial value of not more than £15,000 only if it is also likely that:

(a) the trial is likely to last for no longer than one day; and

(b) oral expert evidence at trial will be limited to one expert in any expert field per party and limited to two fields of expertise (r 26.6(5)).

Features of the fast track

Although claims allocated to the fast track are heard at a formal trial, the procedure is more limited than for cases heard on the multi-track (see below). In most instances, the trial is set down for one day, a trial timetable will usually be set in which evidence and cross-examination will be controlled, disclosure of documents will be limited and expert evidence will be presented by way of written report.

Although it is a key feature of a fast track trial that it will last no longer than one day, the mere *possibility* that a trial *may* last longer than one day is not a conclusive reason for the court to allocate a case to the multi-track instead (PD 26, para 9.1(3)(c)). However, where it is clear that the case *will* last longer than a day the fast track will not be appropriate because of the limits on advocates' fees and the provision that the part-heard case will normally be heard the next day.

Where a case involves a counterclaim or other Part 20 claim that will be heard with the main claim and, as a result, the trial will last for more than one day, the court cannot allocate the case to the fast track (PD 26, para 9.1(3)(e)).

THE MULTI-TRACK

Financial value

The multi-track is the normal track for any claim that has a financial value of more than £15,000 (r 26.6(6)). All Part 8 claims are treated as allocated to the multi-track and therefore the rules about allocation do not apply to them (r 8.9(c)).

Features of the multi-track

The multi-track is suitable for complex cases or cases of high value which are likely to involve the most pre-trial preparation and case management directions. The multi-track allows the court the discretion to decide how much case management a case requires. Some cases with a financial limit above the fast track limit may be relatively straightforward and, if the parties will not consent to the case being allocated to the fast track, the court has the discretion to tailor the case management directions on the multi-track so that, in effect, the directions ordered are the same as those for a fast track case.

CIVIL TRIAL CENTRES AND FEEDER COURTS

Certain courts have been designated Civil Trial Centres. Courts that are not Civil Trial Centres will be 'feeder courts'. The case management of a claim allocated to the multi-track, apart from claims involving possession of land in the county court where the defendant has filed a defence and cases dealt with at the Royal Courts of Justice, will be dealt with at a Civil Trial Centre (PD 26, paras 10.1, 10.2(1)).

A claim involving specialist proceedings as defined in Part 49 or Parts 58–62 will be allocated to the multi-track whatever its value, and the case management of such a case must be dealt with at a Civil Trial Centre (PD 26, para 10.2(2)).

Where a judge at a feeder court decides, on the basis of the allocation questionnaires and any other documents filed by the parties, that a claim should be dealt with on the multi-track, he will normally allocate the claim to the multi-track, give case management directions and transfer the claim to a Civil Trial Centre (PD 26, para 10.2(5)). In some areas, however, such as Greater London, following guidance from the designated civil judge, the feeder court will transfer the case, if it is estimated to last longer than one day and is not a possession case, to the Trial Centre at the Central London Civil Justice Centre, often without first giving directions. If the judge at the feeder court decides that an allocation hearing or some pre-allocation hearing is to take place, the hearing will take place at the feeder court (PD 26, para 10.2(6)). If the case proceeds and is allocated to the multi-track, it will then be transferred to a Civil Trial Centre (PD 26, para 10.2(7)). The judge at the feeder court can, however, transfer the case to a Civil Trial Centre for the decision on allocation to be made (PD 26, para 10.2(8)).

If a case allocated to the multi-track is likely to need more than one case management conference, and the Civil Trial Centre is inconveniently located for the parties or their legal representatives, a judge sitting at a feeder court may, with the permission of the designated civil judge, decide that case management should take place at the feeder court for the time being (PD 26, para 10.2(10)).

A designated civil judge may transfer claims from feeder courts to a Civil Trial Centre notwithstanding the track a claim has been allocated to. He may also allow a feeder court to keep for trial a claim, or category of claims, usually allocated to the multi-track. Whether such permission is granted will depend on the ability of the feeder court in relation to the Civil Trial Centre to provide suitable and effective trial within an appropriate trial period (PD 26, para 10.2(11)).

GENERAL RULES FOR ALLOCATION

It would seem that in most cases, the court will allocate a claim to a track according to whether its financial value falls within the scope of a track (as set out above). In any event, a court cannot allocate a claim to a track if its financial value exceeds the normal limit of that track, unless all the parties consent to the allocation of the claim to that track (r 26.7(3)).

Factors relevant to allocation

However, not all claims have a financial value, and it would also not be appropriate to allocate some claims, having a financial value falling within the normal scope of a track, to the normal track. Therefore, the rules provide a list of matters to which the court must have regard when deciding which track to allocate a case to. These are:

- the financial value, if any, of the claim;
- the nature of the remedy sought;
- the likely complexity of the facts, law or evidence;
- the number of parties or likely parties;
- the value of any counterclaim or other Part 20 claim and the complexity of any matters relating to it;
- the amount of oral evidence which may be required;
- the importance of the claim to persons who are not parties to the proceedings;
- the views expressed by the parties; and
- the circumstances of the parties (r 26.8(1)(a)–(i)).

Therefore, for a claim with no financial value, the court will decide which track would be most suitable for it by considering the other non-financial considerations set out above (r 26.7(2)). This is particularly true of residential possession cases which, as Part 8 proceedings, would normally be allocated to multi-track but where the reality is that, depending on the size and complexity of the case, they might be more suitable for the fast or even the small claims track.

The value of any counterclaim or other Part 20 claim

Where there is more than one money claim, for instance, where the defendant counterclaims, in order to assess the financial value of the claim the court will not usually simply aggregate the amount of the claim and counterclaim but will instead regard the largest claim as determining the financial value of the claim (PD 26, para 7.7), although it is not bound to.

Multiple claimants

Where two or more claimants start a claim against the same defendant using the same claim form, but each claimant has a claim against the defendant separate from the other claimants, the court will consider the claim of each claimant separately when it assesses the financial value of the claim (r 26.8(3)).

The parties' views as to allocation

The parties' views will be treated as an important factor by the court when making its decision, but those views cannot prevent the court from allocating the case to the track it considers most appropriate, even if all the parties have agreed on a different track (PD 26, para 7.5).

NOTICE OF ALLOCATION

When the court allocates a claim to a track, it will serve a notice of allocation on each party along with a copy of the allocation questionnaires and any additional information filed by the other parties to the claim (r 26.9).

The court will send a notice of allocation in Form N154 if the case is allocated to the fast track, Form N155 if the case is allocated to the multi-track, and one of Forms N157–160 if the case is allocated to the small claims track (PD 26, para 4.2). The practice directions dealing with the different tracks give details about the case management directions which will be made at the allocation stage for each track.

The court will generally give brief reasons for its allocation decision in the notice of allocation, unless all the allocation questionnaires have expressed the wish for the claim to be allocated to the track to which the court has allocated it (PD 26, para 4.2(4)).

RE-ALLOCATION

Once the court has allocated a claim to a track, it is not precluded from re-allocating the claim to a different track (r 26.10). This may be appropriate if there has been a change in the circumstances since the case was allocated to a track. The court may re-allocate the case on application by a party, or of its own initiative (PD 26, para 11.2).

Once a claim has been allocated to a track there needs to be a good reason to allocate it to a different track. Re-allocation may cause disruption to the progress of the litigation, especially if it occurs late in the process. The amount by which the financial value of the claim exceeds the normal limit for a track as a result of the amendment is a highly relevant consideration. If the amount by which the limit is exceeded is small, it will usually be a factor of little weight, and may well not lead to a re-allocation, particularly if it could not reasonably have been foreseen at the time when the claim was first formulated and allocated to track. If the amount is large then it will be a factor of very great importance, and will usually require a re-allocation, even if that means causing considerable delay to the completion of the litigation (*Maguire v Molin* [2002] EWCA Civ 1083).

Although r 26.7(3) provides that the court will not allocate proceedings to a track if the financial value of the claim exceeds the limit for that track unless all the parties agree, this rule only determines to which track a claim should be allocated *in the first place*. The question of re-allocation of a claim from one track to another does not necessarily raise the same issues as those when the initial allocation decision is made, and r 26.10 gives the court an unfettered discretion. There is nothing in the rules to suggest that a district judge or Master does not have jurisdiction to continue to hear a fast track claim if it is amended so that its financial value exceeds £15,000, if in all the circumstances it is just to do so (*Maguire v Molin*).

In *Maguire v Molin*, the claimant originally claimed damages limited to £15,000 and the claim was allocated to the fast track. After liability was determined in favour of the claimant, and during an adjournment of the final hearing, the claimant made an application to amend her statement of case to include an additional claim for loss of earnings which the claimant's solicitors had negligently failed to include when the claim was originally pleaded. The proposed amendments increased the value of the claimant's claim to approximately £80,000.

The Court of Appeal held that in light of the substantial increase in value of the claim, the district judge was entitled to take the view that if he had allowed the amendments, it would have been wrong for him to continue with the trial and that he would have no alternative but to re-allocate the claim to the multi-track and order a re-hearing before a circuit judge. However, the decision to re-allocate at this very late stage would have caused considerable disruption to the progress of the litigation. On the other hand, the need for the amendment arose from the claimant's solicitors' failure to make a proper appraisal of the true value of the claim in due time, and the court felt that this was a cogent reason for holding that the defendant should not be prejudiced by the amendment. The defendant would suffer substantial prejudice if the amendment were allowed because he would have deployed more resources to his defence if he had known from the outset that he was facing a claim for approximately £80,000 on the multi-track. In the circumstances, the Court of Appeal held that the district judge was entitled to exercise his discretion to refuse to allow the amendments so as to avoid the need to abort the trial at this late stage.

If the court allocates a claim to a track without an allocation hearing, a party who is dissatisfied with the track the claim has been allocated to should apply to the court to re-allocate the claim. The application should be made in accordance with Part 23. However, if an order was made allocating a claim to a track at a hearing at which a party was present or represented, or of which he had due notice, the dissatisfied party must appeal against the order for allocation (PD 26, para 11.1).

JURY TRIAL

High Court

Where a claim brought in the Queen's Bench Division of the High Court involves an issue against a party of fraud, libel, slander, malicious prosecution or false imprisonment, an application can be made by either party for trial with a jury. If the court is satisfied that such an allegation is in issue, the party has the right to have the claim tried with a jury unless the court is of the opinion that the trial requires any prolonged examination of documents or accounts, or any scientific or local investigation which cannot conveniently be made with a jury (s 69 of the Supreme Court Act 1981 (SCA)).

County courts

Similar provisions apply to cases proceeding in the county courts (s 66 of the County Courts Act 1984 (CCA)).

Application for trial by jury

In both the High Court and the county courts, an application for a claim to be tried with a jury must be made within 28 days of service of the defence (r 26.11).

The right to trial by jury under s 69 of the SCA and s 66 of the CCA has been held to be a fundamental (as opposed to a procedural) right which is beyond the power of the Civil Procedure Rule Committee to limit (*Safeway Stores plc v Albert Tate* [2001] QB 1120; [2001] 2 WLR 1377; [2001] 4 All ER 193).

In *Oliver v Calderdale MBC* (1999) *The Times*, 7 July, a case decided under a similar provision of the former rules, it was held that an application made wholly out of time could be rejected on the grounds that it was unreasonable. It is submitted that the same decision could be made under the CPR, and it is not inconsistent with the exercise of a fundamental right that a party should comply with reasonable time limits and other restrictions, but all will depend on the facts of the particular case.

CHAPTER 17

THE SMALL CLAIMS TRACK

INTRODUCTION

In talking about the small claims track, Lord Woolf said:

> I see the small claims scheme as the primary way of increasing access to justice for ordinary people. It is expressly intended for litigants in person. I believe that the interventionist approach of the small claims scheme provides the most effective protection for litigants who do not have the resources to pay for legal advice and representation and who are not eligible for legal aid. (*Access to Justice*, Interim Report (IR), Chapter 15, paras 3 and 4, www.dca.gov.uk/civil/interfr.htm.)

In the light of this, Lord Woolf recommended an increase in the small claims jurisdiction from £1,000 to £3,000, but in fact it was subsequently increased to £5,000.

SCOPE OF THE SMALL CLAIMS TRACK

The small claims track is the normal track for claims with a financial value of not more than £5,000, subject to the special rules for personal injury and housing disrepair claims (r 26.6). However, just because a claim falls within the financial limit of the small claims track does not mean that it will be allocated to this track if, for instance, the complexity of the law or issues involved would make it unsuitable for hearing on the small claims track with its relative informality and limited procedural framework.

The decision as to the value of the claim is that of the court (r 26.7). Any dispute will be resolved by the court prior to allocation, as it will affect the allocation of the case to track. The intentional overstatement of the amount involved to avoid the claim being referred to the small claims track is a clear abuse of process and may lead to sanctions under Part 3 (the court's case management powers; and see *Afzal v Ford Motor Co Ltd* [1994] 4 All ER 720, a case decided under the former rules).

Where a case involves fraud it is probably not suitable for the small claims track, even where the amount is within the limit, as a full hearing is more appropriate together with a proper award of costs (*Wheen v Smithmann European Homes and Another* (2000) LTL, 25 September, CA). Also, the small claims track is unlikely to be suitable for the trial of a claim where the facts are bitterly disputed and the applicable law potentially complex (*Gregory v Turner* [2003] EWCA Civ 183 at [14]).

A claim against a landlord of residential premises that includes a remedy for harassment or unlawful eviction cannot be allocated to the small claims track whatever the financial value of the claim (r 26.7(4)). This is to enable public funding to be available to the claimant if appropriate.

Where judgment is entered for an amount to be decided by the court following the defendant's admission, the case will not have been allocated to a case management track. The court will then need to decide what directions are necessary for the assessment of the amount claimed. If the financial value of the claim falls within the small claims track jurisdiction the court will allocate it to that track for the amount to be decided (PD 26, para 12.3(1)(b)).

REMEDIES AVAILABLE ON SMALL CLAIMS TRACK

The court has the power to grant any final remedy on the small claims track that it could grant if proceedings were on the fast track or the multi-track (r 27.3). Therefore, the fact that a claimant is seeking a remedy such as an injunction or specific performance would not preclude the claim from being allocated to the small claims track if the value and/or complexity are such that it is suitable for hearing on that track.

FEATURES OF THE SMALL CLAIMS TRACK

In summary, the hallmarks of the small claims track are as follows:

- certain parts of the Civil Procedure Rules (CPR) do not apply – for example, Part 36 offers and payments;
- standard directions are usually given;
- trials are usually heard by the district judge in an informal setting in which the strict rules of evidence do not apply;
- the district judge can decide on an appropriate procedure for the trial and the judge's role is usually interventionist;
- a party is entitled to have a lay representative present his case at a small claims hearing;
- the 'no costs rule' applies (see Chapter 11, 'Costs on the small claims track').

Generally small claims will be dealt with by the district judge, but the functions of the court may be carried out by the circuit judge (PD 27, para 1). This will, however, affect the route of any appeal (see Chapter 37, 'Appeals').

Parts of the CPR that do not apply to small claims

In recognition of the fact that the small claims track is meant to provide a more informal forum in which to decide a dispute, in proportion to the amount at stake and complexity of the dispute, a number of parts of the CPR, or certain rules within a part, do not apply to the small claims track once the case has been allocated to that track. Also, because legal costs are not usually awarded for small claims cases, certain parts of the CPR, such as Part 36 offers to settle and payments in, are not applicable.

The following parts, therefore, are completely excluded:

- Part 18 (further information);
- Part 31 (disclosure and inspection);
- Part 33 (miscellaneous rules about evidence); and
- Part 36 (offers to settle and payments into court) (r 27.2(1)).

The following parts are excluded *except* for the rules indicated:

- Part 25 (interim remedies), except for interim injunctions;
- Part 32 (evidence), except r 32.1 (power of court to control evidence);
- Part 35 (experts and assessors), except rr 35.1 (duty to restrict expert evidence), 35.3 (experts – overriding duty to the court), 35.7 (court's power to direct that

evidence is to be given by a single joint expert) and 35.8 (instructions to a single joint expert); and

- Part 39 (hearings), except r 39.2 (general rule – hearing to be in public) (r 27.2(1)).

Directions on the small claims track

If a defence is filed and the case is allocated to the small claims track, in most cases the court will then give directions for the further conduct of the proceedings. Having made directions, the court can then add to them, vary them or revoke them if it is necessary to do so (r 27.7).

Standard directions

For most claims allocated to the small claims track, the court will give standard directions and fix a date for the final hearing. If a case is suitable for standard directions, these will consist of:

- a direction for each party to file at court, and serve on every other party, copies of all documents (including any expert's report) on which he intends to rely at least 14 days before the date of the hearing;
- a date for the hearing and the time allowed for the hearing;
- a warning that the court must be informed immediately if the case is settled by agreement before the hearing date; and
- any other standard direction set out in the relevant practice direction (r 27.4(1)).

Practice Direction 27 sets out a variety of standard directions for different types of claims, such as road accidents, building disputes and contract claims, landlord and tenant disputes about the return of deposits, and ruined holiday and wedding claims. The practice directions for such claims contain the standard directions and additional directions that are likely to be necessary depending on the nature of the dispute. The practice directions should be consulted for the details, but they cover such additional matters as the provision of photographs and plans and witness statements.

Special directions

If standard directions are unsuitable for a case, the court will give special directions and fix a date for a hearing. Special directions are directions instead of or in addition to standard directions (r 27.4(1)(b)). Examples of special directions are: a direction that the hearing will take place at a venue other than the court, for instance, at one of the parties' business premises; or a direction that expert evidence is necessary and should be obtained by way of a single joint expert (see PD 27, Form F).

In some cases, the court will give special directions and direct that the court will consider what further directions are to be given no later than 28 days after the date special directions were given (r 27.4(1)(c)).

Expert evidence

If the court does not make a direction permitting expert evidence, none will be admissible at the hearing, whether written or oral (r 27.5). This is in keeping with the general rule as to the admissibility of expert evidence for all types of hearing.

Expert evidence is permitted on the small claims track to a limited extent (r 27.2(1)(e)), not all the rules in Part 35 applying to the small claims track. This allows expert evidence to be presented in a more informal way, as there is no requirement to present it in the form of a written report as detailed in PD 35. The rules that do apply are r 35.1 (duty to restrict expert evidence), r 35.3 (expert's overriding duty to the court), r 35.7 (single joint experts) and r 35.8 (instructions to single joint expert). In most claims heard on the small claims track it will not be proportionate to rely on oral expert evidence, and if a party wishes to rely on such evidence he will have to make an application for permission to do so. The court can award up to a maximum of £200 to a party for the cost of obtaining expert evidence (r 27.14(3)(d); PD 27, para 7.3(2)). This is important to bear in mind as, when sanctioning the use of an expert, the court may omit to mention the limit on recoverable fees. In a case where an expert is definitely required but his fees are likely to exceed the £200 maximum, the court may well consider re-allocating the case to another track to enable the fees to be covered.

Preliminary hearings

In some cases, rather than give directions for the further conduct of the claim, the court will fix a date for a preliminary hearing instead. The court has the power to order a preliminary hearing in the following circumstances:

(a) where the court considers that special directions are needed to ensure a fair hearing, but it appears necessary for a party to attend at court to ensure that he understands what he must do to comply with the special directions. This is likely to apply only where the party is a litigant in person. If, for instance, a litigant in person brings a case and the court considers that expert evidence is necessary to decide the case, but the litigant in person has not provided for any, the court may decide to hold a preliminary hearing so that this can be explained to the party and for directions to be given for a single joint expert to be instructed; or

(b) to enable the court to dispose of the claim on the basis that one or other of the parties has no real prospect of success at a final hearing (similar to the provisions for summary judgment as set out in Part 24); or

(c) to enable the court to strike out a statement of case or part of one on the basis that it discloses no reasonable grounds to bring or defend the claim (r 27.6(1)).

The court *must* consider the desirability of limiting the expense for the parties involved in attending court when deciding whether to hold a preliminary hearing (r 27.6(2)). This will obviously be an important factor for a case allocated to the small claims track, where the amount involved will usually be no more than £5,000 and where legal costs are not usually recoverable.

Preliminary hearing to be final hearing

The court can treat the preliminary hearing as a final hearing if all the parties agree (r 27.6(4)) and if there is time.

If a party indicates on his allocation questionnaire that he intends to apply for summary judgment and/or an order to strike out the other party's statement of case, the court may order that this matter be decided at a preliminary hearing, and if the parties agree to this the preliminary hearing can be treated as the final hearing. However, given the limited and proportionate nature of small claims hearings, and the risk that a summary judgment or striking out application may not dispose of the whole claim, it is likely to be rare, and only in very obvious and straightforward cases, that the court will take the step of holding a preliminary hearing rather than allowing the case to proceed to a small claims hearing.

Notice of the preliminary hearing

The court will give the parties at least 14 days' notice of the date of the preliminary hearing (r 27.6(3)).

Directions following a preliminary hearing

If the case is not concluded at the preliminary hearing, at or after the preliminary hearing the court will give directions for the further conduct of the case. This will include a direction fixing the date of the final hearing (if this has not already been fixed) and informing the parties of the time allowed for the hearing, as well as any other appropriate directions, such as the filing and serving of documents (r 27.6(5)).

THE SMALL CLAIMS HEARING

Notice of the final hearing

The court will give the parties at least 21 days' notice of the date fixed for the final hearing, unless the parties agree to accept less notice than this. The notice will also inform the parties of the time allowed for the final hearing (r 27.4(2)).

Hearing before the district judge

In most cases a small claims trial will be heard by the district judge; however, it may be heard by a circuit judge (PD 27, para 1). In most county courts, a small claims trial takes place in the district judge's room in an informal setting (PD 27, para 4.2). The district judge sits behind a desk at the head of a table, while the parties sit at tables arranged at each side. However, the hearing may take place in a court room or in any other appropriate venue, such as the home or business premises of a party (PD 27, para 4.1(3)).

In accordance with the general rule and Art 6 of the European Convention on Human Rights, a small claims hearing should be held in public unless the interests of justice demand that it should be heard in private (r 39.2(1); PD 27, para 4.1(1)). There are certain types of claim where privacy is important, and for those cases the general rule is that the hearing will be in private, for example, mortgagee possession claims (PD 27, para 4.1(2)). The court may also decide to hold the hearing in private if both parties agree to it (PD 27, para 4.1(2)).

In practice, small claims hearings held in public are not attended by many members of the public because they normally take place in the district judge's room, which is not usually readily accessible to the public. In those courts where the district judge's room is inaccessible, there is often a notice inviting those who wish to observe the proceedings to inform the court usher so that arrangements for access can be made. However, r 39.2(2) provides that the court does not have to make special arrangements to accommodate members of the public at a hearing. Notwithstanding the absence of a duty to accommodate, PD 39, para 1.10 gives the judge the power to adjourn proceedings to a larger room or court if it is not practicable to accommodate members of the public who want to observe the proceedings.

Form of the hearing

The judge holding the small claims hearing has discretion to adopt any method of proceeding that he considers to be fair (r 27.8(1)). However, this is within the context of the following rules that:

- the hearing will be informal;
- the strict rules of evidence do not apply;
- the court does not need to take evidence on oath;
- the court may limit cross-examination; and
- the court must give reasons for its decision (r 27.8(2)–(6)).

In practice, it is often the case that district judges adopt a varying approach depending on whether the parties are legally represented or not. If both parties are legally represented, the district judge can be expected to conduct the hearing more formally and rely on the legal representatives to protect their clients' interests. However, where one or both parties are acting in person, the district judge can be expected to be much more interventionist. Lord Woolf described the district judge's role in these circumstances as:

> ... not only that of an adjudicator. It is a key safeguard of the rights of both parties. In most cases, the judge is effectively a substitute for legal representation. He must also hold the ring and ensure that each party has a fair chance to present his own case and to challenge that of his opponent. (IR, Chapter 16, para 26.)

Limiting cross-examination

Practice Direction 27 refers to the court's power to limit cross-examination. This includes the power of the judge to:

(a) ask questions of any witness himself before allowing any other person to do so;

(b) ask questions of all or any of the witnesses himself before allowing any other person to ask questions of any witnesses;

(c) refuse to allow cross-examination of any witness until all the witnesses have given evidence-in-chief;

(d) limit the cross-examination of a witness to a fixed time and/or to a particular subject or issue (PD 27, para 4.3).

Reasons for the decision

Most small claims trials are tape recorded by the district judge. If the hearing is tape recorded, the district judge will usually also tape record his judgment and the reasons for it (PD 27, paras 5.1, 5.4). A party to the proceedings can obtain a transcript of the recording on payment of the transcriber's charges (PD 27, para 5.1).

If the judge does not tape record the hearing and his judgment, he will make a written note of the central points of the oral evidence and the central reasons for his judgment. A party to the proceedings will then be entitled to obtain a copy (PD 27, paras 5.3, 5.4, 5.7).

The reasons for the judge's decision can be given as briefly and simply as the nature of the case allows (PD 27, para 5.5). The judge will normally give his reasons orally at the hearing, but he can decide to send them to the parties in writing at a later stage, or fix a hearing in order to give his reasons (PD 27, para 5.5).

Where there is a right of appeal, or a right to seek leave to appeal any proceedings in a county court, nothing in PD 27 affects the duty of the judge under s 80 of the County Courts Act 1984 (CCA), if so requested by a party, to make a note:

(a) of any question of law raised at the hearing; and

(b) of the facts in evidence in relation to any such question; and

(c) of his decision on any such question and of his determination of the proceedings.

Where such a note has been taken, the judge shall, on the application of a party, and on payment of the prescribed fee, furnish the party with a signed copy of the note, and that signed copy shall be used at the hearing of the appeal (s 80 of the CCA; PD 27, para 5.8).

Representation at a small claims hearing

Small claims proceedings are designed so that litigants in person can act for themselves. In accordance with the Lay Representatives (Rights of Audience) Order 1999 (SI 1999/1225), a party to a small claims hearing may present his own case at the hearing, or a lawyer or lay representative may present it for him (PD 27, para 3.2(1)). A lay representative is defined as a person other than a barrister, solicitor or a legal executive employed by a solicitor (PD 27, para 3.1). A party may, therefore, have any person present his case at a small claims hearing. A lay representative cannot exercise a right of audience in the following circumstances:

(a) if his client does not attend the hearing;

(b) at any stage after judgment; or

(c) on any appeal against a decision of the district judge in the proceedings (Lay Representatives (Rights of Audience) Order 1999; PD 27, para 3.2(2)).

However, these exceptions are not absolute, as PD 27, para 3.2(3), referring to the court's general discretion to hear anybody, states that the court may hear a lay representative even in the circumstances excluded by the Order. Note that the court also has the power to refuse to hear from a lay representative provided cogent reasons are given.

A party may choose to have assistance from a *McKenzie* friend instead (see Chapter 32, 'Hearings').

Any officer or employee may represent a company at a small claims hearing (PD 27, para 3.2(4)).

NON-ATTENDANCE OF PARTIES AT SMALL CLAIMS HEARING

Party electing not to attend final hearing

A party can elect not to attend the hearing and ask the court to decide the claim in his absence instead. In those circumstances, the court will take that party's statement of case and any other filed documents into account when it decides the case at the final hearing, as long as that party has made such a request and notified the court that he will not attend the hearing at least seven days before the date of the hearing (r 27.9(1)). On reaching a decision in a case where a party has given such notice, the judge will send a note of the reasons for his judgment to both parties (PD 27, para 5.6).

However, if a party, for good reason, cannot attend on the date fixed for the hearing, he can apply to the court for it to exercise its case management powers under r 3.1(2)(b) to adjourn the date fixed for the hearing, rather than ask for it to be decided in his absence.

Claimant failing to attend final hearing

If a claimant fails to notify the court that he will not attend in accordance with r 27.9(1) (above) and fails to attend the hearing, the court may strike out the claimant's claim (r 27.9(2)).

Defendant failing to attend final hearing

If the defendant fails to notify the court that he will not attend in accordance with r 27.9(1) (above) and fails to attend the hearing, and the claimant does attend or gives the notice specified in r 27.9(1), the court has the power to decide the claim on the basis of the evidence of the claimant alone (r 27.9(3)).

Both parties fail to attend final hearing

If both parties fail to notify the court that they will not attend in accordance with r 27.9(1) (above) and neither party attends the hearing, the court can strike out the claim and any defence and counterclaim (r 27.9(4)).

Setting judgment aside and rehearing

Where a judgment is given following a small claims hearing in which one of the parties did not attend or give the notice in r 27.9(1), on the application of that party the court has the power to set the judgment aside and order a rehearing so long as certain conditions are met (r 27.11(1)). These are if the applicant can satisfy the court that:

(a) he had good reason for not attending or being represented at the hearing or giving notice under r 27.9(1); and

(b) he has a reasonable prospect of success at a hearing (r 27.11(3)).

Moreover, the party must make the application not more than 14 days after the day on which the judgment was served on him (r 27.11(2)). This is a similar test to that under r 39.5 for a case not allocated to the small track, where a party seeks to set aside judgment following a trial in his absence. It was held in *Barclays Bank plc v Ellis* (2000) *The Times*, 24 October, that the applicant needed to satisfy all three grounds of that test, and if all the grounds were not satisfied the court had no residual discretion to set judgment aside. It is submitted that r 27.11(3) will be interpreted in the same way (see Chapter 32, 'Hearings').

If the court grants the application and sets aside the judgment, it must fix a date for a new hearing of the claim. The judge may order that the hearing take place immediately after the hearing of the application to set the judgment aside and that it be heard by the same judge who set the judgment aside (r 27.11(4)).

The rules giving the court the power to set aside judgment do not apply where the court, with the agreement of all the parties, in accordance with r 27.10 (see below, 'Disposing of a small claim without a hearing'), has dealt with the claim without a hearing (r 27.11(5)). In those circumstances, the correct procedure for a party who wishes to challenge the judgment is for him to make an appeal in accordance with Part 52.

DISPOSING OF A SMALL CLAIM WITHOUT A HEARING

The court has the power, but only if all the parties agree, to dispose of the claim without a hearing (r 27.10).

Once a claim has been allocated to the small claims track, if the court deems it suitable for disposal without a hearing, it will notify the parties of this proposal and invite them to notify the court by a specified date whether they agree to it (r 27.4(1)(e)).

If the parties agree to disposal of the claim without a hearing, the court will decide the case on the parties' statements of case and other relevant documents. Once the judge has decided the matter, he will send a written note of his judgment and reasons for it to both parties (PD 27, para 5.6).

Although active case management includes 'dealing with the case without the parties needing to attend at court' (r 1.4(2)(j)), the judge cannot insist that the final hearing be dealt with in the absence of the parties, even if he believes it would be a suitable case for disposal in this way. Moreover, it is likely that most litigants would not agree to disposal of the case without a hearing.

COSTS ON THE SMALL CLAIMS TRACK

One of the most important features of the small claims track is the so called 'no costs rule'. This rule is an exception to the indemnity principle of our civil litigation system and provides that a party will not be able to recover the legal costs of a small claims case from his opponent (apart from certain limited costs), even in the event of success. The small claims track is designed to provide a simpler, quicker and more informal procedure for bringing and defending a claim so that a litigant in person can deal with the matter himself, and therefore the policy behind the no costs rule is to discourage the instruction of legal representatives, whose use is felt to be disproportionate to the matter being litigated. However, it should be noted that there is no express restriction on legal representation for small claims.

Costs in the discretion of the court

Rule 44.3, which provides that costs are in the discretion of the court, applies to small claims as it does to proceedings on any other track and, although provision is made for certain limited costs to be awarded on the small claims track, whether a party is awarded those costs depends on whether the court is prepared to exercise its discretion to order costs.

Costs of issuing proceedings

The restriction on recovering costs from an opponent does not apply to the fixed solicitor's costs attributable to issuing a claim payable under Part 45, and therefore the claimant can usually recover these if the claim is successful (r 27.14(2)(a)).

Proceedings for an injunction or specific performance

If a party is successful in bringing a claim for an injunction or specific performance on the small claims track, the court may order the opponent to pay a sum not exceeding £260 for legal advice and assistance involved in bringing such a claim (r 27.14(2)(b); PD 27, para 7.2).

Costs of an appeal

A successful party can also apply for the costs of an appeal from a decision on the small claims track. Those costs will be summarily assessed (r 27.14(2)(c)).

Unreasonable behaviour

If a party is held to have behaved unreasonably, the court may order him to pay costs to his opponent. The costs will be assessed summarily (r 27.14(2)(d)). It is rare for the judge to order that a party has behaved unreasonably, but an example might be where a party has unnecessarily caused a late adjournment of the hearing, unreasonably refused to negotiate, or failed to turn up at the hearing.

Under the former rules a similar provision applied, and in *Taylor v Ashworth* (1978) 128 NLJ 737, CA, a last-minute decision by a defendant not to proceed with his defence was held to be unreasonable behaviour, as was the overstatement of the amount of damages claimed and the raising of a speculative and unsupportable defence in *Afzal v Ford Motor Co Ltd* [1994] 4 All ER 720, CA.

Other fees and expenses

The court has a discretion to order a party to pay any court fees paid by their opponent (r 27.14(3)(a)). This may include such fees as the court issue fee and the allocation fee.

Party and witness expenses

The court also has a discretion to order one party to pay another party's or their witnesses' reasonable travel and accommodation expenses in attending the hearing (r 27.14(3)(b)).

Party's and witnesses' loss of earnings

Alternatively, the court can order one party to pay a sum up to a maximum of £50 per day for another party's, or their witnesses', loss of earnings in attending the hearing (r 27.14(3)(c); PD 27, para 7.3). The judge may apportion the amount ordered in relation to the length of the hearing. The principle of 'proportionality' would appear to support this.

Experts' fees

The court also has a discretion to order one party to pay the costs of the other party's expert fees up to a maximum of £200 (r 27.14(3)(d); PD 27, para 7.3). The standard form of directions sent out by the court does not contain a note as to the limit on experts' fees. If the maximum is exceeded, it may not be recoverable. Some courts are making this clear in their directions.

Lay representatives' fees

The restriction on recovering legal costs applies to the fees of a lay representative acting for a party as well as to lawyers' costs (r 27.14(4)).

Pre-allocation costs

If a claimant brings a claim for an amount exceeding the financial scope of the small claims track, but the defendant makes a part admission which reduces the value of the claim such that it comes within the scope of the small claims track, the claimant can, before allocation, apply for judgment with costs on the part admission, and the court has a discretion to allow costs in respect of the proceedings down to the date judgment is entered (PD 44, para 15.1(2)). This rule therefore allows a claimant to recover the costs for the part of the claim that exceeds the small claims limit.

The limitation on costs recoverable in small claims matters applies both before and after the claim is allocated to the small claims track, unless the court or a practice direction provides otherwise (r 44.9(2)). But note r 44.11(1): 'Any costs orders made before a claim is allocated will not be affected by allocation.'

Costs in cases allocated to the small claims track by agreement

If a case is outside the financial limits of the small claims track but the parties agree to the case being heard on the small claims track, the case will be treated, for the purposes of costs, as if it had been allocated to the fast track. However, the trial costs will be in the discretion of the judge, and shall not in any event exceed the fixed trial costs provided for fast track trials (r 27.14(5)).

Claims re-allocated to another track

If a claim, having originally been allocated to the small claims track, is re-allocated to another track, the 'no costs' rule will cease to apply to the claim from the date of re-allocation, but this will not include any costs incurred before that date. The costs rules for either the fast track or multi-track will then apply to the proceedings instead, depending on which track the case was subsequently allocated to (r 27.15).

APPEALS AGAINST JUDGMENT IN SMALL CLAIMS

The rules for appeals in Part 52 apply to appeals from judgments in cases heard on the small claims track in the same way as for hearings on the fast track and multi-track. The previous ground of 'serious irregularity' has now gone and permission to appeal must be obtained. An appeal from a district judge's decision is made to the circuit judge. An appeal from a circuit judge's decision is made to a High Court judge. The procedural requirements for an appeal from a small claims case are less onerous than those for other appeals (see PD 52, paras 5.8A–5.8D and Chapter 37, 'Appeals').

CHAPTER 18

THE FAST TRACK

INTRODUCTION

The fast track is an innovation of the Civil Procedure Rules (CPR) designed to provide expeditious and economic justice in cases between £5,000 and £15,000 where the trial will not last longer than a day. Expert evidence is limited and in most cases will be in the form of a written report prepared by a single joint expert. The fast track features 'a guaranteed and virtually immovable trial date within 30 weeks of allocation'.

The rules and practice directions make it clear that adherence to the timetable and the preservation of the set trial date are an essential feature of the fast track, and that failure to comply with the requirements of the court by specified dates will result in sanctions being imposed unless an extension has been previously granted by way of a prospective application. Sanctions may include striking out, debarring evidence, and various costs orders. The judge can lay down a strict timetable for the hearing itself, which is also expected to be adhered to. As there are fixed costs for the hearing, any adjournment from one day to another means that there will be no extra costs for any subsequent day. Advocates should bear this in mind.

District judges and circuit judges have concurrent jurisdiction in the fast track, with the likelihood that district judges will eventually have sole jurisdiction.

The rate of settlement in fast track trials has proved to be very high, influenced no doubt by the relatively short period for preparation, standard directions for the instruction of a single joint expert, and the application of proportionality to costs. The original proposals were for fixed costs for the whole of the preparation and trial of fast track matters, and considerable research was carried out to see if this was feasible. The limitation of fixed costs to the trial itself is a compromise and it is expected that eventually fixed costs will be introduced for the whole of the proceedings (see Chapter 5, 'Pre-Action Protocols', for a summary of the new scheme for pre-issue fixed fees introduced for low value road traffic accident cases).

ALLOCATION TO THE FAST TRACK

The fast track is the normal track for a claim:

(a) with a financial value of more than £5,000 but not more than £15,000;

(b) where the trial is likely to last for no longer than one day; and

(c) where oral expert evidence at trial will be limited to one expert per party in relation to any expert field and where there will be no more than two fields of expertise (r 26.6(4), (5)).

The claim will *not* be allocated to this track if the court considers that the trial is likely to last longer than five hours (one day) (PD 26, para 9.1(3)(a)). When considering whether the trial can be heard in one day the court will take into account the case management directions that are likely to be given (including the fixing of a trial timetable), as well as the court's powers to control evidence and limit cross-examination (PD 26, para 9.1(3)(b)). Where a case involves a counterclaim or other Part 20 claim that will be tried with the claim, and as a result the trial will last more than a day, the court may not allocate the case to the fast track (PD 26, para 9.1(3)(e)).

The *mere possibility* that the trial may last longer than five hours, or the fact that there is to be a split trial, will not prevent allocation to this track (PD 26, para 9.1(3)(c) and (d)). However, if a case is *likely* to last more than one day then the judge will consider allocating it to the multi-track even though it is within the financial value for the fast track limit.

For the court's discretion to re-allocate a case to another track, see Chapter 16, 'Judicial Case Management: Allocation'.

DIRECTIONS ON ALLOCATION

Case management of cases allocated to the fast track will generally be by directions given at two stages in the proceedings – on allocation to the fast track and on the filing of pre-trial checklists (previously known as listing questionnaires) (PD 28, para 2.1). The intention is for directions to be given on paper at those stages only, without a hearing. In accordance with the ethos of the CPR, the parties are expected to co-operate with each other, and with the court, so that appropriate directions can be agreed (PD 28, para 2.2). Parties often send proposed directions to the court with their allocation questionnaires. These are often useful to the court, but there is no guarantee that the orders suggested will be granted.

On allocation the court's first concern will be to ensure that the issues between the parties are identified and that the necessary evidence is prepared and disclosed (PD 28, para 3.3). In order to achieve this, directions can be tailored to a particular case, but subject to the general limitations on procedures for cases allocated to the fast track.

Court ordered directions on allocation

When it allocates a case to the fast track, the court will give directions for the management of the case and set a timetable for the steps to be taken between the giving of directions and the trial (r 28.2(1)). When it gives directions the court will fix the trial date or fix a trial window (r 28.2(2)).

The matters to be dealt with by directions include:

(a) disclosure of documents;

(b) service of witness statements; and

(c) expert evidence (r 28.3(1)).

Where the court is not aware of any steps taken by the parties other than the service of statements of case, its general approach will be to give directions for the following matters:

*   the filing and service of any further information (under Part 18) required to clarify either party's case;

*   standard disclosure between the parties;

*   disclosure of witness statements by way of simultaneous exchange;

- instruction of a single joint expert, unless there is good reason not to do so;
- where a single joint expert is not to be instructed, disclosure of experts' reports by way of simultaneous exchange; and
- if experts' reports are not agreed, directions for a discussion between the experts (under r 35.12) to identify the issues on which they agree and on which they disagree and for the preparation of a statement on these matters (PD 28, para 3.9).

In most cases the court will order directions based on those set out in Appendix A of PD 28 (PD 28, para 2.7).

Compliance with pre-action protocols

The court will seek to tailor its directions to the needs of the case and the steps it is aware the parties have already taken to prepare their case. In particular it will have regard to the extent to which any pre-action protocol has, or has not, been complied with (PD 28, para 3.2). The parties are expected to have complied with any relevant pre-action protocol or, if there is no applicable pre-action protocol, with the requirements for pre-action behaviour set out in the Practice Direction to the Protocols (see Chapter 5, 'Pre-Action Protocols').

If the parties have complied with the requirements then relevant documents should already have been exchanged, the issues in dispute should have been narrowed and the parties may even have agreed upon, or instructed, a single joint expert. In those circumstances, if the court considers that some or all of the steps in the standard timetable are not necessary, it may omit them and direct an earlier trial (PD 28, para 3.13).

Disclosure of documents

The usual order is for standard disclosure (r 31.5). However, as part of active case management the court will consider whether any other order for disclosure is necessary. If the nature of the case does not require it, the court may direct that no disclosure take place. Alternatively, the court may limit the requirements of disclosure by specifying the documents or classes of documents which the parties must disclose, for example, to damages only where liability is not in dispute (r 28.3(1)).

Expert evidence

Although expert evidence on the fast track is generally limited to one expert per party in relation to any expert field and to expert evidence in two fields of expertise (r 26.6(5)), in reality expert evidence on the fast track is usually by means of a written report from a single joint expert.

In accordance with the general rule, expert evidence is to be given by means of a written report and, indeed, for claims allocated to the fast track, the court will not direct an expert to attend a hearing unless it is necessary to do so in the interests of justice (r 35.5(2)). Further, the court will generally give directions for a single joint expert, unless there is good reason not to do so (PD 28, para 3.9(4)). Accordingly, even if the parties agree that each side should have its own expert evidence, the court can direct that a single joint expert be instructed instead (r 35.7).

In any event, given the limited duration of a trial on the fast track (one day), in most cases there will be insufficient time for parties to call separate experts to give oral evidence. Therefore, in those cases where it is appropriate to call expert oral evidence, and for each party to call separate expert evidence, it will usually be inappropriate to allocate it to the fast track, even if the claim is within the financial limits for cases allocated to that track.

Trial date/trial window

A key feature of the fast track is that on giving directions the court will fix a trial date, or (more likely) fix a trial period (trial window) of not more than three weeks within which the trial will take place, and the standard period between the giving of directions and the trial will be not more than 30 weeks (r 28.2(2) and (4)). The parties will be notified of the trial date or the trial window with the notice of allocation to the fast track (r 28.2(3)). At this stage, the court is more likely to fix a trial window rather than the trial date, with the trial date being fixed after pre-trial checklists have been filed.

'Typical' standard timetable

A typical, standard timetable, starting from the date of service of the order for directions, will provide for:

- disclosure – four weeks;
- exchange of witness statements – 10 weeks;
- exchange of experts' reports – 14 weeks;
- dispatch of pre-trial checklists by the court – 20 weeks;
- filing of completed pre-trial checklists – 22 weeks;
- hearing – 30 weeks (PD 28, para 3.12).

This is only a timetable based on the maximum period of 30 weeks between allocation and trial. In practice, the timetable may be based on a shorter period, particularly if the parties have already complied with the requirements of a pre-action protocol, so that compliance with some standard directions is unnecessary.

Agreed directions on allocation

The parties have an opportunity to agree directions prior to filing allocation questionnaires, and if they submit those agreed directions when filing their allocation questionnaires, and those directions are considered suitable by the court, the court will approve them and give directions in the terms agreed (PD 28, para 3.5). The parties should base their agreed directions on the form of directions at Appendix A to PD 28 (PD 28, para 2.7).

In order to obtain the court's approval the agreed directions must:

(a) set out a timetable by reference to *calendar dates* for the taking of steps for the preparation of the case;

(b) include a proposed date for the trial (or alternatively give a trial period of not more than three weeks), which is not later than 30 weeks (or, in the case of a trial period, which does not end later than 30 weeks) from the date the directions order is made;

(c) include provision about disclosure of documents; and

(d) include provision about both factual and expert evidence (PD 28, para 3.6).

Where appropriate the parties should also include agreed directions about:

(a) the filing of any reply or amended statement of case that may be required;

(b) dates for the service of requests for further information under Part 18; and

(c) the disclosure of evidence (PD 28, para 3.7).

The fact that the parties agree directions does not guarantee that the court will confirm all or any of them.

Disclosure

The proposed directions about disclosure of documents may limit disclosure to standard disclosure, and indeed this is the usual order the court will make in most cases (PD 28, paras 3.6(4)(a), 3.9). Alternatively the parties may propose that disclosure will take place by the supply of copy documents without a list. If that is proposed then the direction must either direct that the parties serve a disclosure statement with the copies, or record that they have agreed to disclosure in that way without such a statement (PD 28, para 3.6(4)).

Expert evidence

In the case of directions about expert evidence, this may include a direction that no expert evidence is required (PD 28, para 3.6(5)). However, where expert evidence is to be relied upon, the parties should include provision about the use of a single joint expert. Alternatively, where a single joint expert has not been agreed, provision should be made for simultaneous or sequential exchange of expert evidence and for without prejudice discussions between experts (PD 28, para 3.7(4)). The parties should also be aware that the court has the power to order the appointment of a single joint expert even if both parties agree to separate experts, and even if those separate experts have already been instructed (r 35.7).

In the case of both a single joint expert and separate experts, the parties should also agree dates for the service of questions to experts and the date by which those questions should be dealt with (PD 28, para 3.7(2)).

Allocation/case management hearings

If it appears to the court that the claim is one which will be allocated to the fast track but that it cannot properly give directions on its own initiative or approve agreed directions that have been filed by the parties, the court may either:

(a) allocate the claim to the fast track, fix a trial date or trial window, list a case management hearing and give directions at that hearing; or

(b) list an allocation hearing and give directions at that hearing (PD 28, para 3.10).

The court may hold an allocation hearing if, for instance, the parties have indicated in their allocation questionnaires that the case should be allocated to different tracks.

On allocating a case to the fast track the court may decide to hold a hearing to give directions if it is desirable to do so. If a hearing is necessary because of the default of a party or his legal representative, the court will usually impose a sanction (PD 28, para 2.3). If the court decides to hold a hearing it will give the parties at least three days' notice of the hearing (PD 28, para 2.6). The court will make arrangements to ensure that applications and hearings are listed promptly so as to avoid delay in the conduct of the case (PD 28, para 2.9).

Where any hearing has been fixed it is the duty of the parties to consider what directions the court should be asked to give and to make any application that may be appropriate to be dealt with at that hearing (PD 28, para 2.6).

DIRECTIONS ON LISTING

Pre-trial checklists

Unless the court dispenses with the need for pre-trial checklists, one of the directions given by the court on allocation to the fast track will include a date for the court to send pre-trial checklists to the parties and a date for the parties to file them at court (r 28.5; PD 28, paras 3.12, 6.1).

The court will send the pre-trial checklist, in Form N170, to the parties at least two weeks before the date specified for their return in the allocation notice, or that specified by any later direction of the court for the return of the completed pre-trial checklists (PD 28, para 6.1(2)). The date specified for filing a pre-trial checklist will not be more than eight weeks before the trial date or the beginning of the trial window (r 28.5(2)).

A fee of £200 is payable by the claimant on filing the listing questionnaire (County Court Fees Order 1999 (SI 1999/689), Sched 1, para 2.1). The fee is £400 in the High Court (Supreme Court Fees Order 1999 (SI 1999/687), Sched 1, para 2.1), although it is highly unlikely, given the financial limits of the track, that a fast track matter will be dealt with by the High Court.

The listing questionnaire requires the parties to provide the following information.

Directions

Whether:

- the party has complied with previous directions; and
- if not why, and to what extent further directions are required; and
- if so which and why.

Experts

Whether:

- the court has already given permission for the use of written expert evidence and if so, for which experts and in which fields;

- reports have been agreed;
- the experts have met;
- the court has already given permission for the use of oral expert evidence and if so, for which experts and in which fields;
- such permission is sought and if so, for which experts and in which fields;
- there are dates *within the trial window* when the experts are not available.

Other witnesses

- How many?
- Names and addresses.
- Availability details *within the trial window.*
- Whether:
  - any statements are agreed;
  - special facilities or an interpreter are required and if so, what.

Legal representation

Whether, and if so by whom, the party is to be represented, together with availability details.

Other matters

The estimated:

- length of the case; and
- number of pages of evidence in the trial bundle.

Costs estimate

The parties are also required to file a costs estimate with their pre-trial checklist in the same form as that to be filed with the allocation questionnaire (PD 43, para 6.4).

Trial timetable

The parties should also file a proposed trial timetable with their pre-trial checklists (see Form N170).

Failure to file pre-trial checklist

If neither party returns the listing questionnaire within 14 days of service then, according to PD 28, para 6.5(1), the court may make an order requiring return of the questionnaire within three days, in default of which the claim and any counterclaim will be struck out. If only one party returns the listing questionnaire then PD 28, para 6.5(2) provides that the judge shall usually give listing directions or fix a listing hearing.

Court fees

Unless he obtains an exemption or a remission, the claimant must pay a court fee when filing the pre-trial checklist. The fee is still payable even if the court dispenses with the need for pre-trial checklists (Supreme Court Fees Order 1999, Sched 1, para 2.1; County Court Fees Order 1999, Sched 1, para 2.1). If the claimant does not pay the fee, the court may send out a notice in Form N173 requiring payment within a specified time and warning the claimant that if he does not pay, his claim will be struck out and he will be liable for the costs of the defendant (r 3.7).

Court ordered directions on listing

As soon as practicable after the date specified for filing a completed pre-trial checklist, the court will make directions to deal with the following matters:

- If a trial date has not already been fixed, fix a date for trial, or confirm the date previously fixed for trial.
- Give directions about evidence, for example, that witness statements are to stand as evidence-in-chief.
- Give directions for trial, including a trial timetable.
- Give a time estimate for the trial.
- Give directions for the preparation of the bundle.
- Specify any further steps that need to be taken before trial (r 28.6; PD 28, para 7.2).

The parties must be given three weeks' notice of the trial date unless, in exceptional circumstances, the court directs that shorter notice will be given (r 28.6(2); PD 28, para 7.1(2)). The notice of hearing will be in Form N172 (PD 28, para 7.1(3)).

Apart from fixing or confirming the trial date, the court will also specify the place of trial and give a time estimate. The trial date must be fixed on the basis that the hearing will end on the same calendar day as that on which it commenced (PD 28, para 7.1).

The court may give directions as to the issues on which evidence is to be given, the nature of the evidence it requires on those issues and the way in which it is to be placed before the court, and may thereby exclude evidence which would otherwise be admissible (r 32.1). A direction giving permission to use expert evidence will say whether it is to be by report or oral, and will name the experts whose evidence is permitted. Permission may be made conditional on the experts discussing their differences and filing a report on the discussion (PD 28, para 7.2(4)).

The usual direction in respect of bundles is for the claimant to lodge an indexed bundle of documents contained in a ring binder with each page clearly numbered, not more than seven and not less than three days before the start of the trial.

Agreed directions on listing

The parties should attempt to agree directions and file them at court with the pre-trial checklists. The court will take the agreed directions into account and may make an order in those terms, or may make a different order (PD 28, para 7.2(1)).

The agreed directions should include provision for:

(a) evidence;

(b) a trial timetable and a trial estimate;

(c) the preparation of a trial bundle; and

(d) any other matters needed to prepare the case for trial (PD 28, para 7.2(2)).

Listing hearing

If a party fails to file the completed pre-trial checklist by the date specified, or if a party fails to give all the information requested in the pre-trial checklist, the court is likely to order a listing hearing, to enable it to decide what directions to give in order to complete preparation of the case for trial (r 28.5(3)). In those circumstances the party at fault is at risk of being ordered to pay the costs of the listing hearing, potentially on the indemnity basis.

The court has a general power to hold a listing hearing if necessary for the purposes of deciding what directions to give for trial (r 28.5(3)).

Where the court decides to hold a listing hearing, the parties will be given at least three days' notice (in Form N153) of the date (PD 28, para 6.3).

Alternatively, if a party fails to file a pre-trial checklist by the date specified, some courts may make an 'unless' order with threats of a sanction in default.

VARIATION OF CASE MANAGEMENT TIMETABLE

Additional directions

Where a party needs to apply for a direction not included in the case management timetable (for example, to amend his statement of case, or for an order that another party provide further information), he must do so as soon as possible so as to minimise the need to change the timetable (PD 28, para 2.8). In accordance with general principle, a party should first seek the agreement of the other party to the additional direction required and file a consent order at court recording the party's agreement. If the other party does not agree then an application will need to be made to the court, in accordance with Part 23, for the court to order the additional direction.

Variation of directions

The parties may vary the case management timetable by written agreement, unless the rules or a practice direction provide otherwise (r 2.11). For instance, the parties may agree that there should be additional time for the service of witness statements, or agree to dispense with or limit standard disclosure. In those circumstances there is no need to file the written agreement at court.

However, the parties cannot agree to vary the case management timetable if the variation would make it necessary to vary any of the dates the court has fixed for:

(a) the filing of the completed allocation questionnaire;

(b) the filing of the completed pre-trial checklist;

(c) the trial; or

(d) the trial period (rr 26.3(6A), 28.4).

If a party wishes to vary any of the dates fixed for the above, he must make an application to the court (r 28.4).

Practice Direction 28 states that it is essential that any party who wishes to have a direction varied take steps to do so as soon as possible. Also, the court will assume, for the purposes of any later application, that a party who did not appeal and who made no application to vary within 14 days of service of the order containing the directions was content that they were correct in the circumstances then existing (PD 28, para 4.2). A party who makes an application outside of this time period should therefore be prepared to explain the reasons for the delay.

If the parties agree that the above dates should be varied, they should apply for an order by consent and file at court a draft of the order sought and an agreed statement of the reasons why the variation is sought. The court may make an order in the agreed terms, or in other terms without a hearing, or it may direct that a hearing be listed (PD 28, para 4.5(2)).

If a party is dissatisfied with a direction given by the court, he may appeal or apply to the court for it to reconsider its decision. A party should appeal if the direction was given or the order was made at a hearing at which he was present or represented, or of which he had due notice (see Chapter 37, 'Appeals', for the restrictions imposed upon appealing case management decisions). In any other case he should apply to the court to reconsider its decision. If an application is made for the court to reconsider its decision, it will usually be heard by the judge who gave the directions or another judge of the same level, and the court will give all parties at least three days' notice of the hearing. The court may confirm its decision or make a different order (PD 28, para 4.3).

The rules allow the court the flexibility to set aside or vary directions where there has been a change in the circumstances since the order was given. This power can be exercised on an application, or by the court acting on its own initiative (PD 28, para 4.4).

In *Jameson v Lovis* [2001] EWCA Civ 1264, the case management judge ordered that expert evidence on two areas of expertise was to be adduced by single joint experts. At a case management conference the claimant sought permission to rely on expert evidence from other experts instead, separately instructed by the claimant. The district judge refused the claimant's application. The claimant's appeal against the judge's decision was dismissed and permission to appeal to the Court of Appeal refused. The claimant did not apply to the Court of Appeal for permission to appeal. However, at a subsequent case management conference the claimant unsuccessfully sought the same orders that had already been rejected by the district judge at the earlier case management conference. The claimant then appealed to the Court of Appeal against this refusal to change the case management decisions. The Court of Appeal criticised the claimant for seeking to 'air [his] case management points all over again at a later case management conference'. The court noted that there were clear and detailed procedures for bringing appeals against interim orders that were not mere technicalities, their purpose being to achieve finality and certainty within the processes of civil litigation. Although it was accepted that if there were a change of circumstances the flexibility of the CPR would allow a change of view as to the procedural orders that had been made, where there was no such change of circumstances the proper approach was, if possible, to appeal the case management decision.

It should be noted that the court will vary the date fixed for trial only in exceptional circumstances and only as a last resort (PD 28, para 5.4(6); and see below, 'Failure to comply with case management directions').

Failure to comply with case management directions

Where one party has failed to comply with a court direction the other party may apply to the court for an order to enforce compliance or for a sanction to be imposed, or both, but he must make the application without delay, and before doing so he should warn the other party of his intention to do so (PD 28, paras 5.1, 5.2).

If the party seeking to enforce compliance with the court direction delays before applying to the court, the court will take this delay into account when considering whether to impose a sanction on the other party, or when considering whether to grant the other party relief from a sanction imposed by the rules or a practice direction (PD 28, para 5.3).

The court will not allow a party's failure to comply with directions to lead to the postponement of the trial unless the circumstances are exceptional (PD 28, para 5.4(1)). Where the trial date is in jeopardy due to a party's failure to comply with directions, the court will exercise its case management powers so as to ensure that essential steps are taken to prepare the case for trial within the shortest possible time, and impose a sanction for non-compliance. Such a sanction may, for instance, deprive a party of the right to raise or contest an issue or to rely on evidence to which the direction relates (PD 28, para 5.4(2), (3)).

If some issues can be made ready for trial at the time fixed while others cannot, the court may direct that the trial proceeds on the issues which are ready, and order that no costs be allowed for any later trial of the remaining issues, or order that those costs be paid by the party in default (PD 28, para 5.4(1), (4)).

Where the court has no option but to postpone the trial, it will do so for the shortest possible time and will give directions in the meantime for the necessary steps to be taken as quickly as possible (PD 28, para 5.4(5)).

It is expressly stated that litigants and their lawyers must be in no doubt that the court will regard the postponement of the trial as an order of last resort. If an application is made to postpone the trial, the court may exercise its powers to require a party, as well as his legal representative, to attend the hearing of the application at which such an order is sought (PD 28, para 5.4(6)).

In *Matthews v Tarmac Bricks & Tiles Ltd* (1999) 143 SJLB 196, CA (incidentally, the first case in which the Court of Appeal was asked to take into account the CPR), the Court of Appeal refused to interfere with a designated civil judge's order fixing a trial date despite both parties' wish to defer the trial to meet the convenience of experts. The judge had fixed a date for trial despite the fact that one of the party's expert witnesses was unavailable on that date, on the grounds that the barrister instructed by the party was unable to explain why the expert was unavailable on that date. The Court of Appeal indicated that if a party is able to explain to the judge that an expert is abroad or already due to attend another hearing, the case management judge can give that information proper consideration when deciding which date to fix for trial. However, if the date is simply inconvenient for an expert, the parties cannot always expect the courts to meet their convenience, particularly if a date is being fixed for trial at a late stage in the proceedings.

The Court of Appeal said that the previous practice under the former rules, whereby it was thought that all that was required was to tell the court the dates that would not be convenient for the doctors instructed by the parties and the court would find a date which would allow the case to be heard to meet their convenience, would no longer be appropriate. Instead, the right course is for the parties to attempt to reach agreement between themselves as to the dates that could be met; they should then consult with the court, and with the court's co-operation find a date within a reasonable time for the hearing. Lord Woolf stated:

> I hope the message that will be understood by both the medical profession and the legal profession, is that it is essential that if parties want cases to be fixed for hearing in accordance with the dates which meet their convenience, those dates should be fixed as early as possible. The parties cannot always expect the courts to meet their convenience. If they hold themselves out as practising in the medico-legal field doctors must be prepared to arrange their affairs to meet the commitments of the courts where this is practical. If there is no agreement as to the dates which are acceptable to the court, the lawyers for the parties must be in a position to give the reasons why certain dates are not convenient to doctors ...

THE TRIAL

The trial will usually take place at the court where the case is being managed, but it may be at another court if appropriate, depending on the needs of the parties and the availability of court resources (PD 28, para 8.1).

Preparation for trial is two-sided:

- The judges should have properly digested the papers *before trial* (PD 28, para 8.2).
- The trial bundle must be so put together as to assist such preparation (PD 28, para 7.2(2)(c); and see PD 39, para 3).
- The parties should attend all hearings with updated costs details, both of costs expended and those likely to be expended. As there is now a requirement for costs estimates to be provided, it is important that those estimates are realistic, as the parties may be held to them in any future assessment of costs.

The court may set a timetable for the trial (r 28.6(1)(b); PD 28, para 7.2(2)(b)). No 'typical' timetable is suggested by the rules or practice directions, but a possible trial timetable for a one-day fast track case may look something like this (*note*: a court day should normally be regarded as five hours (see PD 26, para 9.1(3)(a)):

Judge's reading time	30 minutes
Opening (may be dispensed with – PD 28, para 8.2)	10 minutes
Cross-examination and re-examination of claimant's witness(es)	90 minutes
Cross-examination and re-examination of defendant's witness(es)	90 minutes
Defendant's submissions	15 minutes

Claimant's submissions	15 minutes
Judge's 'thinking time' and judgment	30 minutes
Summary assessment of costs and consequential orders	20 minutes
Total:	5 hours

If the case has to go over from one day it should, if possible, be heard the next day (PD 28, para 8.6).

As can be seen from the above, evidence-in-chief is not included because it is expected to be provided by witness statement (r 32.5(2)) and cross-examination can be curtailed (r 32.1(3)). The strict timetabling of the trial and the lack of refresher fee or additional costs make it clear that it is incumbent on the parties or their legal representatives to ensure that the timetable is kept to by proper preparation prior to trial, taking into account the imposed constraints. The judge is likely to cut off a party if its time is being exceeded, and he will be watching for deliberate prevarication.

Fast track cases are likely to be 'block listed' among a number of judges and courts, so last-minute changes of venue are possible. No other business will normally be listed before a one-day trial and, since there will be no margin for delay, the court will require a prompt start. The new regime encourages parties to negotiate long before trial, and those who leave it until the last moment should arrive at court with plenty of time to spare before the start.

COSTS

The costs of fast track proceedings will usually be summarily assessed at the conclusion of the trial (PD 28, para 8.5). Each party who intends to claim costs must file at court and serve on every other party a statement of costs (PD 44, para 13.5(1)). The statement of costs should follow as closely as possible model Form N260 (PD 43, para 3.2; PD 44, para 13.5(3)). The statement of costs must be filed at court and copies served on any party as soon as possible, and in any event not less than 24 hours before the date fixed for the hearing (PD 44, para 13.5(4); see Chapter 34, 'Costs of Proceedings', for further detail about, and the consequences of failure to file, a statement of costs).

There are fixed costs for the advocate on the trial, varying between £350 and £750 depending on the amount awarded in relation to the claimant and the amount claimed in relation to the defendant, but this is not dependent on the length of the trial (r 46.2; see Chapter 34, 'Costs of Proceedings', for detailed consideration of fast track trial costs).

When the rules for fast track were introduced, the provisions as to conditional fee agreements had not yet been brought into effect, including as they do the question of disputes over the success fee. The added factor of a challenged success fee is likely to breach the timetabling arrangements as set out above, and may make it necessary for an adjournment or reference of the argument to a detailed assessment, which is somewhat against the spirit of the fast track hearing.

CHAPTER 19

THE MULTI-TRACK

INTRODUCTION

The multi-track is suitable for complex cases, or cases of high value which are likely to involve the most pre-trial preparation and case management directions. The multi-track allows the court the discretion to decide how much case management a case requires. In order to provide 'hands-on' case management the court may fix a case management conference or a pre-trial review, or both, with the latter being conducted by the judge before whom the case will be listed for trial. The hallmarks of the multi-track are said to be the ability of the court to deal with cases of widely differing values and complexity, and the flexibility given to the court to manage a case in a way appropriate to its particular needs (PD 29, para 3.2).

ALLOCATION TO THE MULTI-TRACK

The multi-track is the normal track for any claim for which the small claims track or the fast track is not the normal track (r 26.6(6)). The multi-track will therefore encompass claims where the financial value exceeds £15,000, or where the trial is likely to last more than one day, or where there will be more than one expert per party called to give evidence at trial, or for claims where expert evidence in more than two fields of expertise is required.

Claims commenced using the Part 8 procedure are automatically allocated to the multi-track (r 8.9(c)). Also, a claim to which any of Part 49 (specialist proceedings) or Parts 58–62 (specialist lists, for example, commercial court, mercantile courts) apply will be allocated to the multi-track irrespective of its value (PD 26, para 10.2(2)).

VENUE FOR ALLOCATION AND CASE MANAGEMENT

Where the case is one commenced in the Royal Courts of Justice and over which it has jurisdiction then case management will usually be carried out there (PD 29, para 3.1(1)).

Apart from cases proceeding in the Royal Courts of Justice, case management of other cases allocated to the multi-track will normally be undertaken at Civil Trial Centres (PD 29, para 3.1(2)). Civil Trial Centres are regionally situated and are supplemented by 'feeder courts', usually smaller, local county courts that usually transfer multi-track cases to the Civil Trial Centres. The Centres are presided over by designated civil judges, who give guidance to the courts within their responsibility as to the application of the Civil Procedure Rules (CPR) and oversee their operation (see Chapter 16, 'Judicial Case Management: Allocation', for further details). In the London area, for example, the designated civil judge has allowed the feeder courts to keep multi-track possession cases and those multi-track cases which are estimated to last no longer than a day. He has no objection to the feeder courts giving directions in appropriate multi-track cases prior to their transfer to the Trial Centre – the

Central London Civil Justice Centre. Other areas may well have their own, similar arrangements.

DIRECTIONS ON ALLOCATION

On allocation, and after considering the parties' statements of case and allocation questionnaires and other documents filed at court, the court will consider whether it is desirable or necessary to hold a case management conference (CMC) straight away, or whether it is appropriate instead to give directions on its own initiative (PD 29, para 4.5).

The procedural judge may do any or all of the following:

- issue written directions for the management of the case and set a timetable for the steps to be taken between the giving of directions and trial (r 29.2(1)(a));
- set a timetable to fix, as appropriate:
  - a CMC;
  - a pre-trial review (PTR) (r 29.2(1)(b));
  - a date for the filing of a completed pre-trial checklist (r 29.2(3)(b));
- set a trial date or a trial window as soon as practicable and give notice to the parties of the trial date or trial window (r 29.2(2) and (3)(a); PD 29, para 4.10).

Court ordered directions

It is of the essence of the multi-track that directions, given at or without a hearing, will be tailored to the needs of the case and the steps already taken by the parties. At this stage the court's first concern will be to ensure that the issues are identified and that the necessary evidence is prepared and disclosed (PD 29, para 4.3). The court will have regard to the parties' compliance or non-compliance with any relevant pre-action protocol (PD 29, para 4.2). If, due to compliance with the requirements of a relevant pre-action protocol, there is no need for a usual direction to be ordered, for example, disclosure, the court may tailor its directions accordingly.

Where the court decides to give directions on its own initiative without holding a CMC and it is not aware of any steps taken by the parties other than the exchange of statement of case, its general approach will be to direct:

- filing and service of any further information needed to clarify a party's case;
- standard disclosure;
- simultaneous exchange of witness statements;
- the instruction of a single joint expert on any appropriate issue; otherwise, simultaneous exchange of experts' reports (unless it is appropriate for reports on the amount of damages to be disclosed subsequently to those on liability); the court will not, however (except where the parties agree), require instruction of a single expert nor appoint an assessor without fixing a CMC;
- discussion between experts and a statement thereon, if they are not agreed;
- a CMC after the time for compliance with directions; and
- the fixing of a trial period (PD 29, para 4.10).

Agreed directions

The court will expect the parties to co-operate in the giving of directions; and if the parties agree directions, including a proposed trial date or trial window, and the court considers the directions are suitable, it may approve them without a hearing and give directions in the terms proposed (r 29.4; PD 29, para 4.6).

In order to obtain the court's approval the agreed directions must:

(a) set out a timetable by reference to *calendar dates* for the taking of steps for the preparation of the case;

(b) include a date or a trial window when it is proposed the trial will take place;

(c) include provision about disclosure of documents; and

(d) include provision about both factual and expert evidence (PD 29, para 4.7).

Where appropriate the parties should also include agreed directions about:

(a) the filing of any reply or amended statement of case that may be required;

(b) dates for the service of requests for further information under Part 18;

(c) dates for the service of questions to experts under r 35.6 and dates when those questions are to be dealt with;

(d) the use of a single joint expert or, in cases where it is not agreed, the exchange of expert evidence and provisions for without prejudice discussions between experts; and

(e) the disclosure of evidence (PD 29, para 4.8).

The court will scrutinise the parties' proposed timetable carefully, and in particular will be concerned to see that any proposed date or period for the trial and (if provided for) a CMC is no later than reasonably necessary (PD 29, para 4.7(2)).

If the court does not approve the parties' agreed directions and decides to give directions of its own initiative without fixing a CMC, it will take the parties' directions into account in deciding the directions to give (PD 29, para 4.9).

Case management conference

The purpose of the CMC is to set the agenda for the case at the earliest possible stage to ensure that the procedures followed and costs incurred are proportionate to the case. The court will fix a CMC if it appears that it cannot properly give directions on its own initiative and no agreed directions have been filed which it can approve (PD 29, para 4.12). The CMC will be listed as promptly as possible and at least three days' notice will be given (PD 29, para 3.7).

At the CMC the court will review the steps the parties have taken in preparation of their case, and in particular whether the parties have complied with any directions the court may have given. The court will also ensure, as far as it can, that all agreements that can be reached between the parties about the matters in issue and the conduct of the claim are made and recorded (PD 29, para 5.1).

At the CMC, the following matters are likely to be dealt with:

• whether the claimant has made clear the claim he is bringing, in particular the amount he is claiming, so that the other party can understand the case he has to meet (PD 29, para 5.3(1));

- whether any amendments are required to a statement of case (PD 29, para 5.3(2));
- directions on the future conduct of the case, including issues such as disclosure (PD 29, para 5.3(3));
- establishing the likely timescale of the case – this may include setting dates for the milestone events, for example, any further CMC, the return of the pre-trial checklist, or any pre-trial review (PD 29, para 5.4);
- setting the trial date or trial window (if this has not already been done) (PD 29, para 5.4);
- agreeing a case summary (PD 29, para 5.7);
- exploring with the parties:
  - the scope for settlement at this stage, or the possibility of disposing of any particular issues;
  - the extent to which experts will be needed, including the scope for using a single or joint expert, but the court will not at this stage give permission to use expert evidence unless it can identify each expert by name or field and say whether his evidence is to be given orally or by the use of his report (PD 29, para 5.5);
  - the extent to which non-experts will be needed, and the need for oral evidence;
  - whether there should be a split trial or trial of a preliminary issue (in which case any directions would need to indicate to which aspect of the case they referred) (PD 29, para 5.3(7)); and
  - whether the case should be tried by a High Court judge or a specialist judge (PD 29, para 5.9).

If a party intends to apply for a direction not routinely made at a CMC and which he believes may be opposed, he should issue and serve the application in time for it to be heard at the CMC. If the time allowed for the CMC is likely to be insufficient for the application to be heard, the party should inform the court at once so that a fresh date can be fixed. If a party fails to comply with these requirements, and as a result there is insufficient time to deal with all relevant matters at the CMC, a costs sanction may be imposed upon him (PD 29, para 5.8).

If a party has legal representation, a representative familiar with the case and with sufficient authority to deal with any issues which may arise must attend the CMC (r 29.3(2)). That person must be someone personally involved with the conduct of the case, able to deal with fixing the timetable, identification of issues and matters of evidence (PD 29, para 5.2(2)). A wasted costs order will usually be made if the inadequacy of the person attending or his instructions leads to an adjournment (PD 29, para 5.2).

Parties must ensure that all relevant documents (including witness statements and experts' reports) are available to the judge and that all parties know what directions the other seeks (PD 29, para 5.6). The parties and their legal advisers should consider whether the parties personally should attend and whether it would be useful to provide a *case summary* (prepared by the claimant and agreed with the other parties if possible) setting out in 500 words a brief chronology, facts agreed and in dispute, and evidence needed (PD 29, para 5.7).

VARIATION OF CASE MANAGEMENT TIMETABLE

Additional directions

Where a party needs to apply for a direction not included in the case management timetable (for example, to amend his statement of case, or for an order that another party provide further information), he must do so as soon as possible so as to minimise the need to change the timetable (PD 29, para 3.8). In accordance with general principle, a party should first seek the agreement of the other party to the additional direction required and file a consent order at court recording the party's agreement. If the other party does not agree then an application will need to be made to the court, in accordance with Part 23, for the court to order the additional direction.

Variation of directions

The parties may vary the case management timetable by written agreement, unless the rules or a practice direction provide otherwise (r 2.11). For instance, the parties may agree that there should be additional time for the service of witness statements, or agree to dispense with or limit standard disclosure. In those circumstances there is no need to file the written agreement at court.

However, the parties cannot agree to vary the case management timetable if the variation would make it necessary to vary any of the dates the court has fixed for:

(a) the filing of the completed allocation questionnaire;

(b) a CMC;

(c) a pre-trial review;

(d) the filing of the completed pre-trial checklist;

(e) the trial; or

(f) the trial period (rr 26.3(6A), 29.5(1)).

If a party wishes to vary any of the dates fixed for the above, he must make an application to the court (r 29.5).

Practice Direction 29 states that it is essential that any party who wishes to have a direction varied take steps to do so as soon as possible. Also, the court will assume, for the purposes of any later application, that a party who did not appeal and who made no application to vary within 14 days of service of the order containing the directions was content that they were correct in the circumstances then existing (PD 29, para 6.2). A party who makes an application outside of this time period should therefore be prepared to explain the reasons for the delay.

If the parties agree that the above dates should be varied, they should apply for an order by consent and file at court a draft of the order sought and an agreed statement of the reasons why the variation is sought. The court may make an order in the agreed terms, or in other terms without a hearing, or it may direct that a hearing be listed (PD 29, para 6.5).

If a party is dissatisfied with a direction given by the court, he may appeal or apply to the court for it to reconsider its decision. A party should appeal if the direction was given or the order was made at a hearing at which he was present or represented, or of which he had due notice (see Chapter 37, 'Appeals', for the restrictions imposed upon appealing case management decisions). In any other case he should apply to the court to reconsider its decision. If an application is made for the court to reconsider its decision, it will usually be heard by the judge who gave the directions or another judge of the same level, and the court will give all parties at least three days' notice of the hearing. The court may confirm its decision or make a different order (PD 29, para 6.3).

The rules allow the court the flexibility to set aside or vary directions where there has been a change in the circumstances since the order was given. This power can be exercised on an application, or by the court acting on its own initiative (PD 29, para 6.4).

In *Jameson v Lovis* [2001] EWCA Civ 1264, the case management judge ordered that expert evidence on two areas of expertise was to be adduced by single joint experts. At a case management conference the claimant sought permission to rely on expert evidence from other experts instead, separately instructed by the claimant. The district judge refused the claimant's application. The claimant's appeal against the judge's decision was dismissed and permission to appeal to the Court of Appeal refused. The claimant did not apply to the Court of Appeal for permission to appeal. However, at a subsequent case management conference the claimant unsuccessfully sought the same orders that had already been rejected by the district judge at the earlier CMC. The claimant then appealed to the Court of Appeal against this refusal to change the case management decisions. The Court of Appeal criticised the claimant for seeking to 'air [his] case management points all over again at a later case management conference'. The court noted that there were clear and detailed procedures for bringing appeals against interim orders that were not mere technicalities, their purpose being to achieve finality and certainty within the processes of civil litigation. Although it was accepted that if there were a change of circumstances the flexibility of the CPR would allow a change of view as to the procedural orders that had been made, where there was no such change of circumstances the proper approach was, if possible, to appeal the case management decision.

It should be noted that the court will vary the date fixed for trial only in exceptional circumstances and only as a last resort (PD 29, para 7.4(6); and see below, 'Failure to comply with case management directions').

Failure to comply with case management directions

Where one party has failed to comply with a court direction, the other party may apply to the court for an order to enforce compliance or for a sanction to be imposed, or both, but he must make the application without delay, and before doing so he should warn the other party of his intention to do so (PD 29, paras 7.1, 7.2).

If the party seeking to enforce compliance with the court direction delays before applying to the court, the court will take this delay into account when considering whether to impose a sanction on the other party, or when considering whether to grant the other party relief from a sanction imposed by the rules or a practice direction (PD 29, para 7.3).

The court will not allow a party's failure to comply with directions to lead to the postponement of the trial unless the circumstances are exceptional (PD 29, para 7.4(1)). Where the trial date is in jeopardy due to a party's failure to comply with directions, the court will exercise its case management powers so as to ensure that essential steps are taken to prepare the case for trial within the shortest possible time, and impose a sanction for non-compliance. Such a sanction may, for instance, deprive a party of the right to raise or contest an issue, or to rely on evidence to which the direction relates (PD 29, para 7.4(2), (3)).

If some issues can be made ready for trial at the time fixed while others cannot, the court may direct that the trial proceeds on the issues which are ready, and order that no costs be allowed for any later trial of the remaining issues, or order that those costs be paid by the party in default (PD 29, para 7.4(4)).

Where the court has no option but to postpone the trial, it will do so for the shortest possible time and will give directions in the meantime for the necessary steps to be taken as quickly as possible (PD 29, para 7.4(5)).

It is expressly stated that litigants and their lawyers must be in no doubt that the court will regard the postponement of the trial as an order of last resort. If an application is made to postpone the trial, the court may exercise its powers to require a party, as well as his legal representative, to attend the hearing of the application at which such an order is sought (PD 29, para 7.4(6)).

The court will not postpone any other hearing without a very good reason, and for that purpose the failure of a party to comply on time with directions previously given will not be treated as a good reason (PD 29, para 7.4(7)).

In *Holmes v SGB Services* [2001] EWCA Civ 354, the Court of Appeal upheld the trial judge's decision to allow a late amendment to the claim and adjourn the trial on being satisfied that the judge had taken into account a possible tension between the importance of maintaining a trial date and the interests of justice. In making that decision the judge had carried out a balancing exercise and had concluded that the making of the orders sought resulted in the case being dealt with justly. The Court of Appeal emphasised that the judge was exercising a discretion and making a case management decision, and as such the appellant would need to show that the judge erred in principle, not simply that he could have reached another decision. In the circumstances the Court of Appeal found that the judge correctly applied the overriding objective and concluded that the claimant should have the opportunity to instruct his expert on further matters, and therefore his decision to vacate the date fixed for trial and re-list the matter for a new trial date should be upheld.

PRE-TRIAL CHECKLISTS

In practice, listing questionnaires are used only in cases in which the timetable is thought likely to give rise to difficulty. In most cases, the direction given will frequently be 'That there be no pre-trial checklist, save where required by the Listing Office, in which case the completed pre-trial checklist must be filed within 10 days after receipt by the party required to complete it, or within such other period as the court may direct'.

Where the court considers a pre-trial checklist necessary, in accordance with the procedural judge's directions, it will send pre-trial checklists to the parties (r 29.6(1)) no later than two weeks before they are to be returned (PD 29, para 8.1(4)), which will be no later than eight weeks before the trial date or trial period (PD 29, para 8.1(3)). The parties are encouraged to exchange copies of their questionnaires before filing them, to avoid the court being given conflicting or incomplete information (PD 29, para 8.1(5)).

The listing questionnaire will help the court in deciding whether to fix a PTR (r 29.7). Where such a hearing has already been fixed, it will inform the court as to whether that hearing is still required. The form of questionnaire is in Form N170, the same as for fast track. Thus, the listing questionnaire will ask for confirmation that:

(a) directions with regard to disclosure have been complied with;

(b) witness statements and expert reports have been exchanged;

(c) any other directions have been complied with.

If directions have not been complied with, the parties will be required to give reasons why.

The parties will also be asked for:

(a) confirmation of the remaining issues outstanding to be tried;

(b) an estimate of the length of trial;

(c) details of:

- witnesses who will be attending to give evidence;
- any special needs of anyone involved with the trial;
- any other information which the court should know at this stage.

On the basis of the information provided, the court will:

(a) fix a pre-trial review (giving at least seven days' notice);

(b) cancel a previously fixed pre-trial review (r 29.7);

(c) give listing directions;

(d) fix or confirm the trial date; and/or

(e) give any directions for the trial itself (including a trial timetable) which it considers appropriate (r 29.8; PD 29, para 8.2).

Costs estimate

The parties are also required to file a costs estimate with their pre-trial checklists in the same form as that to be filed with the allocation questionnaire (PD 43, para 6.4).

Trial timetable

The parties should also file a proposed trial timetable with their pre-trial checklists (see Form N170).

Failure to file pre-trial checklist

If neither party returns the pre-trial checklist within 14 days of service then, according to PD 29, para 8.3(1), the court may make an order requiring return of the pre-trial checklist within three days, in default of which the claim and any counterclaim will be struck out. If only one party returns the pre-trial checklist then

PD 28, para 8.3(2) provides that the judge shall usually give listing directions or fix a listing hearing. If a listing hearing is directed, the court will fix a date which is as early as possible, giving the parties at least three days' notice (PD 28, para 8.4).

Court fees

Unless he obtains an exemption or a remission, the claimant must pay a court fee when filing the pre-trial checklist. The fee is still payable even if the court dispenses with the need for pre-trial checklists (Supreme Court Fees Order 1999 (SI 1999/687), Sched 1, para 2.1; County Court Fees Order 1999 (SI 1999/689), Sched 1, para 2.1).

If the claimant does not pay the fee, the court may send out a notice in Form N173 requiring payment within a specified time and warning the claimant that if he does not pay, his claim will be struck out and he will be liable for the costs of the defendant (r 3.7).

Pre-trial review

The PTR may be held by the eventual trial judge about 8–10 weeks (variable) before the trial itself in order to:

(a) resolve any discrepancies between the pre-trial checklists;

(b) check that directions have been complied with;

(c) finalise the statement of issues to be tried (at the CMC the court will already have endeavoured to narrow the issues to those relevant to be tried (see r 1.4));

(d) confirm the hearing date;

(e) set the parameters for the trial, including:

- to confirm which documents and case summaries need to be produced for the trial;

- where appropriate, to fix the date by which any trial bundles should be lodged (usually seven days before the trial);

- its length and budget.

The court will give at least seven days' notice of its intention to hold a PTR (r 29.7). It is advisable that the eventual advocates should attend, together with their lay clients or persons authorised on their behalf, as they may need to take instructions, including on the question of settlement. The dates for the CMC, PTR and the trial date will not be capable of alteration without leave of the court (r 29.5).

Listing directions

The court may give directions as follows:

- as to the issues on which evidence is to be given, the nature of the evidence it requires on those issues and the way in which it is to be placed before the court, and may thereby exclude evidence which would otherwise be admissible (r 32.1);

- a direction giving permission to use expert evidence, which will say whether it is to be by report or oral and will name the experts whose evidence is permitted (PD 29, para 9.2(4));

- setting a timetable for the trial, which will confirm or vary the trial date or week, the time estimate for the trial and the place of trial (r 29.8(c)(i); PD 29, para 9.1);
- for the preparation of a trial bundle (PD 29, para 9.2(2)(c)).

The parties should seek to agree the directions and file the proposed order (which will not bind the court) (PD 29, para 9.2(1)), making provision for the matters referred to above and any other matter needed to prepare for the trial (PD 29, para 9.2(2)).

At the moment, it is common for appeals against interim decisions in multi-track cases concerning case management directions to go to the designated civil judge, except where the decision was made by a district judge at a feeder court and there is a circuit judge at the feeder court who is available to deal with the appeal. This is provided that the appeal does not concern novel matters of principle on procedure, in which case the designated civil judge may prefer to deal with it (see also Chapter 37, 'Appeals').

THE TRIAL

Trial windows given in multi-track cases, instead of a fixture, are curiously for a period of just one week only, rather than the possible three-week period which applies in fast track cases (r 29.8(c)(ii)).

The trial will normally take place at a Civil Trial Centre, but it may be at another court if it is appropriate having regard to the needs of the parties and the availability of court resources (PD 29, para 10.1).

The judge will usually have read the papers in the trial bundle and may therefore dispense with an opening address (PD 29, para 10.2). The judge may confirm or vary any timetable given previously or, if none has been given, set his own. Further, if there has been a sufficient change of circumstances, the judge due to hear a trial may vary directions for the hearing of the trial previously made by another judge. In *Umm Qarn Management Co Ltd v Bunting and Another* [2001] 1 CPLR 20, CA, the Court of Appeal upheld the trial judge's decision to order that there be a single trial of all the issues between the parties, notwithstanding that a judge had previously ordered that some of the issues be heard separately at a hearing under Part 24 for summary judgment.

In accordance with general principle the court has the power to control evidence and to restrict cross-examination to that which is necessary (r 32.1). The usual direction will be for witness statements and reports to stand as evidence-in-chief (r 32.5(2)).

Once the trial of a multi-track claim has begun, the judge will normally sit on consecutive court days until it has been concluded (PD 29, para 10.6).

COSTS

There are no limits on costs on multi-track matters once they have been allocated to that track, as there are in small claims and fast track cases. However, they are still subject to full scrutiny by the court in the light of the overriding objective and the principle of proportionality (see Chapter 34, 'Costs of Proceedings').

Costs will be assessed either summarily or by way of detailed assessment, and issues such as misconduct with regard to the proceedings can be raised (see Chapter 35, 'Procedures for Assessing the Amount of Costs').

CHAPTER 20

MAKING APPLICATIONS FOR COURT ORDERS

INTRODUCTION

During the course of proceedings, and even before proceedings are begun, there are many instances when a party might wish to apply for a court order, over and above the usual directions made for the management of the progress of the case from commencement to trial. For instance, an application may be made for an interim remedy such as an interim payment, or it may be made for final relief such as judgment in default or summary judgment.

An application might also be made against a dilatory opponent to force him to proceed with or defend the claim by asking the court to order that, unless the respondent takes the next step in the proceedings, the claim be struck out or judgment be entered against him. Yet still, it may be necessary to apply for an interim remedy before a claim has even started, by way of, for instance, an interim injunction to preserve the status quo until the court can determine disputed rights.

Under the former rules, parties were free to make as many applications for court orders in the course of the progress of the case to trial as they wished. Lord Woolf believed that one of the evils to beset our civil justice system was the culture, particularly amongst the legal profession, of making successive applications for court orders for purely tactical reasons in order to run up costs and wear an opponent down (see *Access to Justice*, Interim Report, Chapter 5, para 41, www.dca.gov.uk/civil/interfr.htm). A classic example was the use of oppressive requests for further and better particulars of pleadings, which were not motivated by a genuine need for clarification of an opponent's case, but in order to cause inconvenience and cost to a party in the process of replying to them.

Under the Civil Procedure Rules (CPR), the court, with its powers of active case management, has more control over the making of applications. On the one hand there is less opportunity to make applications for court orders, because court imposed timetables truncate the time between starting proceedings and trial. On the other hand, procedural judges actively consider not just the merits of an application but also whether the cost and time involved in pursuing it is proportionate to the value of the case. Also, the general rule that the court should make a summary assessment of costs at the conclusion of any hearing that has lasted not more than one day (PD 44, para 13.2) acts as a deterrent to the making of unnecessary or unmeritorious applications.

Simplifying procedure

Lord Woolf identified one of his five overall objectives for the drafting of the CPR as being:

> ... to provide procedures which apply to the broadest possible range of cases and to reduce the number of instances in which a separate regime is provided for a special type of case. (See *Access to Justice*, Final Report (FR), Chapter 20, para 2, www.dca.gov.uk/civil/final/index.htm.)

One aspect of this was the introduction in the CPR of Part 23, which sets out the requirements for making applications. So, rather than separately set out in each rule, under which applications can be made, requirements as to parties, forms, time limits, notice, courts' powers, and so on, Part 23 contains all these matters and applies to all interim applications.

However, despite the intention to have one procedure for all applications for court orders, there are in fact still variations in procedure for different applications. It is therefore also necessary to examine the separate rules for the particular application in question to see if there are any additional or different procedural requirements to those set out in Part 23. For example, PD 25 must be considered when making an application for an interim injunction, freezing injunction or search order. Furthermore, some specialist divisions, such as the Chancery Division and Commercial Court, have their own Court Guides and detailed practice directions which must be followed and which specify more detailed requirements than any in Part 23.

Thus, again, it can be seen that attempts at simplification and unification come up against an insurmountable problem: different processes require different procedures. So, it would be misleading to say that there is a single procedure for all applications. The most that can be said is that there is a single form for all applications and that, although there are some rules common to all applications, these are subject to variations to fit different types of application, different types of proceedings and different circumstances.

WHERE TO MAKE AN APPLICATION

The general rule is that the application must be made to the court where the claim was started (r 23.2(1)). So, if proceedings were started in a county court, the application must be made to that court. However, this general rule will not be appropriate in all circumstances. If proceedings were started in one court but then transferred to another, the application must be made to the court to which the claim was transferred (r 23.2(2)). If the parties have been notified of a fixed date for trial, an application must be made to the court where the trial is to take place (r 23.2(3)).

If an application is made before a claim is started, it must be made to the court where it is likely that the claim to which the application relates will be started unless there is good reason to make the application to a different court (r 23.2(4)). This may be the case where a claim is started in a county court, but a certain type of interim relief is available only from the High Court. For instance, the county courts have no general jurisdiction to grant freezing injunctions or search orders (County Courts Remedies Regulations 1991 (SI 1991/1222)). Therefore, if proceedings are begun in a county court, but the applicant wishes to apply for a freezing injunction, that application should be made to the High Court. The proceedings will then be transferred back to the county court once that application has been dealt with.

Lastly, if an application is made after proceedings to enforce judgment have begun, it must be made to any court that is dealing with the enforcement of the judgment unless any rule or practice direction provides otherwise (r 23.2(5)).

Although, generally, most interim applications will be dealt with by a Master or a district judge, they may refer to a judge any matter which they think should be decided by a judge. This may be the case if the application is particularly substantial or raises matters of public importance. The judge may either deal with the matter, or refer it back to the Master or district judge (PD 23, para 1). Also, apart from in limited circumstances, a Master or district judge does not have the jurisdiction to grant an injunction and this must be dealt with by a judge (PD 25, paras 1.2, 1.3).

PROCEDURAL REQUIREMENTS

General rules

The title to Part 23 is 'General Rules about Applications for Court Orders'. It sets out the general rules for making applications, but also the circumstances when the general rules are or can be modified or not followed. (However, as was stated at pp 279–80 above, 'Simplifying procedure', it may not be enough simply to follow the requirements of Part 23, and reference should also be made to the rule or practice direction (if any) dealing with the application in question, as well as to any relevant specialist practice direction, or Court Guide, to ensure that the correct procedure is being followed for each application.)

In summary, the general rules provide that a party wishing to make an application should file an application notice, along with any supporting evidence, at the court office where the claim was started. The court issues the application notice and allocates a hearing date for the application. The court then serves the application notice, along with any supporting evidence, on the respondent, who is given at least three clear days' notice of the application hearing.

The application notice

The general rule is that in order to make an interim application, the applicant must file and serve an application notice. This is defined in the rules as a document in which the applicant states his intention to seek a court order (r 23.1). There is no prescribed form, but Form N244 may be used for making applications. However, in some cases, some other form, such as a letter (see *Miller v Allied Sainif (UK) Ltd* (2002) *The Times*, 31 October, Ch D), will suffice, for example, an application to extend a stay or to correct a court order under the 'slip rule' (see Chapter 33, p 505, 'The slip rule'). Parties to an application are known as 'applicant' and 'respondent' (r 23.1).

Contents of an application notice

Part 23 simply provides that an application notice must state what order the applicant is seeking and, briefly, why the applicant is seeking the order (r 23.6). The practice direction supplementing Part 23 specifies further formal details that must be provided, namely, that the application notice must be signed and include:

- the title of the claim;
- the reference number of the claim;
- the full name of the applicant;
- where the applicant is not already a party, his address for service; and

- either a request for a hearing, or a request that the application be dealt with without a hearing (PD 23, para 2.1).

It is also stated that Form N244 *may* be used.

An applicant who makes an application using Form N244 must also indicate how any supporting evidence will be presented by ticking one of three options provided on Form N244, that is: witness statement or affidavit; statement of case; or a written summary set out on the back of the application notice itself. Form N244 also states that the application should provide a time estimate for the hearing and say whether this is agreed to by all the parties; state which level of judge is required, for example, district judge; and set out all the parties who need to be served. The parties can also indicate on Form N244 whether they want the matter dealt with by way of a telephone conference (see Practice Form N244).

Form N244 includes a box for the applicant to sign a statement of truth. An application notice is not one of the documents which by Part 22 *must* be verified by a statement of truth. However, if an applicant wishes to rely on matters set out in his application notice as evidence, it must be verified by a statement of truth (r 22.1(3) and PD 23, para 9.7; and see Chapter 12, 'Statements of Case', for consideration of the requirements for statements of truth).

Filing the application notice

The general rule is that in order to make an application for a court order, the applicant must *file* an application notice at court (r 23.3(1)). Filing means delivering the application notice by post or otherwise to the court office (r 2.3(1)). If the court is to serve the application notice (and it usually does unless a request is made by one of the parties to serve), sufficient copies should be filed so that a copy can be retained at court, with enough copies for service of a sealed copy on the party making the application and for service on the other parties to the application (r 6.3(3)). The applicant must also file a copy of any witness statement in support of the application and a copy of any draft order (with sufficient copies) to be served by the court (r 23.7; PD 23, para 9).

When a limited time is provided by the rules for the making of a particular application, receipt at the court office of the application notice will constitute the making of the application (r 23.5). Further, if the specified time ends on a day on which the court office is closed, the application will be made in time if it is received on the next day when the court office is open (r 2.8(5)).

Filing a document at court can be achieved by a number of methods, the most common being by post, but it can also be delivered by hand or by fax. 'Delivery to the court' involves a unilateral, not a transactional, act as it is delivery to a place not a person, so no reciprocal act of acceptance is required. Therefore, if a document must be filed by a certain date it will be sufficiently filed if posted through the court's letter-box after the court office has closed (*Van Aken v Camden LBC* [2002] EWCA Civ 1724).

Applications made without filing an application notice

The rules provide for a party to make an application orally, without filing an application notice, if this is permitted by a rule, practice direction, or the court dispenses with the requirement for an application notice (r 23.3(2)).

If the application is extremely urgent, there may not be enough time to file an application notice before making the application. For instance, a party may need to apply for an urgent interim injunction. In such a situation an application can be made without filing an application notice, but after the hearing the applicant is obliged to file the application notice at the court office on the same or next working day, or within another time ordered by the court (PD 25, para 4.3(2)).

There is also the flexibility for the court to dispense with the need for an application notice. This might be appropriate where, for instance, during the course of a case management conference, a party discovers that it needs to make an application for a particular remedy. If no injustice would be caused to the respondent, the court may allow the applicant to apply orally for the order during the course of the case management conference without the need for an application notice to be filed first.

Notifying the opponent of the application

The general rule is that if an application is sought against another person, the respondent, that person should be notified and served with a copy of the application notice (r 23.4(1)).

Serving the application notice

Part 6 of the CPR sets out the permissible methods for the service of documents (see Chapter 10, 'Service of Documents').

The general rule is that the court will serve the application notice (r 6.3(1)). If the court is to serve the application notice, sufficient copies of the application notice, any supporting evidence and any draft order should be filed so that a copy can be retained at court, with enough copies for service of a sealed copy on the party making the application and for service on the other parties to the application (r 6.3(3)).

The method of service the court will normally use is ordinary first class post (PD 6, para 8.1). Once the application notice is filed, the court will serve the application notice on the respondent and notify the parties of the date of the hearing (if any). Under r 6.3(1)(b) a party is free, however, to notify the court that he will serve the document himself. Also, the court will attempt service once; if it is not effective it will serve a notice of non-service on the applicant, who will then be responsible for serving the application notice (r 6.11).

Time limits for service

Rule 23.7(1) sets out the time limits for serving an application notice. This states, first, that it must be served as soon as practicable after it has been filed. The rule then goes on to state that in any event, except where another time limit is specified by a rule or practice direction, it must be served at least three days (under r 2.8(2) this means clear days) before the court is to deal with the application.

If an application notice is served without giving the specified amount of notice, r 23.7(4) gives the court power, if the circumstances of the case warrant it, to reduce the amount of notice that the applicant is required to give the respondent (sometimes known as 'abridging the time for service'). In such a case, the court can treat whatever notice has been given as sufficient and hear the application. However, where an application should be served but there is not sufficient time to do so, informal notification of the application should be given unless the circumstances of the application require secrecy (PD 23, para 4.2; and see below 'Applications made without notice').

Filing supporting evidence

If a party is relying on supporting evidence, it must be filed at court as well as served on the other parties (PD 23, para 9.6). However, exhibits should not be filed unless a party is specifically directed to do so (PD 23, para 9.6). Rule 23.7(2) states that if the court is serving the application notice, the applicant must also file a copy of any written evidence in support of his application at the same time as he files his application notice. If a party is relying on evidence for an application that has already been filed or served, there is no need to file or serve another copy of such evidence (r 23.7(5)).

The rules also provide powers for the court to exercise active case management functions when dealing with applications, in the sense that there is also provision for the court to direct what evidence should be filed, the form it should take and when it should be served on the other party (PD 23, para 9.2).

Respondent's evidence

Where a respondent to an application wishes to rely on evidence that has not yet been served, he should file it at court and serve it on the other parties as soon as possible, and in any event in accordance with any directions the court may have given (PD 23, paras 9.4, 9.6). The court may give such directions when serving a copy of the application notice on the respondent and notifying him of the date and time of the application hearing.

Evidence in reply

If the applicant decides it is necessary to serve evidence in reply to the respondent's evidence, he should file it at court and serve it on the respondent as soon as possible, and in any event in accordance with any directions the court may have given (PD 23, paras 9.5, 9.6).

Applications made without notice

In general, respondents are notified of the application and given an opportunity to attend and oppose it. Exceptionally, an application can be made without notice in the following circumstances.

If permitted by a rule, practice direction or court order

An application can be made without notice if this is permitted by a rule, practice direction or court order (r 23.4(2); PD 23, para 3(6)). An example of a rule permitting such an application is r 7.6(4)(b), which specifically provides that an application by the claimant to extend the period of time in which to serve the claim form may be made without notice. The reason why this is permissible is because at that stage, the defendant to the claim has not even been served with the proceedings and if the order is refused, the claimant may not be able to bring the claim at all. Moreover, if the order is granted, the defendant is then given the opportunity to apply for the order to be varied or set aside (r 23.10(1)).

In Part 25, which deals with interim remedies, r 25.3(1) provides that the court may grant an interim remedy on an application made without notice 'if it appears to the court that there are good reasons for not giving notice'. An example of a good reason for not giving notice to the respondent would be if the type of remedy needed required secrecy, such as a freezing injunction, which relies on a pre-emptive strike in order to be effective. The rationale for a freezing injunction is that the applicant believes that if the respondent has notice of court proceedings against him, he will try to hide or dissipate his assets in order to avoid paying any judgment debt. In such circumstances, the applicant has to secure and enforce the order for the freezing injunction before the respondent even knows that one has been applied for.

Urgent applications

An application can be made without notice where there is exceptional urgency (PD 23, para 3(1)). An example might be where an interim injunction is needed urgently to stop a person acting so as to cause another irreparable harm. If the application is really urgent, it may even be made before the claimant has issued a claim form against the defendant. There may not be time to attend court for a hearing and so there is provision to make an emergency application over the telephone to the judge and, if it is necessary, to do so outside the normal court hours (see Chapter 21, 'Interim Remedies').

Where an urgent application is made without giving notice to the respondent, although there may not be enough time to give the respondent formal notification of the application in accordance with the rules, the applicant must give the respondent as much notice as he can, unless the application is of a type which requires secrecy (PD 23, para 4.2). This may be limited to giving the respondent telephone notification on the day that an application is being made so that the respondent can attend the hearing, even if there is not enough time to prepare evidence to rebut the applicant's contentions or to provide any instructions apart from those to resist the application.

Other circumstances

Other circumstances in which an application can be made without notice are where the overriding objective is best furthered by doing so (PD 23, para 3(2)). This obviously allows the court to exercise its discretion to deal with particular circumstances. Also, if all the parties consent, or with the permission of the court (PD 23, paras 3(3) and 3(4)). There is also the further situation where a date for a hearing has been fixed and a party wishes to make an application at that hearing, but he does not have sufficient time to serve an application notice. In such circumstances, the applicant may be permitted to make the application orally at the hearing, but he must notify the respondent and the court (if possible in writing) as soon as he can of the nature of the application and the reason for making it (PD 23, paras 2.10 and 3(5)).

Opportunity to set aside or vary orders made without notice

It is recognised that if the court grants an order after hearing only one side, there are obvious risks that injustice will be done. Therefore, if an order is granted on an application made without notice, the respondent has the right to return to court to try to vary or set aside the order (r 23.10(1)). However, this right must be exercised by the respondent within seven days after the order was served on him (r 23.10(2)).

Service of application notice and evidence on the respondent where application is made without notice

In those cases where an application is made without notice, even where the order applied for is not granted, the application notice and any supporting evidence must be served with the order on the respondent unless the court orders otherwise (r 23.9(2)).

If the order is granted, the respondent should be notified of it, as he may wish to apply to set it aside, and often it is in the applicant's interests to notify the respondent of the order in any event, as to be effective the order may well require the co-operation of the respondent.

However, the rule requiring service on the respondent where the order applied for is *not* granted was introduced because it was felt that where an applicant applied for a stringent order, such as a search order, which requires proof of the respondent's wrongdoing, the respondent has an interest in knowing the basis on which the application was made. Judicial concern had been expressed that such remedies are applied for on improper grounds, that is, not because the respondent is threatening to misuse the applicant's property but in order to stifle legitimate competition (see *dicta* of Hoffmann J in *Lock International plc v Beswick* [1989] 1 WLR 1268; [1989] 3 All ER 373).

Court fees

The County Court Fees Order 1999 (SI 1999/689) and the Supreme Court Fees Order 1999 (SI 1999/687) currently set the fees for an application with notice at £60, and for an application by consent, or without notice, at £30. In both cases this is subject to a different fee being specified. The fee is payable on filing the application notice at court.

However, an individual in receipt of income-based state benefits (income support, working families tax credit, disabled person's tax credit or income-based job seeker's allowance), who is not represented by a solicitor with the benefit of legal aid or Community Legal Service Funding, may apply for an exemption from payment of the fee. Even if not in receipt of those benefits, an individual can apply for a reduction or remission of the whole fee if he can show that payment of the fee would cause him undue hardship owing to the exceptional circumstances of his case.

SUPPORTING EVIDENCE

Witness statements and other documents verified by a statement of truth

The general rule is that at hearings other than trials, evidence should be presented by way of witness statements (r 32.6(1)). However, a party may also rely on his statement of case or the application notice itself, as long as these documents are verified by a statement of truth (r 32.6(2)). So, if the evidence relied on is fully set out in the application notice, by including a statement of truth the party does not need to prepare any other document containing evidence for use at the hearing. However, it is likely to be only in very simple and straightforward applications that such a course can be followed.

Affidavits

Under the former rules, evidence supporting interim applications had to be in the form of an affidavit. This is a sworn statement of facts that can be relied on as evidence. Affidavits are a relatively expensive way of presenting evidence for an application, as they need to be sworn before a commissioner for oaths (this includes solicitors, barristers, and public notaries) who charges a fee for each person swearing an affidavit and a fee for each exhibit referred to in the affidavit (see s 81 of the Solicitors Act 1974; s 113 of the Courts and Legal Services Act 1990; s 65 of the Administration of Justice Act 1985). Also, a solicitor or barrister involved in a case cannot swear an affidavit for a party for whom he is acting, so the party must go to the trouble of finding another commissioner for oaths before whom he can swear the affidavit.

It is still permissible to use affidavits under the CPR – and in fact for certain types of applications (such as search orders and freezing injunctions) there is a requirement to support the application with affidavit evidence – however, under the CPR, for all proceedings other than the trial, there are the other methods of presenting evidence detailed above.

The reason for the removal of the requirement to use a sworn affidavit is to reduce the costs involved in proceedings. If a party does choose to use an affidavit where its use is not compulsory, he is unlikely to recover the extra costs involved in doing so (r 32.15(2)). Yet there remains a distinction between sworn evidence in an affidavit and other forms of evidence verified by a statement of truth. Swearing false evidence in an affidavit is punishable as perjury, whereas verifying a statement that the person knows to be false is punishable as contempt of court. Although both are ultimately punishable by imprisonment, only perjury is a criminal offence. The orders for which affidavit evidence is required under the CPR provide drastic remedies, which presumably warrant the use of sworn evidence carrying with it the sanction of a criminal penalty if falsely made (see Chapter 21, 'Interim Remedies').

Function of supporting evidence

The purpose of supporting evidence is to prove the facts relied on in support of or in opposition to the application. Although for certain applications there is a specific requirement for evidence – for example, in order to obtain judgment in default a party must prove that particulars of claim were properly served on the defendant – for others there are no specific requirements for evidence. For those other cases, PD 23 warns that, as a practical matter, the court will often need to be satisfied by evidence of the facts that are relied on in support of or for opposing the application (PD 23, para 9.1).

For some types of application, supporting evidence may not be necessary by way of a separate witness statement. For example, on an application to strike out the other party's statement of case as an abuse for disclosing no claim or defence, there is usually no need to serve supporting evidence where the application is based on a legal submission that the facts pleaded do not disclose a cause of action or defence.

Although, obviously, the court will need to be satisfied by evidence of the facts put forward in support of or against the application, this does not mean that the court will aim to resolve disputed contentions at this stage and there will not usually be, for instance, cross-examination of any witnesses. Even though the CPR place a greater emphasis on pre-trial resolution of issues in the case, what that means is that the court will strive to identify the real issues in the case and eliminate those which are not really being relied upon. It does not mean that during the course of an interim application, the court will attempt to resolve disputed questions of fact and hear detailed argument on points of substantive law underlying the issues in the case (see also Chapter 23, 'Summary Judgment' and Chapter 24, 'Striking Out').

Skeleton arguments

There are additional requirements for bundles of documents and skeleton arguments in the specialist divisions of the court. So, for instance, in the Chancery Division, the general rule is that for applications made to a judge and any substantial applications made to the Master, the parties must prepare a skeleton argument and submit it to the court in advance of the hearing (see the Chancery Guide, 7.20).

A skeleton argument is intended to identify for both the parties and the court the points in issue and the nature of the arguments in support of those points in issue. It is not meant to be a substitute for oral argument. A skeleton argument should be as brief as the nature of the issues allows; it should not normally exceed 20 pages of double-spaced A4 paper and in many cases it should be much shorter than this. It should avoid arguing the case at length, avoid formality and make use of abbreviations, for example, C for claimant (see the Chancery Guide, 7.27, Appendix 3). Reference should be made to the relevant specialist division guides and practice directions for further details.

Although there is no specific requirement for a skeleton argument or bundles of documents for applications in Part 23, if the application is substantial then their use is advisable.

The draft order

Unless the application is extremely simple, the applicant should bring a copy of the draft order to the hearing. Also, if the case is proceeding in the Royal Courts of Justice, and the order is unusually long or complex, it should also be supplied on disk for use by the court office (PD 23, para 12.1). The draft order should also be served on the respondent along with the application notice and any supporting evidence (r 23.7(3)).

METHODS OF DEALING WITH APPLICATIONS

Active case management includes 'dealing with the case without the parties needing to attend at court' (r 1.4(2)(j)) and 'making use of technology' (r 1.4(2)(k)). The CPR provide a number of options, apart from an oral hearing, for dealing with an application. As well as dealing with the application without the expense of an oral hearing, there is also provision for telephone and video conferencing. Lord Woolf envisaged these as vital tools for case management. He was not proposing that telephone conferencing would replace existing hearings or meetings, but instead that it would encourage greater, proactive communication where, in the past, there would have been silence (see FR, Chapter 21, paras 7, 21).

There is nothing in the rules to suggest that telephone and video conferencing are limited to certain types of application or case management functions of the court. Yet, despite their availability for a number of years, and even in the light of a number of pilot schemes to promote them, telephone and video conferencing are not regularly used for contested applications, such as applications for summary judgment. Nevertheless, telephone conferencing is quite commonplace for case management conferences and other hearings dealing with matters such as directions. Indeed, suitable equipment for telephone conferences is now being supplied to more judges' chambers.

Applications dealt with without a hearing

Rule 23.8 sets out the circumstances in which an application may be dealt with without a hearing:

(a) if the parties agree as to the terms of the order sought;

(b) if the parties agree that the application should be dealt with without a hearing; or

(c) the court considers that a hearing would not be appropriate.

Consent orders

A respondent may agree to or not oppose the making of an order in the case. In fact this is the most common instance where an application will be dealt with without a hearing. For instance, an applicant may seek an interim injunction, but before the hearing the respondent agrees to the terms of the injunction. In those circumstances, the respondent can undertake to abide by agreed terms without the need for a contested application hearing (see Chapter 21, 'Interim Remedies'). Or a party may agree that the other party should be able to amend his statement of case without the need to apply to the court for permission (see Chapter 12, 'Statements of Case'). There is therefore provision for the court to enter and seal judgment by consent of the parties. In some circumstances, this can be achieved simply by presenting the agreed order to a court official without the need for the court to approve the consent order (r 40.6(2)). Otherwise, the party must apply for a consent order and the matter must be brought before the court for the order to be approved (r 40.6(5)). The consent order must be drawn so that the judge's name and judicial title can be inserted (PD 23, para 10.3). However, such a consent order can be dealt with without the need for a court hearing (r 40.6(6)).

Where all the parties affected by an order have written to the court consenting to the making of the order, a draft of which has been filed with the court, the court will treat the requirement under r 40.6(7) for the consent order to be signed by a party or his legal representative as having been fulfilled (PD 23, para 10.2). This is a very practical provision that avoids the need to forward the actual consent order to each relevant party for signing before filing it at court where there is limited time for doing so. Instead the parties can agree the terms of the draft order and separately write to the court confirming their agreement, whilst at the same time the applicant files the draft order at court.

The parties to the consent order must ensure that they provide the court with any material it needs to be satisfied that it is appropriate to make the order. In most cases, subject to the requirements of any rule or practice direction, a letter will generally be acceptable for this purpose (PD 23, para 10.4). In accordance with active case management, the court will take a more active role in ensuring that the terms of any order agreed are consistent with the ethos of the new CPR and, in particular, the overriding objective. Moreover, the parties cannot agree between themselves to the terms of an order which would have the effect of varying the 'case milestones', for example, the date for return of the allocation questionnaire, pre-trial checklist, trial period or trial date (rr 26.3(6A), 28.4, 29.5). Practice Direction 23 reminds the parties of this, as well as of the fact that if a consent order is made, the parties must inform the court so that any date fixed for the hearing of the application can be vacated (PD 23, para 10.5).

Agreement that application be dealt with without a hearing

The parties may agree that the application should be dealt with without a hearing. This may arise when the parties decide that the application would not justify the time and cost of a hearing and that their position can be protected by means of a written application and supporting evidence alone. If that is the case, the parties should inform the court in writing, and each should confirm that all evidence and other material on which he relies has been disclosed to the other parties to the application (PD 23, para 11.1).

Court considers that a hearing would not be appropriate

The first request for information made to the applicant when filling out the application notice Form N244 is whether he would like the application dealt with at a hearing. Indeed, this information must be provided whether Form N244 is used or not (see PD 23, para 2.1(5)). When making an application, the applicant therefore has to indicate his preference as to whether the application is dealt with at a hearing or on paper, or by way of telephone conference.

However, in the absence of agreement with the other parties, the applicant cannot insist that the application be dealt with without a hearing. If the applicant makes that choice, the application notice will be sent to the Master or district judge, who must consider whether the application is suitable for consideration without a hearing (PD 23, para 2.3). The Master or district judge then has to be satisfied that it is suitable for the application to be dealt with without a hearing. If that decision is made, the court will inform the applicant and respondent and may give directions for the filing of evidence (para 2.4). If the Master or district judge is not so satisfied, the court will notify the applicant and respondent of the time, date and place for the hearing of the application (para 2.5).

If the court decides that the application is suitable to be dealt with without a hearing, it will treat the application as if it were proposing to make an order on its own initiative (PD 23, para 11.2). The court also has the power under r 3.3 to make an order of its own initiative, and it can do so without hearing the parties or giving them an opportunity to make representations.

Applications by telephone or video conference

Making use of technology, an application can be heard without the parties being physically present before the court. Instead, an application can be made by means of a telephone or video conference. The evidence suggests that such methods are becoming more commonplace. However, the *Admiralty and Commercial Court Guide* positively discourages such applications, stating that 'in most cases (apart from limited exceptions) applications in the Commercial Court are more conveniently dealt with in person' (see para F1.9 of the *Admiralty and Commercial Court Guide*).

Telephone hearings

Practice Direction 23, para 6.1, provides that the court may order an application, or part of one, to be dealt with by a telephone hearing. The application notice was amended to include the opportunity for the applicant to request that the application be heard by telephone conference. Although the court has the power to order that the application is heard in this way, it is unlikely to be ordered unless all the parties consent (PD 23, para 6.2). Also, if a party is acting in person, a telephone conference will not be ordered unless that party is accompanied by a responsible person who is known to the party and who confirms the identity of the party at the beginning of the hearing (PD 23, para 6.3(1)). A responsible person includes a barrister, solicitor, legal executive, doctor, clergyman, police officer, prison officer or other person of comparable status (PD 23, para 6.3(2)).

The telephone hearing is set up by the applicant arranging a telephone conference through BT's (or other comparable telecommunications provider's) 'call out' system, which allows a three-way (or more) telephone conversation, for precisely the time ordered by the court (PD 23, para 6.5(1)). Each party will then be able to participate in the hearing as if he was before the court. The applicant must then arrange for the conference to be recorded on tape by the telecommunications provider whose system is being used and must send the tape to the court (PD 23, para 6.5(5)). The costs of the telephone charges will be treated as part of the costs of the application (PD 23, para 6.5(9)).

Video conferencing

Part 23 also refers, in very general terms, to the availability of video conferencing facilities. Such facilities exist in some courts and can be used to make a live video application to another, more distant court. No detail is provided in the practice direction apart from the information that if the parties wish to use this facility, they should apply to the Master or district judge for directions (PD 23, para 7).

CASE MANAGEMENT

Review of the whole case

In accordance with the court's obligations for active case management, the parties must expect that whenever the case comes before the court, even for a specific remedy, the procedural judge may well take an opportunity to review the conduct of the case as a whole and give directions for its future conduct.

Practice Direction 23 warns the parties that the court may well wish to make case management directions when an application is dealt with, and that they should be ready to assist the court with this function and answer any questions the court may ask for this purpose (PD 23, para 2.9). Thus, it is important that the person who attends court is competent in this regard, failing which there may be a danger of a wasted costs order being made (see *Baron v Lovell* (1999) *The Times*, 14 September).

Timing of the application hearing

Active case management by the court includes 'dealing with as many aspects of the case as it can on the same occasion' (r 1.4(2)(i)). In accordance with this, a party intending to make an application for summary judgment or other early termination of a case should do so before or when filing his allocation questionnaire. Any hearing set to deal with the application will also serve as an allocation hearing if allocation remains appropriate (PD 26, para 5).

For other types of application, the applicant should make the application so that it can be considered at any other hearing for which a date has already been fixed, or for which a date is about to be fixed. If the court has fixed a case management conference, an allocation or a listing hearing, or a pre-trial review for the case, the application should be heard at one of those hearings (PD 23, para 2.8).

Obviously, if none of those hearings has been fixed for the case, if the application has to be made before any of those events occurs (for example, extending the time for service of the claim form), or the application is urgent, then the application will be heard at a separate hearing. Although the application should, if possible, be considered at the same time as any other scheduled interim court hearing in the case, the application itself should be made, and notified to the other party, as soon as it becomes apparent that it is necessary or desirable to make it (PD 23, para 2.7). A party who delays making an application when the need for one has arisen may be penalised in costs or other sanctions.

Duration of the application hearing

Even before the introduction of the CPR, there was judicial criticism of the use of interim applications for detailed consideration of evidence and extended legal argument (see the case of *Derby and Co Ltd v Weldon (No 1)* [1990] Ch 48, CA, where the hearing of the interim application took 26 days and the documents to appeal the judge's order consisted of several thousand pages of affidavits and exhibits). In that case, Parker LJ referred with approval to Lord Templeman's comments in *Spiliada Maritime Corp v Cansulex Ltd* [1987] AC 460, where he said 'that [interim applications] should be measured in hours not days, that appeals should be rare and that [the Court of Appeal] should be slow to interfere' (at 465). He also advocated costs orders being made against parties who used interim applications to try to persuade the court to resolve disputed questions of fact, or against those who made detailed arguments on difficult points of law relating to the underlying claim (at para 58F–G).

Such sentiments have now been incorporated into the CPR. Part 1 of the CPR, the overriding objective, which governs the application and interpretation of all the rules, includes saving expense (r 1.1(2)(b)), dealing with cases in proportion to their value, importance, complexity and the financial position of each party (r 1.1(2)(c)). It is also recognised that court resources are limited and so, rather than allow the parties to decide how much time and money to expend on proceedings, the court will control this by only allotting an appropriate share of the court's resources to a case and taking into account the need to allot resources to other cases (r 1.1(2)(e)).

In *Barrett v Universal-Island Records Ltd* [2003] EWHC 625, Ch, Laddie J held that the process of proper case management demands that the time given to summary applications is not disproportionate to the benefits to be achieved. He said, for example, that spending a few days on a summary application which, if successful, may avoid the need for, or significantly reduce the expected duration of, a trial due to last some months, is likely to be a worthwhile use of court time and is proportionate. However, 'spending that sort of time when trying to short-circuit a trial due to last, say, two weeks, is likely to be disproportionate' (at [44]).

On the other hand, in *Swain v Hillman and Gay* [2001] 1 All ER 91, Lord Woolf stated that the appropriate use of the court's powers under Part 24 to order summary judgment against a party gave effect to the overriding objective by ensuring that only an appropriate share of the court's resources were allotted to a particular case. If a claimant's case is bound to fail, entering summary judgment against the claimant 'saves expense; it achieves expedition; it avoids the court's resources being used up on cases where this serves no purpose, and … generally … it is in the interests of justice' (for the facts of this case see Chapter 23, 'Summary Judgment').

What is clear is that with the court's new powers of case management, the procedural judge will be actively considering whether the time and money spent on each step of a case is proportionate and whether it is likely to produce a justifiable benefit.

OTHER PROCEDURAL MATTERS

Applications to be heard in public

Now, the general rule is that all hearings are held in public (r 39.2(1)). This includes interim applications and is, on the face of it, a major change from the old system where most interim applications were held in private. However, although technically in public, the court does not have to make special arrangements for accommodating members of the public (r 39.2(2)). Therefore, just on this basis alone, it is unlikely that many members of the public will observe interim applications, the majority of which will be heard in Masters' or district judges' rooms which, owing to their size and location in court buildings, are not readily accessible.

Further, there are a number of circumstances in which the court can hold a hearing in private. These include when publicity would defeat the object of the hearing (r 39.2(3)(a)) and when the court considers it necessary in the interests of justice (r 39.2(3)(g)). Therefore, if the nature of the application relies on it being made secretly, such as a freezing injunction or search order, this would justify the court ordering that the application be heard in private.

Power of the court to proceed in the absence of a party

The court has the power to proceed with an application and make any order it thinks fit, even if one of the parties fails to attend the hearing. There is then provision for the court to re-list the application, to be heard again, either of its own initiative or by application of one of the parties (r 23.11).

In *Riverpath Properties Ltd v Brammall* (2000) *The Times*, 16 February, Neuberger J held that r 23.11(2) contained no fetter on the court's discretion, so its effect was to give the court a very flexible power in relation to setting aside and ordering a rehearing in respect of an order that it made in the absence of a party. The court therefore has the power to rehear the application in full and make such different order as it thinks appropriate. However, Neuberger J warned that it would be a very rare case where the court exercised this jurisdiction to set aside an order that it had made if it was satisfied that there was no real prospect of any new order being different from that which it originally made. Also, there may be circumstances where the order has been acted on in such a way as to make it more unjust to set aside the order than to refuse to do so. He also held that the court had a fairly wide discretion as to the terms upon which it may grant or refuse the application. If a party is at fault in not attending the hearing the court may impose conditions to the rehearing of the application, such as the payment of a sum of money into court (r 3.1(3); and compare the court's powers where a party fails to attend the trial under r 39.3).

COSTS OF THE APPLICATION HEARING

Summary assessment

The general rule is that for application hearings lasting less than one day, the procedural judge should make a summary assessment of costs at the end of the hearing unless there is good reason not to do so. A good reason can include where there is not enough time to make a summary assessment (PD 44, para 13.2). This general rule does not apply if the receiving party is legally aided or a Legal Services Commission funded client, or is a child or patient whose solicitor has not waived the right to further costs (PD 44, paras 13.9, 13.11).

Further, the parties have a duty to assist the judge in making a summary assessment of costs. In order to do so, if a party intends to claim costs, he must prepare a written statement of those costs (statement of costs), including specified information as to how they are calculated, file that statement at court and serve it on the party against whom he is claiming costs at least 24 hours before the hearing of the application (PD 44, para 13.5). Failure to do so may result in the court awarding only nominal costs or no costs at all. The court may also take that failure into account when deciding what order to make about the costs of any further hearing or detailed assessment hearing that may be necessary as a result of that failure (PD 44, para 13.6).

However, if the court decides to make an order for 'costs in the case' at the end of the application hearing, the costs of the application will not be assessed until the end of the proceedings (PD 44, para 8.5). Such an order will be made when the court thinks it is appropriate to suspend its judgment as to who should pay the costs of the application until the end of the case. An order for 'costs in the case' means that the party in whose favour the court makes an order for costs at the end of proceedings is entitled to his costs of the application for which the order was made (PD 44, para 8.5).

If an order for the summary assessment of costs is not made, the court may make an order for the detailed assessment of costs under Part 47. Alternatively, the parties may agree the costs themselves. However, if at the end of the application the order made does not mention costs, no party is entitled to the costs of that application (r 44.13). A party should ensure, therefore, that an appropriate application for costs is made at the end of the hearing.

See Chapter 35, 'Procedures for Assessing the Amount of Costs', for further details about summary assessment and about the types of court orders that may be made at interim applications.

Additional liabilities

The fact that a party may have entered into a conditional fee agreement (CFA) or other funding arrangement is not by itself sufficient reason for not carrying out a summary assessment (PD 44, para 14.1). However, if a summary assessment of costs is made, it will not include the additional liability, which must be decided by detailed assessment in the absence of agreement (PD 44, para 14.2).

CHAPTER 21

INTERIM REMEDIES

INTRODUCTION

The court has extensive powers to make interim orders to facilitate the obtaining of final judgment. For instance, a party may require access onto another party's land in order to inspect or take samples of property which are the subject matter of, or relevant to, the dispute.

In some instances a party may require the court's assistance to preserve property which is the subject matter of a dispute, or to preserve evidence or assets prior to final judgment being obtained where there is a risk that it will be destroyed or dissipated with the intention of thwarting the claim. In such circumstances the court has extensive powers to make orders for interim injunctions to maintain and regularise the position between the parties until a trial of the dispute can be heard.

In certain circumstances, and where specific requirements are met, the court has other powers to protect a party's position until trial. In the case of a claimant, this is through the making of an order for an interim payment where it is expected that the claimant will recover a substantial sum at trial. In the case of a defendant, this is through an order for security for costs where there is a risk that the claimant will not be in a position to pay the defendant's costs if he is successful.

All interim remedies are now contained within Part 25. However, it is expressly stated that the fact that a particular interim remedy is not listed in r 25.1 does not mean that the court does not have the power to grant that remedy (r 25.1(3)).

This chapter is divided into three parts: Part A deals with interim injunctions and interim property orders; Part B deals with interim payments; Part C deals with security for costs orders. First, though, we look at the availability of interim remedies before a claim is issued.

INTERIM REMEDIES BEFORE CLAIM IS ISSUED

It is a general principle that before the court will grant an interim remedy it must be satisfied that there is an underlying cause of action between the applicant and respondent. This is because a right to an interim remedy does not usually exist in isolation but is granted in order to facilitate in some way the obtaining of a substantive remedy. Accordingly, an interim remedy will usually be granted only once proceedings have started, but if an interim remedy is required urgently, or it is otherwise necessary to do so in the interests of justice, an order for an interim remedy may be granted before a claim has been issued (r 25.2(2)(b)). An example is where an interim injunction is required to restrain a person from causing irreparable harm. The nature of the remedy for an interim injunction is such that if not granted urgently, the harm which it is intended to prevent will have been caused before an injunction can be put in place.

Where an interim remedy is granted before proceedings are commenced, the court usually gives directions requiring a claim to be commenced (r 25.2(3)). In practice, a party applying for an interim remedy in such circumstances provides a draft of the proposed claim as part of its application for the interim remedy. However, where a party seeks pre-action disclosure, the court does not usually direct that proceedings must be commenced when granting the order (r 25.2(4); see Chapter 29, 'Disclosure of Documents').

A defendant must seek leave to make an application for an interim remedy if he wishes to make such an application before he has filed an acknowledgment of service or a defence (r 25.2(c)). However, the nature of interim remedies is such that it is usually the claimant who applies for most of them, an exception being an order for security for costs.

PART A: INTERIM INJUNCTIONS AND INTERIM PROPERTY ORDERS

Interim injunctions

Injunctions – definition and jurisdiction

The Glossary to the Civil Procedure Rules (CPR) defines an injunction as 'a court order prohibiting a person from doing something or requiring a person to do something'. Interim injunctions include freezing injunctions and search orders.

Under s 37 of the Supreme Court Act 1981 (SCA), the High Court has jurisdiction to grant a final or an interim injunction where the court is satisfied that it is just and convenient to do so. Under s 38 of the County Courts Act 1984 (CCA), the county courts are given the power to make any order which may be made in the High Court, and this therefore includes the power to make a final or an interim injunction.

In the High Court an interim injunction must be made by a circuit judge (PD 2B, para 2.2). A Master or district judge may make an injunction only in limited circumstances, such as where the terms are agreed by the parties (PD 2B, para 2.3). In the county courts, an interim injunction must be granted by a circuit judge, apart from the limited circumstances mentioned in PD 2B, paras 8.1 and 8.2, where a district judge may grant an injunction. For example, a district judge may grant an injunction in a case which is within his jurisdiction to try.

An interim injunction can be applied for in a case allocated to the small claims track, although the other interim remedies specified in Part 25 are not available in such proceedings (r 27.2(1)(a)).

See Chapter 2, 'Sources of Civil Procedure: Structure and Jurisdiction of the Civil Courts' for further details about the jurisdiction of the High Court and county courts to grant injunctions.

Principles upon which an interim injunction will be granted

It must be remembered that standing over all the principles for the granting of an interim injunction is the principle of the overriding objective (r 1.2).

The nature and purpose of an interim injunction was considered by the House of Lords in *Attorney-General v Punch Ltd* [2002] UKHL 50. In that judgment, Lord Hope cited with approval the *dictum* of Lord Oliver in *Attorney-General v Times Newspapers Ltd* [1992] 1 AC 191, in which he said, 'Interlocutory injunctions are designed to ensure the effective administration of justice, so that the rights which it is the duty of the courts to protect can be fairly determined and effectively protected and enforced by the courts' (at para 216A–B). The purpose of an interim injunction is therefore that of a temporary measure to preserve the status quo until the disputed rights of the parties can be fully determined at trial.

As the jurisdiction to grant interim injunctions is to be found in the SCA and the CCA, the leading authority is still the House of Lords' decision in *American Cyanamid Co v Ethicon Ltd* [1975] AC 396, notwithstanding the introduction of the CPR. In that case the House of Lords laid down the following principles to be applied when the court is deciding whether or not to grant an interim injunction:

- The court must be satisfied that there is a serious question to be tried between the parties.

- The court must consider whether the *balance of convenience* lies in favour of granting or refusing an interim injunction.

- The court must not attempt at that stage to resolve conflicts of evidence or questions of law that require detailed argument.

- If the balance of convenience falls equally between the parties the court should preserve the status quo in the meantime until the rights of the parties can be determined at trial.

The *balance of convenience* test may be expressed in terms of whether the risk of injustice if the injunction is refused outweighs the risk of injustice if the injunction is granted (*Nottingham Building Society v Eurodynamics Systems* [1993] FSR 468), or whether damages would provide adequate compensation instead (*Birmingham CC v In Shops* [1992] NPC 71) or the wrong would be irreparable (*Woodford v Smith* [1970] 1 All ER 1091).

Interim injunctions and freedom of expression

The *American Cyanamid* test of whether there is a 'serious issue to be tried' does not apply to applications for interim injunctions made to restrain media publications prior to trial (*Cream Holdings Ltd v Banerjee* [2003] EWCA Civ 103). In *Cream Holdings Ltd v Banerjee*, a company was granted an interim injunction preventing a newspaper from publishing information about it obtained by a former employee. The newspaper and former employee appealed to the Court of Appeal against the order for the interim injunction on the grounds that the company had not satisfied the test in s 12(3) of the Human Rights Act (HRA) 1998 relating to the circumstances in which the court can, in the light of the right to freedom of expression, restrain publication before trial.

Section 12(3) of the HRA 1998 prevents the court from restraining publication before trial unless it is satisfied that the applicant is likely to establish at trial that publication should not be allowed. The Court of Appeal held that the existence of this provision meant that it was not enough for the court simply to be satisfied, in accordance with the test in *American Cyanamid*, that there was a serious issue to be tried. Instead, s 12(3) required the court to put *American Cyanamid* firmly to one side and look at the merits and not just the balance of convenience. The appropriate test in such cases is therefore whether the applicant for an interim injunction has convincingly established a real prospect of success at trial.

However, the court recognised that it was possible in certain cases for an interim injunction to be granted if there were compelling reasons why the applicant's ultimate chance of victory should be preserved rather than pre-empted at the interim stage, even though at that stage the applicant looked more likely to lose than to win at trial. An example of when this may occur is if publication would endanger the applicant's life.

Mandatory interim injunctions

A mandatory injunction requires the party subject to it to take a positive step to carry out an action or to undo what he has done. It was described by Laddie J in *Psychometric Services Ltd v Merant International Ltd* [2002] FSR 8 as 'obliging a party to do things for which he has no enthusiasm'. In general, mandatory injunctions are felt to carry more risk than prohibitive injunctions at the interim stage. This is because such injunctions go further than simply preserving the status quo. Also, in requiring the person to undertake or undo an act, a mandatory injunction is likely to involve the expenditure of more time and money than a prohibitive injunction. Further, a mandatory injunction may well deal with the whole of the relief sought by the applicant and therefore make the full hearing of the dispute at trial unlikely.

In determining whether to grant a mandatory injunction, the Court of Appeal in *Zockoll Group Ltd v Mercury Communications Ltd* [1998] FSR 354, approved the test formulated by Mr Justice Chadwick in *Nottingham Building Society v Eurodynamics Systems*. In summary, therefore, the court must consider the following factors when deciding whether to grant a mandatory interim injunction:

(a) The overriding consideration (as with any interim application) is which course is likely to involve the least risk of injustice if it turns out to be wrong.

(b) An order requiring a party to take a positive step at the interim stage may well carry a greater risk of injustice if it turns out to be wrong than one prohibiting action and thus preserving the status quo.

(c) It is legitimate for the court to expect a high degree of assurance that the claimant will be able to establish his right at trial. The greater the degree of assurance, the less risk of injustice if the injunction is granted.

(d) But even in those cases where the court does not feel a high degree of assurance that the claimant will establish his right at trial, it may still be appropriate to grant the injunction where the risk of injustice if the injunction is refused outweighs the risk of injustice if the injunction is granted.

This test was applied by the court in *Psycometric Services Ltd v Merant International Ltd*, when granting the claimant an interim mandatory injunction. The claimant had very limited assets but substantial potential in the provision of a service involving psychometric testing to an internet-based recruitment company. The claimant had purchased the software for this purpose from the defendant. The claimant encountered problems with the software and sought an interim mandatory injunction compelling the defendant to hand over the source code for the software so that the claimant could continue to develop it with another company. The defendant refused to do so on the ground that the claimant owed it substantial unpaid fees.

The court held that the claimant would suffer a greater injustice than the defendant if the injunction were refused. The claimant had very limited assets but the potential to earn substantial sums utilising the computer software. Also, if the injunction was refused the claimant's employees were at risk of losing their jobs and third party interests would be harmed. The court held that refusing the injunction would worsen the defendant's position because the claimant would have no assets to pay its fees and no potential to earn any income to do so. Indeed, the granting of the injunction was the defendant's best chance of recovering those fees, because without the source code the claimant would go into liquidation. The court therefore found that it was appropriate to grant the claimant a mandatory interim injunction, and to do so carried the least risk of causing injustice.

Terms of an injunction

The terms of an injunction must be clear and precise. The injunction must define precisely what acts are prohibited and which acts are permitted. In *Attorney-General v Punch Ltd*, Lord Hope referred with approval to the *dictum* of Lord Deas in the Scottish case of *Kelso School Board v Hunter* (1874) 2 R 228, 230, in which he said 'if an injunction is to be granted at all, it must be in terms so plain that he who runs may read'. Lord Hope explained that this is because of the penal consequences that will follow if it is breached (at [111]). The principle is that a person should not be put at risk of being in contempt of court if the terms of the injunction are ambiguous or open to dispute. In that case an example given of ambiguous terms was an order that was simply expressed to restrain publication of 'confidential information' or 'information whose disclosure risks damaging national security'.

Further, the prohibition contained within the injunction must extend no further than is necessary to serve the purpose for which the order is made. In *Attorney-General v Punch Ltd*, the House of Lords agreed that although clear, the terms of the injunction were wide. However, the court held that this was not a reason for a party, or third party, not to obey the terms of the order, and if expressed in terms that were too wide the remedy for a party affected by the order was to apply to the court for the terms of the injunction to be varied.

Penal notice

In order to enforce breach of an interim injunction by contempt of court proceedings, it must be endorsed with a penal notice in the following form (PD 40B, para 9.1):

> If you the within-named [ ] do not comply with this order you may be held to be in contempt of court and imprisoned or fined, or [in the case of a company or corporation] your assets may be seized.

See also the examples of a freezing injunction and a search order attached to PD 25 for the suggested form of penal notice.

Effect of an interim injunction

A party who wilfully disobeys the terms of an interim injunction will be liable for contempt of court. This will also apply to someone who is acting for the party or at his direction (PD 40B, para 9). All that has to be proved is that the order was served on that person and he has failed to do that which he was compelled to do, or has done that which the order prohibited (*Attorney-General v Times Newspapers Ltd* [1992] 1 AC 191). However, a person who is not a party to the litigation, or acting on behalf of or at the direction of a party to the litigation, may also be in contempt of court if he acts in a way which constitutes a wilful interference with the terms of the injunction. It has to be shown that there was an intention on his part to interfere with or impede the administration of justice, and this has to be established to the criminal standard, that is, beyond reasonable doubt. An example is where a stranger to the litigation deliberately publishes information which the court has ordered someone else to keep confidential. This would obviously interfere with the administration of justice because once the information has been published the court can no longer do justice between the parties by enforcing the obligation of confidentiality (*Attorney-General v Punch Ltd* [2002] UKHL 50).

Attorney-General v Punch Ltd arose out of the interim injunction imposed in the proceedings against David Shayler, a former member of the Security Service, MI5. Mr Shayler's terms of engagement included an undertaking that he would preserve the confidentiality of information which he obtained in the course of his employment. In August 1997, after leaving the Service, he wrote or provided information for newspaper articles in breach of his undertaking. On 4 September 1997, on the application of the Attorney-General, the High Court granted an injunction until trial or further order restraining Mr Shayler from disclosing any information obtained in the course of his employment.

Mr Shayler was subsequently employed by the satirical magazine, *Punch*, to write about the Security Service. He first wrote for *Punch* in February 1999. Mr Steen, the editor of *Punch*, was aware of the terms of the interim non-disclosure orders made against Mr Shayler. Mr Steen intended that the column in *Punch* would criticise the performance of the Security Services, expose their alleged errors and inefficiencies, and show that their alleged incompetence led to serious and sometimes tragic results. On Friday, 21 July 2000, Mr Steen received from Mr Shayler a draft article, with a view to publication on Wednesday of the following week. The draft dealt with the Bishopsgate bomb in 1993 and the death of WPC Yvonne Fletcher outside the Libyan Embassy in 1984. It was the published version of this article that led to contempt proceedings against *Punch* and Mr Steen.

The House of Lords overturned the Court of Appeal's decision and re-affirmed the High Court judge's decision at first instance that the defendants, *Punch* and Mr Steen, were liable for contempt of court in publishing the articles notwithstanding the terms of the injunction against Mr Shayler. The House of Lords held that the purpose of the interim injunction was to restrain publication of confidential material before trial. The publication of the article in *Punch* did precisely what the order was intended to prevent and had interfered with the administration of justice. The House of Lords therefore held that *Punch* and Mr Steen were in contempt of court as the court's decision must be respected by third parties as well as by the parties to the proceedings.

Discharge, cesser or variation of an interim injunction

A party served with an interim injunction may apply to have the injunction discharged or varied if he can establish that the claimant is not entitled to the order or has failed to comply with the relevant procedure (for example, failed to provide full and fair disclosure). However, where the application is made shortly before trial, the defendant is protected by an undertaking in damages and, if there is no evidence that additional damage may be suffered, the court may apply the overriding objective and refuse to hear the application (*Stephenson Ltd v Mandy* (1999) *The Times*, 21 July). Indeed, Nourse LJ said in that case that expense could be saved by not dealing with the appeal against the order at that stage, and in any event it would not be an appropriate allotment of the court's resources to do so.

An interim injunction (except for a freezing injunction) ceases if the claim is stayed other than by agreement between the parties, unless the court orders otherwise (r 25.10).

If the court has granted an interim injunction and the claim is struck out under r 3.7 (sanctions for non-payment of certain fees), the interim injunction ceases to have effect 14 days after the date that the claim is struck out unless the claimant applies to reinstate the claim before the interim injunction ceases to have effect. The injunction shall continue until the hearing of the application unless the court orders otherwise (r 25.11).

Where a claimant has obtained an interim injunction, this is one of the circumstances in which he will need to seek the court's leave if he wishes to discontinue the claim (r 38.2(2)(a)(i); and see Chapter 36, 'Discontinuance').

A person who is not a party but who is directly affected by an interim injunction may apply to have the judgment or order set aside or varied (r 40.9). This provision has particular significance for third parties who are affected by a freezing injunction or search order.

Procedure for applying for an interim injunction

An application for an interim injunction must be made in accordance with Part 23. However, this is subject to compliance with any specific requirements of PD 25 Interim Injunctions and the requirements of any relevant practice direction or guide produced by the court of a specialist division, for example, the Chancery Guide or the *Admiralty and Commercial Court Guide*. Indeed, the specialist Court Guides provide detailed guidance for applications in their division for interim injunctions, freezing injunctions and search orders. Also, there are additional requirements in respect of applications for freezing injunctions and search orders.

Interim injunctions before proceedings are commenced

If an application is made for an interim injunction before the issue of proceedings, the applicant must undertake, subject to the court ordering otherwise, to issue a claim form immediately. Otherwise, the court will give directions for the issue of the claim (r 25.2(3)).

The claim form should also be served on the respondent with the court order for the interim injunction. The order will then state in the title after the names of the applicant and respondent, 'the Claimant and Defendant in an Intended Action' (r 25.2(3); PD 25, para 4.4).

The application notice

The application notice must state the order sought and the date, time and place of the hearing (PD 25, para 2.1).

Where the court is to serve the application on the respondent, sufficient copies of the application notice and evidence in support for the court and for each respondent should be filed for issue and service (PD 25, para 2.3).

It is important to file a draft of the order sought with the application notice. Further, a disk containing the draft should also be available to the court in a format compatible with the word processing software used by the court. This will enable the court officer to arrange for any amendments to be incorporated and facilitate speedy preparation and sealing of the order (PD 25, para 2.4).

The application notice and evidence in support must be served as soon as practicable after issue and in any event not less than three days before the hearing (PD 25, para 2.2). This means three clear days (r 2.8(2)). When computing the three clear days, the day on which the period begins and the day of the hearing are not included (r 2.8(3)).

Evidence

The application must be supported by evidence, unless the court orders otherwise (r 25.3(2)). The evidence must set out the facts on which the applicant relies for the claim being made against the respondent, including all material facts of which the court should be aware (PD 25, para 3.3).

In hearings, other than at trial, the general rule is that evidence is to be adduced by witness statement, and this applies to application for an injunction (r 32.6(1); PD 25, para 3.2). However, a party may rely upon his statement of case, or application notice if verified by a statement of truth (r 32.6(2); PD 25, para 3.2).

However, it should be noted that applications for search orders and freezing injunctions are some of the few remaining applications that must be supported by affidavit evidence (PD 25, para 3.1).

Applying for an injunction without notice

If the requirement for an interim injunction is extremely urgent, application may need to be made immediately by attendance on a judge by telephone out of court hours. Practice Direction 25 provides details of telephone numbers to ring and the procedure to follow in order to make an emergency application in the High Court (PD 25, para 4.5). Further, injunctions such as freezing injunctions or search orders rely for their success on the element of surprise. Freezing injunctions and search orders can be obtained only if the court is satisfied that, in the case of the former, the respondent will dissipate assets to avoid judgment or, in the case of the latter, that he will destroy evidence, so that advance notification of the application would defeat its purpose. There is therefore provision, where there are good reasons for not giving notice, for an application for an injunction to be made without service of the application upon the respondent (r 25.3(1)). However, if an application is made without giving notice, the evidence in support of the application must state the reasons why notice has not been given (r 25.3(3); PD 25, para 3.4). The application notice, evidence in support and a draft order should be filed with the court two hours before the hearing wherever possible (PD 25, para 4.3).

If an application is made before the application notice has been issued, a draft order should be provided at the hearing and the application notice and evidence in support must be filed with the court on the same or next working day, or as ordered by the court (PD 25, para 4.3). Further, in all cases, except where secrecy is essential, the applicant should take steps to notify the respondent informally of the application, for example, by telephone (PD 25, para 4.3(3)).

Full and fair disclosure

A party applying for an urgent, without notice order for a freezing injunction, search order, or other form of interim injunction, has a high duty to make full, fair and accurate disclosure of all the material information to the court and draw the court's attention to significant factual, legal and procedural aspects of the case (*Memory Corp plc v Sidhu (No 2)* [2000] 1 WLR 1443, *per* Mummery LJ).

This requirement to make full and fair disclosure has been described as the 'golden rule' for urgent applications for injunctions without notice to the opponent (*The Arena Corp Ltd v Schroeder* [2003] EWHC 1089).

The applicant must make proper inquiries before making the application. The duty of disclosure therefore applies not only to material facts known to the applicant, but also to material facts which he should have known if he had made proper inquiries (*Brinks Mat Ltd v Elcombe* [1988] 1 WLR 1350). However, the duty to provide full and fair disclosure does not extend to an obligation to refer to, or disclose the contents of, without prejudice or privileged documents or conversations (*Somatra Ltd v Sinclair Roche & Temperley* [2000] 1 WLR 2453). Indeed, it was held in *Somatra Ltd v Sinclair Roche & Temperley* that where a party deploys evidence of what was said on a without prejudice occasion in support of its case on the underlying merits on an application for a freezing injunction, that party loses the right it would otherwise have had to object to the admissibility of any admissions made in the course of the same without prejudice discussions. The Court of Appeal held that it would be unjust to allow one party to use such material in order to obtain a freezing injunction, where the merits of the case are important to the court's decision, while preventing the other party from using the same material to defeat the case on the merits at trial. This is because a party who is attempting to defeat a case at trial is also seeking to demonstrate that the injunction granted on an interim basis should not have been granted in the first place, and will be seeking an order for an inquiry as to damages which flow from the undertaking given to the court.

The duty involves a requirement on the applicant to summarise his case and the evidence in support; he should identify crucial points for and against the application and not rely on general statements; he should identify any defence that may be put forward; and he should disclose all facts which could reasonably be taken into account by the judge in deciding whether to grant the injunction (*Siporex Trade SA v Comdel Commodities Ltd* [1986] 2 Lloyd's Rep 428).

In *The Arena Corp Ltd v Schroeder* [2003] EWHC 1089 at [213], Boyle J summarised the principles that the court would take into account where a party has failed to comply with his duty of full and fair disclosure:

- the general rule is that the court should discharge the injunction obtained in breach and refuse to renew it before trial;

- notwithstanding the general rule the court has a discretion to continue or renew the injunction;

- the jurisdiction should be exercised sparingly and take into account the need to protect the administration of justice and the requirement to uphold the public interest in requiring full and fair disclosure;

- the court should assess the degree and extent of the culpability with regard to the non-disclosure, but there is no general rule that an innocent failure will not attract the sanction of discharge of the order, nor a general rule that a deliberate breach will attract the sanction;

- the court should assess the importance and significance of the matters which were not disclosed to the court, but in making this assessment the fact that the judge might have made the order anyway is of little, if any, importance;

- the court should take into account the merits of the claimant's claim, but this should not be done on the basis that the strength of the claim is allowed to undermine the policy objective of the principle;

- the application of the principle should not be carried to extreme lengths or allowed to become an instrument of injustice;

- the jurisdiction is penal in nature and the court should therefore have regard to the proportionality between the punishment and the offence;

- there are no hard and fast rules as to when the discretion to continue the injunction should be exercised and the court should take into account all relevant circumstances.

In *The Arena Corp Ltd v Schroeder*, the court refused to continue the freezing injunction in the light of the claimant's failure to comply with the duty of full and fair disclosure on the grounds that the breaches, although not deliberate, showed the lack of care with which the claimant made the application.

It should also be noted that the court will be alert to the potential for respondents to base applications for discharge of injunctions on slender grounds of material non-disclosure where there is little prospect of obtaining a discharge on the substantial merits of the case or on the balance of convenience. If such a tactic is suspected, the court should refuse the application (see the observations of Slade LJ in *Brinks Mat v Elcombe* at 1359).

Undertaking as to damages

An interim injunction will be made subject to an undertaking from the applicant to pay damages to the defendant for any loss sustained by reason of the injunction if it is subsequently held at trial that the applicant was not entitled to restrain the respondent from doing what he was threatening to do (*American Cyanamid v Ethicon* [1975] AC 396).

In *Hoffman La Roche v Secretary of State for Trade and Industry* [1975] AC 295, Lord Diplock explained the basis of an undertaking as to damages as follows. Although the court has no power to compel the applicant to provide an undertaking as to damages, it will refuse the application if he declines to provide one. The undertaking is made to the court, not to the respondent. Accordingly, any failure to comply with the undertaking is not a breach of contract and will be punished by the court by the remedies available for contempt. However, the court extracts the undertaking for the benefit of the respondent. Although the court has a discretion whether or not to enforce the undertaking, if it decides to do so the measure of damages payable is not discretionary.

Inquiry as to damages

If it transpires at trial that the interim injunction was not justified, and the court exercises its discretion to enforce the undertaking as to damages, it will hold an inquiry as to damages, the principles of which are fixed and clear. The calculation is the same as for a breach of contract, as if the applicant had contracted not to prevent the respondent from doing that which he was restrained from doing by the terms of the injunction. The defendant will therefore be compensated for any loss he has suffered as a result of being temporarily prevented from doing that which he was legally entitled to do (*Hoffman La Roche v Secretary of State for Trade and Industry*).

If the claim does not proceed to trial the court still has a discretion to order an inquiry as to damages if, for instance, the claimant discontinues the proceedings. The court also has the power, in accordance with its general case management powers, summarily to dismiss the hearing of the inquiry as to damages if, for instance, the evidence relied on by the party seeking to recover damages does not establish any loss (*FSL Services Ltd v Macdonald* [2001] EWCA Civ 1008).

The usual practice in respect of interim injunctions is not to order an inquiry as to damages until the merits of the claim have been finally decided at trial. However, if a freezing injunction is discharged at any stage, the defendant may be granted an inquiry into damages on the basis that, regardless of the merits of the claim, the injunction was wrongly granted (*Yukong Line Ltd (SK Shipping Ltd) v Rendesbury Investments Corp* [2001] 2 Lloyd's Rep 113).

Although the court has a discretion whether or not to order an inquiry as to damages, the undertaking ought to be given effect except where there are special circumstances. Those special circumstances can include the conduct of the defendant at the time the injunction was obtained or subsequently (*Hoffman La Roche v Secretary of State for Trade and Industry* [1975] AC 295). However, where the reason for the discharge of the injunction is that the court lacked jurisdiction to grant it, for example, where a freezing injunction is granted where there is no substantial risk of dissipation of assets, it is extremely unlikely that the court would refuse to order an inquiry into damages where there is some evidence of loss (*Norwest Holst Civil Engineering Ltd v Plysius Ltd* (1987) *The Times*, 23 July).

The order for an injunction

The general rule, unless the court orders otherwise, is that all orders for an injunction must contain:

(a) an undertaking as to damages;

(b) if made without notice to any other party, an undertaking by the applicant to the court to serve on the respondent the application notice, evidence in support and any order made as soon as practicable;

(c) if made without notice to any other party, a return date for a further hearing at which the other party can be present;

(d) if made without filing the application notice, an undertaking to file and pay the appropriate fee on the same or next working day; and

(e) if made before the issue of the claim form, an undertaking to issue and pay the appropriate fee on the same or next working day, or alternatively, directions for the commencement of the claim.

(PD 25, para 5.1.)

Freezing injunctions

A freezing injunction is an order restraining a party from removing from the jurisdiction assets located there, or from dealing with assets whether located in the jurisdiction or not (r 25.1(f)). A freezing injunction was formerly known as a *Mareva* injunction (after the name of the case in which such a remedy was first granted, *Mareva Compañia Naviera SA v International Bulkcarriers SA* [1975] 2 Lloyd's Rep 509).

Freezing injunctions, together with search orders, have been described as the law's two 'nuclear weapons' (*Bank Mellat v Nikpour* [1985] FSR 87, *per* Donaldson J). However, of the two, the freezing injunction is felt to be more draconian, being described by Jacob J as 'thermo-nuclear' in *Alliance Resources plc v O'Brien* (unreported). Jacob J said in that case that a freezing injunction has 'the on-going effect of judicial chains on a defendant's financial affairs' and it is likely to destroy or severely damage the defendant's credit. He warned that as a freezing injunction gave the claimant an enormous initial advantage in the litigation and put the defendant under tremendous pressure, the court must be vigilant in ensuring that it is granted only when necessary and that it is executed in a fair manner.

The purpose of a freezing injunction is not to provide a claimant with security for his claim but to restrain a defendant from evading justice by disposing of assets otherwise than in the ordinary course of business so as to make himself judgment proof. A claimant does not therefore have an interest in the assets that are subject to the freezing injunction (*Gangway Ltd v Caledonian Park Investments (Jersey) Ltd* [2001] 2 Lloyd's Rep 715).

Jurisdiction to grant a freezing injunction

An application for a freezing injunction must usually be made to a High Court judge, the county court having limited jurisdiction to grant freezing injunctions. However, nominated circuit judges sitting in patents' county courts and mercantile courts do have jurisdiction to grant such an injunction. Also, a High Court judge sitting in a county court may do so (County Court Remedies Regulations 1991 (SI 1991/1222); PD 25, para 1.1). Further, a county court judge may grant a freezing injunction in the following circumstances (reg 3 of the County Court Remedies Regulations 1991):

- In respect of family proceedings under Part V of the Matrimonial and Family Proceedings Act 1984.
- Where an order is necessary in order to preserve property which is the subject matter of the proceedings.
- In aid of execution of a judgment or order made in county court proceedings in order to preserve assets until execution can be levied upon them.

In those circumstances where the county court does not have jurisdiction, if a freezing order is required in a county court case, the case will be transferred to the High Court to obtain the order. Unless the court orders otherwise, after the application has been disposed of, the case will be transferred back to the county court if it was one which should have been commenced in a county court (reg 5 of the County Court Remedies Regulations 1991).

Principles for granting a freezing injunction

To succeed in such an application, the claimant must show:

(a) a 'good arguable case' in relation to his substantive claim – it is not enough to show merely that there is 'a serious question to be tried' (see, for example, *Derby v Weldon* [1990] Ch 48, CA, *per* Parker LJ, at 57);

(b) that the defendant has assets, whether in or outside the jurisdiction;

(c) that there is a real risk that, if the court does not grant an order, the defendant will take the opportunity to dissipate those assets or otherwise put them beyond the reach of the court.

Evidence of intention to dissipate assets

The applicant must have evidence that the respondent is dishonest, or other evidence from which an intention to dissipate assets in order to avoid judgment may be inferred. It will not be enough to show that the respondent is short of money; something more is required; shortness of money does not equate with an intention to dissipate assets (*Midas Merchant Bank plc v Bello* [2002] EWCA Civ 1496).

A person subject to a freezing injunction is not prevented from paying debts incurred in the ordinary course of business (*The Angel Bell* [1981] QB 65; [1980] 1 Lloyd's Rep 632). Similarly, it does not prevent an individual from paying ordinary living expenses, even if they are incurred on a grand scale (*PCW (Underwriting Agencies Ltd) v PS Dixon* [1983] 2 Lloyd's Rep 197). In fact Lloyd LJ indicated that this principle extended to ordinary transactions in the course of business and, indeed, in the course of life (*Normid Housing v Ralphs* [1989] 1 Lloyd's Rep 274).

Balance of prejudice

If a freezing injunction inflicts hardship on the defendant this may be a ground for refusing or discharging the order. The court will take this into account and will generally allow the defendant's legitimate interests to prevail over those of the claimant who seeks to obtain security for a claim which may appear to be well founded but which still remains to be established at trial (*The Niedersachen* [1983] 1 WLR 1412).

In *Midas Merchant Bank plc v Bello* [2002] EWCA Civ 1496, the defendant's only asset in the jurisdiction, his matrimonial home, which was occupied by his wife and four children, one of whom had disabilities, was subject to a freezing injunction. There was a mortgage on the property in respect of which the mortgagee had obtained a possession order, which was suspended pending the defendant's application to discharge the freezing injunction. If the defendant was successful in his application he intended to remortgage the property to raise finance to meet the possession proceedings so that his wife and children could continue living in the property.

The freezing injunction was discharged on the grounds that there was no evidence to show that the defendant had an intention to dissipate assets to avoid judgment. However, the Court of Appeal also considered it relevant, when considering whether to discharge the injunction, that in the circumstances the potential harm to the defendant if the injunction remained far outweighed the potential harm to the claimant if it was removed. If the freezing injunction remained, the defendant's wife and children, one of whom had disabilities, would inevitably lose their home. If the freezing injunction was removed, the defendant could remortgage the property and avoid it being repossessed. The court found that in such circumstances the prejudice to the defendant outweighed the prejudice to the claimant who, if the freezing injunction was removed, might be unable, ultimately, to enforce a judgment debt.

Terms of order for a freezing injunction

The usual order for a freezing injunction provides that the respondent is restrained from disposing of or otherwise dealing with the assets until 'further order of the court'. A party can avoid the imposition of a freezing injunction by providing the claimant with security for his claim.

The terms of a freezing order usually include provision for the respondent to spend a specified amount towards living expenses and business expenses, and a specified amount on legal advice and representation.

The purpose of a freezing injunction is not to interfere with the respondent's ordinary business or his ordinary way of life. Therefore, when specifying amounts that can be spent on such expenses, the court does not consider whether the business venture is reasonable, or whether particular business or living expenses are reasonable. Also, the court does not balance the respondent's claim to spend such moneys against the strength of the applicant's case, or take into account that any moneys spent by the respondent will not be available to the applicant if it obtains judgment (*Halifax plc v Chandler* [2001] EWCA Civ 1750).

Effect of a freezing injunction on third parties

It is a contempt of court for any person notified of the terms of the freezing injunction to knowingly assist in or permit a breach of the order (*Attorney-General v Punch Ltd* [2002] UKHL 50).

A third party notified of the freezing injunction is bound by it as soon as he is notified of it, even though the defendant may not yet be aware of it. Such a third party, if he does anything to assist the defendant to thwart the injunction, will be guilty of a contempt of court (*Z Ltd v A* [1982] 1 QB 558).

However, in order to protect third parties, such as banks, affected by freezing orders, the terms of a freezing injunction in respect of assets located outside of the jurisdiction do not prevent the third party from complying with what it reasonably believes to be its obligations, whether under the criminal law, or contractual law or otherwise, of the country or State in which those assets are situated (*Bank of China v NBM LLC* [2001] EWCA Civ 1933).

Order to provide information about assets

The court may make an order, in support of a freezing order, directing a party to provide information about the location of relevant property or assets, or to provide information about relevant property or assets which are or may be the subject of an application for a freezing injunction (r 25.1(1)(g)).

Freezing injunction against a co-defendant

The court has jurisdiction to grant a freezing injunction over someone against whom the claimant has no direct cause of action, provided that the claim is ancillary and incidental to the cause of action against the defendant. The court must also be satisfied that the person has possession or control of assets and is involved in an attempt to make the principal defendant judgment proof (*TSB Private Bank International SA v Chabra* [1992] 1 WLR 231). In *TSB v Chabra*, Mr Chabra was alleged to be the alter ego of the co-defendant company against whom the claimant had no direct cause of action, but in respect of which there was a good arguable case that assets vested in its name were in fact the beneficial property of Mr Chabra. The court therefore granted a freezing injunction against the company restraining it from disposing or dealing with its assets until it was established whether the claimant was entitled to a judgment against Mr Chabra and until it was established which, if any, of the assets apparently vested in the company were available to satisfy any judgment obtained against Mr Chabra.

Form of order for a freezing injunction

An example of a freezing injunction is annexed to PD 25. The example may be modified in an appropriate case (PD 25, para 6).

Search orders

The court may make an order under s 7 of the Civil Procedure Act 1997 requiring a party to admit another party to premises for the purposes of preserving evidence or property relevant to intended proceedings (r 25.1(h)). Search orders, along with freezing injunctions, have been described as the law's two 'nuclear weapons' (*Bank Mellat v Nikpour* [1985] FSR 87, *per* Donaldson J).

Search orders are most commonly used in breach of copyright or passing off cases in order to seize the infringing articles, or in breach of confidence cases against former employees where confidential processes or lists of customers may have been taken by those former employees who have set up in a competing business.

A search order compels the respondent to permit the applicant to enter and search his premises. It differs from a search warrant in that it is directed not at the premises themselves but at the respondent or other person appearing to be in control of the premises and having authority to permit the search. If the respondent refuses to obey the order, the applicant is restricted to bringing proceedings for contempt of court. The European Court of Human Rights has held that the making of such an order in an appropriate case is not a breach of the right to respect for private life under Art 8 of the European Convention on Human Rights (*Chappell v UK* [1989] FSR 617).

Search orders were formerly known as *Anton Piller* orders after the name of the case in which the nature of the jurisdiction was explained (*Anton Piller KG v Manufacturing Processes Ltd* [1976] Ch 55). There are three essential preconditions for the making of a search order:

(a) an extremely strong *prima facie* case;

(b) the damage, potential or actual, must be very serious for the applicant;

(c) there must be clear evidence that the defendants have in their possession incriminating documents or things, and there must be evidence of a real possibility that they may destroy such material before any application on notice can be heard (*Anton Piller KG v Manufacturing Processes Ltd*).

Given the draconian nature of the remedy, application should not be made without notice to the defendant unless it is essential that the claimant should have inspection of property so that justice can be done between the parties in the circumstances where, if the defendant is forewarned, there is a grave danger that vital evidence will be destroyed and so the ends of justice will be defeated (*Anton Piller KG v Manufacturing Processes Ltd* at 61B, *per* Lord Denning MR).

The reason why the applicant has to show an extremely strong *prima facie* case is that the court is asked to make the order in the absence of, and without notice to, the person against whom it is made and so without hearing his side of the case; and if the order is made it requires the defendant, if he is not to be at risk of contempt of court, to give access to his premises (which may be his home) and to permit those premises to be searched. This therefore gives the basis for an invasion of the defendant's property and his privacy (*Elvee Ltd v Taylor and Others* [2001] EWCA Civ 1943).

Form of order for a search order

An example of a search order is annexed to PD 25. The example may be modified in an appropriate case (PD 25, para 8.6).

Supervising Solicitor

A search order must be executed by a Supervising Solicitor experienced in the operation of search orders (PD 25, para 7.2). The Supervising Solicitor must be independent of the applicant, not being an employee or member of the applicant's firm of solicitors (PD 25, para 8.1). A list of Supervising Solicitors can be found via the Law Society or, in the London area, through the London Solicitors Litigation Association (PD 25, para 7.2). The affidavit in support of the application must state the name of the firm and its address and the experience of the Supervising Solicitor (PD 25, para 7.3(1)).

When serving the search order the Supervising Solicitor may be accompanied only by the persons mentioned in the order, and he must explain the terms and effect of the order to the respondent in everyday language. He must also advise the respondent of his rights to obtain legal advice and to apply to vary or discharge the order (PD 25, para 7.4(4)).

Where the Supervising Solicitor is a man and the respondent is likely to be an unaccompanied woman, at least one other person named in the order must be a woman and must accompany the Supervising Solicitor (PD 25, para 7.4(5)).

The Supervising Solicitor must make a list of all material removed from the premises. The respondent must be given a reasonable opportunity to check the list before any material is removed, and then a copy of the list should be supplied to the respondent (PD 25, para 7.5(6), (7)).

The Supervising Solicitor has to provide the applicant's solicitors with a report on the carrying out of the order (PD 25, para 7.5(11)). The applicant must serve a copy of the report on the respondent and file a copy at court as soon as it is received (PD 25, para 7.5(12)).

Evidence for application for a search order

The evidence in support of an application for a search order must be contained in an affidavit (PD 25, para 3.1). The affidavit must disclose in full the reason the order is sought, including the probability that relevant material will disappear if the order is not made (PD 25, para 7.3(2)). It must also give the address of the premises to be searched and whether they are private or business premises (PD 25, para 7.3(1)).

Service of a search order

Unless the court orders otherwise, the search order must be served personally by the Supervising Solicitor. If the court has ordered that the Supervising Solicitor need not serve the order, the reason for this must be set out in the order (PD 25, paras 7.4(1), 8.2).

The search order must be accompanied by the evidence in support and any documents capable of being copied. This does not include an obligation to serve confidential exhibits, but such exhibits must be made available for inspection by the respondent, in the presence of the applicant's solicitors, while the order is carried out. Afterwards the confidential exhibits can be retained by the respondent's solicitors on their undertaking not to permit the respondent to see them except in the presence of the respondent's solicitors, and on the undertaking that the respondent will not be permitted to make or take away any note or record of them (PD 25, para 7.4(1), (2)).

Unless the court orders otherwise, a search order may be served only between 9.30 am and 5.30 pm, Monday to Friday (PD 25, para 7.4(6)). In *Elvee Ltd v Taylor* [2001] EWCA Civ 1943, the data to be seized was stored on computer. The court ordered that the search order could be executed from 7.30 am because there was evidence that the respondents started their working day at 7.30 am, and it was more practical and would avoid the data being lost or destroyed if the order was executed before the computers were in use.

The respondent's premises can be searched and items removed only in the presence of the respondent or a person who appears to be a responsible employee of the respondent (PD 25, para 7.5(2)).

The search order must not be carried out at the same time as a police search warrant (PD 25, para 8.3).

Documents seized

The documents and other materials to be removed must be identified in the order and only those documents can be removed (PD 25, para 7.5(1)).

Where the order provides for copies of documents to be made, the documents should be retained for no more than two days before being returned to the owner (PD 25, para 7.5(3)).

Where the order provides for material in dispute to be removed pending trial, if appropriate it should be insured and placed in the custody of the respondent's solicitors on their undertaking to retain it in safekeeping and to produce it to the court when required (PD 25, para 7.5(4), (5)).

If any of the material exists only in computer readable form, the respondent is obliged to give the applicant's solicitors immediate access to the computers, with all necessary passwords, to enable the computers to be searched and the listed items to be printed out (PD 25, para 7.5(8)).

Intellectual property cases

Applications for search orders in intellectual property cases must be made in the Chancery Division (PD 25, para 8.5). The reason for this is that judges in this division have the relevant expertise to deal with the difficulties which may arise on such applications (*Elvee Ltd v Taylor and Others*).

As a general principle, a person (or a person's spouse) may refuse to answer any question or produce any document or thing if to do so would tend to expose that person to proceedings for an offence or the recovery of a penalty (*Rank Film Distributors Ltd v Video Information Centre* [1982] AC 380, HL). The privilege against self-incrimination may be withdrawn by statute (s 14(3) of the Civil Evidence Act 1968). It has been so withdrawn in respect of proceedings for infringement of intellectual property rights or for passing off by s 72 of the SCA. Section 72 provides that in such proceedings, a person shall not be excused from answering any question put to him or from complying with any order made, on the grounds that to do so would tend to expose him, or his spouse, to criminal proceedings. However, no statement or admission made by a person in answering any question put to him in such proceedings or in complying with any order shall be admissible in evidence against him, or against his spouse, in criminal proceedings for any related offence for infringement or passing off (s 72(3) of the SCA).

Interim declarations

Under r 25.1(b), the court may grant an interim declaration. An interim declaration may be appropriate in a number of circumstances, for instance, in judicial review proceedings as a means to control the abuse of executive power. It may also be used by doctors and hospitals to obtain an advisory declaration as to whether treatment is appropriate in particular circumstances.

Originally the court's power to make a declaration was restricted to declarations as to existing private rights (*Guaranty Trust Co of New York v Hannay* [1915] 1 KB 536). However, the court now has the power to make a binding declaration whether or not any other remedy is claimed (r 40.20).

In *Bank of Scotland v A Ltd* [2001] EWCA Civ 52, the Court of Appeal explained that the use of interim declaratory relief may be of assistance to banks where a customer's account is being investigated by the Serious Fraud Office (SFO) on suspicion of money laundering. In that case the claimant bank suspected that the defendant's bank account was being so used. It was subsequently informed that the SFO was undertaking investigations involving the defendant. Under s 93D of the Criminal Justice Act (CJA) 1988, the claimant was prevented from notifying or 'tipping off' its customer that it was subject to such an investigation. However, the bank was concerned that if the money in the account was the proceeds of crime and it paid sums out at the defendant's direction, it would be liable to the rightful owner on the grounds of knowingly assisting in a breach of trust. The claimant therefore applied to the court for relief without notice to the defendant and obtained an interim injunction preventing it from paying any sums out of the account until further order. In the light of s 93D of the CJA 1988, the claimant did not serve a copy of the injunction on the defendant. Instead the claimant wrote to the defendant informing it that it was investigating its account and, until it was in receipt of counsel's advice, it would not make any payments out of the defendant's account.

The defendant began proceedings against the claimant and sought an order for the money in its account to be held by its solicitors. It subsequently became established that the defendant was not guilty of money laundering. In the course of the proceedings the defendant became aware of the existence of the interim injunction. The claimant paid the money in the account to the defendant's solicitors, but the parties applied to the court for the issue of costs and a potential inquiry as to damages on the usual undertaking as to damages to be determined.

The Court of Appeal held that it was not appropriate for the claimant to have obtained an interim injunction preventing it from paying sums out of the defendant's account, and indeed it could not see any circumstances in which a court could grant an injunction against the only party who was seeking relief. Instead, the appropriate course would have been for the claimant to attempt to resolve with the SFO what information it was entitled to disclose to the defendant. If the claimant and the SFO could not reach agreement then the claimant could have applied for an interim declaration under r 52.1(1)(b) in proceedings against the SFO. In the circumstances there would be grounds for the hearing to be in private and the defendant would not need to be served because it would not be a party to the proceedings. The declaration could set out what information it would be proper for the bank to rely on and the court would take into account the views of the SFO as to what might prejudice its criminal investigation. The Court of Appeal recognised that the duration of the interim declaration would probably be short, because in most cases it would be necessary to conceal the existence of the criminal investigations for only a fairly limited period.

In the circumstances of that case the court held that the interim injunction should be discharged, and the defendant was entitled to its costs of the proceedings notwithstanding that the claimant was justified in taking action to protect its position. The difficulty for the claimant was that it had applied for the wrong remedy, an interim injunction restraining itself rather than declaratory relief against the SFO.

Interim property orders

The court has the power to make orders in respect of 'relevant property', that is property, including land, which is the subject of the claim or as to which any question may arise on the claim (r 25.1(2)). An order can be made, therefore, in respect of the property which is in dispute between the parties, or property which is relevant evidence in respect of the dispute.

Order for the detention, custody or preservation of relevant property

Under r 25.1(c)(i), the court has the power to make an order for the detention, custody or preservation of relevant property. Such an order may be made where one of the parties to a dispute owns the relevant property and there is a risk that he may dispose of it in the ordinary course of business. However, where there is a risk that the party with the property may dispose of it in order to thwart the claim, it may be appropriate to consider applying for a search order (r 25.1(h)).

Order for the inspection, etc, of relevant property

The court has the power to make an order for the inspection of relevant property, for samples of it to be taken and for experiments to be carried out on it (r 25.1(1)(c)(ii), (iii) and (iv)). Such orders may be appropriate in a wide variety of circumstances where there is an issue about the quality or nature of property.

The purpose of such orders is to facilitate a party in preserving, inspecting and taking samples of property which may be the subject matter of the dispute, or evidence relevant to the dispute. There is also power for the court to order in appropriate circumstances that the property be sold, or income paid from it or that it be delivered up into safekeeping.

Sale, etc, of relevant property

The court has the power under r 25.1(1)(c)(v) to make an order for the sale of relevant property which is of a perishable nature, or which for any other good reason it is desirable to sell quickly. For instance, where there is a dispute about commercial goods of a perishable nature or whose value may fluctuate, it may be desirable to sell the property and hold the proceeds of sale until the dispute can be determined.

The court also has the power to make an order for the payment of income from relevant property until the claim is decided (r 25.1(1)(c)(vi)).

Order authorising entry onto land

The court has the power to give a person authority to enter any land or building in the possession of a party to the proceedings for the purposes of carrying out any of the above orders in respect of relevant property (r 25.1(1)(d)). The existence of such a power is obviously necessary to give effect to the above rules where the party in possession of the property may be unwilling to allow access voluntarily.

Delivery up of goods under the Torts (Interference with Goods) Act 1977

Under s 4 of the Torts (Interference with Goods) Act 1977, the court has the power to make an interim order for the delivery up to the claimant, or a person appointed by the court, on such terms and conditions as may be specified, of goods which are the subject of present or future proceedings for wrongful interference. An application may be appropriate if there is a risk that the goods may be destroyed or disposed of before trial, but it is not confined to such situations.

Inspection, etc, of property before proceedings commenced

The court has the power under s 33(1) of the SCA 1981 s 52(1) of the CCA to make an order for the inspection, photographing, preservation, custody and detention of property which may become the subject matter of subsequent proceedings, or which is relevant to the proceedings. Those provisions also give the court the power to make an order for the taking of samples of, or the carrying out of experiments on, that property.

Inspection, etc, of non-party's property after proceedings commenced

Under s 34(3) of the SCA and s 53(3) of the CCA, the court also has the power to make similar orders to those specified above (see etc 'Inspection of property before proceedings commenced') against a non-party, once proceedings have been commenced.

See also Chapter 29, 'Disclosure of Documents', for further discussion of the court's powers in respect of pre-action disclosure and disclosure against non-parties.

PART B: INTERIM PAYMENTS

Definition

Section 32 of the SCA and s 50 of the CCA provide the statutory basis for the rules of court relating to interim payments.

An interim payment is defined as a payment on account of any debt or damages or other sum, excluding costs, which a defendant may be held liable for to the claimant if judgment is made in the claimant's favour (s 32(5) of the SCA; s 50(5) of the CCA; r 25.1(1)(k)). An interim payment may be made, prior to the court's assessment of the claimant's damages, where the claimant has obtained judgment on liability against the defendant, or the defendant has admitted liability, or where the claimant has a very strong claim against the defendant.

Interim payments were introduced in order to alleviate the hardship that could arise for claimants awaiting compensation in the light of the delay between commencement of proceedings and final judgment being ordered. They are regularly made in personal injury claims where defendants are often covered by insurance and where liability is often easily established.

Orders for interim payments

Time when an application for an interim payment may be made

The earliest a claimant may apply for an order for an interim payment is when the period for the defendant to file an acknowledgment of service has expired (r 25.6(1)).

Conditions to be satisfied for making an interim payment

The court may make an order for an interim payment *only* if:

(a) the defendant admits liability either in whole or in part; or

(b) judgment has already been obtained for damages to be assessed; or

(c) the court is satisfied that if the matter went to trial, the claimant would obtain a 'judgment for a substantial amount of money' (see position as to more than one defendant below); or

(d) it is a claim for possession and the defendant would be liable to pay for use and occupation (r 25.7(1)).

In addition to one of the above being satisfied, in a claim for personal injury, an interim payment may be ordered *only* if:

(a) the defendant is insured; or

(b) the Motor Insurers' Bureau are dealing with the claim; or

(c) the defendant is a public body (r 25.7(2)).

Rule 25.7 has to be interpreted and the powers granted by it exercised in accordance with the overriding objective. The overriding objective includes ensuring that parties are on an equal footing. Depriving a party of money which one party has but which is rightfully the other's does not place the latter on an equal footing with the former. Nevertheless, it might be equally wrong to order an interim payment to a party who might not be able to repay it if an adjustment was required under r 25.8 (*Harmon CFEM Facades (UK) Ltd (In Liquidation) v The Corporate Officer of the House of Commons* (2000) *The Times*, 15 November).

Further, r 25.7 does not provide for an order for an interim payment to be made on conditions. Therefore the court's function is to decide what is or may be due, and it is not concerned with what the claimant might do with the award when it is received. However, notwithstanding this, in an appropriate case the court would have power to attach conditions if it was necessary to do so in accordance with the overriding objective of the CPR (*Harmon CFEM Facades (UK) Ltd (In Liquidation) v The Corporate Officer of the House of Commons*).

Interim payments in personal injury claims where there are two or more defendants

In a claim for personal injuries, where there are two or more defendants (as long as r 25.7(2) is satisfied; see above, 'Conditions to be satisfied for making an interim payment') the court may make an order for an interim payment against any defendant if it is satisfied that the claimant would obtain substantial damages against at least one of the defendants, even if the court has not yet determined which defendant is liable (r 25.7(3)).

Interim payments in claims for possession of land

Where a claimant is bringing proceedings for the possession of land, if the court is satisfied that if the claim went to trial the defendant would be found liable (even if the claim for possession fails) to pay the claimant a sum of money for the defendant's use and occupation of the land prior to the claim for possession being heard, the court may make an order for an interim payment of the sum owed to the claimant (r 25.7(1)(d)).

Procedure for applying

An application is made in accordance with Part 23. The application notice must be served on the defendant at least 14 days before the hearing of the application and must be supported by evidence (r 25.6(3)).

Practice Direction 25B sets out the matters which must be dealt with by the evidence in support. This includes such matters as the sum sought by way of interim payment, the sum in which judgment is likely to be given and the reasons for believing that the conditions in r 25.7 are satisfied (PD 25B, para 2.1).

If the respondent wishes to rely on written evidence at the hearing he must file and serve it at least seven days before the hearing of the application (r 25.6(4)). The applicant then has an opportunity to file evidence in reply to the respondent's evidence, which must be filed and served at least three days before the hearing (r 25.6(5)).

The claimant may make more than one application for an interim payment (r 25.6(2)).

Amount of interim payment

The court may order an interim payment in one sum or in instalments (r 25.6(7)). The amount of the interim payment must not exceed a reasonable proportion of the likely amount of the final judgment (r 25.7(4)).

When deciding on the amount to order the court must take account of contributory negligence and any relevant set off or counterclaim (r 25.7(5)).

The fact that any sum paid might be irrecoverable, if it is subsequently found that the defendant is not liable to the claimant, is irrelevant to the court's discretion whether to make an order for an interim payment. However, where the amount or an element of it may be a matter of judgment or discretionary, care should be taken not to over-compensate the claimant (*Harmon CFEM Facades (UK) Ltd (In Liquidation) v The Corporate Officer of the House of Commons* (2000) 72 Con LR 21).

Restriction on disclosure of interim payment

The fact that a defendant has made an interim payment, whether voluntarily or by court order, shall not be disclosed to the trial judge until all questions of liability and the amount of money to be awarded have been decided, unless the defendant agrees (r 25.9). The reason for this rule is to ensure that there is no risk that the judge will be influenced by the fact that an interim payment has been made or ordered when reaching his decision in the case.

Orders for the adjustment of an interim payment

The court has a wide discretion under r 25.8 to make orders to adjust the interim payment. In appropriate circumstances, for instance if the claimant is unsuccessful at trial, the court has the power to order that the interim payment is repaid to the defendant. Similarly, if the claimant recovers less in damages than the amount of the interim payment the court has the power to order that the excess be repaid (r 25.8(1), (2)). Further, if the court makes such an adjustment in favour of the defendant, it can also award the defendant interest on the overpaid amount running from the date when he made the interim payment (r 25.8(5)).

The court also has the power to vary or discharge an order for an interim payment (r 25.8(2)). The court may do so if good reason is shown, for instance a change in circumstances since the order was made. However, where a party is arguing that the order for an interim payment into court is wrong, the proper step is to appeal and not apply for a variation (*Moore v Sahota* (2000) LTL, 1 March, Ch D).

Where there is more than one defendant, and one defendant has been ordered to make an interim payment to the claimant, the court may order the other defendant to reimburse, either wholly or in part, the defendant who has made the interim payment (r 25.8(2)). However, the court may make such an order only if the defendant seeking reimbursement made a claim in the proceedings against the other defendant for a contribution or indemnity or other remedy (r 25.8(3)).

PART C: SECURITY FOR COSTS

Under r 25.12, a defendant to any claim may apply for security for his costs of the proceedings from the claimant. If the order is granted, a sum of money will usually be ordered to be paid into court, out of which the defendant can enforce any award of costs he may obtain against the claimant.

The purpose of the jurisdiction to provide orders for security for costs is not to protect defendants completely against the risk that their costs might not be paid if the claimant is unsuccessful. The jurisdiction is exercisable in limited circumstances, and even then only if it is just to do so. The rules and the court have to balance the interests of claimants against those of defendants, and in particular the claimant's right to a fair trial under Art 6 of the European Convention on Human Rights.

Part 20 claim

A defendant to a Part 20 claim may apply for security for costs under r 25.12 (r 20.3). Therefore, if a claimant brings a claim against a defendant who then counterclaims against the claimant, the claimant may apply for an order for security for costs against the defendant in his capacity as claimant to the Part 20 claim. However, if the defendant's counterclaim is in effect not much more than a defence to the claimant's claim the court is unlikely to exercise its jurisdiction to make an order for security for costs against such a defendant.

In *Kazakhstan Investment Fund Ltd v Aims Asset Management* (2002) LTL, 23 May, the claimant brought a claim against the defendant for the recovery of fees on the defendant's failure to give the requisite period of six months' notice to terminate a contract. The defendant denied that it was obliged to give such notice and brought a counterclaim for a substantial sum for alleged breaches of the contract by the claimant. Both the claimant and the defendant were resident outside of the jurisdiction and outside of European Union (EU) and European Free Trade Area (EFTA) territories. The court ordered the claimant to provide security for costs of the claim in the sum of £37,500, and the counterclaiming defendant to provide security for costs of the counterclaim in the sum of £125,000.

The appeal court upheld the judge's order on the grounds that the defendant's counterclaim raised facts, matters and issues going completely beyond those needed to be proved by the claimant. Whereas the court found the claimant's claim to be straight-forward, it found that the defendant's counterclaim consisted of a series of detailed allegations and raised complicated matters involving factual and expert evidence. The much larger sum for security for costs for the counterclaim was therefore justified.

Grounds for ordering security for costs

In order to make an order for security for costs the court must be satisfied of both of the following:

- that having regard to all the circumstances it is just to make the order; and
- that one or more of the specified conditions are satisfied (r 25.13(1)).

Conditions to be satisfied

The court must find that one or more of the following conditions are satisfied (r 25.13(2)):

(a) The claimant is:

- ordinarily resident out of the jurisdiction; and

- not resident in a Brussels Contracting State, a Lugano Contracting State or a Regulation State as defined by s 1(3) of the Civil Jurisdiction and Judgments Act 1982.

(b) The claimant is a company or other body (whether incorporated inside or outside Great Britain) and there is reason to believe that it will be unable to pay the defendant's costs if ordered to do so.

(c) The claimant has changed his address since the claim was commenced with a view to evading the consequences of the litigation.

(d) The claimant failed to give his address in the claim form, or gave an incorrect address in that form.

(e) The claimant is acting as a nominal claimant, other than as a representative claimant under Part 19, and there is reason to believe that he will be unable to pay the defendant's costs if ordered to do so.

(f) The claimant has taken steps in relation to his assets that would make it difficult to enforce an order for costs against him.

Court's discretion to order security for costs

It is not sufficient for the court simply to find that one of the specified conditions is satisfied. The remedy is discretionary and the court must properly exercise its discretion when deciding whether or not to order security for costs by having regard to all the circumstances of the case and being satisfied that it is just to make the order.

The purpose for the exercise of the power to order security for costs where the claimant is a company is to avoid any injustice to a defendant who is sued by an impecunious claimant such as would arise if the claim were to fail. However, it is also necessary to avoid, at the other extreme, injustice to a claimant who has a meritorious claim and who may be prevented from bringing the claim if he is required to provide advance security for the defendant's costs. The overall requirement in the exercise of the court's discretion is that the result should be a just one (*Fernhill Mining Ltd v Kier Construction Ltd* (2000) LTL, 27 January, CA, *per* Evans LJ).

In *Fernhill Mining Ltd v Kier Construction Ltd*, the Court of Appeal set aside the judge's order that the claimant provide security for the defendant's costs. The court held that the judge had incorrectly exercised his discretion in ordering security by failing to give sufficient weight to the fact that the claimant had a very high probability of succeeding in its claim against the defendant and that the claimant's impecuniosity was caused by the defendant's actions in wrongfully repudiating its contract with the claimant. Although the Court of Appeal was prepared to assume that the claimant was impecunious, it held that in the circumstances it would cause a high degree of injustice to impose an order for security for costs on the claimant.

The Court of Appeal also held in that case that as far as possible the court should avoid having to form a view on the merits of the case when deciding whether to order security for costs. However, in the circumstances, as the claimant's prospects of success were very strong, it was appropriate to take the merits of the claimant's claim into account.

Claimant resident outside of the jurisdiction or the EU or EFTA

The fact that the claimant is resident outside of the jurisdiction, but is not resident in an EU or EFTA country, is one of the conditions on which jurisdiction to order security for costs is conferred on the court. This applies whether the claimant is an individual, or a company or other body (r 25.13(2)(a)).

A claimant may have two ordinary residences, one within the jurisdiction and one outside. The fact of residence outside the jurisdiction is enough to give the court jurisdiction to make the order; it is not precluded by the fact that the claimant is also ordinarily resident inside the jurisdiction (*Leyvand v Barasch* (2000) *The Times*, 23 March).

However, Lightman J made clear in *Leyvand v Barasch* that an order for security for costs cannot now be ordered as a matter of course against a foreign claimant. Further, the claimant does not have the burden of establishing the ownership of fixed and permanent property within the jurisdiction to avoid the making of such an order. Instead Lightman J stressed that the single criterion for ordering security is what is just in the circumstances of the particular case.

In *Leyvand v Barasch*, the claimant was an Israeli national, ordinarily resident in Israel. However, he also had a home and other property in England, had business activities here and stayed in England on average for 80 days a year. The claimant brought proceedings against the defendant in respect of disputed partnership assets. There was no evidence to suggest that there was any risk that the claimant's assets in the jurisdiction would be dissipated or moved abroad so that they would not be available to satisfy a judgment for costs in the defendant's favour. The court therefore held that due to the claimant's long residence in the jurisdiction, his ownership of a home and his long-established business activities here, it was not just to make an order for security for costs against him.

The connection of the claimant with this country is relevant to the exercise of the court's discretion whether to order security, and the closer the connection the greater the relevance. If the claimant has an established home and is resident here, security is unlikely to be ordered. If the claimant has an established home and is *ordinarily* resident here an order for security for costs is even more unlikely to be made (*Leyvand v Barasch*). However, if there is reason to question a foreign claimant's probity, the nature of any assets within the jurisdiction will be relevant. Accordingly, the risk may be greater if the property is cash, or immediately realisable or transportable, and less if fixed and permanent, such as land (*Leyvand v Barasch*).

The United Kingdom is not entitled to discriminate in its laws against nationals of Member States covered by the Brussels Convention (EU) or the Lugano Convention (EFTA). Accordingly, there is no jurisdiction to order security for costs against a claimant resident in one of those Convention countries. However, the mere fact that a claimant has assets located within a Convention territory is not enough to deprive the court of jurisdiction to order security for costs (*De Beer v Kanaar and Co* [2001] EWCA Civ 1318; [2003] 1 WLR 38; [2002] 3 All ER 1020). In *De Beer v Kanaar and Co*, the Court of Appeal ordered a claimant, who had assets in Convention States but who was ordinarily resident outside, to provide security for the defendant's costs. The court held that it was just to make the order because the claimant gave materially misleading evidence about his assets, which appeared to be deliberate and which put a question mark over the reliability of the rest of his evidence. Also, the court took into account that the claimant had a lack of available assets within the jurisdiction and that it would be difficult to enforce any order for costs against his assets located in Florida.

Effect of the HRA on residence outside the jurisdiction of the EU or EFTA

Article 14 of the European Convention on Human Rights provides that enjoyment of the rights and freedoms of the Convention is to be secured without discrimination on any ground such as sex, race and so on, and this includes national origin. It has long been accepted that orders for security for costs involve issues of access to justice, including the right to a fair trial under Art 6 of the Convention.

After the introduction of the HRA 1998 and the CPR, in *Nasser v United Bank of Kuwait* [2002] 1 WLR 1868, the Court of Appeal had occasion to reconsider the general principle which provided that orders for security for costs would be made automatically where the claimant was resident outside the jurisdiction and outside an EU or EFTA State. In that case the claimant was resident in the United States. Her claim against the defendant was struck out for want of prosecution. She appealed against the striking out of her claim and permission was granted subject to her providing security for the defendant's costs of the appeal. The claimant appealed against the order for security for costs to the Court of Appeal.

The Court of Appeal held that the discretion to order security for costs must be exercised in a manner which is not discriminatory under Art 14. It would be discriminatory and unjustified if the mere fact of residence outside of any EU or EFTA State could justify the exercise of the discretion to make orders for security for costs to protect defendants or respondents to an appeal. This is because such defendants or respondents would be subject to the same risks, against which they would have no protection, if the claimant or appellant was a resident of an EU or EFTA State.

The court said that the rationale for the rule allowing security for costs to be ordered against foreign claimants was the potential difficulties or burdens of enforcement in States which were not party to the Brussels or Lugano Conventions. Therefore the discretion should be exercised in a manner which reflected its rationale and should be based on difficulties of enforcement and not so as to put residents outside EU and EFTA States at a disadvantage compared to those within.

The court emphasised that merely because a person was resident outside the EU or EFTA States did not *necessarily* mean that enforcement would be more difficult. It pointed to the reciprocal enforcement treaties which the UK had with many Commonwealth and common law countries. There would therefore have to be a proper basis for submissions that there was an extra obstacle or burden to enforcement in such other countries. Even then any order for security for costs should be tailored to reflect the obstacles and burdens which did exist.

In *Nasser v United Bank of Kuwait*, the Court of Appeal noted that no country had any reciprocal enforcement treaties with the USA, but this was not generally thought to be a problem because that country was seen to be willing to enforce foreign judgments. The court did recognise that there would be additional costs and delay involved in bringing an action in the US to enforce any English order for costs before enforcements steps could be taken. There would also be additional steps necessary to investigate whether the claimant had assets to enforce against given her alleged impecuniosity. The court also took into account the determined nature of the claimant which might well increase the costs of enforcement. In all the circumstances the Court of Appeal held that it was appropriate to make an order for security for costs against the claimant in the sum of £5,000, which reflected the additional cost and delay that would be involved in enforcing any order for costs against her in the USA.

However, when considering whether it will be difficult to enforce an order for costs against a foreign claimant the court will consider the difficulties of enforcement in the country where the assets are located, not the place of incorporation or residence of the claimant (*Kazakhstan Investment Fund Ltd v Aims Asset Management* (2002) LTL, 23 May). In *Kazakhstan Investment Fund Ltd v Aims Asset Management*, the counterclaiming defendant was a company incorporated in the Cayman Islands but its assets were located in Kazakhstan. The court accepted that enforcement against assets in Kazakhstan, if not impossible, would be extremely difficult and expensive. It held that as a matter of practicality and common sense the court had to consider the difficulties of enforcement in the country where the assets were located, not where the claimant was incorporated or resided. Otherwise the court would be forced to exercise its discretion in a wholly unrealistic and impractical manner because often, particularly in the case of companies, the place of incorporation or residence was simply a matter of convenience, for tax and regulatory reasons.

Impecunious company

Rule 25.13(2)(c) gives the court jurisdiction to make an order for security for costs against a company or other body, whether incorporated inside or outside Great Britain, where there is reason to believe that it will be unable to pay the defendant's costs if ordered to do so. There is overlapping jurisdiction under s 726(1) of the Companies Act 1985 to make such an order against limited companies incorporated in England and Scotland which are claimants in proceedings.

An order for security for costs under s 726 of the Companies Act 1985 is not the inevitable result of the court concluding under that section 'that there is reason to believe that the company will be unable to pay the defendant's costs if successful in his defence' where the claimant's case is meritorious and it is arguable that the claimant's impecuniosity is a direct result of the defendant's allegedly wrongful repudiation of its contract with the claimant (*Fernhill Mining Ltd v Kier Construction Ltd* (2000) LTL, 27 January, CA).

Evidence of claimant company's financial position

The court has to be satisfied by evidence that the claimant company will be unable to pay the defendant's costs if he is successful in his defence. Further, the question is whether the claimant '*will* be unable' to pay, not '*may* be unable' to pay (*Re Unisoft Group Ltd (No 2)* [1993] BCLC 532).

In *Guinle v Kirreh* (1999) LTL, 3 December, the court appointed a single joint expert chartered accountant to provide a report as to whether the claimant would be able to pay the defendant's costs, based on a number of costs outcomes, if the defendant were successful in its defence. The court was satisfied from the expert's evidence that if the costs payable to the defendant exceeded £350,000, the claimant would be unable to pay them. The court therefore directed a further hearing to determine the appropriate amount for the defendant's costs for the purposes of security for costs and whether, and if so in which amount, security for costs should be ordered.

Claimant's behaviour

The court has jurisdiction, where it is just to do so, to order security if it is shown that the claimant has changed his address since the claim was commenced with a view to evading the consequences of the litigation (r 25.13(2)(d)). The reference to change of address is not limited to a change of address from the one shown in the claim form, it is any change of address since the claim was commenced (*Aoun v Bahri* [2002] EWHC 29; [2002] 3 All ER 182). The court also has jurisdiction if the claimant fails to give his address in the claim form, or gives an incorrect address in the claim form (r 25.13(2)(e)).

More generally, the court has jurisdiction where the claimant has taken steps in relation to his assets which would make it difficult to enforce an order for costs against him (r 25.13(2)(g)). Three requirements need to be met under this rule:

(a) the claimant must have taken steps;

(b) the steps must have been taken in relation to his assets;

(c) the steps must be steps which would make it difficult to enforce an order for costs against him.

If r 25.13(2)(g) is to apply, the steps which the claimant has taken in relation to his assets must themselves be matters which, if he loses the case and a costs order is made against him, will make it difficult to enforce the order. Rule 25.13(2)(g) does not provide that security may be ordered if the claimant has taken steps in the past and, if he took similar steps before the end of the case, those similar steps would make enforcement difficult. It has to be the actual steps that he has taken which themselves make enforcement difficult (*Chandler v Brown* (2002) LTL, 5 August, *per* Park J).

In *Chandler v Brown*, the claimant was an individual resident within the jurisdiction. The defendant adduced evidence of the claimant's past conduct which the court acknowledged was seriously unsatisfactory and disturbing. The claimant had a conviction for fraudulent trading and obtaining services by deception. He had also been shown in other proceedings to have misled the court about his assets. The court accepted that the claimant had been dishonest and deceitful in the past. The court understood why the defendants were concerned that their costs might not be paid by the claimant and why they wished to obtain an order for security for costs against him. However, the court held that that was not a sufficient ground for their being granted such an order and it was not enough to bring their application within r 25.13(2)(g).

Rule 25.13(2)(g) is worded objectively, and refers to the effect of the steps in relation to the assets rather than the claimant's motivation in taking those steps (*Aoun v Bahri* [2002] EWHC 29; [2002] 3 All ER 182). In *Aoun v Bahri*, the claimant sold a property he owned in Australia for personal reasons. However, the sale of that property, which represented the bulk of his assets, would make it difficult to enforce an order for costs against him. The court therefore found that this gave it jurisdiction to make an order for security for costs against him. In the circumstances of that case the court found it just to make an order for security for costs against the claimant.

Nominal claimant

If the claimant is a nominal claimant, other than a representative claimant under Part 19, the court may make an order for security for costs against him if there is reason to believe that he will be unable to pay the defendant's costs if ordered to do so (r 25.13(2)(f)). An example of a nominal claimant is a claimant who has had a claim assigned to him.

Stifling a genuine claim

The court may refuse to exercise its discretion to order security for costs if it will mean the stifling of a genuine claim. This applies especially to first instance hearings. This factor does not operate quite so strongly in the context of an appeal, where the party against whom security is sought has already had one hearing and lost.

In *Nasser v United Bank of Kuwait* [2002] 1 WLR 1868, the Court of Appeal noted that the claimant had already been granted permission to appeal which indicated that the court granting permission was satisfied that she had real prospects of success. The court was conscious that the claimant was appealing against an order striking out her claim for delay. If through her impecuniosity the claimant was unable to provide the security for costs ordered by the lower court this would mean that there would be no trial of the merits of her claim. Furthermore, the security for costs was in respect of the appeal against the order for striking out, so her inability to provide that sum would mean that there would not even be any appeal against the decision that there would be no trial of her claim. There was therefore a risk that an order for security would stifle a genuine claim. However, the court found on the evidence that the claimant could afford to provide security for costs and ordered security in the sum of £5,000.

However, in *Monticello plc v Your TV and Radio plc and Others* [2002] All ER (D) 204, Ch D, it was held that a court will not be prevented from ordering security simply on the ground that it would stifle a valid claim. Moreover, the burden is on the party against whom security for costs is sought, to prove that it is impossible for him to fund the litigation. In this case the claimant complained that an order for security of costs would stifle its claim. However, the court found that the claimant was bound to succeed to a fairly substantial amount and that, presumably, making the order for security ought not to mean stifling the claim.

Court's powers to order sums to be paid into court

The court has the power to order sums to be paid into court under r 3.1 when making an order subject to conditions (r 3.1(3)), and if a party fails, without good reason, to comply with a rule, practice direction or relevant pre-action protocol (r 3.1(5)).

It was accepted in *Olatawura v Abiloye* [2002] EWCA Civ 998 that the court's powers under r 3.1 were tantamount to orders for security for costs outside the provisions of Part 25 (Section II). However, it was accepted that under the CPR the court has an altogether wider discretion than under the former rules to ensure that justice can be done in a particular case, including making such orders (see Chapter 6, 'Judicial Case Management: The Overriding Objective', for further discussion of r 3.1).

Procedure for applying for an order for security for costs

The application must be made in accordance with Part 23. It must also be supported by written evidence (r 25.12(2)).

Chapter 20, 'Making Applications for Court Orders', should be consulted for details of the procedure under Part 23, including the requirements of and form of evidence.

Amount of the security

The court has a discretion as to the amount of security to order (r 25.12(3)(a)). The applicant is expected to submit costs estimates, which may be challenged by the respondent.

The court may determine the amount of security by reference to the costs estimate for the whole of the proceedings, or take a point in time, for example, filing of pre-trial checklists, up to which security will be ordered. The defendant can then make a further application for security if this point is reached.

The court is likely to be proportionate when deciding on the amount a party must pay into court and should ensure that the imposition of this penalty does not make it impossible for a party to continue with the litigation (*Chapple v Williams* (1999) LTL, 8 December). However, a party cannot complain that the amount ordered is difficult for him to pay and is likely to have to be prepared to provide full and frank disclosure of his financial circumstances in order to avoid or reduce the amount ordered to be paid into court (*Training in Compliance Ltd (t/a Matthew Read) v Dewse (t/a Data Research Co)* (2000) LTL, 2 October, CA).

Training in Compliance Ltd (t/a Matthew Read) v Dewse (t/a Data Research Co) involved the exercise of the court's discretion under r 3.1 to order that the defendant make a payment into court for its failure to comply with the requirements of the CPR. The Court of Appeal considered authorities decided under the former rules, *Allen v Jambo Holdings* [1980] 1 WLR 1252 and *Yorke (MV) Motors v Edwards* [1982] 1 WLR 444, and held that the clear and salutary principles established in those cases still applied to cases decided under the CPR. The principle was that once the court has exercised its discretion to order a payment in (or indeed security for costs), it is open to the paying party to seek to avoid the order. However, he must be able to demonstrate that he cannot pay, or cannot pay the full amount, and that he has sufficient prospects of success in his claim or defence that the court should not stifle what would otherwise be an arguable claim or defence simply because of default in paying.

Stage of the proceedings at which security may be ordered

As with all applications for interim relief, an application for security for costs should be made as soon as it becomes apparent that it is necessary or desirable to make it (PD 23, para 2.7).

The court should take into account the stage at which an application for security for costs is made, and if it is made too close to the hearing of the trial the application may be dismissed as oppressive (*Vedatech Corp v Crystal Decisions (UK) Ltd* [2002] EWCA Civ 357). In *Vedatech Corp v Crystal Decisions (UK) Ltd*, the Court of Appeal set aside a judge's order that the claimant provide further security in the sum of £200,000 three weeks before the trial was due to be heard. The court noted that, given the late stage in the proceedings, the judge was obliged to make an unless order that the claim be dismissed unless the security was provided. The Court of Appeal found that the judge had erred in failing to consider whether at that late stage the claimant should be ordered to pay security at all. The court held that to dismiss the claimant's claim at this stage for failing to provide security of £200,000 was so oppressive that it went beyond the principle of proportionality that underpinned the judge's exercise of discretion.

Form of the security

If an order for security for costs is made, it usually specifies that the claimant pay a sum of money into court or that he provides a bank guarantee as security. Alternatively, an undertaking from the claimant's solicitor may be acceptable.

In *AP (UK) Ltd v West Midlands Fire & Civil Defence Authority* [2001] EWCA Civ 1917, the Court of Appeal upheld the judge's refusal to accept that the claimant could satisfy an order for security by means of a charge on the claimant's property in favour of the defendant. The court said that the usual alternatives to a payment into court were a solicitor's undertaking or a bank guarantee, those methods of compliance with the order being both simple and straightforward if enforcement becomes necessary.

The court rejected the idea that a charge over property would be a satisfactory form of security. It did not think it appropriate to expect someone entitled to security to wait an extended period for its realisation. Also, when the security came to be realised arguments might be raised as to whether reasonable care had been taken to realise it at its best value. In general, therefore, the court felt that it would be too problematic and unsatisfactory for security to be provided by way of a charge over property.

The court also felt in particular that the reason why such a form of security is not usually suggested in a commercial or mercantile claim is that if property is sufficiently valuable to stand as security, there will be no difficulty in the claimants procuring a bank guarantee for the purpose of security for costs by granting a charge to the bank. In this case, in the absence of the claimant's explanation why money or a guarantee could not be raised from its bank by charging its property to the bank, the court found it impossible to conclude that the security offered by the claimant was adequate security.

However, in *Chandler v Brown*, the court was prepared (although it did not actually make an order for security for costs) to order that the security be provided in the form of a charge over a property owned by the claimant. The court acknowledged that this would be an unusual form in which to order security, but it took into account that the claimant had tried unsuccessfully to obtain a loan and that it would take him approximately nine months to sell the property. In *AP (UK) Ltd v West Midlands Fire & Civil Defence Authority*, the Court of Appeal did indicate that a different view might be taken if the case was not of a commercial nature, but it is submitted that as a general principle the court will not accept a charge over property as satisfactory security in commercial cases.

Failure to provide security for costs

The consequences of the claimant's failure to provide security by the time stipulated will depend on the terms of the court order. In some cases the court will direct that the claim will be struck out if security is not provided within the stipulated time. In other cases the court will simply order that the claim will be stayed. If the claimant's claim is not struck out, it will be open to the defendant to apply under r 3.1 for the claimant's claim to be struck out on its failure to comply with the order for security.

Security for costs of an appeal

The court has the power to order security for the costs of an appeal against an appellant and a respondent who also appeals, on the same grounds as it may order security for costs against a claimant under r 25.13 (r 25.15).

Security for costs other than from the claimant

Where a third party, who is not a party to the litigation, has agreed to contribute to the claimant's costs in return for a share of any money or property which the claimant may recover in the proceedings, and the court considers it just to do so, it may order that the third party provide security for the defendant's costs (r 25.14(1), (2)(b)).

Similarly, where a person has assigned the right to the claim to the claimant (for example, a company assigning a right to a director who can apply for public funding) with a view to avoiding the possibility of a costs order being made against him, and the court considers it just to do so, it may order that that person provide security for the defendant's costs (r 25.14(1), (2)(a)).

In both instances the person concerned must be a person against whom a costs order can be made (r 25.14).

The court's power to award costs includes the power to award costs against a person who is not a party to proceedings (s 51(1) of the SCA). See Chapter 34, 'Costs of Proceedings', for further consideration of the circumstances in which the court will make an award of costs against a person who is not a party to the proceedings.

CHAPTER 22

JUDGMENT IN DEFAULT

INTRODUCTION

If a defendant fails to respond to proceedings, the claimant can apply for judgment to be entered in default. As judgment is entered in these circumstances without there being any trial of the merits, and is purely as a result of the defendant's failure to comply with the procedural requirements of the rules, the court has a discretion to set the judgment aside if good reason is shown, and particularly if the defendant has a good defence on the merits. However, the court may well make setting aside of the judgment conditional on the defendant complying with a condition, such as the payment of money into court or on the immediate payment of the claimant's costs incurred in entering and setting aside judgment.

TYPES OF CLAIM WHERE JUDGMENT IN DEFAULT NOT AVAILABLE

Judgment in default is available for most types of claim. However, there are some notable exceptions. Judgment in default is not available:

- if the claim is for the delivery of goods where the agreement is regulated by the Consumer Credit Act 1974;
- if the claim is brought under Part 8;
- if the claim is a possession claim;
- if a practice direction provides that judgment in default is not available in, for example, claims for provisional damages, or in some specialist proceedings such as admiralty proceedings, arbitration proceedings and contentious probate proceedings (r 12.2; PD 12, paras 1.2 and 1.3).

JUDGMENT IN DEFAULT

A claimant may obtain either:

(a) judgment in default of an acknowledgment of service: if a defendant has not filed an acknowledgment of service or a defence to the claim (or any part of the claim) and the time limit for doing so has expired, the claimant may obtain judgment in default (r 12.3(1)). The time limit for filing acknowledgment of service is 14 days after service of particulars of claim on the defendant; or

(b) judgment in default of a defence: if a defendant has filed an acknowledgment of service, but has not filed a defence and the time limit for doing so has expired, the claimant may obtain judgment in default (r 12.3(2)). The time limit is 28 days after service of the particulars of claim.

Therefore, if a defendant does not respond at all, judgment will be entered in default of an acknowledgment of service rather than in default of defence even if judgment is entered at a time when the time limit for filing the defence has expired.

If a defendant files and serves a document that purports to be a defence within the requisite time limits, he will avoid judgment being entered against him in default (PD 12, para 1.1). However, if the document filed does not satisfy the requirements for a defence it is liable to be struck out either on an application by the claimant, or by the court acting of its own initiative (rr 3.4, 24.2).

Late filing of an acknowledgment of service/defence

In *Coll v Tattum* (2001) *The Times*, 3 December, the defendant failed to acknowledge service or file a defence and the claimant applied for judgment in default. On the return day for the hearing of the application for judgment in default the defendant purported to file an acknowledgment of service and a defence. The court found that such a situation was not clearly dealt with by the Civil Procedure Rules (CPR) but was of the opinion that it was a question for the exercise of the court's discretion in the circumstances of the case.

The court took into account the fact that the defendant's delay was unsatisfactory, but on the other hand accepted that he had an arguable defence. The court found in the circumstances that it would be disproportionate to enter judgment in default, with the effect of throwing the onus onto the defendant to justify his being given permission to defend. The defendant was therefore given an extension of time until the date of the hearing to file his defence and it was left to the claimant to apply for summary judgment if he was so advised.

Judgment in default of a defence to a counterclaim

If a defendant makes a counterclaim to the claimant's claim and the claimant does not file a defence to counterclaim within the time limit for doing so, the defendant may apply for judgment in default (r 12.3(2)). The time limit for the claimant to respond to the defendant's counterclaim is 14 days after service of the counterclaim (rr 15.4 and 20.3). For the purposes of judgment in default, a defendant who has made a counterclaim is in the same position as a claimant to a claim (r 20.3), and references in this chapter to claimant and defendant include claimant and defendant to a counterclaim. However, it should be noted that there is no procedure for a claimant to acknowledge service of the defendant's counterclaim (r 20.4(3)).

Circumstances in which a claimant cannot obtain judgment in default

In those claims where it is possible to obtain judgment in default, it will *not* be available where:

- the defendant has applied to have the claimant's statement of case struck out under r 3.4 and that application has not been disposed of;
- the defendant has applied for summary judgment under Part 24 and that application has not been disposed of;
- the defendant has satisfied the whole claim (including any claim for costs); or

- the defendant has admitted liability to pay the *whole* of a money claim but requested time to pay (r 12.3(3)).

PROCEDURE FOR APPLYING FOR JUDGMENT IN DEFAULT

Filing a request for judgment in default

So long as none of the provisions of r 12.3(3) applies (see above), where a claimant is seeking the following remedies he can apply for judgment in default by simply filing a request in the relevant practice form. That is where the claim is for:

- a specified amount of money (Form N205A or N225);
- an amount of money to be decided by the court (unspecified amount of money) (Form N205B or N227);
- delivery of goods where the claim form gives the defendant the alternative of paying the value of the goods (if value specified – Form N205A or N225; if value unspecified – Form N205B or N227);
- any combination of the above remedies; or
- a claim for costs only, being fixed costs (Form N205A or N225) (rr 12.4 and 12.9(1); PD 12, para 3).

Making an application for judgment in default

For those claims where the claimant is seeking a discretionary remedy rather than damages, or where the parties fall into certain categories of litigant, the claimant must make an application for judgment in default. Therefore, the claimant must make an application (in accordance with Part 23) for judgment in default where:

- the claim consists of or includes a non-monetary remedy such as an injunction;
- the claim is for costs only, *not* being fixed costs;
- the claim is against a child or patient;
- the claim is in tort by one spouse against the other;
- the claim is against the Crown;
- where the defendant is resident outside the jurisdiction and has been served with the claim without leave under the Civil Jurisdiction and Judgments Act 1982;
- the defendant is domiciled in Scotland or Northern Ireland or in any other Convention territory or Regulation State;
- where the defendant is a State;
- where the defendant is a diplomatic agent who enjoys immunity from civil jurisdiction by virtue of the Diplomatic Privileges Act 1964; or
- the claim is against persons or organisations who enjoy immunity from civil jurisdiction under the provisions of the International Organisations Acts 1968 and 1981 (rr 12.4(2), 12.9 and 12.10; PD 12, para 2.3).

If a claimant expressly abandons his claim for any of the above, by so declaring in his request for judgment in the relevant practice form, he can obtain judgment in default by filing a request (r 12.4(3)).

The application for default judgment under Part 23 must be made on notice to the defendant, except where the following circumstances apply:

(a) the defendant has failed to file an acknowledgment of service;

(b) where the defendant was served outside the jurisdiction without leave under the Civil Jurisdiction and Judgments Act 1982; or

(c) where any other rule specifies that notice does not need to be given (r 12.11(4); PD 12, para 5.1).

When the claimant makes an application for judgment to be entered, the judgment that is entered in default is such judgment that it appears the claimant is entitled to on his statement of case (r 12.11(1)). That is, the court will not make any inquiry into the merits of the case and will simply grant such judgment as it appears the claimant is entitled to on his statement of case, so long as the statement of case sets out the necessary facts to establish the claimant's claim and the procedural requirements of Part 12 have been complied with. The judgment in default is therefore conclusive of issues of liability in the statement of claim. However, this is subject to the exception that if an application is made for judgment in default against a child or a patient, the claimant must satisfy the court by evidence that he is *entitled* to the judgment claimed (PD 12, para 4.2). There are also special requirements for evidence where a defendant is served out of the jurisdiction and for applications against a State (PD 12, paras 4.3 and 4.4).

ESTABLISHING ENTITLEMENT TO JUDGMENT IN DEFAULT

In all types of claim where the court is requested to enter judgment in default, whether through the filing of a request or by application, the court must be satisfied that the requirements of Part 12 have been fulfilled. However, in all cases (except for claims against a child or patient), even the type of case where an application must be made under Part 23 and supported by evidence, the evidence required to enable the court to enter judgment on liability does not have to prove the merits of the substantive claim itself, but instead the particulars of claim must show on their face that the necessary facts to establish the cause of action have been pleaded, that the correct procedure has been followed to serve the particulars of claim and show that the defendant has not responded to them.

Therefore, both on a request and on an application for default judgment, the court must be satisfied that:

• the particulars of claim have been served on the defendant;

• the defendant has not filed either an acknowledgment of service or a defence and the relevant period for doing so has expired;

• the defendant has not satisfied the claim; and

• the defendant has not admitted liability to pay the whole of a money claim, but requested time to pay (PD 12, para 4.1).

When necessary, a party should provide a witness statement covering all these matters along with his application under Part 23. Also, where the claimant has served particulars of claim the court will not enter judgment in default unless and until the claimant has filed a certificate of service (see rr 6.10, 7.4(3)).

Where an application is made for judgment in default, the claimant need not serve evidence in support of his application on a party who has failed to file an acknowledgment of service (r 12.11(2)).

In the case of an application for judgment against a child or patient, a litigation friend must be appointed to act on behalf of the child or patient before judgment can be obtained and the claimant must satisfy the court by evidence that the claimant is entitled to the judgment claimed (PD 12, para 4.2).

On an application for judgment for delivery up of goods where the defendant will not be given the alternative of paying their value, the evidence must identify the goods and state where the claimant believes the goods to be situated and why their specific delivery up is sought (PD 12, para 4.6).

In those cases where the defendant was served with the claim either outside the jurisdiction without leave under the Civil Jurisdiction and Judgments Act 1982, or within the jurisdiction but when domiciled in Scotland or Northern Ireland or in any other Convention territory, and the defendant has not acknowledged service, evidence, in the form of an affidavit, must establish that the claim is one the court has power to hear and decide, no other court has exclusive jurisdiction under the Act to hear and decide the claim, and the claim has been served properly in accordance with Art 20 of Sched 1, 3C or 4 to the Civil Jurisdiction and Judgments Act 1982 (PD 12, paras 4.3, 4.5).

JUDGMENT FOR A FINAL AMOUNT OR AN AMOUNT TO BE DECIDED

Default judgment obtained by filing a request

If a claimant obtains judgment in default by filing a request in the relevant practice form, the judgment will be either for a final amount, if the claim is for a specified amount or value, or for an amount to be decided by the court at a hearing, if the claim is for an unspecified amount or value.

Judgment for a final amount obtained after filing a request

Where the claim is for a specified amount of money, if judgment in default is entered, the claimant may specify in the request whether he wants payment to be made immediately or by a specified date, or may specify the time and rate of payment by instalments (r 12.5(1)). As a judgment in default for a specified amount will entitle the claimant to seek immediate payment of the amount claimed from the defendant, without the need for any further assessment, it is often referred to as judgment for a 'final amount'.

Judgment will be entered for the amount of the claim (less any payments made), interest (if entitled) and fixed costs, as shown on the claim form, to be paid at the time and rate requested by the claimant, or, if the claimant has not specified the time and rate of payment, judgment will be for payment to be made immediately (r 12.5(2)).

However, it should be noted that a default judgment obtained by filing a request in a claim for delivery of goods, where the claim form gives the defendant the alternative of paying their value, will be judgment requiring the defendant to deliver the goods or (if he does not do so) to pay the value of the goods as decided by the court (less any payments made) and costs (r 12.5(4)).

Interest

On entering judgment in default, a claimant who is claiming a *specified* amount of money will be able to include an amount for interest up to the date of judgment when filing his request as long as the following conditions are met. These are:

(a) that the claimant has given the requisite details about interest in his particulars of claim;

(b) that the request includes a calculation of interest from the date of issue of the claim form to the date of the request for judgment; and

(c) if interest is claimed under s 35A of the Supreme Court Act 1981 or s 69 of the County Courts Act 1984, so long as the rate claimed is no higher than that which was available under those provisions when the claim form was issued (r 12.6(1)).

Where the claimant is claiming an unspecified amount of money, or the above conditions are not met, judgment will be for an amount of interest to be decided by the court (r 12.6(2)).

Judgment for an amount to be decided by the court obtained after filing a request

If a claimant claims an unspecified amount of money and applies for judgment in default, the judgment will be for an amount to be decided by the court and costs (r 12.5(3)).

The court will also enter judgment in default for an amount to be decided by the court when a request is made for judgment for the value of goods to be decided by the court or an amount of interest to be decided by the court.

When the court enters judgment in default for an amount to be decided by the court it will give any directions it considers appropriate, which may include listing the claim for a disposal hearing, allocating the claim to a track, directing the parties to file allocation questionnaires by a specified date, and staying the claim while the parties try to settle the case by alternative dispute resolution (ADR) or other means (r 12.7; PD 26, para 12).

Disposal hearings

If the financial value of the claim falls within the small claims track jurisdiction, the court will allocate it to that track for the amount to be decided. However, where the financial value exceeds the jurisdiction of the small claims track, the court will order that the amount be decided at a disposal hearing, unless the amount payable appears to be genuinely disputed on financial grounds, or the dispute is not suitable to be dealt with at a disposal hearing (PD 26, para 12.3(2)).

For further details about disposal hearings, see Chapter 9, 'Responding to a Claim'.

Jurisdiction of Masters and district judges

A Master or district judge has jurisdiction to decide the amount to be paid to the claimant whatever the financial value of the claim, unless the court orders otherwise (PD 26, para 12.6). However, in *Sandry v Jones* (2000) *The Times*, 3 August, CA, it was stated that where a personal injury claim involves substantial and complex issues on damages, it is not normally appropriate for a district judge to assess damages.

Challenging the amount of damages

Where there is a default judgment for damages to be assessed, the default judgment is conclusive on the issue of liability of the defendants as pleaded in the statement of case. However, on the assessment of damages any point which goes to quantification of those damages can be raised by the defendant provided it is not inconsistent with any issue settled by the judgment (*Lunnun v Singh* (1999) *The Times*, 19 July). Therefore, although the defendant may decide not to apply to set aside the default judgment itself, he may attend the damages hearing to contest the amount of damages to be awarded to the claimant.

In *Lunnun*, the claimant brought a claim for damage caused by leakage of water and sewage onto his premises from the defendant's premises next door. Although the Court of Appeal found that it was inherent in the default judgment that the defendant must be liable for some damage, all questions going to quantification, including the question of causation in relation to particular heads of loss, could be challenged by the defendant at the damages hearing. Accordingly, in that case, although the defendant could not dispute that there had been a leakage of water and sewage from his premises onto the claimant's premises which had caused some damage, at the damages hearing he could challenge how much water leaked, how much damage such water caused, and what loss the claimant suffered as a result.

CLAIMS AGAINST MULTIPLE DEFENDANTS

As a general rule, if a claimant is bringing a claim for money or delivery of goods against one of two or more defendants, and the claim against one defendant can be dealt with separately from the claim against the other defendant, if the claimant applies for default judgment against one of the defendants, the court can enter default judgment against that defendant and the claimant can continue the proceedings against the other defendant (r 12.8(1), (2)(a)). However, if the claim cannot be dealt with separately from the claim against the other defendants, the court will not enter judgment in default against only one of the defendants and must deal with the application for judgment in default at the same time as it disposes of the claim against the other defendants (r 12.8(2)(b)).

Also, a claimant may not *enforce* judgment for possession of land or delivery of goods unless the judgment is obtained against all of the defendants or the court gives permission (r 12.8(3)).

Defendants liable in the alternative

It was established in the House of Lords case of *Morel v Earl of Westmoreland* [1904] AC 11 that where a claim is brought against more than one defendant in the *alternative*, for instance, against the principal and in the alternative against the agent *on mutually inconsistent allegations of fact*, if a claimant enters judgment against one only of the defendants he will have elected to take his remedy against that defendant and cannot afterwards sue the other defendant who is not jointly but alternatively liable. However, if defendants are sued as jointly liable, the claimant can enter judgment against one defendant and continue to pursue the other defendant as jointly liable. In the Privy Council decision of *Bonus Garment Co v Karl Rieker & Peh Poh Cheng* (1997) LTL, 21 July, a plaintiff was held not to have made an election to sue one of two alternatively liable defendants in the circumstances where the claims against the defendants were not in fact alternative claims.

The facts of the *Bonus Garment* claim were that the plaintiff manufactured garments in Hong Kong. It sold garments to Rieker, agreeing to deliver them by a particular date. The plaintiff alleged that Reiker's agent in Hong Kong, Peh Poh Cheng, agreed with the plaintiff that the delivery date could be extended. The garments were duly delivered to Reiker who sold them in the course of its business. However, Reiker refused to pay the plaintiff for the garments on the grounds that it had suffered loss due to late delivery and that Peh Poh Cheng had no authority to agree any extension of the delivery period. The plaintiff brought an action against Rieker for the price of the goods, but in the alternative claimed against Peh Poh Cheng for breach of warranty of authority. Peh Poh Cheng failed to respond to the proceedings and the plaintiff entered judgment in default against her for damages for breach of warranty to be assessed. However, the plaintiff recovered nothing from her under that judgment.

The Privy Council found that the claims against the two defendants were not alternative claims in the circumstances where the plaintiff alleged that Rieker had accepted the garments. If at trial the plaintiff established that Rieker accepted the garments, the question whether delivery was out of time or not would be irrelevant. Rieker would be liable for the price of the garments and the only relevance of the late delivery would be that Rieker might have a cross-claim if it could show damages for late delivery. Accordingly, the Privy Council found that the factual assumption underlying the judgment against Peh Poh Cheng, that she had no authority to vary the delivery date, was not inconsistent with the factual allegation that Rieker had accepted the goods and was therefore liable for payment. It found that the basic requirement to bring the *Morel* principle into play – two claims against two defendants based on mutually inconsistent assumptions of fact – had not been shown to arise in this case.

Morel was distinguished in *Pendleton v Westwater & Swingware Ltd* [2001] EWCA Civ 1841. In that case the claimants, who were husband and wife, were employed as managers of a hotel on the Isle of Wight. The hotel was owned by the second defendant, a company, exclusively owned and controlled by the first defendant. The hotel ran into financial trouble. The claimants helped out with their own money. The claimants brought proceedings against both defendants to recover the sums they had loaned. The claimants obtained default judgment against the second defendant for the sums loaned following its failure to file a defence. However, the second defendant had no assets to pay the judgment debt. There was subsequently a trial of the claim at which the court found that the claimants had paid the loans to the first defendant personally and not to the second defendant. Further, the trial judge rejected the defendants' argument that by entering default judgment against the second defendant the claimants had made an irrevocable election to go against the second defendant in respect of the loans which barred any claim against the first defendant (in accordance with the *Morel* principle).

The Court of Appeal held that on the particular facts of this case, and without laying down any general rule, the claimants did not make a conclusive, unequivocal election by entering default judgment against the second defendant. The court was of the opinion that the merits were all in the claimants' favour and took into account: that the substantive case brought by the claimants, as it emerged in their evidence at trial, was that the debt was owed by the first defendant; that the judgment against the second defendant was a default judgment entered without the court having to consider the merits at all; that the second defendant was merely the vehicle for the first defendant's activities; and that the judgment against the second defendant remained unsatisfied. The Court of Appeal did not accept that the entering of a default judgment, without more, amounted to an election and distinguished *Morel v Earl of Westmoreland* on this basis, as that case involved summary judgment. In deciding whether an election had been made the court had to see the basis upon which the claims were made and the basis upon which the judgment was given, and in the circumstances of this case no election had been made.

SETTING ASIDE DEFAULT JUDGMENT

Default judgment set aside as of right

Where judgment has been entered against a defendant in default in circumstances in which the necessary preconditions for the entry of judgment under Part 12 have not been satisfied, the court *must* set the judgment in default aside (r 13.2). The court cannot therefore impose conditions (such as payment of a sum into court) when judgment in default must be set aside as of right, even if the defendant does not have real prospects of successfully defending the claim.

Therefore, the court must set default judgment aside if:

(a) in the case of a judgment in default of acknowledgment of service, an acknowledgment of service has been filed, or if the time limit for filing an acknowledgment of service has not yet expired;

(b) in the case of a judgment in default of defence (whether to a claim or counterclaim) a defence has been filed, or if the time limit for filing a defence has not yet expired;

(c) the defendant has applied to have the claimant's statement of case struck out under r 3.4 or applied for summary judgment under Part 24 and the application has not been disposed of;

(d) the whole of the claim was satisfied before judgment was entered; or

(e) the defendant admitted liability for the whole of a money claim and requested time to pay (r 13.2).

It was held in *Credit Agricole Indosuez v Unicof Ltd and Others* [2003] EWHC 77, a case involving service of proceedings out of the jurisdiction, that a defendant is entitled to have judgment set aside as of right where a claim form is not served on a defendant either by the method claimed or at all. Rule 13.2 is mandatory, so if the claim form is not served on the defendant, time for filing an acknowledgment of service will not expire and the conditions of r 12.3(1) will not be satisfied.

Further, in *Southern Aluminium & UPVC Windows Ltd v Clare* (1999) LTL, 22 June, where service of proceedings had not been effected, in that case because they were not served at the defendant's home address or his address for service, it was held that the defendant was entitled to have judgment in default set aside as of right and to defend the claim without any conditions, such as payment of a sum into court, being imposed. (This case was started under the former rules but decided after the CPR came into force.)

The circumstances in which the court *must* set aside judgment in default are limited to those set out in r 13.2. Rule 13.3(1) says that *in any other case* the court has a discretion to set aside or vary a default judgment if either:

(a) the defendant has a real prospect of successfully defending the claim; or

(b) there is some other good reason why the judgment should be set aside or varied, or the defendant should be allowed to defend the claim.

Therefore, if the claim form was properly served but did not in fact come to the defendant's attention, the defendant is not entitled to have judgment in default set aside as of right under r 13.2 and must instead make an application under r 13.3.

Circumstances in which claimant must set aside default judgment

If the claimant has purported to serve particulars of claim and enters judgment in default against the defendant to whom the particulars of claim were sent, but subsequently has good grounds to believe that the particulars of claim did not reach the defendant before judgment was entered, the claimant must either:

(a) file a request for judgment to be set aside; or

(b) apply to the court for directions (r 13.5(2)).

The claimant must take no further steps in the proceedings to enforce judgment until the judgment has been set aside or the court has disposed of the application for directions (r 13.5(3)).

It is submitted that this rule applies where the claimant believes that service of the particulars of claim was effective and sufficient time passes for judgment in default to be entered against the defendant, but after judgment is entered it is clear that service was not effective, for instance, because the particulars of claim are returned undelivered by the postal service. In those circumstances the claimant must not take any steps to enforce the judgment but instead must either file a request for judgment to be set aside, and, if so advised, re-serve the particulars of claim, or apply to the court for directions. The latter option may be taken where the claimant has grounds to believe that the defendant is evading service and so seeks an order that service be deemed to have occurred, or perhaps an order for service by an alternative method (see Chapter 10, 'Service of Documents').

However, this rule would not seem to be applicable to the situation where service was effective but the defendant alleges that he did not receive the particulars of claim. In those circumstances the onus would appear to be on the defendant, in accordance with r 13.3, to apply to the court to exercise its discretion to set judgment aside (see below, 'Court exercising discretion to set aside or vary default judgment').

Court exercising discretion to set aside or vary default judgment

In all other cases, apart from those where the court must set aside default judgment, the court has a *discretion* to set aside or vary default judgment if:

(a) the defendant has a real prospect of successfully defending the claim; or

(b) it appears to the court that there is some other good reason why the judgment should be set aside or varied, or the defendant should be allowed to defend the claim (r 13.3(1)).

It is also expressly provided that the court, when deciding whether to exercise its discretion to set aside default judgment, must consider whether the person seeking to set aside default judgment applied to do so promptly (r 13.3(2)).

Real prospect of successfully defending the claim

The provision in r 13.3 that a judgment will be set aside if the 'defendant has a real prospect of successfully defending the claim' mirrors the provisions in relation to resisting applications for summary judgment under Part 24. The rule requires a case to be better than merely arguable before a default judgment can be set aside (*ED & F Man Liquid Products Ltd v Patel & Patel International* [2003] EWCA Civ 472; *Finance Corp v Utexafrica Sprl* [2001] CLC 1361, QBD (Comm Ct)). In *Finance Corp v Utexafrica Sprl*, it was said that in ordinary language to say that a case has no realistic prospect of success is generally much the same as saying that it is hopeless. Further, that 'A person who holds a regular judgment, even a default judgment, has something of value and in order to avoid injustice he should not be deprived of it without good reason. Something more than a merely arguable case is needed to tip the balance of justice in favour of setting judgment aside' (*per* Moore-Bick J). Moreover, it would seem contrary to the overriding objective, as it would simply cause undue expense and delay for both parties and the court system, to set aside judgment entered in default if the defendant has no defence to the claim and will therefore inevitably be found liable to the claimant.

In the case of *Regency Rolls Ltd v Carnall* [2001] All ER (D) 1417, the Court of Appeal found the defendant's defence to be risible, and because it was so wholly inconsistent with all the probabilities it required the most cogent objective evidence (which was not put forward) before it could be preferred to the claimant's case. The court therefore refused to set aside judgment entered against the defendant in default of his attendance at the hearing (under r 39.3) because his defence had no real prospects of success.

In *ED & F Man Liquid Products Ltd v Patel & Patel International*, judgment in default of acknowledgment of service was obtained against two defendants. The claim was for payment of two deliveries of industrial alcohol to the defendants trading as Quickstop. The second defendant was successful in having judgment in default set aside on the grounds that he was not a partner but merely an employee of Quickstop Limited. However, as for the first defendant, in the light of a series of unqualified admissions of the claimant's debt over a prolonged period prior to judgment, the Court of Appeal held that his defence (that title in the alcohol never passed to Quickstop) had no real prospect of success. The court held that for judgment in default which has been regularly obtained to be set aside the defence sought to be argued must carry some degree of conviction and the defendant must have a case which is better than merely arguable. In this case the court found that there was no real substance in the factual assertions made by the first defendant which were contradicted by contemporaneous documents.

Burden of proof as to real prospects of success

When applying to have judgment in default set aside, the burden of proof rests upon the defendant to satisfy the court that there is good reason why a judgment regularly obtained should be set aside (*ED & F Man Liquid Products Ltd v Patel & Patel International*).

In *ED & F Man Liquid Products Ltd v Patel & Patel International*, the Court of Appeal held that the phrase 'real prospect of successfully defending the claim' in r 13.3(1) is a similar test to that when a claimant applies for summary judgment under r 24.2. It found that the only significant difference between the two rules is that on an application for summary judgment the overall burden of proof rests upon the claimant to establish that there are grounds for his belief that the defendant has no real prospect of success; whereas on an application to set aside judgment entered in default the burden rests upon the defendant to satisfy the court that there is good reason why a judgment regularly obtained should be set aside.

Although the court recognised that in practice the burden of proof is only of marginal importance in relation to the assessment of evidence, it was of the opinion that a defendant applying under r 13.3 may find the court less receptive to applying the test in his favour than if he were a defendant advancing a timely ground of resistance to an application for summary judgment under r 24.2.

Delay in applying to set aside default judgment

In the exercise of its discretion whether to set aside judgment entered in default the court must have regard to whether the application to set aside was made promptly (r 13.3(2)). The discretion must be exercised in accordance with the overriding objective and the weight to be given to this factor will depend on the circumstances of the case.

In *Regency Rolls Ltd v Carnall* [2001] All ER (D) 1417, the Court of Appeal said that 'promptly' is to be defined in accordance with its dictionary meaning, that is, 'with alacrity'. This means that the defendant is to display all reasonable celerity in the circumstances. Although the court was of the opinion that, in the circumstances of that case, 30 days was too long for the defendant to delay before making an application, the decision not to set aside the judgment was based on the defendant's failure to establish that he had reasonable prospects of success.

In *Thorn plc v MacDonald* (1999) *The Times*, 15 October, the defendant failed to file and serve a defence within the time limits and the claimant entered judgment in default. The defendant made an application to set aside the judgment nine days after judgment in default had been entered. The defendant gave no reasons for the delay in applying to set aside default judgment. The Court of Appeal held that the failure to give a reason for the delay was something the judge was entitled to take into account when exercising his discretion whether to set aside judgment in default. However, in the circumstances of this case, as the defendant had shown a triable defence, the claimant had suffered minimal prejudice and the delay was only of nine days, and taking into account that the defendant had given no reason for the delay, the court found that justice demanded that the default judgment be set aside. Brook LJ emphasised, *obiter*, that a defendant's failure to give any reason for delay would not be a 'knockout blow' to an application to set aside default judgment. Instead, this would be one consideration for a judge, applying the overriding objective, in deciding whether to exercise his discretion to set aside judgment in default.

Thorn plc v MacDonald was applied in *Sahidur Rahman v Rahman & Bose* (1999) LTL, 26 November. In that case it was found that the delay in applying to set aside default judgment was extremely long and wholly unexplained, that the defence had no real prospect of success and there would be prejudice to the claimant if the case was reopened. The court was of the opinion that there came a point when mere delay caused prejudice: time eroded recollection and there were no documents in the case as they had been lost. The court was also of the opinion that the overriding objective meant that matters had to be dealt with expeditiously and fairly and there had already been a great deal of court time spent on this case. Taking all these factors into account the court held that judgment in default would not be set aside.

Some other good reason for setting default judgment aside

This is not defined but is similar to the provisions under r 24.2(b), which provides that, when dealing with an application for summary judgment, the court must also consider whether there is any compelling reason why the case or issue should be disposed of at trial. The overriding objective will also be relevant.

In *Credit Agricole Indosuez v Unicof Ltd* [2003] EWHC 77, the court found this case to be an example of where there would be some other good reason for setting aside default judgment, because judgment had been entered on a false basis as to service of proceedings. In that case the court found that the claimant knew the defendant was likely to challenge the jurisdiction of the court to hear the claim. Therefore, if judgment was not set aside, or set aside on conditions, the defendant would lose the opportunity to contest jurisdiction. The court found that this would cause real prejudice to the defendant regardless of the merits of any defence to the proceedings it might have.

Court's discretion to impose conditions when exercising its discretion to set aside judgment

The court may impose conditions, such as the payment of a sum of money into court, when it grants an order setting aside judgment in default (r 3.1(3)).

It should be noted that the court has no discretion to impose conditions when judgment in default is set aside as of right, or where the claimant has failed properly to serve proceedings and therefore has a duty to set judgment aside or apply for directions (see pp 339–40 above, 'Default judgment set aside as of right', and pp 340–41 above, 'Circumstances in which claimant must set aside default judgment').

An order should not be made making it a condition of setting aside a judgment that the defendant should pay moneys that he clearly cannot afford (*Chapple (James) v (1) Williams (David) (2) Emmett (Guy) (t/a Global Windows & Conservatories) (A Firm)* (1999) LTL, 8 December, CA).

Procedure for applying to set aside or vary default judgment

An application to set aside or vary default judgment must be made by notice of application in accordance with Part 23.

An application to the court to exercise its discretion to set aside or vary default judgment must be supported by evidence (r 13.4(3)). In accordance with the general principle for evidence at hearings other than trial, the evidence should be in the form of a witness statement rather than oral (r 32.6(1)). Moreover, if a party's statement of case or application notice is verified by a statement of truth, this can be used as evidence at the hearing (r 32.6(2)).

The evidence should set out an explanation for the failure to respond to the particulars of claim in time and demonstrate that the defendant has a real prospect of successfully defending the claim.

Automatic transfer

The application to set aside or vary default judgment will be automatically transferred to be heard at the defendant's home court if the following conditions are met:

(a) the claim is for a specified amount of money;

(b) the judgment was obtained in a court which is not the defendant's home court;

(c) the claim has not been transferred to another defendant's home court either for the court to determine the rate of payment following an admission under r 4.12, or as a result of the operation of the rule of automatic transfer under r 26.2; and

(d) the defendant is an individual (r 13.4).

The defendant's home court is the county court or district registry for the district in which the defendant resides or carries on business, or, if there is no district registry, the High Court (r 2.3).

The above rules on automatic transfer will not apply if the claim was commenced in a specialist list.

Abandoned claim restored when default judgment is set aside

If a claimant abandoned a remedy for which judgment in default could be obtained only by making an application in order to apply for judgment in default by filing a request, and that judgment is set aside, the abandoned claim is automatically restored when the default judgment is set aside (r 13.6).

CHAPTER 23

SUMMARY JUDGMENT

INTRODUCTION

In some cases a party will have no prospect of succeeding in bringing or defending a claim and, in those circumstances, it will be open to his opponent to apply, or for the court acting on its own initiative, to dispose summarily of an issue or issues, or sometimes the whole case, without the need for a full trial.

In *Access to Justice*, Final Report, Lord Woolf stated that part of his aims in making his recommendations was to encourage settlement 'by disposing of issues so as to narrow the dispute' (p 16, para 7(d)). Under the Civil Procedure Rules (CPR), the court, as well as the parties, has the power to initiate a summary judgment hearing (Part 24). Also, part of the ethos of the CPR is to discourage the tendency, particularly of lawyers, to include every possible issue as part of a party's case, meritorious or not. Accordingly, the court has a duty, as part of active case management, to '[identify] the issues at an early stage' and to '[decide] promptly which issues need full investigation and trial and accordingly [dispose] summarily of the others' (r 1.4(2)(b) and (c)).

TYPES OF PROCEEDINGS WHERE SUMMARY JUDGMENT AVAILABLE

An application under Part 24 for summary judgment can be made by either a claimant or a defendant, or by the court of its own initiative. The availability of summary judgment against a claimant is a major innovation of the CPR, not being formerly available under the old rules, and reflects the importance the CPR place upon weeding out unmeritorious claims, defences and issues.

Application by defendant

A defendant can make an application for summary judgment against a claimant in any type of proceedings (r 24.3(1)). However, see pp 346–47 below, 'Defamation proceedings'.

Application by claimant

A claimant can make an application for summary judgment against a defendant in any type of proceedings except residential possession proceedings against a mortgagor or a person with security of tenure under the Rent Act 1977 or the Housing Act 1988, or in proceedings for an admiralty claim *in rem* (r 24.3(2)). Although summary judgment is not available to a claimant in these types of claim, a claimant can apply for an order striking out such a claim under r 3.4.

Specific performance of agreements relating to land

Notwithstanding the exceptions referred to in r 24.3(2), an application can be made under Part 24 in a claim which includes a claim for:

(a) specific performance of an agreement for the sale, purchase, exchange, mortgage or charge of any property, or for the grant or assignment of a lease or tenancy of any property, whether damages are claimed in the alternative or not; or

(b) the rescission of such an agreement; or

(c) the forfeiture or return of any deposit made under such an agreement (PD 24, para 7.1(1)).

An expedited procedure is provided for claimants seeking summary judgment in such claims. The claimant can apply for summary judgment at any time after the claim form has been served, even if particulars of claim have not been served, and even if the defendant has not acknowledged service, whether the time period for acknowledging service has expired or not (PD 24, para 7.1(2)).

This special procedure is available for such claims as, in most cases, as long as an enforceable agreement is in existence, the defendant will have no defence to such a claim.

Accounts and inquiries

If a claimant seeks a remedy in his claim form which includes, or necessarily involves, taking an account or making an inquiry (for example, an account of the profits made from the sale of articles infringing copyright), any party to the proceedings can make an application under Part 24 for a summary order directing any necessary accounts or inquiries to be taken or made (PD 24, para 6).

Defamation proceedings

Although an application for summary judgment in defamation proceedings is not expressly precluded, Part 24 does not override the statutory right under s 69(1) of the Supreme Court Act 1981 (and see s 66 of the County Courts Act 1984) to trial by jury in a defamation claim. The right to trial by jury in defamation claims is a fundamental (as opposed to a procedural) right, connected with freedom of speech, which is beyond the power of the Civil Procedure Rule Committee to limit (*Safeway Stores plc v Albert Tate* [2001] QB 1120; [2001] 2 WLR 1377; [2001] 4 All ER 193).

Safeway Stores plc v Albert Tate arose out of a boundary dispute in which the defendant alleged that the claimant deliberately encroached on his boundary when developing their land. The defendant displayed a sign that said 'Safeway Where Fraud Ideas Come Naturally'. The claimant brought a claim against the defendant for damages and an injunction for libel. On the day fixed for the hearing, due to an administrative error on the court's behalf, no jury panel had been arranged. The defendant applied for the trial to be adjourned on the ground of his ill health but, without any proper notice, the claimant applied for summary judgment against the defendant on the ground that there was no defence of substance to the claim. The judge granted the claimant's application and entered judgment for the claimant for damages for libel to be assessed by a jury, and granted an injunction against the defendant to restrain publication of the words 'Safeway Where Fraud Ideas Come Naturally'. The Court of Appeal set aside the judge's decision and held that the question whether the words complained of were, as a matter of fact, defamatory of the claimant was one for a jury, and it was not open to the judge to rule that the words complained of were defamatory and to enter judgment for the claimant. The Court of Appeal remitted the case to the county court for a short jury trial, at which the issues of the meaning of the words and damage to the claimant could be decided by a jury.

However, an application under Part 24 can properly be made in order to determine certain questions which fall within the jurisdiction of the judge in defamation proceedings, for example, whether the words complained of were published on an occasion of qualified privilege (*Safeway Stores plc v Albert Tate*).

The Defamation Act 1996, which came into force on 28 February 2000, provides for summary disposal of defamation claims and for that disposal to be determined without a jury, although there are specific limitations on the amount of damages that can be recovered under that procedure. Part 53 sets out the procedure relating to such summary disposals in defamation proceedings.

A party cannot make a concurrent application under the Defamation Act 1996 and Part 24, and if a party makes an application under both he will be put to his election as to which provision he wishes to rely upon (r 53.2(3); *Clarke v Davey* [2002] EWHC 2342).

Part 20 proceedings

An application for summary judgment under Part 24 can be made in respect of a Part 20 claim (for example, counterclaim) as a Part 20 claim is treated as if it were a claim for these purposes (r 20.3).

Part 8 claims

In principle, the Part 24 procedure applies to claims commenced under Part 8. However, given the nature of such claims, it is less likely that summary judgment will be applied for in respect of them (see Chapter 15, 'Part 8 Claims').

Summary judgment in small claims proceedings

Summary judgment is available for proceedings on any track, including those allocated to the small claims track. However, in practice, an application for summary judgment should be made before the case is allocated to the track.

Under the small claims procedure the court has the power to hold a preliminary hearing, in order to decide whether to dispose of the claim on the basis that one or other of the parties has no real prospect of success at a final hearing (r 27.6(1)(b)).

Summary judgment for single issue or whole claim

Summary judgment is available in respect of a whole claim or defence, or part of a claim or defence, or in respect of a particular issue or issues forming part of the claim or defence (r 24.2).

SUMMARY JUDGMENT ON COURT'S OWN INITIATIVE

The court has unlimited powers to make orders of its own initiative, whether following a hearing or without a hearing, even if neither party has applied for an order (*James v Evans* [2001] CP Rep 36; (2000) *The Times*, 2 August). This therefore includes deciding whether to dispose summarily of issues, or to order summary judgment against one of the parties.

In accordance with its duty of active case management, the court has the power to decide which issues need full investigation at trial and which issues can be disposed of summarily (r 1.4(2)(b) and (c)). In *Harris v Bolt Burdon* (2000) *The Times*, 8 December and *Swain v Hillman and Gay* [2001] 1 All ER 91, the Court of Appeal reminded judges of the court's power summarily to dispose of cases which had no real prospect of success and urged them to exercise this power in appropriate cases.

Further, in *Peter John O'Donnell and Others v Charly Holdings Inc (A Company Incorporated Under the Laws of Panama) and Another* (2000) LTL, 14 March, Lord Woolf reminded judges that in an appropriate case, in accordance with the overriding objective, they should consider, of their own initiative, the merits of a case, and if it has no prospects of success it should not be allowed to continue.

In *James v Evans* (above), there had been no application for summary judgment throughout the proceedings. On the first day of the trial the judge invited the parties to address him on the basis of summary judgment and proceeded to give judgment for the claimant without hearing oral evidence, a procedure upheld by the Court of Appeal. However, the intention is that active case management and identification of issues should result, where appropriate, in summarily disposal of issues at an early stage. In *James v Evans*, although the Court of Appeal confirmed that the trial judge was correct in finding, on the first day of a trial listed for three days, that there was no defence to the claim, Dame Elizabeth Butler-Sloss was of the opinion that active case management should have been exercised at the directions stage to identify the issues earlier, so as to avoid witnesses being called for a trial unnecessarily.

The *dictum* of Dame Elizabeth Butler-Sloss was cited with approval in *Orford v Rasmi Electronics and Others* [2002] EWCA Civ 1672, where the trial judge was criticised by the Court of Appeal for summarily determining the claimant's claim at the opening of the trial. In that case both parties acted in person and the court emphasised that its decision could not be considered authoritative in the absence of legal argument. However, the court found that the trial judge should not have summarily determined the claimant's claim, when the claimant was acting in person, without giving him prior notice or a proper opportunity to resist such an application, and therefore remitted the matter for a retrial.

SUMMARY JUDGMENT AND HUMAN RIGHTS

An order summarily determining a case in accordance with Part 24 will not in itself be a breach of Art 6 (right to a fair trial) of the European Convention on Human Rights. In *Kent v Griffiths* [2000] 2 WLR 1158, [2000] 2 All ER 474; a case about the liability of the London Ambulance Service answering an emergency call, Lord Woolf MR said that when the legal position is clear and an investigation of the facts would provide no assistance, the courts should not be reluctant to dismiss cases which have no real prospect of success and there would be no contravention of Art 6 in doing so. He explained that under the CPR courts are now encouraged, where an issue or issues can be identified which will resolve or help to resolve litigation, to determine those issues at an early stage of the proceedings so as to achieve expedition and save expense, and that this was an important part of ensuring a fair trial.

In supporting Lord Woolf's opinion in that case, May LJ, in *S v Gloucestershire CC; L v Tower Hamlets LBC* [2001] 2 WLR 909, [2000] 3 All ER 345, added that in an appropriate case a summary hearing can be a fair hearing for the purpose of Art 6 because a defendant is entitled to a fair summary hearing of a case which, when properly investigated, has no real prospect of success.

GROUNDS FOR SUMMARY JUDGMENT

Lord Woolf proposed that the test for summary judgment under the CPR should be easier for applicants to satisfy than the test under the old rules (see Interim Report, Chapter 6, para 21, www.dca.gov.uk/civil/interfr.htm). The old test was for the claimant to satisfy the court that the defendant had 'no defence to the claim'. Thus, summary judgment was available only where there was plainly no defence to a claim, and if the defendant could show a 'triable issue' he would succeed in avoiding summary judgment. The new test is for the applicant to satisfy the court that there is 'no real prospect of succeeding in bringing or defending the claim or issue' (r 24.2).

The test the court will apply when deciding whether to grant summary judgment is whether it is satisfied, in the case of an application against the claimant, that he has no real prospect of succeeding on the claim or issue, and, for an application against the defendant, that he has no real prospect of successfully defending the claim or issue, *and*, in both cases, that there is no other compelling reason why the case or issue should be disposed of at a trial (r 24.2).

An application for summary judgment may be based either on a point of law (including the construction of a document), or on the absence of evidence to prove a party's case or a combination of these (PD 24, para 1.3).

Prospects of success at trial

On an application for summary judgment against a claimant under r 24.2, the correct test is not whether the claim is bound to fail, but whether the claimant has no real prospect of succeeding on the claim or issue (*Peter Robert Krafft v Camden LBC* (2000) LTL, 24 October, CA).

In *Swain v Hillman and Gay*, Lord Woolf MR said: 'The words "no real prospect of being successful or succeeding" do not need any amplification, they speak for themselves. The word "real" distinguishes fanciful prospects of success.' Pill LJ said: 'This is simple language, not susceptible to much elaboration, even forensically.'

In *Swain*, the claimant was injured while working on a construction site, when a plank, which was standing upright, fell on him suddenly without warning. It was not disputed that the plank had been in that position for three days before it fell on the claimant. The defendant applied for summary judgment on the grounds that in the absence of any explanation as to how the plank was dislodged, the claimant had no real prospect of succeeding in establishing that the defendant was negligent. However, summary judgment was refused on the basis that the claimant was entitled to argue that the plank should not have been left where it was and the defendant had a responsibility to explain what had occurred.

In *Harris v Bolt Burdon (A Firm)* (2000) *The Times*, 8 December, the claimant brought a claim on the grounds that she had suffered an infection caused by retaining products of conception as a result of the negligence of the local health authority in delivering her baby. The claimant instructed the defendant solicitors to pursue her claim. The claimant obtained legal aid and two medical reports, but the expert evidence did not establish that the health authority had failed to maintain an acceptable clinical standard. The defendants issued proceedings on the claimant's behalf but without serving them, and the time limit for doing so expired. The claimant brought proceedings for professional negligence against the defendants. The Court of Appeal found that in the light of the expert evidence and/or on the grounds that the limitation period had expired before the claimant issued proceedings, the claimant's case was 'absolutely unwinnable'. The Court of Appeal was of the opinion that it would be wrong to let the claimant's case go on without any possible ultimate benefit to the claimant and entered summary judgment against the claimant.

However, in *Three Rivers DC v Governor and Co of the Bank of England* [2001] UKHL 16, although it was accepted that the claimant would have great difficulty in establishing its claim, the House of Lords held that it could not be said at that stage that the claimant had no real prospect of succeeding on the claim at trial. The case concerned a complicated claim for misfeasance in public office against the Bank of England for authorising the Bank of Credit and Commerce International SA (BCCI) to carry on the business of banking. The House of Lords held (by a majority) that as the issues raised were far from easy, and as it was a complex case, it should not be decided on the documents without hearing oral evidence and should be heard at trial instead. Their Lordships therefore overturned the Court of Appeal's decision upholding the judge's decision at first instance to enter summary judgment in favour of the defendant.

In *Chan U Seek v Alvis Vehicles Ltd* [2003] EWHC 1238, although the court found the claimant's case to be very weak, it was not able to hold that there was no real prospect of the claim succeeding and reluctantly refused the defendant's application for summary judgment. The claim was based on commission claimed by the claimant for negotiating contracts for the sale of military equipment to the Indonesian Ministry of Defence. It was alleged that one of the claims was statute-barred and that the claimant had not been the effective cause of the other contracts. In refusing an application by the defendant for summary judgment or strike out, the court said:

> If the court considers that the claim, though very weak, stands a chance of success it is not consonant with basic principles of English justice or ... Human Rights law for a party seeking to pursue such a claim, to be barred from proceeding with it. However much one may seek to apply the rules of proportionality, it is not and cannot be the court's function to stifle a claim merely because it looks very weak and unlikely to succeed. (At 20, *per* Neuberger J.)

The court felt that it might be that after disclosure and cross-examination the claim was justified, and it was not the function of the court to carry out a mini-trial at an interim stage of the proceedings.

This decision seems somewhat at odds with the concept of a 'claim which stands no real prospect of success' set out in r 24.2(a) and r 13.3(1)(a). However, the court was of the opinion that it could not assess the efficacy of the claim without hearing further evidence, and that it was not the court's role on an application for summary judgment to try the facts (and see *Somerset-Leeke v Kay Trustees Ltd* [2002] All ER (D) 37 below, 'Issues to be investigated at trial'). Further, Neuberger J accepted that the court should be slow to permit a claim to proceed beyond an interim stage where it involves the hope that something will turn up. However, he was also of the opinion that each interim application to dismiss a claim on the basis that there is no evidence to support it must be judged by reference to the particular facts of the case.

Prospects of success of the claim

Where the court is considering an application for summary judgment against a claimant it should decide whether the claimant has a real prospect of succeeding on the claim before investigating the likelihood of establishing causation and damages (*Kumarth Khalagy and Another v Alliance and Leicester plc* (2000) LTL, 23 October, CA).

In *Kumarth*, the Court of Appeal was of the opinion that on a construction of the contractual documents the claimants had no prospect of establishing that the bank was in breach of contract by not advancing a loan to them. The Court of Appeal held that the judge in the court below was wrong to refuse to grant summary judgment on the grounds that the claimants would be able to establish causation and loss without first deciding whether the claimants had a real prospect of succeeding on the claim.

Summary judgment and the 'cheque rule'

In most cases a claimant will be entitled to summary judgment against a defendant in a claim on a dishonoured cheque. There are only a limited number of defences, namely: fraud, invalidity, illegality, or failure of consideration (*Nova (Jersey) Knit Ltd v Kammgarn Spinnerei GmbH* [1977] 1 WLR 713; [1977] 2 All ER 463). The reason for the rule is that payment by cheque is treated as equivalent to payment by cash.

Issues to be investigated at trial

The court's power to order summary judgment under Part 24 is not meant to dispense with the need for a trial where there are issues that should be investigated at trial. Accordingly, where there are issues to be investigated, or where it is clear that cross-examination of witnesses is necessary, it would not be appropriate for the court to conduct a mini-trial to decide the matter at an application for summary judgment (*Somerset-Leeke v Kay Trustees Ltd* [2002] All ER (D) 37).

In a highly complex case, where an application relies on inferences of fact, the overriding objective may well require the claim to go on to trial. The same approach also applies in a case where the issues involve mixed questions of fact and law and the application of the law is complex because it depends crucially on detailed findings of fact (*Yeheskel Arkin v Borchard Lines Ltd (No 2)* [2001] CP Rep 108).

In *Esprit Telecoms UK Ltd v Fashion Gossip Ltd* [2000] All ER (D) 1090, the Court of Appeal overturned the judge's decision to enter summary judgment in favour of the claimant in a claim involving allegations of fraudulent and deceitful misconduct and criminal offences under the Telecommunications Act 1984. Although the court stressed that it was not suggesting that it would never be appropriate to enter summary judgment where there were allegations of fraud, it held that where there were such allegations there must be a firm foundation of fact, and all the facts, every nuance, need exploration and need to be firmly established. It would not be right to make such findings on the documents alone, without an oral hearing. The court also concluded that as the case raised issues concerning the law of restitution and conspiracy which were not straightforward, summary judgment was not appropriate. Further, the case involved the possible development of legal principles, and such an analysis should not take place until the facts had been established at a trial, and it would not be appropriate to proceed on the basis of assumptions and summary conclusions about the facts. The court was of the opinion that summary procedures are meant to deal with the plain and obvious cases, and this case was not one of them.

Other reason for disposing of the case at trial

The final aspect of the test leaves the court with a wide discretion to decide whether it is appropriate to grant summary judgment. For instance, it may be that although a respondent cannot establish a claim or defence at the time of the application, he may be able to do so if he can obtain discovery of documents from the applicant or trace a key witness who is not immediately available. In such circumstances, the court is likely to decide that the case should be disposed of at trial rather than summarily.

Summary judgment and the overriding objective

In *Swain v Hillman and Gay*, Lord Woolf expressed the view that it was important for a judge in an appropriate case to make use of the powers contained in Part 24 and said that in doing so the judge would be giving effect to the overriding objective in Part 1. He explained that Part 24 was in the interests of justice and furthered the overriding objective by saving expense, achieving expedition and avoiding the court's resources being used up on unmeritorious cases.

Relationship between r 3.4 and Part 24

A party may make an application both to strike out a party's case under r 3.4 and for summary judgment under Part 24 and the court, acting of its own initiative, may exercise its powers under both these provisions (PD 3, para 1.2). An application under r 3.4 is more technical, as the court is generally concerned only with deficiencies with the statement of case, while the court has wider powers under Part 24 and will consider the evidence supporting the claim or defence.

In *Taylor v Midland Bank Trust Co Ltd* [1999] All ER (D) 831, a dispute that arose over the administration of two discretionary settlements, an application was made by the defendants under r 3.4 to strike out the claim. The application failed and the defendants appealed. The Court of Appeal held that it had the power to treat the application to strike out as though it had been made for summary judgment under

Part 24 (approved by the House of Lords in *Three Rivers DC v Governor and Co of the Bank of England*). In reaching its decision in *Taylor*, the court held that 'the question the court had to consider was whether (a) the claimants had failed to show a case which, if unanswered, would entitle them to judgment, or (b) the defendants had shown that the claimants' claim would be bound to be dismissed at trial.' As it was, the appeal was dismissed.

In *S v Gloucestershire CC; L v Tower Hamlets LBC*, the Court of Appeal declared that for an application for summary judgment to succeed where a strike out application under r 3.4 would not succeed, three conditions must be satisfied, namely:

(a) all substantial facts relevant to the claimant's case which were reasonably capable of being before the court must be before the court;

(b) those facts must be undisputed or there must be no reasonable prospect of successfully disputing them; and

(c) there must be no real prospect of oral evidence affecting the court's assessment of the facts.

The court will then need to be satisfied that, upon those facts, there is no real prospect of the claim succeeding and that there is no other reason why the case should be disposed of at a trial.

In *S v Gloucestershire CC; L v Tower Hamlets LBC*, the claimants, when children, had been in the care of their respective local authorities. The defendant local authorities had placed them with foster parents and the claimants claimed that they had been sexually abused by the foster father in each case. Each of the foster fathers had been subsequently convicted of sexual offences with children. The appellants claimed damages for physical suffering and long-term psychological damage caused by the abuse, which they claimed was caused by the negligence of the defendants who had placed them with foster parents and had monitored their placement. It was held that although the court can consider evidence when deciding an application under r 3.4(2)(a), the Court of Appeal recognised that an application under r 3.4(2)(a) primarily relates only to the statement of case. Therefore the court was of the opinion that because cases of this kind required 'anxious scrutiny', the court would strike out such a claim under r 3.4(2)(a) only in the clearest case, given the nature of the subject matter and the components of the claim.

If an applicant makes a 'double-barrelled' challenge under both r 3.4 and Part 24, the court will normally start by considering the first challenge, for which it will not need to consider any evidence. If the other party's statement of case contains a coherent set of facts which disclose a legally recognisable claim or defence, the applicant is then entitled to try to persuade the court that notwithstanding that fact the other party has no real prospect of success. It is at this second stage that the court will normally have to consider any evidence the parties may adduce (*Rixon v Chief Constable of Kent* (2000) *The Times*, 11 April).

Relationship between summary judgment and setting aside default judgment

The same test, 'real' prospect of success, is applied by the court when a defendant applies to have judgment in default set aside, in a case in which the court has a discretion to set judgment aside (r 13.3). In *ED & F Man Liquid Products Ltd v Patel & Patel International* [2003] EWCA Civ 472, the Court of Appeal held that the phrase 'real prospect of successfully defending the claim' in r 13.3(1) is a similar test to that when a claimant applies for summary judgment under r 24.2. It found that the only significant difference between the two rules is that on an application for summary judgment the overall burden of proof rests upon the claimant to establish that there are grounds for his belief that the defendant has no real prospect of success; whereas on an application to set aside judgment entered in default, the burden rests upon the defendant to satisfy the court that there is good reason why a judgment regularly obtained should be set aside.

PROCEDURE FOR APPLYING FOR SUMMARY JUDGMENT

Stage when an application for summary judgment can be made

Given the nature of the application, a defendant will be able to apply for summary judgment as soon as proceedings are served on him. However, a claimant cannot apply for summary judgment until the defendant has filed an acknowledgment of service or a defence, unless the court gives permission or a practice direction provides otherwise (r 24.4(1)).

In certain cases for specific performance of agreements relating to land, the claimant can apply for summary judgment at any time after the claim form has been served (see p 346 above, 'Specific performance of agreements relating to land'). Also, applications for summary disposal under the Defamation Act 1996 may be made by either party at any time after service of the particulars of claim (PD 53, para 5.2; and see pp 346–47 above, 'Defamation proceedings').

Normally, a file will not come to the judge's attention until allocation, unless a vigilant clerk spots something amiss, but on allocation, or possibly earlier, the court will always consider its powers under r 3.4(1) to consider sanctions or to dispose of a claim summarily.

Claimant making an application before defence has been filed

If a claimant does make an application for summary judgment against a defendant before the defendant has filed a defence, the defendant does not need to file a defence before the hearing (r 24.4(2)).

In most cases, it will be more sensible for a claimant to apply for summary judgment only after a defence has been filed, as it is easier to make an application armed with the knowledge of what the defendant's defence will be. Also, if a defendant has a weak case, he may well not file a defence after acknowledging service, and then the claimant can apply for judgment in default of defence to be entered instead. Judgment in default of defence can, in some cases, be entered simply on the basis of the filing of a request by the claimant in the prescribed form. However, even if it is the type of case where an application must be made, in both types of request for judgment in default, unlike an application for summary judgment, the court will not consider the merits of the claim or defence (see Chapter 22, 'Judgment in Default').

The application notice

An application for summary judgment is made in accordance with Part 23. The applicant should fill in a general form of application and the application notice must include a statement that it is an application for summary judgment under Part 24 (PD 24, para 2(2)).

The application notice or the supporting evidence, whether contained in the notice, or referred to by the notice or served with the notice, must set out concisely the basis of the application (PD 24, para 2(3)). Therefore, the application must state:

(a) the point of law or provision in a document on which the applicant relies; and/or

(b) that the applicant believes that, on the evidence, the respondent has no real prospect of succeeding on the claim or issue or of successfully defending the claim or issue (as the case may be); and

(c) in all applications, state that the applicant knows of no other reason why the claim or issue should be disposed of at trial (PD 24, para 2(3)).

The application notice should also draw the respondent's attention to r 24.5, which provides details as to how and when the respondent can file and serve evidence in reply to the claimant's evidence (PD 24, para 2(5)).

Evidence relied on to support application

There is no general requirement for the applicant to serve evidence in support of an application for summary judgment. Further, existing evidence, such as that in a statement of case, can be relied upon, if appropriate.

Under r 32.6(1), if there is evidence at a summary judgment application, it should usually be in the form of witness statements, unless the court orders otherwise. The witness statement should comply with r 32.8, which includes the requirement that if letters, documents and other evidence are also relied upon, they should form exhibits to the witness statement. However, as with all other applications made under Part 23, if all the evidence on which a party wishes to rely is contained within the application notice or a statement of case, a party can rely on these documents instead, as long as the document is verified by a statement of truth (r 32.6(2)).

If the evidence to support the application is contained in a document other than the application notice itself, for example, a witness statement or statement of case, the application notice should identify the written evidence on which the applicant relies (PD 24, para 2(4)).

In most applications for summary judgment, therefore, there will be no oral evidence at the hearing and no cross-examination on the content of witness statements. It can therefore be seen that if a party's case is based on the type of evidence which can only be challenged through cross-examination at trial, such as oral factual statements that the other party denies, it is likely to prove difficult to establish that the other party's claim or defence has no real prospect of success in the context of a summary hearing.

Notice of hearing

The applicant must give the respondent at least 14 days' notice of the hearing and the issues which it is proposed that the court will decide at the hearing. If the court fixes a hearing of its own initiative it must give the parties the same notice (r 24.4(3)).

However, if a practice direction provides for a different period of notice to be given for applications in certain types of proceedings, that notice period must be followed instead (r 24.4(4)). The time is reduced to four days for a claimant's application in a claim for specific performance of agreements relating to land (PD 24, para 7.3). As a result of PD 24, para 7.1, a respondent to an application in respect of specific performance will not be entitled to rely on the provisions in r 24.4(3), and r 24.5 (see below, 'Filing and serving evidence in reply') will clearly have no application. The reason for this shorter period is that in cases of this type there is usually no other evidence apart from the agreement of which the claimant seeks specific performance.

Filing and serving evidence in reply

If the respondent wishes to rely on written evidence at the hearing in reply, he should file a copy of the evidence at court and on every other party to the application at least seven days before the hearing (r 24.5(1)).

On receiving the respondent's evidence, if the applicant wants to rely on written evidence in reply, he should file a copy of the evidence at court and on every other party to the application at least three days before the hearing (r 24.5(2)).

However, if a party intends to rely on his application notice or statement of case as evidence at the hearing, and these documents have already been filed at court and served on the other parties in the course of the proceedings, there is no need for a party to re-file or re-serve those documents for the purposes of the summary judgment hearing (r 24.5(4)).

Timing of application for summary judgment

As with all applications made in accordance with Part 23, an application for summary judgment should be made as soon as it becomes apparent that it is necessary or desirable to make it (PD 23, para 2.7). Although not restricting applications for summary judgment to certain stages of the proceedings, in *Access to Justice*, Interim Report, Lord Woolf warned that:

> [In] keeping with the new ethos which my recommendations will bring about, applicants will be expected to apply promptly as soon as they have sufficient information on which to act [and] [w]here an application is made late in the course of proceedings the courts would impose sanctions on the applicant if he has delayed unnecessarily and allowed costs to escalate [and] the court itself will be in a position to direct a hearing and determine issues summarily. There should, therefore, be only a few cases in which an opportunity for summary disposal is overlooked. (Chapter 6, para 20.)

A party is asked to indicate whether he intends to apply for summary judgment when completing his allocation questionnaire and will be expected to make the application before or when filing his allocation questionnaire (PD 26, para 5.3(1)). If a party makes an application for summary judgment before the case has been allocated to a track, the court will not normally allocate the case before the hearing of the application (PD 26, para 5.3(2)).

If a party indicates in his allocation questionnaire that he intends to make an application for summary judgment, but he has not yet made the application, the judge will usually direct that an allocation hearing is listed (PD 26, para 5.3(3)), the intention being that the application is heard at the allocation hearing, so long as the application has been issued and served giving the other party the requisite notice (PD 26, para 5.3(4)).

Where the court decides, at a hearing in which a party is applying for summary judgment, or where the court has ordered such a hearing of its own initiative, that the claim should continue, it will either treat the hearing as an allocation hearing, allocate the claim and give case management directions or give other appropriate directions (PD 26, para 5.5).

A defendant can apply for summary judgment at any time after the proceedings have been commenced; he is not required to file an acknowledgment of service or a defence before doing so. Further, if the defendant makes an application under this Part, the claimant may not obtain default judgment against him until it is disposed of (r 12.3(3)(a)).

Court convening a summary judgment hearing of its own initiative

If the court decides to convene a hearing of its own initiative for the purposes of deciding whether to dispose summarily of issues or to enter summary judgment against one of the parties, it must give both parties at least 14 days' notice of the hearing and details of the issues that it is proposed the court will decide at the hearing (r 24.4(3); but see *James v Evans* [2001] CP Rep 36; (2000) *The Times*, 2 August, where no notice was given, see p 348 above, 'Summary judgment on court's own initiative').

If the court sends the parties notice of a summary judgment hearing fixed of its own initiative, any party who wishes to rely on written evidence must file a copy of it at court and on every other party to the proceedings at least seven days before the hearing (r 24.5(3)(a)). Also, if a party wishes to reply to a party's evidence, he must file a copy of the written evidence in reply at court and on every party to the proceedings at least three days before the hearing (r 24.5(3)(b)). However, the court may make a different order about the requirement of the parties to serve their evidence on each other (r 24.5(3)).

Jurisdiction of Masters and district judges

The Master or district judge has jurisdiction to hear the application. However, the Master or district judge can also refer the matter to be heard by a High Court judge or circuit judge respectively, if the nature of the case is such that the Master or district judge thinks this appropriate (PD 24, para 3).

COURT'S POWERS ON SUMMARY JUDGMENT APPLICATION

Judgment for the claimant

If the applicant is the claimant and the court is satisfied that the respondent's defence (or any issues within it) has no real prospect of success and there is no other compelling reason why the case should proceed to trial, it can enter judgment for the claimant for the whole claim, or on a particular issue or issues (PD 24, para 5.1(1)).

Judgment for the defendant

If the applicant is the defendant and the court is satisfied that the respondent's claim (or any issues within it) has no real prospect of success and that there is no other compelling reason why the case should proceed to trial, the court can strike out or dismiss the whole claim, or a particular issue or issues within it (PD 24, para 5.1(2)).

Dismissal of the application

If the court decides that the application is an unsuitable one for summary judgment, it can dismiss the application (PD 24, para 5.1(3)).

On dismissing the application, the court will give case management directions as to the future conduct of the proceedings (PD 24, para 10), for example, direct that allocation questionnaires be filed.

Conditional orders

If it appears to the court that it is possible, but improbable, for the claim or defence to succeed, the court is likely to make a conditional order (PD 24, para 4). Such an order will be appropriate when the court is doubtful about the merits of a claim or 'shadowy' defence but is unable to decide conclusively that it has no real prospect of success without proper testing of the evidence at trial.

The conditions the court can impose in such circumstances are an order for the party to:

(a) pay a sum of money into court; or

(b) take a specified step in relation to his statement of case;

and in both cases providing for the party's claim to be dismissed or statement of case struck out if he does not comply (PD 24, para 5.2).

In *Chapple v Williams* (1999) LTL, 8 December, May LJ said, *obiter*, that where a judge is considering imposing conditions, it should, generally speaking, be reasonably possible for the person upon whom the condition is imposed to comply with it. In that case the defendant was legally aided and asserted that there was no reasonable prospect of him paying the sum ordered, £4,000, into court. Although not technically necessary to decide the case, May LJ expressed his opinion that in the circumstances imposing such a condition was not correct. In any event, any conditional order has to be reasonable in order to comply with the payer's European Convention right to a fair trial (*Anglo-Eastern Trust Ltd v Kermanshahchi; Alliance v Kermanshahchi* [2002] EWCA Civ 198).

However, in the case of *Foot & Bowden v Anglo Europe Corp Ltd* (2001) LTL, 15 January, a company was ordered to pay the sum in dispute into court as a condition of defending even though the company was no longer trading and claimed not to have the sum required. The Court of Appeal found that the imposition of the condition was entirely appropriate in the circumstances, because although the company claimed to have no assets and not to have traded for several years, whenever the company was in need of money to sustain litigation the record showed that the money became available from one source or another.

Case management directions

If an unsuccessful application for summary judgment is made, the court can give directions about the future management of the case at the hearing (r 24.6(b)). If the defendant has filed a defence but the case has not yet been allocated, the next direction would be for the claim to be allocated. If the court has enough information at this stage, it can allocate the case there and then, or it can treat the rest of the hearing as an allocation hearing. Alternatively, the court might make an order for allocation questionnaires to be filed by a specified date.

If the claimant makes an unsuccessful application for summary judgment and the defendant has not yet filed a defence, the most likely direction for the court to make is for the filing and service of a defence (r 24.6(a)).

Costs of the application

In accordance with the general rule, the costs of a summary judgment application are in the discretion of the court. However, the most likely order is for the unsuccessful party to the application to pay the successful party's costs (r 44.3).

Part 45 sets out the fixed costs that the court will award to the applicant on the entry of judgment following an application for summary judgment (r 45.4). If the court does not order fixed costs, it is likely to order summary assessment of the costs of the application (r 43.3).

However, it should be noted that, in accordance with the general rule, if the order for summary judgment does not mention costs, none will be payable (r 44.13). The onus is therefore on the successful party to ensure that costs are applied for.

SETTING ASIDE AN APPLICATION FOR SUMMARY JUDGMENT

If the applicant or respondent fails to attend the hearing, the court can proceed in his absence (r 23.11(1)). If the court makes an order at that hearing it may, on an application or of its own initiative, set aside the order and re-list the application for hearing (r 23.11(2)).

Practice Direction 24, para 8.1, also specifically provides that if an order for summary judgment is made against a respondent who did not appear at the hearing of the application, the respondent may apply for the order to be set aside or varied.

The court is likely to consider setting aside or varying an order for summary judgment only where the respondent can demonstrate a real prospect of successfully bringing or defending the claim. Also, the court has the power to impose conditions such as the payment of a sum of money into court or the payment of costs on the indemnity basis as the price for setting aside the order (r 3.1(3)).

APPEAL AGAINST AN ORDER FOR SUMMARY JUDGMENT

If an order for summary judgment is made following a hearing at which both parties attended, a party who wishes to challenge the order must appeal against the order following the procedure in r 52.

SUMMARY POSSESSION OF LAND AGAINST SQUATTERS

Introduction

In many cases, proceedings for the recovery of land are lengthy and costly, with the court having wide powers to suspend orders for possession. However, where squatters occupy land in circumstances where there could be no question of having the permission of the landowner to do so, it would be inequitable to require the landlord to pursue the usual route to regain possession even if accelerated possession procedures were utilised (such as that available in the case of an assured shorthold tenancy where the contractual term has expired and a notice requiring possession has been served; see r 55.11). Therefore, in such situations, a landowner can use a summary procedure to obtain possession in a short period of time.

The summary procedure can be used against persons who enter onto or remain in occupation of land without the licence or consent of the owner, but is not available against a tenant who is holding over after the expiration of his tenancy (r 55.1(b)) other than an unlawful sub-tenant (*Moore Properties (Ilford) Ltd v McKeon* [1976] 1 WLR 1278). However, as the procedure is available against a person who entered into occupation with the permission of the owner but remains in occupation of land without his licence or consent, it may be available against a licensee where the licence has been terminated (eg, against a service occupier).

Summary possession proceedings

The procedure for summary possession of land is contained in Part 55.

Where summary possession proceedings are brought, the court will fix a day for the hearing when it issues the claim form (r 55.5(1)). The proceedings must be commenced in the county court for the district where the land or any part of the land is situated (r 55.3(1)). In exceptional circumstances a claim may be commenced in the High Court (r 55.3(2); PD 55, paras 1.1 and 1.3).

Even if the dispossessed landowner does not know the name of the occupants (which is likely to be the case in respect of squatters), he can still issue summary possession proceedings. In these circumstances, the occupiers are described as 'persons unknown' (r 55.3(4)).

The proceedings are commenced by way of a claim form in Form N5. In the High Court, the Part 8 claim form is used in Form N208.

The applicant must file particulars of claim (Form N121) which state:

(a) the applicant's interest in the land on the basis of his right to claim possession;

(b) the circumstances in which the land has been occupied without licence or consent and in which his claim to possession arises (PD 55, para 2.6).

An acknowledgment of service is not required and Part 10 does not apply (r 55.7(1)); neither does the requirement under r 15.2 to file a defence (r 55.7(2)); nor default judgment under Part 12 (r 55.7(4)).

Service of the proceedings

Service is in accordance with Part 6. The claim form and any witness statements must be filed and served together (r 55.8(5)).

Where all or any of the occupants are not named as respondents, the claim form must be served either by affixing a copy of the documents on the main door or other conspicuous part of the premises, and if practicable inserting a copy through the letter-box at the property in a sealed transparent envelope addressed to 'the occupiers', or by placing copies, addressed to the occupiers, in sealed transparent envelopes, on stakes in the ground at conspicuous parts of the occupied land (r 55.6; PD 55, para 4.1).

Hearing of claim

In most cases, the day fixed for the hearing by the court will, in the case of residential premises, be not less than five days after the day of service and, in the case of other land, not less than two days after service (r 55.5(2)). However, these periods can be shortened in the case of urgency or by permission of the court (r 3.1(2)(a)).

If there is no substantive defence to the claim for possession, the court must make an order for possession, which is usually to have immediate effect (see *McPhail v Persons (names unknown); Bristol Corp v Ross and Another* [1973] 3 All ER 393).

The court has power to make an order for possession of the whole of land owned by the claimant even though trespassers may be occupying only part of the land, particularly where there is a threat of further trespass (*University of Essex v Djemal* [1980] 1 WLR 1301, CA).

Order of possession

The order for possession, in Form N36, will be an order *in rem*, that is, an order that the applicant recover possession of the land rather than an order for the occupants to give possession.

If an order for possession is made against squatters (but not where the occupiers originally entered the land with permission), the court is bound to make an order for possession to be given forthwith and has no discretion to suspend the order (see *McPhail v Persons (names unknown); Bristol Corp v Ross and Another*).

Warrant of possession

Once an order for possession is made, a warrant of possession to enforce the order, in Form N325, can be issued without the court's permission (CPR Sched 2 CCR Ord 24, r 6(1)). However, after the expiry of three months from the making of the order for possession, the permission of the court must be obtained to issue a warrant of possession (CPR Sched 2 CCR Ord 24, r 6(2)).

As the order for possession is an order *in rem*, it is effective against all the occupiers of the premises, and the bailiff is entitled to evict everyone he finds on the premises even though that person was not a party to the proceedings for possession (*R v Wandsworth County Court ex p London Borough of Wandsworth* [1975] 3 All ER 390).

INTERIM POSSESSION ORDERS

In respect of summary possession proceedings in the county court (an interim possession order is not available in the High Court), if certain conditions are fulfilled the applicant can apply for an interim possession order ('IPO', introduced by ss 75 and 76 of the Criminal Justice and Public Order Act 1994).

The conditions that must be fulfilled are:

- the only claim in the proceedings is for the recovery of premises;
- the claim is made by a person with an immediate right of occupation and who has had such a right throughout the period of unlawful occupation;
- the claim is made against a person who entered the premises without consent and has not subsequently been granted consent;
- the claim is made within 28 days of the date when the applicant first knew, or ought reasonably to have known, that the respondent was in occupation (r 55.21).

The meaning of 'premises' is that given in s 12 of the Criminal Law Act 1977, which does not include open land.

Issue of the application

The applicant files a claim form in Form N5 (PD 55, para 9.1). The particulars of claim must state the claimant's interest in the land or the basis of his right to claim possession and the circumstances in which it has been occupied without licence or consent (PD 55, para 2.6). When the claimant files his claim form he must also issue an application notice seeking interim possession in Form N130 (r 55.22(3); PD 55, para 9.1). If possible the claimant should include all the evidence that he wishes to present in his statement of case.

Service of the application

The proceedings should be served by fixing a copy of the documents on the main door or other conspicuous part of the premises and, if practicable, inserting them through the letter-box at the premises in a sealed transparent envelope addressed to 'the occupiers' (r 55.6, PD 55, para 4.1). Additionally, but not alternatively, the applicant can fix copies of the documents, in sealed transparent envelopes, on stakes in the ground at conspicuous parts of the premises (r 55.6; PD 55, para 4.1).

The applicant must file a witness statement or affidavit of service in Form N135 at or before the time fixed for consideration of the application (r 55.23(3)).

The respondent to the order may file a witness statement or affidavit in Form N133 in opposition to the making of the interim possession order at any time before the hearing (r 55.24).

The making of an interim possession order

Under r 55.25(2), the court will make an IPO if:

(a) the claimant has:

- filed a certificate of service of the documents (Form N215) referred to in r 55.23(1); or
- proved service of those documents to the satisfaction of the court; and

(b) the court considers that:

- the conditions set out in r 55.21(1) are satisfied; and
- any undertakings given by the claimant as a condition of making the order are adequate.

The interim possession order

If the court makes the IPO, it is in prescribed Form N134 and compels the respondent to vacate the premises within 24 hours of the service of the order on him (r 55.25(3)). The IPO must be served on the respondent by the applicant within 48 hours of the court approving the terms of the order (r 55.26(1)).

On making the IPO, the court will fix a return date for the hearing of the claim which is not less than seven days after the date on which the IPO is made (r 55.25(4)). In the meantime, the applicant can act on the IPO, and if the respondent does not vacate the premises the applicant must ask the police to enforce the order. The order cannot be enforced by the bailiffs under a warrant of possession.

The IPO expires on the return date (r 55.27(2)), and on that date the judge must either make a final order for possession, or dismiss the claim or direct that the proceedings continue as summary possession proceedings under Part 55, Section I (r 55.27(3)).

If the court holds that the applicant was not entitled to an IPO, the respondent may apply for enforcement of the undertakings given by the applicant, which can include an assessment of any damages suffered (r 55.27(3)(d)).

If the defendant has left the premises, he may apply on grounds of urgency for the IPO to be set aside before the date of the hearing of the claim (r 55.28(1)). The application must be supported by a witness statement (r 55.28(2)). On receipt of the application, the court will give directions as to:

(a) the date for the hearing; and

(b) the period of notice, if any, to be given to the claimant and the method of service of any such notice (r 55.28(3)).

Note that there is no provision for a defendant to appeal the making of an IPO without having first vacated the premises.

Where no notice is required under r 55.28(3)(b), the only matters to be dealt with at the hearing of the application to set aside are whether:

(a) the IPO should be set aside; and

(b) any undertaking to reinstate the defendant should be enforced;

and all other matters will be dealt with at the hearing of the claim (r 55.28(5)). Where notice is required under r 55.28(3)(b), the court may treat the hearing of the application to set aside as the hearing of the claim (r 55.28(7)).

The court will serve on all the parties:

(a) a copy of the order made under r 55.28(5); and

(b) where no notice was required under r 55.28(3)(b), a copy of the defendant's application to set aside and the witness statement in support (r 55.28(6)).

CHAPTER 24

STRIKING OUT

INTRODUCTION

The court has the power to strike out a party's statement of case either on the application of a party or on its own initiative. Striking out is a draconian step as it usually means that either the whole or part of the party's case is at an end and final judgment can be entered against him. However, where it is apparent on the face of a statement of case that it does not establish a sustainable claim or defence in law, it is in most cases in accordance with the overriding objective for it to be struck out at an early stage rather than allow it to proceed incurring unnecessary costs for the parties and wasting the court's resources. The court also has the power to strike out a statement of case which is an abuse of the court's process because, for instance, it seeks to re-litigate issues which have already been fully decided or where the claim is vexatious. Further, the court can also use the sanction of striking out a party's statement of case in order to compel compliance with rules, practice directions and court orders, and in order to ensure that a party does not, by his conduct, prejudice his opponent or other court users who wish to share in the court's limited resources. The exercise of the court's powers to strike out a statement of case is discretionary in nature and will depend on the circumstances of the particular case.

POWER TO STRIKE OUT A STATEMENT OF CASE

Rule 3.4 sets out specific circumstances where the court has the power to strike out a statement of case. These are where it appears to the court:

(a) that the statement of case discloses no reasonable grounds for bringing or defending the claim;

(b) that the statement of case is an abuse of the court's process or is otherwise likely to obstruct the just disposal of proceedings; or

(c) that there has been a failure to comply with a rule, practice direction or court order (r 3.4(2)).

These powers are in addition to any other power the court may have to strike out a statement of case (r 3.4(5)). So, for instance, the court could strike out a statement of case in the exercise of its inherent powers to protect its own process from abuse, this inherent jurisdiction of the court being expressly preserved by r 3.1.

Statement of case

'Statement of case' is defined in the rules to mean a claim form, particulars of claim (where these are not included in a claim form), defence, Part 20 claim or reply to defence. The term also refers to any further information given in relation to a statement of case, whether it is given voluntarily or in response to a court order (r 2.3(1)).

Any reference in the rules relating to the power to strike out a statement of case includes the power to strike out part of a statement of case (r 3.4(1)).

Striking out

The Glossary at the end of the Civil Procedure Rules (CPR) defines 'striking out' to mean the court ordering written material to be deleted so that it may no longer be relied upon.

STRIKING OUT UNMERITORIOUS CASES

As part of case management, the court has an active role in ensuring that those issues, whether pleaded as part of a claim or a defence, which can or should be disposed of summarily before trial, should be disposed of at as early a stage as possible rather than continue to go forward for full investigation at trial (r 1.4(2)(c)). However, as Laddie J said in *Barrett v Universal-Island Records Ltd* [2003] EWHC 625, Ch: 'If it appears that there is a real, as opposed to fanciful, prospect of the claim or defence succeeding at the trial, a trial there must be, even if the court has a strong suspicion that the claim or defence will fail.' See also *Chan U Seek v Alvis Vehicles Ltd* [2003] EWHC 1238, where a 'weak' claim was allowed to continue because only a trial could determine whether or not it would succeed at trial.

Further, the process of proper case management demands that the time given to summary applications is not disproportionate to the benefits to be achieved. As Laddie J explained in *Barrett v Universal-Island Records Ltd*, just because the longer the time spent on a summary application the more confidence a court may have as to the likely outcome at trial, does not mean that it is appropriate to spend whatever time it will take on a summary application to reach confidence as to the outcome at trial. He said, for example, that spending a few days on a summary application which if successful may avoid the need for, or significantly reduce the expected duration of, a trial due to last some months, is likely to be a worthwhile use of court time and is proportionate. However, 'spending that sort of time when trying to short-circuit a trial due to last, say, two weeks, is likely to be disproportionate' (at [44]).

Laddie J also warned that if a case is not appropriate for summary determination, the savings in time and costs to be made on an application for a strike out or summary judgment may be illusory. In his opinion, an application which fails, and which involves an appeal, will result in the parties having spent more time and money on the litigation and may well delay the trial. Although this may be an acceptable risk where a comparatively short summary application carries a reasonable prospect of disposing of, or significantly shortening, a much longer trial, it is less likely to be so where the summary application itself is likely to be comparatively lengthy and complex.

To obtain summary determination of a claim or defence, the applicant must show that the other party's case is fanciful, and he must be able to do this without the need for a mini-trial. If the issues appear complex and difficult to unravel even after a prolonged hearing then the case is not suitable for summary determination (*Three Rivers DC v Governor and Co of the Bank of England* [2001] UKHL 16; [2001] 2 All ER 513; *Barrett v Universal-Island Records Ltd*; *Chan U Seek v Alvis Vehicles Ltd* [2003] EWHC 1238).

Relationship between r 3.4 and Part 24

The court has two distinct powers to dispose summarily of claims and defences before trial. One is under r 3.4, where the court can strike out a statement of case (or part of one) if it discloses no reasonable grounds for bringing or defending a claim, or is an abuse of process of the court, or is otherwise likely to obstruct the just disposal of the proceedings. The other is under Part 24, which gives the court the power to enter summary judgment against a claimant or defendant where that party has no real prospect of succeeding on his claim or defence. There is a substantial overlap between the two powers and an application can be made under both rules (PD 3, para 1.7).

An application to strike out a statement of case under r 3.4(1)(a) and (b) is more technical than an application for summary judgment under Part 24. Under the former, the court is generally concerned only with deficiencies with the statement of case itself, while the court has wider powers under Part 24 and will consider the evidence supporting the claim or defence. Indeed, for the purposes of a strike out, the court will assume that what is pleaded can be established, and then go on to consider whether, notwithstanding this, the case should be struck out (see *Swain v Hillman* [2001] 1 All ER 91; *Carnduff v Rock and Chief Constable of West Midlands Police* [2001] EWCA Civ 680).

No reasonable grounds for bringing or defending the claim

The practice direction accompanying r 3.4 gives examples of the types of case when the court may strike out a statement of case on the basis that it fails to disclose any reasonable grounds for bringing or defending the claim (PD 3, paras 1.4–1.6). For instance, if a claimant's statement of case states 'Money owed £5,000', and does not set out any facts indicating what it is about, it is liable to be struck out. In the same way, if the defendant's defence is simply a bare denial without any facts in support, that too is liable to be struck out. Thus, 'the defendant denies the claimant's claim and puts the claimant to strict proof' will not be acceptable.

A party's statement of case is also liable to be struck out if it is based on incoherent facts which make no sense, or if based on facts which are coherent but which even if true would not amount to a legally recognisable claim or defence. It is stressed in the practice direction that these examples are given by way of illustration only (PD 3, para 1.8).

In an area of the law which is uncertain and developing it is not normally appropriate to strike out a claim or defence under r 3.4 (*Health and Safety Executive v Thames Trains Ltd* [2003] EWCA Civ 720). In *Health and Safety Executive v Thames Trains Ltd*, the Court of Appeal held that there was no arguable case against the HSE for breach of statutory duty to victims of the Ladbroke Grove train crash. However, the court was unable to say, without a full examination of the facts, whether or not the HSE owed a common law duty of care to those victims and whether it was in breach of it. Therefore an application to strike out the claimant's application failed.

In *Farah and Others v British Airways plc and The Home Office* (2000) *The Times*, 26 January, the claimants were Somali nationals who purchased air tickets from British Airways plc to fly from Cairo to London. British Airways refused to fly them to

London on the grounds that the claimants did not have valid entry documents. As a result the claimants were initially detained in Cairo airport and then deported to Ethiopia. The claimants brought proceedings against British Airways for breach of contract, contending that they all had valid visas granting them leave to enter Britain and they suffered loss and damage as a result of British Airways' refusal to transport them, including distress and injury to feelings. One of British Airways' defences was that it had a reasonable basis for its belief that the claimants did not have valid entry documents having relied on the advice of a representative of the Home Office's immigration service who was present at the airport. The claimants therefore brought a claim against the Home Office on the grounds that the immigration service negligently gave British Airways incorrect advice, in breach of its duty of care to provide correct and accurate information, and as a result the claimants suffered loss and damage when British Airways refused to carry them to this country.

At first instance the judge struck out the claimants' particulars of claim that alleged negligence against the Home Office on the grounds that there was insufficient proximity between the claimants and the Home Office to create a duty of care. The Court of Appeal set aside the decision to strike out the claimants' particulars of claim on the grounds that the claimants contended there was a lacuna in the law which should be filled, and as this was a developing area of jurisprudence, which involved the issue as to whether an analogous situation gave rise to a duty of care, it had to be explored further. It was also not appropriate to determine the issue before the full facts had been established at trial.

Abuse of process

The type of case where a statement of case is likely to be held to be an abuse of the court's process or as otherwise likely to obstruct the just disposal of proceedings is said to be where the claim is vexatious, scurrilous or obviously ill-founded (PD 3, para 1.5). An example of this may be where proceedings are started to pursue a claim which has already been dealt with by way of full and final settlement between the parties.

In exercising its power whether to strike out a claim under r 3.4(2)(b) the court must seek to give effect to the overriding objective. The overriding objective includes taking into account the court's need to allot its own limited resources to other cases which must be weighed against the claimant's wish to have a 'second bite at the cherry' (*Securum Finance Ltd v Ashton* [2000] 3 WLR 1400). In *Securum Finance Ltd v Ashton*, the Court of Appeal decided not to strike out part of the claimant's claim as an abuse of process where the claim was indistinguishable from an earlier claim brought by the claimant which had been struck out for inordinate and inexcusable delay. Although the court held that it was an abuse of process to seek to pursue the same claim in a second claim, when it could and should have been pursued properly and in compliance with the Rules of Court in the first claim, the court did not strike out the claim because the claimant also brought other claims in the same proceedings which had not been litigated in the earlier proceedings. The court was of the opinion that to strike out part of the claim on those grounds would be an incorrect exercise of discretion in this case, because whether or not part of the claim was struck out would make no difference to the court's resources needed to try the rest of the litigation.

In *Carnduff v Rock and Chief Constable of West Midlands Police* [2001] EWCA Civ 680, the claimant was a registered police informer. He brought a claim against the West

Midlands Police to recover payment for information he supplied to them in his role as informer. The defendant made an application to strike out the claimant's claim. Although the court was not prepared to strike out the claimant's claim on the grounds that the agreement was unenforceable, or that the claimant had not earned any remuneration, the court held that the claim should be struck out under r 3.4, or under the court's inherent jurisdiction, because the hearing of a fair trial would necessarily require the police to disclose information which it was not in the public interest to disclose. The court said that where reliance is placed on considerations of public policy, various competing interests and considerations may have to be taken into account before a judgment can be made as to where the overall public interest lies. In this case there was, on the one hand, the fundamental public interest in ensuring that justice is done and is seen to be done. There was also the public interest in the enforcement of contractual obligations. However, competing with those interests was the public interest that the effectiveness of the law enforcement agencies in investigating and preventing crime should not be adversely affected by an obligation to make public information or material of a sensitive or confidential nature.

In *Clark v University of Lincolnshire and Humberside* [2000] 3 WLR 752; [2000] 3 All ER 752, the defendant was a new university and therefore had no charter and no provision for a visitor (ie, an official with the right or duty of occasionally inspecting and reporting). It was a statutory corporation with legal personality and a capacity to enter into contracts within its powers. The court found that the arrangement between the claimant, a fee-paying student, and the defendant was that of contract. The claimant brought proceedings against the defendant for breach of contract. The Court of Appeal found that as the defendant was also a public body, proceedings should have been commenced by way of judicial review (see Part 54). It held that such disputes should be resolved internally. If that was not possible and there was no visitor, the court might have no alternative but to become involved, but this should be by way of judicial review. However, in this case, although it would have been more appropriate for the claimant to bring proceedings by way of judicial review, the court would not strike out a claim solely on this ground, unless there was an abuse of process, which it did not find in this case.

In *Barrett v Universal-Island Records Ltd*, the court said that in order to strike out a claim or defence, or enter summary judgment without a full trial of the claim or defence, the court must have a high degree of confidence that the claim or defence will not succeed at trial. The court held that applications for summary relief on the grounds of abuse of process should not be treated any differently from other summary applications for final relief. The rule that such applications should not be allowed to develop into mini-trials applied as much to one type as the other. Every court has an inherent jurisdiction to prevent its procedure being abused. This includes the power to stay or strike out vexatious proceedings, and also includes the power to grant a *quia timet* injunction restraining a party from commencing proceedings so as to prevent serious loss being caused by anticipated but unidentified proceedings (*Ebert v Birch* [1999] 3 WLR 670).

The court will strike out a claim as an abuse of process if it is brought not to vindicate a right but to cause expense, harassment or commercial prejudice going beyond that normally encountered in properly conducted litigation (*Wallis v Valentine and Others* [2002] EWCA Civ 1034). Wallis's (W's) claim arose out of a long history of neighbour disputes between himself and the defendants, in which the latter had succeeded in obtaining injunctive and other relief against W. W alleged that three documents, most notably an affidavit sworn by the first defendant, contained defamatory statements about him which had been posted both to him and to G (his partner) at their home. W further alleged that, when the defendants subsequently sold their property, the affidavit had been disclosed by them 'to others', namely, the new owners of the defendants' property. Both the new owners and the solicitor who had acted for them on their purchase gave evidence that the affidavit had not been disclosed to them at any time and that they were wholly unaware of its contents. On the basis of that evidence the judge struck out W's plea of publication 'to others'. Having found that there had been publication only to G, who had been living with W throughout the entirety of his dispute with the defendants and who was fully aware of all that had transpired in the course of that dispute, the judge further held that, having regard to the overriding objective, the claim was an abuse of process. The judge's decision was upheld by the Court of Appeal.

Abuse of process and delay

Where a party has suffered substantial prejudice as a result of another party's delay such that a fair trial is no longer possible, as, for example, where a primary witness has died, the court may, in the exercise of its discretion, strike out a claim or defence whether under r 3.4(2)(c) or its general case management powers under r 3.1(2)(m), or under the court's inherent jurisdiction to protect its own process from abuse, expressly preserved by r 3.1(1) (*Purdy v Cambran* (1999) LTL, 17 December).

Where there has been inordinate and inexcusable delay in bringing or defending proceedings, this in itself can constitute an abuse of process and justify the striking out of a claim or defence, even if the other party has not been prejudiced by the delay. The court will take into account the effect on other litigants and the court system of a party's inordinate delay in bringing or defending proceedings, and the need to protect its own processes from abuse (*Shikari v Malik* (1999) *The Times*, 20 May).

The decisions about inordinate and inexcusable delay are mainly based on transitional cases, that is, those cases which were commenced under the old rules but finally decided under the CPR. Under a system of active judicial case management, it is thought that there will be limited opportunity for parties to cause inordinate and inexcusable delay in bringing or defending proceedings, and most of the transitional cases will now have been decided. However, there is still scope for a party, in the course of litigation, repeatedly to fail to comply with rules, practice directions and court orders. In such circumstances the court has the power to strike out a party's case on those grounds under r 3.4(2)(c).

In *Re McHugh Southern Ltd (In Liquidation)* (2003) *The Times*, 30 January, Ch D, the court held that a strike out of proceedings where there has been excessive delay can, in appropriate cases, violate a litigant's right to a fair trial under Art 6 of the European Convention on Human Rights. The result is that other penalties ought to be considered in all cases where it is still possible for a fair trial to take place.

The court's powers to sift out unmeritorious claims and defences

When a claim form is presented for issue or when a defence is filed, it will first be received by a court officer. A court officer is a member of the court staff, but has no judicial function (see r 2.3). However, in order to further the process of case management at all levels, court officers presented with documents by parties with a request for a step to be taken can, instead of taking that step, consult a judge instead. The judge can then decide whether that step should be taken (r 3.2).

Claims

Where it appears to a court officer that the claim form which is being presented for issue falls within r 3.4(2)(a) or (b) above, he is obliged to issue the claim form but can then consult a judge before further steps are taken in the case. If the judge is satisfied that the claimant's statement of case is such that it does fall within r 3.4(2)(a) or (b), he has the power to order that the claim be stayed until further order. This can include an order that the claim form be retained by the court and not served on the defendant until the stay is lifted (PD 3, para 2).

The judge can also order that no application to lift the stay be heard unless the claimant files further documents such as a witness statement or particulars of claim. The judge has the power to make such orders of his own initiative, or after giving the claimant the opportunity to attend a hearing before deciding whether to do so (PD 3, paras 2.1–2.4).

Defences

In the same way, the court officer may consult a judge about a defence filed which appears to fall within r 3.4(2)(a) or (b) (PD 3, para 3.1). If satisfied that the defence does fall within those provisions, the judge can make an order of his own initiative striking it out; however, he may also extend the time for the defendant to file a proper defence (PD 3, para 3.2). The judge may also allow the defendant a hearing before deciding whether to strike out the defence (PD 3, para 3.3).

The judge can also make an order that unless a defendant clarifies his defence or provides further information about it within a specified time, his defence will be struck out (PD 3, para 3.4). Note that a defence which admits liability but disputes the amount of damages (rather than damages as a whole) is likely to be treated by the judge as no defence at all, resulting in judgment being given to the claimant with an order for damages to be assessed.

STRIKING OUT FOR FAILURE TO COMPLY WITH A RULE, PRACTICE DIRECTION OR COURT ORDER

Under r 3.4(2)(c), the court has the power to strike out a party's case if that party has failed to comply with a rule, practice direction or court order. In most circumstances, the court is unlikely to order the striking out of a statement of case on a single occasion of failure to comply. Instead, the court is more likely to make an order that unless the party in default take the required step by a specified date, his statement of case will be struck out (an 'unless order'). Note that there will be many occasions where it will not be appropriate to strike out a claim where the claimant is absent but is represented through the attendance of his lawyers (*Rouse v Freeman* (2002) *The Times*, 8 January, QBD (Div Ct)).

In the case of *Biguzzi v Rank Leisure plc* [1999] 1 WLR 1926; [1999] 4 All ER 934, Lord Woolf gave some general guidance on the operation of the court's powers to strike out a statement of case under r 3.4(2)(c). He emphasised that while the court must not be lenient towards a party who has failed to comply with a rule, practice direction or court order, as the court had the scope to impose a wide range of sanctions to punish default, it should not be driven to resort to striking out when another sanction would be more appropriate. He believed that the drastic remedy of striking out would be most appropriate for the most serious breaches of the rules. Lord Woolf was also mindful that a lesser sanction than striking out was less likely to result in an appeal of the order. Other sanctions include the power to order a party to pay indemnity costs and to pay a sum of money into court.

This decision should be considered in the light of *UCB Corporate Services v Halifax* (1999) unreported, 6 December, CA, where the court made it clear that just because the court had available a wide range of other sanctions short of striking out that did not mean that the court could not order the striking out of a statement of case if it was justified in all the circumstances of a case.

It should be borne in mind that the above two decisions were both transitional cases where the conduct complained of, being the 'wholesale disregard of the rules' which led to the case being struck out, occurred under the old civil procedure rules but the appeal against the striking out was heard after the CPR came into force. With active judicial case management, it is unlikely for a party to have the opportunity to indulge in 'wholesale disregard of the rules' and '[t]he delays which used to disfigure the conduct of litigation ought not to occur in future'. Under the CPR, at each stage of the proceedings the court is likely to impose an unless order threatening striking out if a party fails to carry out the required action within a specified time. If such an order is made and not complied with, the striking out of the statement of case will apply automatically, leaving a party to resort to applying for relief from that sanction (rr 3.8, 3.9).

Also, it would seem that the court is unlikely to exercise its power under this rule to strike out a statement of case where there has been a technical failure to comply with the rules but the party in default has provided all the necessary information about his case to the other party. In the case of *Hannigan v Hannigan* [2000] All ER (D) 693, a party started proceedings in the wrong form and committed many other breaches of the rules in presenting his case. The Court of Appeal held in that case that as the defendant knew precisely what was being claimed, and as the interests of the administration of justice would have been better served if the defendant had pointed out the procedural defects to the claimant in accordance with the duty of the parties to help the court further the overriding objective, it would not be just to strike out the claimant's claim, notwithstanding the claimant's catalogue of procedural errors, as in the circumstances such a response would be disproportionate. Where a middle course, such as limiting interest or damages, is more appropriate than strike out, that course should be followed.

Consideration should also be given to the impact of the Human Rights Act 1998 and a possible contention that striking out a statement of case for a single technical misdemeanour might amount to a breach of Art 6(1) of the European Convention on Human Rights – the right to a fair trial. In *Mody v Zaman* (2001) LTL, 13 November, QBD, the Court of Appeal re-affirmed its guidance that the imposition of sanctions must be proportionate to the default. Where the default is a failure to observe a technical requirement, striking out the claim may be too drastic. In this case it was the breach of an order to lodge in the appeal court an agreed note of the judgment below. Striking out was held not to be warranted.

In *Whittaker v Soper* [2001] EWCA Civ 1462, the defendants applied, at a very late stage in proceedings, for permission to rely on fresh expert evidence in place of the expert evidence they had originally sought to rely on. The defendants' conduct in the proceedings had already resulted in two previous trial dates being vacated, and if this application were granted the new trial date would also be vacated. Accordingly, the court granted the defendants' application only on condition that they paid the sum of £100,000 into court. This order was subsequently varied, on the defendants' application, so that the defendants were each ordered to execute legal charges over their properties as security for the sums claimed by the claimants in the proceedings. The court also expressly ordered that if the defendants failed to comply with this order they would be debarred from defending the claim. Although the defendants had executed the charges, it subsequently transpired that they had failed to register the charges with the Land Registry. On the morning of the first day of the trial, the claimants applied, without prior notice, for the defendants' defence to be struck out for their failure to comply with the court order. The trial judge granted the claimants' application and subsequently entered judgment for the claimants in the sum of £241,000 plus interest and costs.

The Court of Appeal overturned the judge's order on the grounds that he had overlooked the utmost seriousness of debarring a defendant from defending on the day of the trial itself and had failed to consider whether the claimant would suffer any prejudice if the trial went ahead without any strike out. The judge had failed to consider the matters listed in r 3.9 when deciding whether the defendants should be granted relief from the sanction imposed by the order and did not consider whether a strike out was ultimately proportionate to the circumstances. In the light of the judge's errors, the Court of Appeal exercised its own discretion whether to grant relief under r 3.9. The court considered all the relevant factors under r 3.9 in the light of the circumstances of the case, including the fact that the claimants were not prejudiced because new or amended charges could have been entered into that morning and the claimants' position protected at the Land Registry. Weighed against this was the injustice to the defendants of preventing them from defending the claim on the morning of the trial itself.

In accordance with *Biguzzi v Rank Leisure plc* [1999] 1 WLR 1926, the court emphasised that the ultimate sanction of strike out should be viewed against the backdrop of the other powers and sanctions available to the court. In this case the court was of the opinion that the judge should not have barred the defence on the day of trial itself, unless he felt that the claimants could not have a fair trial on that occasion or were otherwise prejudiced in ways that he could not correct by the use of the wide powers at his disposal.

PROCEDURE FOR APPLYING FOR AN ORDER TO STRIKE OUT A STATEMENT OF CASE

An application for striking out a statement of case should be made in accordance with Part 23 and should be made as soon as possible and before allocation if possible (PD 3, para 5.1). The application should be made on Form N244, the general form of application, and supported by evidence if necessary. Some applications to strike out – those, for instance, based on the grounds that a party's case does not disclose a legally recognised cause of action – should not require evidence to support them, as it should be clear from the face of the statement of case (PD 3, para 5.2).

CONSEQUENTIAL ORDERS

As well as striking out the statement of case, the court can make other orders consequential on the striking out (r 3.4(3)). For instance, it is usually ordered that the costs of the other party are to be paid by the party whose case was struck out. Also, the court has the power to enter judgment for the other party.

Restrictions on resurrecting a struck out claim

If a claimant's statement of case is struck out and the court has also made an order for the claimant to pay the defendant's costs of the proceedings, if the claimant fails to pay those costs, and in fact starts another claim against the same defendant based on facts which are the same or substantially the same as those relied on in the struck out statement of case, the defendant can apply for the subsequent claim to be stayed until his costs of the original proceedings are paid (r 3.4(4)).

It is likely to be treated as an abuse of process in itself to start another claim based on the same or substantially the same facts as the claim that was struck out if the original claim was struck out on the grounds that it disclosed no reasonable cause of action or was an abuse of process. Moreover, given the court's obligation, in furtherance of the overriding objective, to consider the interests of all court users, it may well decide that it is not an appropriate use of court resources to allow a claimant to bring a fresh claim based on the same grounds as one that has already been struck out on the grounds of delay even though the limitation period has not expired (*Securum Finance Ltd v Ashton* [2000] 3 WLR 1400).

In considering this question in the case of *Securum Finance Ltd v Ashton*, the Court of Appeal held that the court must consider, when deciding whether to allow a second claim to proceed in those circumstances, whether the claimant's wish to have a second bite at the cherry outweighs the need to allot the court's own limited resources to other cases.

Also, if a claimant's statement of case is struck out and the limitation period for the cause of action has expired, if the claimant starts a new claim against the defendant for the same matter, the defendant will be able to have that claim struck out, either under r 3.4(2)(a) or under Part 24, on the grounds that the statement of claim discloses no reasonable grounds for bringing or defending the claim, or the claim has no real prospect of success.

Appealing order striking out statement of case

If a party's statement of case is struck out under r 3.4, and that party wishes to challenge that order or any consequential order, such as the entry of judgment in the other party's favour, this should be done by way of appeal of the order in accordance with the appropriate procedure under Part 52.

ORDERS THREATENING STRIKING OUT

The court has the power to make an order for a party to do something backed by the sanction that if the party fails to comply, his statement of claim will be struck out. Such an order is commonly known as an 'unless order'. In the first instance, the court will make an unless order where a party has failed to comply with a rule, practice direction or court order, and in effect gives the party a second chance to comply before his statement of case is struck out.

Judgment by request following striking out for non-compliance with an order

If an order is made warning a party that if he does not comply by a specified time his statement of case will be struck out, and if he does not comply, the statement of case will be automatically struck out. The other party can then, if certain conditions are met, apply for judgment to be entered for him with costs by simply filing a request for judgment (r 3.5).

For all parties, in order to be able to enter judgment by filing a request, the order threatening to strike out the statement of case must relate to the whole of the other party's statement of case (r 3.5(2)(a)). Where the party wishing to obtain judgment is the claimant, he can only do that by request if his claim is for one of the following remedies:

- a specified amount of money;
- an amount of money to be decided by the court;
- delivery of goods where the claim form gives the defendant the alternative of paying their value; or
- a combination of any of the above claims (r 3.5(2)(b)).

The request must state that the right to enter judgment has arisen because the court's order has not been complied with (r 3.5(4)).

Judgment by application following striking out for non-compliance with an order

If either the order threatening to strike out the statement of case does not refer to the whole of a party's statement of case, or, where the party seeking to enter judgment is a claimant, his case is not one set out in the list set in r 3.5(2)(b), the party must instead make an application to the court under Part 23 to enter judgment (r 3.5(5)).

Setting aside judgment entered after striking out

Where judgment has been entered after a party's statement of case has been struck out for non-compliance with a specified order, the party against whom judgment has been entered may apply to the court for judgment to be set aside (r 3.6(1)). An application should be made on Form N244 in accordance with Part 23. However, in order to apply for judgment to be set aside, the party must apply not more than 14 days after the judgment was served on him (r 3.6(2)).

If judgment was entered in circumstances where the right to enter judgment in fact had not yet arisen, the court has no discretion and must set the judgment aside (r 3.6(3)). However, if judgment had been rightfully entered in accordance with the procedure set out in r 3.5, the party must apply to the court to exercise its discretion to set judgment aside, in accordance with its powers under r 3.9 to grant relief from sanctions (r 3.6(4)).

VEXATIOUS LITIGANTS

A vexatious litigant is a person who habitually and persistently and without any reasonable cause brings vexatious civil proceedings, or makes vexatious applications in civil proceedings or brings vexatious criminal prosecutions, whether against the same person or different persons (*Attorney-General v Covey and Matthews* [2001] EWCA Civ 254).

Vexatious proceedings or applications include those that are frivolous and without any reasonable grounds. An order can be made under s 42 of the Supreme Court Act 1981 (a 's 42 order') against a vexatious litigant which prevents him from bringing or continuing with civil proceedings, or from making applications within civil proceedings or from bringing criminal proceedings without first obtaining the leave of the High Court to do so.

The order may be a 'civil proceedings order', a 'criminal proceedings order' or an 'all proceedings order' depending on whether civil, or criminal or all proceedings are involved. Such an order can be obtained only on the application of the Attorney-General. If a civil proceedings order is in place against such a vexatious litigant, he will be unable to begin, or continue or make any application in any civil proceedings without seeking the permission of the High Court (s 42(1A) of the Supreme Court 1981). If such proceedings are brought without permission the court will be entitled to strike them out as an abuse of process.

A s 42 order may be unlimited in time and so prevent a vexatious litigant from bringing any proceedings for an indefinite period without first obtaining the permission of the court (*Attorney-General v Covey and Matthews*).

Attorney-General v Covey and Matthews was a conjoined appeal brought by vexatious litigants in respect of different proceedings. The main issue the Court of Appeal had to decide was whether the proceedings brought by the appellants fell within the definition of vexatious proceedings under s 42 of the 1981 Act in the light of the fact that the proceedings in question were brought against different individuals rather than the same individual. Mr Covey brought separate proceedings against a family, the Surrey Constabulary and his employers, while Mr Matthews brought 33 actions against separate defendants.

The Court of Appeal had no difficulty in holding that it was not necessary for there to be an element of repetition in the proceedings *against a particular defendant* for the proceedings to fall within the provisions of s 42. In making the determination as to whether there is the necessary element of repetition the court has to look at the whole history of the applicant's litigious activity. The court recognised that in some cases the activity will focus upon a particular defendant, but it may also focus upon a particular grievance or be represented by numerous claims against a wide range of defendants in circumstances where no reasonable cause of action exists. In this case the court found that a s 42 order was fully justified. The appellants had caused a variety of defendants to suffer some disadvantage by their litigation. The court considered that the cumulative effect of the appellants' litigation, both against the individuals who were drawn into the proceedings and on the administration of justice generally, had to be taken into account.

It was also held in *Attorney-General v Covey and Matthews* that because a vexatious litigant can apply for permission to bring or continue proceedings which are justified, a s 42 order does not restrict or reduce access to justice. It was also held that there were a number of other safeguards for a vexatious litigant. These were that a s 42 order has to be made on behalf of the Attorney-General, acting in his long-established constitutional role as the guardian of the public interest. The involvement of the Attorney-General was held to be an acknowledgment that an application should be made only where there are good grounds to justify curtailing the right of an individual to have unlimited access to the courts. Further, the Attorney-General's application for a s 42 order has to be heard and determined by a Divisional Court (a court consisting of at least two High Court judges) (and see *Ebert v Birch* [1999] 3 WLR 670).

Application for permission to bring civil proceedings

If a person is subject to a civil proceedings order he must apply for permission to bring, or continue or make any application in civil proceedings. The procedure for making such an application is set out in PD 3B, paras 7.1–7.10.

The application is made under Part 23 using an application notice (Form N244). The application notice must contain the relevant matters set out in PD 3B, paras 7.3–7.5, and the application must be decided by a High Court judge (PD 3B, para 7.6).

The High Court judge may, without a hearing, either make an order dismissing the application or grant the permission sought. Alternatively he may give directions for further written evidence to be supplied before an order is made, or give directions for the hearing of the application. An order for a hearing of the application may include an order that the application notice is served on the Attorney-General and on any other person against whom the litigant wishes to bring proceedings (PD 3B, paras 7.6–7.7).

If permission is granted, allowing the litigant to bring or continue proceedings or make an application against a person, that person can apply to set aside the grant of permission if it was given other than at a hearing of which that person was given notice (PD 3B, para 7.9).

Grepe v Loam order

The court has an inherent jurisdiction to prevent further applications being made without the leave of the court in existing proceedings that are already before the court. Such orders are known as *Grepe v Loam* orders, after the case that decided that matter (*Grepe v Loam* (1887) 37 Ch D 168).

A *Grepe v Loam* order is not as wide as a s 42 order which can prevent a litigant from issuing any civil proceedings without the leave of the High Court. However, the existence of s 42 orders has not supplanted the power of the court to make a *Grepe v Loam* order, which can be made by a single High Court judge and can be made in the county court (see judgment of Woolf LJ in *Ebert v Birch*).

In *Ebert v Birch*, the Court of Appeal held that the court (both the High Court and the county courts) also has the power, in the exercise of its inherent jurisdiction, and where there is sufficient cause, to make an 'extended *Grepe v Loam* order', restraining a litigant from bringing anticipated but unidentified proceedings against defendants without the leave of the court.

Vexatious litigants and human rights

In *Ebert v Official Receiver* [2001] EWCA Civ 340, the Court of Appeal held that the making of a s 42 order was not in contravention of Art 6 of the European Convention on Human Rights (right to a fair trial).

In *Attorney-General v Covey and Matthews*, the Court of Appeal also held that the imposition of a s 42 order was not in contravention of Art 6. The court referred to well-established jurisdiction of the European Court which confirmed that the right of access secured by Art 6 may be subject to limitations as long as they do not impair the very essence of the right of access to the courts and as long as the restrictions pursue a legitimate and proportionate aim (*Tolstoy Miloslavsky v UK* (1999) 20 EHRR 442). In applying that jurisdiction the Court of Appeal held that the order made in that case pursued a legitimate aim in the light of the cumulative effect of the vexatious litigants' proceedings both against the individual defendants and on the administration of justice. It found that in making such an order there was a reasonable relationship and proportionality between the means employed and the aims sought to be achieved.

Further, in *Ebert v Birch* [1999] 3 WLR 670, it was held that as long as the court's inherent power to make *Grepe v Loam* orders is exercised only when it is appropriate to be exercised, there would be no contravention of Art 6.

Restraining unauthorised representatives

The court also has the power, in the exercise of its inherent jurisdiction to protect its processes from abuse, to restrain a person from conducting litigation, or exercising rights of audience on behalf of another person, where he is not authorised to do so under the Courts and Legal Services Act 1990 (*Noueiri v Paragon Finance plc* [2001] EWCA Civ 1402).

CHAPTER 25

OFFERS TO SETTLE AND PAYMENTS INTO COURT

INTRODUCTION

The system of Part 36 offers to settle and payments into court is designed to put pressure on parties to settle disputes rather than litigate them. Lord Woolf said, in his Final Report (FR):

> My approach to civil justice is that disputes should, wherever possible, be resolved without litigation. Where litigation is unavoidable, it should be conducted with a view to encouraging settlement at the earliest appropriate stage. (*Access to Justice*, FR, Chapter 10, para 2, www.dca.gov.uk/civil/final/index.htm.)

Lord Woolf described Part 36 as 'one of the cornerstones of the reforms of procedure made by the CPR' (*Petrotrade Inc v Texaco Ltd* [2001] 4 All ER 853).

Avoiding litigation and early settlements fall within the 'saving expense' part of the overriding objective (r 1.1(2)(b)), and Part 36 offers and payments can be seen as one of the main tools in bringing these results about. Part 36 provides a mechanism for a party, the offeror, to make an offer or payment to settle a dispute which, if rejected by the opponent, the offeree, and the case proceeds to trial, can be used as an indicator as to whether those proceedings were a waste of time and money.

If at trial judgment is given for the claimant which is the same as, or less than, the terms or amount of the defendant's Part 36 offer or payment then, on the face of it, the claimant will have wasted expense for both parties in litigating the matter rather than accepting the Part 36 offer or payment. Similarly, if at trial judgment is given for the claimant which is more than the terms or amount of the claimant's Part 36 offer to settle, the defendant will have wasted expense for both parties in litigating the matter rather than accepting the claimant's Part 36 offer. Therefore, Part 36 provides that such a party will be penalised for the wasted expense in taking the case to trial through costs or interest penalties, unless it would be 'unjust to do so'. The nature of the penalties imposed depends on whether the party is claimant or defendant. The risk of incurring those penalties operates as a tremendous pressure on parties to settle rather than litigate disputes.

In order to ensure that parties have an incentive to make Part 36 offers and payments, Part 36 provides that the successful offeree *will* be entitled to the costs and other benefits of having made a Part 36 offer or payment which is more generous than the amount or terms awarded at trial, *unless* it would be unjust to make such an order. However, as might be expected under the ethos of the new rules, the decision of the court as to whether a party should be subject or entitled to the costs and other penalties provided by Part 36 is not simply based on a 'mathematical' test of whether the offer or payment is better or worse than that ordered at trial. Rather, a Part 36 offer or payment will be viewed against the backdrop of the litigation as a whole and the conduct of the parties, particularly relevant in this context being the behaviour of the parties in disclosing material matters. Therefore, a party can be confident of obtaining the advantages provided by the system of Part 36 offers to settle and payments into court only if he has given full disclosure of all relevant evidence and information about his case so that the other side can make an informed decision whether to make or accept such an offer (see *Ford v GKR Construction* [2000] 1 All ER 802).

The position relating to Part 36 offers has been complicated somewhat by the fact that, under Part 44, the court, when dealing with costs, can consider any offer (or lack of offer) made in the proceedings (not just as to costs) whether or not it is Part 36 compliant.

Definitions and terminology

The types of offers that can be made under Part 36 are referred to as 'Part 36 offers' and 'Part 36 payments' (r 36.2(1)). A clear distinction should be made between a Part 36 offer to settle and a Part 36 payment into court and the circumstances in which each can be used.

A Part 36 payment is made only by parties in the position of a defendant and involves the payment of a sum of money into the Court Funds Office with notification to the claimant that this is the amount by which the defendant is prepared to settle the claim (r 36.2(1)(a); PD 36, para 1.1(1)). Parties in the position of a defendant include a claimant in his capacity as defendant to a counterclaim or other claims under Part 20, and the reference to a defendant in this chapter should be taken to include these parties (r 20.3).

A Part 36 offer involves a written offer to settle the claim on terms which may include the offer of a sum of money, but without actually paying that sum of money to the party or into court. A Part 36 offer may also consist of or include a non-monetary remedy, such as the giving of an undertaking (r 36.2(1)(b); PD 36, para 1.1(2)). Part 36 offers can be made by both claimants and defendants; for the latter, only in respect of non-money claims (r 36.3(1)).

The party who makes a Part 36 offer or payment is known as the 'offeror' and the party to whom it is made is known as the 'offeree' (r 36.2(2), (3); PD 36, para 2.2).

General overview of Part 36

Part 36 payments and Part 36 offers can be made only once proceedings have started (r 36.2(4)). However, there is also provision to make a pre-action offer to settle, which will be taken into account by the court when it comes to make an order as to costs, as long as it complies with the provisions of r 36.10. Once proceedings have started, a party can make a Part 36 offer or a Part 36 payment at any time, including in respect of appeal proceedings (r 36.2(4)(b)).

Part 36 provides that a party may make a Part 36 offer or payment in respect of first instance proceedings and a Part 36 offer or payment in respect of an appeal. If a claimant makes a Part 36 offer in respect of first instance proceedings which the defendant seeks to appeal, the claimant must make a separate Part 36 offer in respect of the appeal proceedings in order to obtain the benefits of Part 36 for the appeal proceedings. A party cannot make a 'portmanteau' offer which would provide him with protection both at first instance and on a subsequent appeal (*P & O Nedlloyd BV v Utaniko Ltd* [2003] EWCA Civ 174).

If the defendant makes a Part 36 offer or payment which is accepted by the claimant, or the claimant makes a Part 36 offer which is accepted by the defendant (in both cases within the specified timescale), the claimant will be entitled to his costs of the proceedings up to the date of acceptance of the Part 36 offer or payment (rr 36.13–36.15).

If a party makes a pre-action offer to settle or Part 36 offer or payment there is nothing to stop the other party making a counter-offer in response. Each offer or payment will then separately have the potential consequences provided for by Part 36 as long as it fulfils the necessary formalities.

Small claims

A Part 36 offer or payment will not have the costs or other consequences provided for by that Part while the claim is being dealt with on the small claims track, unless the court orders otherwise (rr 27.2 and 36.2(5)). Therefore, although a party is not prohibited from making a Part 36 offer or payment in cases dealt with on the small claims track, it will depend on the exercise of the court's discretion whether the costs or other consequences will be ordered against an offeree who fails to better the offer. It is submitted that in the light of the 'no costs rule' applicable to cases heard on the small claims track, the court is likely to make such an order only in exceptional circumstances, perhaps when a party is guilty of unreasonable behaviour such as would justify the court making a costs order against the unreasonable party in any event (r 27.14(2)(d)).

Rule 36.2(5) provides that the restriction on Part 36 applying to small claims hearings applies only while the claim is 'being dealt with' on the small claims track. This suggests that this restriction will cease to apply if the claim is subsequently re-allocated to another track.

PRE-ACTION OFFERS TO SETTLE

Before proceedings have started, parties can make pre-action offers to settle which the court will take into account when making any order as to costs as long as the offer complies with the provisions of r 36.10. The provisions of r 36.10 are that the offer must:

(a) be expressed to be open for at least 21 days after the date it was made;

(b) if made by a person who would be a defendant if proceedings were started, include an offer to pay the costs of the offeree incurred up to the date 21 days after the date it was made; and

(c) otherwise comply with Part 36 (r 36.10(2)).

Rule 36.10 provides that the offer is made on the date it was received by the offeree (r 36.10(5)). Therefore, this will be the actual date of receipt without taking into account any deemed time for service. There is no requirement that a pre-action offer to settle must be in writing, although in practice most will be.

Formal rules for service do not apply to the making of Part 36 offers to settle, which can therefore be made by sending the document by fax to the offeree's solicitors even where the solicitors have indicated on their writing paper that they do not accept service by fax (*Denise Charles v NTL Group Ltd* [2002] EWCA Civ 2004).

Rule 36.10 also provides that where proceedings are started, if the offeror is a defendant to a money claim, in order for his pre-action offer to settle to be taken into account by the court on the question of costs he must, within 14 days of service of the claim form, make a Part 36 payment into court of an amount which is not less than the sum offered before the proceedings began (r 36.10(3)).

Significance of pre-action offer once proceedings started

If a pre-action offer to settle is made in accordance with r 36.10 but rejected by the offeree and proceedings are started, the offer to settle will be taken into account by the court when any order for costs is made, even if no further Part 36 offer or payment is made.

The purpose of r 36.10 is to enable a party to make an offer which complies with Part 36, and has all the consequences of a Part 36 offer, before proceedings are commenced. Where an offer has been made before the commencement of litigation, which complies with r 36.10 and the remainder of Part 36, the court will take that offer into account as a Part 36 offer. Part 36 provides the claimant with an incentive to make an offer of settlement before proceedings are commenced in the same way as the claimant is provided with an incentive to make an offer to settle after proceedings have commenced (*Huck v Robson* [2002] EWCA Civ 398 at [51]–[56], *per* Parker LJ).

However, if the offeror is a defendant to a money claim, in order to have the consequences specified by Part 36, he must turn that offer to settle into a Part 36 payment within 14 days of service of the claim form. Further, the Part 36 payment must be for at least the same amount or more than the sum specified in the offer to settle (r 36.10(3)).

If the defendant makes a pre-action offer to settle and the claimant subsequently starts proceedings, the claimant is restricted in his freedom to accept the offer or any Part 36 payment (made in accordance with r 36.10(3)) without the permission of the court (r 36.10(4)). The claimant would therefore need to have a good reason for wanting to accept the offer or payment after he had implicitly rejected it by starting proceedings, with all their attendant cost both to the parties and the court system. This rule gives the court the opportunity to decide whether starting proceedings was an unreasonable step for the claimant to take rather than accepting the offer or payment which he now seeks to take. In these circumstances, the claimant would have to make an application to the court in accordance with Part 23 to accept the offer or payment, thus giving the court the opportunity to decide whether the claimant should be deprived of his costs or ordered to pay some or all of the defendant's costs.

If the claimant simply thinks better of carrying on with proceedings, having originally rejected the defendant's pre-action offer to settle, the likely order the court will make is an order that the defendant be awarded costs from the time when the claimant rejected the pre-action offer to settle (although the claimant is likely to be awarded the costs incurred before then). On the other hand, it may be that a defendant discloses relevant documents only at a late stage after proceedings have been commenced, which if revealed earlier would have caused the claimant to accept the offer. In the latter situation, it may well be reasonable for the claimant to seek to accept the offer after proceedings were commenced and be entitled to an award of costs on the basis that it was not unreasonable for the claimant to reject the earlier offer in the absence of the subsequently disclosed documents.

MAKING A PART 36 PAYMENT INTO COURT

The general rule is that, once proceedings have started, if the claimant's claim is for money and the defendant would like to make an offer to settle which will have the costs consequences provided by Part 36, if not accepted by the claimant the offer must be made by way of a Part 36 payment (r 36.3(1); PD 36, para 3.1). This is a strict rule subject to only two minor qualifications (see pp 385–86 below, 'Exceptions to requirement to make Part 36 payment in money claims').

However, in exercising its general discretion as to costs, the court is entitled to take into account any payment into court or admissible offer to settle, whether or not made in accordance with Part 36 (r 44.3(4)(c)). In *Amber v Stacey* [2001] 2 All ER 88, the claimant brought a claim for an unpaid invoice. After proceedings were commenced, by letter dated 1 October 1997, the defendant made an offer to settle the claimant's claim for £4,000. This offer was not accepted, and on 7 August 1998 the defendant made a payment into court in the sum of £2,000 and on 20 January 1999 a further payment into court in the sum of £1,000. At trial the claimant failed to recover more than the amount of the payment in. The trial judge ordered the claimant to pay the defendant's costs incurred from 1 October 1997 until 20 January 1999.

The Court of Appeal held that it was a proper exercise of the judge's discretion for him to make an order depriving the claimant of his costs over that period of time even though a Part 36 payment which exceeded the amount of the judgment was not made until 20 January 1999. The judge was entitled to take into account the claimant's unreasonable behaviour in refusing to accept the much higher offer to settle, as well as his precipitous conduct in commencing the proceedings when he did. However, the Court of Appeal held that the judge erred in law, and exceeded the wide discretion under r 44.3, when he ordered the claimant to pay the defendant's costs over the same period of time, as if the defendant had made a Part 36 payment into court on 1 October 1997 which exceeded the amount awarded at trial. The court was firmly of the view that a written offer to settle should not be treated as a precise equivalent to a payment into court. Although the court found that such an order should not have been made, it did not find the judge's order wholly wrong, and in order to give effect to the judge's views on relevant matters affecting the court discretion, the Court of Appeal ordered the claimant to pay a proportion, namely, one half of the defendant's costs, for the period 1 October 1997 to 20 January 1999.

Where the claimant's claim includes both a monetary and a non-monetary element, and the defendant wants to settle the whole claim, there is a special procedure which must be followed, but basically the defendant must make a Part 36 payment in respect of the monetary element (r 36.4(2)).

Like a Part 36 offer, a Part 36 payment can be made only once proceedings have started, but one can be made at any time after proceedings have started and can be made in appeal proceedings (r 36.3(2)). A Part 36 payment can be improved at any time and as many times as required.

Part 36 payment notice

A defendant who wishes to make a Part 36 payment must serve a Part 36 payment notice on the offeree. He must also file at court a copy of the Part 36 payment notice and a certificate of service confirming service on the offeree (PD 36, para 4.1(1), (2)). The defendant should also send the payment, usually a cheque, made payable to the *Accountant General of the Supreme Court*, to the Court Funds Office, along with a sealed copy of the claim form and a completed Court Funds Office Form 100 (PD 36, para 4.1).

However, different provisions apply for a litigant in person who does not have a current account, who may, in a claim proceeding in a county court or District Registry, make a Part 36 payment by lodging the payment in cash with the court and filing at the court the Part 36 payment notice and a completed Court Funds Office Form 100 (PD 36, para 4.2).

Form N242A may be used for the Part 36 payment notice, but it is not a prescribed form. However, in order to be a valid Part 36 payment notice, the notice must comply with the following requirements. It must:

- state the amount of the payment (r 36.6(2)(a));
- state that it is a Part 36 payment (PD 36, para 5.1(1));
- be signed by the offeror or his legal representative (PD 36, para 5.1(2)). If the Part 36 payment is made by a company or other corporation, in accordance with the general scheme under the Civil Procedure Rules (CPR), a person holding a senior position in the company or corporation may sign on the offeror's behalf, but that person must state what position he holds (PD 36, para 5.5);
- state whether the payment relates to the whole claim or to part of it, or to any issue that arises in it and, if so, to which part or issue (r 36.6(2)(b)). Therefore, the defendant can make a payment which relates either to the whole of the claimant's case or to just part of it. However, the defendant must state whether the payment is in whole or part settlement of the claimant's case and, if it is in part settlement, he must specifically identify which issue or issues he is offering to settle;
- state whether it takes into account any counterclaim (r 36.6(2)(c)). If the defendant is making a counterclaim, the claimant would obviously need to know if the defendant is also offering to settle the counterclaim at the same time and whether the amount paid in is only in respect of the claimant's claim or is the difference between the claimant's claim and the defendant's counterclaim. If the defendant did not have to so specify, as a counterclaim is treated as an independent claim in its own right (r 20.3), the claimant might unwittingly accept the sum paid in without realising that this does not bring the dispute to an end, as he still has to defend the defendant's counterclaim against him;
- if an interim payment has been made, state that the defendant has taken into account the interim payment (r 36.6(2)(d)). If the defendant has already made an interim payment, a claimant would need to know if the sum paid in is a clear sum in addition to the interim payment, or if it is a sum which includes the amount already paid by way of interim payment;
- if it is expressed not to be inclusive of interest, give the details relating to interest set out in r 36.22(2) (r 36.6(2)(e)). If the Part 36 payment notice is silent as to

interest, the sum offered will be treated as inclusive of all interest up until the last day it could be accepted without needing the permission of the court (r 36.22(1)). However, if the sum offered is expressed not to include interest, the Part 36 payment notice must state whether interest is offered and, if it is, give the amount offered, the rate or rates offered and the period or periods for which it is offered (r 36.22(2));

- provide certain additional information when benefit received by the claimant is recoverable under the Social Security (Recovery of Benefits) Act 1997 (r 36.23).

Deduction of benefits

In those cases where a claimant has received certain State benefits covering losses for which a defendant is liable, for example, where a claimant has been unable to work due to a personal injury and has been receiving income support, if the defendant makes a payment into court to settle the claim which is accepted by the claimant, the defendant will be liable to repay the benefit received by the claimant to the Secretary of State in accordance with the Social Security (Recovery of Benefits) Act 1997.

Therefore in those cases, if the defendant makes a Part 36 payment, the Part 36 payment notice must specify the amount of gross compensation paid, the name and amount of any benefit by which that gross amount is reduced and that the sum paid in is the net figure after deduction of the amount of the benefit (r 36.23(3)). If the claimant does not accept the Part 36 payment in, it will be the gross figure that the claimant has to beat in order to avoid the costs consequences under Part 36 (r 36.23(4)). In those cases where a claimant has or may have obtained recoverable State benefits, the defendant must obtain from the Secretary of State a certificate of recoverable benefits which specifies the type and amount of recoverable benefit the claimant has received. When making the Part 36 payment in, the defendant must file in court the certificate of recoverable benefits with the Part 36 payment notice (PD 36, para 10.1(2)).

Service of a Part 36 payment notice

The offeror must serve the Part 36 payment notice on the offeree; it will not be served by the court (r 36.6(3)). The offeror must also file a certificate of the service of the notice at court (r 36.6(3)). The usual methods of service apply to service of the Part 36 payment notice (r 36.8(2)).

Exceptions to requirement to make Part 36 payment in money claims

As was stated at p 383 above, the almost invariable rule is that where the claimant is making a monetary claim and the defendant wants to rely on the costs consequences provided by Part 36, he must make a Part 36 payment (r 36.3). However, this general rule is subject to two minor qualifications.

Interim payments

First, if a defendant has made an interim payment to the claimant and decides not to offer any further sum in settlement of the claim, he can make a Part 36 offer based on the interim payment (r 36.5(5)). Clearly, this exception will be of limited use as, almost by definition, an interim payment is of a sum that is less than the amount for which the defendant believes he is liable. Also, if the defendant wants to offer more than the amount provided by the interim payment, he must make a Part 36 payment of that additional sum in order to comply with r 36.3 and the payment in must state that it takes into account the interim payment (r 36.6(2)(d)). Thus, when a defendant has already made an interim payment to the claimant and decides to make that payment the final offer in settlement, the defendant can make an offer to settle by reference to that interim payment without making any further payment into court. That offer to settle will, for all intents and purposes, be treated as if it were a payment into court in the sum of the interim payment.

Certificate of recoverable benefits

Secondly, in those cases where recoverable benefits have been paid to the claimant and the defendant has applied for, but not yet received, a certificate of recoverable benefits (see p 385 above, 'Deduction of benefits'), the defendant can make a Part 36 offer to settle a monetary claim which will have the costs consequences provided by Part 36 as long as he makes a Part 36 payment of that amount not more than seven days after he receives the certificate (r 36.23(2)).

Split trial on liability and quantum

Where liability is denied by a defendant, the court can order that there be a separate trial on liability and then (if the claimant is successful) a separate assessment of the quantum of damages. This will often save expense, as time and costs will not have to be spent on the issue of the amount of damages until it is established whether the claimant will be successful. Where such an order is made, a defendant can make a Part 36 offer limited to accepting liability up to a specified proportion (r 36.5(4)). However, once (or even before) the trial on liability has been decided, in a money claim, the defendant must make a Part 36 payment in order to claim the consequences under Part 36 if the claimant fails to better the payment at any subsequent hearing to determine the amount of damages to which the claimant is entitled (r 36.3).

Provisional damages

Where there is a risk that as a result of personal injury the claimant may develop a serious disease or suffer some serious deterioration in his physical or mental condition, the claimant may seek additional damages to compensate for this risk. Alternatively, the claimant may make a claim for provisional damages against the defendant (see Chapter 26, 'Provisional Damages'). These apply where the claimant seeks a sum in damages from the defendant on the basis that he will not develop the disease or suffer the deterioration, but with the opportunity to return to court for further damages to be assessed if, within a specified timescale, in fact he goes on to develop the disease or suffer the deterioration. A defendant may make a Part 36 payment even when the claimant is also seeking provisional damages (r 36.7(1)). However, when making a Part 36 payment in this type of case, the Part 36 payment notice must specify whether or not the defendant is offering to agree to the making of an award for provisional damages (r 36.7(2)).

If the defendant is offering to agree to the making of an award for provisional damages, the Part 36 payment notice must also state:

(a) that the sum paid into court is in satisfaction of the claim for damages on the assumption that the injured person will not develop the disease or suffer the type of deterioration specified in the notice;

(b) that the offer is subject to the condition that the claimant must make any claim for further damages within a limited period and state what that period is (r 36.7(3)).

If the claimant does accept the Part 36 payment, he will also be entitled to his costs of the proceedings as provided by r 36.13 (r 36.7(4)). However, if the claimant accepts a Part 36 payment which includes an offer to agree to the making of an award for provisional damages, he must apply to the court within seven days of accepting the payment for the court to make an order for the award of provisional damages under r 41.2 (r 36.7(5)). At the same time as making the order, the court will also direct which documents are to be filed and preserved as the case file, which will be the basis for any future application for further damages (PD 41, para 2.1). The money in court will not be paid out until the court has dealt with the claimant's application for an award of provisional damages (r 36.7(6)).

Court Funds Office deposit account

If a Part 36 payment is made but not accepted by the claimant within the time specified, the money paid into court will be automatically placed on deposit by the Court Funds Office (Court Funds Rules 1987 (SI 1987/821), r 31(1)). On any later payment out of the money, unless the parties agree otherwise, interest accruing up to the date of acceptance will be paid to the defendant and interest accruing as from the date of acceptance until payment out will be paid to the claimant (PD 36, para 7.10). However, money paid into court which is accepted within the time specified will not be placed on deposit and will not accrue interest (Court Funds Rules 1987, r 32(4)).

Treating money paid into court as a Part 36 payment

The court has power to order a party to pay money into court in a variety of circumstances. It may be on the grounds that a party has without good reason failed to comply with a rule, practice direction or pre-action protocol (r 3.1(5)), or it may be as a condition for defending the claim (r 3.1(3)).

Where a defendant has been ordered to pay money into court under r 3.1(3) or r 3.1(5), he is entitled to treat the whole or any part of that sum as a Part 36 payment (r 37.2(1)). In order to do this, the defendant must file a Part 36 payment notice and then serve it on the other parties (r 37.2(2)). The payment into court will then be treated like any other Part 36 payment into court which the claimant can accept in settlement of the claim (r 37.2(3)).

The same provisions apply to a payment in made in accordance with a defence of tender before claim, that is, the defendant can elect to treat the whole or any part of the money paid into court as a Part 36 payment (r 37.3).

MAKING A PART 36 OFFER

Part 36 offers to settle can be made by both the claimant and the defendant once proceedings have started. As stated above, however, if the defendant is defending a money claim, he must make a Part 36 *payment* rather than a Part 36 offer (r 36.3). If the claim is not for a monetary remedy but instead for another remedy, such as an injunction or a declaration, a defendant can make a Part 36 offer on terms which, if not accepted by the claimant who goes on to receive an order on the same or less advantageous terms at trial, will, unless it is unjust to do so, have the costs and other consequences provided for by Part 36 (r 36.20).

A claimant can make a Part 36 offer to settle his own claim. That is, the claimant can offer to accept less money or less advantageous terms than he is claiming in his claim and, if the defendant rejects this offer, the consequences provided for by Part 36 will apply unless the court considers it unjust to make such an order (r 36.21).

Procedural requirements

In order to have the consequences specified by Part 36, a Part 36 offer must fulfil the following requirements:

- it must be in writing (r 36.5(1)). There is no prescribed form and it could be contained in a letter;
- the Part 36 offer must state that it is a Part 36 offer and be signed by the offeror or his legal representative (PD 36, para 5.1);
- it must state whether it relates to the whole of the claim or to part of it, or to an issue that arises in it and, if so, to which part or issue (r 36.5(3)(a)). Like a Part 36 payment, a Part 36 offer must state whether it is an offer to settle the whole claim or just part of it and, if only part of the claim, it must specifically identify which issue or issues it relates to;
- it must state whether it takes into account any counterclaim (r 36.5(3)(b)). Again, if the defendant is counterclaiming, the offeror must expressly state whether the terms offered take the counterclaim into account;
- if it is expressed not to be inclusive of interest, it must give the details relating to interest set out in r 36.22(2) (r 36.5(3)(c));
- if the Part 36 offer is silent as to interest, the sum offered will be treated as inclusive of all interest up until the last day it could be accepted without needing the permission of the court (r 36.22(1)). However, if the sum offered is expressed not to include interest, the Part 36 offer must state whether interest is offered and, if it is, give the amount offered, the rate or rates offered and the period or periods for which it is offered (r 36.22(2));
- if the Part 36 offer is made at least 21 days before the start of trial, it must state that it remains open for 21 days from the date it is made and also that if the offeree does not accept it within those 21 days, the offer can be accepted only if the parties agree the liability for costs or the court gives permission (r 36.5(6));
- if the Part 36 offer is made less than 21 days before the start of the trial, it must state that it can be accepted only if the parties agree the liability for costs or the court gives permission (r 36.5(7)).

In *Neave v Neave* [2003] EWCA Civ 325, the offer made by the claimant failed to specify, in accordance with r 36.5(6), that after 21 days the offer could be accepted only if the parties agreed the liability for costs or the court gave permission. The Court of Appeal held in that case that the requirements of r 36.5 are mandatory and failure to comply with them will mean that the offer to settle is not made in accordance with Part 36. However, where the offer to settle is expressed to be made pursuant to Part 36 and the failure to comply with the requirements of r 36.5 is a technical defect, which would not mislead a legally represented party, the court will readily relieve the offeror from the consequences of the mistake by exercising its discretion under r 36.1(2) to hold that, despite failing to comply with its requirements, the offer will have the consequences specified in Part 36. Although decided on other grounds, the Court of Appeal also indicated in *Mitchell v James* [2002] EWCA Civ 997 that it would have been prepared to use its power in r 36.1(2) to order that an offer had the consequences specified in Part 36 where there had been a failure to comply with r 36.5(6) in the circumstances where the defendants were legally represented and there was no evidence that they were misled. However, it should be noted that it is a question of the exercise of the court's discretion in the circumstances of a particular case and if, for instance, the offeree has been misled, or otherwise prejudiced by the defect, the court is unlikely to use its power under r 36.1(2) to waive the defect.

Terms as to costs

Where a claimant's offer to settle contains a term offering concessions on the claimant's costs, the court will not take that term into account when deciding under r 36.21 whether the defendant is liable for more, or the judgment against the defendant is more advantageous to the claimant, than the offer to settle (*Mitchell v James*). In *Mitchell v James*, the Court of Appeal was of the opinion that the terms of r 36.14 (which provide that the claimant will be entitled to his costs where the defendant accepts his Part 36 offer without needing the permission of the court) are inconsistent with a term as to costs being part of a Part 36 offer. Also, as there will have been no assessment of costs at that stage, it could not have been intended that the trial judge when giving his judgment would have to evaluate the quantum of his costs order, if the Part 36 offer includes a term as to costs. The Court of Appeal was further of the opinion that there would be a real risk of abuse if a term as to costs could be included in a Part 36 offer. This is because every claimant could make a Part 36 offer containing the terms sought in his claim, plus an offer as to costs, in the hope that if he succeeded in his substantive claim he would obtain indemnity costs in place of the ordinary award of costs on the standard basis.

Although a term as to costs is not within the scope of a Part 36 offer, that is not to say that a claimant cannot make an offer that includes a term as to costs which the court will have regard to when exercising its usual discretion in relation to inter-party costs at the end of the case (see Chapter 34, 'Costs of Proceedings').

Terms as to interest

A Part 36 offer or payment may include an offer as to interest on the debt or damages claimed (r 36.22). However, the court will not take into account any concession made by the claimant as to the uplift interest which may be awarded to him if the defendant fails to better the claimant's Part 36 offer when deciding whether the claimant has recovered more than, or the judgment against the defendant is more advantageous than, the terms of the claimant's Part 36 offer (*Ali Reza-Delta Transport Co Ltd v United Arab Shipping Co SAG* [2003] EWCA Civ 811).

CLARIFICATION OF A PART 36 OFFER OR PART 36 PAYMENT NOTICE

The offeror must provide certain prescribed information when making a Part 36 offer or payment. This includes such matters as whether the offer or payment is in settlement of the whole of the claimant's case or is made only in respect of certain issues in the case, and whether the offer or payment includes interest. It may be that the Part 36 offer or Part 36 payment notice is not entirely clear as to the basis on which it is made. In these circumstances, the offeree can request the offeror to clarify the offer or payment as long as he makes this request within seven days of the offer or payment being made (r 36.9(1)).

If the offeror does not voluntarily provide the information in clarification, as long as the trial has not started, the offeree can apply to the court for an order that such information is provided (r 36.9(2)). An application for clarification should be made in accordance with Part 23 (PD 36, para 6.2) and should state in what respects the Part 36 offer or Part 36 notice of payment needs clarification (PD 36, para 6.3).

If the court makes an order that the offeror clarify the offer or payment, it will also specify the date when the Part 36 offer or payment is treated as having been made (r 36.9(3)). Therefore, if the offer needs to be clarified and the court makes an order to this effect, the court is also likely to order that the offer or payment be treated as having been made from the date when the clarified Part 36 offer was received, or the clarified Part 36 payment served, on the offeree.

CLAIMS FOR A MONEY AND A NON-MONEY REMEDY

A claimant may claim both a money remedy and a non-money remedy such as an injunction. It would be open to a defendant to make a Part 36 payment to settle just the monetary part of the claim, or a Part 36 offer to settle just the non-monetary part of the claim. As set out above, the defendant's intentions as to whether it was the whole or part of the claim, and which part, that he was offering to settle must be specified in the Part 36 payment notice or Part 36 offer. However, a defendant may, on the other hand, wish to settle the whole claim by means of both a Part 36 payment in respect of the monetary element of the claim and a Part 36 offer in respect of the non-monetary element of the claim. If so, the defendant must follow the procedure set out in r 36.4 in order for the offer to settle to have the consequences set out in Part 36.

Procedure

In order to settle the whole claim by means of a money offer in respect of the money claim and a non-money offer in respect of the non-money claim, the defendant must make a Part 36 payment in relation to the money claim and a Part 36 offer in relation to the non-money claim (r 36.4).

The Part 36 payment notice must identify the document that sets out the terms of the Part 36 offer and state that if the claimant gives notice of acceptance of the Part 36 payment, he will be treated as also accepting the Part 36 offer (r 36.4(3)). Then, if the claimant gives notice of acceptance of the Part 36 payment, he will also be taken as giving notice of acceptance of the Part 36 offer in relation to the non-money claim (r 36.4(4)). In other words, the claimant cannot accept the Part 36 payment without also accepting the Part 36 offer.

Rule 36.4(4) does not expressly provide the same consequences if a claimant accepts the defendant's Part 36 offer (that is, that the Part 36 payment is also automatically accepted). However, the practice direction to Part 36 states that if the claimant accepts a Part 36 offer which is part of a defendant's offer to settle the whole of the claim, the claimant will be deemed to have accepted the offer to settle the whole of the claim (PD 36, para 7.11).

TIME WHEN A PART 36 OFFER OR PAYMENT IS MADE AND ACCEPTED

Part 36 puts a time limit on the ability of the offeree to accept a Part 36 offer or payment without the need either for the parties to reach an agreement as to the liability for costs, or for the permission of the court to be obtained. It is therefore important to know when the time limit starts to run and when acceptance has occurred.

Time when a Part 36 payment is made

Rule 36.8(2) states that a Part 36 payment is made when written notice of the payment into court is served on the offeree. This is further explained in PD 36 as meaning that the Part 36 payment is made when the Part 36 payment notice is served on the claimant (PD 36, para 3.2). The defendant must serve the Part 36 payment notice on the claimant and file a certificate of service of the notice at court (r 36.6(3)). The usual rules as to service will apply (see Chapter 10, 'Service of Documents').

If the defendant increases the amount paid into court, the increase in the Part 36 payment will be effective when notice of the increase is served on the offeree (r 36.8(4) and PD 36, para 3.3).

Time when a Part 36 offer is made

A Part 36 offer is made when received by the offeree (r 36.8(1)), that is, whenever the written document setting out the Part 36 offer is actually received by the offeree. Therefore, the rules for service of documents and deemed dates for service set out in Part 6 do not apply – the Part 36 offer is simply made when the document containing it is received by the offeree (*Charles v NTL Group Ltd* [2002] EWCA Civ 2004).

In *Charles v NTL Group Ltd*, the defendant sent a Part 36 offer for £50,000 to the claimant's solicitors, which was received by fax more than 21 days before the commencement of the trial. The defendant was entitled to make a Part 36 offer rather than a Part 36 payment because, at the time the Part 36 offer was made, the defendant had not received a certificate of recoverable benefits (r 36.23(2)). The defendant paid the sum offered (minus an interim payment and the recoverable benefits) into court two days after receipt of the certificate of recoverable benefits. At trial the claimant received less than the amount offered by the defendant in its Part 36 offer. However, the claimant argued that the Part 36 offer had not been validly served 21 days before trial because, contrary to Part 6, it had been served by fax even though the claimant's legal representative's letterhead made it clear that they were not willing to accept service by fax. The trial judge accepted the claimant's arguments and refused to take the Part 36 offer into account when he decided costs because he held the Part 36 offer had not been made 21 days before the start of the trial.

In setting aside the judge's order as to costs and substituting it with the usual costs order under r 36.20, the Court of Appeal held that a Part 36 offer was effected when received by the offeree without any need to comply with the provisions as to service contained in Part 6. The court noted that the formal rules for service did apply to Part 36 payments into court but understood the distinction as being that the whole question of offer and acceptance is based in contract law without the need for the involvement of the court, whereas a payment into court of necessity involves the court in the process and therefore the more formal requirement for service can be understood in that context.

If the offeror decides to improve the Part 36 offer, the improvement to the offer will be effective when its details are received by the offeree (r 36.8(3); PD 36, para 2.5).

In *Neave v Neave*, the claimant's offer to settle provided that it was open for acceptance for 21 days 'from today'. The offer to settle was sent to the defendant by fax the day after the date on the letter. The defendant argued that as an offer to settle is not made until it is received by the offeree, and the reference to 'today' meant the date of the letter, the offer did not comply with r 36.5(6)(a) because it was open for acceptance for only 20 days rather than 21 days as prescribed by the rules. However, the Court of Appeal held that, as a matter of construction, a letter which is expressed to be open 'for 21 days from today and is made pursuant to CPR 36' is intended to comply with r 36.5(6)(a) and ought to be read accordingly. Furthermore, a letter which is received by fax will ordinarily bear two dates – the date typed on the letter and the date of transmission supplied automatically by the sender's fax machine. The court held that if the dates differ then 'today' is more likely to mean, in the context of a letter which purports to contain a Part 36 offer, the date upon which the letter is sent and received, that is, the date of the fax transmission.

Acceptance of a Part 36 offer or payment

A Part 36 offer or Part 36 payment is accepted when notice of its acceptance is received by the offeror (r 36.8(5)). A notice of acceptance must be sent to the offeror and filed at court (PD 36, para 7.6). Court Form N243A can be used to accept the Part 36 payment, but it is not a prescribed form and there is no court form for acceptance of a Part 36 offer. What is prescribed is the information that must be contained in the notice of acceptance. The notice of acceptance must:

(a) set out the claim number;

(b) give the title of the proceedings;

(c) identify the Part 36 offer or Part 36 payment notice to which it relates; and

(d) be signed by the offeree or his legal representative (PD 36, para 7.7).

TIME LIMITS FOR ACCEPTANCE OF A PART 36 OFFER OR PAYMENT

If the offeror makes a Part 36 offer or payment into court at least 21 days before the start of the trial, the offeree can accept it without the court's permission if the offeree gives the offeror written notice of acceptance not later than 21 days after the offer or payment was made (r 36.11(1) and r 36.12(1)).

If the offeree does not accept the offer or payment within this 21-day time period, the offeree cannot subsequently accept it unless the parties agree the liability for costs, or, failing that, the offeree obtains the permission of the court (r 36.11(2)(b) and r 36.12(2)(b)).

Further, if the offeror makes a Part 36 offer or payment less than 21 days before the trial, the offeree cannot accept it without the permission of the court unless the parties agree what the costs consequences of acceptance will be (r 36.11(2)(a) and r 36.12(2)(a)).

If the court's permission is needed, it is obtained either by an application under Part 23 if made before trial, or by an application to the trial judge if made once the trial has started (PD 36, para 7.4). The court will also make an order regarding the costs of the proceedings. The court has a discretion to make any order as to costs, and this expressly includes the usual costs order which results when the claimant accepts a Part 36 offer or payment in (PD 36, para 7.5).

In *Barclays Bank plc v Martin & Mortimer* (2002) LTL, 19 August, it was confirmed that the court has a discretion whether or not to grant permission for a claimant to accept a Part 36 payment out of time, and it was not just a question of the court fixing the costs consequences of giving permission to accept a Part 36 payment out of time. In that case, the claimant brought a claim against the defendants for a negligent valuation. The defendants defended on substantial grounds, but also made an early payment into court of £52,000 that was not accepted by the claimant. Following the claimant's late disclosure of relevant documents the defendants obtained permission to re-amend their statement of case to plead a further ground for their defence. The claimant then applied for permission to accept the Part 36 payment out of time. The court held that when deciding whether to grant the claimant permission to accept a Part 36 payment out of time, it is necessary to consider the position of the defendant as well as that of the claimant, and in particular whether the circumstances had changed since the Part 36 payment was made and, if so, what caused the change in circumstances. The court had to decide, having regard to the relevant factors, what justice required as between the claimant and the defendant in the circumstances of each case.

In refusing the claimant permission to accept the Part 36 payment out of time, the court took into account:

(a) that the defendants had denied liability throughout;

(b) that the defendants had made a Part 36 payment at an early stage;

(c) that the defendants made the payment into court at a time when they were unaware of the points that were subsequently pleaded in the re-amended defence;

(d) that the defendants were not at fault in not raising the points before they had received disclosure of relevant documents; and

(e) that since that time the defendants' position had improved.

In the circumstances the court was of the opinion that it would be wholly inappropriate to grant the claimant permission to accept the Part 36 payment out of time, particularly as there was no way that the court could make an order for costs which would compensate the defendants for the consequences of having to pay over the sum of £52,000 to the claimant.

In the case of an offer or payment made less than 21 days before the start of the trial, the practical effect of the rule is that it prevents a claimant from offering or accepting a relatively low sum at a late stage after substantial costs may have been incurred, and also being automatically entitled to recover the whole costs of the claim on acceptance. The rule allows the court to consider the circumstances of each case and whether it was reasonable for a claimant to pursue a claim so far and perhaps incur substantial costs for a relatively small sum. Of course, it may be that the circumstances are such that the claimant should be entitled to his costs of the claim on acceptance in the usual way, but the rule operates as a safeguard in those cases where it would cause injustice if the usual rule were to apply.

Obtaining payment out of a Part 36 payment

If a claimant accepts a Part 36 payment, the claimant obtains payment out of the sum paid into court by filing a request for payment with the Court Funds Office in Courts Funds Office Form 201 (r 36.16; PD 36, para 8.1).

Certain information must be provided on Court Funds Office Form 201, such as the name, address and bank details of the legal representative acting on behalf of the claimant, or, if the claimant does not have a legal representative, his own details. If the claimant is legally represented, the payment out can be made only to the legal representative (see PD 36, paras 8.2–8.5 for details).

Children and patients

In the case of litigants acting under a disability, namely, a child or a patient, the court must approve any settlement made on their behalf (r 21.10). Therefore, if a Part 36 offer or payment is made in such proceedings, the court's permission must be obtained before it can be accepted. Further, a court order is needed before the sum paid into court can be paid out (r 36.18).

The application for approval is made in accordance with Part 23 (PD 36, para 7.8).

PRIVILEGE OF OFFER OR PAYMENT

There are restrictions on disclosure to the court of the fact that a Part 36 offer or payment has been made, or its contents, until all relevant questions of liability and quantum have been decided. The basis for this rule is that it is public policy to encourage parties to settle disputes rather than litigate them, and it is thought that a party would be reluctant to try to compromise a claim if statements or offers made in the course of such negotiations for settlement could be relied upon at trial as admissions of liability and quantum. Negotiations for settlement are, therefore, protected from disclosure by privilege.

The details of any offer or payment are usually put in a sealed envelope in the court file so that any judge dealing with the matter, especially the trial judge, will not be aware of it, although, by seeing the envelope, he may well be aware that an offer or payment has been made. At a case management conference the judge is likely, in any event, to ask if any offers or payments in have been made as part of his general case management powers and with a view to encouraging the parties to settle. If details are given, the judge should then disqualify himself from dealing with any trial if the claim is not settled. Similarly, the court's computerised history of the proceedings, a copy of which is often on the court file or called for by the judge, will not contain any details of any offer or payment.

Part 36 offer

A Part 36 offer is to be treated as 'without prejudice except as to costs' (r 36.19(1)). The Glossary to the CPR is not very illuminating and explains the phrase as meaning 'the circumstances in which the content of those negotiations may be revealed to the court are very restricted'. This phrase has been held to mean that the privilege by which such an offer to settle is protected from disclosure is modified so that there is a right to refer to the offer on the issue of costs (see *Cutts v Head* [1984] 2 WLR 349). Further, it has also been established that such offers, not being unreservedly 'without prejudice', can also be admissible in other circumstances if the fact that such an offer had been made was relevant, for instance, in interim matters such as an application for security for costs (see *Simaan General Contracting Co v Pilkington Glass Ltd* [1987] 1 All ER 345).

The nature of the protection given to such offers should be distinguished from fully 'without prejudice' offers. As a rule of evidence, the latter cannot be revealed to the court at all, at any stage of the proceedings, except with the consent (or by waiver) of both parties or to prove that a settlement has been reached if this is disputed (*Unilever v Procter & Gamble* [1999] 2 All ER 691).

Therefore, if a party makes a Part 36 offer, although it will not be admissible to the trial judge until all questions of liability and quantum have been determined, it will be admissible when the issue of costs comes to be decided. It is also likely that it will be admissible at interim hearings, even before the questions of liability and quantum have been decided, if it would be appropriate and relevant for it to be revealed to the court.

Part 36 payment

Rule 36.19(2) provides that the fact that a Part 36 payment has been made shall not be communicated to the trial judge until all questions of liability and the amount of money to be awarded have been decided. This restriction is equivalent to that applied to disclosure of an offer made 'without prejudice except as to costs'.

Therefore, as the rule specifically refers only to the trial judge, it would seem there is no general restriction on communication to a judge at an interim hearing where the fact of a payment in may be relevant to such matters as whether security for costs should be ordered or the size of an interim payment. This would be consistent with the former practice under the old rules and the position with Part 36 offers.

Rule 36.19(3) also expressly modifies any privilege from disclosure in the following circumstances:

(a) where the defence of tender before claim has been raised;

(b) where the proceedings have been stayed because a Part 36 offer or payment has been accepted;

(c) where the issue of liability has been determined before any assessment of the money claimed and the fact that there has or has not been a Part 36 payment may be relevant to the question of the costs of the issue of liability.

COSTS CONSEQUENCES OF ACCEPTANCE OF A PART 36 OFFER OR PAYMENT

Where the defendant makes a Part 36 offer or payment, or the claimant makes a Part 36 offer that is of a type which can be freely accepted within a 21-day period, and it is accepted by the claimant or defendant respectively, the claimant will be entitled to his costs of the proceedings up to the date of service of the notice of acceptance (rr 36.13(1) and 36.14). In these circumstances, a costs order will be deemed to have been made in the claimant's favour which, if necessary, the claimant can apply to enforce (r 44.12(1)(b) and (c)).

If the Part 36 offer or payment can be accepted only if the parties agree the liability for costs or the court gives permission, and the parties fail to reach an agreement, if the offeree applies for permission which is granted, the court will also make an order as to costs (r 36.11(3) and r 36.12(3)). The court will have a discretion as to the costs order to be made in all the circumstances of the case (see Part 44).

If the Part 36 offer or payment relates to part only of the claim and the claimant abandons the rest of the claim, although usually the claimant will still be entitled to the costs of the claim up to the date of service of the notice of acceptance, in the circumstances the court can make another order as to costs (r 36.13(2)). This will cover the situation where a claimant abandons a substantial part of his case, as it may well not be reasonable to do that without incurring any costs liability if substantial costs have been incurred pursuing that part of the claim.

The costs will include the claimant's costs in defending a counterclaim (if any) if the Part 36 offer or Part 36 payment notice states that it takes into account the defendant's counterclaim (r 36.13(3)). Obviously, if the counterclaim is not also settled at the same time, this will continue as a separate claim with an independent costs liability.

If the parties cannot agree a figure for the claimant's costs, on acceptance of a Part 36 offer or payment, the claimant will be entitled to costs on the standard basis (r 36.13(4)). In those cases where the court's permission is needed to accept the Part 36 offer and the court makes an order for costs, the court will also decide whether those costs are to be payable on the standard or indemnity basis (see Part 44).

Interest on costs

The claimant is also entitled to interest on costs paid on acceptance of a Part 36 offer or payment under s 17 of the Judgments Act 1838 (for High Court cases) and s 74 of the County Courts Act 1984 (for county court cases) at the statutory rate of interest which is currently 8% (see the Judgment Debts (Rate of Interest) Order 1993 (SI 1993/564)).

THE EFFECT ON THE PROCEEDINGS OF ACCEPTANCE OF A PART 36 OFFER OR PAYMENT

If a Part 36 offer or payment that relates to the whole claim is accepted, the claim will be stayed (r 36.15(1)). As the Glossary to the rules states, a stay imposes a halt on proceedings.

Although the claim has been stayed, it is expressly provided that this will not affect the courts' power to enforce the terms of a Part 36 offer, order payment out of the sum paid into court, or to deal with any question of costs relating to the proceedings (r 36.15(5)).

Although the claim has been halted, it must be remembered that it is not a final judgment in the claim and a stay can always be lifted. However, it would only be in exceptional circumstances that the court would allow a claimant to lift the stay and continue pursuing a claim once an offer or payment in compromise of the claim has been accepted, an example being where an agreement to settle has been induced by fraud.

Part 36 payment

In the case of a Part 36 payment, as the money is securely in court, on acceptance the Court Funds Office will simply pay the money out to the claimant (r 36.16; PD 36, para 8). Having accepted money paid into court and the proceedings having been stayed, the claimant would be unable to continue pursuing the claim unless the court lifted the stay. As stated above, this would be granted only in exceptional circumstances. Moreover, if the claimant started fresh proceedings based on the same claim, the defendant would, in most cases, be able successfully to apply for the new proceedings to be struck out as an abuse of process (see Chapter 24, 'Striking Out').

Part 36 offer

If a Part 36 offer that relates to the whole claim is accepted, the claim will be stayed (r 36.15(1)). Both parties can seek to enforce the terms of a Part 36 offer by simply applying to the court without the need to start a separate claim to enforce the compromise (r 36.15(2)). Somewhat repetitively, r 36.15(6) provides that where a Part 36 offer has been accepted and one party alleges that the other has not honoured the terms of the offer, and he is therefore entitled to a remedy for breach of contract, he may apply to the court for the remedy without having to start a new claim (unless the court orders otherwise). Therefore, although the Part 36 offer and acceptance will be binding as a contract between the parties, if either side fails to abide by the terms, the other party can apply to the court to enforce them without having to start entirely separate proceedings based on breach of contract.

Acceptance of Part 36 offer or payment relating to part only of the claim

If the Part 36 offer or payment relates to part only of the claimant's claim, the claim will be stayed as to that part only, and unless the parties agree the liability for costs these will be decided by the court (r 36.15(3)). The court has a discretion as to the costs and can make an appropriate order for costs depending on the relative importance of those issues which have been compromised and those which have not (*Clark Glodring & Page Ltd v ANC Ltd* (2001) LTL, 28 February).

MULTIPLE DEFENDANTS

Where a claimant is suing more than one defendant and the defendants jointly make a Part 36 offer or payment which the claimant accepts, the usual costs and other consequences will apply as if there was only one defendant to the claim. Therefore, the claimant will be able to enforce the Part 36 offer and the deemed costs order against one or all of the defendants. However, the position is more complicated when the claimant wishes to accept a Part 36 offer or payment made by one or more, but not all, of a number of defendants. The relevant rules that apply depend on whether, on the one hand, the defendants are sued jointly or in the alternative, or, on the other hand, whether they are sued on the basis of several liability.

If the defendants are sued *jointly* (that is, both deemed to be liable) or in the *alternative* (that is, either claimed to be liable), the claimant can accept the Part 36 offer or payment (within the specified timescale) without needing the permission of the court as long as he:

(a) discontinues his claim against those defendants who have not made the offer or payment; and

(b) those defendants give written consent to the acceptance of the offer or payment (r 36.17(2)).

On the other hand, if the defendants are sued on the basis of *several* liability, the claimant can accept a Part 36 offer or payment (within the specified timescale) made by one or more, but not all, of the defendants without needing the permission of the court and continue with his claims against the other defendants, if he is still entitled to (r 36.17(3)). If the claimant wants to accept a Part 36 offer or payment made by one or more, but not all, of the defendants in circumstances other than those set out in r 36.17(2) and (3), or outside of the specified timescale for acceptance, the claimant must apply to the court for an order permitting a payment out to him of any sum in court and such order as to costs as the court considers appropriate (r 36.17(4)).

WITHDRAWING A PART 36 OFFER OR PAYMENT

An offeror is free to withdraw a Part 36 offer before it has been accepted, but if it is withdrawn it will not have the consequences provided by Part 36 (r 36.5(8); see

Scammell v Dicker [2001] 1 WLR 631). In *Scammell v Dicker*, the Court of Appeal confirmed that a Part 36 offer can be withdrawn at any time prior to acceptance: a Part 36 offer is an offer to enter into a contract with the offeree, and Part 36 does not exclude the general law of contract that an unaccepted offer can be withdrawn.

However, a Part 36 payment can be withdrawn by the defendant only with the permission of the court (r 36.6(5)). A defendant should therefore consider very carefully the timing and amount of any payment into court as, once made, the presumption is that the claimant will be free to accept it (within the time limits) along with payment of his costs. In the usual course of events, it will be very unlikely for a defendant to have any desire to withdraw his payment in. The most likely reason why a defendant would wish to do so is if new evidence comes to light, or there is a change in the law which puts a different complexion on the claimant's case than it had at the time when the defendant made the payment in. In the case of new evidence, it is likely that the court will have to be persuaded that it is new evidence and not simply evidence that the defendant could have obtained, but did not obtain, before he made the payment in. Whatever the reason for wanting to withdraw a payment in, the court will have to be persuaded that, in accordance with the overriding objective, it would be fair to allow a defendant to withdraw money previously paid into court (*Marsh v Frenchay Healthcare NHS Trust* (2001) LTL, 3 August).

In *Marsh v Frenchay Healthcare NHS Trust*, the claimant brought a personal injury claim against the defendant for clinical negligence in carrying out an operation to remove a tumour from the claimant's brain. The defendant paid approximately £450,000 into court, which the claimant accepted in settlement of his claim. However, the defendant then applied to withdraw the whole or part of the payment in after it had obtained secret video evidence that, the defendant maintained, showed that the claimant had exaggerated the severity of his symptoms and misrepresented the extent of his capabilities. On appeal the court held that it would not be constrained by case law decided under the former rules and instead would adopt a flexible approach and consider the application in accordance with the overriding objective. After watching the video evidence, the court was not persuaded that it supported the defendant's contentions. Instead, the court was of the opinion that the payment into court was a calculated, across the board decision for good tactical reasons, which indeed brought forth the claimant's acceptance. The court therefore concluded that it would be unjust to hold that the video evidence entitled the defendant to withdraw the whole or any part of the payment in.

The defendant must seek the court's permission to withdraw a payment in even if the claimant does not accept the payment in within the time allowed without needing the permission of the court. However, if the claimant has not accepted within that timescale, it will be easier for a defendant to justify withdrawing a payment, as the claimant cannot accept it in any event unless the parties agree the liability for costs or the court gives permission.

REJECTION OF A PART 36 OFFER OR PAYMENT

If the offeree rejects a Part 36 offer or payment, the claim is pursued to trial and the offeree fails to better the offer or payment, the costs and other consequences as provided by Part 36 will then come into play. What those consequences may be will depend on whether the offeree is claimant or defendant. Often, both claimant and defendant will have made a Part 36 offer or payment and then various outcomes may be possible, depending on which party has beaten what.

Claimant fails to better defendant's Part 36 offer or payment

If, at trial, the claimant is successful, but in a money claim is awarded a sum in damages the same as or less than the defendant's Part 36 payment, or in a non-money claim the judgment is for the same or a less advantageous remedy than that offered by the defendant's Part 36 offer, the defendant will usually be entitled to the costs consequences provided by Part 36. Rule 36.20 provides that, unless the court considers it unjust to do so, the court will order that the claimant pay all of the defendant's costs incurred from the latest date on which the claimant could have accepted the Part 36 offer or payment without needing the permission of the court.

This is often referred to as a 'split' order as to costs. This means that although the defendant is likely to be ordered to pay the claimant's costs incurred up to the last date for acceptance of the Part 36 offer or payment, the claimant will usually be ordered to pay the defendant's costs incurred thereafter. As the defendant's costs will, at this stage, include the costs of trial, they are likely to be substantial.

Although the rule is in mandatory terms, that is, that the court 'will' order the claimant to pay the defendant's costs in these circumstances, this is subject to the qualification '[u]nless [the court] considers it unjust to do so'. This gives the court the scope to make a different costs order in relation to the defendant's costs incurred after the claimant rejected the defendant's Part 36 offer or payment.

An example of a case where the defendant made a Part 36 payment which exceeded the claimant's award of damages, but was nevertheless ordered to pay the claimant's costs and was not granted a 'split' order for costs under r 36.20 because the court decided that it would be unjust to grant the defendant such an order, is *Ford v GKR Construction* [2000] 1 All ER 802. This was a personal injury claim where the defendants took the opportunity, during an adjournment of the trial, to employ inquiry agents to carry out secret video surveillance of the claimant. This video evidence clearly showed that the claimant was able to do more things than she had admitted in her testimony. The defendants were given leave to adduce this evidence at trial and, as a result, the judge awarded the claimant less damages than the amount of the defendants' payment into court. However, when it came to making an order for costs, the judge refused to grant the defendants the split order as to costs provided by r 36.20. The judge decided – and his decision was upheld by the Court of Appeal – that it would be unjust to make the costs order provided by r 36.20 in the defendants' favour because the defendants had behaved unreasonably in obtaining and disclosing evidence which undermined the claimant's case only at a late stage in the proceedings. In the absence of this evidence, the claimant was not in a position to assess whether she should accept the defendants' payment into court at the time when it was made.

The Court of Appeal emphasised in this case that the parties must provide each other with as much information about their case as possible as early as possible, so that an offeree can make an informed decision as to whether to accept a Part 36 offer or payment. This case underlines the philosophy behind the CPR for openness and co-operation between the parties. It also places an onus on parties to prepare their cases fully at an early stage, or run the risk of being effectively penalised under the rules for late preparation.

However, it should be stressed that the presumption is that it will be quite rare for a defendant to be deprived of the costs penalties against a claimant under r 36.20 when the claimant fails to better a Part 36 offer or payment. Lord Woolf, in *Ford v GKR*, stated that the provisions of rr 36.20 and 36.21 provide the 'usual consequences of not accepting an offer which, when judged in the light of the litigation, should have been accepted'.

Claimant betters his Part 36 offer

If at trial the defendant is held liable to the claimant for more, or the judgment against the defendant is more advantageous to the claimant, than the proposals contained in a claimant's Part 36 offer, the court will order the consequences against the defendant provided by r 36.21 unless it considers it unjust to do so (r 36.21(4)). It should be borne in mind that the successful claimant will be entitled to damages, or a non-monetary remedy, from the defendant in any event, and in most cases to interest and costs as well if he is successful at trial, but when a defendant also fails to better the claimant's Part 36 offer, the defendant also becomes subject to the penalties provided by Part 36. The defendant may be liable for all or any of the following:

(a) an order to pay the claimant's costs on the indemnity basis from the latest date when the defendant could have accepted the offer without needing the permission of the court (r 36.21(3)(a));

(b) interest on those costs at a rate not exceeding 10% above base rate (r 36.21(3)(b)); and

(c) in a money claim, the defendant may be ordered to pay the claimant interest on any sum of money awarded (not including interest) at a higher rate than usual but not exceeding 10% above base rate, for some or all of the period starting with the latest date on which the defendant could have accepted the offer without needing the permission of the court (r 36.21(2)).

Rule 36.21 contains a list of what the court may take into account when considering whether it would be unjust to make the order. It provides that the court will take into account all the circumstances of the case, including:

(a) the terms of any Part 36 offer;

(b) the stage in the proceedings when any Part 36 offer or payment was made;

(c) the information available to the parties at the time when the Part 36 offer or Part 36 payment was made; and

(d) the conduct of the parties with regard to the giving or refusing to give information for the purposes of enabling the offer or payment into court to be made or evaluated (r 36.21(5)).

An order under r 36.21 should be the usual consequence where a Part 36 offer has been made, has not been accepted and has been beaten at trial. The trial judge must therefore start from the basis that the claimant is entitled to an order for costs, and on the indemnity basis, unless he considers it unjust not to make such an order (*Neave v Neave* [2003] EWCA Civ 325 at [10], [41], *per* Chadwick LJ). It was said in *Mitchell v*

James [2002] EWCA Civ 997 that 'Injustice in the eyes of the court is therefore the only basis on which the court could refuse to make an order for indemnity costs and interest. That does not confer a general discretion on the court' (at [33], *per* Gibson LJ).

In *Neave v Neave*, Chadwick LJ held that where there has been a Part 36 offer, the court will fail properly to exercise its discretion as to costs unless it considers whether r 36.21 is applicable (that is, whether the defendant is held liable for more, or the judgment against the defendant is more advantageous to the claimant, than the proposals contained in the claimant's Part 36 offer) and, if relevant, whether in the circumstances of the case it would be unjust to make an order in favour of the claimant.

Neave v Neave was a claim brought by a mother against her son for the recovery of nine historic vehicles the claimant alleged had been transferred to her under her late husband's will. At trial the judge awarded the claimant damages for the defendant's trespass in coming onto the claimant's property to take some of the vehicles, and held that the claimant was entitled to six out of the nine vehicles she claimed. The trial judge expressed the view, in strong terms, that the litigation should never have been brought or defended and was critical of both parties' behaviour, commenting that the motivation for the litigation was not an interest in historic vehicles but 'another chapter in an appalling family rift giving rise to the mutual desire to hurt and wound'.

In deciding the issue of costs, the trial judge acknowledged the general rule that the unsuccessful party should be ordered to pay the successful party's costs, but held that in the light of the parties' conduct, taking into account all the circumstances of the case in accordance with r 44.3(4) and (5), the claimant should receive only one-third of her costs from the defendant. However, in making that order the judge did not take into account whether the claimant had obtained a more advantageous judgment than her Part 36 offer, in which she offered a compromise on the basis that she should have five vehicles and the defendant should have four.

The Court of Appeal found that the judge was wrong not to address the question whether his judgment was more advantageous to the claimant than her Part 36 offer to settle and, if so, whether he should make a costs order in her favour under r 36.21. The Court of Appeal did conduct that exercise and found that the judgment was at least £2,500 more advantageous to the claimant than the terms of her Part 36 offer to settle. The court therefore made an order under r 36.21 for payment of the claimant's costs on the indemnity basis from the latest date on which the defendant could have accepted the claimant's Part 36 offer without needing the permission of the court. The court also awarded interest on those costs at 4% over base rate.

The court further found that there were no factors in *Neave*, arising either from the particular matters which the court is required to take into account under r 36.21(5), or more generally, which would make it unjust to make the orders provided by r 36.21. This was because the requirement to take all the circumstances into account must be read in context. In the context of this case, where litigation should never have been brought or defended, 'steps taken to bring the litigation to an end should be encouraged and not discouraged; should be rewarded and not disappointed' (at [43]).

It is accepted that the consequences of r 36.21 are draconian for a defendant, and they are intended to be so in order to discourage defendants from rejecting reasonable Part 36 offers. It is also felt that unless the powers to award indemnity costs and additional interest conferred by r 36.21 are exercised in a way that makes a material, albeit proportionate, difference to the outcome of the case, the rule will become otiose (*Richard Little and Others v George Little Sebire and Co* (1999) *The Times*, 17 November).

The purpose of r 36.21 is to encourage a claimant to make a Part 36 offer, in the same way that r 36.20 encourages a defendant to make a Part 36 payment or offer. In *Neave v Neave*, Chadwick LJ explained that the benefit to a claimant in making a Part 36 offer lies in the costs consequences that follow if the offer is not accepted. The risk in making the offer is that if the offer is accepted the claimant will lose the opportunity to argue the case and risk doing worse than if no offer were made. He stressed that it was therefore important that where the claimant's offer is not accepted, the claimant should not be deprived, without good reasons, of the benefit which has been held out to him as an inducement to make the offer. He felt that if claimants and their advisers come to think that Part 36 offers will not have the costs consequences which r 36.21 provides, they will be much less likely to make such offers, whereas the making of Part 36 offers, which, if accepted, lead to the settlement of litigation and the saving of costs, is to be encouraged (at [41]).

In *Huck v Robson* [2002] EWCA Civ 398, the claimant made an offer to settle her personal injury claim arising out of a narrow road collision on the basis that she would accept a 95%:5% split on liability. That offer was rejected and at trial the claimant succeeded in establishing that the defendant was 100% liable for the accident. However, the trial judge refused to order that the claimant was entitled to indemnity costs under r 36.21 on the grounds that the claimant's offer to settle was derisory and was not a genuine attempt at settlement as it was inevitable that the defendant would reject it. The Court of Appeal allowed the claimant's appeal and ordered the claimant's costs to be assessed on the indemnity basis. It was held that where a claimant has bettered his Part 36 offer he has a *prima facie* entitlement to indemnity costs, the general presumption that a successful claimant only receives costs on the standard basis being displaced by r 36.21.

Although it was accepted that if it was self-evident that the offer made was merely a tactical step designed to secure the benefit of the incentives provided by r 36.21, for example an offer to settle for 99.9% of the full value of the claim, the judge would have a discretion to refuse indemnity costs, the court found that this was not the case with this offer. The offer in this case provided the defendant with a real opportunity for settlement even though it did not represent any possible apportionment of liability. The court held that the fact that it was inevitable that the defendant would reject the offer made by the claimant was an irrelevant factor in deciding whether the award of costs to the claimant on the indemnity basis would be unjust. The Court of Appeal emphasised that when deciding whether it would be unjust to award the claimant his costs on an indemnity basis the court must take into account justice in the individual case it has to decide, not justice in general between claimants and defendants, or views as to social policy in general.

Although only r 36.21 specifies this list of circumstances which the court will take into account when deciding whether it is unjust to make the order, it seems, in the light of *Ford v GKR* [2000] 1 All ER 802, that the court will in fact carry out this exercise whenever it has to decide whether it is unjust to apply the costs or other penalties under either Part 36.20 or Part 36.21.

The powers to award such penal interest on sums recovered or indemnity costs are in addition to the court's usual powers to award interest to the claimant (r 36.21(6)). However, r 36.21(6) makes it clear that where the court awards interest under this rule on the same sum and over the same period as it awards interest under a different power, the total rate of interest awarded may not exceed 10% over base rate.

In *All-in-One Design and Build Ltd v (1) Motcomb Estates Ltd (2) Whiteswan (Worldwide) Ltd* (2000) *The Times*, 4 April, the claimant made an offer to settle which was not accepted by the defendant. The claimant then went on to recover more than the amount of its Part 36 offer at trial. As part of its order for costs under r 36.21, the court ordered interest on the judgment sum at 10% over base rate. The defendant argued that awarding the claimant such a rate of interest was more than was required to compensate the claimant and was punitive and therefore unjust, and that as a result r 36.21 was *ultra vires* the Civil Procedure Act 1997. On appeal, the court held that r 36.21 was not *ultra vires* the Civil Procedure Act 1997. The court accepted that the function of an award of interest under s 35A of the Supreme Court Act 1981 and s 69 of the County Courts Act 1984 is to compensate a claimant for being kept out of his money. However, it found that the function of the power under r 36.21 to award enhanced interest is to sanction a party for failing to accept a reasonable offer and thereby unnecessarily prolong the litigation. The court found that there were many instances of powers to impose sanctions throughout the CPR. Indeed, imposing such sanctions would give effect to the express purpose of the Civil Procedure Act 1997, which is to make the justice system accessible, fair and efficient.

The interaction of Part 36 and Part 44

Rule 36.1(2) states that:

> Nothing in this Part prevents a party making an offer to settle in whatever way he chooses, but if that offer is not made in accordance with this Part, it will only have the consequences specified in this Part if the court so orders.

Those last words make it clear that the court has a discretion to waive Part 36 requirements. This is reinforced by r 44.3, which deals with the circumstances to be taken into account by the court when exercising its discretion as to costs. Rule 44.3(4)(c) states that in deciding what order (if any) to make about costs, the court must have regard to all the circumstances, including any payment into court or admissible offer to settle made by a party which is drawn to the court's attention (whether or not made in accordance with Part 36).

This rather wide approach to the court's discretion has been tempered somewhat by the Court of Appeal in *Amber v Stacey* [2001] 2 All ER 88, in which it stated that there are compelling reasons of both principle and policy why those prepared to make genuine offers of monetary settlement should do so by way of Part 36 payments rather than by way of written offers. The Court of Appeal said that Part 36 payments offer greater clarity and certainty about:

(a) genuineness;

(b) ability to pay;

(c) whether the offer was open or without prejudice; and

(d) the terms on which the dispute could be settled.

Effect of claimant's Part 36 offer to settle where summary judgment is obtained

It has been held in the case of *Petrotrade Inc v Texaco Ltd* [2001] 4 All ER 853 that r 36.21 does not apply where summary judgment is given, as the provisions of that rule have effect only 'where at trial' the defendant is liable for more than the proposals contained in a claimant's Part 36 offer. In giving the judgment of the Court of Appeal in this case, Lord Woolf recognised that this may act as a temptation to claimants not to seek summary judgment in cases where it could be obtained, with the objective of obtaining higher rates of interest at the conclusion of a trial. However, he warned that such a course would be 'entirely contrary to the whole ethos and policy of the CPR' and he was confident that if it was shown that such a tactic had been used, the court would use its ample powers to ensure that the claimant did not benefit from it.

Lord Woolf also stressed that the court always had power to order costs on an indemnity basis and to award interest at such rate as it considered just, this power being re-enacted in Part 44. If this case had been decided by Lord Woolf at first instance, he would have been inclined to award additional interest at the rate of 4% above base rate for a period of 12 months, as well as making an order for indemnity costs from the time of the Part 36 offer.

As the wording of r 36.20 is the same as r 36.21 in referring to 'trial', it would appear that the same provisions would apply if the claimant obtained summary judgment against the defendant but was awarded terms less favourable or a sum less than the defendant's Part 36 offer or payment into court. In such circumstances, it seems a defendant could not rely on obtaining the costs benefit provided by r 36.20.

Claimant betters defendant's Part 36 offer or payment but fails to better own Part 36 offer

Under the terms of Part 36, as long as the claimant betters the defendant's Part 36 offer or payment, he will not be subject to any penalty under Part 36 if he does not also better his own Part 36 offer. In those circumstances, the usual costs order is likely to apply, namely, that the defendant pay the claimant's costs of the proceedings.

A claimant therefore has this advantage over a defendant. If a defendant makes his Part 36 offer or payment too low and it is not accepted by the claimant, he will suffer a disadvantage as he will fail to secure the 'split' order as to costs and, in all likelihood, end up paying the claimant's costs of the claim. However, the claimant suffers no similar disadvantage if he makes his Part 36 offer too high. If the defendant rejects the claimant's Part 36 offer and the claimant does not better his offer at trial, there is no adverse consequence provided by Part 36 for the claimant.

As the claimant will have succeeded at trial, he is likely to recover his costs of the claim from the defendant regardless of whether he also betters his Part 36 offer. However, this is not to say that the court will not take into account the fact that the claimant recovered less than his own Part 36 offer when exercising its discretion as to the making of costs orders under Part 44, although it is expressly provided in para 8.4 of PD 44 that this circumstance alone will not lead to a reduction in costs awarded to the claimant.

CHAPTER 26

PROVISIONAL DAMAGES

INTRODUCTION

Definition

Under s 32A of the Supreme Court Act 1981 (SCA) and s 51 of the County Courts Act 1984 (CCA), in a claim including a claim for damages for personal injury in which there is a chance that at some time in the future the injured person will, as a result of his injuries, develop some serious disease or suffer some serious deterioration in his physical or mental condition, the court has the power to make a judgment awarding damages to the injured person on the assumption that he will not develop the disease or suffer the deterioration, but with an order that further damages will be awarded in the future if he does so. Such an award of damages is known as provisional damages (r 41.1(2)(c)).

If a claimant in a personal injury case obtains evidence to show that a consequence of his injuries caused by the defendant is that he runs a risk of developing another disease or of suffering a deterioration in the future, he can either claim damages on a 'once and for all basis', which includes a sum in compensation for carrying this risk, or he can seek an order for provisional damages. A claimant in such circumstances will have to weigh up the advantages and disadvantages in seeking damages in full and final settlement, which include an element to compensate him for this risk, or in seeking an order for provisional damages, which will not give him any additional sum immediately but which would allow him to make an application for further compensation if the disease or deterioration occurs in the future.

OBTAINING AN AWARD OF PROVISIONAL DAMAGES

Conditions for making an award of provisional damages

The court may make an order for an award of provisional damages if the particulars of claim include a claim for them and if the court is satisfied that s 32A of the SCA or s 51 of the CCA applies (r 41.2(1)). Therefore, it is important when drafting proceedings to consider whether a claim for provisional damages should be included (see Chapter 12, 'Statements of Case', for the matters that must be pleaded when making a claim for provisional damages).

Terms of the order for provisional damages

The order for provisional damages must specify the disease or type of deterioration in respect of which an application for compensation can be made at a future date, and specify the period of time within which the application can be made (r 41.2(2)(a) and (b); PD 41, para 2.1). The time period must be specified but can be expressed as being for the duration of the claimant's life (PD 21, para 2.3).

An award of provisional damages can be made in respect of more than one type of disease or deterioration, and for each can specify different time periods within which an application can be made (r 41.2(2)(c)).

The Annex to PD 21 sets out a form for the terms of a provisional damages judgment (PD 21, para 2.6).

The case file

If an order for provisional damages is made, the court will make an award of immediate damages for the claimant's existing injuries and specify which documents are to be filed and preserved as the case file in respect of any application for further damages (PD 41, para 2.1).

The case file is likely to include such documents as a copy of the judgment, the statements of case, medical reports and a transcript of relevant parts of the claimant's evidence. If further orders are made, for instance, extending the time within which an application for further damages can be made, a copy will be added to the case file (PD 41, paras 3.2, 3.4). The associate or court clerk will endorse the court file to show that it contains the case file documents and in order to identify the period of time within which the case file documents must be preserved, and preserve them in the court office where the proceedings took place (PD 41, para 3.3).

The practice direction expressly reminds legal representatives of their duty to preserve their own case file, which is sensible given the time period which may elapse before an application for further damages may be made (PD 41, para 3.6).

Agreeing provisional damages by consent

If the parties agree to compromise a claim on grounds that include provisional damages, they should apply under Part 23 for an order to approve judgment by consent (PD 41, para 4.1).

The order for judgment by consent should contain the matters which would be specified in any court order for provisional damages following judgment, and a direction should be given specifying the documents to be preserved as the case file, and the documents specified should be lodged at court by the claimant or his legal representative (PD 41, paras 4.2, 4.3).

Applying for further damages

Once the time period specified by the order has expired, the claimant cannot apply for further damages in respect of the disease or deterioration under the order for provisional damages (r 41.3(1)). However, the claimant can make a number of applications to extend the time period originally specified (r 41.2(3)).

It is likely that the claimant will have to establish grounds to justify making an extension of time, and a current medical report should be filed at the time of making the application (PD 41, para 3.5).

A claimant is limited to making one application for further damages under the order for provisional damages (r 41.3(2)).

Procedure for applying for further damages

The claimant must give the defendant (and his insurers, if known) at least 28 days' written notice of his intention to apply for further damages (r 41.3(3) and (4)). Within 21 days after the end of the 28-day notice period, the claimant must apply to the court for directions (r 41.3(5)).

An application for further damages is made under Part 23 and follows the same procedure as that for applications for an interim payment (r 41.3(6)). Therefore, a copy of the application notice must be served on the respondent at least 14 days before the hearing of the application and must be supported by evidence. The evidence must establish the claimant's entitlement to the further damages. The respondent to the application must file and serve any written evidence on which he intends to rely at least seven days before the hearing of the application. If the applicant wishes to rely on written evidence in reply, he must file and serve a copy at least three days before the hearing (see r 25.6).

JUDGMENT IN DEFAULT WHERE PROVISIONAL DAMAGES CLAIMED

If the defendant fails to respond to the claimant's particulars of claim, which include a claim for provisional damages, the claimant cannot enter judgment in default under Part 12 unless he abandons his claim for provisional damages.

Instead, if the claimant wishes to continue his claim for provisional damages, he should make an application under Part 23 to the Master or district judge for directions (PD 41, para 5.1). The Master or district judge will then direct the issues to be decided, being, in most cases, whether the claim is an appropriate one for an award of provisional damages and the amount of immediate damages. If an award of provisional damages is made, provisions for the preservation of the case file will be made (PD 41, paras 5.2 and 5.3).

CHAPTER 27

SPECIAL RULES FOR CHILDREN AND PATIENTS

INTRODUCTION

There are special rules governing proceedings involving children and patients that take account of the fact that such parties are usually not able to act on their own behalf and to ensure that any settlement is in their interests and for their benefit. In general, a child or patient acts through a litigation friend, who is usually a parent or guardian or someone else who is responsible for their welfare. If there is no such party, the Official Solicitor will be appointed to act as litigation friend.

Under the old rules, children were referred to as 'infants' and a distinction was made between a 'next friend' and a 'guardian *ad litem*', the former acting for a plaintiff and the latter for a defendant. In accordance with the ethos of the reforms, the Civil Procedure Rules (CPR) introduced simplified and modernised terminology for the rules relating to children and patients, so, for instance, both now act through a litigation friend, whether they are bringing or defending proceedings.

DEFINITIONS

Child

A child is a person under 18 (r 21.1(2)(a)), replacing the expressions 'infant' and 'minor'. It is possible for a child also to be a patient, which may be relevant if the condition persists after he has ceased to be a child, especially with regard to any money awarded to the child.

Patient

A patient is a person who, by reason of a mental disorder within the meaning of the Mental Health Act 1983, is incapable of managing and administering his own affairs (r 21.1(2)(b)). 'Mental disorder' is defined by s 1(2) of the Mental Health Act 1983 as 'mental illness, arrested or incomplete development of mind, psychopathic disorder and any other disorder or disability of mind'. Thus the definition is very wide. There are basically three categories of people who come within the definition: those with a mental illness; those with learning disabilities; or those with brain damage.

The evidence of a medically qualified person is required for a diagnosis of a mental disorder, and the court should not take that burden upon itself just because someone appears to be a difficult litigant. It may be necessary to stay proceedings until this issue has been resolved, with the court conducting an inquiry, on notice to the party in question, with appropriate medical evidence. Where there are difficulties in obtaining such evidence, the Official Solicitor may be consulted.

Litigation friend

A litigation friend is a person who brings or defends proceedings on behalf of a child or patient. There may not be more than one litigation friend for the child or patient in any particular proceedings.

A litigation friend has a duty to conduct proceedings fairly and competently on behalf of the child or patient. He must not have any interest in the proceedings adverse to the child or patient, and every step and decision he takes in the proceedings must be for the benefit of the child or patient (PD 21, para 2.1). He is required by para 2.3 of PD 21 to state in the *'certificate of suitability'* that he consents to act and knows or believes that party to be a child or patient.

A litigation friend may be a parent or guardian, the person with whom a child or patient resides or who has care of him, or a person who is authorised under Part VII of the Mental Health Act 1983 to conduct proceedings on behalf of a patient. Alternatively, the litigation friend may be the Official Solicitor (as long as provision is made for his charges) (PD 21, para 3.6).

PROCEEDINGS BY OR AGAINST PATIENTS

A patient *must* have a litigation friend to bring or defend proceedings on his behalf (r 21.2(1)).

Title of proceedings involving a patient

The title of any proceedings involving a patient should give the name of the patient followed in brackets by the name of the litigation friend and the words, 'his/her litigation friend' (PD 21, para 1.3).

PROCEEDINGS BY OR AGAINST CHILDREN

A child must have a litigation friend to conduct proceedings on his behalf unless the court makes an order allowing the child to act on his own behalf (r 21.2(2) and (3)).

Application for an order permitting a child to act on his own behalf

The application for an order permitting the child to act on his own behalf may be made by the child himself. The application should be made in accordance with Part 23 and, if the child already has a litigation friend, must be made on notice to him, otherwise it should be made without notice (r 21.2(4)).

However, if the court makes an order permitting a child to act without a litigation friend, but it subsequently becomes apparent that it is desirable for the child to have a litigation friend, the court may appoint a person to be the child's litigation friend (r 21.2(5)).

Title of proceedings involving a child

If the child has a litigation friend, the title of the proceedings should give the name of the child followed in brackets by the words, 'a child by [name] his/her litigation friend' (PD 21, para 1.5(1)).

If the child is conducting proceedings on his own behalf, the child should be referred to in the title by his name followed in brackets by the words 'a child' (PD 21, para 1.5(2)).

BECOMING A LITIGATION FRIEND

A person may not become a litigation friend for either a child or a patient, whether by court order or under any other entitlement, unless he satisfies the following conditions:

(a) he can fairly and competently conduct proceedings on behalf of the child or patient;

(b) he has no interest adverse to that of the child or patient; and

(c) where the child or patient is a claimant, he undertakes to pay any costs which the child or patient may be ordered to pay in relation to the proceedings (subject to any right he may have to be repaid from the assets of the child or patient) (rr 21.4(3), 21.6(5)).

Order appointing a litigation friend

Under r 21.6, the court has the power to appoint a person to be a litigation friend, of either a child or a patient, as long as it is satisfied that the person meets the requirements set out in r 21.4(3) (above). An application to appoint a litigation friend should be made in accordance with Part 23 and may be made either by the person who wishes to be the litigation friend, or by a party to proceedings (r 21.6(2), (4); PD 21, para 3.2). The application must be supported by evidence, which can be in the form of a witness statement, or within the application notice itself if it contains a statement of truth that the person consents to act as a litigation friend and which satisfies the court of the matters referred to in r 21.4(3).

In the event of difficulty in finding a suitable litigation friend, it may be necessary to approach the Official Solicitor. He can be appointed to act only if he consents, and he will consent only if there is no one else suitable to take up the post. The Official Solicitor to the Supreme Court may be contacted at 81 Chancery Lane, London WC2A 1DD, tel 020 7911 7127.

The application notice must be served on the following specified people:

(a) in the case of a child, one of the child's parents or guardians, or, if there is no such person, the person with whom he resides or in whose care the child is (PD 21, paras 2.4(1) and 3.3(1));

(b) in the case of a patient, on the patient, unless the court orders otherwise (r 21.8(2); PD 21, para 3.3(2)), and on the person authorised under Part VII of the Mental Health Act 1983 to conduct proceedings on his behalf, or, if there is no such person, on the person with whom he resides or in whose care the patient is (PD 21, paras 2.4(2) and 3.3(1)).

Stage when litigation friend becomes necessary

A claimant must apply for an order appointing a litigation friend for a child or patient against whom he is proceeding if the child or patient has no litigation friend (and the court has not made an order allowing a child to act for himself) and either someone who is not entitled to be a litigation friend files a defence, or the claimant wishes to take some step in the proceedings (apart from issuing and serving a claim form) (rr 21.3(2)(b) and 21.6(3)).

If a party becomes a patient during proceedings, no party may take any step in the proceedings without the permission of the court until the patient has a litigation friend (r 21.3(3)). Also, a person may not make an application against a child or patient before proceedings have started without the permission of the court (r 21.3(2)(a)).

If a party takes any step in the proceedings before a litigation friend has been appointed, it shall be of no effect, *unless the court orders otherwise* (r 21.3(4)). Thus, it is possible for the court to make an urgent order in proceedings involving a child or patient before the appointment of a litigation friend, taking into account all the relevant circumstances and provided there will be no prejudice to the child or patient.

Procedure for becoming a litigation friend without a court order

If a person is authorised under Part VII of the Mental Health Act 1983 to conduct legal proceedings in the name of, or on behalf of, a patient, he is entitled to be the litigation friend of the patient in any proceedings to which his authority extends (r 21.4(2)). Such a person must file an official copy of the order or other document which constitutes his authorisation to act (r 21.5(2)).

A person who is not so authorised under the Mental Health Act 1983, or who wishes to act for a child, may become a litigation friend for a child or patient without a court order by filing a certificate of suitability stating that he satisfies the conditions set out in r 21.4(3) (r 21.5(3)).

In either case, if he is acting for the claimant, the person who wishes to act as the litigation friend must file the authorisation or certificate of suitability at the same time the claim form is issued; if he is acting for the defendant, at the time when he takes a step in proceedings on behalf of the defendant (r 21.5(4) and (5)).

The certificate of suitability must also be served on every person on whom the claim form should be served, and a certificate of service must be filed at the same time (rr 21.5(6) and 6.6). The specified persons are those referred to above under PD 21, para 2.4.

Contents of a certificate of suitability

The certificate of suitability must be signed in verification of its contents and contain the following statements by the person wishing to be the litigation friend:

• that he consents to act;

• that he knows or believes that the litigant is a child or patient;

- in the case of a patient, the grounds of his belief as to why he is a patient and attaching any relevant medical opinion;
- that he can fairly and competently conduct proceedings on behalf of the child or patient and that he has no adverse interest to that of the child or patient; and
- where the child or patient is the claimant, an undertaking to pay any costs which the child or patient may be ordered to pay (subject to any right he may have to be repaid from the assets of the child or patient) (PD 21, para 2.3(2)).

Form N235 (Certificate of Suitability of Litigation Friend) can be used.

Changing a litigation friend or preventing a person from acting as a litigation friend

The court has the power to terminate the appointment of a litigation friend, or substitute a different person as litigation friend or make an order that a person may not act as litigation friend (r 21.7(1)).

An application for the court to exercise its powers in that way must be made in accordance with Part 23, giving the reasons why the order is sought, and be supported by evidence (r 21.7(2); PD 21, para 4.2).

Under r 21.7(3), the court may not substitute a new litigation friend unless it is satisfied that the proposed person is a suitable person to act as such in accordance with the requirements of r 21.4(3).

The application must be served on the persons specified in para 2.4 of PD 21, the person who is currently the litigation friend, or purporting to act as the litigation friend, as well as the person who it is proposed should be the litigation friend (unless he is the applicant) (r 21.8(3); PD 21, para 4.4).

The court may appoint the person proposed or any other person who complies with the conditions specified in r 21.4(3) (r 21.8(4)).

PROCEDURE WHERE A LITIGATION FRIEND IS NO LONGER NECESSARY

Children

Where a litigant who was formerly a child, who is not also a patient, reaches the age of 18, a litigation friend's appointment automatically ceases (r 21.9(1)).

Notice that appointment of litigation friend for a child has ceased

The litigant who was formerly a child must then serve notice on the other parties stating that he has reached full age, that the appointment of the litigation friend has ceased, giving his own address for service and stating whether or not he intends to carry on with the proceedings (r 21.9(4); PD 21, para 5.2). When the litigant who was formerly a child reaches 18, the litigation friend may also serve a notice on all the other parties stating that his appointment has ceased, whether or not the former child does so (PD 21, para 5.4). The litigation friend may do so in order to avoid any further liability for the costs of the former child.

Title of proceedings after litigation friend's appointment ceases

On reaching full age, if the child carries on with the proceedings he will subsequently be described in the proceedings by adding the following words in brackets after his name, 'formerly a child but now of full age' (PD 21, para 5.3).

Consequences of failure to serve the notice

If the child does not serve such a notice on the other parties within 28 days of the appointment of the litigation friend ceasing, an application can be made for the court to strike out the child's claim or defence (r 21.9(5)).

Litigation friend's liability for costs

Once the litigation friend's appointment has ended, he has an incentive to ensure that the other parties are notified of this because until such time as they are, he will remain liable for the child's or patient's costs of the proceedings (r 21.9(6)). The litigation friend's liability for costs will end only when the child or patient serves the notice referred to in r 21.9(4), or the litigation friend serves notice on the other parties that his appointment to act has ceased (r 21.9(6)).

Patients

When a patient recovers and ceases to be a patient, the litigation friend's appointment will not cease until it is ended by court order (r 21.9(2)).

The former patient, the litigation friend or a party may make the application to the court for an order ending the litigation friend's appointment (r 21.9(3)). The application must be supported by evidence in the form of a medical report indicating that the patient has recovered and is capable of managing and administering his property and affairs. If the patient's affairs were under the control of the Court of Protection, the application must include a copy of the order or notice discharging the receiver. If the application is made by the patient, it should include a statement indicating whether or not he intends to carry on with or continue to defend proceedings (PD 21, para 5.7).

Notice that appointment of litigation friend for a patient has ceased

If the order is made, it must be served on the other parties to the proceedings and the former patient must file and serve on the parties a notice stating that his litigation friend's appointment has ceased, giving his own address for service and stating whether or not he intends to carry on with or continue to defend the proceedings (r 21.9(4); PD 21, para 5.8).

The same potential consequences apply to the former patient who fails to serve such a notice as apply to a similar failure by a former child, and the litigation friend's liability for costs continues in the same way until such a notice is filed and served (r 21.9(5) and (6)).

COMPROMISE BY OR ON BEHALF OF A CHILD OR PATIENT

In the light of the potential vulnerability of a litigant who is a child or patient, any settlement or compromise of proceedings, whether brought by or against such a litigant, will not be valid unless approved by the court (r 21.10(1); PD 21, para 1.6). It should be noted that this includes an agreement for the apportionment of a sum to a dependent child under the Fatal Accidents Act 1976 (PD 21, para 1.6 and paras 7.1–7.3). This will enable defendants to obtain a valid discharge from the claim, and will protect children and patients from any lack of skill and experience on the part of their legal representatives (*Black v Yates* [1999] 4 All ER 722). It will also ensure that the legal representatives are paid a proper and reasonable amount for their fees.

A settlement will include where the child or patient accepts a Part 36 offer to settle, or payment into court or provisional damages, for which, therefore, the court's approval must also be sought.

Also, under the common law, in many instances, a contract between a child and another person is not binding unless the child ratifies the contract on reaching the age of 18. As a result of this, if a claim made by or against a child is compromised before proceedings are started, there is a procedure for the court to approve the settlement; and if it is approved, the settlement is binding and enforceable (r 21.10(2)).

Court approval of compromise or settlement of proceedings

An application should be made in accordance with Part 23 and should include the following information:

- whether and to what extent the defendant admits liability;
- the age and occupation (if any) of the child or patient;
- the litigation friend's approval of the proposed settlement or compromise; and
- in a personal injury claim arising from an accident, details of the accident, copies of any medical reports, information required under Part 16 for statements of case in personal injury claims, evidence and details of police reports and criminal prosecutions (if applicable) (PD 21, para 6.2).

Counsel's opinion

Unless it is a very straightforward case, counsel's opinion should also be obtained as to the merits of the settlement or compromise. A copy of the opinion, including the instructions sent to counsel, should also be supplied to the court when the application for approval is made (PD 21, para 6.3).

Court approval of compromise or settlement before proceedings have started

The same information and requirement for counsel's opinion as are required once proceedings have started are necessary for an application for approval of a compromise or settlement made before proceedings have started. However, the application is made in accordance with Part 8. The Part 8 application must include a request for approval of the settlement or compromise and, in addition to the details of the claim, set out the terms of the settlement or compromise or attach a draft consent order in Practice Form N292 (r 21.10(2)(b); PD 21, para 6.1).

Judge hearing the application

The application for approval of the compromise or settlement, both before and after proceedings have started, is normally heard by a Master or district judge (PD 21, para 6.4). The hearing should normally be attended by the litigation friend and child or patient, unless this is not practical or there is some other good reason.

Hearing in public or private

The general rule is that all hearings are to be held in public (r 39.2(1)). This accords not only with the CPR, but is also in accordance with Art 6 of the European Convention on Human Rights as incorporated into the Human Rights Act 1998. However, this general rule is subject to a power to order that proceedings be heard in private if a private hearing is necessary to protect the interests of any child or patient (r 39.2(3)(d); PD 39, para 1.6).

Although the court has the power to direct that a hearing be held in private where it involves the interests of a child or patient, including the approval of a compromise or settlement or an application for the payment out of court of money to such a person, there is no presumption that such a hearing will be in private. In fact, in *Beatham v Carlisle Hospitals NHS Trust* (1999) *The Times*, 20 May, Buckley J held that the approval of a settlement on behalf of a child or patient and the reasons for that decision would normally be given in public, but any part of the hearing which requires details of the negotiation to be given to the court to justify the approval should be dealt with in private. It was stated in that decision that in order to avoid the need for a private hearing, counsel's opinion, as required under PD 21, para 6.3, should be provided to the court in advance of the hearing.

COURT CONTROL OF MONEY RECOVERED BY OR ON BEHALF OF A CHILD OR PATIENT

The court will take steps to ensure that money paid by or on behalf of a child or patient is administered for the benefit of the child or patient (r 21.11(1)). In the exercise of this power, the court may order that the money be paid into court and invested, or otherwise dealt with (r 21.11(2)).

Investment on behalf of a child

The money is usually transferred to the Investment Division of the Public Trust Office to be applied for the benefit of the claimant as the court sees fit. The court will normally give directions as to the investment of the money on Form CFO320. There is usually a choice between high interest or equity investment, or, more popularly, a combination of the two.

Application may be made from time to time for payment out of moneys in the fund but moneys should be paid out only if they are clearly for the maintenance, education or benefit of the child (PD 21, para 12.1). This may include, for example, money to buy a computer or to pay for a school holiday, but close scrutiny will be given by the court to ensure that the payment out is to benefit the child and not as an indirect means of benefiting the parent.

Where a child reaches full age, his fund in court, if it is money, will be paid out to him, and if it is in the form of investments such as shares or unit trusts it will be transferred into his name (PD 21, para 12.2).

Rule 21.12 and PD 21, paras 8.1–12.3, should be consulted for details as to the court's power to order investments and as to the appointment of the Official Solicitor to be guardian of a child's estate.

Investment on behalf of a patient

The Court of Protection is responsible for protecting the property of patients and is given extensive powers to do so under the Mental Health Act 1983. Fees are charged for the administration of funds by the Court of Protection, and these should be provided for in any settlement (PD 21, para 11.1).

In the case of a patient, if the moneys are substantial (over £30,000), the question of the administration of them should be left to the Court of Protection (PD 21, para 11.2(1)). If the sum is less than £20,000 it may be retained in court and invested in the same way as for a child, and in the case of sums between these two amounts the advice of the Master or the Court of Protection should be sought (PD 21, para 11.2(2), (3)).

Applications can be made for payment out of money in the fund in the same way as for a child (PD 21, para 12.1; see above).

COSTS PAYABLE TO OR BY A CHILD OR PATIENT

There are special rules as to the assessment of costs payable by or to a child or patient (r 48.5). This will usually be a detailed assessment (r 48.5(2)), but the court may decide that this should be dispensed with (PD 48, para 51.1).

SERVICE OF DOCUMENTS ON A CHILD OR PATIENT

The claim form

The claim form must be served on the following specified people:

(a) in the case of a child, one of the child's parents or guardians, or, if there is no such person, the person with whom he resides or in whose care the child is;

(b) in the case of a patient, on the person authorised under Part VII of the Mental Health Act 1983 to conduct proceedings on his behalf, or, if there is no such person, on the person with whom he resides or in whose care the patient is (r 6.6(1)).

Any other document

Apart from the claim form, a party wishing to serve a document on a child or patient in proceedings must serve it on the child's or patient's litigation friend (r 6.6(1)). Obviously, if the court has made an order giving a child permission to act on his own behalf, a party should serve the document on the child.

STATEMENTS OF TRUTH IN PROCEEDINGS INVOLVING A CHILD OR PATIENT

The rules require that certain documents *must* be verified by a statement of truth, such as a statement of case or a witness statement, and certain documents *may* contain a statement of truth, such as an application notice (see r 22).

Statement of truth by a litigation friend

If a litigation friend is appointed, a statement of truth in a statement of case, a response under r 18.1 providing further information, or an application notice is a statement that the litigation friend (as opposed to the child or patient) believes that the facts stated in the document being verified are true (r 22.1(5)). The statement of truth must be signed by the litigation friend or his legal representative (r 22.1(6)(a)). However, it should be noted that the statement of truth in a witness statement should be made and signed by the person making the statement (r 22.1(6)(b)). Therefore, this will be the child or patient if he makes a witness statement.

JUDGMENT IN DEFAULT AGAINST A CHILD OR PATIENT

If proceedings are brought against a child or patient, but he fails to respond to the particulars of claim within the time period specified by the rules, the claimant can obtain judgment in default only by making an application to the court under Part 23 (rr 12.4, 12.10). If a litigation friend has not been appointed for the child or patient, or the court has not made an order permitting a child to act on his own behalf, the claimant will have to apply for a litigation friend to be appointed before making the application to enter judgment in default (rr 21.3(2)(b) and 21.6(3)).

CHAPTER 28

CHANGE OF SOLICITOR

INTRODUCTION

If a client retains a solicitor to act in a matter, a solicitor acting for another party, who knows the other party has retained a solicitor to act, should not communicate directly with the other party except with the consent of the other solicitor (see The Law Society, *Guide to the Professional Conduct of Solicitors*, 8th edn, Chapter 19, www.guide-on-line.lawsociety.org.uk).

If a solicitor has notified the other party that he is acting for his client and confirmed that he is authorised to accept service of proceedings, that solicitor must be served with proceedings. A solicitor so acting for his client is known colloquially (but not in the Civil Procedure Rules (CPR)) as being 'on the record'. If a solicitor ceases to act for the client, there is a requirement to notify the court and the other parties accordingly; similarly if a party instructs a solicitor having formerly acted in person.

SOLICITOR ACTING FOR A PARTY

A solicitor is treated as acting for a party when the address for service of documents is the business address of the solicitor (r 42.1).

The address for service is that defined by r 6.5. Rule 6.5(2) requires a party to give an address for service within the jurisdiction. Where a solicitor is acting for a party, the address for service is the solicitor's business address. However, where the document to be served is the claim form, the address for service will be the solicitor's business address if the solicitor is authorised to accept service (r 6.13). Where the defendant is a company and its solicitor has agreed to accept service, if nevertheless service is effected on the defendant itself, in accordance with the Companies Act 1985, service is still good (*Cranfield v Bridgegrove Ltd and Other Cases* [2003] EWCA Civ 656; see Chapter 10, 'Service of Documents', for details about the rules for service on a party's solicitor).

Where a party or his solicitor changes his address for service, a notice of that change should be filed and served on every party (PD 42, para 2.3).

Duty to give notice of a change of solicitor

A party or his solicitor (where one is acting) must serve on every party notice of a change of solicitor, or that a solicitor has ceased to or started to act, in the following circumstances:

(a) a party for whom a solicitor is acting wants to change his solicitor;

(b) a party, having conducted the claim in person, appoints a solicitor to act on his behalf (except where the solicitor is appointed only to act as an advocate for a hearing); or

(c) a party, after having conducted the claim by a solicitor, intends to act in person (r 42.2(1)).

Where a party changes his solicitor or, having conducted the claim by a solicitor, intends to act in person, the party or his solicitor (where one is acting) must also serve the notice on his former solicitor (r 42.2(2)).

It is only after the notice has been served on all the parties (and any former solicitor) that it should then be filed at court (PD 42, para 1.2).

Notice of change of solicitor

Practice Form N434 should be used. This contains the following information:

(a) that a party has changed solicitor, or that a solicitor has ceased to or started to act for the party, as the case may be;

(b) the party's new address for service;

(c) that the notice has been served on all the parties and, where applicable, the former solicitor (r 42.2(3) and (4)).

The notice should be filed in the court office in which the claim is proceeding (PD 42, para 2.5).

Solicitor 'on record' until notice is served or court order made

Where a party has changed his solicitor or intends to act in person, the former solicitor will be treated as the party's solicitor unless and until a notice of change of solicitor is served, or the court makes an order that the solicitor has ceased to act (r 42.2(5)).

Order that a solicitor has ceased to act

Whether a solicitor's retainer has ended is a question of fact. It usually continues either until the solicitor discharges himself or until death. However, in *Donsland Ltd v Van Hoogstraten* [2002] EWCA Civ 253, where the client was the claimant company and it was the sole director who died, the court held that the company's solicitors still had instructions to act as the company still existed.

A solicitor may apply for an order that he has ceased to be the solicitor acting for a party (r 42.3(1)). The solicitor may do this when he has terminated the retainer in circumstances when he can show just cause to do so, for example, when the client fails or refuses to provide instructions or money on account, or to pay an interim bill, but the client fails or refuses to file and serve a notice that his solicitor has ceased to act for him.

A solicitor will be obliged to seek such an order if the client refuses to file and serve the necessary notice as, in these circumstances, the solicitor cannot sign the notice on the client's behalf but is still treated as the solicitor on the record for that client until a notice is served by the former client or his new solicitor, or the court makes an order.

The former client must be served with notice of the application, unless the court orders otherwise. The application should be made in accordance with Part 23 and supported by evidence (r 42.3(2); PD 42, para 3.2). In straightforward cases, this can be dealt with by the court without the need for a hearing (see *Miller v Allied Sainif*

(UK) Ltd (2000) *The Times*, 31 October, Ch D, *per* Neuberger J). However, the application should not be served on any other party to the proceedings, as this may injure the client's interests.

If the court makes an order that the solicitor has ceased to act, a copy of the order must be served on every party to the proceedings. In accordance with the usual rule, service will be effected by the court; but if the party or the solicitor serves notice instead, a certificate of service in Practice Form N215 must also be filed (r 42.3(3); PD 42, para 4.3).

If the court makes such an order, the party must give a new address for service within the jurisdiction (PD 42, para 5.1). If the party does not notify the other parties of a new address, the address for service of that party will be determined in accordance with the table in r 6.5(6).

Legal Services Commission (LSC) funded client or assisted person

If the certificate of an LSC funded client or an assisted person is revoked or discharged, the solicitor's retainer ends on receipt of the notice of revocation or discharge of the certificate (reg 4 of the Community Legal Service (Costs) Regulations 2000 (SI 2000/441); reg 83 of the Civil Legal Aid (General) Regulations 1989 (SI 1989/339)).

If the LSC funded or assisted person wishes to continue with the proceedings, if he appoints a solicitor to act on his behalf he must file and serve a notice of change of solicitor in accordance with r 42.2(2). If he wishes to act in person, he must give an address for service (r 42.2(6)).

Where the LSC funded or assisted person's certificate is revoked or discharged and the solicitor therefore ceases to act, and the former client wishes to act in person or to appoint another solicitor to act on his behalf, the former solicitor must also file and serve on every other party a notice of the change giving the last known address of the former LSC funded or assisted person (PD 42, para 2.2).

APPLICATION BY ANOTHER PARTY TO REMOVE A SOLICITOR

Where a solicitor who has acted for a party has died, become bankrupt, ceased to practise or cannot be found, and the party has not given notice of a change of solicitor or notice of intention to act in person in accordance with r 42.2(2), any other party may apply for an order declaring that the solicitor has ceased to be the solicitor for the other party in the case (r 42.4(1)).

The application should be made in accordance with Part 23 and supported by evidence and served on the party to whose solicitor the application relates, unless the court orders otherwise (PD 42, para 4.2). Where the court makes an order, the same provisions apply as to service of the order as where the court makes an order following a solicitor's application for a declaration that he has ceased to act (see pp 422–23 above, 'Order that a solicitor has ceased to act').

Where a party seeks to remove solicitors acting for its opponent on the grounds of a conflict of interest, the court has the power to order the solicitors be removed from the record (*Re L (Minors) (Care Proceedings: Cohabiting Solicitors)* (2000) *The*

Times, 27 July), but it does not have jurisdiction to order a party to instruct further solicitors (*SMC Engineering (Bristol) Ltd v Alastair Duff Fraser and Another* (2001) *The Times*, 26 January, CA; and see below, 'Court's inherent power to remove a solicitor').

COURT'S INHERENT POWER TO REMOVE A SOLICITOR

The court has an inherent power to remove a solicitor from the record where it is in the interests of fairness and justice to do so. However, it is recognised that the exercise of this power is in conflict with the right of a litigant to choose his legal representatives and it is therefore exercised only with extreme caution.

The court exercised this power to remove solicitors from the record in the case of *Re L (Minors) (Care Proceedings: Cohabiting Solicitors)* by making a declaration that those solicitors were no longer acting. The grounds for the declaration were that the solicitors on the opposing sides were cohabiting and it was felt that on discovering this an unsuccessful lay client might believe that there would therefore be bias. Wilson J said in that case: 'It was not disputed that the court had power to determine whether a particular firm of solicitors should play a role in the forensic exercise of which it was the director.' Striking features in that case which led to the exercise by the court of this power included the fact that the application was for care orders and that one of the cohabitants had conduct of the case on behalf of the local authority exercising powers as the arm of the State.

Where a party is entitled to proceed in person, the court has no jurisdiction to order that he instructs a firm of solicitors to act for him (*SMC Engineering (Bristol) Ltd v Alastair Duff Fraser and Another*).

Court's power to refuse to hear a particular advocate

The court has an analogous power under s 27(4) of the Courts and Legal Services Act 1990 to refuse to hear a particular advocate.

In *Noueiri v Paragon Finance plc* [2001] EWCA Civ 1402, the court made an order restraining an unqualified advocate from exercising rights of audience and rights to conduct litigation on behalf of any other party, apart from himself, except with the permission of the High Court or Court of Appeal, on the grounds that, in the circumstances of that case, it was in the public interest to do so.

CHAPTER 29

DISCLOSURE OF DOCUMENTS

INTRODUCTION

Prior to the introduction of the Civil Procedure Rules (CPR) there had been a long tradition in our jurisdiction of an extensive obligation to disclose relevant documents in the course of proceedings. This included disclosing not only documents which would be evidence of an issue in the action, but also those 'which it was reasonable to suppose, contained information which *may*, either directly or indirectly, lead the party seeking disclosure to a train of inquiry which enabled him to advance his own case or to damage that of his adversary' (paraphrasing Brett LJ in *Compagnie Financière et Commerciale du Pacifique v Peruvian Guano Co* (1882) 11 QBD 55). Moreover, a distinctive feature of our common law system, in comparison to that on the continent for instance, is an obligation to disclose documents damaging to one's own case.

The rules on disclosure were substantially reformed with the introduction of the CPR in an attempt to limit the extent of the process. Therefore, although in appropriate circumstances extensive orders for disclosure can be made, most orders made under the CPR will be limited to *standard disclosure*. Also, whereas under the former rules an order for disclosure was made in every case as a matter of course, this is not the position under the CPR. Furthermore, when an application for more extensive disclosure than standard disclosure is made, the court applies a cost–benefit analysis when deciding whether to grant the order in a particular case.

It will be noted that the old expression 'discovery' has been replaced with 'disclosure' and that added to the obligation to disclose is the obligation to search for relevant documents. Proportionality and reasonableness have also been added to the duty to search and disclose.

Proportionality and disclosure

Rule 31.3(2) enables a party to refuse to give inspection of documents if it would be disproportionate to do so. This may apply, for example, where extricating requested documents from a vast quantity of documents may not be reasonably viable having regard to all the circumstances of the case. Similarly, the duty to search contained in r 31.7 is tempered by the factors to be taken into consideration under r 31.3(2). In the disclosure statement, reference may also be made to the question of proportionality when explaining why some documents were not searched for and disclosed.

Proportionality is an important principle in the area of disclosure (*Simba-tola v Elizabeth Fry Hostel* [2001] EWCA Civ 1371). In *Simba-tola*, the claimant brought a claim under the Race Relations Act 1976 that she had been a victim of racial discrimination by other residents at a bail hostel. It was further alleged that staff at the hostel had failed to prevent the abuse and had victimised the claimant. The defendant denied racial discrimination. It contended either that no member of staff was present during the alleged incidents of abuse by other residents, or that staff warned the resident concerned and took appropriate action. The defendant also alleged that at times the claimant behaved in an aggressive way.

The claimant applied for full and proper disclosure of documents held by the hostel, including specific disclosure of the personal files of the residents she alleged abused her. In response the defendant disclosed the log book, message book and the personal file that was held for the claimant.

The Court of Appeal upheld the judge's decision to refuse an order that the defendant disclose the personal files of the other residents on the grounds that the defendant's log book recounted the day-to-day occurrences in the hostel, including individual incidents involving particular persons, and therefore the personal files of residents would not contain any additional material of relevance. The court held that in accordance with the principle of proportionality, in exercising its discretion under Part 31 the court may properly take into account the fact that the document sought would provide no additional information, or no significant amount of additional information, beyond that already available to the other party and the court. It would not therefore be proportionate in this case to order the disclosure and inspection of documents which, in so far as they were relevant at all, very largely duplicated what was already available.

Disclosure on the small claims track

The rules about disclosure in Part 31 apply to all claims except a claim allocated to the small claims track (r 31.1(2)). The usual direction in relation to documents on the small claims track, if any, is for a party to file at court and serve only copies of those documents on which he intends to rely (r 27.4(3)).

Definition of document /copy of a document

A document is defined as 'anything in which information of any description is recorded' (r 31.4). The definition of a document in Part 31 is therefore much wider than the ordinary meaning of the word would suggest. It is not confined to paper documents and will include such things as photographs, videos, computer disks and CDs.

A copy of a document means anything onto which information recorded in the document has been copied, by whatever means, whether directly or indirectly (r 31.4).

Definition of disclosure

A party discloses a document by stating that it exists or has existed (r 31.2). It should be noted, therefore, that unless the court orders otherwise, it is not necessary for a party to provide a copy of the document or allow a party to inspect it in order to comply with disclosure. However, the obligation to disclose a document is usually accompanied by the right of the other party to inspect or obtain a copy of the document (r 31.3).

Control of a document

Where a party is required to disclose documents, he is obliged to disclose documents which are or have been in his control (r 31.8(1)). This covers not just documents in his actual physical possession, but also those that were in his physical possession, documents of which he has or has had a right to possession, or documents he has or has had a right to inspect or take copies of (r 31.8(2)). It should be remembered that disclosure involves a statement that a document exists or has existed, and so the mere fact that a document has been sent to or is held by someone else or no longer exists does not mean that a party is excused from disclosing it.

Copies of documents

If there is more than one copy of a document, a party need disclose only one of it (r 31.9(1)). However, if a copy of a disclosable document contains a modification, obliteration or other marking or feature, it will be treated as a separate document and be disclosable in its own right (r 31.9(2)).

NATURE OF DISCLOSURE

Disclosure in stages

The court may direct, or the parties may agree in writing, that disclosure or inspection, or both, shall take place in stages (r 31.13). Such an order may be made, for instance, when there is an order for a split trial on liability and quantum.

Duties of legal representatives in respect of disclosure

A legal representative acting for a party must endeavour to ensure that the party understands his duty to comply with disclosure (PD 31, para 4.4). A party is often surprised at the obligation to disclose documents adverse to his case, and a legal representative must fully explain this to his client.

In *Rockwell Machine Tool Co Ltd v Barrus* [1968] 2 All ER 97, Sir Robert Megarry VC emphasised that it was a legal representative's professional responsibility to ensure that his client appreciated at an early stage of the litigation not only the duty of disclosure and its width, but also the importance of not destroying documents which might by any possibility have to be disclosed. He said that this duty extended to ensuring that in any corporate organisation knowledge of this burden is passed on to any who may be affected by it.

In *Douglas and Zeta-Jones v Hello! Ltd* [2003] EWHC 55, it was held that this duty applies in respect of electronic messages in the same way as it applies to hard copies.

Continuing duty of disclosure

A party has a continuing duty of disclosure throughout the course of the proceedings. If further disclosable documents come to a party's attention, he must disclose them to the other party immediately (r 31.11; PD 31, para 3.3).

Consequences of failure to disclose documents or allow inspection

If a party fails to disclose a document or fails to allow inspection of it, he cannot rely on that document in the proceedings, unless the court gives permission (r 31.21).

Deliberate destruction or forgery of disclosable documents

The purpose of the rules of disclosure is to secure the fair trial of the proceedings in accordance with the due process of the court. If a party deliberately destroys documents which he should disclose, even if this amounts to a contempt or defiance of the court, he will not be deprived of the opportunity to bring or defend the claim unless his conduct puts the fairness of the trial in jeopardy (*Douglas and Zeta-Jones v Hello! Ltd* [2003] EWHC 55).

In *Douglas and Zeta-Jones*, it was established that the defendants had prepared false witness statements and destroyed relevant documents. Notwithstanding the defendants' conduct, which called into question the veracity of their evidence and the adequacy of their disclosure, the court was not persuaded that a fair trial was no longer possible or that the conduct of the defendants justified an order striking out the whole or any part of their defence. However, the court said that in evaluating the evidence the trial judge would be able to consider whether the documents which should have been produced to the claimants would have provided material for the cross-examination of the defendants.

The court must also draw a distinction between documents destroyed before and those destroyed after proceedings are commenced. The former conduct would justify the intervention of the court only if it was satisfied that the documents were destroyed in an attempt to pervert the course of justice (*Douglas and Zeta-Jones v Hello! Ltd*). In *Douglas and Zeta-Jones*, for instance, the court accepted that the defendants' practice of deleting emails after they were read would not justify the intervention of the court when the emails in question were deleted before the commencement of the proceedings and there was no evidence that they were deleted with the intention to pervert the course of justice.

However, where a party has forged documents and persists in deception on a large scale, it will result in him forfeiting his right to continue to be heard (*Arrow Nominees Inc v Blackledge* (2000) *The Times*, 7 July, CA). In *Arrow Nominees*, the defendant forged letters to support his defence. The letters were discovered to be forgeries by the claimant's solicitors because the letterhead included a telephone number with an area code which was not yet in use at the time the letters were purported to have been written. The claimant was unsuccessful in obtaining an order before trial to strike out the defendant's defence because the court was not satisfied that a fair trial was no longer possible. However, the judge expressly stated that a further application might be appropriate if the defendant's dishonest conduct persisted.

After the forgeries were discovered the defendant was unwilling to make a frank disclosure of the extent of his fraudulent conduct and persisted in his attempts to deceive. The claimant made a further application at the trial to have the defendant's defence struck out but the trial judge refused to do so on the grounds that the defendant's conduct did not preclude a fair trial of the claim.

The Court of Appeal held that the trial judge was wrong not to strike out the defendant's defence, and he should have done so in order to prevent the court's process from being used as a means of achieving injustice. The court found that the defendant had demonstrated that he was determined to pursue proceedings with the object of preventing a fair trial and had therefore forfeited his right to take part in a trial. It held that where, as here, there was a flagrant and continuing affront to the court, striking out would not be a disproportionate remedy for such an abuse.

The Court of Appeal found that the trial judge regarded the risk of a fair trial not being possible as the factor of crucial – even overriding – weight, and the court accepted that it is a factor of considerable weight which may often be determinative. However, the court said that the question of a fair trial is not the only material factor. When considering this issue the court must also take into account the overriding objective. This includes the consideration that attempted perversion of justice is the very antithesis of parties coming before the court on an equal footing. The court must also allot the case an appropriate share of the court's resources while taking into account the need to allot resources to other cases. Further, the case must be dealt with in a way which is proportionate to the amount of money involved in the case, its importance and the financial position of the parties.

As a result of the defendant's behaviour the court found that the trial was 'hijacked' by the need to investigate which documents were false and which had been destroyed. The result was that the case occupied far more of the court's time than was necessary for the purpose of deciding the real points in issue between the parties. This was held to be unfair to the claimant and unfair to other litigants who needed to have their disputes tried by the court.

In the light of its conclusions the Court of Appeal in *Arrow Nominees* suggested that it would be preferable for a judge faced with an application to strike out a statement of case in such circumstances to resolve the matter whether full disclosure of fraudulent conduct has been made before the trial begins or as a preliminary issue at the start of the trial. If the judge is satisfied, in the light of what he accepts is full disclosure, that there is no substantial risk that the admitted forgery or destruction of documents will lead to a result which is unsafe then he will allow the trial to proceed. However, if he is not satisfied that there has been full and frank disclosure of the fraudulent conduct then the correct response is to refuse to allow the party in default to take any further part in the proceedings.

Subsequent use of disclosed documents

The general principle, subject to exceptions, is that a party to whom a document has been disclosed may use the document only for the purposes of the proceedings and not for any other purpose (r 31.22). The exceptions are where:

(a) the document has been read to or by the court, or referred to at a public hearing;

(b) the court gives permission; or

(c) the person who disclosed the document and the person to whom the document belongs agree (r 31.22(1)).

Document read out or referred to in court

Once a document has been read out or referred to in open court, the general principle is that there will no longer be any restriction on the use that can be made of that document either by the parties or by third parties (r 31.22(1)(a)). This principle was established following the successful challenge in the European Court of Human Rights (ECtHR) to the House of Lords' decision in *Home Office v Harman* [1983] 1 AC 280. The House of Lords had held in that case that a lawyer was in contempt of court for allowing a journalist to inspect confidential documents provided to her on disclosure after they had been read out in court. The ECtHR held that the decision infringed the journalist's right under Art 10 of the Convention (freedom of expression) to receive and impart information.

Rule 31.22(1)(a) also reflects the principle of orality of the English trial. The reason for the principle is to ensure that justice is done in public. In order that those attending a trial held in public should be able to understand the case, the confidentiality of a document is released once it is read or used in court.

In order to adapt to modern practice, namely, the presentation of evidence and arguments in writing, yet keeping the principle of orality of the English trial, the release of confidentiality will apply to documents referred to in writing at trial as well as those read out in open court. Also, any document pre-read by the judge or referred to in a witness statement which stands as evidence-in-chief will be treated as if it were read out or referred to in open court (*SmithKline Beecham v Connaught* [1999] 4 All ER 498).

However, as r 31.22(1)(a) is based on the principle of orality of the English trial, if there is no trial, perhaps because the claim is disposed of by consent before trial, disclosed documents will remain confidential however much they were pre-read by the judge (*SmithKline Beecham v Connaught*).

Order restricting the use of a disclosed document

Notwithstanding the exceptions in r 31.22(1), the court has the power, on the application of a party or any person to whom the document belongs, to make an order restricting or prohibiting the use of a document which has been disclosed, even where it has been read to or by the court or referred to at a public hearing (r 31.22(2) and (3)).

In *Lilly Icos Ltd v Pfizer Ltd* [2002] EWCA Civ 2, the Court of Appeal laid down some guidelines for the application of r 31.22(2) and (3). The starting point is the normal rule of publicity for the trial and any documents read or referred to at trial. There must therefore be a very good reason to depart from this principle, which reflects English jurisdiction and is reinforced by Arts 6 (right to a fair trial) and 10 (freedom of expression) of the European Convention on Human Rights. When considering an application in respect of a particular document the court must consider the role the document played at trial. Accordingly, the court will be less inclined to allow the application where the document was central to the issues between the parties. The court must also be provided with specific reasons why a party will be damaged by publication of the document. On the other hand, a court considering such an application should take into account the other general rule that trials should be held in public. The court will therefore be better able to resist an application for the hearing of a trial in private in order to protect confidential information if it makes an order providing confidentiality to sensitive documents which will be read out or referred to at trial.

In *Lilly Icos Ltd*, the applicant applied for an order under r 31.22(2) in respect of a document containing figures for advertising and promotion which, it alleged, were highly commercially sensitive and could not be obtained other than from the applicant's confidential records. In making an order to preserve the confidentiality of the document the Court of Appeal said that the most important feature of that case was the limited role the document played in the case. The document was referred to only in passing and was not part of any submissions. Indeed, the court was satisfied that if the document was in a separate document, rather than being exhibited to a witness statement, it would not have been referred to in court at all. However, the court stressed that the decision in that case was not authority for a general rule that advertising figures can be kept confidential; each application must be decided on its own merits.

Extent of disclosure

In most cases, a party will be required to give *standard disclosure* only. An order requiring a party to give 'disclosure' means that the party is required to give *standard disclosure* only unless the court expressly orders otherwise (r 31.5(1); PD 31, para 1.1). Therefore, although where disclosure is ordered it is usually *standard disclosure*, the court has the power to make a more extensive order for disclosure than *standard disclosure* if required, but it must expressly do so.

A party does not have the right to insist that an order for *standard disclosure* is made in proceedings as the court has the power to dispense with the need for *standard disclosure* altogether, or limit its extent (r 31.5(2)).

The parties may agree to dispense with or limit *standard disclosure*. If the parties agree to this, they should record their agreement in writing and lodge it at court (r 31.5(3); PD 31, para 1.4).

Disclosure under pre-action protocols

Although a party will not be obliged to give disclosure unless ordered to do so, in some types of proceedings, for example, personal injury or clinical negligence claims, a prospective defendant should have already provided disclosure of a significant number of documents without an order in accordance with the pre-action protocol applicable to these types of claim (see Chapter 5, 'Pre-Action Protocols').

A party's non-compliance with a relevant pre-action protocol can be taken into account by the court when making orders for costs (r 44.3).

STANDARD DISCLOSURE

Scope of standard disclosure

Standard disclosure imposes an obligation on a party to disclose the following documents that are or have been in his control:

- documents on which a party relies;
- documents which adversely affect his own case;
- documents which adversely affect another party's case;
- documents which support another party's case; and
- any documents which he is required to disclose by a relevant practice direction (r 31.6).

Thus, documents which are purely 'neutral' need not, and should not, be disclosed, otherwise costs consequences may apply.

The limitation of standard disclosure to the above categories of documents reflects a deliberate intention to curtail the process of disclosure; to get away from the traditional approach based on 'telling the story' or 'leading to a train of inquiry', as exemplified by the decision in *Compagnie Financière et Commerciale du Pacifique v Peruvian Guano Co* (see p 421 above, 'Introduction'). This accords with Lord Woolf's recommendations set out in *Access to Justice*, Final Report, Chapter 12, for the limits of disclosure in most cases (*Three Rivers DC and Others v HM Treasury & Governor & Co of the Bank of England* [2002] EWCA Civ 1182, *per* Chadwick LJ).

Duty of search

A party is required to carry out a reasonable search for documents which he is obliged to disclose as part of standard disclosure (r 31.7(1); PD 31, para 1.2). Such a test leaves considerable scope for deciding what is reasonable in a particular case, and issues of proportionality will obviously be important (PD 31, para 2). If a party decides not to search for a category of documents on the ground that to do so would be unreasonable, he must state this in his disclosure statement and identify the category of document involved (r 31.7(3)). A party who has made this decision should have borne in mind the following factors when reaching a decision that a search was unreasonable:

- the number of documents involved. The more documents involved, the greater the efforts that should be made;
- the nature and complexity of the proceedings. A large sum or complex proceedings would justify more effort being made than in proceedings for a smaller sum in a straightforward matter;
- the ease and expense of retrieval of any particular document. It may be disproportionate to go to a great deal of effort and expense in searching for a document even if the dispute involves a large sum or complex issues; and
- the significance of any document which is likely to be located. Obviously, the more important the document, the more effort should be made (r 31.7).

Although the disclosing party does not have to apply to the court for permission to limit his search in this way, the court will take these factors into account when hearing any application for specific disclosure made by a party who challenges the disclosing party's decision not to conduct a search on the grounds of reasonableness.

Procedure for standard disclosure

List of documents

In order to comply with disclosure, a party should compile a list of disclosable documents in Practice Form N265 and serve it on every other party (r 31.10; PD 31, paras 1.3 and 3.1).

The documents must be identified in a convenient order and manner, and a concise description of each document (or category of document) should be provided (r 31.10(3)). Practice Direction 31 sets out how a party can comply with these requirements. This provides that the documents should be listed in date order, numbered consecutively and given a concise description such as, 'letter, claimant to defendant'. If there is a large number of documents falling into the same category, for example, bank statements, a party can list those documents as a category, rather than individually, for example, by saying '50 bank statements relating to account number x, at bank x, dated x to x' (PD 31, para 3.2).

The list must indicate those documents in respect of which the party claims a right or duty to withhold inspection (r 31.10(4)(a)). It must also indicate those documents which are no longer in the party's control, and what has happened to those documents (r 31.10(4)(b)).

Form N265 is divided into three sections. In the first section, the disclosing party must list the documents in his control which he has no objection to the other side inspecting. In the second section, the disclosing party must list the documents in his control which he objects to the other side inspecting. In the third section, the disclosing party must list the documents he once had, but no longer has in his control.

Disclosure statement

Under r 31.10(5) and PD 31, para 4.1, the list of documents *must* include a disclosure statement containing specified information. The disclosure statement *must* be made by the party personally (or by a representative or employee of a party in the case of a company or firm) and *not* by his legal representative on his behalf. The form of the disclosure statement is set out in the Annex to PD 31. The disclosure statement should:

- set out the extent of the search that has been made to locate disclosable documents. The party should specify the earliest date of the documents involved in the search, the locations of the search and the categories of documents searched for. The party should also draw attention to any particular limitations on the extent of the search and the reasons for the limitations based on the ground of proportionality;

- expressly state that the party believes the extent of the search to have been reasonable in all the circumstances;

- in the case of a party which is a company, firm, association or other organisation, give the name, address and position or office of the person making the disclosure statement and an explanation as to why that person is the most appropriate person to make the statement;

- if applicable, state that the party claims a right or duty to withhold an identified document from inspection, or part of a document to which it relates, and give the grounds on which he claims that right or duty;

- if applicable, identify documents which are no longer in the party's control and state what has happened to them;

- if applicable, state that the party considers it would be disproportionate to the issues in the case to permit inspection of identified documents within a certain category;

- certify that the party understands the duty to disclose documents; and

- certify that to the best of his knowledge, the party has carried out that duty (rr 31.3(2), 31.10(4), (6), (7), 31.19(3), (4); PD 31, paras 4.1–4.7 and Annex).

False disclosure statements

If a person makes, or causes another person to make, a false disclosure statement, without an honest belief in its truth, he is liable to be proceeded against for contempt of court (r 31.23).

Disclosing documents without a disclosure statement

The parties may agree in writing to disclose documents without making a list and to disclose documents without the disclosing party making a disclosure statement (r 31.10(8)).

Supplemental list

A party has a continuing duty of disclosure throughout the course of the proceedings (r 31.11(1)). If, therefore, the existence of further disclosable documents comes to the attention of a party after he has served a list of documents, he should prepare a supplemental list of these further documents and serve it on every other party (PD 31, para 3.3). A party should comply with this obligation as soon as these additional documents come to his attention (r 31.11(2)).

SPECIFIC DISCLOSURE

A party to whom disclosure has been made may have grounds to believe that the disclosure is inadequate on the basis that documents or a category of documents which should have been disclosed have not been, or that a party has not properly searched for disclosable documents. Moreover, in some cases, a party may believe that disclosure wider than standard disclosure is necessary to do justice in a particular case. In those circumstances, a party can apply to the court for an order for *specific disclosure* of a document or category of documents (r 31.12(1); PD 31, para 5.1).

In *Rigg v Associated Newspapers Ltd* [2003] EWHC 710, the court held that there was no limitation as to the stage during the proceedings when an application for specific disclosure under r 31.12 could be made. It held that it had a discretion whether to make the order but that the applicant must satisfy the court that it should make 'accelerated disclosure', that is, disclosure earlier than would normally take place.

In *Rigg*, the court held that it was just for it to make an order for specific disclosure of a document which had a direct bearing on an issue raised in the pleadings. The document in question was the journalist's notes of an interview with the claimant from which the defendant had quoted extensively in its defence (see pp 436–37 below, 'Right to inspect document mentioned in statement of case, etc', for the facts and further consideration of this case). The issue raised in the pleading was whether the defendant had made deliberate falsehoods and was malicious. This had a direct bearing on whether the claimant should accept an offer of amends made by the defendant under s 2 of the Defamation Act 1996. This is because if the claimant accepted the offer of amends she would be deprived of an opportunity to have a jury trial, and the journalist's notes would assist the claimant in deciding whether the defendant knew the words complained of were false and defamatory.

In making its order the court took into account that the claimant was present at the interview and had already alleged in her particulars of claim that the article contained deliberate falsehoods and that the defendant was malicious in publishing it. The court was therefore satisfied that the claimant was not conducting a fishing expedition in seeking disclosure on the off chance that something might turn up. The court was aware that the claimant could press on with her claim and obtain disclosure of the notes in some months' time, but accepted that this would be time-wasting and disproportionately expensive. In the circumstances of that case the court saw no reason to postpone the time when disclosure had to be made and ordered that the defendant disclose the interview notes.

Procedure for applying for specific disclosure

In the first instance, the party should request that the disclosing party provide such disclosure voluntarily. However, if the disclosing party refuses to comply, the other party can apply to the court for an order.

The application should be made in accordance with Part 23 and must be supported by evidence justifying the applicant's belief that documents have not been disclosed which should have been, or why wider disclosure than standard disclosure is necessary in this case, in order to satisfy the court that the application is not a 'fishing expedition'. The grounds must be set out either in the application notice itself, or in any supporting evidence (PD 31, paras 5.2, 5.3).

The court will consider all the circumstances of the case in the light of the overriding objective, but if the court is satisfied that a party has failed to comply with his obligation to give disclosure, whether through a failure to conduct a proper search or otherwise, it is likely to make an order remedying this failure (PD 31, para 5.4).

If the application is successful, the court may order a party to:

(a) disclose documents or classes of documents specified in the order;

(b) carry out a search to the extent stated in the order;

(c) disclose any documents located as a result of that search (r 31.12(2); PD 31, para 5.5).

When making the order, the court is likely to make it subject to or conditional on a sanction, such as striking out of the party's statement of case, if it is not complied with.

INSPECTION

Right to inspect a disclosed document

A party has a general right to inspect a document which has been disclosed to him (r 31.3(1)).

The court has the power to order a disclosing party to permit another party to inspect any document which that party has a right to inspect (*Bennett v Compass*

Group UK [2002] EWCA Civ 642). In *Bennett*, the claimant brought a claim against the defendant for personal injury. The claimant had given disclosure of medical records and the defendant asked to inspect those documents. The claimant's solicitors did not reply to the defendant's solicitor's correspondence requesting inspection of the claimant's medical records.

At a case management conference the district judge ordered the claimant to supply the defendant with all necessary authority to enable it to obtain copies of the claimant's medical records. The claimant appealed against the order. The matter came before the Court of Appeal as a second tier appeal under r 52.13 because it was held to raise an important point of principle or practice. The important point of principle or practice was whether the district judge had jurisdiction to order the claimant to produce medical records for inspection.

The Court of Appeal held that where documents relevant to issues in litigation between the claimant and defendant are in the physical possession of a third party, but are documents in respect of which one of the parties has a right to inspect or take copies so as to bring those documents in the control of that party for the purposes of r 31.8(2), the court can require that party to give the other party authority which enables him to obtain inspection of those documents. An example of when relevant documents may be in the possession of a third party is when such documents are held by a bank.

Inspection of medical records

In *Bennett v Compass Group UK*, the Court of Appeal held that the court should be very cautious before making an order that a party must produce his medical records for inspection by the opponent. Indeed, Pill LJ, in a dissenting judgment, held that in that case the district judge had wrongly exercised his discretion to make such an order. Although Pill LJ did not exclude the possibility that there might be circumstances in which such an order was appropriate, he believed instead that apart from in exceptional cases, the disclosure should be organised and managed by the disclosing party's solicitor. He said that if the disclosing party's solicitor organises disclosure of medical records, this will ensure proper protection for the disclosing party's interests in this sensitive area. If disclosure is not made, the CPR contain ample and proportionate sanctions for the court to apply, including the power to stay a claim and to strike out a claim.

In *Bennett*, the Court of Appeal also cautioned that where an order is made authorising a third party to permit an opposing party to inspect medical records, the order must be very clearly and carefully drafted to ensure that none of the claimant's rights, whether under the European Convention on Human Rights or otherwise, are or could be infringed. Accordingly, the precise nature of the authority must be very carefully delineated so that the person given authority to disclose is in no doubt what records the other party is permitted to see.

Right to inspect document mentioned in statement of case, etc

Even if not formally disclosed to him, a party may inspect a document *mentioned* in:

(a) a statement of case;

(b) a witness statement;

(c) a witness summary; or

(d) an affidavit (r 31.14(1)).

Document mentioned in an expert's report

A party may also apply for an order for inspection of any document *mentioned* in an expert's report which has not already been disclosed in the proceedings (r 31.14(2)). In *Bennett v Compass Group UK*, the Court of Appeal confirmed that where a document is referred to in an expert's report, in that case the claimant's GP and hospital records, the defendant is entitled to inspect those documents.

However, r 31.14(2) is subject to r 35.10(4), which provides that in respect of *instructions* to an expert, a court will not order disclosure of any specific document unless it is satisfied that there are reasonable grounds for considering that the statement of instructions set out in the expert's report is inaccurate or incomplete (r 31.14(2)).

Meaning of 'mentioned' in r 31.14

In *Rigg v Associated Newspapers Ltd*, the court explained the scope and meaning of the word 'mentioned' in r 31.14. In order for a document to be 'mentioned' there must be a direct allusion to it; quoting from a document does not amount to mentioning or directly alluding to it.

In the *Rigg* case, the claimant, the actress Dame Diana Rigg, brought proceedings against the publisher of the *Daily Mail* for defamation in respect of an article it published based on an interview given by the claimant. The claimant alleged that the article was defamatory because it suggested that she had chosen to reveal herself in public as a lonely, embittered, rejected and vengeful woman who had attacked British men and was bitter about her husband's adultery and her failed marriage, and about not having a man in her life. The claimant claimed aggravated damages on the grounds that the article included deliberate falsehoods and that the words were published maliciously.

In its defence the defendant denied deliberate falsehoods or that it was malicious, and set out in its defence, at length and detail and in quotation marks, the words that it contended were spoken by the claimant in the course of the interview. These quotations were based on the interview notes of the journalist conducting the interview and so the claimant sought disclosure of those notes under r 31.14. However, the court held that the journalist's notes were not *mentioned* in the defence so as to give rise to the right to inspect under r 31.14. A document will not be mentioned if there is no reference to it. The court found in this case that there was no mention in the defence to the notes as such, and there was certainly no direct and specific reference to them, and that quoting from the notes did not amount to mentioning them or directly alluding to them (the court ordered disclosure of the notes to the claimant on other grounds; see pp 434–35 above, 'Specific disclosure').

Exceptions to right to inspect disclosed document

A party will have no right to inspect a disclosed document if:

(a) the document is no longer in the control of the party who disclosed it;

(b) the party disclosing the document has a right or duty to withhold inspection; or

(c) it falls into a category of documents of which the disclosing party has stated in his disclosure statement that to permit inspection would be disproportionate to the issues in the case (this *cannot* include any documents the disclosing party is relying upon) (r 31.3).

Inspection and copying of documents

Often, a party will send copies of the disclosed documents to the other parties with the disclosure list. Strictly, however, a party need only send the disclosure list, and it will be for the other party to request inspection or copying of the documents on the list that are available or to inspection of which the other party has no objection.

A party served with a disclosure statement who has a right to inspect documents must send the disclosing party written notice of his wish to do so. The disclosing party must then permit inspection no more than seven days after the date of receiving the request. If a party prefers to receive copies rather than physically inspect the documents, the disclosing party must comply with this request as long as the other party has undertaken to pay his reasonable copying charges (r 31.15).

A party can choose to inspect the documents and also request copies, which should be provided as long as there is an undertaking to pay reasonable copying charges (r 31.15).

Order for specific inspection

If the disclosing party has indicated that he objects to the other party inspecting a document or documents falling into a certain category on the grounds that it would be disproportionate to the issues in the case to allow inspection, the other party can apply to the court for an order for specific inspection of that document or category of documents (r 31.12(3)).

The application should be made in accordance with Part 23 and should indicate the grounds on which the party maintains it is important that he be allowed to inspect the document or documents.

PRIVILEGE FROM DISCLOSURE OR INSPECTION OF A DOCUMENT

There are certain types of document which a party can usually withhold from disclosure or inspection. These may be divided into three broad categories:

- public interest immunity;
- legal professional privilege; and
- privilege against self-incrimination.

Privilege from disclosure

Public interest immunity

There is a well-established principle that a party can claim to protect a document from disclosure on the grounds that, otherwise, disclosure would damage the public interest (see *Burmah Oil Co Ltd v Governor and Co of the Bank of England* [1980] AC 1090 and *Conway v Rimmer* [1968] AC 910). Such a ground is obviously more likely to be used by the Government and public bodies rather than private parties. However, it is not restricted to such bodies, and a claim to such immunity was successfully made by a charity (see *D v NSPCC* [1978] AC 171).

If a party believes that disclosure of a document, which would otherwise be disclosable, would damage the public interest he may apply to the court, without notice, for an order permitting him to withhold disclosure (r 31.19(1)). The court will balance the public interest in concealment against the public interest that the administration of justice should not be frustrated when deciding whether to grant the order. Given the nature of the application, the order of the court must not be served on, or be open to inspection by, any other person, unless the court specifically orders otherwise (r 31.19(2)).

Confidential documents

A document will not be privileged from disclosure merely because it is confidential. However, where the court is impressed with the need to preserve confidentiality in a particular case, it will consider carefully whether the necessary information can be obtained by other means not involving a breach of confidence. In order to reach a conclusion whether disclosure is necessary notwithstanding confidentiality, the tribunal should inspect the documents (*Science Research Council v Nasse* [1980] AC 1028).

In *Simba-tola v Elizabeth Fry Hostel*, the Court of Appeal held that *Nasse* remained the leading authority where the court is dealing with documents which are said to be confidential but not protected by public interest immunity. Although that case was decided on the issue of proportionality rather than confidentiality (see pp 425–26 above, 'Proportionality and disclosure'), the Court of Appeal confirmed that where disclosure is sought of confidential documents, where there is additional relevant information contained in those confidential documents, the court must conduct the balancing exercise described in *Nasse* and inspect the documents concerned.

'Without prejudice' communications

Communications between the parties genuinely aimed at settlement, known as 'without prejudice' communications, are privileged and therefore inadmissible as evidence at trial (*Rush & Tompkins Ltd v Greater London Council* [1989] AC 1280).

It is a rule of evidence that fully 'without prejudice' communications cannot be revealed to the court at all, at any stage of the proceedings, except with the consent (or by waiver) of both parties or to prove that a settlement has been reached if this is disputed (*Unilever v Procter & Gamble* [1999] 2 All ER 691). However, communications which are 'without prejudice save as to costs' can be referred to once all issues as to liability and quantum are decided in respect of the issue of costs (see *Cutts v Head* [1984] Ch 290; [1984] 2 WLR 349). Also, such offers, not being unreservedly 'without prejudice', are also admissible in other circumstances if the fact that such an offer had been made is relevant, for instance at interim hearings such as an application for security for costs (see *Simaan General Contracting Co v Pilkington Glass Ltd* [1987] 1 All ER 345).

As the communications are made between the parties, each party will obviously have a copy of without prejudice communications. Any documents relating to without prejudice communications are disclosable between the parties although not admissible as evidence at court. Also, without prejudice communications between some but not all of the parties to a dispute are not disclosable to any other party to the dispute who was not a party to the communications (*Rush & Tompkins Ltd v Greater London Council*).

There are two grounds upon which without prejudice communications are privileged: one is the public policy of encouraging parties to negotiate and settle disputes out of court; the other is that there is an implied agreement that communications in the course of negotiations are not admissible in litigation (*Muller v Linsley & Mortimer* [1996] 1 PNLR 74).

The absence of the caption 'without prejudice' does not prevent the communications from being treated as without prejudice if it is clear from surrounding circumstances that the parties were seeking to compromise an existing dispute, whether it has given rise to proceedings or not. On the other hand, simply marking a document 'without prejudice' will not make it privileged if the substance of the communication is not a genuine approach to attempt settlement of the dispute (*Rush & Tompkins Ltd v Greater London Council*). However, where parties agree to negotiate on a without prejudice basis, the court will not dissect out identifiable admissions and withhold protection from the rest of the communications. Otherwise parties conducting, for instance, a without prejudice meeting would not be able to speak freely and openly for fear that part of their communications would be admissible against them (*Unilever v Procter & Gamble*).

Where without prejudice communications are justified on the basis of an implied contract, English courts can give extra-territorial effect to the restraint (ie, in respect of proceedings in other jurisdictions) by an order enforcing the contract. However, where the only reason for the without prejudice protection is the public policy of encouraging negotiations between the parties, for example, where the communications are between other parties to the dispute, an English court cannot order a person not to make use of without prejudice communications in a foreign court by seeking to impose in foreign proceedings a restraint which is justified only by its own perception of what public policy requires (*Prudential Insurance Co of America v The Prudential Assurance Co Ltd* [2002] EWCA Civ 1154).

Privilege from inspection

Legal professional privilege

Legal professional privilege is regarded as a fundamental human right guaranteed by Art 8 of the European Convention on Human Rights (right to respect for private and family life) and long established in the common law. It is a necessary corollary of the right of any person to obtain skilled advice about the law. It is not merely a rule of evidence; it is a substantive right founded on an important public policy (*R (Morgan Grenfell & Co Ltd) v Special Commissioner of Income Tax* [2002] UKHL 21, [7], [31]; [2002] 2 WLR 1299, *per* Lord Hoffmann).

Legal professional privilege may be divided into two types:

(a) legal advice privilege; and

(b) litigation privilege.

Legal advice privilege

Legal advice privilege covers communications between a lawyer and client for the purposes of obtaining legal advice; such communications are privileged whether or not litigation is contemplated. The reason for the protection of such communications is to enable a person to consult a lawyer and tell him the whole truth knowing that what he reveals in confidence cannot be disclosed without his consent. It is regarded as a fundamental principle for the proper administration of justice and as a human right (*R v Derby Magistrates' Courts ex p B* [1996] AC 487; [1995] 4 All ER 526, HL).

Legal advice privilege extends to all communications between solicitor and client on matters within the ordinary business of the solicitor and referable to the relationship (*Balabel v Air India* [1988] Ch 317). However, it does not protect communications that relate to the furtherance of criminal or fraudulent acts (*O'Rourke v Darbishire* [1920] AC 581).

Legal advice privilege is not an interest that falls to be balanced against competing public interests. This is because once any exception to the general rule is allowed, the client's confidence is necessarily lost. If a lawyer is to be able to give his client an absolute and unqualified assurance that what he tells him will not be disclosed without his consent in any circumstances, the assurance must follow and not precede the undertaking of any balancing exercise (*B and Others v Auckland District Law Society* [2003] UKPC 38).

The privilege stems from the confidential relationship of client and solicitor and attaches only to communications between the client and the solicitor. It does not extend to documents obtained from third parties to be shown to a solicitor for advice (*Three Rivers DC and Bank of Credit and Commerce International SA (In Liquidation) v Governor & Co of the Bank of England* [2003] EWCA Civ 474). In the *Three Rivers* case, the Court of Appeal held that material prepared by Bank of England employees for submission to the Bingham Inquiry, set up to investigate the collapse of BCCI, was not covered by legal advice privilege. The court held that this was the case even though the documents prepared by the employees were sent to the Bank's solicitors. The Bank's employees were in the position of a third party, sending documents to the solicitor so that the solicitor could give advice to his client. On the other hand, the documents would not be protected by litigation privilege because that protection applies only to adversarial proceedings and the Bingham Inquiry was not adversarial.

In the *Three Rivers* case, the Court of Appeal referred to earlier authority which clearly established the limits of legal advice privilege. It was recognised that the privilege was possessed by a client only in relation to his communications with his lawyer and no other adviser, not even a medical adviser. It was for this reason that it was important to keep legal advice privilege confined to its proper limits and not extend it to all communications between a lawyer and third parties (at [26]).

Litigation privilege

Litigation privilege applies to communications between a client or his lawyer and third parties which come into existence, after litigation is contemplated or commenced, with the sole or dominant purpose of obtaining advice, information or evidence for the purposes of the litigation. The communication will be privileged only if it can be shown that the dominant purpose for the existence of the document is to obtain advice, information or evidence for actual or contemplated litigation (*Waugh v British Railways Board* [1980] AC 521). Litigation privilege is a creature of adversarial proceedings and cannot exist in the context of non-adversarial proceedings, for example, a private, non-statutory inquiry (*Three Rivers DC and Bank of Credit and Commerce International SA (In Liquidation) v Governor & Co of the Bank of England*).

Although not relevant for its decision in *Three Rivers*, because it was accepted that the proceedings in question were non-adversarial, the Court of Appeal held that it could not be said that the dominant purpose of the preparation of documents in that case was the obtaining of legal advice. Instead, the documents were the raw material for presentation to the Inquiry and the dominant purpose for which they were prepared was to enable the Bank to comply with its primary duty of putting all relevant factual material before Bingham LJ who was conducting the Inquiry (at [35]).

The question of dominant purpose is a matter for the court to determine after consideration of the relevant evidence (*Three Rivers District Council and Bank of Credit and Commerce International SA (In Liquidation) v Governor & Co of the Bank of England* at [35]). As a general principle, privilege does not attach to a document obtained by a party or his adviser for the purpose of litigation if the document did not come into existence for that purpose (*Ventouris v Mountain* [1991] 3 All ER 472, CA).

Statutory exclusion of legal professional privilege

Legal professional privilege may be excluded or abrogated by statute, but where an Act does not expressly do so, such a result will not be implied unless it necessarily follows from the express provisions of the statute construed in their context (*R (Morgan Grenfell & Co Ltd) v Special Commissioner of Income Tax* [2002] UKHL 21; [2002] 2 WLR 1299).

In *R (Morgan Grenfell & Co Ltd) v Special Commissioner of Income Tax*, the Inland Revenue demanded, under s 20(1) of the Taxes Management Act 1970, to see documents relating to advice which the claimant had received from lawyers about the efficacy of a proposed tax avoidance scheme. The issue in the case was a question of construction of the Act, namely, whether it empowered the Inland Revenue to require the disclosure of documents notwithstanding that they were covered by legal professional privilege. It was accepted that s 20(1) made no express reference to documents protected by legal professional privilege. The House of Lords also held that s 20(1) did not create a necessary implication that legal professional privilege was intended to be excluded. It therefore held that the Inland Revenue was not entitled to demand disclosure of such privileged documents. This was held to be the case notwithstanding that liability under the Act turned on the purpose for which the taxpayer entered into the transaction to avoid tax.

In *B and Others v Auckland District Law Society*, the Privy Council held that the New Zealand Law Practitioners Act 1982, which required lawyers to produce documents to the Auckland District Law Society when investigating complaints of professional misconduct, did not expressly, or by necessary implication, exclude legal professional privilege. Therefore, the lawyers subject to the investigation could not be compelled to produce privileged documents to the Law Society's complaints committee.

However, the ECtHR held, in *Foxley v UK* (2001) 31 EHRR 25, that legal professional privilege is a fundamental human right which can be invaded only in exceptional circumstances. Therefore, any statutory provision which purports to exclude or abrogate legal professional privilege must be compatible with the Convention, and may be compatible only if it can be shown to have a legitimate aim which is necessary in a democratic society (*R (Morgan Grenfell & Co Ltd) v Special Commissioner of Income Tax*).

'Trend of advice' privilege

Where a solicitor has copied or assembled a selection of *third party* documents, the selection will be privileged if its production would 'betray the trend of advice which he is giving the client' (*Ventouris v Mountain* [1991] 3 All ER 472, CA, *per* Bingham LJ, applying the principle established in *Lyell v Kennedy (No 3)* (1884) 27 Ch D 1, CA).

In *Lyell v Kennedy*, the plaintiff claimed to be entitled to land as purchaser from the heir-at-law of an intestate, who had died many years earlier. The land was in the possession of the defendant and the central issue in the action was whether the defendant's possession barred the plaintiff's claim. This raised further issues as to the intestate's pedigree and as to the heirship of her estate. For the purposes of his defence, the defendant's solicitor obtained copies of certain burial certificates and other records, and made copies of the inscriptions on certain tombstones and obtained photographs of certain houses. The plaintiff sought disclosure of these documents. The court refused to order disclosure on the grounds that the documents were privileged. The court held that the documents were obtained for the purposes of the defence, and it would deprive a solicitor of the means afforded for enabling him fully to investigate a case if he was required to produce such documents. This would be the case even if the documents were public records, because the very fact of the solicitor having identified certain documents and obtained copies of them meant that to order disclosure of them might show the solicitor's view as to the case of his client in respect of the claim made against him.

In *Lyell v Kennedy*, Bowen LJ explained that a collection of records may be the result of professional knowledge, research and skill, just as a collection of curiosities is the result of the skill or knowledge of the antiquarian. He said that if it was the solicitor's mind which selected the materials then those materials, when chosen, represent the result of the solicitor's professional care and skill, and to order disclosure of them would be 'asking for the key to the labour which the solicitor has bestowed in obtaining them' (at 31).

However, a distinction must be drawn between a selection made from *third party* documents, the disclosure of which may reveal the trend of advice (as in *Lyell v Kennedy*), and a selection made from *own client* documents (*Sumitomo Corp v Credit Lyonnais Rouse Ltd* [2001] EWCA Civ 1152). In the *Sumitomo Corporation* case, the claimant brought a claim arising out of the unauthorised trading activities of one of its former employees during the period 1985–96. This unauthorised trading had caused the claimant to incur substantial losses. The claimant brought proceedings against the defendant alleging that by clearing the unauthorised transactions, and in providing lines of credit for them, the defendant dishonestly assisted the claimant's former employee's breaches of duty and/or knowingly procured breaches of his contract of employment. In order to prepare its case, the claimant assembled a large amount of documentation from its offices, consisting of 6.9 million pages, mostly in Japanese. The claimant's solicitors, assisted by translators, reviewed each document to determine whether it might be relevant to the litigation. If a document was found to be relevant it was translated into English.

In its list of disclosure, the claimant disclosed some 89,000 pages of documentation which included 3,400 documents in Japanese. Of the documents in Japanese, 725 had been translated into English. The claimant claimed privilege in the translated documents. It claimed that disclosure of the translations would indicate which documents the claimant's solicitors considered sufficiently important to require translation and would therefore betray the general trend of their advice to the claimant. The court held that the translations were not privileged. It held that there was no reason why translations of documents should be treated differently from copies of documents. The rules governing legal professional privilege applied equally to all reproductions of original documents, whether the process of reproduction consisted of copying or translation. In the context of legal professional privilege, there was no relevant distinction between a translation of an unprivileged document in the control of the party claiming privilege and a copy of such a document. Each document derives solely from the original document and each is directed at reproducing the sense of, and the information contained in, the original document as exactly and precisely as is reasonably practicable. In particular, neither process in itself introduces any element of confidentiality that does not or did not exist in the original document (at [44], [46]).

Further, the court held that the translations did not fall into the *Lyell v Kennedy* exception. The claimant had contended that the translations were the product of the lawyers' knowledge, research and skill, and that the minds of the lawyers chose which documents to translate. The court distinguished the case from *Lyell v Kennedy* on the basis that the documents in *Lyell v Kennedy* were a selection of third party documents the disclosure of which would betray the trend of advice to the client, whilst in this case the documents were own client documents which were not privileged. The *Lyell v Kennedy* principle did not extend to copies or translations which represented the 'fruits of a selection made for litigious purposes from own client documents' (at [77]).

Privilege from self-incrimination

A party is not compelled to disclose documents that may tend to expose him or his spouse to a criminal penalty. However, this right has been withdrawn in relation to compliance with orders for disclosure relating to infringement of industrial property rights, such as patents and copyright, by s 72 of the Supreme Court Act 1981 (SCA). Also, if the person can be adequately protected by some other means, such as an undertaking by the Crown Prosecution Service (CPS) not to prosecute, the privilege will not apply (*ATT Istel Ltd v Tully* [1993] AC 45).

Disclosure of privileged documents

A party who wishes to claim that he has a right or duty to withhold inspection of a document must identify the document and state that he has this duty or right and the grounds on which he claims it either in his disclosure list, or, in a case where there is no disclosure list, in a written statement to the other party (r 31.19(3) and (4)).

In the first instance, the party making the claim merely has to assert the right or duty; it will then be up to the other party to apply to the court, if need be, in order to challenge the disclosing party's claim to be able to withhold inspection of the document (r 31.19(5); PD 31, para 6.1).

Application to withhold disclosure or permit inspection

An application by a disclosing party to withhold disclosure under r 31.19(1) on the ground that disclosure would damage the public interest, or by the other party to permit inspection under r 31.19(5), should be made in accordance with Part 23 and supported by evidence (r 31.19(7)).

In order to decide the application, the court may order that the document in question be produced to the court, or invite any other person, whether or not a party, to make representations about the application (r 31.19(6)).

The court has a discretion whether to order production of documents. In *Ventouris v Mountain*, the court also held that the production and inspection of documents was not automatic once relevance and the absence of entitlement to privilege was established. It said that while the court's ultimate concern is to ensure the fair disposal of the claim, it can also take into account other legitimate concerns, and it can control the terms upon which production and inspection may be ordered (at 485e, *per* Bingham LJ). An example of where production or inspection may be refused or limited is where it is established that there is a risk that production of documents could lead to violence, intimidation, interference with witnesses or destruction of evidence.

Waiver of privilege

A client expressly waives his legal professional privilege when he elects to disclose communications which the privilege would entitle him not to disclose *(Paragon Finance plc v Freshfields (A Firm)* [1999] 1 WLR 1183; [1999] 1 WLR 1463).

Unless privilege is waived, a document will remain privileged after the occasion for the privilege has passed; 'once privileged, always privileged' *(R v Derby Magistrates' Court ex p B* [1996] AC 487 at 503G–H, *per* Taylor CJ).

It is well established that the privilege belongs to the client and not to his lawyer, and that it may not be waived by the lawyer without his client's consent *(R v Derby Magistrates' Court ex p B)*.

Privileged material may be disclosed for a limited purpose, with the result that it can be used for that purpose but no other. A privileged document can therefore be disclosed for a limited purpose without completely waiving privilege in the document. It is in the interests of the administration of justice that a partial or limited waiver of privilege should be made by a party who would not contemplate anything which might cause privilege to be lost, and it would be most undesirable if the law could not accommodate it (*B and Others v Auckland District Law Society*).

A party who waives privilege in relation to one communication is not taken to waive privilege in relation to all communications. However, a party is not entitled to waive privilege in such a partial and selective manner that unfairness or misunderstanding may result (*Paragon Finance plc v Freshfields (A Firm)*).

When a client sues a solicitor who has formerly acted for him, alleging negligence, he invites the court to adjudicate on questions directly arising from the confidential relations that formerly subsisted between the solicitor and his client. Since court proceedings are public, the client brings that formerly confidential relationship into the public domain. The client thereby waives any right to claim the protection of legal professional privilege in relation to any communication between them so far as necessary for the just determination of his claim. The rationale for this principle is that a party cannot deliberately subject a relationship to public scrutiny and at the same time seek to preserve its confidentiality (*Paragon Finance plc v Freshfields (A Firm)*).

In *Paragon Finance plc v Freshfields*, the claimants sued their former solicitors, Freshfields, for alleged negligence in the handling of a commercial transaction between the client and a third party. The claimants accepted that in bringing proceedings against their former solicitors they had impliedly waived legal professional privilege in communications between them. However, the defendants, Freshfields, asserted that the clients' waiver of privilege applied not only to those communications, but also to confidential communications between the clients and different solicitors whom they later instructed to purse and settle their claim against the third party.

The Court of Appeal held that the claimants had not waived privilege in those other communications. The claimants were not suing those other solicitors and so had not brought that confidential relationship into the public domain. Further, unlike the situation where a defendant solicitor seeks to rely on communications between it and its former client of which it is aware, in this situation the defendants were seeking disclosure of communications of which they had no knowledge.

In *Lillicrap v Nalder and Son* [1993] 1 WLR 94, property developers sued their solicitors for negligence in failing to advise of a problem relating to title in a conveyancing transaction. The solicitors denied causation because they contended that even if they had given the advice they should have given, the client would still have gone ahead with the transaction. In order to provide evidence for their defence, the defendants wanted to rely on other cases in which they had acted for the claimants and given adverse advice, but which had not deterred the claimants from proceeding with a transaction.

The Court of Appeal held that the defendants were entitled to rely on evidence from other retainers with the client. The court held that where a client sued his former solicitor there was not a general principle to allow a roving search into anything else in which the solicitor, or any other solicitor, may have happened to have acted for the client. However, it held that the waiver must go far enough to enable the defendant to establish a defence to the claim. Therefore, it would extend to matters under earlier retainers where the experience of the client was, to the knowledge of the solicitor, such that the solicitor was not in breach of duty as alleged.

Inadvertent release of privileged document

If a party inadvertently allows a privileged document to be inspected, the party inspecting the document may use it or its contents only with the permission of the court (r 31.20).

When the court is considering whether to make an order to allow a party to use a privileged document which has been inadvertently disclosed, or to grant an injunction to restrain its use, the court must do what is just and equitable in all the circumstances of the case (*Al Fayed and Others v Commissioner of Police for the Metropolis and Others* [2002] EWCA Civ 780).

In *Al Fayed and Others v Commissioner of Police for the Metropolis and Others*, the defendant, as part of the process of inspection of disclosed documents under r 31.1, sent the claimant, by mistake, copies of two opinions from counsel. However, this occurred against a background in which the defendant had already deliberately provided the claimant with a copy of another opinion from counsel, and where the claimant and defendant had communicated about the documents to be disclosed by the defendant. It was therefore not a case where there was no sensible reason why the defendant should not disclose the opinions. The defendant had previously expressed itself unprepared to disclose the other two opinions from counsel but on the grounds that they were irrelevant, not because they were privileged. Also, the documents were sent in circumstances where there had appeared to be a careful approach to disclosure; it was not a case where disclosure was done in a hurry.

The court found that it would not be obvious to a reasonable solicitor in the position of the solicitors in this case that a mistake had been made. The Court of Appeal therefore held that the claimants should be permitted to make proper use of the documents on the basis that they were no longer subject to legal professional privilege as between the parties to the proceedings.

The Court of Appeal summarised the relevant principles to be taken into account by the court in deciding whether to exercise its discretion to make an order permitting use of documents disclosed by mistake, or to grant an injunction to restrain their use. These principles include the fact that a solicitor, considering documents made available by the other party to the litigation, owes no duty of care to that party and is in general entitled to assume that any privilege which might otherwise have been claimed for such documents has been waived. In those circumstances, where a party has given inspection of privileged documents by mistake, it will in general be too late for him to correct the mistake by obtaining injunctive relief. Standard disclosure is an important aspect of any proceedings, and the Court of Appeal warned that it is an important part of the duty of any solicitor to put in place a system which ensures that it is carried out properly and with care.

However, the court has the jurisdiction to intervene to prevent the use of documents made available for inspection by mistake where justice requires, for example, where inspection is procured by fraud. In the absence of fraud, it all depends on the circumstances, but the court may grant an injunction if the documents have been made available as a result of an obvious mistake. A mistake is likely to be held to be obvious if the solicitor appreciates that a mistake has been made before making use of the documents, or it would be obvious to a reasonable solicitor in his position that a mistake had been made. However, the court is exercising an equitable jurisdiction which depends on the circumstances of each case. In some cases where there has been an obvious mistake, it may nevertheless be held to be inequitable or unjust to grant relief. An example is where the documents are sent to the client for consideration before being considered by the solicitor, and the client learns a fact from the documents which it would be unjust to prevent him from using in the litigation, even though it would have been apparent to the solicitor that a mistake had been made.

PRE-ACTION DISCLOSURE AND DISCLOSURE AGAINST NON-PARTIES

Pre-action disclosure

Normally, a party is obliged to provide disclosure only once proceedings have started. However, under s 33 of the SCA and s 53 of the County Courts Act 1984 (CCA), in appropriate circumstances a person can apply for disclosure of documents from another person even before any proceedings have started. Previously, this power was only available for potential claims in personal injury and clinical negligence claims, but with the introduction of the CPR, the power was extended to potential claims in all areas of law.

An order for pre-action disclosure may be made in relation to any type of matter as long as the following conditions are satisfied:

(a) the respondent to the application is *likely* to be a party to subsequent proceedings;

(b) the applicant is also *likely* to be a party to those proceedings;

(c) the document or classes of document for which the applicant seeks disclosure would be disclosable by the respondent in accordance with standard disclosure if proceedings had started (r 31.16(3)(a), (b), (c)); and

(d) pre-action disclosure is desirable in order to:

- dispose fairly of the anticipated proceedings; or
- assist the dispute to be resolved without proceedings; or
- save costs (r 31.16(3)(d)).

There are two conditions that must be satisified before an order for pre-action disclosure can be made. One is a condition of a jurisdictional nature where the requirements of r 31.16(3)(a)–(c) must first be satisfied, and the other is of a discretionary nature where the requirements of r 31.16(3)(d) must be satisfied. The court must not confuse the two types of conditions (*Black v Sumitomo Corp* [2001] EWCA Civ 1819; [2002] 1 WLR 1562).

In *Snowstar Shipping Co Ltd v Graig Shipping plc* [2003] EWHC 1367, Morison J warned that it was 'important, if not essential, that every application for pre-action disclosure should be crafted with great care, so that it is properly limited to what is strictly necessary' (at [35]). The court refused the application in that case because the claim was 'thin and fragile' and the application too widely drawn. Also, the court was of the opinion that the applicant was 'fishing for disclosure of documents which would either be privileged or subject to considerable commercial sensitivity' (at [35]).

Disclosure against a non-party

A party can compel a non-party to attend court to give relevant evidence or produce relevant documents (r 34.2). However, if a non-party holds relevant documents which may support a party's case, it may well be to that party's advantage to obtain those documents before any hearing. The party may, for instance, need the document to prove a vital part of his case, or in order to persuade his opponent to settle. Therefore, under s 34 of the SCA or s 53 of the CCA, if the following conditions are met, the court can make an order for disclosure of documents against a person who is not a party. These are:

(a) the documents are *likely* to support the case of the applicant or adversely affect the case of one of the other parties to the proceedings; and

(b) disclosure is necessary in order to dispose fairly of the claim or to save costs (r 31.17(3)).

In *Three Rivers DC and Others v HM Treasury & Governor & Co of the Bank of England*, the claimants sought an order against the Treasury, under r 31.17, for the disclosure of the documents or classes of documents listed in a schedule to their application. Those were documents provided to, or generated by, Bingham LJ in the course of his inquiry into the Bank of Credit and Commercial International (BCCI). The Court of Appeal upheld the judge's order at first instance that the Treasury should provide the documents requested by the claimant.

The court took into account that an applicant under r 31.17 cannot be expected to specify which documents under the control of another, which he may never have seen, will support his case or adversely affect that of another party, or to know whether he will wish to rely upon them. Similarly, the person against whom disclosure is sought, being a stranger to the dispute, cannot be expected to decide this matter for himself. Further, the court cannot be expected to decide whether documents which it has not seen will satisfy this test. Accordingly, the test has to be one of probability, that is, whether the document is *likely* to fulfil these requirements.

The Court of Appeal held that the structure of r 31.16 and that of r 31.17 were very similar, being complementary provisions which extend the court's powers in relation to disclosure. In each case the rule imposed threshold conditions. In the case of r 31.17, this was that the documents of which disclosure is sought are *likely* to support the case of the applicant or adversely affect the case of one of the parties to the proceedings (r 31.17(3)(a)). The court held that the word '*likely*' meant 'may well', and that it was not as high a test as 'more likely than not' but was higher than 'more than merely fanciful' which was what the words 'real prospect of success' were held to mean in *Swain v Hillman* [2001] 1 All ER 91, in respect of applications for summary judgment under Part 24 (see Chapter 23, 'Summary Judgment'). The court also expressed the view that properly understood, the word '*likely*' presented no difficulties and that the temptation to gloss the language of the rule should be resisted. The court said that the word 'likely' took its meaning from its context. In the case of r 31.17, the context is a jurisdictional threshold to the exercise of a statutory power. Although the threshold may appear to be a modest one, the judge then has properly to exercise his discretion whether to grant the application in the particular circumstances of the case.

In applying the threshold test it has to be accepted that some documents which may then appear likely to support the case of the applicant or adversely affect the case of one of the other parties will turn out not to do so. Also, when applying the test to individual documents, it is important to bear in mind that each document has to be read in context, so that a document which considered in isolation does not appear to satisfy the test, may do so if viewed as one of a class. Further, there is no objection to an order for disclosure of a class of documents, provided that the court is satisfied that all the documents in the class do meet the threshold condition. Moreover, as long as the court is satisfied that all the documents in the class meet the threshold condition, it is immaterial that some of the documents will turn out, in the event, not to support the case of the applicant or adversely affect the case of one of the other parties. In all the circumstances, the Court of Appeal held that the documents sought by the claimant, being documents relating to the Bingham Inquiry, satisfied the relevant threshold test in r 31.17.

In *Clark v Ardington Electrical Services and (1) Helphire (UK) Ltd (2) Angel Assistance Ltd (Respondents to Non-Party Disclosure)* [2001] EWCA Civ 585, the Court of Appeal held that when considering whether to make an order for disclosure against a non-party the court ought not to determine disputes of substance in order to decide whether documents are or are not relevant. *Clark* was concerned with the Helphire Group, which ran accident repair and car hire schemes for innocent motorists arising out of car accidents. The innocent motorists paid a modest fee and the schemes involved providing credit for the cost of car hire and repair until such costs were recovered from the insurers of the negligent defendant motorist.

The Helphire Group schemes met with similar resistance from the defendants' insurers as did the 'credit hire' schemes considered by the House of Lords in *Giles v Thompson* [1994] 1 AC 142 and *Dimond v Lovell* [2000] 2 WLR 1121. In this case the dispute was concerned with the contention that the amounts claimed were not the amounts actually paid by Helphire on behalf of the claimants. The discovery against the non-party, Helphire, related to this issue and was directed at the arrangements which Helphire had with repairers and engineers.

The judge at first instance ordered the claimant and/or the non-party, Helphire, to disclose all documents indicating when and what repair and engineer charges were invoiced and paid both by them and to them. The claimant appealed on the grounds that the documents were irrelevant, because the claim was hers and what Helphire paid did not matter. However, the defendants contended that only amounts paid by Helphire were recoverable, and the documents sought would show what these amounts were and when they were paid, and this information might shed light upon whether the schemes were a sham.

The Court of Appeal held that when an order for disclosure was sought against a non-party, the court should not proceed to resolve disputed issues between the parties when deciding whether the documents sought are relevant. In this case the issue to which the disclosure related was raised by the defendants in their defence and no attempt had or could be made to strike it out. It is for the judge to decide those disputed issues at trial based on the evidence, some of which will come from the non-party disclosure. The court held that the judge was right not to enter into the merits of the debate in any detail for the purpose of making the disclosure decision under r 31.17, and the documents sought did satisfy both limbs of the threshold test.

Further, in exercising his discretion whether to make the order, the judge was entitled to take into account that the case was a test case, and it was therefore important for the court to have as full a picture as possible as to how the Helphire schemes worked.

Applications for pre-action disclosure and disclosure against a non-party

The application should be made in accordance with Part 23 and must be supported by evidence (rr 31.16(2), 31.17(2)).

If the application is successful, the order must specify the document or classes of document which the respondent is obliged to disclose, and require the respondent to specify, when making disclosure, whether any of those documents are no longer in his control, or whether he claims a right or duty to withhold inspection of any of those documents (rr 31.16(4), 31.17(4)).

The court may also order the respondent to indicate what has happened to any documents no longer in his control and specify a time and place for disclosure and inspection (rr 31.16(5), 31.17(5)).

Therefore, in the case of a non-party, if the order is made he will be required to give disclosure of these documents in the same way as if he was a party to the proceedings.

Costs of an application for pre-action disclosure or disclosure against a non-party

The court will usually allow the person against whom such an order is made the costs of the application, as well as the costs of complying with any order which is made for disclosure. However, if the court considers it unreasonable for a party not to have voluntarily disclosed a document, particularly if the document should have been disclosed in compliance with a pre-action protocol, and unreasonable for the party to oppose the application for disclosure, the court may make a different order for costs, including one which provides that the party applying for the order be allowed the costs (r 48.1).

COURT'S INHERENT POWER TO ORDER PRE-ACTION DISCLOSURE AND DISCLOSURE AGAINST A NON-PARTY

The rules as to pre-action disclosure and disclosure against a non-party do not limit any other powers the court may have, in the exercise of its inherent jurisdiction to control proceedings, to order pre-action disclosure or disclosure against a non-party (r 31.18).

Rule in *Norwich Pharmacal*

If a person, through no fault of his own, whether voluntarily or not, has got mixed up in the tortious acts of others so as to facilitate their wrongdoing, he may not incur any personal liability but he comes under a duty to assist the person who has been wronged by giving him full information and by disclosing the identity of the wrongdoers.

This principle, laid down in the case of *Norwich Pharmacal v Customs & Excise* [1974] AC 133, gives the court the power to make an order for disclosure, known as a *Norwich Pharmacal* order, against a so called 'innocent wrongdoer'. This power of the court, based on the court's exercise of its inherent jurisdiction to control proceedings, has been expressly preserved by r 31.18.

In *Totalise plc v Motley Fool Ltd* [2001] EWCA Civ 1897, a *Norwich Pharmacal* order was made against the defendant which operated a website providing financial information to investors. Part of the service provided by the defendant consisted of a 'discussion board' relating to particular companies, in which users of the website could post information and opinions likely to be of interest to other investors. The user was obliged to register and enter into a contract with the defendant containing the defendant's standard terms before being able to make a posting on the discussion board.

The defendant was contacted by solicitors acting for the claimants, complaining about a number of postings on the defendant's website by a person using the nickname 'Zeddust', which were defamatory of the claimant. The claimant's solicitors requested confirmation that the postings would be removed, that Zeddust's posting rights would be immediately withdrawn, and that the identity and registration details of Zeddust would be disclosed to the claimant's solicitors. The defendant responded to these requests by confirming that the postings had been removed and that the account of Zeddust had been suspended. However, the defendant refused voluntarily to provide contact details of Zeddust on the grounds that it was restrained from doing so by the terms of the Data Protection Act 1998 and its terms of business with Zeddust. The claimant therefore made an application for a *Norwich Pharmacal* order against the defendant, requesting disclosure and production in a witness statement of the full name and address of Zeddust and all documents which were or had been in the possession, custody or power of the defendant relating to the identity of Zeddust.

The court granted a *Norwich Pharmacal* order obliging the defendant to provide the information requested of Zeddust's identity. The court held that there was no reason under the Data Protection Act 1998 for the defendant to withhold the information sought. It found that the balance weighed heavily in favour of granting the relief sought. It said that to find otherwise would be to give a clear indication to those who wish to defame that they can do so with impunity behind the screen of anonymity made possible by the use of websites on the internet.

Costs incurred in complying with a *Norwich Pharmacal* order

It was confirmed in *Totalise plc v Motley Fool Ltd* that the court has a discretion as to the order for costs when deciding a *Norwich Pharmacal* application. However, the court stressed that such applications are not ordinary adversarial proceedings where the general rule is that the unsuccessful party pays the costs of the successful party. Instead they are akin to proceedings for pre-action disclosure where costs are governed by r 48.3. Accordingly, in most cases where there has been a successful application for a *Norwich Pharmacal* order, the applicant should be ordered to pay the costs of the innocent party, including the costs of making the disclosure.

The court in *Totalise* acknowledged that there may be cases where the circumstances required a different order, but held that this did not include the following circumstances, where:

- the party required to make the disclosure had a genuine doubt whether the person seeking the disclosure was entitled to it;

- the party was under a legal obligation not to reveal the information, or where the legal position was not clear, or the party had a reasonable doubt as to the obligations;

- the party could be subject to proceedings if disclosure was voluntary;

- the party would or might suffer damage by voluntarily giving the disclosure; or

- the disclosure would or might infringe a legitimate interest of another (at [30]).

However, the above provisions as to costs apply only to defendants who are classed as 'innocent wrongdoers', that is, defendants who become mixed up in tortious acts and are only concerned that rights and duties, such as duties of confidence and legitimate interests of privacy, are considered by the court. Those provisions would not apply to a party who supports or is implicated in a crime or tort, or who seeks to obstruct justice being done. The court will require such parties to bear their own costs and, if appropriate, pay the other party's costs (at [31]).

CHAPTER 30

EXPERTS AND ASSESSORS

INTRODUCTION

Lord Woolf was particularly concerned with the role of experts in civil proceedings. He felt there were several issues that needed to be addressed:

- there was a perception of a lack of objectivity on the part of experts. The concept had developed of 'hired guns' – experts who would tailor their evidence to the requirements of those instructing and paying them;

- cases often had unnecessary experts;

- the fees of experts were often unreasonable and/or out of proportion with the size of the dispute;

- the availability of experts to attend court, or even carry out examinations or inspections, was often very doubtful, resulting in considerable delays (see *Access to Justice*, Interim Report (IR), Chapter 23).

As a result of the introduction of the Civil Procedure Rules (CPR), the adversarial nature of expert evidence in litigation is mitigated and now the expert's paramount duty is to help the court, and this overrides any obligation he may have to those who instruct or pay him. Experts instructed to prepare a report for the purposes of proceedings will, by their nature, be expected to be neutral. The previous practice of having one's own 'tame' experts will not be acceptable, the suggestion being that it distorts the true administration of justice.

The rule that expert evidence cannot be adduced without the leave of the court is re-asserted, so that no party may call an expert, or put in evidence an expert's report, without the court's permission. The court now has a duty to restrict expert evidence, which may mean an order for the appointment of a single joint expert, even if both parties have already obtained their own expert reports. This is particularly so in fast track matters where oral evidence by experts is the exception. In such matters, the expert's report is likely to be decisive, rather like the family welfare officer's report in children matters. The judge will not be bound to follow the conclusions in the report, but will have to give good reasons for not doing so.

In those cases where strict time limits have been set down, for example, cases allocated to the fast track, the 'elusive' expert is on his way out and the response by the court to a request for more time is likely to be 'get another expert'.

The process of limiting the use of expert evidence begins even before litigation starts where there are protocols, for example the personal injury pre-action protocol, which encourage the joint selection of experts (see Chapter 5, 'Pre-Action Protocols').

EXPERT EVIDENCE

Nature of expert evidence

In order to be adduced at trial, expert evidence must be admissible expert evidence under s 3 of the Civil Evidence Act 1972. To qualify as expert evidence within s 3, the party seeking to call the evidence must satisfy the court of the existence of a body of expertise governed by recognised standards or rules of conduct capable of influencing the court's decision on any of the issues that it has to decide. Further, the witness to be called must have sufficient familiarity with and knowledge of the expertise in question to render his opinion potentially of value in resolving any of those issues (see judgment of Evans-Lombe J in *Liverpool Roman Catholic Archdiocese Trust v Goldberg* [2001] 1 WLR 2337; [2001] 4 All ER 950, and his earlier judgment in *Barings plc v Coopers and Lybrand* [2001] EWCA Civ 1163).

Expert instructed for the purpose of court proceedings

A distinction should be drawn between an expert instructed to prepare evidence for the purpose of court proceedings and an expert instructed to advise or inform a party about the subject of his expertise, which may include advice about the expert evidence obtained for the court proceedings. It is only an expert instructed to give or prepare evidence for the purposes of court proceedings who has an obligation to be independent of the party instructing him and who owes an overriding duty to the court (r 35.2).

Shadow expert

In a complex case a party may feel it appropriate to instruct a separate expert to advise him on such matters as the questions to be put to a single joint expert. Such an expert is often referred to as a 'shadow expert'. A shadow expert will not be subject to the rules in Part 35, but neither will he be permitted to give evidence to the court, and his fees and expenses are unlikely to be recoverable from the other party.

Expert's overriding duty to the court

An expert instructed to give or prepare evidence for the purposes of court proceedings owes a paramount duty to help the court on matters within his expertise (r 35.3(1); PD 35, para 1.1). This duty overrides any obligation the expert may have to the person who instructed him or by whom he is paid (r 35.3(2); PD 35, para 1.1). The expert should address his report to the court and not to the instructing party. Also, at the end of his report the expert must include a statement that he understands his duty to the court and has complied, and will continue to comply, with that duty (r 35.10(2); PD 35, paras 2.1, 2.2(9)).

In the light of the court's duty under r 1.1, the expert's role is therefore to assist the court, on matters within his expertise, to further the overriding objective to deal with cases justly.

Independent and impartial expert evidence

The role of an expert instructed to give or prepare evidence for the purposes of court proceedings is to provide an independent, objective and unbiased opinion on matters within his expertise in order to assist the court to decide the expert issues in the case. An expert should therefore ensure that he is unaffected by the pressures of litigation and not assume the role of an advocate seeking to persuade the court to make a decision favourable to the party instructing him (PD 35, paras 1.2, 1.3).

It is a long-established principle of civil procedure that 'expert evidence presented to the court should be and should be seen to be the independent product of the expert uninfluenced as to form or content by the exigencies of litigation' (see *dictum* of Lord Wilberforce in *Whitehouse v Jordan* [1981] 1 WLR 246). However, in introducing the reforms to expert evidence under the CPR, Lord Woolf's intention was to 'increase the independence of experts and to reduce their partisan use by the parties' (see IR, Chapter 23, para 4, www.dca.gov.uk/civil/interfr.htm). It is thought that ensuring that an expert owes an overriding duty to the court and not to the party instructing him will increase the independence and impartiality of experts.

In *Liverpool Roman Catholic Archdiocesan Trustees Inc v Goldberg*, a claim for professional negligence against a barrister, the defendant's expert, a barrister, had known the defendant for 28 years and was his good friend; they were also in the same chambers. In his report, the expert referred to his relationship with the defendant and said: 'I should say that my personal sympathies are engaged to a greater degree than would probably be normal with an expert witness.' The court held that this admission rendered the evidence unacceptable as the evidence of an expert, on grounds of public policy, in accordance with the principle in *Whitehouse v Jordan*, that justice must be seen to be done as well as done. The court accepted that expert evidence from a friend of one of the parties would not be automatically excluded. However, where it is demonstrated that there exists a relationship between the proposed expert and the party calling him which a reasonable observer might think was capable of affecting the views of the expert so as to make them unduly favourable to that party, his evidence should not be admitted however unbiased the conclusions of the expert might be. The question is one of fact, namely, the extent and nature of the relationship between the proposed witness and the party.

There is no overriding objection to calling as an expert a person who is employed by the party calling him, as long as that person is suitably qualified to give expert evidence and it can be demonstrated that he is aware of his primary duty to the court (*Field v Leeds CC* (2000) 17 EG 165).

Field v Leeds CC involved a claim by tenants against their local authority landlord for disrepair. The issue in the case was whether the disrepair was caused by condensation or rising damp. If the disrepair was caused by condensation then the local authority would have no responsibility, but if it was caused by rising damp then it could be responsible. The local authority wished to call one of its employees as an expert witness on this issue. The court held that there was no general rule excluding an employee from acting as an expert as long as that person was suitably qualified and could demonstrate that he was aware of his duty to the court and his duty to be objective. However, it was recognised that the fact of such a person's employment might go to the weight of his evidence.

Experts cannot be appointed on a 'no win, no fee' basis. In *R v Secretary of State for Transport ex p Factortame and Others* [2002] EWCA Civ 932, the Court of Appeal did not find an agreement champertous which provided for a firm of accountants to be paid in fees 8% 'of the final settlement received'. This was because the accountants did not perform the role of expert witnesses – other experts were retained for that purpose who were entirely independent – and the accountants' work consisted largely of important back-up services for the two independent experts. However, it is likely to be contrary to public policy for an expert witness to give evidence on a contingency fee basis. An expert witness owes an overriding duty to the court, and it would give the expert a significant financial interest in the outcome of the case which would undermine his independence were he to give evidence on a contingency fee basis.

Under PD 35, para 1.6, an expert who has prepared a report for the purpose of court proceedings is required to inform all parties (that is, not just the instructing/ paying party) as well as the court, if appropriate, without delay, if, after producing a report, he changes his view on any material matter. Obviously this duty will apply only if the instructing party wishes to rely on the expert's report and it has been disclosed in the proceedings.

Expert's access to the court

An expert is entitled to file a written request to the court for directions to assist him in carrying out his functions as an expert (r 35.14(1)). However, an expert must, unless the court orders otherwise, provide a copy of any proposed request for directions to the party instructing him at least seven days before he files the request, and to all other parties at least four days before he files the request (r 35.14(2)).

When the court gives directions it may also direct that a party be served with a copy of those directions (r 35.14(3)).

An example where an expert may seek directions from the court may be where he is unable to obtain the co-operation of another expert to hold a discussion and prepare a statement of issues. An expert may also experience difficulties in relation to the party instructing him due to the overriding duty he owes to the court and the obligation to be impartial and independent of any party.

Expert evidence at trial

The general rule is that expert evidence is to be given in a written report (r 35.5). A party will need to seek permission to call an expert to give oral evidence at trial.

Where each party has an expert, the trial judge must give reasons for preferring one expert's evidence over the other (*Dyson v Leeds CC* (1999) LTL, 22 November). In *Dyson*, the claimant was the executor of the estate of a plumber who died of mesothelioma caused by exposure to asbestos. The principal issue in the case was whether occupiers of property should have realised and taken precautions against asbestos dust in the 1950s or the 1970s. The judge preferred the evidence of the defendant's expert and therefore found in favour of the defendant. The claimant appealed on the grounds that the judge gave no reasons for preferring the defendant's expert evidence. The Court of Appeal held that a judge must give reasons for preferring one side's expert evidence over the other, and in this case it would have been perfectly possible for the judge to have set out in sufficient detail why it seemed more likely that knowledge would have come to occupiers in the 1970s rather than in the 1950s. As the appeal court was faced with disputed evidence which was not necessarily compelling on one side or the other, it held that the only way that the injustice could be corrected was by remitting the case back to the county court for a retrial.

A judge is entitled to form a conclusion based on a consideration of the expert evidence adduced by both parties. In *Coker v Barkland Cleaning Ltd* (1999) LTL, 6 December, the claimant sustained an injury to his back when he was struck by a cleaning machine while working in a supermarket. Each party adduced expert evidence. The claimant's expert attributed the claimant's symptoms to the accident, while the defendant's expert said that the claimant's symptoms were not as a result of the accident but arose from a pre-existing disability. The defendant's expert found that the claimant suffered an exacerbation of his pre-existing symptoms for a maximum period of one year after the accident. The judge preferred the evidence of the defendant's expert, except that he found that the symptoms had been exacerbated for a period of two years rather than one year. The claimant appealed on the ground that the judge should not have preferred the defendant's expert's evidence, and the defendant cross-appealed on the ground that there was no evidential basis for the judge to extend the period of exacerbation from one year to two. The Court of Appeal found that the judge was entitled to accept the general effect of the defendant's expert's evidence, namely, that based on his knowledge and experience, a person would be expected to recover from an accident of this nature within one year. The court further found that the judge was entitled to form a conclusion, taking into account both the claimant's and the defendant's expert evidence, that a longer period of exacerbation was more likely and to assess that as a period of two years rather than one.

In *Britannia Zinc Ltd v Southern Electric Contracting Ltd and Another* [2002] EWHC 606 (TCC), the court held that once litigation has been commenced and has come to trial, there is very limited scope for the court to derive help from the evidence of a loss adjuster. The nature of the expertise of a loss adjuster is essentially in evaluating evidence of loss, and, by the time a claim has come to trial, the evaluation of such evidence is the function of the court. It is the assessment of the trial judge, having heard or seen relevant evidence of loss, that matters once the claim comes to trial, not the opinion of a loss adjuster.

Expert evidence at small claims hearings

Expert evidence is also restricted for claims allocated to the small claims track (rr 27.2(1)(e), 35.1). A party must seek permission to adduce expert evidence, whether written or oral, at a small claims hearing (r 27.5). However, in accordance with the proportionate nature of such proceedings, under r 27.2(1)(e) only certain sections of Part 35 apply to expert evidence on the small claims track, namely:

(a) the court's duty to restrict expert evidence (r 35.1);

(b) the expert's overriding duty to the court (r 35.3);

(c) the court's power to direct the appointment of a single joint expert (r 35.7); and

(d) the rule governing instructions to a single joint expert (r 35.8).

If a party is given permission to adduce expert evidence for a hearing allocated to the small claims track, the amount of costs that can be recovered from an opponent for the expert's fees is limited to £200 for each expert (r 27.14(3)(d); PD 27, para 7.3(2)). Courts should bear this in mind when ordering experts' reports in such matters. If the small claim requires an expert's report to decide issues in the case and the expert's fees are likely to exceed the £200 limit, the parties should consider applying to the court to allocate the matter to a higher track where the limitation on recoverable fees will not apply.

Codes of Guidance for experts

The Civil Procedure Working Party, led by the Expert Witness Institute Chair, Sir Louis Blom Cooper, QC, has produced a *Guide for Experts and Those Instructing Them for the Purpose of Court Proceedings* which is intended to assist in the interpretation of the rules relating to expert evidence and to 'promote better communication and dealings both between the expert and the instructing party and between the parties' (see the preamble to the *Guide* available at www.ewi.org.uk).

The Academy of Expert Witnesses, the self-proclaimed 'largest professional body for expert witnesses in the UK and around the world', produces the *Code of Guidance for Experts and Those Instructing Them* (available at www.academy-experts.org). The Academy's guide is designed to give practical guidance on all aspects of the use of experts both before and after proceedings are commenced. The Academy's guide is quoted with approval in the cases of *Smith v Stephens* (2001) LTL, 16 October and *Peet v Mid-Kent Healthcare NHS Trust* [2001] EWCA Civ 1703 as providing an appropriate standard for experts to follow. The Working Party's *Guide* is criticised by the Academy for 'falling short of the kind of practical, user-friendly guide required by expert witnesses and lawyers' (see Academy's press release, 20 December 2001, available at www.academy-experts.org).

COURT'S DUTY TO RESTRICT EXPERT EVIDENCE

The court has a duty to restrict expert evidence to that which is reasonably required to resolve the proceedings (r 35.1). Under its duty actively to manage cases, the court should therefore identify what expert evidence is needed, if any, to resolve the issues in the case. The court should then go on to make directions for expert evidence that is limited to deciding those issues. It would also appear that this duty places an obligation on the court to limit the amount of expert evidence admitted by directing, in appropriate cases, that the evidence be given by a single expert jointly instructed by the parties rather than two experts separately instructed by each party.

In *MMR and MR Vaccine Litigation (No 4)* [2002] EWHC 1213, QB, the court held that Part 35 of the CPR, which deals with expert evidence, is not intended to permit reports prepared for interim applications to be the basis of questions for use at trial. This is particularly so when the reports themselves are not to be relied on at trial either because the experts will be serving new reports, or because the experts who prepared the reports are not the experts whose reports would be relied on at trial.

Permission to adduce expert evidence

A party must apply for the court's permission to adduce expert evidence (r 35.4(1)). A party should, if possible, identify the actual expert he wishes to rely upon before seeking the court's permission to adduce expert evidence. If a party has not identified a particular expert at that stage, he must in any event identify the field of expertise he wishes to rely upon (r 35.4(2)). A party will usually apply for permission when filing his allocation questionnaire. As the court will also be making other directions at that stage for the management of the proceedings, including fixing a trial window, if the party has identified a particular expert he wishes to rely upon and there is a prospect that that expert may attend trial to give evidence, he should ensure that the expert has provided him with details of any dates he wishes to avoid.

If the court gives permission for expert evidence to be relied upon, it will be restricted to the expert named or the particular field identified (r 35.4(3)). A party will therefore need to make a further application to the court if, for any reason, he wishes to rely upon the evidence of a different expert or in another field.

The court also has the power to limit the amount of the expert's fees and expenses that a party wishing to rely on expert evidence may recover from any other party (r 35.4(4)).

FORM AND CONTENT OF EXPERTS' REPORTS

The presumption is that expert evidence will be given in the form of a written report unless the court orders otherwise (r 35.5(1)). Although a party can seek permission for their expert to attend trial to give evidence, for cases allocated to the fast track this will be permitted only where it is necessary in the interests of justice (r 35.5(2)).

An expert's report prepared for the purpose of court proceedings must comply with the requirements set out in PD 35, which specifies the form and content of experts' reports (r 35.10(1)).

Statement of duty to the court

An expert's report should be addressed to the court, not the party from whom the expert received his instructions (PD 35, para 2.1). Also, at the end of his report there must be a statement that the expert understands his duty to the court and has complied with that duty (r 35.10(2); PD 35, para 2.2(9)).

In *Stevens v Gullis* [2001] 1 All ER 527, the defendant's expert was debarred from giving evidence because the court found that the defendant's expert had no concept of the requirements placed upon an expert witness and did not understand his duty to the court or set out in his report that he understood that duty. Also, the report prepared by the expert did not comply with the requirements of PD 35 in a number of respects.

Expert's qualifications

The expert must give details of his qualifications in his report (PD 35, para 2.2(1)). An expert should be suitably qualified and have relevant expertise in an area in issue in the case, and be aware of his primary duty to the court and his duty to be objective (*Field v Leeds CC* (2000) 17 EG 165).

Expert's instructions

An expert's report must include a statement of the substance of all material instructions, whether written or oral, on which the report was based (r 35.10(3); PD 35, para 2.2(3)). In many cases an expert will annex a copy of his instructions to his report, and a party should therefore be careful not to include privileged material that he does not want to disclose to the other party in his instructions to the expert.

Although instructions to the expert are not privileged from disclosure, the court will not order a party to disclose specific documents forming those instructions or allow the opponent to question the expert in court on those instructions, unless there are reasonable grounds to consider that the statement of instructions is inaccurate or incomplete (r 35.10(4); PD 35, para 4).

Morris and Others v Bank of India [2001] All ER (D) 21; (2001) LTL, 16 November, is an example of a case where the court was satisfied that the statement of instructions was inaccurate or incomplete. In that case factual witness statements were not due to be exchanged until after exchange of experts' reports. However, there were reasonable grounds to suppose that one party's expert was supplied with draft witness statements as part of his instructions, but he did not make this clear in his statement of the substance of his instructions. The court recognised that if the expert was supplied with draft witness statements for the purposes of his instructions then those draft witness statements would lose their privileged character. Further, because the statement of instructions was inaccurate or incomplete the party instructing the expert was obliged to disclose the instructions, including the draft witness statements, to the opponent. The court suggested that in order to avoid such an outcome the instructing party should have formulated certain assumptions of fact for the expert to use for the basis of his report, rather than actually send him the draft witness statements.

Parties will need to exercise extra judgment in respect of all communications with 'their' experts: there is no privilege in any such matters if they are material to the opinion and it will be for the expert to judge (with or without help from the court under r 35.14) what to disclose.

Content of expert's report

In general terms, an expert must make it clear which facts are within his own knowledge and justify the opinions he has reached in his report. Accordingly, PD 35 specifies that an expert's report must:

(a) give details of any literature or other material on which the expert has relied in making the report;

(b) make clear which of the facts stated in the report are within the expert's own knowledge;

(c) say who carried out any examination, measurement, test or experiment which the expert has used for the report, giving the qualifications of the person and saying whether or not the test or experiment has been carried out under the expert's supervision;

(d) where there is a range of opinion on the matters dealt with in the report, summarise the range of opinion and give reasons for the expert's own opinion; and

(e) if the expert is not able to give his opinion without qualification, he must state the qualification (PD 35, para 2.2(2)–(6), (8)).

An expert's report must also contain a summary of the conclusions reached in the report (PD 35, para 2.2(7)).

Statement of truth

An expert's report must be verified by a statement of truth in the following form:

> I confirm that in so far as the facts stated in my report are within my own knowledge I have made clear what they are and I believe them to be true and that the opinions I have expressed represent my true and complete professional opinion. (PD 35, para 2.4.)

Written questions to experts

A party is entitled, as of right, to one opportunity to put written questions to a single joint expert or an expert instructed by another party for the purpose only of clarification of his report, as long as the questions are put within 28 days of service of the expert's report (r 35.6(2)). Where a party sends written questions to the expert, a copy should at the same time be sent to the other parties (PD 35, para 5.2).

If a party wishes to put further questions, or where it is later than 28 days after service of the expert's report, or where the questions are to be put for any other purpose other than clarification of the report, a party can do so only if the court gives permission or the other party agrees (r 35.6(2)). If an opponent will not agree, the court is likely to grant permission readily for relevant questions to be put which seek more than mere clarification of an expert's report. The rationale behind questions is to seek to avoid the need for experts to attend trial and be available for cross-examination. Therefore the court is likely to allow questions to be put which would be appropriate questions to put to an expert in cross-examination.

In *Mutch v Allen* [2001] EWCA Civ 76, the claimant was involved in a road traffic accident while travelling as a backseat passenger in a car driven by the defendant. He was not wearing a seat belt at the time, and as a result was thrown out of the vehicle and sustained serious injuries. The defendant alleged contributory negligence on the part of the claimant for not wearing a seat belt, which failure has been a criminal offence for backseat passengers since 1989. In practice, in most cases the failure to wear a seatbelt can reduce a claimant's damages by 50% or more. The claimant's medical expert's report noted that the claimant was not wearing a seat belt but said nothing about the consequences of this in respect of the injuries suffered by the claimant. The defendant put a written question to the claimant's expert asking him whether the severity of the claimant's injuries would have been materially reduced, or prevented altogether, if he had been wearing a seat belt. The claimant's expert answered the question in the affirmative.

Although the question was not strictly for the purposes of clarification, the defendant was entitled to put it because the court gave him permission to do so. The Court of Appeal was of the opinion that the defendant was entitled to rely on the expert's answers to his question in support of his case for contributory negligence. However, in the circumstances it also indicated that the claimant's expert should be called to give oral evidence at trial and that both sides be permitted to cross-examine him. It further indicated that this might be a case where the claimant should be entitled to call other expert evidence on this issue.

An expert's answers to such written questions are treated as part of the expert's report (r 35.6(3)).

If a party puts a written question to an expert instructed by another party in accordance with r 35.6 and the expert does not answer the question, the court has the power to order that the party who instructed the expert may not rely on the evidence of that expert, or may not recover the fees and expenses of that expert from the other party, or both (r 35.6(4)).

The party instructing the expert must pay any fees charged by the expert for answering questions put by the other party. However, this does not affect the court's decision as to who is ultimately liable to pay the expert's costs (PD 35, para 5.3).

Disclosure of expert's report

The court will usually make directions about disclosure of expert evidence on giving permission for the use of expert evidence. The most usual direction is for simultaneous exchange of expert reports. However, this does not apply to personal injury cases, where the claimant must annex a copy of a medical report about his injuries to his particulars of claim (PD 16, para 4.3). Therefore, if the defendant has permission to rely on separate expert evidence in response, this will necessarily be disclosed after the defendant has been served with the claimant's report.

If a party obtains an expert report which is not a single joint expert report, it is privileged from disclosure and a party cannot be compelled to disclose it if he does not wish to do so (*Carlson v Townsend* [2001] EWCA Civ 511). However, if a party fails to disclose an expert's report to his opponent, he may not use the report at trial or call the expert to give evidence orally unless the court gives permission (r 35.13).

Also, if a party wishes to substitute one expert for another, in most cases a condition of the order granting permission to instruct a fresh expert will be that the party must disclose the earlier expert report to the opponent (*Beck v Ministry of Defence* [2003] EWCA Civ 1043). In *Beck v Ministry of Defence*, the claimant brought a high value claim for damages against his employer for negligent psychiatric treatment. The claimant contended that the treatment provided by the defendant not only failed to cure him but exacerbated his condition, turning it into a major depressive illness resulting in his discharge from his post with the RAF and causing the long term destruction of his employment prospects for the rest of his life. The parties had permission to obtain expert reports, but the defendants lost confidence in their expert psychiatrist despite the fact that his report was favourable to them.

The Court of Appeal considered that the case management judge had properly exercised his discretion when deciding that it was just to allow the defendants to instruct a fresh expert; the claimant would suffer no prejudice and it would have no impact on the timing of the trial. The Court of Appeal also upheld the judge's decision to order that the defendants must disclose the earlier expert's report as a condition of the granting of permission to instruct a fresh expert. The reason for the condition was held to be to discourage 'expert shopping', that is, seeking to find a fresh expert when the conclusions of the earlier expert are unfavourable to a party.

The court felt that to be required to disclose the earlier report would act as a check against this possible abuse and ensure that justice was seen to be done.

In *Baron v Lovell* (1999) *The Times*, 14 September, the defendant was refused permission to call expert evidence at trial when he disclosed his expert report at a very late stage in the proceedings. The claimant's claim was a personal injury claim arising out of a road traffic accident. The claimant's medical reports were annexed to his particulars of claim. The defendant failed to comply with the court timetable for service of experts' reports and served his report at a late stage. The defendant then failed to attend a pre-trial review at which directions for expert evidence at the trial were considered by the judge. The judge found that there was very little difference of opinion between the claimant's and the defendant's experts, and in the light of the late disclosure of the evidence held that the defendant was not allowed to rely on expert evidence at trial. The judge's decision was upheld by the Court of Appeal.

Where a party has disclosed an expert's report it will no longer be privileged and any other party may use that report as evidence at the trial (r 35.11).

SINGLE JOINT EXPERT

Where two or more parties wish to submit expert evidence the court has an unrestricted power, exercisable in accordance with the overriding objective, to decide that the expert evidence should be given by a single joint expert rather than by the parties' individual experts (r 35.7). Lord Woolf, in *Peet v Mid-Kent Healthcare Trust* [2001] EWCA Civ 1703, emphasised that the court has the power to make such a direction and it was not a matter of choice for the parties. He also said in that case, 'unless there is a reason for not having a single expert, there should only be a single expert' (at [28]).

In practice, the court should appoint a single joint expert only where it is appropriate to do so. A single joint expert will usually be appropriate where the amount involved is relatively low and where the issue for the expert is simple to identify. However, in fast track cases, where the trial is limited to a period of one day and oral expert evidence at trial will be permitted only where it is necessary in the interests of justice (r 35.5(2)), a direction for a single joint expert will be the rule rather than the exception.

A challenge to an order for a single joint expert can be made only by an appeal, not by seeking different directions as to the expert at a subsequent case management conference before a different judge (see r 35.7(1); *Jameson v Lovis and Another* [2001] EWCA Civ 1264). In *Jameson v Lovis*, the claimant's attempt to challenge the order for a single joint expert, by seeking instead to obtain permission to use his own expert evidence at a subsequent case management conference, was described by the Court of Appeal as 'a full-frontal assault on the whole notion of court-imposed single joint experts [which was] an integral part of the civil justice reforms' (at [29], *per* Simon Brown LJ).

It is recognised that it may not be appropriate to order the appointment of a single joint expert in clinical negligence cases where there is often more than one school of thought as to proper medical practice. In *Oxley v Penwarden* (2001) LTL, 6 March, the claimant sued his doctor for negligence in failing to diagnose a condition, which failure he alleged led to his leg being amputated above the knee. Both parties wished to instruct their own expert on the issue of causation. At a case management conference, the district judge ordered that this was an appropriate case in which the parties should agree a single expert vascular surgeon on the issue of causation. However, the Court of Appeal, in overturning that decision, found that this was eminently a case where it was necessary for the parties to have the opportunity of investigating causation through an expert of their choice and to have the opportunity to call that evidence at trial. The court recognised that it was inevitable in cases such as these that parties would find the greatest difficulty in agreeing the appointment of a single expert. If there was more than one school of thought on this issue, the selection of an expert from one particular school of thought would effectively decide an essential question in the case without the opportunity for challenge.

However, in respect of any aspect of a clinical negligence case that involves non-medical expert evidence, such as that of an employment consultant or a nursing specialist, the court will usually order that such evidence be given by a single joint expert (see *dicta* of Woolf LCJ in *Peet v Mid-Kent Healthcare NHS Trust* [2001] EWCA Civ 1703 at [5]).

Jointly selected experts

A single joint expert is jointly selected and instructed by both parties. However, this should be distinguished from the situation where the parties jointly agree the identity of an expert whom only one party goes on to instruct. The Pre-Action Protocol for Personal Injury Claims promotes the practice of the parties agreeing the selection of an expert mutually acceptable to both parties but who is then instructed by only one party (see Chapter 5, 'Pre-Action Protocols'). Where the parties merely agree the identity of the expert but do not jointly instruct the expert, any report prepared by that expert will remain privileged and the other party will not be entitled to see it unless the instructing party agrees (see *Carlson v Townsend*; Chapter 5, 'Pre-Action Protocols').

Selecting a single joint expert

Where there is a direction for the appointment of a single joint expert, in the first instance the parties should attempt to agree the identity of the expert. In practice the parties exchange lists of names of suitable experts and attempt to agree a mutually acceptable one. However, if the parties cannot agree who the expert should be, the court may either select the expert from a list prepared or identified by the parties, or make an order that the expert be selected in another manner, for instance, from a list prepared by the court (r 35.7(3)).

Instructing a single joint expert

Where the court has directed that a single joint expert should be appointed by the parties, each party is entitled to give instructions to the expert (r 35.8(1)). In practice the parties usually attempt to agree the instructions to be sent to the expert, but if that is not possible each party should send its own instructions to the expert. The court has no jurisdiction to order that there be a single letter of instruction to a single joint expert and one party is not bound by instructions given to the expert by the other party (*Yorke v Katra* [2003] EWCA Civ 867).

If separate instructions are sent, each party must send a copy of those instructions to the other party (r 35.8(2)).

The single joint expert's report

Each instructing party will be entitled to receive a copy of the single joint expert's report. In most cases, the very nature of a single joint expert's report will mean that the findings of the report will favour only one of the instructing parties. A party is entitled to put written questions to the expert seeking clarification of his report, and questions for purposes other than clarification with the permission of the court or the consent of the other party (r 35.6(2)).

It should be noted that just because a single joint expert's findings are adverse to one of the parties, this does not mean that that party is effectively bound by his conclusion (*Layland v Fairview New Homes plc & Lewisham LBC* [2002] EWHC 1350). In *Layland*, the claimants bought a flat from Fairview but were unaware that Lewisham LBC had plans to build an incinerator and power plant on land nearby. The claimants brought proceedings against the defendants for misrepresentation based on their failure to disclose Lewisham's plans in relation to the power plant. A single joint expert was appointed whose report concluded that there was no diminution in the value of the flat as a result of the proximity of the power plant. In the light of the findings of that report the defendants applied for summary judgment of the claimant's claim. The court held that as long as there was a prospect of the expert through cross-examination, or the court through submissions, being persuaded to reach a different conclusion to that contained within the report, summary judgment should not be entered against the claimant on the basis of the expert's report.

Attendance of the single joint expert at trial

The intention behind the rules for the appointment of a single joint expert is that that expert's evidence should be by way of written report, and that this should be the evidence in the case on the issues covered by that expert's report. There is therefore usually no order for the single joint expert to attend trial. However, this is not to say that a party cannot obtain such an order if it would be in accordance with the overriding objective for that party to be permitted to amplify the expert's opinion, or to cross-examine the expert on his opinion at trial.

Separate meeting with single joint expert

When a single joint expert is instructed, he owes an equal duty of openness and confidence to both parties, as well as an overriding duty to the court. Both parties should know what information has been placed before the expert. It would therefore be totally inconsistent with the concept of a single joint expert for one party, without the agreement of the other party, to conduct a separate conference with the expert in order to test his views in the absence of the other party (see *dicta* of Lord Woolf LCJ in *Peet v Mid-Kent Healthcare NHS Trust; Smith v Stephens* (2001) LTL, 16 October, QBD).

The fees of a single joint expert

The instructing parties will be jointly and severally liable for the payment of the expert's fees and expenses unless the court orders otherwise (r 35.8(5)). On making an order for a single joint expert to be instructed, but before he is instructed, the court can give directions limiting the amount that can be paid by way of fees and expenses to the joint expert and directing that the instructing parties pay that amount into court (r 35.8(4)). In *Kranidiotes v Paschali* [2001] EWCA Civ 357, the judge limited the amount of the expert's fees to a proportionate figure in the light of the value of the claim. The single joint expert appointed to prepare a report quoted a fee that was substantially higher than that allowed by the court and the court therefore ordered that a different expert should be appointed instead.

Permission for a second expert's report

Where a single joint expert has been instructed, it is almost inevitable that his findings will support one party's case over the other. In appropriate circumstances, where it would be unjust not to do so, a party who disagrees with the findings of a single joint expert will be given permission to obtain and rely upon his own separate expert evidence (see *Daniels v Walker* [2000] 1 WLR 1382; *Cosgrove v Pattison* (2001) LTL, 7 February).

In *Daniels v Walker*, the parties agreed jointly to instruct an expert to give an opinion on the care requirements of the injured claimant. The defendant did not accept the findings of the single joint expert and wished to instruct his own separate expert. As the case was substantial, and the defendant's reasons for objecting to the findings of the single joint expert report were not 'fanciful', the Court of Appeal gave the defendant permission to obtain his own separate expert. However, the court indicated that where a modest sum was involved it was likely to be disproportionate to obtain a second report 'in any circumstances', and instead questions should be put to the expert who has already prepared the report.

Cosgrove v Pattison involved a boundary dispute between neighbours. The parties jointly instructed a surveyor to provide an opinion on a number of issues, including the precise location of the boundary line between the two properties. The single joint expert's report favoured one of the parties and the other applied for permission to rely on a separate report from another expert. The court found in this case that it was a sufficient reason to grant that permission where the party had found a new expert who had a contrary view to the joint expert which gave grounds for believing that the single joint expert was wrong. It should be noted that the court indicated that this would not be a sufficient reason in every case and it would depend on all the circumstances of the case.

DISCUSSION BETWEEN EXPERTS AND STATEMENT OF ISSUES

The court may direct discussion between experts so as to identify the issues and, where possible, reach an agreed opinion on those issues (r 35.12(1)). The court may specify the issues that the experts must address when they meet (r 35.12(2)). This may include directions on the need to deal with drafting of agendas for expert meetings and guidelines for expert meetings. The court may also direct that the experts prepare a statement of issues after they have met, showing those issues on which they agree and those on which they disagree, with a summary of their reasons for disagreeing (r 35.12(3)).

In *Hubbard and Others v Lambeth Southwark and Lewisham HA and Others* [2001] EWCA Civ 1455, CA, the court extolled the virtues of pre-trial discussions between experts, stating that in almost every case experts are able to narrow the issues to be determined at trial, even in very complex cases, and that an obvious time and cost benefit flowed from this. The court held that the court is not prevented from making such an order, even if both parties object, and should do so if it thinks something will come of it. The court saw nothing wrong with a general approach by case management judges to making an order for such discussions to take place where there has been an exchange of expert reports. A mere objection by one party would not be sufficient; some very good reason for not having a meeting would have to be shown. The court also held that an order for such a meeting does not raise any issues under Art 6 of the European Convention on Human Rights.

Where there is a meeting of experts, any communications associated with that meeting are without prejudice and protected by privilege (r 35.12(4)). However, any statement of issues prepared by the experts as a result of that without prejudice meeting is not privileged (*Robin Ellis Ltd v Malwright Ltd* [1999] 2 WLR 745). It was recognised in *Robin Ellis Ltd v Malwright Ltd* that after giving his initial privileged advice an expert may honestly change his opinion either as a result of further research and thought, or as a result of discussions with other experts. If so, the expert should record that change either in the joint statement of issues, or in a supplementary report. In confirming that the statement of issues was not privileged, the court explained that the purpose of a statement of issues was to assist the court in the case management of the claim. Further, it was only as an open document that the joint statement of issues could serve its purpose, which in the interests of public policy was to narrow the issues in dispute and thus increase the prospects of the claim settling.

The purpose of a meeting of experts is not to achieve a settlement and any agreement reached, even if contained in a statement of issues, will not be binding on the parties (r 35.12(5)). However, in practical terms a party wishing to present a case inconsistent with such an agreement will face considerable difficulties.

In *Smith v Stephens*, the court refused to grant permission for there to be a joint meeting between experts at which the claimant's representative would attend but not the defendant's. The court held that to allow otherwise would favour one side over the other, which would not accord with the overriding objective and would fail to secure an 'even playing field' (see also *Peet v Mid-Kent Healthcare NHS Trust* [2001] EWCA Civ 1703).

ACCESS TO INFORMATION

Where a party has access to information which is not reasonably available to the other party, the court may direct that the party who has access to the information must prepare and file a document recording the information and serve a copy of that document on the other party (r 35.9). A party seeking such information from another party should apply to the court for an order if the other party does not agree to provide the information voluntarily. This provision may perhaps be used by a party seeking data or test results from another party, particularly where one party has substantially more resources than the other, for example, in a claim by an individual against a hospital or a large company.

COURT APPOINTED ASSESSOR

The court has the power under s 70 of the Supreme Court Act 1981 and s 63 of the County Courts Act 1984 to appoint an assessor to assist it to dispose of proceedings. Assessors are commonplace in admiralty proceedings, where they are appointed to advise the court on nautical matters. If the court exercises its power to appoint an assessor the provisions of r 35.15 will apply. The role of an assessor must be distinguished from that of an expert. The purpose of an assessor is to advise and assist the court where the subject matter of the proceedings involves technical or scientific matters (r 35.15(2)). An assessor does not decide any issue; he advises the judge so as to enable him to reach a decision. The assessor will not give evidence in the proceedings and is not available for questioning or cross-examination (PD 35, para 7.4).

If the court intends to appoint an assessor it will give the parties 21 days' notice in writing of the name of the proposed assessor, of the matter in respect of which the assistance of the assessor will be sought, and of the qualifications of the assessor to give that assistance (PD 35, para 7.1). The parties have an opportunity to object to the appointment of the proposed assessor, either personally or in respect of his qualifications, by filing a written objection within seven days of receipt of the court's notification of the proposed appointment of an assessor. The court will take any objection into account when deciding whether or not to make the appointment (PD 35, paras 7.2, 7.3).

The court may direct the assessor to prepare a report for the court on any matter at issue in the proceedings (r 35.15(3)(a)). If the assessor prepares a report before the trial has begun, the court will send a copy of it to the parties who may use it at trial (r 35.15(4)). The court may also direct that the assessor attend the trial to advise the court on any matter in the proceedings (r 35.15(3)(b)).

The court will determine how much the assessor is to be paid for his services, and this will form part of the costs of the proceedings (r 35.15(5)). The court may also order any party to deposit a sum of money in court in respect of the assessor's fees, and where it does so the assessor will not be asked to act until the sum has been deposited (r 35.15(6)). However, the appointment of an assessor will be justified only in a substantial case, and r 35.15 does not apply to cases allocated to the small claims track (r 27.2(1)(e)).

EXPERT IMMUNITY

An expert witness who gives evidence at trial cannot be sued for anything that he says in court. This immunity from suit extends to the contents of the report that he adopts as, or incorporates into, his evidence (*Raiss v Palmano* [2001] PNLR 21; *Stanton v Callaghan* [2000] QB 75; [1999] 2 WLR 745; [1998] 4 All ER 961). The reason for the rule is one of public policy to ensure that the administration of justice is not impeded. Witnesses, including expert witnesses, should not be deterred from giving evidence from fear that they might be sued by a dissatisfied party.

In *Stanton v Callaghan*, the parties' experts had a meeting and prepared a joint statement of issues. As a result of matters agreed with the opponent's expert, the claimants' expert drastically changed his position regarding the value of the claimants' claim and amended his draft report to reflect this. In the light of that revised evidence the claimants were advised to accept a payment into court of a much lower amount than the claimants previously expected to obtain, with resulting adverse costs consequences. The claimants brought a claim against their expert for negligence for this change of opinion. The Court of Appeal held that any joint statement prepared by an expert following a meeting of experts was immune from suit on the public policy grounds of ensuring that there was no tension between an expert's duty to assist the court and fear of the consequences of departure from previous advice.

In *Raiss v Palmano*, the court held that an expert witness is entitled to immunity for reasons of public policy even in respect of evidence that turns out to have been dishonest. In that case the expert falsely stated in his report that he was on the Royal Institute of Chartered Surveyors' Panel of Arbitrators, but was subsequently discredited in court when he was forced to admit that this statement was untrue.

However, an expert's immunity does not extend to protect an expert, who has been retained to advise as to the merits of a party's claim in litigation, from a claim by that party in respect of that advice, notwithstanding that it was anticipated when the advice was given that the expert would be a witness at the trial if that litigation were to proceed (*Stanton v Callaghan*). Therefore, a claimant who launches proceedings on the basis of negligent advice from an expert, and who would not have brought proceedings if he had obtained advice from a competent expert, may be able to bring proceedings against the expert in negligence even if the claimant expected to call that expert as a witness at the court proceedings.

Note also that, although the CPR do not specify a sanction for an expert's failure to comply with his duty to the court, it is appropriate to refer 'biased and irrational' conduct of an expert to his professional body (*Pearce v Ove Arup Partnership Ltd and Others* (2001) LTL, 8 November, Ch D).

CHAPTER 31

EVIDENCE

INTRODUCTION

The Civil Procedure Rules (CPR) enhanced the court's powers to control evidence and those powers are to be applied in accordance with the overriding objective. The application of the overriding objective, and in particular the requirements to save expense and to deal with a case in ways which are proportionate, may result in the court restricting the scope and type of evidence that is to be adduced to prove the issues in a case. Further, the general intent of the CPR is that litigation should be conducted with as little technicality as possible, and this has particular significance for the rules of evidence (see *dictum* of Lord Woolf in *Douglas and Zeta-Jones v Hello! Ltd* [2003] EWCA Civ 332 at [9]).

In furtherance of the overriding objective the court may therefore order the appointment of a single joint expert (see Chapter 30, 'Experts and Assessors'), and in order to save costs witness statements generally replace affidavits in most instances where witness evidence is required. There is also now provision for a party to rely on a statement of case or application notice as evidence in a case where such documents are verified by a statement of truth.

The CPR do not alter the law of evidence, which is a separate subject in its own right, full consideration being outside the scope of this book (the reader is referred to Alan Taylor, *Principles of Evidence*, 2nd edn, 1998, London: Cavendish Publishing).

Court's power to control evidence

The court has the power to control the evidence to be adduced in the proceedings by giving directions as to the issues on which it requires evidence; the nature of the evidence it requires to decide those issues; and as to the way in which the evidence is to be placed before the court (r 32.1(1)).

The court's powers in r 32.1(1) can be seen as a reflection of its general case management powers and its duty actively to manage cases in accordance with the overriding objective under r 1.4. In furtherance of its powers to control evidence the court may exclude evidence that would otherwise be admissible, and may also limit cross-examination (r 32.1(2), (3)). Directions as to the control of evidence may be given at any stage, but more usually on allocation or at a pre-trial review. The court's decision as to the admissibility of evidence is a matter of case management and of what is just in accordance with the overriding objective (*Burstein v Times Newspapers Ltd* [2001] 1 WLR 579, *per* May LJ). *Burstein* concerned the assessment of damages to be awarded to a claimant in defamation proceedings. The trial judge excluded evidence that gave background context to the defamatory publication. The Court of Appeal said that to keep that evidence away from the jury was in effect to put them 'in blinkers', particularly as the evidence was directly relevant to the damage the claimant claimed was caused by the defamatory publication. Although the Court of Appeal accepted that the court has the power to confine evidence, both in its subject matter and its duration, to that which is directly relevant to the issues, it held that the trial judge had erred in excluding this relevant evidence which justice required should have been considered.

In *Gregory v Turner* [2003] EWCA Civ 183; [2003] 1 WLR 1149; [2003] 2 All ER 114, the Court of Appeal severely criticised the district judge's case management decisions for the hearing of a small claim, which included a refusal to allow any oral evidence or cross-examination of witnesses. Although the district judge was purporting to give effect to the overriding objective by limiting the evidence in this way, the Court of Appeal found her decision to be wrong and unjust because it meant that there was no proper hearing of the claimants' evidence.

Rule 32.1 is seen as a power to restrict the evidence that the parties wish to rely upon. It is not interpreted as giving the court the power to dictate to a litigant what evidence he should tender (*The Society of Lloyd's v Jaffray* (2000) *The Times*, 3 August). It was also said by the Court of Appeal in *Douglas and Zeta-Jones v Hello! Ltd* [2003] EWCA Civ 332 that, although r 32.1 gives the court very wide powers to control evidence, it does not entitle the judge to 'look for evidence', it being the obligation of the parties to produce the evidence on which they rely to support their case and to rebut the case of the other side (at [10]).

Evidence in cases allocated to the small claims track

The court's power to control evidence under r 32.1 applies to proceedings allocated to the small claims track. However, the rest of Parts 32 and 33, containing rules about evidence, do not apply to small claims (r 27.2(1)(c), (d)) and the approach to evidence is dictated by the district judge.

Relevance and admissibility of evidence

Evidence, for the purposes of civil proceedings, can be described as information that may be properly presented to the court to support the probability of facts being asserted before it. Evidence can be presented only if it is relevant, meaning logically probative or disprobative of the matter for which proof is required.

Evidence that is relevant is admissible, meaning receivable, by the court *unless* it is by some rule excluded from being received. Apart from public security, this comes down to 'privilege', that is, the exclusion of communications between a party and his legal advisers, or communications between a client or his lawyer and third parties for the purposes of the litigation, or exclusion by agreement between the parties. An agreement by the parties to exclude evidence may arise where there have been communications between parties where a dispute has arisen, or is likely to arise, and the parties have written letters or continued negotiations in the knowledge that the courts will not order disclosure of them if a concluded agreement is not reached. That is, they are expressly or by implication 'without prejudice'. However, admissible evidence may be excluded by the court in accordance with its general power to control evidence (r 32.1).

The court does have jurisdiction to strike out material in a witness statement that is irrelevantly prejudicial, but the power should be exercised sparingly. Parties typically include such material in the course of interim proceedings, and the conduct of the court's business would be seriously impeded if every instance of inclusion were to lead to an application to strike out (*Sandhurst Holdings Ltd v Grosvenor Assets Ltd* (2001) LTL, 25 October, Ch D). In *Sandhurst*, one of the defendant's witness statements served in support of an interim application stated that the claimant was subject to a restraint order made by the court under the Drug Trafficking Act 1994. The claimant submitted that this information was included with a view to poisoning the mind of the court and was scandalous and irrelevant. The court held that its inclusion could not embarrass the court because the matter consisted of an order made by the court itself. Also, it could not embarrass the claimant because he did not dispute that the order was made. The court accepted that the inclusion of this material was irrelevantly prejudicial, but found that it was inevitable in the course of interim proceedings that parties would typically include this sort of matter in evidence and it would take up too much of the court's time hearing applications to strike it out. However, the court said that if a party continues to rely upon such material in the course of proceedings and it is demonstrated to be irrelevant, the court can deal with it by an appropriate order as to costs at an appropriate time.

EVIDENCE OF WITNESSES

As a general rule, any evidence that needs to be proved by a witness at trial must be proved by their oral evidence given in public, but in any other hearing is to be proved by their evidence in writing (r 32.2(1)). This general rule usually applies so that at most trials witness evidence is given orally, whilst at interim hearings it is usually given by means of witness statements, or even a statement of case or application notice verified by a statement of truth (see also r 32.6).

The general rule will not apply if there is any provision to the contrary in the rules (r 32.2(2)). So, for instance, for Part 8 claims, where there is no substantial dispute of fact, the court is unlikely to order the attendance of witnesses at the trial and will instead rely on their written evidence (r 8.6).

The court has no power to order that a party must call a witness it has identified but decided not to call so that the witness is available for cross-examination by the other party. The court has no discretion to require a party to call evidence which it was not minded to call (*The Society of Lloyd's v Jaffray* (2000) *The Times*, 3 August).

Witness evidence by video link

Provision is made for witnesses, in appropriate circumstances, to give evidence through a video link, or by other means (r 32.3). Annex 3 to PD 32 gives guidance on the use of video conferencing in the civil courts, both in respect of its use by witnesses to give evidence at trial and in respect of its use at interim applications, case management conferences and pre-trial reviews. The guidance is based in part on the protocol of the Federal Court of Australia (PD 32, para 29.1 and Annex 3).

Although the Video Conferencing Guidance (VCF) in PD 32 Annex 3 provides that the court's permission is required for the use of video conferencing for any part of any proceedings, it does not specify in what circumstances such permission will be granted (VCF, para 8).

In *Rowland v Brock* [2002] EWHC 692; [2002] 4 All ER 370, a case decided before the introduction of VCF in PD 32 Annex 3, the court held that no limits should be placed upon the exercise of the court's power to permit video link evidence. In *Rowland*, an application was made to use video link evidence because the witness was resident abroad and would be arrested on criminal charges if he came to England. The Master refused to make an order for video link evidence, holding that its use should be ordered only in cases of 'pressing need' or where a witness is too ill to attend. The appeal court found that this approach was too restrictive and conflicted with the broad and flexible purpose of allowing such facilities to be used in order to achieve justice. The judge referred to r 1.1 and r 1.4 as support for his view that considerations of costs, time and inconvenience were relevant considerations for the court's exercise of its discretion whether to allow evidence by such means.

The judge also held that it was consistent with Art 6 (right to a fair trial) of the European Convention on Human Rights to allow a witness to give evidence by video link so that a party was on an equal footing with the other party. This would be so where the only other alternative would be for one party to be present at trial and subject to cross-examination, whilst the other party's evidence was confined to the reading of a statement pursuant to a Civil Evidence Act notice. He was further of the view that access to justice in a civil matter should not be at the price of the litigant losing his liberty and facing criminal proceedings. However, the judge recognised that a refusal to attend court that could be characterised as an abuse of process or contemptuous, or in order to gain a collateral advantage, would be a good reason for the court to refuse to exercise its discretion to grant permission. Further, where evidence is given by video link the court will be able to make due allowances for any technological consequences on the demeanour and the delivery of evidence (at [9]).

In *Douglas and Zeta-Jones v Hello! Ltd* [2003] EWCA Civ 332, Lord Woolf took the opportunity to remind the parties that the court has the power to receive evidence by video link if necessary in order to reduce inconvenience to witnesses and to help to control costs (at [21]).

Witness statements

A witness statement is a 'written statement signed by a person which contains the evidence, and only that evidence, which a person will be allowed to give orally' (r 32.4(1)).

In *Alex Lawrie Factors Ltd v Morgan* (1999) *The Times*, 18 August, the Court of Appeal explained that witness statements and affidavits are there for the witness to say in his or her own words what the relevant evidence is, and they are not to be used as a vehicle for complex legal argument. The court also warned of the dangers that occur when lawyers put into witnesses' mouths, in the witness statements they settle for them, a sophisticated legal argument which in effect represents the lawyers' arguments in the case and to which the witnesses would not be readily able to speak if cross-examined on their witness statements.

Requirement to serve witness statements for use at trial

Where evidence is to be adduced by witnesses at trial, the court will order the parties to serve on each other any witness statement of the oral evidence which the party serving the statement intends to rely on in relation to any issue of fact to be decided at the trial (r 32.4(2)). In order to rely on witness evidence at trial, a party must therefore disclose before trial a witness statement containing the witness's evidence. The reason for this rule is to prevent surprise, save costs and to promote settlement. However, a party is not obliged to call a witness to give evidence at trial merely because a witness statement has been served (*Douglas and Zeta-Jones v Hello! Ltd* [2003] EWCA Civ 332).

Failure to serve witness statement in time

If a witness statement is not served in respect of an intended witness within the time specified by the court then the witness may not be called to give oral evidence at trial unless the court gives permission (r 32.10). A party who has failed to serve a witness statement within the time specified should apply for relief from the sanction imposed by r 32.10. The court will also have to have regard to the provisions of Art 6(1) of the European Convention on Human Rights as to the effect on a 'fair trial' of allowing or disallowing evidence in a particular case.

In considering whether to grant relief from that sanction the court should apply the checklist in r 3.9 (*Jones v Williams* (2002) LTL, 27 May). In *Jones*, the dispute between the parties turned on which version of events was believed by the court. However, the defendant, who was acting in person, failed to serve witness statements in accordance with the court's directions or in a proper form, and the judge ordered that the defendant was not entitled to rely upon oral evidence at trial. The Court of Appeal held that the judge's decision was wrong because he had not taken into account that the effect of failing to grant relief from this sanction would be a disaster for the defendant. In a case where the dispute centred on oral transactions between the parties, if the judge heard only one side's evidence the inevitable result would be that the court would decide the case in favour of the party who gave evidence. In ordering a retrial the Court of Appeal said that in order for the court to try the case properly it was of paramount importance that it heard the parties give evidence and for them to be cross-examined, and it would need the strongest reasons, which were not present in that case, to exclude the defendant's evidence.

In *Mealey Horgan plc v Horgan* (1999) *The Times*, 6 July, the defendants delayed in serving witness statements. In granting the defendants extra time to serve their witness statements, the court held that it would be wholly unsatisfactory and unjust, save in fairly extreme circumstances, for a court to deal with a case in effect on one side's evidence. The court gave examples of circumstances that might justify an order excluding one party's evidence as including where there has been deliberate flouting of court orders or such inexcusable delay so that the only way the court could fairly entertain that party's evidence would be by adjourning the trial. In *Mealey Horgan plc,* the court found that the claimants could properly prepare for trial and do their case justice notwithstanding the defendants' delay in serving witness statements. In the circumstances the court granted the defendants extra time to serve their witness statements and relief from the sanction imposed for failing to serve them in time.

Directions in relation to witness statements for use at trial

The court can give directions as to the order in which witness statements are to be served and whether or not witness statements are to be filed at court (r 32.4(3)). The normal requirement is that if a party wishes to rely at trial on the evidence of a witness contained in a witness statement, he must call the witness to give oral evidence, unless the court orders otherwise (r 32.5(1)).

Also, the usual rule is that a witness statement will stand as the evidence-in-chief of the witness called to give evidence at trial unless the court orders otherwise (r 32.5(2)).

Form of witness statements

A witness statement must comply with the requirements of PD 32 (r 32.8). The relevant provisions are contained in PD 32, paras 17–22, which provide detailed requirements for the contents and presentation of witness statements. Failure to comply with the formalities may result in a refusal of the court to admit the document or allow the costs of preparation (PD 32, para 25(1)).

A witness statement must also be verified by a statement of truth in the following form: 'I believe that the facts stated in this witness statement are true' (PD 32, paras 20.1, 20.2).

Hearsay evidence in witness statements

See pp 485–87 below, 'Hearsay evidence', for the definition of and requirements in relation to hearsay evidence in civil proceedings. Where a witness statement which is to be adduced at trial contains hearsay evidence, notice of the use of hearsay evidence under s 2(1)(a) of the Civil Evidence Act 1995 is given by serving the witness's witness statement in accordance with directions from the court (r 33.2(1)).

False statements of truth

A person who makes a false statement of truth in a witness statement, a statement of case or application notice without an honest belief in its truth is guilty of contempt of court (r 32.14).

If a party alleges that another person has made a false statement of truth, he must refer the allegation to the court dealing with the proceedings in question (PD 32, para 27.2(1)). The court may exercise its powers under the CPR (for example, impose sanctions); initiate steps to consider if there is a contempt of court and, where there is, punish it; or direct the party making the allegation to refer the matter to the Attorney-General with a request for him to consider whether he wishes to bring proceedings for contempt of court (PD 32, para 27.2(2)).

It is only flagrant breaches of the obligation to be responsible and truthful in verifying a statement of case or witness statement that should be enforced if necessary by committal proceedings (*Malgar Ltd v RE Leach (Engineering) Ltd* (2000) *The Times*, 17 February). In *Malgar*, the claimant made an application under r 32.14 for permission to bring proceedings to commit the defendant company and two of its officers for contempt of court in making false statements in documents verified by a statement of truth, namely, the defendant's defence and witness statements. The defendant had submitted to summary judgment in respect of part of its defence. The claimant brought the application asserting that the defendant made false statements about that part of its defence for which summary judgment had been entered.

The court held that in order to establish contempt of court for signing a false statement of truth, it must be shown that the individual knew that what he was saying was false and that his false statement was likely to interfere with the course of justice. However, in this case the court found that the false statement was not persisted in because the defendant had submitted to summary judgment over that part of its defence. The court did not find that there was therefore an attempt to interfere with the course of justice of a sufficient seriousness to warrant committal proceedings. Indeed, the court found in those circumstances that committal proceedings were tenuous. The court did accept that if the defendant had persisted in the statements it would be a different matter.

The court also found that a further reason why committal proceedings would be highly undesirable was that there were still substantial proceedings on foot between the parties. The committal proceedings would obstruct the sensible disposal of what was outstanding between the parties. In the circumstances the court found the application for permission to bring contempt proceedings to be disproportionate.

Contempt proceedings are public law proceedings and permission is needed to bring them because what is involved is an allegation of public wrong. The court is therefore concerned to see that the public interest requires that committal proceedings should be brought. The public nature of such contempt proceedings should be compared with contempt proceedings brought to protect or further private rights, for example, an application for an order that a party is in contempt where he fails to comply with an injunction (*Malgar Ltd v RE Leach (Engineering) Ltd*).

Role of witness statements at trial

As a general rule, if a party has served a witness statement and he wishes to rely at trial on the evidence of the witness who made the statement, he must call that witness to give oral evidence (r 32.5(1)). However, a party is not obliged to call that witness to give evidence and may instead adduce the statement as hearsay evidence (*Douglas and Zeta-Jones v Hello! Ltd* [2003] EWCA Civ 332; and see below, 'Adducing witness statement as hearsay evidence').

The usual rule, unless the court orders otherwise, is that where a witness is called to give oral evidence his witness statement stands as his evidence-in-chief (r 32.5(2)). This rule is now almost universally applied, being considered to reduce the length and cost of the trial.

Where a witness is called to give evidence at trial he may be cross-examined on his witness statement, whether or not the statement or any part of it was referred to during the witness's evidence-in-chief (r 32.11).

Adducing witness statement as hearsay evidence

If a party who has served a witness statement does not call the witness to give evidence at trial or put in the witness statement as hearsay evidence, any other party may put in the witness statement as hearsay evidence (r 32.5(5)). However, the other party is not *entitled* to put the witness statement in evidence, the court having a discretion whether to allow him to do so (*McPhilemy v The Times Newspapers Ltd (No 2)* [2000] 1 WLR 1732).

In *McPhilemy*, the trial judge exercised his discretion to refuse the claimant permission to put in as hearsay evidence one of the defendant's witness statements, being a witness who the defendant did not call to give evidence. The Court of Appeal held that the trial judge was correct because the claimant intended to rely only on part of the witness's evidence, and as for the rest it wished to say that it was untrue. The court held that the CPR did not change the basic rules of evidence, one of which was that a party cannot assert (save for limited exceptions such as hostile witnesses) that his own witness's evidence is untrue. It said that a party cannot put in evidence a statement of a witness knowing that his evidence conflicts to a substantial degree with his case on the basis that he will say straight away, in the witness's absence, that the court should disbelieve as untrue a substantial part of that evidence.

Where a party decides not to call a witness whose witness statement has been served, prompt notice should be given to the other parties. The party should say whether he wishes to put the witness statement in as hearsay evidence. This will give the other party an opportunity to decide whether he wishes to rely on the witness statement instead (*The Society of Lloyd's v Jaffray* (2000) *The Times*, 3 August).

If one party serves a witness statement on the other party but does not call the witness to give evidence, and the other party adduces the witness's statement as a hearsay statement under r 32.5(5), the party serving the witness statement may apply for permission to have the witness called in order to cross-examine him on his witness statement (*Douglas and Zeta-Jones v Hello! Ltd* [2003] EWCA Civ 332).

In the *Douglas* case, the Court of Appeal upheld the trial judge's decision to allow the claimant (the party serving the witness statement) to have the witness called to be cross-examined even though the witness was effectively the claimant's witness. The Court of Appeal held that r 33.4 (power to call witness for cross-examination on hearsay evidence) read with r 32.5(5) allowed the party serving the witness statement to cross-examine his own witness in these circumstances. The Court of Appeal also supported the trial judge's view that it would assist in the achievement of justice for this witness to be called to give evidence, because she played a central role in the negotiations which were part of the subject matter of the dispute.

In *Douglas*, the Court of Appeal drew attention to the fact that r 33.4 allowed the maker to be cross-examined only as to the contents of his witness statement and did not allow cross-examination as to matters that did not arise out of the witness statement. However, the court recognised that the extent of cross-examination is ultimately a decision for the trial judge in the exercise of his powers to control cross-examination.

Further evidence from witness at trial

A witness giving oral evidence at trial may, with the permission of the court, *amplify* his witness statement (r 32.5(3)(a)). Also, the court may give permission for the witness to give evidence in relation to new matters that have arisen since his witness statement was served on the other parties (r 32.5(3)(b)).

The test the court will apply when deciding whether to allow such new or amplified evidence is where there is good reason not to confine the evidence of the witness to the contents of his witness statement (r 32.5(4)).

The balance between confining a witness to what is in the statement and permitting departure (save in respect of 'new' material) is in effect a balance between unnecessarily expensive and elaborate statements on the one hand, and the potential for 'ambush' on the other. Substantial injustice caused by the latter should result in the new evidence simply being excluded, and this is an adjunct to the wide general powers under r 32.1.

In *Mancini v Telecommunications UK Ltd* [2003] EWHC 211, the claimant served a one-page witness statement on the defendant which did not address the allegations raised by the defendant against the claimant. The defendant applied for the claimant's case to be struck out for failure to comply with court orders and on the grounds that on the basis of the claimant's evidence in his witness statement his claim was bound to fail. The claimant contended that his case should not be struck out because he intended to expand upon his witness statement at trial. The appeal court held that the judge at first instance was not wrong in coming to the conclusion that on the basis of the claimant's witness statement his claim did not have a reasonable prospect of success. The court said that the whole point of a witness statement was to set out the entirety of the witness's evidence relevant to the case. It was not acceptable for the witness to say a few things and then seek to amplify them in the witness box.

Use of witness statements for other purposes

The general rule is that a witness statement may be used only for the purposes of the proceedings in which it is served (r 32.12(1)). However, there are exceptions to this general rule, which are where:

(a) the witness gives consent in writing to some other use of it;

(b) the court gives permission for some other use; or

(c) the witness statement has been put in evidence at a hearing held in public (r 32.12(2)).

In accordance with the principle of orality in an English trial, once a witness statement has been put in evidence at a hearing held in public any privilege contained in the statement will be waived.

Public access to witness statements

A witness statement that stands as evidence-in-chief is open to inspection during the course of the trial unless the court orders otherwise (r 32.13(1)). This rule is consistent with the principle of orality at trial and public access to witness statements and documents referred to at trial.

Any person may apply for an order that the witness statement is not open to inspection, or that words or passages are not open to inspection (r 32.13(2), (4)). However, in order to grant such an order the court must be satisfied that the application falls within one of the exceptions set out in r 32.13(3) that justify the court in making such an order. The exceptions are:

(a) the interests of justice; or

(b) the public interest; or

(c) where it is justified given the nature of any medical evidence in the statement; or

(d) because of the nature of any confidential information in the statement; or

(e) in order to protect the interests of any child or patient (r 32.13(3)).

Witness summaries

Witness summaries may be served with the court's leave on an application without notice where it is not possible to obtain a witness statement (r 32.9(1)). A witness summary is a summary of the evidence, if known, which would otherwise be included in a witness statement. The intention is to be able to refer to brief notes obtained and prepared which do not go quite so far as the full statement. Alternatively, if the evidence is not known, it is a summary of the matters about which the party serving the witness summary proposes to question the witness (r 32.9(2)). This will therefore apply where a witness is hostile. The rules as to service, amplification and form are the same as for witness statements, but a witness summary does not include a statement of truth (r 32.9(4), (5)).

Evidence at hearings other than trials

The general rule is that evidence at hearings other than the trial is by witness statement rather than oral evidence (rr 32.2(1)(b), 32.6(1); PD 32, para 1.2). A witness may give evidence by affidavit instead if he wishes to do so, but is unlikely to recover the additional costs of doing so unless he is required to use an affidavit (r 32.15(2); PD 32, para 1.2). Indeed a party may rely on the matters set out in his statement of case or application notice, if verified by a statement of truth (r 32.6(2); PD 32, para 1.3).

However, a party may apply to the court for permission to cross-examine the person on his witness statement (r 32.7(1)). For most hearings, other than the trial, the court will not resolve disputed issues of fact and so it will not usually be appropriate for the court to allow cross-examination of witnesses at such applications.

Affidavits

An affidavit is a written, sworn statement of evidence (Glossary; and see Chapter 20, 'Making Applications for Court Orders', for further considerations about the nature of affidavits). Apart from a few exceptions, witness statements now replace affidavits as the normal way of giving evidence. However, evidence is to be given by affidavit if sworn evidence is required by an enactment, rule or practice direction, or if it is ordered by the court (r 32.15(1); PD 32, paras 1.4, 1.6). For instance, a party applying for a freezing injunction or search order must provide supporting evidence in an affidavit (PD 25, para 3.1).

An affidavit may be used in circumstances where a statement would have sufficed, but the party putting it forward may not recover any additional costs of preparing it unless the court orders otherwise (r 32.15(2)). For the format of affidavits see PD 32, paras 2–16. Failure to comply with the formalities may have the same result as with witness statements (see p 478 above, 'Form of witness statements').

Witness summons

If a party wishes to secure the attendance of a witness at a hearing, a *witness summons* may be served upon the witness compelling him to attend court to give evidence, or produce documents or both (r 34.2(1); PD 34, para 1.1). Under the former rules the witness summons was known in proceedings in the Supreme Court as a *writ of subpoena ad testificandum* (order to attend to give evidence, usually abbreviated to *subpoena*) and a *writ of subpoena duces tecum* (order to attend with documents), and in proceedings in the county courts as a *witness summons*. The title *witness summons* was adopted, and the Latin names abandoned, in favour of the principle of plain English that runs throughout the CPR.

A witness summons may be required where a witness is reluctant to attend trial to give evidence, or may be of assistance to a witness where he needs to demonstrate to another person, for instance an employer against whom he is giving evidence, that he is not giving evidence voluntarily but is obliged to do so. However, a witness summons can be issued even against a witness who has not indicated that he is reluctant to attend, and a party may simply wish to serve witness summonses on all his witnesses as a formality.

The court has the power to set aside a witness summons in appropriate circumstances (r 34.3(4)).

Issue of a witness summons

In most cases a witness summons may be issued without permission, except where a party wishes to have a summons issued less than seven days before the date of the trial and in certain other exceptional cases, such as where a party wishes a witness to attend at a hearing other than the trial (r 34.3(1), (2)). A witness summons is to be issued in the court where the case is proceeding, or where the hearing will be held (r 34.3(3)).

Two copies of the witness summons should be filed with the court for sealing, one of which will be retained on the court file (PD 34, para 1.2).

Service of witness summons

A witness summons is served by the court, unless the party on whose behalf it is issued indicates in writing, when he asks the court to issue, that he wishes to serve it himself (r 34.6(1); PD 34, para 3.4). The court will use the usual method of service when serving the witness summons, that is, ordinary first class post (rr 6.2, 6.3).

A witness summons is binding if it is served at least seven days before the date on which the witness is required to attend court (r 34.5(1)). The court also has the power to order that the witness summons shall be binding even if it is served less than seven days before the date on which the witness is required to attend court (r 34.5(2)).

Once a witness summons has been served it will be binding on the witness until the conclusion of the hearing at which the attendance of the witness is required (r 34.5(3)).

Compensation for travelling and other expenses

At the time of service of the witness summons the witness must be offered or paid a reasonable sum to cover travelling expenses and a sum by way of compensation for loss of time as specified by PD 34 (r 34.7; PD 34, paras 3.1, 3.4).

Where the court is to serve the witness summons, the party on whose behalf it is issued must deposit in the Court Office the money to be paid or offered to the witness under r 34.7 (r 34.6(2); PD 34, para 3.2).

The amount to be offered or paid is a sum reasonably sufficient to cover the witness's expenses in travelling to and from the court and a sum in respect of the period during which earnings or benefits are lost, or such lesser sum as it may be proved the witness will lose as a result of his attendance at court (r 34.7; PD 34, para 3.2). The sum for loss of earnings or benefits is based on the sums payable to witnesses attending the Crown Court, which are fixed by the Prosecution of Offences Act 1985 and the Costs in Criminal Cases (General) Regulations 1986 (SI 1986/1335) (PD 34, para 3.3).

Depositions

The court has the power to order a person to be examined on oath before the hearing takes place. The person being examined is known as the *deponent* and the evidence is referred to as a *deposition*. The deponent may be examined before a judge, an examiner of the court or such other person as the court appoints (r 34.8(1), (2), (3)).

An application for an order to take evidence by deposition may be made if, for instance, the witness is unable to attend trial, perhaps because he is too ill to do so. However, where a witness is unable to attend trial it may be preferable and cheaper for his evidence to be given by video link instead (r 32.3).

The deponent gives evidence before the examiner as if the examination were being conducted at trial. There is therefore provision for all parties to be present and for the deponent to be cross-examined (r 34.9).

A party who wishes to rely on the deposition at a hearing must serve notice of his intention to do so on every other party at least 21 days before the date fixed for the hearing (r 34.11).

Letter of request

Where a party wishes to take a deposition from a person outside the jurisdiction, an application can be made to the High Court for the issue of a *letter of request* to the judicial authorities of the country in which the deponent is (r 34.13(1)). The letter of request is a request to a judicial authority to take the evidence of the deponent or arrange for it to be taken (r 34.13(2)). Although the order must be made by the High Court, it can be made in respect of county court proceedings (r 34.13(3)).

The deponent may be examined either on oath or affirmation, or in accordance with any procedure permitted in the country in which the examination is to take place (r 34.13(5)).

HEARSAY EVIDENCE

Definition of hearsay

Hearsay is defined as 'a statement made otherwise than by a person while giving oral evidence in the proceedings which is tendered as evidence of the matters stated' (s 1(2) of the Civil Evidence Act (CEA) 1995; r 33.1(a)). Hearsay is therefore not the direct evidence of a witness himself, but what someone else has been heard to say. References to hearsay under the CEA 1995 and in the CPR include hearsay of whatever degree, that is, whether first hand or second hand hearsay (r 33.1(b)).

If a statement is made – other than by a witness in the course of giving his evidence – evidence of it can be given to prove that the statement was made, and then the statement would not be hearsay; but if it is offered as proof of its contents, that would be hearsay. For a full discussion, see *Subramaniam v Public Prosecutor* [1956] 1 WLR 965.

The CEA 1995 abolished the rule against the admissibility of hearsay evidence in civil proceedings. The aims of the 1995 Act were to make all relevant hearsay evidence admissible whilst avoiding the need for complex notice provisions. Section 1 of the CEA 1995 provides that in civil proceedings, evidence shall not be excluded on the grounds that it is hearsay. Section 2(1)(a) of the CEA 1995 says that a party intending to adduce hearsay evidence 'shall' give notice of that fact. However, although there is a requirement to give notice of the intention to adduce hearsay evidence, the notice provisions are much simpler than those specified under the Civil Evidence Act 1968.

Also, s 2(4) of the CEA 1995 goes on to say that *failure* to give notice goes to costs, and weight, and not so as to make the hearsay evidence inadmissible. Thus, there is now no power actually to exclude evidence on the grounds that it is hearsay in any circumstances. However, although evidence may not be excluded on the grounds that it is hearsay, it may be excluded on other grounds, say, because it is irrelevant or as a result of the court's exercise of its power to control evidence under r 32.1.

Hearsay evidence to be given orally or in a witness statement

Where a party intends to rely on hearsay evidence at trial but the hearsay evidence is to be adduced by a witness giving oral evidence, or it is contained in a witness statement of a person who is not being called to give oral evidence, notice of the intention to rely on hearsay evidence will be given in accordance with s 2(1)(a) of the CEA 1995 by serving a witness statement on the other party (r 33.2(1)). Thus, no separate hearsay notice is required. There is also no requirement when serving the witness statement to indicate which parts of it contain the hearsay evidence. However, the witness statement must indicate which of the statements made in it are made from the witness's own knowledge and which are matters of information or belief, and in the case of the latter the source for any matters of information and belief must be identified (PD 32, para 18.2).

Also, where the hearsay evidence is contained in a witness statement of a witness who is not being called to give oral evidence at trial, the party intending to rely on the hearsay evidence must, when he serves the witness statement, inform the other parties that the witness is not being called to give oral evidence and give the reasons why the witness will not be called (r 33.2(2)).

The 'hearsay notice'

In all other cases apart from where the hearsay evidence is to be given by a witness orally at trial or is contained in a witness statement, a party who intends to rely on hearsay evidence at trial must serve a hearsay notice on the other parties (r 33.2(3)).

There is no prescribed form for a hearsay notice but the hearsay notice must:

(a) identify the hearsay evidence; and

(b) state that the party serving the notice proposes to rely on the hearsay evidence at trial; and

(c) give the reason why the witness will not be called (r 33.2(3)).

The party proposing to rely on the hearsay evidence must serve the notice no later than the latest date for serving witness statements and, if the hearsay evidence is in a document, supply a copy to any party who requests him to do so (r 33.2(4)).

Hearsay evidence at hearings other than trials

There is no requirement to give notice of intention to rely on hearsay evidence at hearings other than trials (r 33.3(a)). Indeed, at hearings other than trials the usual rule is that evidence is to be adduced in writing rather than orally, which thereby results in all witness evidence being hearsay evidence at hearings other than trials.

Failure to give hearsay notice

If a party is required to give a hearsay notice but fails to do so, this does not affect the admissibility of the evidence but the failure may be taken into account by the court when exercising its discretion in relation to costs and the course of proceedings (for example, may result in an adjournment). It is also likely adversely to affect the weight of the evidence (s 2(4) of the CEA 1995).

Cross-examination of witness where witness statement adduced as hearsay statement

If a party proposes to rely on hearsay evidence and does not propose to call the person who made the original statement to give oral evidence, the other party may apply for permission to call the witness to be cross-examined on the contents of the statement (r 33.4(1)). An application for permission to cross-examine the witness under r 33.4(1) must be made not more than 14 days after the day on which notice of intention to rely on the hearsay evidence was served on the applicant (r 33.4(2)).

In *Douglas and Zeta-Jones v Hello! Ltd* [2003] EWCA Civ 332, the defendant took the claimant by surprise when, at the conclusion of its oral evidence at trial, it notified the court that it wished to rely on a witness statement served on it by the claimant as a hearsay statement. The defendant then proceeded to address the court on inferences to be drawn from the evidence contained in that witness statement. However, the defendant was in turn surprised when the claimant then applied under rr 32.5(5) and 33.4 for permission to call the witness to be cross-examined on the contents of her witness statement. The Court of Appeal upheld the trial judge's decision to allow the claimant to call the witness for cross-examination even though the witness was effectively the claimant's own witness.

Credibility of witness not called to give evidence

Where a party proposes to rely on hearsay evidence without calling the maker of that statement to give oral evidence, if the other party wishes to call evidence to attack the credibility of that witness he must give notice of his intention to do so not more than 14 days after the day on which the witness statement was served on him (r 33.5).

ADMISSIONS

Where a fact is admitted and is therefore not in dispute between the parties, it is unnecessary to prove that fact at trial.

A fact may be admitted in a party's statement of case, and an opponent may make use of the admittance by himself averring it with a different interpretation. Admissions may also be made in answer to a request for further information (Parts 16 and 18; and see Chapter 12, 'Statements of Case').

A party may apply for judgment to be entered on an admission (r 14.3).

Admissions may be made at any stage, as well as at the trial itself. Formal admissions made in civil proceedings are binding only for the purpose of those proceedings.

Notice to admit facts

A party may serve a *notice to admit facts* on another party requiring him to admit the facts, or part of the case of the serving party as specified in the notice (r 32.18(1)). A notice to admit must be served no later than 21 days before the trial (r 32.18(2)).

Where the other party makes any admission in response to the notice, the admission may be used against him only in the proceedings in which the notice to admit is served and only by the party who served the notice (r 32.18(3)).

The court also has a discretion to allow a party to amend or withdraw any admission made by him on such terms as it thinks just (r 32.18(4)).

Withdrawing an admission

It should be noted that once a party has made an admission in proceedings, whether in response to a notice to admit facts or in his statement of case or even more informally, for instance by letter, the court's permission is required to amend or withdraw it (rr 14.1(5), 32.18(4)).

The application to amend or withdraw an admission should be made in accordance with Part 23. The court will balance the prejudice to each party when exercising its discretion whether to grant permission to withdraw an admission (*Sollitt v DJ Broady Ltd* (2000) LTL, 23 February).

In *Bird v Bird's Eye Walls Ltd* (1987) *The Times*, 24 July, a decision under the former rules, it was held that in an appropriate case the court may permit a party to withdraw an admission made in error during the course of proceedings and before trial if no injustice would result. In *Bird*, the defendant to a personal injury claim admitted liability in a letter, so that the only issue between the parties was the quantum of the claimant's damages. However, the defendant subsequently informed the claimant 18 months later that it was withdrawing the admission. The Court of Appeal held that having made that admission in the proceedings the defendant required the court's permission to withdraw it. Further, in that case the Court of Appeal refused to grant permission because the claimant was prejudiced as documents relevant to liability were no longer in existence and neither was the original machinery which had caused the claimant's injuries.

DOCUMENTS

Authenticity of documents

A party is deemed to admit the authenticity of a document disclosed to him under Part 31 (see Chapter 29, 'Disclosure of Documents') unless he serves notice that he wishes the document to be proved at trial (r 32.19(1)).

A notice to prove a document must be served by the latest date for serving witness statements, or within seven days of disclosure of the document, whichever is the later (r 32.19(2)).

Evidence of title to land

Under s 113 of the Land Registration Act 1925, office copies of the register and of documents filed in the Land Registry, including original charges, are admissible in evidence to the same extent as the originals. Section 113 applies to all proceedings, including proceedings for the possession of land (PD 33B, paras 1, 2).

Bundles for hearings

The court may give directions requiring the parties to use their best endeavours to agree a bundle or bundles of documents for use at the hearing (PD 32, para 27.1).

If a bundle is agreed, all documents contained in the bundle are admissible at that hearing as evidence of their contents, unless the court orders otherwise or a party gives written notice of objection to the admissibility of particular documents (PD 32, para 27.2).

Plans, photographs and models, etc

Where a party intends to put in an item such as a plan, photograph or model as evidence of any fact and it is not contained in a witness statement, affidavit or expert's report, and is not to be given orally at trial, he must give notice that he intends to use that evidence not later than the latest date for serving witness statements (r 33.6(1), (4)).

Where no witness statements are to be adduced at a hearing, or where a party intends to put in the evidence solely in order to disprove an allegation made in a witness statement, he must give notice that he intends to use that evidence at least 21 days before the hearing (r 33.6(5)).

If a party fails to provide the necessary notice of intention to use that evidence, the evidence shall not be receivable at trial unless the court orders otherwise (r 33.6(3)).

In *Orford v Rasmi Electronics* [2002] EWCA Civ 1672, the defendant presented the claimant with a layout plan of its premises on the day of the hearing. The claimant wished to challenge the accuracy of the plan but did not have a proper opportunity to do so in the absence of prior notice of the use of the plan. The trial judge found in favour of the defendant. The Court of Appeal found that the defendant's failure to provide proper notice of the use of the plan was a serious procedural unfairness which had caused the claimant prejudice as it was relevant to an important issue in the case. The Court of Appeal therefore allowed the claimant's appeal against the judge's finding and ordered a retrial so that the claimant could adduce new evidence to challenge the accuracy of the plan.

CHAPTER 32

HEARINGS

INTRODUCTION

Part 39 deals with the rules relating to hearings. This includes the trial (r 39.1) but will also include the hearing of interim applications. In some circumstances, the court can deal with an interim application without a hearing, but in practice this will usually occur only where a party makes an application without notice to his opponent or the parties agree the terms of the order sought (r 23.8; Chapter 20, 'Making Applications for Court Orders', should be consulted for the detailed rules regarding interim applications).

HEARINGS

Hearings to be in public

The general rule is that hearings are to be in public (r 39.2). This general rule applies both to interim applications and trials, and accords with established principles of natural justice as well as Art 6 of the European Convention on Human Rights, which provides for an entitlement to a fair and *public* hearing.

The general rule is not absolute and r 39.2 and its accompanying practice directions contain a list of circumstances in which the general rule may not apply and a hearing may be held in private (formerly known as 'in chambers' or '*in camera*') (PD 39, para 1.5). For instance, a hearing may be held in private if it is necessary to protect the interests of any child or patient (r 39.2(3)(d)). Also, it may be held in private if publicity would defeat the object of the hearing (r 39.2(3)(a)), for instance, in the case of an application for a freezing injunction or search order (see Chapter 21, 'Interim Remedies'). A hearing may also be held in private if it involves confidential information, and indeed PD 39 contains a list of hearings that necessarily involve information relating to personal financial matters, such as mortgage possession proceedings and proceedings for the repossession of residential tenancies for non-payment of rent, which should in the first instance be listed as hearings in private (PD 39, para 1.5). Further, the court has a general discretion to hold a hearing in private if it is in the interests of justice to do so (r 39.2(3)(g)).

The intention to hold hearings in public may be frustrated by the layout of court buildings. Many have district judge chambers (where, for example, small claims trials are heard) in suites behind locked doors for security. This may be circumvented by a notice inviting members of the public who wish to be present to ask the usher to allow them access. In any event, the court does not need to make special arrangements for accommodating members of the public (r 39.2(2)).

Rights of audience

The Courts and Legal Services Act (CLSA) 1990 governs rights of audience before the courts. If the representative is not a barrister or solicitor, or a member of any other authorised body, and does not have rights granted by some other statute, he may have a right of audience in respect of any proceedings only if the court hearing the matter gives permission (s 27 of the CLSA 1990). However, the court will grant permission only in exceptional circumstances to individuals who do not meet the stringent requirements of the 1990 Act, particularly those who make a practice of seeking to represent otherwise unrepresented litigants (*D v S (Rights of Audience)* [1997] 1 FLR 724, pp 728C–729A, *per* Lord Woolf MR).

Where a representative has a right of audience (for example, barrister or solicitor) the court has the power to refuse to hear that person (s 27(4) of the CLSA 1990). It is a criminal offence, and also a contempt of the court concerned, to purport to exercise a right of audience where none exists (s 70(1) of the CLSA 1990).

At any hearing, the court should be provided with a written statement containing information about each advocate; his name and address; his qualification (for example, barrister) or entitlement to act as an advocate; and the party for whom he acts (PD 39, para 5.1).

In *Noueiri v Paragon Finance plc* [2001] EWCA Civ 1402, Mr Alexander, who was not qualified as a barrister or solicitor, or a member of any other authorised body, was given permission under s 27 of the CLSA 1990 to exercise rights of audience in order to represent the claimant in proceedings, having previously been given such permission in respect of parties in other cases. The Court of Appeal considered Mr Alexander's conduct in the case, in which he made a repeated number of hopeless applications for permission to appeal, to have been inappropriate and incompetent. The court also considered his previous conduct in representing litigants in other cases, from which it concluded that he was a 'menace' to the administration of justice. It therefore held that it was in the public interest for an order to be made restraining Mr Alexander from exercising rights of audience (and rights to conduct litigation) on behalf of any other party, apart from himself, except with the permission of the High Court or Court of Appeal. The court also expressed the view that the courts who had granted him a right of audience seemed to have done so in ignorance of Lord Woolf's guidance in *D v S (Rights of Audience)* that (in the light of dangers to the administration of justice where unqualified representatives are given rights of audience) they should be given only in exceptional cases.

Representation at trial of companies or other corporations

A company may be represented by an authorised employee, provided the court gives permission (r 39.6; and see PD 39, paras 5.2 and 5.3). Rule 39.6 is intended to enable a company or other corporation to represent itself as a litigant in person; permission should therefore be given unless there is a particular and sufficient reason for withholding it (PD 39, para 5.3). The company does not have to be represented by a director, but may be represented by an authorised employee, subject to the court's permission (*Watson v Bluemoor Properties Ltd* [2002] EWCA 1875). The court will be entitled, when considering whether or not to grant permission, to take into account the difficulty of the case and the individual's experience and position in the company (PD 39, para 5.3).

The court's permission for an employee to represent the company should, if possible, be obtained in advance of the hearing, and preferably from the judge who is to hear the case (PD 39, para 5.4). The permission may be obtained informally and without notice to the other parties. The judge who gives permission should record in writing that he has done so and supply a copy to the company and to any other party who asks for one (PD 39, para 5.5).

Where an employee is to represent the company, the written statement providing information for the court about the representative (see pp 491–92 above, 'Rights of audience') should also include details of the full name of the company, as stated in the certification of registration; its registered number; the position or office held in the company by the representative; and the date and manner in which the representative was authorised to act for the company (for example, date of board resolution) (PD 39, para 5.2).

Small claims hearings

Under the Lay Representatives (Rights of Audience) Order 1999 (SI 1999/1225), a party to a claim allocated to the small claims track is entitled to be represented by a lay representative at the small claims hearing. A lay representative is defined as a person other than a barrister, solicitor or legal executive employed by a solicitor (PD 27, para 3.1).

McKenzie friends

A party in any proceedings may choose to have assistance from a so called *McKenzie* friend. Such a person does not act for the litigant but provides assistance during the conduct of the proceedings, and will usually sit beside the litigant at the trial, take notes and advise *sotto voce* on the conduct of the case.

The Court of Appeal reviewed the status of, and entitlement of the litigant to, a *McKenzie* friend in the case of *R v Bow County Court ex p Pelling* [1999] 1 WLR 1807; [1999] 4 All ER 75. The court held in that case that, as regards hearings in public, a litigant in person should be allowed the assistance of a *McKenzie* friend unless the judge is satisfied, in accordance with the overriding objective, that fairness and the interests of justice are such that the litigant should not have such assistance. However, a *McKenzie* friend is not entitled to address the court, and if he does so he becomes an advocate and requires the grant of a right of audience under s 27 of the CLSA 1990. A court can also prevent a *McKenzie* friend from continuing to act where the assistance given is contrary to the administration of justice, for instance, where the *McKenzie* friend is indirectly running the case or using the litigant as a puppet.

Also, for hearings held in private, the nature of the proceedings which makes it desirable for them to be heard in private may mean that it is inappropriate for a *McKenzie* friend to assist, and the court has a discretion to exclude a *McKenzie* friend from such proceedings. Moreover, in *ex p Pelling* the court held that the *McKenzie* friend has no right to provide the assistance and cannot therefore complain about being excluded, the right to assistance being that of the litigant in person.

Recording of proceedings

At any hearing, whether in the High Court or a county court, the judgment, and any summing up given by the judge, will be recorded, unless the judge directs otherwise. Usually, the evidence will also be recorded (PD 39, para 6.1).

Any party or person may request a copy of a transcript of any trial or hearing upon payment of relevant charges (PD 39, para 6.3). However, where the person requesting the transcript is not a party to the proceedings, and the trial or hearing was held in private, the provision of a transcript is in the discretion of the court (PD 39, para 6.4).

It is a contempt of court under s 9 of the Contempt of Court Act 1981 for a party or member of the public to use unofficial recording equipment in any court or judge's room without the permission of the court (PD 39, para 6.2).

Human Rights Act authorities

Section 2 of the Human Rights Act (HRA) 1998 provides that a court or tribunal determining a question which has arisen in connection with a Convention right must take account of any judgment, decision, declaration or advisory opinion of the European Court of Human Rights, opinion or decision of the Commission, or decision of the Committee of Ministers, whenever made or given, so far as, in the opinion of the court or tribunal, it is relevant to the proceedings in which the question has arisen. The court is therefore not entitled to decide questions relating to Convention rights in accordance only with domestic precedent or its own discretion.

Section 2(2) of the HRA 1998 goes on to provide that evidence of any judgment, decision, declaration or opinion which may be taken into account is to be given in the proceedings in accordance with rules of court. Practice Direction 39 specifies that any authority cited should be an authoritative and complete report, and the party must give to the court, and to any other party, a list of the authorities he intends to cite and copies of the reports not less than three days before the hearing (PD 39, para 8.1(1), (2)). Copies of the complete original texts issued by the European Court and Commission, either paper-based or from the Court's judgment database (HUDOC), available on the internet, may be used (PD 39, para 8.1(3)).

In *Barclays Bank plc v Ellis* (2000) *The Times*, 24 October, the Court of Appeal criticised counsel who, 'at the last minute and without any warning, either to his opponent or to the court, thought it appropriate to make reference to Article 6 of the European Convention on Human Rights'. At the time the HRA 1998 had not come into force, but the court held that if counsel wished to rely on the provisions of the HRA 1998 then they had a duty to have available, for the information of the court, any material in terms of decisions of the European Court of Human Rights upon which they wished to rely or which would help the court in its adjudication. The position is now expressly governed by s 2 of the HRA 1998 and the procedure set out in PD 39, para 8 (see above).

THE TRIAL

Timetables for trial

For cases allocated to the fast track and the multi-track, the court will give directions for a trial timetable, after the expiry of the date specified for filing a completed pre-trial checklist. The timetable will be fixed in consultation with the parties (r 39.4) and will take into account the draft trial timetable that should be submitted by each party with his pre-trial checklist.

Trial bundles

Unless the court orders otherwise, the claimant must file the trial bundle. The trial bundle must contain documents required by a relevant practice direction and any court order (r 39.5(1)). The court will give any specific directions for the preparation and lodging of the trial bundle after the last date for the return of the pre-trial checklist. In a case where the Court of Appeal commented that the preparation of bundles 'verged on scandalous', the court emphasised the importance of complying with good practice, and the specific requirements of relevant practice directions as to the contents and organisation of bundles, in the context of an appeal to the Court of Appeal (*Governor & Co of the Bank of Scotland v Henry Butcher & Co* [2003] EWCA Civ 67).

Practice Direction 39, para 3.2, which should be consulted for details, provides a list of all the documents that should be included in the trial bundle, unless the court orders otherwise. The contents of the trial bundle should be agreed between the parties where possible. The parties should also agree, where possible, that the documents contained in the bundle are authentic even if not disclosed under Part 31, and that the documents in the bundle may be treated as evidence of the facts stated in them even if a notice under the Civil Evidence Act 1995 has not been served. However, where the parties cannot agree the contents of the bundle, a summary of the points on which the parties are unable to agree should be included in the bundle (PD 39, para 3.9).

The originals of any documents included in the trial bundle should be available at trial (PD 39, para 3.3). If a document to be included in the trial bundle is illegible, a typed copy should be included in the bundle next to it, suitably cross-referenced (PD 39, para 3.8).

The preparation and production of the trial bundle is the responsibility of the legal representative who has conduct of the claim on behalf of the claimant, even if the task is delegated to another person (PD 39, para 3.4). The trial bundle should be paginated continuously throughout and indexed with a description of each document and the page number. Also, where the total number of pages is more than 100, numbered dividers should be placed at intervals between groups of documents (PD 39, para 3.5).

Under r 39.5(2), the trial bundles must be filed at court not more than seven and not less than three days before trial.

The bundle should normally be contained in a ring binder or lever arch file. Where there is more than one bundle, they should be clearly distinguishable, for example, by different colours or letters. If there are numerous bundles, a core bundle should be prepared containing the core documents essential to the proceedings with references to the supplementary documents in the other bundles (PD 39, para 3.6). For convenience, experts' reports may be contained in a separate bundle and cross-referenced in the main bundle (PD 39, para 3.7).

It is important to remember that a claimant will need to compile bundles for each of the other parties, and another for use of the witnesses (PD 39, para 3.10). Practice Direction 39 does not specify when the bundle should be provided to the other parties but this is often dealt with by court directions.

Settlement or discontinuance before trial

If an offer to settle is accepted, or a settlement reached, or a claim is discontinued and this disposes of the whole of a claim for which a date or 'window' has been fixed for the trial, the parties must ensure that the listing officer for the trial court is notified immediately (PD 39, para 4.1). This gives the listing officer the opportunity to allocate the time set aside for trial, or the trial window, to other parties. Indeed, the court office 'overlists' cases on the assumption that most cases settle or are otherwise disposed of before trial.

In *Tasyurdu v Immigration Appeal Tribunal* [2003] EWCA Civ 447, in the context of an application for permission to appeal which was withdrawn at very short notice, the Court of Appeal took the opportunity to remind parties that saving court resources was part of their obligation to help the court achieve the overriding objective, and that this involved notifying the court office as soon as it is known that a hearing will not be effective. Indeed, the Master of the Rolls said: 'It is infuriating to spend the weekend reading Monday's case and then to be told that it was settled on Friday.'

Conduct of the trial

The trial should proceed in accordance with the trial timetable, but the judge may vary or confirm any timetable given previously or, if none has been given, set his own (PD 28, para 8.3; PD 29, para 10.3).

The judge will usually have read the papers in the trial bundle and, both for trials on the fast track or multi-track, opening speeches may be dispensed with (PD 28, para 8.2; PD 29, para 10.2).

The court has the power to control evidence and to restrict cross-examination, and witness statements will stand as evidence-in-chief (Part 32). As for presentation of witness evidence, see Chapter 31, 'Evidence'. Where a fast track trial is not finished on the day for which it is listed, the judge will normally sit on the next court day to complete it (PD 28, para 8.6). In the case of a multi-track trial, the judge will normally sit on consecutive court days until it has been concluded (PD 29, para 10.6). However, this will be subject to the availability of the judge.

Exhibits at trial

Exhibits that are handed in and proved at the trial will be recorded by the court on an exhibit list and kept by the court until the conclusion of the trial, unless otherwise directed. At the conclusion of the trial, it is the parties' responsibility to obtain the return of those exhibits that they handed in and to preserve them for the period in which any appeal may take place (PD 39, para 7).

Failure to attend trial

If a defendant fails to attend the trial, the claimant may prove his claim and obtain judgment and, if there is a counterclaim, seek to have it struck out (r 39.3(1)(c)). Where the claimant fails to attend the trial, the defendant may prove his counterclaim and, similarly, seek the striking out of the claim (r 39.3(1)(b)). In cases where neither party attends, the court may strike out the whole of the proceedings (r 39.3(1)(a)).

Where a party does not attend trial and the court gives judgment or makes an order against him, he may apply for the judgment or order to be set aside (r 39.3(3)). Further, where the court strikes out the proceedings, or any part of them, an application can be made for those proceedings, or part of them, to be restored (r 39.3(2)).

The application to set aside the judgment, or part of it, or to restore the proceedings, should be made in accordance with Part 23 and must be supported by evidence giving reasons for the failure to attend court and stating when the applicant found out about the order against him (r 39.3(4); PD 39, paras 2.3–2.4).

Where an application is made by a party who did not attend trial to set aside the judgment, or to restore the proceedings, the court may grant the application *only if* the applicant:

(a) acted promptly when he found out that the court had exercised its power to strike out, or to enter judgment or make an order against him;

(b) had a good reason for not attending the trial; and

(c) had a reasonable prospect of success at the trial (r 39.3(5)).

The court has no residual discretion to make an order setting aside the judgment or restoring the proceedings if the above three requirements are not satisfied (*Barclays Bank plc v Ellis*). In *Barclays Bank plc v Ellis*, the defendants did not attend the trial of the claimant's claim to recover moneys allegedly due in respect of a joint loan account. The trial proceeded in their absence and judgment was entered against them in the sum of approximately £780,000 plus costs. The defendants, who were acting in person, had misread a letter from the claimant such that they were under the impression that the trial was to start at midday, rather than at 10.30 am. The defendants applied to set aside the judgment that was entered against them. Although the Court of Appeal was satisfied that the defendants had acted promptly when they found out that judgment had been entered against them in their absence, and that they had a good reason for not attending the trial, the court was not satisfied that the defendants had a reasonable prospect of success at the trial. It found the defendants' various defences to be hopeless or incredible, and held that as all three requirements of r 39.3(5) had not been satisfied it had no power to set the judgment aside.

In *Thakerar v Northwick Park and St Mark's NHS Trust and Another* [2002] EWCA Civ 617, a case in which the claimant satisfied all of the requirements of r 39.3(5)(a), (b) and (c), the Court of Appeal said that 'elementary fairness suggests that a party who, when struck out for non-attendance, acts promptly and shows good reason for non-attendance and a reasonable chance of eventual success should have their case restored unless some special further ground exists for doing otherwise' (at [32]). The court went on to say that except where there are special grounds, there is no reason to make those clear and simple rules uncertain by the exercise of judicial discretion.

Such special grounds will *not* include a simple cost-benefit analysis of the claim, since, all other things being equal, there is no reason why a modest claim ought to be treated less favourably than a more sizeable one. Nor should such special grounds include unsatisfied costs orders, as essentially costs can and should be dealt with on their own terms in such cases. Furthermore, r 39.3 is headed 'Failure to attend the trial' and its mechanism is to deal, and deal only, with entire pleadings, that is: a claim; a defence; a counterclaim; a defence to counterclaim. It does not allow the court to say that *part* of a pleading is unsustainable or has no reasonable prospect of success: Part 24 (summary judgment) exists to enable this to be done.

CHAPTER 33

JUDGMENTS AND ORDERS

INTRODUCTION

The Civil Procedure Rules (CPR) did not fundamentally reform the rules relating to judgments and orders, although there are some significant changes (for example, that a judgment or order takes effect from the date it was given or made (unless the court orders otherwise) rather than, as under the former rules, from the date it is sealed or otherwise perfected).

Part 40 deals with both judgments and orders. There is no express distinction between judgments and orders in the CPR, neither term being defined and, indeed, being referred to interchangeably. In very general terms, it may be said that 'judgment' refers to a final judgment, whilst 'order' refers to an interim judgment or case management direction. However, in some circumstances it may be difficult to identify whether a judgment is a final judgment or an interim order.

STANDARD REQUIREMENTS FOR JUDGMENTS AND ORDERS

Every judgment or order must state the name and judicial title of the person who made it. However, the following judgments and orders are entered administratively by the court office and therefore will not contain a name or judicial title:

- a default judgment entered by a court officer under r 12.4 after the filing of a request;
- a default costs certificate obtained under r 47.11;
- a judgment entered by a court officer (under Part 14) after the filing of a request following the defendant's admission;
- a consent order under r 40.6(2) which can be entered by a court officer;
- an order made by a court officer under r 70.5 (to enforce the award of a tribunal or other body or person other than the High Court or a county court); or
- an order made by a court officer under r 71.2 for a judgment debtor to attend court to provide information about his means (r 40.2).

Every judgment or order must bear the date on which it was made and be sealed by the court (r 40.2(2)). The date of the judgment or order is significant, because the judgment or order will take effect from the date it was made and not from the date when it was sealed or otherwise perfected (r 40.7). Accordingly, an appellant must file the appellant's notice at the appeal court within 14 days after the *date of the decision of the lower court* that the appellant wishes to appeal and not 14 days after the judgment or order of the court is *sealed or otherwise perfected* (r 52.4(2); *Sayers v Clarke-Walker (A Firm)* [2002] EWCA Civ 645; [2002] 3 All ER 490).

In *English v Emery Reimbold & Strick Ltd* [2002] EWCA Civ 605, the Court of Appeal said that it is the judge's duty to produce a judgment that gives a clear explanation for his order. It went on to say that an unsuccessful party should not seek to upset a judgment on the ground of inadequacy of reasons unless, despite the advantage of considering the judgment with knowledge of the evidence given and submissions made at trial, that party is unable to understand why it is that the judge has reached an adverse decision. The effect of the human rights legislation and Strasbourg jurisprudence is that a decision should be reasoned; however, the extent of the reasoning does not go any further than that required under domestic law.

DRAWING UP OF JUDGMENTS AND ORDERS

Every judgment or order, including those made at trial, will be drawn up (drafted) by the court unless:

(a) the court orders a party to draw it up;

(b) a party with the permission of the court agrees to draw it up;

(c) the court dispenses with the need to draw it up; or

(d) it is a consent order under r 40.6 (r 40.3(1)).

After the judgment or order is drawn up it will be sealed by the court.

The court has the power to direct that the parties file an agreed statement of the terms of the judgment or order before the judgment or order is drawn up (r 40.3(2)(b)). The parties must file the agreed statement of terms within seven days from the date the court makes the direction, unless the court orders otherwise (PD 40B, para 1.4).

If the court requires the terms of an order, which is being drawn up by the court, to be agreed by the parties, the court may direct that a copy of the draft order is sent to all the parties for their agreement to be endorsed on it and returned to the court before the order is sealed, or give notice of any appointment to attend before the court to agree the terms of the order (PD 40B, para 1.5).

If a judgment or order is drawn up by a party, the court may direct that it is checked by the court before it is sealed (r 40.3(2)(a)). The party responsible must file the draft within seven days of the date the order was made, with a request that the draft be checked before it is sealed (PD 40B, para 1.3).

FILING OF JUDGMENTS AND ORDERS

Where a judgment or order is drawn up by a party, he must file it at court no later than seven days after the date on which the court ordered or permitted him to draw it up, so that it can be sealed by the court (r 40.3(3)(a)). If a party fails to file the judgment or order at court within that period, any other party may draw it up and file it (r 40.3(3)(b)).

SERVICE OF JUDGMENTS AND ORDERS

In accordance with the general rule, the court will serve judgments and orders, unless the court directs otherwise (r 6.3). Where a judgment or order has been drawn up by a party and is to be served by the court, the party who drew it up must file a copy to be retained at court, and sufficient copies for service on himself and on the other parties. Once the judgment or order has been sealed the court must serve a copy on each party to the proceedings (r 40.4(1)).

Any order made otherwise than at trial must be served on the applicant and the respondent and any other person on whom the court orders it to be served (r 40.4(2)).

The court may order a judgment or order to be served on the party as well as his legal representative (r 40.5). Such an order is likely to be made only in exceptional circumstances, for example, where a penal notice has been attached to an order for an injunction, or an order requiring a judgment debtor to attend court. A penal notice warns the party that he must obey the order, and if he does not do so he may be sent to prison for contempt of court.

UNLESS ORDERS

Where the court makes an order requiring an act to be done (except the payment of an amount of money), the order must specify the time within which the act should be done (PD 40B, para 8.1).

If a party fails to comply with a rule, practice direction or court order, the court may make a further order directing that the party comply or face a specified consequence, usually the striking out of the party's claim or defence. Such an order is commonly known as an 'unless order'. An unless order must set out the consequences of failing to do the specified act, and should if possible specify the time and date within which the act should be completed, rather than give a period of time from the date of service of the order within which the act should be completed (PD 40B, para 8.2).

An example of an unless order is as follows:

> Unless the claimant serve his list of documents by 4.00 pm on Friday, January 22, 2004, his claim will be struck out and judgment entered for the defendant.

INJUNCTIONS

An order for an injunction, restraining a party from doing an act, or requiring a party to do an act, can be enforced by proceedings for contempt of court as long as certain requirements are fulfilled, including the endorsement on the order of a penal notice and personal service on the party to be bound by the order (CPR Sched 1 RSC Ord 45, r 5(1); CPR Sched 2 CCR Ord 29, r 1(1)).

BINDING NATURE OF JUDGMENT

A judgment of the court is binding; this is consistent with the fundamental principle of our common law that the outcome of litigation should be final. Where judgment has been given, either in a court of first instance or on appeal, the successful party ought, save in most exceptional circumstances, to be able to assume that the judgment is a valid and effective one (*In Re Barrell Enterprises* [1973] 1 WLR 19).

Where an issue has been determined by a decision of the court, that decision should definitively determine the issue as between those who were parties to the litigation. Furthermore, parties who are involved in litigation are expected to put before the court all the issues relevant to the litigation. If they do not, they will not normally be permitted to have a second bite at the cherry (*Henderson v Henderson* (1843) 3 Hare 100). There are safeguards to this policy of closure: accordingly, the law allows appeals; the law exceptionally allows appeals out of time; the law still more exceptionally allows judgments to be attacked on the ground of fraud; and the law exceptionally allows limitation periods to be extended (*The Ampthill Peerage Case* [1977] AC 547 at 569A–E, *per* Lord Wilberforce).

The Court of Appeal has a residual jurisdiction to re-open an appeal after it has been finally decided in order to avoid real injustice in exceptional circumstances. An example of such a situation would be where the court that made the decision was biased. If a judge is biased this is a breach of natural justice, and the need to maintain confidence in the administration of justice makes it imperative that there should be a remedy. In order to exercise the jurisdiction the court must be satisfied that a significant injustice has occurred and there is no alternative effective remedy (*Taylor v Lawrence* [2002] EWCA Civ 90 at [54]–[55]).

The High Court also possesses an inherent jurisdiction to re-open its decisions if it is clearly established that a significant injustice has occurred and there is no alternative effective remedy (*Seray-Wurie v Hackney LBC* [2002] EWCA Civ 909). In *Seray-Wurie v Hackney LBC*, the Court of Appeal held that the case got 'nowhere near satisfying this extremely tough requirement' (at [17], *per* Brooke LJ). The claimant had obtained a default costs certificate against the defendant. The defendant had attempted to serve points of dispute in time but had failed and made an application within three days to set the default costs certificate aside. In the circumstances the court exercised its discretion under r 47.12(2) to set aside the default costs certificate on the grounds that the overriding objective required that the defendant be entitled to be heard on the merits as to costs and therefore there was a good reason why the detailed assessment proceedings should continue. The claimant was refused permission by the High Court to appeal the order.

Although the claimant had now exhausted his opportunities to appeal the decision, he applied instead for an order that the decision of the High Court refusing permission to appeal be 're-opened for a hearing' in accordance with the principle in *Taylor v Lawrence* (see above). The Court of Appeal found that there was no possibility of any reasonable costs judge reaching any other conclusion and therefore no injustice had occurred, and there were no grounds to re-open the decision.

There is currently no decision as to whether the county courts have similar powers to re-open their decisions. In *Seray-Wurie v Hackney LBC*, the Court of Appeal expressly stated that nothing in its judgment should be interpreted as having any effect in relation to re-opening decisions made by circuit judges sitting as an appeal court in the county court.

DATE FROM WHICH JUDGMENT OR ORDER TAKES EFFECT

A judgment or order takes effect from the day when it was given or made, or such later date as the court may specify (r 40.7), and not (unless the court orders otherwise) from the date that it is sealed or otherwise perfected (*Sayers v Clarke-Walker (A Firm)* [2002] EWCA Civ 645).

However, where a reserved judgment is made available to the parties on a confidential basis in advance of its being handed down, the judgment or order is not made until such time as it is handed down (*Prudential Assurance Co Ltd v McBains Cooper (A Firm) and Others* [2000] 1 WLR 2000; [2001] 3 All ER 1014).

RESERVED JUDGMENTS

At the end of a hearing a judge may give an immediate oral judgment, or reserve judgment and subsequently hand down a written judgment. In the High Court, if the judge reserves judgment he may provide a copy of his judgment to the parties on a confidential basis before formally handing it down (see *Practice Statement (Supreme Court: Judgments)* [1998] 1 WLR 825; *Practice Statement (Supreme Court: Judgments) (No 2)* [1999] WLR 1; and *Practice Note (Court of Appeal: Handed Down Judgments)* [2002] 1 WLR 344). The purpose of this practice is to introduce an orderly procedure for the delivery of reserved judgments, whereby the parties' lawyers can have time to consider and agree the terms of any consequential orders they may invite the court to make, and the process of delivering judgment can be abbreviated by avoiding the need for the judge to read the judgment orally in court. The purpose is not to allow the parties to have more material available to them to help them settle their dispute (*Prudential Assurance Co Ltd v McBains Cooper (A Firm) and Others*).

In *Prudential Assurance Co Ltd v McBains Cooper*, the judge reserved judgment and subsequently sent copies of his judgment to the parties in accordance with the Practice Statement. Just before the judge was due formally to hand down his judgment, the parties asked him to adjourn the hearing with a view to making a Tomlin order recording a settlement of the proceedings agreed by the parties. The parties also invited the judge not to hand down the judgment in open court. In his judgment the judge had decided three disputed issues of law that were of wider interest and application than just to the parties to the dispute, and the judge was of the opinion that there were strong public interest grounds for formally delivering judgment in open court.

It was accepted that the judge had not given judgment within the meaning of r 40.7(1) when he sent the judgment to the parties' lawyers; it was also accepted that it was open to the parties to settle their case at any time, whether before or after judgment was handed down. Further, it is always open to the parties, after hearing or reading a reasoned judgment, to invite the court to make a consent order in some other terms at any time before an order of the court is perfected in pursuance of that judgment. However, the Court of Appeal rejected the parties' argument that, having obtained the judge's judgment, the parties were at liberty to compromise their dispute and to make it a term of their compromise that the judge would not publish the judgment whose terms they had read.

The Court of Appeal held that the judge possessed a discretion to decide whether or not to hand down his judgment, as it may well be in the public interest for the judge to decide to continue to deliver judgment notwithstanding that the parties had settled. Although the wishes of the parties were a factor for the court to take into account when deciding how to exercise that discretion, the judge would not be deprived of the power to decide whether or not to hand down judgment simply because the parties decided to settle their dispute after reading the judgment which was sent to them in confidence. It was held to be in the public interest for judgments to be given which decided points of law of wider interest, and it was also felt that if the court did not have a discretion to decide, the parties could prevent the judge from delivering judgment, even if it contained findings of serious fraud or serious negligence, if one of the parties was willing to pay the other party large sums of money to suppress it.

VARIATION OF JUDGMENTS AND ORDERS

If a judgment is sealed or otherwise perfected this exhausts the jurisdiction of the court to deal with a matter, in accordance with the general principle that the outcome of litigation should be final (*Taylor v Lawrence* [2002] EWCA Civ 90 at [9]). The court has the power to amend or vary a judgment or order at any time before the judgment is sealed or otherwise perfected, but the discretion to do so will be exercised only in exceptional cases and in accordance with the overriding objective (*Stewart v Engel* [2000] 1 WLR 2268; [2000] 3 All ER 518).

In *Royal Brompton Hospital NHS Trust v Frederick Alexander Hammond and Others* [2001] EWCA Civ 778, the judge provided his written judgment to the parties on a confidential basis before formally handing it down. One of the parties submitted that a court would be more inclined to alter its judgment before it was officially handed down than afterwards. The Court of Appeal affirmed the decision in *Stewart v Engel*, and further held that there was no logical reason why a written judgment should be more readily altered after delivery to the parties, but before handing down, than during delivery of an oral argument or immediately after delivery. The same principle applied and there must be exceptional circumstances before a judge would reconsider his judgment, which did not exist in this case.

In *Re Blenheim Leisure (Restaurants) Ltd (No 3)* (1999) *The Times*, 9 November, Neuberger J gave examples of circumstances in which the court might justifiably exercise its jurisdiction to reconsider and amend or vary its judgment before it is sealed. These were:

(a) where there was a plain mistake on the part of the court;

(b) a failure of the parties to draw to the court's attention a fact or point of law that was plainly relevant;

(c) discovery of new facts subsequent to the judgment being given; or

(d) where a party could argue that he was taken by surprise by a particular application from which the court ruled adversely to him and which he did not have a fair opportunity to consider.

Further, the Court of Appeal and High Court have a residual jurisdiction to reopen a decision after it has been finally decided in order to avoid real injustice in exceptional circumstances (*Taylor v Lawrence*).

Court's general power to vary or revoke an order

As part of its general case management powers the court has the power to vary or revoke an *order* (r 3.1(7)). This power gives the court a wide discretion but it will be subject to the fundamental principles referred to above regarding the court's limited jurisdiction to reopen decisions after they have been finally decided and to vary or revoke an order after it has been sealed or otherwise perfected.

There are a number of express rules throughout the CPR that give the court power to set aside or vary judgments or orders. For instance, where an order is made following the application of one party without notice to the other, the other party can apply, within seven days of service of the order, for the order to be varied or set aside (r 23.10). Also, where judgment has been entered against a party after his failure to comply with an unless order, that party can apply, within 14 days of service of the order, for the judgment to be set aside (r 3.6). There are also provisions for a party to apply to set aside judgment entered in default (r 13.3) and limited provision for a party to apply to set aside judgment given at a hearing which he failed to attend (r 39.3).

Non-party applying to set aside judgment or order

A person who is not a party, but who is directly affected by a judgment or an order, may apply to have the judgment or order set aside or varied (r 40.9).

An example of where a non-party may apply for a judgment or an order to be set aside is where there is an order or a judgment relating to land to which he is not a party but in which he claims an interest. So, for instance, where a charging order is made in respect of land in which a non-party claims an interest (s 3(5) of the Charging Orders Act 1979; r 73.9), or where a non-party is entitled to claim relief where a possession order is made (PD 55, para 2.3).

TIME FOR COMPLYING WITH A JUDGMENT OR ORDER

A party must comply with a judgment or an order for the payment of an amount of money, including costs, within 14 days of the date of the judgment or order unless the judgment or order specifies a different date for compliance, or any of the rules specify a different date, or the court has stayed the proceedings or judgment (r 40.11).

THE 'SLIP' RULE

The court may, at any time, correct an accidental slip or omission in the judgment or order and a party may apply for a correction without notice (r 40.12). The court also has an inherent jurisdiction to vary its own orders to make the meaning and intention of the court clear (PD 40B, para 4.5).

The slip rule cannot enable a court to have second or additional thoughts. Once the order is drawn up, any mistakes must be corrected by means of an appeal to an appellate court. However, it is possible under the slip rule to amend an order to give effect to the intention of the court (*Bristol-Myers Squibb Co v Baker Norton Pharmaceuticals Inc & Napro Biotherapeutics Inc* [2001] EWCA Civ 414).

In *Bristol-Myers Squibb Co v Baker Norton Pharmaceuticals Inc & Napro Biotherapeutics Inc*, the claimant was unsuccessful at trial and ordered to pay the defendants' costs of the proceedings. However, the order for costs limited the defendants' costs to one set of costs. In accordance with the general rule, interest was payable on those costs from the date of the court's judgment. The defendants appealed the order for costs and the Court of Appeal set aside the judge's order limiting the defendants' costs to one set of costs. This had the effect that interest on the costs ran from the date of the Court of Appeal's order. This meant that the Court of Appeal's judgment deprived the defendants of interest (estimated at £50,000) that had accrued during the time between the order made by the judge and that made by the Court of Appeal. The Court of Appeal held that the order setting aside the whole of the judge's order on costs was an accidental slip, which it corrected under r 40.12. The court explained that the only issue raised on the appeal was whether the restriction placed by the judge was appropriate. At no time was that part of the judge's order that required the claimant to pay the defendants' costs challenged, and it was not the intention of the Court of Appeal to alter that part of the order. The intention of the court was to remove the restriction, not to alter the general right to costs that had been ordered. The terms of the order did not meet the intention of the court contained in the judgment and had an unexpected legal effect which could be corrected under the slip rule.

In *Markos v Goodfellow and Others* [2002] EWCA Civ 1542, the Court of Appeal confirmed that the slip rule, under r 40.12, is limited to a genuine slip and is not designed to correct a substantive issue. Accordingly, the judge was wrong to have amended an order in circumstances where there had not been an accidental slip or omission in the judgment or order. *Markos* concerned a claim for trespass where the claimant only just succeeded in proving trespass over a distance of about 4 inches – the judge in the court below refused her even nominal damages. On appeal, the judge said that the first instance judge's conclusions were correct that the trespass had caused no harm, but incorrect because any degree of trespass to land, however small, was actionable. The appeal judge therefore ordered that nominal damages of £2 should be added by means of using the slip rule to amend the original judgment. The Court of Appeal made it clear that this was an inappropriate use of the rule.

Application to correct an error in a judgment or order

The application to correct an error in a judgment or order can be by means of an informal document such as a letter (PD 40B, para 4.2). The application should describe the error and set out the correction required. The application may be dealt with without a hearing if:

(a) the applicant so requests;

(b) the parties consent; or

(c) the court does not consider that a hearing would be appropriate (PD 40B, para 4.2).

The judge may deal with the application without notice if the slip or omission is obvious, or may direct that notice of the application is given to the other party (PD 40B, para 4.3). If the application is opposed it should, if practicable, be listed for a hearing before the judge who gave the judgment or made the order (PD 40B, para 4.4).

JUDGMENT ON CLAIM AND COUNTERCLAIM

Where the court gives judgment for a specified amount both for the claimant on his claim and against the claimant on a counterclaim, if there is a balance in favour of one of the parties, the court may order the party whose judgment is for the lesser amount to pay the balance (r 40.13(1), (2)).

However, even if the court orders judgment for the balance in favour of one party, it may still make a separate order as to costs against each party (r 40.13(3)).

INTEREST ON JUDGMENTS

Where interest is payable on a judgment under s 17 of the Judgments Act 1838 or s 74 of the County Courts Act 1984 (CCA), interest begins to run from the date that judgment is given unless there is a rule or practice direction which makes a different provision, or the court orders otherwise, and this includes ordering interest to begin from a date before the date that judgment was given (r 40.8).

In the High Court every judgment debt carries interest from the date that judgment is given (s 17 of the Judgments Act 1838). In the county courts, judgments for the payment of a sum of £5,000 or more carry interest from the date judgment is given (s 74 of the CCA). However, if a debt falls under the Late Payment of Commercial Debts (Interest) Act 1998, any judgment entered will carry interest, whatever the amount of the judgment debt (County Courts (Interest on Judgment Debts) (Amendment) Order 1998 (SI 1998/2400)).

In both the High Court and the county courts, the judgment debt interest rate is currently 8% (Judgment Debts (Rate of Interest) Order 1993 (SI 1993/564)).

Where a contract provides for the payment of interest on a debt, although interest at the contract rate can be ordered up to the date of entry of judgment, interest will be at the judgment debt interest rate once judgment is entered, unless the contract specifically provides that any judgment obtained for recovery of payment under the contract is to carry interest at the contract rate (*Re European Central Railway* (1877) 4 Ch D 33).

BIAS OF JUDGE

If there is an allegation of judicial bias, the appeal court considering the matter must first ascertain all the circumstances that have a bearing on the suggestion that the judge was biased. It must then ask whether those circumstances would lead a fair-minded and informed observer to conclude that there was a real possibility that the tribunal was biased (*Magill v Porter and Weeks* [2001] UKHL 67 at [99]–[104]).

In *Taylor v Lawrence*, the parties litigated a boundary dispute. At the trial the defendants were not represented, but the claimants had both solicitors and counsel. The trial judge informed the parties that he had been a client of the claimants' solicitors in a personal matter, involving the drafting of his will. None of the parties objected to his continuing to hear the trial. The judge found in favour of the claimants. The defendants appealed and one of the grounds was an appearance of bias because of the judge's relationship with the claimants' solicitors. Before the hearing of the appeal it was disclosed to the defendants that the judge and his wife had used the services of the claimants' solicitors to draft a codicil to their wills the night before judgment was given against the defendants. It subsequently became known that the judge had not paid the claimants' solicitors for their services. However, the explanation given was that the work was so modest it would not have been economic for the solicitors to render an account.

In applying the test whether a fair-minded and informed observer would conclude that in those circumstances there was a real danger of bias, the Court of Appeal held that it was unthinkable that an informed observer would regard it as conceivable that a judge would be influenced to favour a party in litigation, with whom he had no relationship, merely because that party happened to be represented by a firm of solicitors who were acting for the judge in a purely personal matter in connection with a will. The court had no reason to doubt the explanation given for a bill not being rendered, and found that there was no evidence that the judge knew this to be the case, but held that even if he did, it would not alter the court's view.

The Court of Appeal noted that in our jurisdiction there is a close relationship between the judiciary and the legal profession, and it is often the case that barristers and solicitors appear before judges with whom they have practised and socialised. It was felt that this did not prejudice but enhanced the administration of justice. The court was of the opinion that judges, solicitors and advocates are entitled to expect from a fair-minded and informed observer a corresponding recognition that they will endeavour to be true to their judicial oath and to the standards set by their respective professional codes. Accordingly, it was not to be assumed, without cogent evidence to the contrary, that a judge's acquaintanceship, whether social or professional, with those conducting litigation before him in a professional capacity, would lead him to reach a decision in that litigation that he would not otherwise reach on the evidence and the arguments.

The Court of Appeal held that if the situation is one where a fair-minded and informed person might regard the judge as biased, it is important that the judge makes disclosure of the relevant circumstances that might give rise to the appearance of bias. Also, if disclosure is made it should be full disclosure. The Court of Appeal warned judges to be circumspect about declaring the existence of a relationship where there is no real possibility of it being regarded by a fair-minded and informed observer as raising a possibility of bias. If such a relationship is disclosed, it unnecessarily raises an implication that it could affect the judgment and approach of the judge.

CONSENT JUDGMENTS AND ORDERS

Even where proceedings are commenced, most disputes settle on agreed terms rather than proceed to be determined at trial. Where the parties reach agreement a consent order can be filed at court recording the terms of the agreement. This will enable the proceedings to be disposed of and allow a party (if necessary) to enforce the terms of the agreement recorded in the consent order simply by making an application to the court, without the need to commence a fresh claim for breach of the compromise agreement.

Entering a consent order without the permission of the court

Part 40 contains a procedure that allows a court officer to enter and seal a consent order as an administrative, rather than a judicial, act. In order to invoke this procedure the following conditions must be satisfied:

(a) the judgment or order is of a type set out in r 40.6(3) (see below);

(b) none of the parties is a litigant in person; and

(c) the approval of the court is not required before an agreed order can be made (for example, the compromise is not by or on behalf of a child or patient under Part 21) (r 40.6(2)).

If those conditions are satisfied a court officer may enter and seal the following orders and judgments, agreed by consent:

• the payment of an amount of money, including unspecified as well as specified damages, as well as the value of goods to be decided by the court at a subsequent hearing;

• the delivery up of goods with or without the option of paying the value of the goods or the agreed value;

• the dismissal of any proceedings, wholly or in part;

• the stay of proceedings on agreed terms, disposing of the proceedings, whether those terms are recorded in a schedule to the order or elsewhere;

• the stay of enforcement of a judgment, either unconditionally or on condition that the money due under the judgment is paid by instalments specified in the order;

• the setting aside under Part 13 of a default judgment which has not been satisfied;

• the payment out of money which has been paid into court;

• the discharge from liability of any party; or

• the payment, assessment or waiver of costs, or such other provision for costs as may be agreed (r 40.6(3)).

However, if the consent order appears to be unclear or incorrect, the court officer may refer it to a judge for consideration (PD 40B, para 3.2).

In *Gerrard Ltd v Michael Read & Christows Asset Management Ltd* (2002) *The Times*, 17 January, Ch D, it was held that there is a public interest benefit in holding a party to the terms of a consent order to which, with the benefit of legal advice, he is evidently willing to be bound. However, the court stated that the jurisdiction to vary either an interim or a final consent order extends to discharging a term of the order that as a matter of general law is void and unenforceable, such as, as in this case, unlawful restraint of trade, while leaving the remainder of the order in force.

Applying for a consent order to be entered at court

In all other cases, where the provisions of r 40.6(2) do not apply, the parties can apply to the court for a consent order to be made in the agreed terms (r 40.6(5)). As the terms of the order or judgment are agreed, the court will usually deal with the application without a hearing (r 40.6(6)).

An application notice, requesting a judgment or an order in the terms of the consent order, should be filed with the consent order, and the consent order must be drawn so that the judge's name and judicial title can be inserted (PD 40B, para 3.3).

Tomlin orders

If the parties agree terms of settlement that include matters outside of the dispute, or orders which the court has no power to make, the parties can record those terms and attach them as a schedule to the consent order, or refer to their existence in another document, and apply for an order staying the proceedings on the agreed terms. Such an order is known as a 'Tomlin order' after the name of the judge who first suggested it.

A Tomlin order allows the parties to agree additional terms, such as a confidentiality clause, which the court has no power to order. The court will not approve the terms in the schedule but will make an order staying the proceedings to enable the agreed terms to be put into effect. If appropriate, the court will also make an order for the payment out of moneys paid into court with orders in respect of accrued interest, and make an order for costs to be assessed if not agreed. It is important to ensure that the provision for payment out of money paid into court or for costs to be assessed is contained in the body of the order, and not in the attached schedule, because a court order is needed for a payment out of court or the assessment of costs.

The court will also usually make an order for 'liberty to apply', so that the parties can apply to the court for an order to enforce the terms without the need for the parties to start fresh proceedings to enforce the terms of the compromise. However, like any other contractual terms, the court will not enforce the agreed terms if they are too vague.

Form of consent order

All consent orders to be filed at court must be drawn up in the terms agreed and must be expressed as being 'By Consent'. A consent order must also be signed by each party's legal representative, or by the party if he is acting in person (r 40.6(7)).

SALE OF LAND AND APPOINTMENT OF CONVEYANCING COUNSEL

In any proceedings relating to land, the court may order the land (or part of it) to be sold, mortgaged, exchanged or partitioned (r 40.16). The court may direct that a deed or document shall be prepared, executed or signed, and make an order as to who is to prepare the deed or document, or approve it, in order to give effect to the order (PD 40B, para 2.1). If the parties are unable to agree the form of the deed or document, any party may apply, in accordance with Part 23, for the form in which the deed or document is to be settled (PD 40B, para 2.2). The court may settle the deed or document itself, or refer it to a Master, district judge or conveyancing counsel of the Supreme Court to settle it (PD 40B, para 2.3). Conveyancing counsel of the Supreme Court are appointed under s 131 of the Supreme Court Act 1981.

Where the court makes an order for the sale, mortgage, exchange or partition of land it also has the power to order that any party deliver up to the purchaser, or any other person, possession of the land, receipt of rents or profits relating to it, or both (r 40.17).

CHAPTER 34

COSTS OF PROCEEDINGS

INTRODUCTION

In his Final Report (FR), Lord Woolf said that costs were 'central to the changes' he wished to bring about and that virtually all his recommendations for reform of the civil procedure system were 'designed at least in part to tackle the problems of costs'. He stated that his reforms were designed to reduce the amount of costs incurred by a party by controlling what was required of a party in the conduct of proceedings, to make the amount of costs more predictable and more proportionate to the nature of the dispute. He also recommended that costs be used more effectively as a method to control unreasonable behaviour, and that litigants should be provided with more information about costs so that they could exercise greater control over their lawyer's expenditure of costs on their behalf (see *Access to Justice*, FR, Chapter 7, para 5, www.dca.gov.uk/civil/final/index.htm).

Although it seems true to say that parties and legal representatives are now much more aware of the incidence of costs when conducting proceedings than they were before the Civil Procedure Rules (CPR) were introduced, and much more afraid of being penalised in costs for their conduct in the course of proceedings, there is no clear evidence that the CPR have in fact reduced the level of costs that are incurred in conducting proceedings. In fact, the limited evidence that there is suggests that, on the contrary, costs have risen (see the Lord Chancellor's Department (now known as the Department for Constitutional Affairs) paper, *Further Findings*, published in August 2002, www.dca.gov.uk/civil/reform/ffreform.htm, discussed in Chapter 1, 'Introduction'). A common criticism made of the CPR is that they cause front-loading of costs, which can result in higher levels of costs than would previously have been the case under the former civil procedure system, particularly if a case settles at an early stage. Complaint is also commonly heard that the requirement to produce costs estimates and statements of costs throughout the course of proceedings, in order to keep the client, the opponent and the court informed of the level of costs being incurred, paradoxically increases the costs burden on a party in conducting litigation.

However, what the courts are very alive to is costs being in some way proportionate to the amount in issue, and they have not hesitated to reduce bills which have fallen foul of this principle. In addition, when making orders for costs the court will readily take into account the conduct of the parties, both before and during the proceedings, and whether any efforts were made to try to resolve the dispute without the need for litigation.

DEFINITIONS AND JURISDICTION

Definition of 'costs'

The term 'costs' in the CPR is defined to include fees, charges and remuneration, including success fees in conditional fee agreements, as well as disbursements, expenses and any insurance premiums for legal expenses insurance. Costs also includes remuneration allowed to a litigant in person and any fee or reward charged by a lay representative for acting on behalf of a party in proceedings allocated to the small claims track (r 43.2).

However, what is not expressed within that definition is whether such fees, charges, remuneration, expenses, etc are confined to those incurred by the party's solicitor in conducting the litigation. The general principle is that only the costs incurred by a party's solicitor (including disbursements such as expert's and counsel's fees) are recoverable and not any sums claimed by the litigant as being incurred in the course of instructing his solicitor. However, where a party's employees carry out work of an expert nature to investigate and obtain evidence for the preparation of a case, such costs may be recoverable as costs of the proceedings (*Admiral Management Service Ltd v Para-protect Europe Ltd* [2002] EWHC 233, Ch D). Further, costs incurred by a party before proceedings were commenced, and before a solicitor was instructed, may be recoverable if the costs were reasonably incurred in order to obtain material that was, or would have been but for the settlement of the proceedings, of use and service in the claim (*Admiral Management Service Ltd v Para-protect Europe Ltd*).

Paying party/receiving party

The CPR use the expression 'paying party' to refer to the party liable to pay costs and 'receiving party' to refer to the party entitled to be paid costs (r 43.2).

Base costs and additional liabilities

Since the statutory changes to the rules regarding conditional fee agreements, to permit recoverability of the success fee and any after the event insurance premium from an opponent, the amounts claimed in success fees and insurance premiums have become known as 'additional liabilities' and all the other costs of the proceedings are known as 'base costs'. An additional liability includes the additional amount for collective conditional fee agreements made by a membership organisation (r 43.2; PD 43, para 2.2).

Funding arrangements

A conditional fee agreement, or a collective conditional fee agreement, which provides for a success fee and after the event insurance policies, is known as a 'funding arrangement' (r 43.2; PD 43, para 2.2).

Proceedings other than court proceedings

The costs rules apply not only to the costs of parties involved in court proceedings, but also, where the court has the power to assess those costs, to the costs of proceedings before an arbitrator, tribunal or other statutory body (r 43.2(2)(a)).

Solicitor/client costs

The costs rules also apply to the costs payable by a client to his solicitor when the client seeks to challenge the amount of those costs (r 43.2(2)(a)).

Costs payable under a contract

The rules will also apply to the costs payable by one party to another under the terms of a contract where the court makes an order for the assessment of those costs (r 43.2(2)(b)).

The indemnity principle

The effect of the indemnity principle is that the costs that the paying party will be ordered to pay the receiving party are no more than an indemnity to the receiving party, that is, the amount which the receiving party has to pay his solicitor and no more (*Gundry v Sainsbury* [1910] 1 KB 99; for a detailed consideration of the indemnity principle, see Chapter 4, 'Funding Litigation'). However, the indemnity principle has been abrogated for certain types of conditional fee agreements (CFAs) entered into after 2 June 2003 following amendments to the Conditional Fee Agreements Regulations 2000 (SI 2000/692) and the Collective Conditional Fee Agreement Regulations 2000 (SI 2000/2988). Where a CFA provides that the solicitor will not seek to recover by way of costs from his client anything in excess of what the court awards, or what is recovered from the opponent, the costs of such an agreement will be recoverable costs for the purposes of CPR Parts 44–48 (r 43.2(3), (4)). Accordingly, a solicitor will now be entitled to agree not to charge the client more than is recovered from the other side in costs without such an agreement being unenforceable for breaching the indemnity principle.

Counsel's fees

Where counsel appears for a party at a hearing the general rule is that, for the purposes of detailed assessment of those costs, there is no need to obtain a certificate expressing the court's opinion whether it was appropriate for counsel to attend the hearing. However, the court will express an opinion as to whether it was appropriate for counsel to attend the hearing if the paying party asks the court to do so, or more than one counsel appeared for a party, or the court wishes to record its opinion on the matter. Where the court expresses such an opinion it will be taken into account by a costs officer conducting a detailed assessment of costs to which that order relates (PD 44, para 8.7).

Costs draftsman's fees

Costs draftsman's fees can be included in the 'reasonable costs of preparing and checking the bill' (PD 43, para 4.18), although this does not apply to publicly funded family matters. Whether a costs draftsman is needed to prepare a summary bill of costs or costs estimate will depend on its complexity.

Who assesses costs?

Costs assessed by the court may be assessed by:

(a) an authorised court officer, being an officer of a county court, a district registry, the Principal Registry of the Family Division or the Supreme Court Costs Office who has been authorised to assess costs;

(b) a costs officer, being a costs judge, a district judge or an authorised court officer; or

(c) a costs judge, being a taxing Master of the Supreme Court (r 43.2(1)).

Authorised court officer

There are jurisdictional limits to the claims for costs that can be assessed by an authorised court officer by way of detailed assessment in the Supreme Court Costs Office and the Principal Registry of the Family Division (PD 47, para 30.1(1)). Also, if all the parties to a detailed assessment hearing agree that it should not be conducted by an authorised court officer, if the receiving party notifies the court of this when requesting a hearing date, the court will list the hearing before a costs judge or a district judge instead (PD 47, para 30.1(3)). If the parties cannot agree, but a party would like to object nevertheless, the party can make an application to the court under Part 23 and the court can decide, if sufficient reason is shown, to list the detailed assessment hearing before a costs judge or a district judge (PD 47, para 30.1(4)).

Moreover, there are certain aspects of the rules relating to detailed assessment where an authorised court officer has no power to act. These are wasted costs orders, orders in relation to misconduct, sanctions for delay in commencing detailed assessment proceedings, detailed assessment of costs payable to a solicitor by his client (unless it relates to costs in proceedings involving a child or patient) and when a party makes an application objecting to an authorised court officer carrying out a detailed assessment (r 47.3).

COSTS ORDERS MADE DURING THE COURSE OF PROCEEDINGS

Prior to the final hearing, a number of costs orders may be made during the life of a case. For example, if one of the parties applies to amend his statement of case, permission is usually granted on terms that the amending party pays the 'costs of and caused by' the amendment. However, if the court makes an order that does not mention costs none will be payable (r 44.13). A party who is, or may become, entitled to costs on the making of a court order, should therefore ensure that provision is made in the order for the payment of costs.

Practice Direction 44 includes a table of costs orders (with definitions) that the court will commonly make in applications made before trial (PD 44, para 8.5).

An order for 'costs' or 'costs in any event' means that the party in whose favour the order is made will be entitled to the costs to which the order relates, whatever other costs orders are made in the proceedings. This type of order may be made, for example, in favour of the innocent party where the other party is obliged to apply for relief from a sanction. Such an order reflects the fact that the party applying for relief from a sanction is blameworthy and should bear the costs incurred by reason of their default, whatever the merits of the substantive case.

An order for *'costs in the case'* or *'costs in the application'* means that the party who obtains an order for costs in his favour at the end of the proceedings is entitled to the costs to which the order relates. Such a costs order applies to matters such as the ordering of directions for the conduct of the proceedings. It reflects the fact that the party who obtains a costs order in his favour at the end of the case is usually entitled to all of the costs inevitably incurred in pursuing the proceedings.

An order for *'costs reserved'* defers, to a later occasion, the decision as to which party is entitled to the costs to which the order relates. This costs order may, for example, be made where one party applies for an interim injunction, as the remedy of an interim injunction will be granted before the merits of the underlying cause of action have been decided. Once the substantive cause of action has been determined, the court will know whether the party granted the interim injunction was entitled to the benefit of it and will then be in a position to decide which party is entitled to the costs of that order. However, if the court does not make a specific order, the costs of such an order will be *costs in the case*.

If an order is made for *'claimant's/defendant's costs in the case/application'*, the party identified will be entitled to recover the costs to which the order relates only if he is awarded costs at the end of the proceedings. Such orders are rarely made these days, but may be appropriate where the court feels that there is some merit in the successful applicant's application but that it all depends on a trial of the evidence and whether the applicant's eventually wins.

An order for *'costs thrown away'* is usually made where one party has had to apply for relief, for example, to set judgment aside, and although he is successful in the application he will have to pay his own and the other party's costs incurred as a result of such an application. This is similar to an order for *'costs of and caused by'* (for example) an amendment, referred to above.

An order for *'costs here and below'* may be made following appeal proceedings where a party is successful in appealing an order made by a lower court. However, where the decision of a Divisional Court is appealed, the party is not entitled to any costs incurred in any court below the Divisional Court (PD 44, para 8.5).

Where the court makes *'no order as to costs'* or orders *'each party to pay his own costs'*, each party must bear his own costs to which the order relates whatever costs order the court makes at the end of the proceedings. Such an order may be made, for example, where the court is critical of the behaviour of both parties, for instance, where due to a failure to co-operate to agree directions, an unnecessary attendance is required at court.

COURT'S DISCRETION AS TO COSTS

By s 51 of the Supreme Court Act 1981 (SCA), the costs of and incidental to proceedings in the High Court and any county courts are in the discretion of the court, and the court has full power to determine by whom and to what extent costs are to be paid.

A successful party is not entitled to recover costs, the court having a discretion in every case as to whether costs are recoverable from another party (r 44.3(1)(a)).

Moreover, although the general rule is that the unsuccessful party must pay the successful party's costs, the court can make a different order (r 44.3(2)). Also, a party cannot rely on the operation of the general rule in the absence of a reference to costs in a court order, because if costs are not expressly mentioned in the order, no party is entitled to any (r 44.13(1)). Further, the general rule does not apply to certain family and probate proceedings in the Court of Appeal (r 44.3(3)).

Therefore, although in most cases the general rule will prevail, behind these rules is the message, running throughout the CPR, that the court is concerned not just with the ends but also with the means to the ends, that is, the court will not simply award costs to the successful party without also considering the conduct of the parties over the course of the proceedings. As Lord Woolf put it in *Phonographic Performance Ltd v AEI Rediffusion Ltd* [1999] 2 All ER 299, the general rule is 'a starting position from which a court can readily depart' (at 313j). However, although the court may make a different order to the general rule (r 44.3(2)), the court must have reason to do so as this 'is a constraint which follows necessarily from the existence of a general rule' (*Spice Girls Ltd v Aprilia World Service BV* [2002] EWCA Civ 15 at [162], *per* Morrit V-C).

The Court of Appeal has stressed that the question of which costs order is appropriate in a particular case is one for the discretion of the judge, and an appellate court will be slow to interfere in the judge's exercise of his discretion (*Verrechia v Commissioner of Police for the Metropolis* [2002] EWCA Civ 605).

Court's reasons for costs order

In the majority of cases there is no need for a judge to give reasons for his decision on costs following a hearing because the decision is implicit from the circumstances in which the award is made, that is, the costs follow the event and the successful party is awarded his costs. However, where the reason for an order for costs is not obvious, the judge should explain why he has made the order (*Verrechia v Commissioner of Police for the Metropolis*). In *Verrechia*, the claimant brought proceedings to recover damages under the Torts (Interference with Goods) Act 1997 in respect of 40 items of property that the police failed to return to him following his acquittal from charges of dishonestly handling stolen property. The trial judge found that the claim succeeded in respect of 20 items but failed in respect of the remaining 20 items. The judge awarded damages in the sum of £37,300 plus interest and, without giving any reasons, made no order as to costs. The Court of Appeal found that although the judge had not given express reasons for this order, a fair reading of that part of the judge's judgment led to the conclusion that the judge considered that that order was the right order in the light of what the claimant had obtained under the judgment. That is, the judge clearly thought that the proceedings had resulted in a 'draw'. The Court of Appeal held that it was open to the judge in the circumstances of that case to reach that conclusion, and said that the judge's reasons for his order could be deduced from his judgment in the case.

Circumstances to be taken into account when ordering costs

When deciding what order to make about costs, the court must take account of all the circumstances (r 44.3(4)). When considering the circumstances, the court must take the following matters into account:

(a) the conduct of all the parties;

(b) whether a party has succeeded on part of his case, even if he has not been wholly successful; and

(c) any payment into court or admissible offer to settle made by a party which is drawn to the court's attention (whether or not made in accordance with Part 36) (r 44.3(4)(a)–(c)).

However, the court is not limited to considering these matters and may consider any other relevant factor as well. In *Home Office v Lownds* [2002] EWCA Civ 365, Lord Woolf described the considerations that are to be taken into account when making an order for costs as 'redolent of proportionality' (at [3]). All of the factors in r 44.3(4) (and any other relevant factors) may persuade the court to make an order as to costs other than one in accordance with the general rule, namely, that the unsuccessful party pay the successful party's costs.

In *Professional Information Technology Consultants Ltd v Jones* [2001] EWCA Civ 2103, the Court of Appeal upheld the trial judge's decision to order the defendant to pay two-thirds of the claimant's costs of the proceedings. The defendant appealed against the order for costs on the grounds that the claimant had made an amendment to her statement of case the day before the trial that substantially altered the case the defendant had to meet, and in the absence of which the claimant's claim would have failed. In those circumstances the defendant submitted that the general rule, set out in the Court of Appeal decision of *Beoco v Alfa Laval Co* [1995] QB 137, should prevail, namely, that the defendant should be awarded its costs of the proceedings down to the date of the amendment and the claimant should be awarded its costs thereafter. However, the Court of Appeal found that the trial judge had proceeded from the correct starting point, namely, that the successful claimant should be awarded its costs, and took into account all the relevant considerations that worked in the defendant's favour. The trial judge was also in the best position to assess whether it was possible for the defendant to make a proper evaluation of the strengths and weaknesses of the case before trial. In those circumstances the trial judge was entitled to take the course of discounting the claimant's costs by one-third, as there were a number of ways, not just one, of making a costs order that reflected the fact that there had been a fundamental amendment of the case.

However, in *Spice Girls Ltd v Aprilia World Service BV*, the Court of Appeal overturned the trial judge's order that the defendant, who had been successful overall, pay 10% of the claimant's costs on the grounds that it had unreasonably pursued two discrete issues on which it had been unsuccessful. The Court of Appeal held that the judge's finding that the defendant had unreasonably pursued two issues could not be supported and that therefore her decision as to the costs of those issues was flawed and must be set aside. In those circumstances the court held that it was entitled to exercise its own discretion as to the costs that the defendant was to be ordered to pay to the claimant. Although the court accepted that the court had jurisdiction to order a party who has been successful overall to pay his own and the other party's costs of discrete issues on which he has not been successful (r 44.3(4)(b)), it was not persuaded that it was appropriate to do so in this case. In the circumstances of the case the court did not think that the costs of the discrete issues should receive special treatment, and set aside the order that the defendant pay 10% of the claimant's costs of the proceedings.

The conduct of the parties

When making a decision as to whether to order costs, the court's view of the conduct of the parties will be informed by the overriding objective and the parties must therefore ensure that they have shown themselves to be open and fair in exchanging information and to have taken steps to avoid the need for litigation (r 1.2). The parties must also show that they have conducted the litigation in a reasonable and proportionate way and that they have concentrated on the real issues in dispute between them.

In accordance with this, r 44.3(5) provides that the conduct of the parties includes:

(a) conduct before as well as during the proceedings and, in particular, the extent to which the parties followed any relevant pre-action protocol;

(b) whether it was reasonable for a party to raise, pursue or contest a particular allegation or issue;

(c) the manner in which a party has pursued or defended his case or a particular allegation or issue; and

(d) whether a claimant who has succeeded in his claim, in whole or in part, exaggerated his claim.

In *Dunnett v Railtrack* [2002] EWCA Civ 302, even though the Court of Appeal dismissed Ms Dunnett's appeal, it refused to order that she pay Railtrack's costs because the court felt the appeal hearing could have been avoided if Railtrack had agreed to resolve the matter by means of mediation or arbitration, particularly as the use of Alternative Dispute Resolution (ADR) had been strongly recommended by the judge below.

In *Jones v University of Warwick* [2003] EWCA Civ 151, although the defendant was successful in appealing the court's decision, the Court of Appeal (subject to hearing argument) was minded to order that the defendant pay the claimant's costs of the appeal hearing because its misconduct in obtaining evidence, by secretly filming the claimant in her own home, caused the challenge to the admissibility of that evidence. The Court of Appeal also indicated to the trial judge that in order to discourage conduct of that sort, when he comes to deal with the question of costs in the substantive hearing he should take into account the defendant's conduct when deciding the appropriate order for costs.

In *Booth v Britannia Hotels Ltd* [2002] EWCA Civ 579, the claimant worked as a chambermaid for the defendant and brought a personal injury claim against the defendant for a crush injury sustained to her left hand. The claimant subsequently reported that the injury had caused a condition known as reflex sympathetic dystrophy, which substantially increased the value of her claim. A month before the trial of the claim the defendant disclosed video evidence that showed that the claimant had full function in her left hand. In the light of the video evidence the claimant accepted £2,500 in damages plus costs to be assessed on the standard basis. The claimant sought costs in excess of £82,000, but the defendant argued that such costs were unreasonable in respect of a claim worth £2,500. On assessment the claimant's costs were assessed as approximately £57,000 and the defendant was ordered to pay 60% of those costs. On appeal, the Court of Appeal held that the judge had wrongly exercised her discretion and set aside that order. The court held that the judge should have asked herself what costs were reasonably incurred and what would be a reasonable amount to allow in respect of each item of costs in order to establish quantum of £2,500. The court held that in the circumstances of this case, where the claimant pursues a claim for personal injury which she knows, or must be taken to know, she has not suffered, the defendants should not be required to bear any part of the costs she expended in that unreasonable pursuit.

Success for part of a case

In recognition of the fact that the parties must aim to identify and concentrate on the real issues in dispute, and in order to discourage the 'scatter gun' approach to litigation (including every possible issue as part of a case regardless of merit), the court is expressly given the power to make costs orders in favour of a party who has been successful on only part of a case, or certain issues in the case. This has been described as 'the most significant change of emphasis of the new [costs] rules' (*Phonographic Performance Ltd v AEI Rediffusion Ltd* [1999] 2 All ER 299 at 313–14, *per* Lord Woolf). Therefore, under r 44.3(6), the court may order that a party must pay:

(a) a proportion of another party's costs;

(b) a stated amount in respect of another party's costs;

(c) costs from or until a certain date only;

(d) costs incurred before proceedings have begun;

(e) costs relating to particular steps taken in the proceedings;

(f) costs relating only to a distinct part of the proceedings; and

(g) interest on costs from or until a certain date, including a date before judgment.

In the interests of a more straightforward calculation, rather than order a party to pay costs relating to a distinct part of the proceedings, the court must, if practicable, order a party to pay either a proportion of another party's costs, or costs from or until a certain date instead (r 44.3(7)). Indeed, in *Verrechia v Commissioner of Police for the Metropolis*, the Court of Appeal emphasised that the CPR require that an order which allows or disallows costs by reference to certain issues should be made *only* if other forms of order under r 44.3(7) cannot be made which sufficiently reflect the justice of the case. The court was of the opinion that there were good reasons for this rule, because an order that allows or disallows costs of certain issues creates difficulties at the stage of the assessment of costs. This is because the costs judge will have to master the issue in detail to understand what costs were properly incurred in dealing with it, and then analyse the work done by the receiving party's legal advisers to determine whether or not it was attributable to the issue the costs of which had been disallowed. Such an analysis would add to the costs of the assessment and make them disproportionate to the benefit gained. The court said that a 'percentage order' under r 44.3(6)(a) will often produce a fairer result than an 'issues based' order under r 44.3(6)(f), and such an order is consistent with the overriding objective.

In *Budgen v Andrew Gardner Partnership* [2002] EWCA Civ 1125, the Court of Appeal affirmed the court's entitlement to make an order that the defendant pay only 75% of the claimant's costs (a percentage costs order) rather than an order that the claimant be deprived of its costs in respect of a particular issue in the proceedings (an issue-based costs order), even where the claimant failed on that issue and where the court found it was unreasonable of the claimant to pursue it.

In *Phonographic Performance Ltd v AEI Rediffusion Ltd* [1999] 2 All ER 299, Lord Woolf explained in the following terms why he thought the approach under the former rules to deciding which party was entitled to costs was wrong:

> The most significant change of emphasis of the [CPR] is to require courts to be more ready to make separate orders which reflect the outcome of different issues. In doing this, the [CPR] are reflecting a change of practice which has already started. It is now clear that a too robust application of the 'follow the event principle' encourages litigants to increase the cost of litigation, since it discourages litigants from being selective as to the points they take. If you recover all your costs as long as you win, you are encouraged to leave no stone unturned in your effort to do so. (At 314a.)

In the case of *Firle Investments Ltd v Datapoint International Ltd* [2001] EWCA Civ 1106, the judge decided that in order to do broad justice in that case, the defendant should be ordered to pay only a modest contribution to the claimant's costs. The judge therefore decided to order that the defendant pay only a third of the claimant's costs up to the date of a realistic offer of settlement made by the defendant and only 15% of the claimant's costs after that date. Such an order was made notwithstanding the fact that the claimant had recovered £3,500 more than the defendant's Part 36 payment into court. The judge described this as a slim victory and criticised the claimant for not responding to this offer of settlement in a more constructive and conciliatory way. Although the Court of Appeal varied the judge's order so as to allow the claimant all of its costs up to the date of payment in and 70% (rather than 15%) thereafter, the court supported the judge's finding that the claimant had made the trial more complicated than it needed to be because of its failure to make factual admissions.

Also, in *Mars UK Ltd v Teknowledge Ltd (No 2)* [1999] TLR 510, Jacob J declared that one of the claims pleaded by the successful claimant had only barely been reasonable and that, therefore, the unsuccessful defendant should be given credit for the costs relating to that issue. The court estimated that on final assessment, the claimant would recover only 40% of its costs as it was also guilty of heavy-handed pre-action conduct.

In *Antonelli v Allen & Kandler* (2001) LTL, 31 August, a successful defendant recovered only three-quarters of his costs from the unsuccessful claimant because he lost on two issues put forward in his defence. The court justified its decision on the grounds that if the defendant had not relied on these two issues it would have significantly cut down the amount of documentary and oral evidence in the case and limited the arguments at trial.

Part 36 offers to settle and payments in

One of the matters that the court must take into account when deciding what order to make about costs is any payment into court or admissible offer to settle which is drawn to the court's attention, whether or not it was made in accordance with Part 36 (r 44.3(4)(c)). Part 36 provides for a number of sanctions and penalties if a party fails to better a Part 36 offer or payment at trial. There is therefore an interrelationship between offers and payments in made in accordance with Part 36 and the general rules about costs in Part 44.

In *Amber v Stacey* [2001] 2 All ER 88, although the Court of Appeal acknowledged that written offers should be encouraged and were relevant to the question of costs, it was of the opinion that they should not be treated as equivalent to a payment into court. The court believed that there were compelling reasons of principle and policy why a defendant prepared to make a genuine offer of monetary settlement should do so by way of a Part 36 payment into court. Part 36 payments into court were said to have a number of advantages over written offers to settle. They were said to answer all questions as to:

(a) genuineness;

(b) the offeror's ability to pay;

(c) whether the offer is open or without prejudice; and

(d) the terms on which the dispute can be settled.

In *Perry Press T/A Pereds v Chipperfield* [2003] EWCA Civ 484, an offer to settle was made which was not in accordance with Part 36 and which was not clear and certain in its terms. The offer was described as an offer 'to enter into serious negotiations' rather than a finalised and clear offer to settle, and there was no defined or limited offer as to costs, simply an offer to pay a *contribution* to the legal costs. In the circumstances the Court of Appeal held that, as the offer was not sufficiently clear and concise, the judge was entitled not to take it into account when considering the costs of the proceedings.

Where a claimant fails to accept a defendant's Part 36 offer to settle or payment, the usual order will be that the claimant must pay any costs incurred by the defendant after the latest date on which the offer or payment could have been accepted without needing the permission of the court (r 36.20(2)). There must be good reason, taking into account all the circumstances of the case, before a judge can depart from the general rule (*Burgess v British Steel plc* (2000) *The Times*, 29 February).

In *Ford v GKR Construction Ltd (and Others)* [2000] 1 All ER 802, the Court of Appeal upheld the trial judge's decision to award the claimant all the costs of a claim even though the claimant had failed to recover more in damages than the defendant's payment into court. In making this decision the court took into account that the defendant had obtained and disclosed further evidence at a late stage in the proceedings, which could have been obtained at a much earlier stage, and as a result the claimant was not in a position properly to assess whether to accept the payment in at the time it was made.

The case of *Firle Investments Ltd v Datapoint International Ltd* [2001] EWCA Civ 1106 is also an example of circumstances in which the court may not follow the general rule as to costs even where judgment is for a greater sum than a Part 36 payment.

Part 36 does not provide any penalty for a claimant where he makes a Part 36 offer to settle but fails to obtain a judgment that is more advantageous than that offer. It seems to be the intention of the rules to encourage claimants to make such offers by protecting them from any adverse consequences if they fail to better them, as PD 44, Section 8.4 specifically provides that those circumstances alone will not lead to a reduction in costs awarded to the claimant.

Paying the balance of costs due

If a party who is entitled to costs is also liable to pay costs, the court may assess the costs the party is liable to pay and either set off the amount assessed against the amount the party is entitled to be paid and direct him to pay any balance, or delay the issue of a certificate for the costs to which the party is entitled until he has paid the amount which he is liable to pay (r 44.3(9)).

TIME WHEN COSTS ORDERS ARE MADE

The court has the power to make an order about costs at any stage of a case (PD 44, para 8.3(1)). Apart from making an order at the conclusion of the proceedings, the court is likely to make costs orders when it deals with any application, makes any order or holds any hearing (PD 44, para 8.3(2)). However, it should be remembered that if the court does not make an order for costs none are payable, and it is therefore incumbent upon a party seeking costs to apply for an order for them (r 44.13(1)). Also, the court cannot assess the amount of any success fee relating to a conditional fee agreement or any other additional liability until the conclusion of the proceedings (PD 44, para 8.3(3)).

Costs of interim applications

There are a number of different orders about costs the court will commonly make when dealing with the case before trial. In relation to an application or a hearing, these range from an order that a particular party is to bear the costs of the application or hearing whatever the outcome of a case, that the party who is successful at trial will be entitled to the costs of it, or that neither party will be entitled to the costs of it, depending on the nature and outcome of the application or hearing (see pp 516–17 above, 'Costs orders made during the course of proceedings'). For instance, a party who fails to file a defence in time and therefore must apply to set aside judgment in default, is likely to have to pay the costs of the other party which have been incurred as a consequence, and the costs order is likely to be for that party's 'costs thrown away'. However, if the court convenes a case management conference, the order for costs following that hearing is likely to be 'costs in the case'.

In the case of *Desquenne et Giral UK Ltd v Richardson* [2001] FSR 1, CA, a case involving an application for an interim injunction, it was held that when deciding whether to make a costs order following a hearing or an application, the court should take account of the effect of the overriding objective to deal with cases justly. Therefore, if the nature of the application or hearing was such that neither party could be said to be the winner or the loser at that stage, because that would depend on the merits of the substantive case at trial, it would not be just for the court to make a costs order in favour of one party or to order summary assessment of those costs. The proper order in such circumstances would be to reserve costs to the trial judge or order costs in the case.

Costs in appeal hearings

A court hearing an appeal has the power to make costs orders in relation to the hearing below as well as in relation to the appeal hearing unless the appeal is dismissed (r 44.13(2)). Therefore, if a party successfully challenges a judgment on appeal which includes an order for the party to pay the other party's costs, the appeal court, when allowing the appeal, may also reverse the costs order made by the court below.

Solicitor's duty to notify client about costs order

If the court makes a costs order against a legally represented party when the party is not present, the party's solicitor must notify his client in writing of the costs order and explain why it was made, no later than seven days after the solicitor receives notice of the order (r 44.2; PD 44, para 7.2).

Such a rule, obliging a legal representative to keep his client informed about the costs that are being incurred in bringing or defending proceedings, is consistent with the ethos of the CPR with its emphasis on proportionality and the saving of expense. It may also serve to make a client aware of any shortcomings in the conduct of his case by his legal representative which have resulted in the client becoming liable for costs. However, this rule should be distinguished from the court's powers to make orders for costs against a party or a legal representative for misconduct (r 44.14) and wasted costs orders made personally against legal representatives (r 48.7).

Practice Direction 44 draws attention to the fact that there is no sanction specified if a legal representative does not abide by this rule, but goes on to state that the court may require the legal representative to produce evidence to the court showing that he took reasonable steps to so notify his client (PD 44, para 7.3). In any event, a failure to comply would very likely be seen as a matter of professional misconduct.

Funding arrangements – court assessment of the additional liability

In order to preserve the confidentiality of the level of the success fee and/or any insurance premium from an opponent, the court will not assess the amount of any additional liability until the conclusion of the proceedings, or part of the proceedings, to which the funding agreement relates (r 44.3A(1)). Proceedings are concluded when the court has finally determined the matters in issue in the claim, whether or not there is also an appeal (PD 43, para 2.4). However, the court may order, or the parties may agree in writing, that although proceedings are continuing, they will nevertheless be treated as concluded (PD 43, para 2.5).

The court may summarily assess both the base costs and the additional liability, make a detailed assessment of both the base costs and the additional liability, or summarily assess the base costs and make a detailed assessment of the additional liability (r 44.3A(2)). Therefore, the court cannot make a detailed assessment of the base costs but summarily assess the additional liability.

If the court decides in assessment proceedings to disallow all or part of the legal representative's success fee which is part of a CFA, the disallowed amount will not be payable by the legal representative's client either, unless the court orders otherwise (Conditional Fee Agreements Regulations 2000 (SI 2000/692), reg 3(2)(b)). If the legal representative wants to continue to claim payment of the disallowed amount of the success fee from his client, he must make an application to the court for such an order. If the legal representative's client is not present at the time the court disallows some or all of the success fee, and the legal representative indicates his wish to apply for such an order, the court may adjourn the assessment hearing so that the client can be notified of the application sought and be separately represented (r 44.16).

DEEMED COSTS ORDERS

In certain circumstances, a party will have a right to receive costs from the other party. Accordingly, unless the court orders otherwise, the defendant will have a right to receive costs where:

(a) the claimant's case is struck out under r 3.7 for non-payment of fees; or

(b) the claimant discontinues his claim (r 38.6).

A claimant will have a right to receive costs where:

(a) he accepts the defendant's Part 36 offer or payment (r 36.13(1)); or

(b) the defendant accepts the claimant's Part 36 offer (r 36.14).

In the event that these steps are taken, and the party becomes entitled to costs, a costs order will be deemed to have been made on the standard basis (r 44.12(1)). Also, interest payable pursuant to s 17 of the Judgments Act 1838 or s 74 of the County Courts Act 1984 (CCA) will begin to run from the date on which the event which gave rise to the entitlement to costs occurred (r 44.12(2)).

Striking out for non-payment of court fees

In most cases the claimant is liable to pay a court fee on the filing of an allocation questionnaire or pre-trial checklist. If the claimant fails to pay the relevant fee, or apply for exemption or remission of the fee, his claim will be automatically struck out and he will be liable for the defendant's costs of the claim, unless the court orders otherwise. Although the claimant's claim will be automatically struck out in such circumstances, he can apply for relief from this sanction (r 3.7).

Claimant discontinuing claim

Where a claimant discontinues a claim, the normal rule is that he is liable for the costs of the defendant incurred on or before the date on which the claimant serves notice of discontinuance on the defendant. However, the court has a discretion to make a different order if it is just to do so (r 38.6).

Part 36 offers and payments

Where a claimant accepts a defendant's Part 36 offer or payment without needing the permission of the court, he is entitled to his costs of the proceedings up to the date upon which he serves notice of acceptance. Similarly, where a defendant accepts a claimant's Part 36 offer to settle without needing the permission of the court, the claimant is entitled to his costs of the proceedings up to the date upon which the defendant serves notice of acceptance (rr 36.13, 36.14).

AMOUNT OF COSTS

Having ordered costs to be paid by one party to another, if the costs to be paid are not fixed costs and if the parties cannot agree on the amount to be paid, the court must then also assess the amount of costs to be paid under the order. There are two bases on which costs can be assessed by the court: either the standard basis or the indemnity basis (r 44.4(1)).

Standard basis

The test for assessing costs on the standard basis is:

(a) only costs which have been reasonably incurred will be allowed;

(b) only costs which are proportionate to the matters in issue will be allowed; and

(c) any doubt about whether costs were reasonably incurred, or were reasonable and proportionate in amount, must be resolved in favour of the paying party (r 44.4(1) and (2)).

This is the basis that the court will order in most cases when assessing the costs that one party must pay to the other. In fact, if, when making an order for costs, the court does not indicate the basis on which costs are to be assessed, or if it orders a basis other than the standard or indemnity basis, the costs will be assessed on the standard basis (r 44.4(4)). It is important to note that the court will take into account the question of proportionality when deciding on the amount of costs to be allowed under the standard basis.

The indemnity basis

The test for assessing costs on the indemnity basis is:

(a) only costs which have been reasonably incurred will be allowed; and

(b) any doubt about whether costs were reasonably incurred or were reasonable in amount must be decided in favour of the receiving party (r 44.4(1) and (3)).

Although the costs must have been reasonably incurred and reasonable in amount, there is no requirement of proportionality for costs assessed on the indemnity basis. In addition, where there is any doubt as to whether the costs were unreasonably incurred or unreasonable in amount, the court will resolve that doubt in favour of the receiving party. This means that costs assessed on the indemnity basis are considerably more generous to the receiving party than costs assessed on the standard basis, and that the party who has such an order made in his favour is more likely to recover a sum which reflects the actual costs in the proceedings.

In *Reid Minty v Taylor* [2001] EWCA Civ 1723, after a 12-day libel trial the jury found in favour of the defendant's defence of justification. The defendant invited the court to award costs against the claimant on an indemnity basis. The trial judge refused to order costs other than on the standard basis, holding that in such circumstances costs could be awarded on an indemnity basis only if there had been 'some sort of moral lack of probity or conduct deserving of moral condemnation on the part of the paying party'. The Court of Appeal held that the trial judge had misdirected himself as to the circumstances necessary for an award of indemnity costs. It held that costs may be awarded on the indemnity basis where a party has conducted the litigation unreasonably. The court has a wide discretion as to whether to order costs on the indemnity basis which must be exercised judicially, in all the circumstances, having regard to the matters referred to in r 44.3(4) and r 44.3(5). It was said in *Reid Minty v Taylor*, 'if one party has made a real effort to find a reasonable solution to the proceedings and the other party has resisted that sensible approach, then the latter puts himself at risk that the order for costs may be on an indemnity basis' (at [37], *per* Kay LJ).

However, in *Excelsior Commercial & Industrial Holdings Ltd v Salisbury Hammer Aspden & Johnson* [2002] EWCA Civ 879, Lord Woolf stressed it was a critical requirement that before an indemnity order could be made there must be some conduct or circumstance which takes the case out of the norm. In that case the Court of Appeal upheld the trial judge's finding that an order for costs on an indemnity basis was justified against the claimant which refused to accept a payment in of £100,000 but which recovered only nominal damages of £2. The circumstances which took the case out of the norm were that the claimant had not relied on the negligent conduct of the defendant in entering into a transaction, had suffered no loss in doing so, and therefore the sum it was seeking from the defendant would have been a windfall. Lord Woolf supported the judge's view that 'this was a speculative claim by the claimant which the defendants had made various attempts to resolve outside the court and in relation to which the Part 36 offer was the final straw' (at [40]).

In *Société Internationale de Télécommunications Aéronautiques SC v The Wyatt Co (UK) Ltd* [2002] EWHC 2401, the claimant rejected the defendant's Part 36 offer to settle made before trial. At the trial the claimant was completely unsuccessful. The defendant applied for indemnity costs against the claimant on the basis that despite being invited by the defendant to abandon its claim, the claimant had proceeded with the claim and pursued it with determination. The court did not regard the claimant's unwillingness to be persuaded to drop its claim as something which justified an award of indemnity costs. Also, although it accepted that the claimant pursued its claim with determination, it found nothing wrong with that because it also found that it pursued its claim scrupulously, fairly and without any impropriety.

In all of the above decisions – *Reid Minty v Taylor*, *Excelsior Commercial & Industrial Holdings Ltd v Salisbury Hammer Aspden & Johnson* and *Société Internationale de Télécommunications Aéronautiques SC v The Wyatt Co (UK) Ltd* – the court held that although a claimant who betters his own Part 36 offer is entitled to recover costs on an indemnity basis, there is no equivalent provision in the rules where a claimant fails to beat a defendant's Part 36 offer, and a defendant must apply to the court to exercise its discretion to make such an order taking into account all the circumstances of the case.

The indemnity basis is the usual basis for assessing the amount of costs to be paid by a client to his solicitor (r 48.8).

Factors to be taken into account when assessing costs

When assessing the amount of costs to be paid on either the standard or the indemnity basis, the court must take all the circumstances of the case into account (r 44.5). The whole ethos behind the CPR is to reduce the amount of time and money spent litigating and to avoid the need for litigation if possible; the parties will, therefore, have to be aware of the need to justify incurring costs and of the amount incurred at every stage of the case, both before and after proceedings have started.

The court must consider the following circumstances (as well as any other relevant circumstances) when assessing the amount:

(a) the conduct of all the parties, including, in particular, conduct before as well as during the proceedings, and any efforts made before and during the proceedings to try to resolve the dispute;

(b) the amount or value of any money or property involved;

(c) the importance of the matter to all the parties;

(d) the particular complexity of the matter, or the difficulty or novelty of the questions raised;

(e) the skill, effort, specialised knowledge and responsibility involved;

(f) the time spent on the case; and

(g) the place where and the circumstances in which work or any part of it was done (r 44.5(3)).

Legal representative's charging rates

Solutia UK Ltd v Griffiths [2001] EWCA Civ 736 was a case involving a group claim by residents living in the vicinity of a chemical works plant for personal injury caused by a gas leak. The Court of Appeal had to decide whether it was reasonable for the claimants to instruct London solicitors who charged at a higher hourly rate as compared to local provincial solicitors. The Court of Appeal held that the test to determine the reasonableness of instructing particular legal advisers involved an objective element, but was one that must be applied in the context of the particular circumstances of the particular litigants in the individual case. In that case the court found that it was reasonable for the claimants to instruct London solicitors rather than provincial solicitors because of a variety of factors, including the fact that the London solicitors had previously dealt with similar claims from other residents; that they had the confidence of the residents; and that some of the residents had been dissatisfied with the inefficiency of local solicitors who had also dealt with the claim.

Proportionality

When assessing the amount of costs to allow on the *standard* basis, the court's test of proportionality will be based on the factors set out in r 1.1(2)(c), namely, the amount of money involved, the importance of the case, the complexity of the issues and the financial position of each party (PD 44, para 11.1). The Court of Appeal emphasised in *Contractreal Ltd v Davies* [2001] EWCA Civ 928 that proportionality 'is not simply a question of comparing the total amount claimed in the bill of costs with the total amount claimed or recovered in the proceedings, there are other considerations to be taken into account, such as the importance of the case and the complexity of the issues' (at [61], *per* Arden LJ).

In *Home Office v Lownds* [2002] EWCA Civ 365, the claimant, a prisoner, brought proceedings against the Home Office for clinical negligence for its failure to diagnose and properly treat his gallstones and his dental condition. The claimant started proceedings before the CPR came into force, but they were settled after the CPR came into force for the sum of £3,000 plus costs. The claimant's costs were assessed by the district judge in the sum of £14,871.30 before VAT. Due to the effect of the transitional provisions on the assessment of costs for proceedings started before the CPR came into force, the Court of Appeal refused to interfere with the judge's assessment. However, Lord Woolf felt that the case raised important issues of principle, namely, that litigation should be conducted in a proportionate manner and, where possible, at a proportionate cost. Accordingly, in his judgment Lord Woolf took the opportunity to give general guidance on the significance courts should attach to the requirement of proportionality when making orders for costs and when assessing the amount of those costs.

Lord Woolf commented that the amount of costs assessed by the judge in this case could not be regarded as proportionate. Senior Costs Judge Hurst, who was sitting as an assessor in the case, indicated that in his experience costs for conducting litigation of this sort up to the stage it was settled should have been in the region of £6,500 to £7,000 instead. However, it was recognised that an additional sum should be added in this case to reflect the fact that the claimant was in prison, which would make it more difficult to obtain instructions.

It has been held that when considering the proportionality of the costs incurred, VAT should be excluded from the starting point figure because it is a percentage tax levied on the cost of the service provided. The impact of the tax has no bearing on the steps taken in the litigation or the cost of them (*Giambrone and Others v JMC Holidays Ltd* [2003] 1 All ER 982).

Two-stage approach

In *Lownds*, Lord Woolf said that the key to how judges assessing costs should give effect to the requirement of proportionality is for them to decide what costs are *necessary* to conduct the litigation. He said that there has to be a 'two-stage approach' – a global approach and an item-by-item approach. The global approach will indicate whether the total sum claimed is, or appears to be, disproportionate, having regard to the considerations in r 44.5(3). This will include, for instance, whether the appropriate level of fee earner or counsel has been deployed, what offers to settle have been made, whether unnecessary experts have been instructed, and other matters referred to in r 44.5(3). In the light of the global approach, if the costs as a whole appear disproportionate then the court must be satisfied that the work in relation to each item was necessary and, if necessary, that the cost of the item is reasonable. However, in deciding what is necessary, the conduct of the other party is highly relevant. If the other party is co-operative this can reduce costs, but if he is unco-operative this can render necessary costs that would otherwise be unnecessary.

If litigation is not conducted in a proportionate manner this does not mean that no costs are recoverable, but it does mean that only those costs which would have been incurred if the litigation had been conducted proportionately will be recoverable. Further, in a case where proportionality is likely to be an issue the costs judge must make a preliminary judgment at the outset as to the proportionality of the costs as a whole.

However, if the costs as a whole are not disproportionate then all that is normally required is that each item should have been reasonably incurred and the cost for that item should be reasonable. If the appropriate conduct of the proceedings makes costs necessary then the requirement of proportionality does not prevent all the costs being recovered either on an item-by-item approach, or by a global approach. However, only a reasonable amount will be recovered for items that are necessary.

It was held in *Giambrone and Others v JMC Holidays Ltd* that if a costs judge has ruled at the outset of a detailed assessment that the bill as a whole is not disproportionate, he is not precluded from deciding that items in the bill appear disproportionate having regard to the matters in issue. The costs judge should consider whether an item is proportionate and reasonably incurred, and proportionate and reasonable in amount.

In *Lloyds TSB Bank plc v Lampert* [2003] EWHC 249, Ch, it was held that the judge's failure to follow the two-stage test for considering proportionality set out in *Home Office v Lownds* was a seriously procedural irregularity. The court found that the judge did consider proportionality on an individual basis but did not consider it on a global basis. The matter was referred back to the judge for him to reconsider whether or not as a preliminary judgment proportionality was relevant. The judge must then proceed to assess the bill in accordance with the guidance set out in *Home Office v Lownds*.

Lord Woolf was of the opinion that the mandatory and unqualified requirement of proportionality, when assessing the amount of costs on the standard basis, should encourage parties to conduct litigation in a proportionate manner and encourage the settlement of disputes without the need to commence proceedings – both being important objectives of the CPR (*Home Office v Lownds* at [8], [9]).

The requirement to conduct litigation in a proportionate manner calls for an assessment, at the outset of the case, of the likely value of the claim and its importance and complexity. In the light of that assessment there is then a requirement to plan in advance the necessary work required; the appropriate level of person to carry out the work; the overall time that will be necessary; and the appropriate spend on the various costs in bringing the claim to trial and the likely overall cost. For instance, Lord Woolf commented that in *Lownds* there were eight visits to the prison which proved to be very expensive, whereas four visits would have been ample ([2002] EWCA Civ 365 at [23]).

However, PD 44 goes on to provide expressly that it is recognised that the relationship between the total costs incurred and the financial value of the claim may not be a reliable guide, and that a fixed percentage should not always be applied to the value of the claim in order to ascertain whether or not the costs are proportionate. It is also expressly stated that solicitors are not required to conduct litigation at rates which are uneconomic, and it is recognised that in a modest claim the proportion of costs is likely to be higher than in a large claim, and may even equal or possibly exceed the amount in dispute (PD 44, para 11.2).

FAST TRACK TRIAL COSTS

Part 46 sets a limit to the amount of costs an advocate can recover for preparing for and appearing in a fast track trial. These are known as fast track trial costs (r 46.1(1)). A maximum set amount is recoverable for the advocate's costs, whether the costs of the proceedings are assessed summarily or by detailed assessment (r 46.2(1)).

However, it should be borne in mind that the usual rule is for the costs of proceedings on the fast track to be assessed summarily (PD 28, para 8.5).

The rules for fast track trial costs apply only where, at the time of trial, the claim is allocated to the fast track. The rules do not apply to trials heard on any other track, whatever the financial value of the claim (PD 46, para 26.2). This restriction also applies to claims heard on the small claims track where the financial value exceeds the small claims track limit but the parties agree that the case should be allocated to the small claims track. In those cases, the costs are in the discretion of the court. However, the amount of those costs cannot exceed the amount of costs that would have been awarded in fast track trial costs if the case had been allocated to the fast track (PD 46, para 26.3(a); r 27.14(5)).

Fast track trial costs of a litigant in person

If a litigant represents himself at trial, if he can prove that he has suffered financial loss in so doing, he can recover two-thirds of the amount that would have been awarded if an advocate had conducted the fast track trial. If the litigant in person cannot show financial loss then he will be entitled to recover an amount in respect of the time he reasonably spent doing the work at the rate specified for litigants in person in the practice direction on costs, which is currently £9.25 per hour (r 46.3(5); PD 48, para 52.4).

Definition of trial

For the purposes of fast track trial costs, the definition of 'trial' includes a hearing where the court is to decide an amount of money or the value of goods following the entry of default judgment or judgment after an admission (r 46.1(2)(c)). However, trial in these circumstances does not include the hearing of an application for summary judgment under Part 24, the court's approval of a settlement or compromise which involves a child or a patient, or a disposal hearing where the amount to be paid under a judgment or order is to be decided by the court (r 46.1(2)(c)(i), (ii); PD 46, para 26.3(b)).

Amount of fast track trial costs

There is a table of amounts of fast track trial costs, which increase in accordance with the value of the claim (r 46.2(1)). This sets the fast track trial costs that can be recovered by a party's advocate, whether acting for a claimant or for a defendant. There are three bands of costs:

*   where the value of the claim does not exceed £3,000, fast track trial costs of £350 may be awarded;
*   currently, where the value is more than £3,000 but not more than £10,000, £500 may be awarded; and
*   where the value is more than £10,000, £750 may be awarded.

The figures provided are for the advocate's costs alone and do not include VAT or any disbursements (r 46.1(2)).

The court cannot award more or less than the amounts specified unless it decides not to award any fast track trial costs, a party is guilty of improper or unreasonable behaviour, or it falls within the circumstances providing for additional amounts. The court can also apportion the amount awarded between the parties if a party is successful on some issues but not others, in order to reflect their respective degrees of success (r 46.2(2)).

Additional amounts

There are a number of circumstances in which the court can award amounts additional to those specified for fast track trial costs in Part 46.

Costs of attendance of legal representative

If, in a particular case, the court considers that it was reasonable for a party's legal representative to attend the trial to assist the advocate, if that party is awarded costs, the court can award an additional amount of £250 in addition to the fast track trial costs for the attendance of the legal representative (r 46.3(2)).

Fast track case settles before trial

If a case allocated to the fast track settles before trial, when assessing the amount of costs to be allowed for a party's advocate for preparing for the trial, the court cannot allow a greater amount than that which the party would have recovered in costs if the trial had taken place (r 44.10(1)). The court will also take into account when the claim was settled and when the court was notified of this when assessing such costs (r 44.10(2)).

Separate trial of an issue

If the court directs a separate trial of an issue, the court can award an additional amount in respect of the separate trial. The additional amount for the separate trial must not exceed two-thirds of the amount of fast track trial costs payable for the claim, but is subject to a minimum award of £350 (r 46.3(3) and (4)).

Success fees

If an advocate in a fast track trial is acting under a CFA that provides for a success fee, the court also has the power to add the amount of the success fee onto the amount allowed for fast track trial costs (r 46.3(2A)). In the event of any dispute between the parties as to the amount of the success fee, in view of the limitation of time that applies to fast track cases, the judge may be tempted to order a detailed assessment. This will have extra costs implications as well as preventing the quick 'finality' which fast track hearings were originally designed to achieve.

Unreasonable and improper behaviour

Where the court considers that the party who is to pay the fast track trial costs has behaved improperly during the trial, the court has a discretion to award an additional amount in costs to the other party as it considers appropriate (r 46.3(8)).

If the court considers that the party who is to receive costs has behaved unreasonably or improperly during the trial, it may award that party a lower amount than the amounts usually paid in accordance with the value of the claim (r 46.3(8)).

Value of the claim for fast track trial costs

Part 46 specifies how the value of a claim is to be calculated. If the claim involves only money, the value of the claim is naturally decided by a different method depending on whether the party to be awarded the costs is the claimant or defendant.

Money claims

In a claim involving the payment of money only, if the claimant is entitled to costs, whether the claim was specified or unspecified, the value of the claim is the total amount of the judgment, but excluding interest, costs and any reduction for contributory negligence (r 46.2(3)(a)).

If the defendant is entitled to costs, the value of the claim is either the amount specified by the claimant in the claim form, excluding interest and costs, or, if the claim is for an unspecified amount, the maximum amount the claimant reasonably expected to recover as stated in his statement of value on the claim form. However, if the claimant had stated in his claim form that he could not reasonably say how much he expected to recover, the value of the claim is deemed to be more than £10,000, which gives rise to the highest amount of fast track trial costs (r 46.2(3)(b)).

Non-money claims

If a claim is for a non-money remedy only, the value of the claim is deemed to be more than £3,000 but not more than £10,000, the middle band of fast track trial costs. However, in an appropriate case, the court can order that a different method of calculating the value is carried out instead (r 46.2(4)).

Mixed claims

If a claim includes a claim for a money and a non-money remedy, the value of the claim is deemed to be the higher of either the money claim (as calculated above) or the non-money claim (as calculated above). However, in an appropriate case, the court can order that a different method of calculating the value is carried out instead (r 46.2(5)).

COSTS OF COUNTERCLAIMS IN FAST TRACK TRIAL COSTS

Claimant successful

If a defendant makes a counterclaim against the claimant which has a higher value than the value of the claimant's claim against him, but the claimant is successful at trial, both on his claim and the counterclaim, the value of the claim for the purposes of fast track trial costs awarded to the claimant will be the value of the defendant's counterclaim, calculated by the same method set out above for claims (r 46.2(6)).

Defendant successful

Where a defendant makes a counterclaim and the claimant is unsuccessful on his claim but the defendant is successful on his counterclaim, as a counterclaim is treated as if it were a claim (r 20.3), if the court awards the defendant costs it is likely to calculate the amount of fast track trial costs by reference to the value of the counterclaim as if it were a claim. However, if the claimant put the value of the claim at a higher amount than the counterclaim, the court may decide to assess the fast track trial costs in accordance with the value of the claimant's claim under the rules referred to above which apply where a claimant is to be awarded costs (r 46.2).

Both parties successful

Where a defendant makes a counterclaim against the claimant and the claimant is successful on his claim but the defendant is successful on his counterclaim, the court will calculate fast track trial costs in the following way. The court will calculate the amount of fast track trial costs the claimant would be entitled to on his claim but for the counterclaim, and calculate what the defendant would be entitled to on his counterclaim but for the claimant's claim, and make one award of fast track trial costs, of the difference, if any, to the party entitled to the higher award of costs (r 46.3(6)).

Fast track trial costs where there are multiple parties

Where the same advocate is acting for more than one party, the court may make only one award of fast track trial costs for that advocate. The parties for whom the advocate is acting are then jointly entitled to the fast track trial costs that are awarded (r 46.4(1)).

Multiple claimants with money only claims

If each of a number of claimants has a separate claim against the defendant, in a money only claim, the value of the claim for the purposes of calculating the claimants' fast track trial costs is the total amount of the judgment made in favour of all the jointly represented claimants. If the defendant is to be awarded costs in these circumstances, the value of the claim is the total amount claimed by the claimants (r 46.4(3)(a)).

Multiple claimants with non-money claims

Where the only claim of each of a number of claimants is for a non-money remedy, the value of the claim is deemed to be more than £3,000 but not more than £10,000 (r 46.4(3)(b)).

Multiple claimants with mixed claims

Where the claims of a number of claimants include both a money and a non-money claim, the value of the claim is deemed to be either more than £3,000 but not more than £10,000, or the total value of the money claims if that is higher (r 46.4(3)(c)).

Multiple defendants

Where there is more than one defendant and any or all of them are separately represented, the court may award fast track trial costs to each party who is separately represented (r 46.4(4)).

Multiple claimants/single defendant

If there is more than one claimant but only one defendant, the court can make only one award of fast track trial costs to the defendant for which the claimants are jointly and severally liable (r 46.4(5)). This means that the defendant can choose to recover the full amount of the costs from just one of the claimants, or from both. The value of the claim is calculated in accordance with the rules for claims by multiple claimants set out above (r 46.4(6)).

COSTS ON THE SMALL CLAIMS TRACK AND FAST TRACK

Where a claim is allocated to the small claims track or the fast track, the special rules about costs that relate to those tracks will apply to work done before as well as after allocation, unless an order in respect of that work was made before allocation (PD 44, para 15.1(2)). However, before a claim is allocated to one of those tracks, the court is not restricted by any of the special rules about costs that apply to that track (PD 44, para 15.1(1)).

Allocation to small claims track following an admission

If a claimant issues a claim for a sum outside the financial limit of the small claims track, but the claim is allocated to that track only because an admission of part of the claim by the defendant reduces the amount in dispute to a sum within the normal scope of that track, on entering judgment for the admitted part before allocation of the balance of the claim, the court may allow costs in respect of the proceedings down to that date (PD 44, para 15.1(2)).

Allocation from small claims track

If the court decides to allocate a claim from the small claims track to another track, before the case is allocated, it must decide whether to make an order that one party is to pay costs to another party in accordance with the rules about costs on the small claims track. If the court decides that such an order for costs should be made, it will also summarily assess those costs (PD 44, para 16).

RE-ALLOCATION OF A CLAIM TO ANOTHER TRACK

If a case is allocated to one track, but then subsequently re-allocated to a different track, any special rules about costs on the track that the claim was originally on will apply to the claim up to the date of re-allocation, but then any special rules about costs applying to the track the claim has been allocated to will apply from the date of re-allocation (r 44.11(2)). An example of a special rule about costs applying to a track is the 'no costs' rule of the small claims track. Also, any costs orders made before a claim is re-allocated will be preserved on re-allocation (r 44.11(1)).

COSTS ORDERS FOR MISCONDUCT

The court may make a costs order disallowing all or part of the costs being claimed by a party, or ordering a party or his legal representative personally to pay the costs which have been incurred by another party, if the party or legal representative is at fault because:

(a) the party or his legal representative fails to comply with a rule, practice direction or court order in relation to a summary or detailed assessment; or

(b) the party or his legal representative has behaved unreasonably or improperly before or during the proceedings which are the subject of the assessment (r 44.14(1) and (2)).

This rule gives the court, whether of its own initiative or at the request of a party, the power to investigate and punish a party or his legal representative for misconduct both before and during the course of proceedings, or in relation to assessment proceedings. Misconduct includes the taking of steps that are calculated to prevent or inhibit the court from furthering the overriding objective (PD 44, para 18.2). The power is in addition to the power to make wasted costs orders (see below).

Moreover, if the court makes such an order and the client is not present, the legal representative has an obligation to notify his client in writing no later than seven days after the solicitor receives notice of the order (r 44.14(3)). Although no sanction is specified for breach of this rule, the court has the power to require the solicitor to produce evidence to the court that he has complied with it (PD 44, para 18.3).

WASTED COSTS ORDERS

The court has the power under s 51(6) of the SCA to disallow a legal representative from recovering costs from his own client or to order that the legal representative personally pay costs to another party. In exercising this power the court may make a wasted costs order, being an order that the legal representative pay a specified sum in respect of costs to a party, or an order disallowing the costs of the legal representative relating to a specified sum or items of work (PD 48, para 53.9). In *Medcalf v Weatherill* [2002] UKHL 27, the House of Lords confirmed that s 51(6) of the SCA empowers the court to make a wasted costs order in favour of a party to the proceedings against the legal representative of any other party and is not limited to an order against a party's own legal representative. Where the court is considering making a wasted costs order, it must be satisfied that:

(a) the legal representative acted improperly, unreasonably or negligently;

(b) such behaviour caused another party to incur unnecessary costs; and

(c) it is just to order him to compensate the party for some or all of those costs (PD 48, para 53.4).

Examples of conduct that may justify a wasted costs order include failing to attend a hearing, causing an unnecessary step to be taken in proceedings, or prolonging a hearing by gross repetition or extreme slowness in the presentation of evidence or argument.

It will not be enough to justify an order that the court considers that an advocate has been arguing a hopeless case. An advocate has a duty to present his client's case even though he may think it is hopeless and even though he may have advised his client that it is. However, it should be noted that if a party is raising issues or is taking steps which have no reasonable prospect of success or are an abuse of process, both the aggrieved party and the court have other powers to remedy the situation by invoking summary remedies such as striking out and summary judgment: 'The making of a wasted costs order should not be the primary remedy; by definition it only arises once the damage has been done. It is a last resort' (*Medcalf v Weatherill* [2002] UKHL 27, *per* Lord Hobhouse).

The conduct complained of must constitute a breach of duty to the court in order to justify a wasted costs order (*Medcalf v Weatherill*). Also, any impropriety must be of a serious nature akin to an abuse of process; negligence on its own will not suffice, however serious that negligence might be (*Persaud v Persaud* [2003] EWCA Civ 394).

A wasted costs order can be made against a barrister for conduct immediately relevant to the exercise of a right of audience but not involving advocacy in open court, for instance, the contents of a statement of case drafted by counsel (*Medcalf v Weatherill*).

If solicitors cease acting before proceedings are commenced, they could not be said to have exercised rights of audience or rights to conduct litigation and therefore they are not legal or other representatives against whom wasted costs orders can be made under s 51(6) of the SCA (*Byrne v South Sefton HA* [2001] EWCA Civ 1904).

In *Medcalf v Weatherill* [2002] UKHL 27, the House of Lords was alert to the danger that the wasted costs jurisdiction may fail to achieve its objective of reducing the costs of litigation and saving court time as it often results in costly and time-consuming satellite litigation. Their Lordships warned that in order to avoid this consequence, the discretionary power to make a wasted costs order should be reserved for those cases where the unjustifiable conduct can be demonstrated without recourse to disproportionate procedures.

An application for a wasted costs order is, like all questions of costs, within the discretion of the judge. However, when deciding whether to allow a wasted costs application, the court should not just take into account the expected length of the hearing without having regard to the prospects of success or whether proper case management could properly control the time and complexity of the dispute (*Wagstaff v Coll* [2003] EWCA Civ 469).

Wasted costs and legal professional privilege

The case of *General Mediterranean Holdings SA v Patel and Another* [1999] 3 All ER 673 led to part of r 48.7 being held to be *ultra vires*. Former r 48.7(3) (which was subsequently revoked) gave the court the power, for the purposes of wasted costs proceedings, to direct that privileged documents be disclosed to the court and to the other party to the application. The reason for the rule was to allow the court fully to investigate the conduct and advice given by the legal representative in the proceedings when considering whether to make a wasted costs order against him, as this might be possible only through access to privileged documents. However, although para 4 of Sched 1 to the Civil Procedure Act 1997 gave the CPR the power to 'modify the rules of evidence as they apply to proceedings in any court within the scope of the CPR', the court held that legal professional privilege was not a mere rule of evidence but a substantive and fundamental common law principle, and one on which the administration of justice rests. The Civil Procedure Rule Committee, exercising as it did a subordinate power in drafting r 48.7(3), could not abrogate or limit a person's right to legal confidentiality. Rule 48.7(3) was accordingly held to be *ultra vires*.

The court cannot, therefore, order that a legal representative disclose privileged documents for the purposes of wasted costs proceedings. The privilege belongs to the client and not the legal representative, and it will often not be in the client's interests to waive the privilege. Further, it may give rise to a conflict of interest, as the legal representative may be obliged to advise the client that it is not in his interests to waive privilege, or advise him to seek alternative legal advice.

Accordingly, where a wasted costs order is sought against a legal representative precluded by legal professional privilege from giving his full answer to the application, the court should not make an order unless, proceeding with extreme care, it is:

(a) satisfied that there is nothing the legal representative could say, if unconstrained, to resist the order; and

(b) satisfied that it is in all the circumstances fair to make the order (*Medcalf v Weatherill*).

In *Medcalf v Weatherill*, the House of Lords endorsed the judgment of Lord Bingham MR in *Ridehalgh v Horsefield* [1994] 3 All ER 848, in which he warned judges considering making a wasted costs order to make full allowance for the lawyer's inability to tell the whole story as a result of the operation of legal professional privilege and therefore to give the lawyer the benefit of any doubt.

In the light of the restrictions on the court having access to the full facts, due to the operation of legal professional privilege, it will be rare for the court in such circumstances to be able to make a sound decision that the legal representative's conduct is such that a wasted costs order should be made against him. However, it is felt that 'it is better that in certain circumstances the wasted costs jurisdiction should be emasculated by the principle of legal professional privilege than vice versa' (Court of Appeal decision in *Medcalf v Weatherill* (2001) *The Times*, 2 January, *per* Wilson J).

Applying for a wasted costs order

A party can apply for a wasted costs order against a legal representative by making an application in accordance with Part 23, or simply by making an application orally in the course of any hearing (PD 48, para 53.3). If an application is made in accordance with Part 23, the application notice and any evidence in support must identify what the legal representative is alleged to have done or failed to do, and the unnecessary costs that he has thereby caused the other party to incur (PD 48, para 53.8).

Although the court has the power to make a wasted costs order of its own initiative (PD 48, para 53.2), a judge should consider whether it is appropriate to do so if the other party has not itself applied for one, and should take into account that the representative whose conduct is impugned will have nobody to recover the potentially substantial costs from if he is successful in resisting the order (*Burt v Wells* (1999) LTL, 26 July).

The wasted costs hearing

The court must give the legal representative a reasonable opportunity to attend a hearing to give reasons why the court should not make a wasted costs order against him (r 48.7(2)).

In general, the hearing will be conducted in two stages. At the first stage, the court must be satisfied that it has evidence that, if unanswered, would lead to a wasted costs order being made and that the wasted costs proceedings are justified notwithstanding the likely cost of them. The court will therefore have to be satisfied that there is a case to answer, as well as considering issues of proportionality, before deciding whether to make a wasted costs order. The court will then usually adjourn the hearing in order to give the legal representative an opportunity to be heard as to why a wasted costs order should not be made against him. At the second stage the court will hear the legal representative, and even if the court is satisfied as to the matters at the first stage, the court must also be satisfied that it is appropriate to make the wasted costs order (PD 48, para 53.6).

If a party makes an application under Part 23 for a wasted costs order against a legal representative, the court may proceed to the second stage without adjourning the hearing if it is satisfied that the legal representative has already had a reasonable opportunity to give reasons why the court should not make a wasted costs order (PD 48, para 53.7).

Orders for wasted costs can be made at any stage of the proceedings, but are usually left until after the end of the trial, as otherwise the proceedings are likely to be sidetracked by the wasted costs matter. Also, if an application is made during the course of proceedings a party's advisers may feel that they can no longer act for their client, so that the party could in effect be deprived of the advisers of his choice (*Ridehalgh v Horsefield* [1994] 3 All ER 848).

Where proceedings between the parties had been settled and stayed on terms contained in a Tomlin order, there was no need to lift the stay in order to pursue a wasted costs application against solicitors acting for one of the parties (*Wagstaff v Colls* [2003] EWCA Civ 469).

The court will give directions about the procedure that will be followed in each case in order to ensure that the issues are dealt with in a way which is fair and as simple and summary as the circumstances permit (PD 48, para 53.5). In *Wagstaff v Coll*, Ward LJ said that 'a wasted costs hearing has perforce to be summary, a bit rough and ready' and that it 'must not be turned into a state trial' (at [82]).

Investigating the circumstances

The court may direct a costs judge or a district judge to inquire into the matter and report to the court as to the nature of the legal representative's behaviour and the unnecessary costs incurred as a result, before it makes a wasted costs order (r 48.7(6)).

Notifying the client

The court may also order that the legal representative notify his client of any proceedings for a wasted costs order being brought against him and of any wasted costs order made against him (r 48.7(5)).

COSTS ORDERS IN FAVOUR OF OR AGAINST A NON-PARTY

Section 51 orders

The court has full power to determine by whom and to what extent the costs of proceedings are to be paid (s 51 of the SCA). This extends to include the power to make an order against a person who is not a party to the proceedings. Such an order is an exceptional order and the court should treat an application for such an order with caution. However, it is exceptional only because normally a party is pursuing or defending a claim for his own benefit through solicitors acting on his instructions, and there will usually not be any justification for ordering someone else to pay the costs. Where that is not the case the judge must exercise his discretion to decided whether the circumstances are such that it would be just to make an order under s 51 of the SCA, a 's 51 order', that a non-party pay the costs of proceedings (*Aiden Shipping Co Ltd v Interbulk Ltd* [1986] AC 965 at 980F, *per* Lord Goff).

If the court is considering making an order for costs in favour of or against a non-party, that person must be added as a party to the proceedings for the purposes of the decision about costs only, and be given an opportunity to attend a hearing for the matter to be considered further (r 48.2(1)). The provisions do not apply where the party against which an order may be made is the Legal Services Commission, when the court is considering making a wasted costs order (see r 48.7) and for applications for pre-action disclosure and disclosure against a non-party (see r 48.1; Chapter 29, 'Disclosure of Documents') (r 48.2(2)).

In *Hamilton v Al Fayed* [2002] EWCA Civ 665, the Court of Appeal confirmed the general principle that a 'pure funder', that is, a person who provides a litigant with funds and who has no interest in the outcome of the litigation other than to obtain reimbursement of the funds which he has provided, is exempt from liability to pay costs under s 51 of the SCA. This principle was held to apply not only to relatives motivated by natural affection, but also to anyone whose contribution is motivated by a wish to ensure that a genuine dispute is not lost by default.

Hamilton v Al Fayed arose out of the unsuccessful libel claim brought by former MP Neil Hamilton against Mohammed Al Fayed in respect of the 'cash for questions' scandal. Having lost his libel claim, Mr Hamilton was ordered to pay Mr Al Fayed's costs of the proceedings, which were assessed in the sum of £1,467,576. Mr Hamilton did not pay anything towards those costs and was made bankrupt. Mr Al Fayed sought s 51 orders against a number of individuals who provided a 'fighting fund' in order to help pay Mr Hamilton's legal costs of the claim. The funds were provided on the understanding that if the claim were successful the money would be returned, but otherwise not. The court held that the contributors were 'pure funders' and that as such they were entitled to the benefit of the general principle that they were exempt from a s 51 order, and there was nothing exceptional in the circumstances to justify denying them that protection. The Court of Appeal held that it was in the public interest that 'the unfunded party's ability to recover his costs must yield to the funded party's right of access to the courts to litigate the dispute in the first place' (at [45], *per* Simon Brown LJ). Otherwise it was felt that 'if pure funders are regularly exposed to liability under section 51, such funds will dry up and access to justice will thereby on occasion be lost' (at [47], *per* Simon Brown LJ). Another benefit of the principle was said to be that it would mean that there were fewer litigants in person.

The involvement of persons as 'pure funders' should be distinguished from a person's involvement in litigation that amounts to unlawful maintenance and champerty (see Chapter 4, 'Funding Litigation'). Also, the general principle will not apply in exceptional cases, for instance, where 'the litigation was oppressive or malicious or pursued for some other ulterior motive' (*Hamilton v Al Fayed* at [86], *per* Hale LJ). In *Fulton Motors Ltd v Toyota (GB) Ltd* (1999) LTL, 6 July, the Court of Appeal held that a s 51 order could be made against an individual who funded an insolvent litigant where he had a personal interest in the outcome and was aware of the risks involved.

In *Blugilt Peterlee Ltd v SLS Engineering Ltd* (2002) LTL, 3 April, the claimant company brought a claim for sums owed by the defendant for the supply of eight storage tanks. The defendant counterclaimed for loss caused by alleged defects in the tanks. The expert evidence was in favour of the defendant and judgment was entered for the defendant with costs. However, the defendant subsequently discovered that the claimant had ceased trading and disposed of all its assets a year earlier. The court held that this was just the sort of exceptional case that justified a s 51 order against the directors of the claimant and against a company connected with the claimant. The connected company had funded part of the claim and stood to benefit from a successful outcome. As for the directors, although they had no financial interest in the claim and were not shareholders in the claimant, they had decided that the claim should continue when they knew that the claimant did not have any assets from which to meet any potential judgment or costs liability, and when it was clear that the claimant could no longer realistically have any interest in the pursuit of the claim.

It should be noted that the mere fact that a director of a company makes the decision for the company to pursue litigation or provides funding for the company to do so is not usually sufficient to justify a s 51 order against him. A director who acts properly in what he considers to be the best interests of the company should not be at risk of having to pay the costs. Further, the fact that the company does not have the means to satisfy any judgment against it will not in itself justify such an order (*Taylor v Pace Developments* [1991] BCC 406).

In *Floods of Queensferry Ltd v Shand Construction Ltd* [2002] EWCA Civ 918, the defendant applied for a s 51 order against the claimant's solicitors on the grounds that they had funded the claimant's claim. The Court of Appeal found that the claimant's solicitors had not funded the claim and held that as long as solicitors offered legal services within the rules of their profession they would not as a general rule be vulnerable to a s 51 order. In giving her judgment, Hale LJ, relying on previous Court of Appeal decisions in *Tolstoy Miloslavsky v Aldington* [1996] 2 All ER 556 and *Hodgson v Imperial Tobacco* [1998] 2 All ER 673, said that there was 'a distinction between those who provide money to pay for legal services and those who provide those legal services' (at [79]). She said that the provision of legal services was of enormous benefit to the proper administration of justice, including securing equality of arms in access to the courts. She also felt that 'it would be a sad day if solicitors could not extend credit, even to their litigation clients, without fear of vulnerability to a Section 51 order' (at [81]).

In *RA & SA (Children) sub nom Re A (Children)* [2001] 1 FLR 723, the court allowed a Family Centre to intervene and be joined in proceedings under r 48.2 in order to recover its costs when, as a result of an attack on its integrity by the father in child contact proceedings, the Centre had had to take part in the proceedings in order to defend its reputation. Although the court was very reluctant to make orders for costs against parents in family proceedings, it found that the father's attack had been unjustified and unacceptable, and so it was appropriate to make a s 51 order that he pay the Centre's costs in attending the hearing to defend its reputation.

Disclosure of identity of party funding litigation

The court has an ancillary power to order a party to proceedings, or solicitors who have been on the record for that party, to disclose, to the opposing party, the name or names of those who financed the litigation for the benefit of that party (*Raiffeisen Zentral Bank Osterreich AG v Crosseas Shipping Ltd* [2003] EWHC 1381). In *Raiffeisen*, the claimant had evidence, in the form of an affidavit sworn by the defendant in respect of a freezing injunction, that the defendant had insufficient money to fund his participation in the proceedings. The court was satisfied that the only inference to be drawn from the evidence was that someone was maintaining the defendant's defence, and funds were being provided by a third party, such as a family trust. The court therefore exercised its discretion to make an order that the defendant, and his former solicitors, disclose the name of the party or parties who maintained the defendant's defence and appeal in the proceedings.

COSTS IN FAVOUR OF A TRUSTEE OR PERSONAL REPRESENTATIVE

A trustee or personal representative acting as such in proceedings on behalf of and for the benefit of the fund over which he has been appointed, in the absence of a right to be paid his costs under a contract, is usually entitled to be paid his costs arising from such proceedings out of the fund and for those costs to be assessed on the indemnity basis (r 48.4(1) and (2)). Obviously, this rule may not apply if the trustee or personal representative is not acting on behalf of the fund.

In *D'Abo v Paget (No 2)* (2000) *The Times*, 10 August, it was held that the guidelines on costs in *Re Buckton* [1907] 2 Ch 405 had survived the introduction of the CPR. In *Re Buckton*, it was said that there were three categories of trust litigation:

(a) proceedings by trustees to have the guidance of the court as to the construction of the trust instrument or some question arising in the course of the administration. The costs of such proceedings are to be treated as necessarily incurred for the benefit of the estate and ordered to be paid out of the fund;

(b) an application by someone other than the trustee which raises the same kind of point as in (a) and would have justified an application by the trustees. The costs of such proceedings are to be treated in the same way as those in (a); and

(c) an application by a beneficiary making a hostile claim against the trustees or other beneficiaries. The costs of such litigation are to be treated in the same way as ordinary litigation, that is, the costs will follow the event.

In *D'Abo*, a beneficiary to a trust brought proceedings to clarify the terms of the trust. The court found that on the true construction of the trust the beneficiary was entitled to the trust fund absolutely. The court confirmed that the normal rule was that the costs of trustees, and also of beneficiaries joined as defendants, would be paid out of the trust fund on the indemnity basis. Although the court accepted that a more robust approach to costs was appropriate now, it held that the CPR did not supersede the *Re Buckton* guidelines. The court found that the proceedings in this case would, in the ordinary course of events, have been brought by the trustees; the trustees were willing and able to bring them, and the only reason why the claimant brought them was to obtain an order for costs against the other beneficiary if she was successful. However, the court was of the opinion that the question of construction of the trust was a difficult one on which three leading counsel had taken different views. It was satisfied that if the claimant had not started the proceedings the trustees would have had to in order to establish the interests of the beneficiaries. In the circumstances, the court was of the opinion that this case fell into category (b) of the *Re Buckton* guidelines and that the trustees were entitled to their costs out of the fund on the indemnity basis, whilst the other beneficiary, who had taken no part in the proceedings except to protect her position on costs, was entitled to her costs out of the fund on the standard basis.

COSTS WHERE MONEY IS PAYABLE BY OR TO A CHILD OR PATIENT

Where a child or patient is a party to proceedings in which money is ordered to be paid to or for the benefit of the child or patient, or to be paid by or on his behalf, as a general rule the court must order a detailed assessment of the costs payable to the child or patient by another party and of the costs payable by the child or patient to his solicitor (r 48.5(1) and (2)). However, the court may make a summary assessment of the costs payable by a child or patient to the other party (PD 44, para 13.11).

The general rule does not apply where there is no need to apply it in order to protect the interests of the child or patient, or where the solicitor acting for the child or patient has agreed to waive the right to claim further costs following an agreement for the payment of a specified sum in costs by another party or the summary assessment of the costs by the court, or where an insurer or other party is liable to pay the child's or patient's costs to his solicitor and the insurer or other party can afford to do so (PD 48, para 51).

LITIGANTS IN PERSON

A litigant in person may be awarded the costs, payable by another person, of acting on his own behalf. The court can decide to assess those costs by either summary or detailed assessment (r 48.6(1)).

Definition of 'litigant in person'

Neither the rules nor the glossary to the CPR define the phrase 'litigant in person', presumably on the grounds that it is self-explanatory. However, r 48.6(6) states that, for the purposes of the rules about costs, a litigant in person includes a company or other corporation which is acting without a legal representative, and a barrister, solicitor, solicitor's employee or other authorised litigator who is acting for himself.

Solicitor acting for his firm or represented by his firm

It should be noted, however, that under the CPR, a solicitor who, instead of acting for himself, is represented in the proceedings by his firm or by himself in his firm's name, is not a litigant in person (PD 48, para 52.5). This means that the solicitor will be able to recover costs as if he had employed a solicitor at the usual rate charged by a solicitor of the appropriate grade to conduct the proceedings, apart for items which the fact of his acting directly rendered unnecessary (*Malkinson v Trim* [2002] EWCA Civ 1273). It was said in *Malkinson* that a partner who is represented by his firm incurs no liability to the firm but suffers a loss for which, under the indemnity principle, he ought to be compensated because the firm, of which he is a member, expends time and resources that would otherwise be devoted to other clients. Also, the solicitor will be able to recover such costs if the work is done on his behalf by the partnership or people employed by the partnership. This principle was established by the case of *London Scottish Benefits Society v Chorley* (1884) 12 QBD 452.

This principle does not apply to an employee of a solicitors' firm acting on behalf of himself who, in accordance with the definition in r 48.6(6), will be a litigant in person.

Amount of costs recoverable by a litigant in person

Financial loss

If a litigant in person can show that he suffered financial loss in acting for himself in the proceedings, he can recover an amount of costs to reflect this, but the amount must not exceed more than two-thirds of the amount that would have been allowed in legal costs if a legal representative had represented the litigant in person (r 48.6(2)).

Evidence of financial loss

A litigant in person should file at court and serve evidence of his financial loss on a party from whom he seeks costs at least 24 hours before any hearing at which his costs may be decided. If a litigant in person seeks detailed assessment, he should file that evidence with his notice of commencement (PD 48, paras 52.2 and 52.3).

Hourly rate

If a litigant in person cannot show that he suffered financial loss in acting for himself, the amount of costs he can be awarded will be based on the amount of time which was reasonably spent doing the work at a rate which is currently set at £9.25 per hour (r 48.6(4); PD 48, para 52.4).

In *R v Legal Services Commission ex p Wulfsohn* [2002] EWCA Civ 250, the Court of Appeal held that if r 48.6(2) and r 48.6(4) are read together, in principle a litigant in person is entitled to compensation for his time, at the rate fixed by statutory instrument (currently £9.25 per hour). However, the amount a litigant in person can claim is subject to a cap, which means that however long a litigant spends, he cannot recover more than two-thirds of the amount that would have been allowed in legal costs if a legal representative had represented the litigant in person. In that case the court accepted that the litigant in person had spent 1,200 hours conducting research on the case which involved complex issues. In those circumstances it held that the right approach was to start with the cap and identify what it would have cost if the litigant in person had instructed a legal representative. On a rough and ready basis the court held that those costs would have been approximately £15,000, which meant that the cap in relation to the litigant in person was £10,000. The court also allowed the cost of additional expenses for photocopying, postage and travel, which came to £460.

However, in *Greville v Sprake* [2001] EWCA Civ 234, the Court of Appeal said that a litigant in person is limited to the time which would reasonably have been spent *by a solicitor* on the preparation of the case. Thus, some degree of legal knowledge on the part of the litigant in person is assumed even if it does not exist.

Other costs

The litigant in person can also recover the costs of disbursements if they would have been incurred by a legal representative on his behalf, and any payments reasonably made by him for legal services relating to the conduct of the proceedings, plus the costs of obtaining expert assistance, from someone who is legally qualified or qualified to calculate legal costs, in order to assess his claim for costs (r 48.6(3); PD 48, para 52.1).

A litigant in person who does not seek costs may apply for a witness allowance for his expenses in attending court. However, a litigant in person is not entitled to claim both his costs for attending court and a witness allowance (r 48.6(5)).

COSTS OF GROUP LITIGATION

Where the court has made a Group Litigation Order (GLO), there will be two aspects of the costs incurred: individual costs, and common costs. Individual costs are those costs that are incurred in relation to an individual claim on the group register, while common costs consist of three elements:

(a) costs incurred in relation to the GLO issues;

(b) individual costs incurred in a claim while it is proceeding as a test case; and

(c) costs incurred by the lead solicitor in administering the group litigation (r 48.6A(2)(a), (b)).

Unless the court orders otherwise, the general rule is that where a group litigant is ordered to pay costs, he will be liable for the individual costs of his claim and be severally liable for an equal proportion, together with all the other group litigants, of the common costs (r 48.6A(3), (4)).

If a GLO is already in place and common costs have been incurred, the court may order that a litigant entered onto the group register at that stage is liable for a proportion of those costs (r 48.6A(6)). This is because a litigant who joins the group register in the future acquires the benefit of work done in the past and so should become potentially liable for costs liabilities going back to the beginning of the GLO.

Where there is a GLO the court will usually make a costs sharing order at an early stage of the group litigation. Such an order is intended to cover, in general terms, the future conduct of the litigation. The costs sharing order will commonly provide for costings at quarterly intervals, whereby parties and their legal representatives provide information on costs already incurred and estimates of costs of proposed further work.

In *Sayers v SmithKline Beecham plc* [2001] EWCA Civ 2027, the Court of Appeal said that a costs sharing order should not determine in advance that the costs will be awarded by reference to the determination of common issues (that is, follow the event) rather than be decided once the fate of each individual litigant's claim is known. This is because such an order would not take into account that the resolution of common issues may turn out to be academic, and the court should be free to make whatever appears to be the most appropriate order in the circumstances.

The Court of Appeal in *Sayers* also held that, as a matter of principle, it would be unjust to claimants, and an inappropriate advantage to defendants, if a costs sharing order were to provide in advance that any discontinuing claimant is to be liable for his individual costs together with his several share of common costs at the end of the quarter at which he discontinues. The court was of the opinion that to have a *prima facie* rule that a discontinuing claimant should have such a costs liability was 'too blunt an instrument and is unnecessarily favourable to defendants when it is as yet unknown whether the claimants as a whole are to be successful in the common issues which are to be tried' (at [19]). The reason for this is that a group claim is essentially different from the typical claim where a single claimant brings a claim. The group claim will continue in the same form as currently constituted even after a claimant, for whatever reason, decides to discontinue. Usually, in the typical claim all issues of liability are tried together, whereas in group claims certain common issues will be tried on their own before it is possible to apply the results to the individual claimants. There are also many different reasons why a claimant in a group claim may wish to discontinue.

CHAPTER 35

PROCEDURES FOR ASSESSING THE AMOUNT OF COSTS

INTRODUCTION

There are two procedures by which the court can assess costs: by *summary* or by *detailed* assessment. The court can decide which mode of assessment to employ unless one of those methods is specifically provided for by a relevant rule or practice direction (r 44.7). An order for costs will be treated as an order for the amount of costs to be decided by detailed assessment, unless the court orders otherwise (PD 44, para 12.2).

The assessment of costs has been described as the 'Achilles heel of the [Woolf] reforms' and criticised on the grounds that 'making a fair assessment of the costs of litigation [often] involves a more intricate process than resolving the issues in the litigation itself' (*per* Lord Phillips, extracted in *Further Findings*, www.dca.gov.uk/civil/reform/ffreform.htm, para 7.25).

Time for payment of costs

If costs are assessed summarily or fixed costs are payable, if the judgment or order ordering payment also states the amount of costs, the paying party must pay them within 14 days of the date of the judgment or order. If costs are to be assessed by detailed assessment, the costs are payable within 14 days of the date of the certificate which states the amount. In either case, the court can specifically order a different period of time for payment of the costs (r 44.8).

Summary assessment

Summary assessment is the procedure whereby the court assesses costs at the end of the hearing and orders payment of a sum of money instead of fixed costs and without a detailed consideration of each item claimed (r 43.3). Summary judgment is a rough and ready process. Research conducted by the Lord Chancellor's Department concluded that summary assessment is universally disliked by practitioners as it is felt to be carried out inconsistently and is unpredictable (see www.dca.gov.uk/civil/reform/ffreform.htm).

The court can use a party's costs estimates provided throughout the hearing to help it decide whether costs claimed are reasonable (PD 43, para 6.6), as well as a statement of costs. The court should give a party an opportunity to address it so as to justify the costs claimed in the statement of costs if necessary (*Edwards v Devon & Cornwall Constabulary* [2001] EWCA Civ 388).

The court has a discretion whether to order a summary assessment of costs. Practice Direction 44, Section 13, provides that whenever a court makes an order about costs which does not provide for fixed costs, it should consider whether to make a summary assessment of costs. In *Contractreal Ltd v Davies* [2001] EWCA Civ 928, the Court of Appeal did not find that the judge was wrong to order a summary assessment of costs because a relatively small amount of damages had been recovered, even though the matters in the case were relatively complex and the proceedings lasted for a long time. The court felt it important that summary assessments are made because they lead to prompt payment of costs in favour of the receiving party. However, it should be noted that the judge's decision was set aside on the grounds that he had erred in his actual assessment of the costs and the claimant's costs were referred for detailed assessment.

However, there are certain circumstances in which summary assessment cannot take place, such as of the costs of a legally aided or Legal Services Commission (LSC) funded client, and others in which summary assessment will not be appropriate. Also, if the court makes an order for costs to be assessed, and decides that this should be by way of summary assessment, this should be specified, as otherwise the order will be treated as an order for detailed assessment (PD 44, para 12.3).

In any event, as a general rule, unless there is a good reason not to do so, the court will make a summary assessment of the costs of the following:

(a) the whole claim following a fast track trial;

(b) any hearing which has lasted no longer than one day (and if the hearing disposes of the whole claim, the court may summarily assess the costs of the whole claim); and

(c) hearings in the Court of Appeal to which para 14 of PD 52 applies (PD 44, para 13.2).

An example of a good reason not to assess costs summarily is where the paying party shows substantial grounds for disputing the sum claimed for costs which cannot be dealt with summarily, or where there is not enough time for summary assessment. Also, the court cannot make a summary assessment of the costs of a receiving party who is an assisted person or LSC funded client (PD 44, para 13.9).

In respect of a hearing that has lasted no longer than one day, although, as a general rule, the court will summarily assess the costs of the hearing, this is likely to be the case only if the order for costs has determined that one party is to receive the costs of the hearing. Therefore, summary assessment will not take place if the order for costs is for costs in the case or some other order where the costs liability depends on which party is successful at trial, or is to be decided at a later date (*Desquenne et Giral UK Ltd v Richardson* [2001] FSR 1, CA).

Statement of costs

Whenever a party is claiming costs that are likely to be assessed summarily, he must assist the judge in making a summary assessment of those costs by filing at court and serving on every other party a statement of costs (PD 44, para 13.5(1)). The statement of costs should follow as closely as possible model Form N260 (PD 43, para 3.2; PD 44, para 13.5(3)). The statement of costs should cover the following matters:

- the number of hours claimed;
- the hourly rate;
- the grade of fee earner;
- disbursements;
- solicitor's costs for attending or appearing at the hearing;

- counsel's fee for attending the hearing; and
- any VAT to be added to these amounts (PD 44, para 13.5(2)).

The statement of costs need not reveal the level of the success fee of any conditional fee agreement, or the amount of any other additional liability (PD 44, para 13.5(5)). It must be signed by the party or by his legal representative (PD 44, para 13.5(3)).

Time for filing and serving the statement of costs

The statement of costs must be filed at court, and copies of it must be served on any party against whom it is intended to seek an order for payment of those costs. It should be filed and served as soon as possible, and in any event not less than 24 hours before the date fixed for the hearing (PD 44, para 13.5(4)).

Consequences of failure to provide a statement of costs

The court will take into account the failure to provide a statement of costs when it is deciding what order to make about the costs of the claim. Therefore, the court may well decide not to award costs to a party who would otherwise be entitled to them if he fails, without reasonable excuse, to file and serve a statement of costs within the time period specified. If, as a result of the failure to provide a statement of costs, the court is unable to assess costs and a further hearing is necessary to do so, or detailed assessment is necessary, the court will take this into account when deciding what order to make as to the costs of the further hearing or detailed assessment proceedings (PD 44, para 13.6).

In *Macdonald v Taree Holdings Ltd* (2000) *The Times*, 28 December, it was held that in a case of mere failure to comply with the requirement to provide a statement of costs, it would not be right to deprive a party, otherwise entitled to summary assessment of costs, of his costs altogether unless there was an aggravating factor. Where there was a failure to comply with the '24 hour rule' the court should take that into account, but its reaction should be proportionate. The court should assess whether prejudice had been caused to the other party and, if no prejudice resulted, go on to assess the costs in the normal way. If prejudice had been caused, the court should address the question of how that prejudice should best be dealt with. There were three possibilities:

(a) give the paying party a brief adjournment to consider the schedule and then proceed to assess costs, in which circumstances, where the paying party had not had as much time as it should have done, the court should err in favour of a light figure in cases of doubt;

(b) stand the matter over for a detailed assessment, in which case the receiving party might have to pay the costs of that assessment; or

(c) stand over the assessment of costs but keep the assessment on a summary basis, which might not require another hearing.

Costs estimates

It is a general principle of the Civil Procedure Rules (CPR) that a party should keep the other party informed as to their potential liability, not only in respect of the claim or counterclaim, but also in respect of costs. In furtherance of this, PD 43 provides for the filing and service of costs estimates at various stages of the proceedings. Costs estimates are also used to assist the court to decide what, if any, order to make about costs and for the purposes of case management. It is also the intention that the exercise of providing a costs estimate encourages parties and their legal representatives to be aware of the costs that are being incurred and to take steps accordingly to limit them, a suggestion which found favour with the court in *Solutia UK Ltd v Griffiths* [2001] EWCA Civ 736. If the court is assessing costs, it may take any previous costs estimate into account when deciding whether the costs claimed are reasonable (PD 43, para 6.6).

Form of costs estimates

A costs estimate is a summary of the costs that a party intends to seek from another party if he is successful in the case. It is divided into two main parts:

(a) an estimate of costs already incurred; and

(b) an estimate of costs to be incurred.

The costs set out in the estimate should be base costs only, that is, those costs other than the amount of any additional liability. An additional liability includes the success fee of a conditional fee agreement and any legal expenses insurance premium. The estimate of costs should also include disbursements (PD 43, paras 2.2 and 6.2). The costs estimate should follow the form illustrated in Precedent H in the Schedule of Costs Precedents annexed to the practice direction supplementing Parts 43–48 (PD 43, para 6.5).

Under PD 43, paras 6.3 and 6.4, unless the court otherwise directs, a party, apart from a litigant in person, must file at court and serve on all other parties a copy of a costs estimate at the following stages:

(a) in a claim outside the financial scope of the small claims track, at the same time as filing the allocation questionnaire;

(b) in a claim on the fast track or multi-track or under Part 8, at the same time as filing the pre-trial checklist (listing questionnaire); and

(c) at any other time that the court orders, within 28 days of the date of the order or within a time specified by the court. The court may also order that a party demonstrate the likely effect on costs of the giving of a particular case management direction that the court is considering, such as an order for a split trial.

When filing and serving the costs estimate with the allocation questionnaire and pre-trial checklist, the legal representative must also serve a copy on his client (PD 43, para 6.4).

DETAILED ASSESSMENT

Detailed assessment is the procedure whereby the costs of the receiving party are assessed in detail by a costs officer (r 43.4). Detailed assessment has replaced the former procedure of taxation, and any reference to taxation in an order will be taken to mean detailed assessment (PD 43, para 3.8).

The general rule is that detailed assessment will not be ordered until the conclusion of the proceedings, that is, when the court has finally determined the matters in issue, whether or not the court's decision is appealed (PD 47, para 28.1(1)). Therefore, it is unlikely that the costs of any interim application will be assessed by way of detailed assessment. However, the court has a discretion to order detailed assessment at any stage (r 47.1).

In some cases, proceedings will reach a stage where, although the matter has not been finally decided, there is no realistic prospect of the claim continuing; for instance, where a party has secured an interim injunction which has effectively determined the issues in dispute between the parties. In such circumstances, the court may order, or the parties may agree in writing, that although the proceedings are continuing, they will nevertheless be treated as concluded so that detailed assessment can take place (PD 47, para 28.1(3)).

Venue for detailed assessment proceedings

An application for detailed assessment should be made in the appropriate office, which is the county court or district registry where the case that gave rise to the right to detailed assessment was being dealt with, or to which proceedings were transferred, and in all other cases the Supreme Court Costs Office (r 47.4; PD 47, para 31.1).

Proceedings may be transferred to another county court for detailed assessment to be carried out (r 30.2). Also, a party may apply for, or the court of its own initiative may direct, that another specified court, registry or office is to be the appropriate office to carry out the detailed assessment. However, the Supreme Court Costs Office is reserved for the largest and most difficult assessments and so, unless this was already the appropriate office for a case, the court will not direct that the detailed assessment be carried out there unless it would be justified given such relevant matters as the size of the bill of costs, the difficulty of the issues involved, the likely length of the hearing and the cost to the parties (r 47.4(2), (3); PD 47, para 31.2(3)).

Payment on account

If detailed assessment is ordered, the court may order a specified amount to be paid on account before the costs are assessed and, in fact, the court should always consider whether to exercise its power to do so when it makes an order for detailed assessment (r 44.3(8); PD 44, paras 8.6, 12.3). A payment on account is often referred to as an interim payment. In *Mars UK Ltd v Teknowledge Ltd (No 2)* [1999] TLR 510, the court held that where a party was successful, the court should normally make an order for an interim payment of a lower amount than the party would almost certainly recover, calculated on a rough and ready basis. However, it was recognised that the court must take all the circumstances into account before deciding to make such an order. Relevant considerations that would indicate that an interim payment should *not* be made may include the unsuccessful party's intention to appeal, the relative financial position of each party and the overriding objective to deal with cases justly.

The decision in *Mars UK Ltd* was distinguished in *Dyson Appliances v Hoover Ltd* [2003] EWHC 624 on the grounds that in *Mars UK Ltd* the judge who ordered the interim payment had heard the whole trial and inquiry into damages and was therefore in a position to make a meaningful assessment of the costs and consider the issue of proportionality. In *Dyson Appliances*, by contrast, the matter had settled, so the judge did not have detailed knowledge of the nature and strength of the arguments that would have been advanced at trial. Although it was held that the court did have the power under r 44.3(8) to order an interim payment even when it had not heard the trial, there was no presumption that an interim payment should be made. The court should simply consider an application for an order for interim payment on its own merits. In that case the judge refused to order an interim payment because he knew very little about the case, except that it had been fought on a grand scale and a very large amount of costs was involved. The judge was also mindful that the claimant could apply to the costs judge to issue an interim costs certificate under r 47.15 once a request for a detailed assessment hearing had been made. The judge was of the opinion that at that stage the costs judge will, in terms of information about the case, be in a similar position to that of the trial judge ordering a payment on account after hearing the trial.

Detailed assessment pending an appeal

Detailed assessment will not be stayed pending an appeal, unless the court so orders (r 47.2). The party who is appealing should apply either to the court whose decision is being appealed, or to the court that is hearing the appeal for an order staying the detailed assessment until after the hearing of the appeal (PD 47, para 29).

Detailed assessment in relation to an additional liability

Detailed assessment proceedings may be in respect of just base costs where there is no additional liability to assess, or where those costs have been agreed. On the other hand, detailed assessment may be in respect of just an additional liability where the base costs have been agreed or assessed summarily. Alternatively, detailed assessment may be in respect of both the base costs and the additional liability (PD 47, para 32.2).

Commencement of detailed assessment proceedings

In order to commence detailed assessment proceedings, the party in whose favour a costs order has been made, known as the receiving party, must serve a notice of commencement in Form N252, a copy of a bill of costs, and copies of evidence in relation to counsel's fees and disbursements on the party who has been ordered to pay costs, known as the paying party (r 47.6; PD 47, paras 32.3 and 32.8). The procedure at this stage does not involve filing any document at court. It is only when a request for a detailed assessment hearing is made that the court is involved and a court fee is payable (see pp 558–59 below, 'Form of request for a detailed assessment hearing').

If the paying party does not respond to the notice of commencement and the receiving party becomes entitled to a default costs certificate, the receiving party will also be able to claim fixed costs and the court fees on obtaining a default costs certificate. The receiving party, therefore, must show on the notice of commencement these extra sums that will be claimed in fixed costs and court fees if a default costs certificate is obtained (PD 47, para 32.8).

Commencement of detailed assessment proceedings in relation to an additional liability

If the detailed assessment proceedings are in relation to an additional liability only, such as the level of success fee in a conditional fee agreement, the receiving party must serve a notice of commencement in Form N252, a copy of the bill of costs, relevant details of the additional liability, and a statement giving the name and address of any person upon whom the receiving party intends to serve the notice of commencement (PD 47, paras 32.4 and 32.5). The relevant details about the additional liability are, in the case of a success fee, a statement showing the amount of costs that has been agreed or summarily assessed, and the percentage increase claimed in respect of them and a statement of the reasons for the level of the percentage increase (as required by reg 3 of the Conditional Fee Agreements Regulations 2000 (SI 2000/692); and see Chapter 4, 'Funding Litigation'). In the case of an insurance premium, the receiving party must serve a copy of the insurance certificate showing the extent of the costs covered and the amount of the premium (PD 47, para 32.5).

If the detailed assessment proceedings are in respect of both the base costs and an additional liability, the receiving party must serve all the documents referred to in PD 47, paras 32.3 and 32.5, as set out above (PD 47, para 32.7).

Service on other relevant persons

The receiving party must also serve these documents on any other relevant person. This is defined as a person who was involved in the court proceedings and is directly liable for any costs orders made against him, a party who has notified the receiving party that he has a financial interest in the outcome of the detailed assessment proceedings and therefore wishes to be a party to them, and any other party the court orders should be served with these documents. A person so served will also become a party to the detailed assessment proceedings (r 47.6(2), (3); PD 47, para 32.10).

Bill of costs

A party applying for detailed assessment should submit a bill of costs. Although model forms of bills of costs should be used (see Precedents A, B, C and D in the Schedule of Costs Precedents), they are not compulsory; however, if a model form is not used, a party must give an explanation in the background information of his bill as to why the appropriate model has been departed from (PD 43, para 3.7). Practice Direction 43, paras 4.1–4.17 cover in detail how a bill of costs should be set out, and which items should be shown and what can be claimed.

Time limit for commencing detailed assessment proceedings

A party must commence detailed assessment proceedings within three months after the date when the right to detailed assessment arose. The circumstances giving rise to a right to detailed assessment are either:

(a) a judgment, direction, order, award or other determination; or

(b) where the claimant discontinues under Part 38, or on the acceptance of an offer to settle or payment into court under Part 36 (r 47.7).

The parties can agree to extend or shorten the time specified for commencement of detailed assessment proceedings, or a party may apply for such an order (PD 47, paras 33.1, 33.2).

Sanction for failure to commence detailed assessment proceedings in time

If the receiving party commences detailed assessment proceedings later than the time period specified, the only sanction the court may impose is to disallow all or part of the interest on the costs otherwise payable to the receiving party under either s 17 of the Judgments Act 1838 or s 74 of the County Courts Act 1984. However, this is subject to the court's powers under r 44.14 to disallow all or part of the costs being assessed or to order a party or his legal representative to pay costs on the grounds of misconduct (r 47.8(3)).

However, if a receiving party fails to commence detailed assessment proceedings within the time period specified by the rules or a direction of the court, the paying party can apply to the court for an order that unless the receiving party commences the application within a further time specified by the court, all or part of the receiving party's costs, to which he would otherwise be entitled, will be disallowed (r 47.8(1) and (2)).

Points of dispute

In order to challenge the amount of costs claimed by the receiving party in his bill of costs, the paying party must serve points of dispute on the receiving party and every other party to the detailed assessment proceedings (r 47.9(1)). Practice Direction 47 provides details as to the contents of the points of dispute. The points of dispute must identify each item in the bill of costs that is disputed and state the nature and grounds of the dispute. Where practicable, a suggested alternative figure that should be allowed instead should be given, and the document must be signed by the party or by his solicitor (PD 47, para 35.3). In any event, the practice direction also provides that the points of dispute should be short and to the point and follow Precedent G of the Schedule of Costs Precedents as closely as possible (PD 47, para 35.2).

Time for service of points of dispute

Points of dispute must be served on the receiving party, and any other party to the detailed assessment proceedings, within 21 days after the date of service of the notice of commencement (r 47.9(2); PD 47, paras 35.4, 35.5). The parties may agree to extend or shorten the time specified for service of points of dispute, or a party may apply for an order to extend or shorten that time under r 3.1(2) (PD 47, para 35.1). However, in the absence of such agreement or order, the paying party may not be heard in the detailed assessment proceedings unless the court gives permission (r 47.9(3)).

Reply to points of dispute

The receiving party has the option of serving a reply to the points of dispute if he thinks it necessary. Such a reply should be served within 21 days after service of the points of dispute on him (r 47.13).

Documents on disk

In recognition of the fact that a bill of costs or points of dispute can be long and detailed, and as a sign of the times, there is provision for the party in receipt of such documents to request a copy on computer disk. A paying party can request that a disk copy of the bill of costs be sent to him by the receiving party, free of charge, within seven days after receipt of such a request (PD 47, para 32.11). Likewise, a receiving party can request, within 14 days of receipt of the points of dispute, that a disk copy of the points of dispute be sent to him, free of charge, within seven days after receipt of such a request (PD 47, para 35.6).

Parties agreeing costs

If the parties agree a figure for costs, they can apply for an order that a certificate be issued in the terms of the compromise agreement. As the judgment is by consent, it can be dealt with by a court officer who can issue the certificate, whether an interim or a final certificate (PD 47, para 36.1).

If the parties agree costs but the paying party will neither pay them nor agree to a consent order, the receiving party can make an application under Part 23 for an interim or final certificate to be issued based on the agreement reached between the parties (PD 47, para 36.2). The receiving party must support the application with evidence, and the paying party can rely on evidence in response which must be filed and served on the paying party at least two days before the hearing date. The application will be heard by a costs judge or a district judge (PD 47, para 36.3).

Default costs certificates

If a receiving party has commenced detailed assessment proceedings but the paying party has not served points of dispute within the time specified (or applied for or agreed extra time for doing so), the receiving party may file a request in Form N254, at the appropriate office, signed by the party or his solicitor, for a default costs certificate (r 47.9(4); PD 47, paras 37.1, 37.2).

On receipt of the application a default costs certificate in Form N255 will be issued, which includes an order to pay the costs to which it relates and which is enforceable by the receiving party (r 47.11(1), (2); PD 47, para 37). This procedure therefore allows the receiving party to obtain an order for payment of his costs in default of the paying party's challenge to the amount of costs detailed in his bill of costs. However, if, before the court has issued a default costs certificate, any party to the proceedings serves points of dispute, the court may not issue a default costs certificate (r 47.9(5)).

If a default costs certificate is obtained, the paying party must still obtain a detailed assessment of any costs payable out of the Community Legal Service Fund (PD 47, para 37.5).

Fixed costs of a default costs certificate

The receiving party will be entitled to fixed costs of £80 plus payment of any court fees in applying for a default costs certificate, which will be included in the default costs certificate when it is issued by the court (PD 45, para 25.1).

Setting aside a default costs certificate

The court also has the power to set aside a default costs certificate. The court must set it aside if the party obtaining it was not entitled to it, for example, if the time period for filing points of dispute had not expired (r 47.12(1)).

The court has a discretion to set aside or vary the default costs certificate if it appears to the court that there is some good reason why the detailed assessment proceedings should continue (r 47.12(2)). The application to set aside must be supported by evidence, and the paying party should file a copy of the bill of costs and default costs certificate and a copy of the points of dispute he proposes to serve, if his application is granted, in order to persuade the court that he has good grounds to challenge the bill of costs. When deciding to exercise its discretion to set aside the order, the court must consider whether the application was made promptly, and the applicant should explain the reason for failing to serve points of dispute in time. If the application to set aside the default costs certificate is successful, the court will give directions for the management of the detailed assessment proceedings (PD 47, para 38).

The court may direct that the order setting aside the default costs certificate is subject to a condition, such as the paying party paying a sum of money into court. The court may also order that the paying party pay a proportion of the costs being claimed to the receiving party on account (rr 3.1(3), 44.3(8); PD 47, para 38.3).

Receiving party applying to set aside a default costs certificate

If, after a default costs certificate has been issued, the receiving party discovers that the notice of commencement did not reach the paying party at least 21 days before the default costs certificate was issued, the receiving party must either file a request for the default costs certificate to be set aside or apply to the court for directions. The receiving party must not attempt to enforce the default costs certificate, or take any further step in the detailed assessment proceedings until the certificate has been set aside or the court has given directions (r 47.12(3)).

If the receiving party simply applies for the default costs certificate to be set aside, this is a purely administrative act and can therefore be carried out by a court officer. However, if the receiving party applies for any other order or for directions, this will be dealt with by a costs judge or a district judge (PD 47, para 38.1).

DETAILED ASSESSMENT HEARING

Form of request for a detailed assessment hearing

Where the receiving party has served a notice of commencement and the paying party has served points of dispute, the receiving party must file a request for a detailed assessment hearing in Form N258 (r 47.14; PD 47, para 40.2). A court fee is payable on the filing of the request (see the Supreme Court Fees Order 1999 (SI 1999/687) and the County Court Fees Order 1999 (SI 1999/689), as amended, for the level of fee).

Form N258 must be accompanied by the following documents:

- a copy of the notice of commencement of the detailed assessment proceedings;
- a copy of the bill of costs;
- a copy of the document giving the right to the detailed assessment (for example, a court judgment or order, a notice of acceptance of a Part 36 offer or payment, a notice of discontinuance);
- a copy of the points of dispute for every party who has served points of dispute (which should be annotated by the receiving party to show which items have been agreed and which are in dispute and the value of these items);
- a copy of any replies served;
- a copy of all court orders relating to the costs which are to be assessed;
- a copy of the required evidence of counsel's fee notes, expert fees and of disbursements claimed exceeding £250;
- where there is a dispute as to the receiving party's liability to pay his solicitor's costs, a copy of any document provided by the solicitor to his client explaining how the solicitor's charges are to be calculated; and
- a statement, signed by the receiving party or his solicitor, giving contact details of the receiving party, the paying party and any other relevant party, as well as an estimate of the length of time the detailed assessment hearing will take (PD 47, para 40.2).

Privilege and documents filed in support of detailed assessment

Chapter 4, 'Funding Litigation', 'The indemnity principle and disclosure' and 'Disclosure of the conditional fee agreement', should be consulted for the position regarding disclosure of otherwise privileged documents in respect of detailed assessment hearings (see Chapter 4, pp 47–49 and p 49 above, respectively).

Time limit for filing request for a detailed assessment hearing

Rules 47.14(2)–(5) set out the time limits for the filing of a request for a detailed assessment hearing, and the sanctions and possible court orders for failure to do so within the time period. These are the same as those provided for the commencement of detailed assessment proceedings (for details, see p 556 above, 'Sanction for failure to commence detailed assessment proceedings in time').

Interim costs certificate

Once a receiving party has filed a request for a detailed assessment hearing, he can apply to the court for an interim costs certificate (r 47.15(1)). The application is made in accordance with Part 23 (PD 47, para 41.1). The court has the power to decide that an appropriate sum should be paid in the interim pending the detailed assessment hearing. The court will take into account whether a payment on account has already been made following the order for detailed assessment.

The costs judge will have sufficient information to be in a position to decide whether or not to issue an interim certificate and, if so, in what amount, having received a fully itemised bill of costs, points of dispute and the information included with the request for detailed assessment.

If the application is granted, the court will issue an interim costs certificate in Form N257 for an amount it considers appropriate. The interim costs certificate will usually include an order that the paying party pay the costs to which it relates (r 47.15(2)). However, the court can decide to order that the amount be paid into court instead (r 47.15(3)). The court may amend or cancel the interim certificate at any time (r 47.15(1)(b)).

Date for the hearing

On receipt of a request for a detailed assessment hearing, the court will either fix a date for the hearing, or, if the costs officer considers it necessary, give directions or fix a date for a preliminary appointment (PD 47, para 40.5).

Only the receiving party and paying party and any other relevant person who has served points of dispute may be heard at a detailed assessment hearing, and the court will give those parties at least 14 days' notice of the time and place of the detailed assessment hearing and a copy of the points of dispute annotated by the receiving party in the way referred to above (r 47.14(6); PD 47, para 40.6(1), (2)).

Documents to be filed

The receiving party must file the papers in support of the bill of costs not less than seven, nor more than 14 days before the date of the detailed assessment hearing (PD 47, para 40.11). Practice Direction 47, para 40.12, sets out detailed provision for the papers to be filed and the order in which they are to be arranged for the purposes of the hearing.

Nature of the hearing

The hearing will be concerned only with considering the items specified in the points of dispute, unless the court gives permission for other items to be considered (r 47.14(7)).

Rights of audience at detailed assessment hearings

Under s 27 of the Courts and Legal Services Act (CLSA) 1990, counsel instructed by solicitors, a solicitor or an employee of a solicitor representing a party to the proceedings have rights of audience in detailed assessment proceedings. Also, if a party is legally represented, costs consultants and costs draftsmen have rights of audience only on the basis that they are temporarily, and for the purpose of the detailed assessment proceedings, employees of the solicitor representing the party. The solicitor employing the costs consultant or costs draftsman will remain responsible for the conduct of the detailed assessment proceedings.

It was held by the Supreme Court Costs Office in *Ahmed v Powell* (2003) LTL, 25 February, that costs negotiators did not have rights of audience under s 27 of the CLSA 1990 because they were employed by an insurance company rather than instructed by the solicitor acting for the insurance company. The costs negotiators had an arrangement with the insurance company by which they were paid a commission at a set rate provided they achieved a monthly average gross saving of a certain percentage of claimants' costs. The judge also held that the agreement between the insurance company and the costs negotiators was not subject to the statutory safeguards in respect of contingency fee agreements and offended against public policy. Arrangements of that type were said to give rise to concerns that the question of costs might be pursued over-vigorously, and therefore disproportionately and in breach of the overriding objective.

Amendment of documents for detailed assessment

A party may vary his bill of costs, points of dispute or reply without seeking permission to do so, but the court may subsequently disallow the variation, or permit it only upon conditions such as the payment of costs caused or wasted by the variation. If a party does vary any of these documents, he must file a copy of the documents showing the variations with the court and serve a copy on every party to the proceedings (PD 47, para 40.10).

Settlement of the detailed assessment proceedings

If the parties settle the detailed assessment proceedings before the hearing, the receiving party must notify the court immediately. In order to ensure that the hearing date can be free for other parties, it is requested that the receiving party notify the court by way of fax if possible (PD 47, para 40.9(2)).

If the parties agree the amount of costs, either party can apply to the court that was due to hear the detailed assessment proceedings for a costs certificate, either interim or final, in the amount agreed (r 47.10).

Final costs certificate

At the detailed assessment hearing, the court will indicate any disallowance or reduction in the sums claimed by making an appropriate note on the bill of costs. The onus is then upon the receiving party to draw up a completed bill of costs which makes clear the correct figures agreed or allowed in respect of each item, and which recalculates the summary of the bill in accordance with what has been agreed or allowed following the detailed assessment. The receiving party must then file the completed bill of costs (along with receipted fee notes and receipted accounts in respect of disbursements) with the court no later than 14 days after the detailed assessment hearing (PD 47, paras 42.1–42.4).

As long as the receiving party has paid all court fees associated with the detailed assessment, the court will then issue a final costs certificate in Form N256 and serve it on the parties to the detailed assessment proceedings (r 47.16(3); PD 47, para 42.5). The final costs certificate will show the amount of costs agreed between the parties or which were allowed on detailed assessment, along with the amount of any VAT if applicable (PD 47, para 42.7).

The final costs certificate will include an order to pay the costs to which it relates unless the court orders otherwise (r 47.16(5)). Payment of the costs ordered is then enforceable in the same way as any other judgment. However, enforcement proceedings for either an interim or a final costs certificate may not be issued in the Supreme Court Costs Office (PD 47, para 42.12).

COSTS OF DETAILED ASSESSMENT PROCEEDINGS

Receiving party generally entitled to costs

As a general rule, the receiving party will be entitled to the costs of the detailed assessment hearing, and the court will assess those costs and add them to the bill of costs (r 47.18(1); PD 47, para 45.1).

Court's discretion as to costs of detailed assessment proceedings

However, when deciding what order to make about the costs of the detailed assessment proceedings, the court must have regard to the conduct of all the parties, the amount by which the bill of costs has been reduced, and whether it was reasonable for a party to claim the costs of a particular item or to dispute a particular item (r 47.18(2); PD 47, para 45.4). If the court orders costs of the detailed assessment to be paid by the paying party, it will either assess those costs summarily, or make an order for them to be decided by detailed assessment (PD 47, para 45.2).

Offers to settle without prejudice save as to the costs of the detailed assessment proceedings

A paying party or a receiving party can make a written offer to settle the costs of the proceedings which gave to the assessment and, if the offer is expressed to be without prejudice save as to the costs of the detailed assessment proceedings, the court will take it into account when deciding who should pay the costs of those proceedings (r 47.19(1)). Therefore, if a paying party offers to settle the claim for costs in a sum which is the same as or greater than the amount ordered by the court, the court is likely to award the paying party the costs of the detailed assessment proceedings. Likewise, if the receiving party offers to settle his claim for costs for a lower sum than that ordered by the court, he is likely to be awarded his costs of the detailed assessment hearing.

Time limits for making the without prejudice offer

Although r 47.19 does not specify a time within which an offer to settle should be made, PD 47 states that an offer made by the paying party should usually be made within 14 days after service of the notice of commencement on that party. If the offer is made by the receiving party, it should normally be made within 14 days after the service of points of dispute by the paying party. Offers made after these periods are likely to be given less weight by the court in deciding what order as to costs to make unless there is good reason for the offer not being made until the later time (PD 47, para 46.1).

As such an offer is without prejudice save as to costs of the detailed assessment hearing, it should not be revealed to the costs officer until the question of costs of the detailed assessment hearing comes to be decided (r 47.19(2)).

Contents of the without prejudice offer

The offer to settle should specify whether or not it is intended to be inclusive of the cost of preparation of the bill, interest and VAT. The offeree may include or exclude some or all of these items as long as this is made clear on the face of the offer. However, unless the offer specifies that these items are excluded, the offer will be treated as being inclusive of them (PD 47, para 46.2).

Acceptance of the offer

Where an offer to settle is accepted, either party may apply for a certificate in agreed terms (PD 47, para 46.3; r 47.10).

LSC funded client or assisted person

Where the receiving party is an LSC funded client or an assisted person, the provisions about without prejudice offers save as to the costs of the detailed assessment proceedings will not apply, unless the court orders otherwise (PD 47, para 46.4).

Discontinuing detailed assessment proceedings

The paying party may discontinue detailed assessment proceedings in accordance with the general rules about discontinuance (PD 47, para 36.5(1)).

The receiving party can discontinue detailed assessment proceedings without permission before he has requested a detailed assessment hearing. However, the paying party can then apply to the appropriate office for an order about the costs of the detailed assessment proceedings (PD 47, para 36.5(2)), the likely order on costs being that the receiving party pay the paying party's costs of the detailed assessment proceedings.

However, where the receiving party has requested a detailed assessment hearing, he must apply to the court for permission to discontinue the proceedings (PD 47, para 36.5(3)). Once a hearing has been requested, if the receiving party wishes to discontinue, it is very likely that he will be ordered to pay the paying party's costs and may be subject to other penalties.

If agreement is reached, a bill of costs can be withdrawn by consent at any time, whether or not a detailed assessment hearing has been requested (PD 47, para 36.5(4)).

COSTS PAYABLE OUT OF THE COMMUNITY LEGAL SERVICE FUND

From 1 July 2003, any publicly funded bill presented for assessment that does not exceed £2,500 and which does not include an *inter partes* element will be assessed directly by the LSC. Accordingly, such bills should be sent there and not to the court (Civil Legal Aid (General) (Amendment) Regulations 2003 (SI 2003/1312)).

As for costs over that sum, where costs are payable only out of the Community Legal Service (CLS) Fund, to a LSC funded client, or the legal aid fund to an assisted person, additional provisions apply where the court is to assess costs.

The LSC funded client or the assisted person's solicitor may commence detailed assessment proceedings by filing a request in Practice Form N258A (r 47.17(1)). Form N258A must be accompanied by the following documents:

- a copy of the bill of costs;
- the document giving the right to the detailed assessment;
- a copy of all orders of the court relating to the costs which are to be assessed;
- a copy of the required evidence of counsel's fee notes, expert fees and of disbursements claimed exceeding £250;
- legal aid certificates, LSC certificates, and any amendments, authorities and certificates of discharge or revocation;
- the relevant papers in support of the bill under PD 47, para 40.12 only if proceeding in the Supreme Court Costs Office; for cases proceeding in a district registry or county court, such papers should be filed only if requested by the costs officer;
- a statement signed by the solicitor giving his contact details and, if the assisted person has a financial interest in the detailed assessment and wishes to attend, giving his postal address to which the court can send a notice of any hearing (PD 47, para 43.3).

Time limits for application for detailed assessment

The solicitor claiming costs from the CLS or legal aid fund must file the request in Form N258A within three months after the date when the right to detailed assessment arose (r 47.17(2); PD 47, para 43.2).

Notifying the client

If the LSC funded client or assisted person has a financial interest in the outcome of the assessment (this will be the case if he has made a contribution to his certificate, or if he has recovered or preserved property in the proceedings), the solicitor must also serve a copy of the request for a detailed assessment on his client (r 47.17(3)).

Provisional assessment

Where the LSC funded client or assisted person does not have an interest in the outcome, or has indicated that he does not wish to attend an assessment hearing, the court will provisionally assess the solicitor's costs on receipt of a request for detailed assessment, without the attendance of the solicitor, unless it considers that a hearing is necessary (r 47.17(5); PD 47, para 43.4).

After provisionally assessing the bill, the court will send a notice in Form N253, setting out the amount of costs the court proposes to allow, as well as the bill of costs to the solicitor (r 47.17(6); PD 47, para 43.5). If the solicitor accepts the amount of costs allowed on provisional assessment, he must complete the bill by entering the correct figures allowed in respect of each item, recalculate the summary of the bill in accordance with what was allowed, and file it along with a completed Community Legal Service Assessment Certificate in Form EX80A (PD 47, paras 43.5, 43.9). If the solicitor does not accept the provisional assessment, he may ask for a detailed assessment.

Detailed assessment of CLS costs

Where the solicitor has certified that the LSC funded client or assisted person with an interest in the outcome wishes to attend an assessment hearing, the court will fix a date for a hearing on receipt of the solicitor's request (r 47.17(4)).

The court will also fix a date for an assessment hearing if the solicitor informs the court within 14 days after he has received a provisionally assessed bill that he wants the court to hold such a hearing (r 47.17(7)). The court will give at least 14 days' notice of the time and place of the detailed assessment hearing to the solicitor and, if appropriate, the solicitor's client (PD 47, para 43.7).

CLIENT'S APPLICATION FOR DETAILED ASSESSMENT OF SOLICITOR'S BILL

In certain circumstances, a client can apply to the court for a detailed assessment of his solicitor's bill under s 70 of the Solicitors Act (SA) 1974. In respect of non-contentious business, the client can challenge the bill by way of detailed assessment, unless he has entered into a non-contentious business agreement with his solicitor under s 57 of the SA 1974. In respect of contentious business, the client can challenge the bill by way of detailed assessment, unless he has entered into a contentious business agreement with his solicitor under s 59 of the SA 1974 (see Chapter 4, 'Funding Litigation').

Solicitor and client costs are assessed on the indemnity basis, so proportionality will not be an issue. There is a presumption that costs were reasonably incurred if they were incurred with the express or implied approval of the client, and that the costs are reasonable in amount if their amount was expressly or impliedly approved by the client. However, if costs are of an unusual nature or amount and the solicitor did not warn his client that, as a result, he might not recover them from his opponent, they are presumed to have been unreasonably incurred. These presumptions may be rebutted by evidence to the contrary (r 48.8(2); PD 48, para 54.2).

Regard should be had to the Solicitors' Practice (Costs Information and Client Care) Amendment Rules 1998, which amended r 15 of the Solicitors' Practice Rules (both available on the Law Society website: www.lawsoc.org.uk) by requiring a solicitor to keep the client informed about costs, with updating at regular intervals (at least every six months). Solicitors are prohibited from recovering any shortfall from their clients in fast track matters as far as fixed trial costs (r 46.2) are concerned, unless there is a written agreement with the client that they may do so (s 74(3) of the SA 1974).

Where the court disallows any amount of the percentage increase of a conditional fee agreement following summary or detailed assessment, the legal representative may apply for an order that the disallowed amount should continue to be payable by his client (r 44.16).

Procedure for assessment

If the court makes an order for the assessment of costs payable to a solicitor by his client, the solicitor must serve a breakdown of costs on his client within 28 days of the order. The client can then serve points of dispute, but must do so within 14 days after service on him of the breakdown of costs. If the solicitor wishes to serve a reply, he must do so within 14 days of service of the points of dispute. Either party can file a request for a hearing date after points of dispute have been served, but no later than three months after the date of the order for costs to be assessed (r 48.10). Reference should be made to PD 48, para 56, for details of the procedure.

In respect of any item of costs relating to proceedings in the county court, the solicitor can recover an amount of costs from his client greater than that which his client could have recovered from another party to the proceedings only if the solicitor and client have entered into a written agreement which permits this (s 74(3) of the SA 1974; r 48.8(1A)).

APPEALS FROM DECISIONS IN DETAILED ASSESSMENT PROCEEDINGS

Right to appeal decision of authorised court officer

Any party to detailed assessment proceedings (apart from an LSC funded client or an assisted person) may appeal the decision of an authorised court officer without leave and by following the procedure laid down in r 47.20 and PD 47, para 47. An authorised court officer is an officer of a county court, a district registry or the Principal Registry of the Family Division or the Supreme Court Costs Office who has been authorised to assess cost (r 43.2).

Court hearing appeal

An appeal from the authorised court officer is to a costs judge or a district judge of the High Court (r 47.21).

Procedure for appealing

If a party wishes to appeal, he must file a notice of appeal in Form N161 along with a record of the judgment appealed against within 14 days after the date of the decision he wishes to appeal. The court will then serve a copy of the notice on the parties involved in the detailed assessment proceedings, and give notice of a date for the appeal hearing to those parties (r 47.22; PD 47, para 48.1).

Court's powers on hearing an appeal

On hearing an appeal from an authorised court officer, the court will rehear the proceedings that gave rise to the decision appealed against, and make any order and give any directions it considers appropriate (r 47.23).

Appeal from a costs judge or district judge

Permission is required to appeal the decision of a costs judge or a district judge, and the appeal will be to a High Court judge. Such an appeal and all other appeals from decisions made in detailed assessment proceedings, apart from decisions made by an authorised court officer, must follow the general procedure for appeals set out in Part 52 (r 47.20).

FIXED COSTS

In certain circumstances set out in Part 45, an amount of costs is specified to be recoverable in respect of solicitor's costs. On making an order for costs, if fixed costs are applicable, there is a presumption that only those costs will be payable and the court will not assess the costs. However, the court has the power to make a different order and may, for instance, order that the costs be assessed instead (r 45.1). The relevant tables in Part 45 should be consulted for details of the amount of costs allowed.

Circumstances where fixed costs payable

Where a party claims a *specified* sum of money (which exceeds £25) and he obtains:

- judgment in default under r 12.4(1);
- judgment on an admission under r 14.4(3);
- judgment on a part admission under r 14.5(6);
- summary judgment under Part 24;
- an order striking out the other party's defence under r 3.4(2)(a) as disclosing no reasonable grounds for defending the claim;
- judgment for delivery of goods where the value of the claim exceeds £25 and this was the only claim and the court gave a fixed date for the hearing on issuing the claim,

the party is entitled to recover an amount of fixed commencement costs, fixed costs on entry of judgment and certain other fixed costs in relation to solicitor's charges in bringing the claim as well as any appropriate court fee (r 45.1). This rule also applies where a judgment creditor has taken steps under Parts 70–73 to enforce a judgment. The fixed costs can be added to the judgment debt.

Also, a defendant will be able to limit his liability to pay only fixed commencement costs, and no other costs, if either:

(a) the claimant claims a specified amount of money which the defendant pays within 14 days after service of particulars of claim on him, as long as he also pays the fixed commencement costs at the same time; or

(b) the claimant claims a specified sum of money and the defendant makes a Part 36 payment into court within 14 days after service of the particulars of claim on him in satisfaction of the whole claim and the claimant accepts it.

However, the court can order that the defendant pay more than those fixed commencement costs in appropriate circumstances (r 45.3).

Fixed commencement costs

In order to recover the fixed costs, they must be specifically claimed. The claim form includes a section into which an amount for fixed commencement costs may be inserted. The amount that can be claimed is regulated by tables set out in Part 45 which provide different levels of costs depending on the value of the claim and the method of service used to serve the claim form. If the court served the claim form, or the claimant served it by a method other than personal service, a lower amount is allowed than if the claimant effected personal service on the defendant (r 45.2).

Fixed costs on entry of judgment

Where the claimant has claimed fixed commencement costs in his claim form, in certain circumstances the claimant may also recover fixed costs on entry of judgment as well as the fixed commencement costs. Those circumstances are where the claimant is able to enter judgment:

- in default of an acknowledgment of service under r 12.4(1);
- in default of a defence under r 12.4(1);
- on an admission under r 14.4 or a part admission under r 14.5 and the claimant accepts the defendant's proposals for payment;
- on an admission under r 14.4 or part admission under r 14.5 and the court decides the date and times of payment;
- following a successful application for summary judgment under Part 24 or the striking out of a defence under r 3.4(2)(a);
- on a claim for delivery of goods under a regulated agreement within the meaning of the Consumer Credit Act 1974.

The amount of the fixed costs on entering judgment is based on an ascending scale in the above order, with different amounts given for each circumstance, depending on the amount of the claim (r 45.4).

Miscellaneous fixed costs

Part 45 also provides an additional amount of fixed costs for a case where there is a requirement that a party serve a document personally, where service by an alternative method is carried out under r 6.8, and where a document is served out of the jurisdiction (r 45.5).

Fixed costs in small claims

If a claim is allocated to the small claims track, a party is unable to recover his legal costs from his opponent even if successful as a result of the operation of the so called 'no costs rule' (r 27.14). However, if the successful party is the claimant, the court can award him fixed commencement costs at the rate set out in Part 45, as well as the court fees paid by the claimant (PD 45, para 24).

COSTS PAYABLE UNDER A CONTRACT

Where the court assesses (whether by the summary or detailed procedure) costs that are payable by the paying party to the receiving party under the terms of a contract (for example, mortgages or leases), the costs payable under those terms are, unless the contract expressly provides otherwise, to be presumed to be costs which have been reasonably incurred and are reasonable in amount, and the court will assess them accordingly (r 48.3(1)). This rule does not apply where the contract is between a solicitor and his client (r 48.3(2)).

Practice Direction 48, para 50.1, provides that the court may make an order that all or part of the costs payable under the contract shall be disallowed if the court is satisfied by the paying party that costs have been unreasonably incurred or are unreasonable in amount.

In *Gomba Holdings UK Ltd v Minories Finance Ltd (No 2)* [1992] 3 WLR 723, it was acknowledged that an order for the payment of costs of proceedings by one party to another party is always a discretionary order (s 51 of the Supreme Court Act 1981). However, the Court of Appeal held in that case that where there is a contractual right to the costs, the discretion should ordinarily be exercised so as to reflect that contractual right.

In *Gomba Holdings*, the Court of Appeal held that a mortgagee is not to be deprived of a contractual or equitable right to add costs to the security, merely by reason of an order for payment of costs made without reference to the mortgagee's contractual or equitable rights, and without any adjudication as to whether or not the mortgagee should be deprived of those costs.

Gomba Holdings was followed in *Fairview Investments v Sharma* (1999) LTL, 9 November, a case that involved proceedings for forfeiture under s 146 of the Law of Property Act 1925, by a landlord against a tenant for breach of covenant. The tenant's lease contained a standard clause in which the tenant agreed to pay all of the landlord's expenses, including solicitors' costs, arising out of the service of a notice under s 146 and related proceedings. The Court of Appeal held that the court's discretion should, in such cases, ordinarily be exercised so as to reflect the landlord's contractual right to costs. Further, those costs should be assessed on the indemnity basis given that the covenant specified that the tenant was to be liable for *all* of the landlord's expenses.

In mortgage possession matters, should the lender not ask for assessment then he is entitled to his costs as of right if the mortgage document so provides, without the court conducting an assessment (*Gomba Holdings*).

PRE-ISSUE FIXED RECOVERABLE COSTS

For road traffic accident disputes arising after 6 October 2003, a Fixed Recoverable Costs Scheme has been introduced, commonly known as 'predictable costs'. The scheme applies to road traffic accident disputes which settle before issue of proceedings and which involve personal injury, personal injury and vehicle damage, and vehicle damage only, where the claim is above the small claims limit and the total damages do not exceed £10,000, including general and special damages and interest, but excluding VAT. The scheme was brokered by the Civil Justice Council, which dealt with submissions from representatives from personal injury lawyers and those from the insurance industry. Details on the background to the scheme may be found on the Civil Justice Council website (www.costsdebate.civiljusticecouncil.gov.uk).

In cases covered by the scheme, the fixed recoverable costs consist of recoverable base costs of £800 plus an amount in costs equivalent to (i) 20% of the damages up to £5,000; and (ii) 15% of the damages from £5,000 to £10,000. The fixed recoverable costs operate on a sliding scale, for example, damages of £7,523 will result in recoverable costs of £2,178.45 calculated as follows: £800 base costs plus 20% of £5,000 (£1,000) and 15% of £2,523 (the remaining amount above £5,000) (£378.45).

The fixed recoverable costs apply to all cases within the definition, except that a party can apply for costs to be assessed if there is an exceptional reason not to apply the scheme (CPR Part 45, Section II).

COSTS-ONLY PROCEEDINGS

A new rule, r 44.12A, was introduced to deal specifically with the issue of costs where a dispute is compromised without the need for proceedings. Therefore, where the parties have settled a dispute before proceedings have been started and have reached agreement, which is made or confirmed in writing, on all issues, *including which party is to pay costs*, but the parties cannot agree the amount of those costs, either party may start costs-only proceedings by issuing a claim form in accordance with Part 8.

In *Bensusan v Freedman* (2001) LTL, 6 November, Senior Costs Judge Hurst gave general guidance on costs-only proceedings. He said that if a claimant is forced to commence proceedings under Part 7, rather than costs-only proceedings under Part 8, the defendant will find himself having to pay not only the reasonable and proportionate costs of the claim itself, but also the costs of the Part 7 proceedings and any related assessment proceedings. Further, if the defendant acts unreasonably in compelling the commencement of Part 7 proceedings, the court will consider making an order for costs on the indemnity basis.

Contents of the claim form

The Part 8 claim form must:

(a) identify the claim or dispute to which the agreement to pay costs relates;

(b) state the date and terms of the agreement on which the claimant relies;

(c) attach a draft of the order which the claimant seeks; and

(d) state the amount of costs claimed and whether they are claimed on the standard or indemnity basis.

The Part 8 claim form must be accompanied by a copy of the compromise agreement, and copies of documents on which the claimant relies to prove the defendant's agreement to pay costs must be filed and served along with the claim form (PD 44, paras 17.3, 17.4).

Once the time period for the defendant to file an acknowledgment of service has expired, the claimant can request that an order be made in the terms of his claim by sending a letter to the court to this effect, and the court will make the order unless the defendant has filed an acknowledgment of service indicating that he intends to contest the claim or seek a different order (PD 44, para 17.6).

The court has the power either to make an order for costs, or to dismiss the claim. The order for costs will be for an amount to be decided by detailed assessment (PD 44, para 17.8(1)).

The court must dismiss the claim if it is opposed. The defendant can oppose the claim by filing an acknowledgment of service stating that he intends to contest the proceedings or seek a different remedy. As soon as such an acknowledgment of service is filed, the court will dismiss the claim (PD 44, para 17.9(1)(a)). However, a claim will not be treated as opposed if the defendant files an acknowledgment of service stating that he disputes the amount of the claim for costs (PD 44, para 17.9(1)(b)).

If the claim is dismissed, the claimant can issue a claim form under Part 7 or Part 8 to sue on the agreement made in settlement of a dispute where the agreement makes provision for costs (PD 44, paras 17.9, 17.11). In order to avoid the defendant being able to contest the application, the party in whose favour the agreement to pay costs is made should ensure that the terms of the settlement include an agreement by the paying party that the amount of costs will be decided by detailed assessment if not agreed.

The nature of costs-only proceedings

Costs-only proceedings involve two distinct steps: first, the Part 8 application seeking an order for costs; and, secondly, detailed assessment of those costs. The intention is that the costs-only proceedings should be brought with the consent of both parties as a simple and convenient means of assessing the costs of the claim where there is a dispute. If the defendant's acknowledgment of service indicates that the application is not opposed, or a consent order is filed, the court may make an order for costs without a hearing.

Senior Costs Judge Hurst also stated in *Bensusan v Freedman* (2001) LTL, 20 September, that in no circumstances should a district judge or costs judge hear the costs-only application and then immediately embark upon a summary assessment of the costs in dispute, because a summary assessment should be made only by a judge who has decided the substantive issues. In costs-only proceedings the only issue decided by the judge is whether or not there should be a detailed assessment of the costs.

Once an order for assessment is made, where the claim for costs includes a success fee of a conditional fee agreement, or an additional amount under a collective conditional fee agreement and/or an after the event legal expenses insurance premium, when assessing the costs the costs judge or district judge should have regard to the time when and the extent to which the claim has been settled and to the fact that the claim has been settled without the need to commence proceedings (PD 44, para 17.8(2)).

Cost of the costs-only proceedings

Where costs-only proceedings are started, either party can make a r 47.19 offer to settle the claim for costs. If the offer is not accepted the court will take the offer into account on the question of the costs of the costs-only proceedings. When considering the costs of the costs-only proceedings, the court must take all the circumstances into account, including the conduct of the parties (r 47.18(2)).

In *Crosbie v Munroe* [2003] EWCA Civ 350, the parties settled a road traffic accident claim without the need to start proceedings. The settlement included an agreement for the defendant to pay the claimant's costs but the amount of the costs could not be agreed and the claimant commenced costs-only proceedings. The claimant accepted the defendant's r 47.19 offer to settle the costs of the claim. The claimant subsequently requested that the defendant pay the claimant's costs of the costs-only proceedings, and failing this indicated that he would seek summary assessment of those costs. At first instance the court held that the defendant's offer to settle the costs of the claim included the costs of the costs-only proceedings. The issue for the Court of Appeal was the meaning of the phrase in r 47.19, 'a written offer to settle the costs of the proceedings which gave rise to the assessment proceedings', in the context of costs-only proceedings. The Court of Appeal held that the 'costs of the proceedings' related only to the costs leading up to the disposal, on this occasion by agreement, of the substantive claim. Accordingly, the issue of the costs of the costs-only proceedings was still outstanding. The court observed that if the costs judge or district judge considers that the receiving party should have accepted an offer made before the Part 8 proceedings commenced, he would be likely to conclude that the paying party should receive all his costs, including any costs involved in the subsequent costs-only proceedings pursuant to r 47.18(2).

CHAPTER 36

DISCONTINUANCE

INTRODUCTION

If a party starts proceedings that for any reason he does not wish to continue, the proceedings can be discontinued in accordance with Part 38. In most cases a claimant will be able to discontinue as of right, but in certain circumstances he must seek the court's permission to discontinue. Where a claimant discontinues, the general rule is that he is liable to pay the defendant's costs up to the time of discontinuance, but the court has a discretion to make a different order.

There is no similar provision for a defendant to discontinue a defence. If a defendant wishes to withdraw a defence, he should make an admission on which a judgment can be entered.

ABANDONING REMEDIES

If a claimant claims more than one remedy in proceedings, such as a money remedy and an injunction, if he wishes to abandon one of those remedies but continue seeking the other remedies, he is not treated as discontinuing his claim (r 38.1). In those circumstances, the claimant should follow the procedure to amend a statement of case under Part 17 in order to abandon the remedy.

In the light of the provisions relating to costs of proceedings, and in particular the court's power to make costs orders that reflect how successful the parties have been, the claimant should give consideration to abandoning a remedy at an early stage if time and costs will need to be spent by the parties in dealing with it, where a claimant believes he will be unsuccessful in achieving it at trial.

DISCONTINUANCE

A claimant may discontinue all or part of a claim at any time, but in some circumstances the court's permission is needed (r 38.2). The same considerations as to the potential costs implications of continuing with an unsustainable claim apply as referred to above in relation to the abandonment of a remedy.

Discontinuance without the permission of the court

In most circumstances, all the claimant needs to do is to file a notice of discontinuance at court and a copy on every other party in order to discontinue the proceedings (rr 38.2(1) and 38.3(1)). Court Form N279 must be used and the notice must state that the claimant has served notice of discontinuance on every other party to the proceedings (r 38.3(2); PD 4, para 3.1).

Multiple defendants

Where there is more than one defendant, the claimant may discontinue all or part of the claim against all or any of the defendants (r 38.2(3)). The notice of discontinuance must specify against which defendants the claim is discontinued (r 38.3(4)).

Multiple claimants

Where there is more than one claimant to the claim, a claimant may not discontinue unless every other claimant consents in writing, or the court gives permission (r 38.2(c)). In these circumstances, a copy of the written consent of the other claimant(s) must be attached to the notice of discontinuance (r 38.3(3)).

Date when discontinuance takes effect

Discontinuance takes effect on the date that the notice of discontinuance is served on the defendant (r 38.5(1); *Jarvis plc v PricewaterhouseCoopers* (2000) *The Times*, 10 October, Ch D). Proceedings will be brought to an end against the defendant on that date, unless the defendant applies to have the notice set aside (r 38.5(2)).

Discontinuance of part of a claim

If the claimant discontinues *part* of a claim, he will only be liable for the costs of the part of the proceedings which he discontinues. The court will not usually assess these costs until the conclusion of the rest of the proceedings (r 38.6(2)).

However, if in these circumstances the parties agree a sum as to costs that the claimant should pay, or the court does in fact order the costs to be paid before the conclusion of the proceedings, the court may stay the remainder of the proceedings until the claimant pays those costs (r 38.8).

Discontinuance with the court's permission

A claimant needs the court's permission to discontinue all or part of a claim in respect of which:

(a) the court has granted an interim injunction;

(b) any party has given an undertaking to the court; or

(c) the claimant has received an interim payment (unless the defendant who made the interim payment consents in writing) (r 38.2(2)(a) and 38.2(2)(b)).

If a court has ordered an interim injunction, or a party has given an undertaking to the court, in the light of the fact that the party obtaining the injunction or undertaking must give an undertaking as to damages if it turns out that the injunction or undertaking was unjustified, permission must be applied for to discontinue the claim, or part of the claim to which it relates, so that the court can discharge the order and make any orders on the undertaking as to damages which might be appropriate.

However, where there are a number of defendants and the claimant obtains an interim injunction against some of the defendants only, the claimant does not need permission to discontinue in respect of a defendant against whom an injunction has not been obtained (*KGM v Generali-Kent Sigorta AS* (2002) LTL, 30 September).

If an interim payment has been made and a claimant subsequently abandons his claim, the court has the power to order repayment, and so the court's permission must be obtained to abandon proceedings in these circumstances.

Where the claimant needs the court's permission to discontinue all or part of the claim, he should make an application in accordance with Part 23.

Right to have notice of discontinuance set aside

If a claimant discontinues proceedings, the defendant can apply, within 28 days of service of the notice of discontinuance on him, to have the notice of discontinuance set aside (r 38.4). This provision gives the court a wide discretion to consider whether discontinuance may cause injustice to the defendant. The defendant should make any application in accordance with Part 23.

In *Gilham v Browning* [1998] 2 All ER 68, a case decided by Lord Woolf under the former rules, the Court of Appeal upheld the judge's order that the counterclaiming defendants' notice of discontinuance of the counterclaim (now known as a Part 20 claim) was an abuse of process and should be set aside. The judge had previously ordered that the defendants could not adduce further evidence in the proceedings because of delay and the prejudice that would be caused to the claimant. The defendants served the notice of discontinuance with the admitted purpose of getting around the court's order disallowing the evidence, by abandoning their counterclaim before it had been adjudicated upon, so that they might start new proceedings in which the disallowed evidence could be called. Lord Woolf was of the opinion in this case that the notice of discontinuance was plainly an abuse of process. The counterclaiming defendants were seeking to use the court process to obtain a collateral advantage which it would be unjust for them to obtain, 'that is to escape by the side door from the first action where their counterclaim was evidentially hopeless in order to start a new action where the evidential problems would not arise, and in circumstances where a long overdue date for trial of the first action was fixed and imminent'.

In *Gilham*, Lord Woolf recognised that the court's jurisdiction to strike out for abuse would be used sparingly and only in plain cases where there had been a misuse of the court's process. However, he also emphasised that the court's power to do so was not constrained by fixed categories of circumstances and would instead be a question of fact and degree in a particular case.

Costs of the proceedings

The usual price a claimant pays for discontinuing all or part of a claim against the defendant is that he must pay the defendant's costs of the proceedings incurred up to the date of discontinuance (r 38.6(1)). The defendant will be automatically entitled to costs, unless the court orders otherwise; and when the claimant discontinues, a costs order will be deemed to have been made in the defendant's favour on the standard basis (r 44.12) to be assessed by detailed assessment if not agreed (r 44.7).

However, the court may deprive a defendant of his costs, or even order him to pay the claimant's costs when the claimant discontinues, if, for instance, the claimant has obtained an advantage from suing the defendant. In *R (Chorion plc) v Westminster CC* [2002] EWCA Civ 1126, the claimant brought proceedings for judicial review for an order quashing the council's policy in respect of public entertainment and late café licences. After proceedings had begun the council resolved to change its policy in such a way as to address the main complaint of the claimant. As a result, the claimant applied to discontinue its claim and was granted an order that the defendant council pay its costs, on the grounds that the claimant had achieved the principal relief it had sought against the council.

Other circumstances that may justify a discontinuing claimant recovering his costs from the defendant are where the claimant has obtained an injunction against the defendant and does not wish to pursue any further claim for damages.

The court's power to make a costs order different to the usual order that the claimant pay the defendant's costs when he discontinues is not limited to particular circumstances, the court having a discretion to make an order in accordance with the justice of the case. In *Everton v WPBSA (Promotions) Ltd* (2001) LTL, 17 December, the court held that it was just and reasonable for the claimant to discontinue his claim against the defendant with no order as to costs. The claimant brought libel proceedings against four defendants. The claimant agreed terms of settlement with the first three defendants. In the meantime the fourth defendant was involved in related libel proceedings brought by another party, as a result of which the fourth defendant went bankrupt.

The fourth defendant argued that if it discontinued, the claimant should pay its costs of the claim, because the fact that the claimant wished to discontinue showed that the claim should not have been brought against the fourth defendant in the first place. The fourth defendant also argued that it had a viable defence to the claimant's claim, which had not been adjudicated upon or dismissed. However, the court held that in the unusual circumstances of the case the claimant was allowed to discontinue with no order as to costs. The discontinuance could not be equated with defeat or an acknowledgment of likely defeat: although the defence had not been shown to be unviable, neither had the claimant's claim against the defendant been shown to be unviable. The court found that the reality was that the claimant had been compelled to abandon his claim against the fourth defendant because it had become worthless, through no fault of the claimant but rather by reason of the supervening bankruptcy of the fourth defendant.

The usual order when a claimant discontinues is that the costs payable to the defendant are assessed on the standard basis. However, the court has a discretion to order costs on an indemnity basis where such an order is justified (*Naskaris v ANS plc* [2002] EWHC 1782; *Atlantic Bar & Grill Ltd v Posthouse Hotels Ltd* [2000] CP Rep 32, Ch D; *Shaina Investment Corp v Standard Bank London Ltd* (2001) LTL, 12 November, Ch D). In *Naskaris*, where the claimant discontinued his claim, the court ordered him to pay the defendant's costs on an indemnity basis for part of the proceedings because of the claimant's unreasonable behaviour. The claimant had made unreasonable attempts to obtain an adjournment of the trial, had rendered himself inaccessible in the critical period up to commencement of the trial, and failed to co-operate with the defendant in preparations for the trial.

If a claim has been allocated to the small claims track, as there is usually no liability to pay an opponent's costs, even if unsuccessful, the provisions on deemed costs orders on discontinuance are specifically excluded (r 38.6(3)). Therefore, where a claim is allocated to the small claims track, the 'no costs' regime will apply, save for any pre-allocation costs and any allegations of unreasonable behaviour pursuant to r 27.14(2)(d).

Subsequent proceedings

If a claimant discontinues proceedings at any stage after the defendant has filed a defence, he will need to seek the permission of the court to make another claim against the same defendant arising out of the same, or substantially the same, facts as those relating to the discontinued claim (r 38.7). The same applies if only part of a claim is discontinued – the balance of the claim may be stayed until the costs of the discontinued part are paid (r 38.8). This is what happened in *Stevens v School of Oriental and African Studies* (2001) *The Times*, 2 February, a case in which the court held that it was not inconsistent with the right to a fair and public hearing under Art 6 of the European Convention on Human Rights for the court to exercise its discretion to prevent further litigation over the same area until the costs occasioned by the original unsuccessful attempt have been paid. The court said that the claimant can indeed pursue the defendant once, but if he fails, and in particular if the claim is struck out, then he may not pursue it again until he has put the defendant back in the position he was before the original claim started by paying his costs.

Although the claimant must seek permission to start fresh proceedings in these circumstances, as there has been no judgment in the original proceedings, the defence of issue estoppel or *res judicata* will not be available in relation to the subsequent proceedings. This will not be the case if the parties have compromised the claim and the claimant discontinues the proceedings. In such circumstances, the defendant will be able to rely on the existence of the contract of compromise to strike out any fresh proceedings as an abuse of process under r 3.4.

However, it is likely that in most cases, the court will consider it an abuse of process to commence fresh proceedings after discontinuing the first, and strike out the subsequent proceedings under r 3.4. The court may also decide, by analogy with the cases on striking out for delay, not to allow the subsequent claim to proceed on the grounds that when applying the overriding objective and considering the interests of all court users, it would not be an appropriate use of court resources to allow a claimant to bring a fresh claim based on the same or substantially the same facts as the discontinued claim.

CHAPTER 37

APPEALS

INTRODUCTION

The introduction of Part 52 on appeals has been described as bringing about 'the most significant changes in the arrangements for appeals in civil proceedings in this country for over 125 years' (*Tanfern v Cameron-MacDonald* [2000] 1 WLR 1311; [2000] 2 All ER 801, *per* Brooke LJ). In general terms these reforms mean that the decision of a judge hearing a first instance appeal takes on much greater importance than it did under the former rules, as now most such appeals will consist of a review rather than a rehearing. Also, in most cases permission to appeal is required, and there is no appeal against a refusal to grant permission made at an oral hearing. Further, the scope for making a second tier appeal is severely restricted; only the Court of Appeal can give permission for a second appeal, and then only when it is satisfied that it involves an important point of principle or practice, or there is some other compelling reason for such an appeal.

In *Tanfern v Cameron-MacDonald*, Brooke LJ warned that litigants and their advisers must pay even greater attention to the need to prepare their cases with appropriate care because, with the reforms to the appeals procedure, they may find it much more difficult to extricate themselves from the consequences of an ill-prepared case before a judge at first instance in a lower court.

Part 52 has unified and simplified the process of appealing which, prior to its introduction, was quite complex with different rules for appeals to different courts.

Scope of Part 52

Part 52 applies to appeals to the civil division of the Court of Appeal, the High Court and a county court (r 52.1(1)). However, the rules as to appeals in Part 52 do not apply to an appeal against a detailed assessment of costs carried out by an authorised court officer (r 52.1(2)). The appeals procedure does apply to all other orders made by judges, including against summary or detailed assessment of costs. Appeals to the House of Lords are governed by a separate procedure (see pp 600–01 below, 'Appeals to the House of Lords').

Part 52 also applies to statutory appeals, that is, rights of appeal specified by statutes governing the operation of a variety of bodies, for example, tribunals, disciplinary and appeals committees of professional bodies (PD 52, para 17.2). However, the requirement under r 52.3 to obtain permission to appeal will not apply to such appeals, unless such permission is already required by the statute in question (*Colley v Council for Licensed Conveyancers* [2001] EWCA Civ 1137).

DESTINATION OF APPEALS

The destination of appeals is governed by the Access to Justice (Destination of Appeals) Order 2000 (SI 2000/1071) (DO 2000). As a general rule, an appeal lies to the next level of judge in the court hierarchy. Therefore, in the county court, an appeal lies from a district judge to a circuit judge, and from a circuit judge to a High Court judge. In the High Court, an appeal lies from a Master or district judge to a High Court judge, and from a High Court judge to the Court of Appeal.

However, the normal route of appeal will not be followed where a district judge or a circuit judge in the county court, or a Master or district judge of the High Court, gives a *final decision* in a Part 7 claim allocated to the multi-track (PD 52, para 2A.2(a)). Also, the normal rule will not apply to specialist proceedings under the Companies Acts 1985 or 1989, or to those to which Sections I, II, or III of Part 57, or any of Parts 58–63 apply (PD 52, para 2A.2(b)). In those circumstances, an appeal lies to the Court of Appeal (Art 4 of the DO 2000).

For second appeals, under Art 5 of the DO 2000, any appeal that was made on an appeal to a county court or the High Court can only be appealed to the Court of Appeal. However, this does not apply to a decision of a court officer authorised to assess costs.

Where a party applies for permission to appeal at the High Court, in circumstances where it is quite obvious that a High Court judge has no jurisdiction to hear the appeal, it will be rejected summarily. Since its rejection is in essence an administrative act (because the court has no jurisdiction) there will not be any kind of reasoned judgment (*Slot v Isaac* [2002] EWCA Civ 481).

In *Slot v Issac*, the claimants appealed to a circuit judge against a case management decision of a district judge. The circuit judge refused the appeal without a hearing. However, rather than exercise their right to request that the circuit judge reconsider his decision at an oral hearing, the claimants sought to appeal his decision to a High Court judge. The claimants' application was summarily dismissed by the High Court on the grounds that it had no jurisdiction to hear it.

Final versus interim decision

A final decision is one that would finally determine the entire proceedings, subject to any possible appeal or detailed assessment of costs, whichever way the court decided the issues before it (Art 1(2)(c) of the DO 2000). A final decision includes the assessment of damages or any other final decision where it is 'made at the conclusion of part of a hearing or trial which has been split up into parts and would, if made at the conclusion of that hearing or trial, be a final decision' (Art 1(3) of the DO 2000). It does not include a decision only on costs.

However, it does mean that if a judge makes a final decision on any aspect of a claim, such as limitation, or on part of a claim which has been directed to be heard separately, this is a final decision within the meaning of this provision. When determining whether a decision made at the conclusion of a trial of a preliminary issue is a final decision, a commonsense test should be applied, namely, whether the issue would have formed a substantive part of the final trial, even if it does not end the claim entirely (*Roerig v Valiant Trawlers Ltd* [2002] EWCA Civ 21; [2002] 1 WLR 2304; [2002] 1 All ER 961).

On the other hand, orders striking out the proceedings or a statement of case, and orders giving summary judgment under Part 24 are not deemed to be final decisions because they are not decisions that would finally determine the entire proceedings whichever way the court decided the issues before it (*Tanfern Ltd v Cameron-Macdonald*). Appeals against such orders should therefore be made to the next level of judge in the court hierarchy in accordance with general principles.

Leap-frog appeals

Where, under the general rules, an appeal would lie to a circuit judge or a High Court judge, but it is considered that the appeal raises an important point of principle or practice, or there is some other compelling reason, the lower court or the appeal court may order the appeal to be transferred directly to the Court of Appeal instead (r 52.14(1)).

Where certain conditions are satisfied and a point of law of general public importance is involved in a decision of the High Court which either:

(a) relates wholly or mainly to the construction of an enactment or of a statutory instrument and has been fully considered by the High Court in its judgment; or

(b) is a point in respect of which the judge is bound by a decision of the Court of Appeal or of the House of Lords and which was fully considered in previous proceedings;

the High Court may grant a certificate allowing a party to appeal directly to the House of Lords. A certificate of the High Court must be obtained and the leave of the House of Lords given before the leap-frog appeal may proceed (s 12 of the Administration of Justice Act 1969).

PERMISSION TO APPEAL

With very few exceptions permission is required to appeal from a judge's decision in a county court or the High Court (r 52.3).

In the case of a committal order, a refusal to grant habeas corpus, or a secure accommodation order made under s 25 of the Children Act 1989, because the liberty of the subject is in issue, permission is not required and appeal lies as of right. Rule 52.3 also specifies that practice directions may provide for other types of claim where permission is unnecessary, but currently no such practice directions are in force.

However, the requirement under r 52.3 to obtain permission to appeal does not apply to statutory appeals unless the requirement to obtain permission is already required by the statute in question (*Colley v Council for Licensed Conveyancers*).

Obtaining permission to appeal

An application for permission to appeal may be made either to the lower court at the hearing at which the decision to be appealed was made, or to the appeal court (r 52.3(2)). Parties should make an oral application for permission to appeal at the hearing at which the decision they wish to appeal against is made (PD 52, para 4.6). However, if no such application is made, or if the lower court refuses permission to appeal, an application for permission to appeal may be made to the appeal court (r 52.3(2), (3); PD 52, para 4.7).

In most cases the application for permission to appeal to the appeal court will be dealt with on paper without a hearing (PD 52, para 4.11). However, where the appeal court refuses permission to appeal without a hearing, the person seeking permission has the right to request that the decision be reconsidered at a hearing (r 52.3(4); PD 52, para 4.13).

A request for the decision to be reconsidered at a hearing must be filed at court within seven days after service of the notice stating that permission has been refused (r 52.3(5)). However, the appeal court has power under r 3.1(2)(a) to extend the seven-day period for requesting an oral hearing (*Slot v Issac*).

Respondent's response to application for permission to appeal

In many cases, unless the court directs otherwise, notice of the hearing of the appellant's application for permission to appeal will not be given to the respondent. However, the court will usually notify the respondent of the hearing if the appellant is asking for a remedy against the respondent pending the appeal, such as a stay of the order of the lower court (PD 52, para 4.15).

Practice Direction 52, para 4.22, specifies that, in most cases, applications for permission to appeal will be determined without the court requiring submissions from or, if there is an oral hearing, attendance by the respondent.

In *Jolly v Jay* [2002] EWCA Civ 277, the Court of Appeal gave general guidance on the respondent's role at this early stage where permission to appeal is being sought. The court said that the respondent should file submissions at this early stage only if they are addressed to the point that the appeal would not meet the relevant threshold test for the granting of permission. Alternatively, if there is some material inaccuracy in the papers placed before the court that might reasonably be expected to lead the court to grant permission when it would not have done so if it had received the correct information on the point.

Further, where the application for permission is to be determined on paper, any submission from the respondent must be in writing. In the event of an oral hearing, a respondent should consider whether he can make his submissions equally well in writing, particularly as he may not be allowed his costs of attending the hearing. In any event the respondent will have no entitlement to address the court unless the court has made a specific written direction that he may do so, or grants him permission to do so at the hearing.

However, the Court of Appeal said in *Jolly v Jay* that if the respondent wishes to advance submissions on the merits of the substantive appeal, the appropriate time for him to do so is at the appeal itself, if permission is granted. The rationale for this guidance is that it is not desirable for the respondent to make submissions on the merits of the substantive appeal at the permission stage, because this may lead to delay in dealing with the permission application and take up the resources of the court unnecessarily if permission is not in fact granted.

It should be borne in mind that if the respondent is present at the hearing at which permission to appeal was granted, he is not entitled to apply subsequently for an order that the court exercise any of its powers under r 52.9(1)(b) to set aside permission to appeal, or under r 52.9(1)(c) to impose or vary conditions upon which an appeal may be brought (r 52.9(3)).

Respondent's costs of the application for permission to appeal

Where the court does not request submissions from or attendance by the respondent, costs will not normally be allowed to a respondent who volunteers submissions or attendance (PD 52, para 4.23). However, where the court does request submissions from or attendance by the respondent, or attendance by the respondent with the appeal to follow if permission is granted, the court will normally allow the respondent his costs if permission is refused (PD 52, para 4.24). The award of costs will, in accordance with usual practice, be a matter for the discretion of the individual judge (*Jolly v Jay*).

Granting of permission to appeal

Permission to appeal will be given only where:

(a) the court considers that an appeal has a real prospect of success; or

(b) there is some other compelling reason why the appeal should be heard (r 52.3(6)).

In the context of an application for summary judgment, Lord Woolf defined the word 'real' as meaning a realistic rather than a fanciful prospect of success (see *Swain v Hillman* [2001] 1 All ER 91). In *Tanfern Ltd v Cameron-MacDonald*, the Court of Appeal said that the same definition would apply to whether an appeal had a real prospect of success.

Permission subject to conditions

When granting permission to appeal the court may make it subject to conditions (r 52.3(7)(b)).

It is clear from r 52.3(7) and r 3.1(3) that the Civil Procedure Rules (CPR) contemplate that one of those conditions may be that a sum of money is paid into court (*Hammond Suddard Solicitors v Agrichem International Holdings Ltd* [2001] EWCA Civ 1915).

Limit of issues to be heard on appeal

The order giving permission to appeal may limit the issues to be heard on appeal (r 52.3(7)(a)). If the court does limit the issues to be raised on appeal, it will expressly refuse permission to appeal in respect of any remaining issues. However, the court may instead limit the issues to be raised on appeal but reserve the question of permission to appeal on any remaining issues to be decided by the court hearing the appeal.

If the court takes this alternative course, the appellant must, within 14 days after service of the court's order, inform the appeal court and the respondent in writing whether he intends to pursue the reserved issues. The parties must then include, in any time estimate for the appeal hearing, their time estimate for the reserved issues (PD 52, paras 4.18, 4.19).

Refusal of permission to appeal

If the appeal court refuses permission to appeal without a hearing, the parties will be notified of that decision with the reasons for it. The appellant is entitled to have the decision reconsidered at an oral hearing. This may be before the same judge (PD 52, para 4.13). If permission to appeal is refused after an oral hearing, no further right of appeal exists and the party's avenues of appeal are exhausted (s 54(4) of the Access to Justice Act 1999; PD 52, para 4.8). The terms of s 54(4) are clear and the Court of Appeal does not retain an inherent, non-statutory jurisdiction to hear appeals whenever it is necessary to correct errors in the court below (*Riniker v University College London* [2001] 1 WLR 13; however, see pp 598–99 below, 'Re-opening an appeal').

Although there is an opportunity (subject to stringent restrictions) to make an application for a second tier appeal of a decision made by a county court or the High Court which was itself made on appeal, there is no opportunity to make a further application for permission to appeal following the refusal of permission by an appeal court after an oral hearing. The Court of Appeal has made it clear that it has no jurisdiction to hear the latter and the Civil Appeals Office will not waste court resources by listing such applications (*Jolly v Jay*).

However, where permission to appeal is refused following an oral application, the appellant is entitled to make an application for permission to appeal against the order for costs made by the judge on the hearing for permission, or some other ancillary order such as an order refusing an adjournment made on that occasion. An appeal against such an order is a 'first appeal' and follows the usual appeal route (*Jolly v Jay*). The same rationale applies to a refusal by the court to extend time for making an appeal (*Foenander v Bond Lewis & Co* [2001] EWCA Civ 759).

Appeal against a case management decision

Separate considerations apply to whether the court will give permission to appeal against a case management decision. Appeals against such decisions are discouraged because they can unduly disrupt the progress of the case and incur disproportionate cost. Therefore, where the application is for permission to appeal against a case management decision, the court dealing with the application may take into account whether:

(a) the issue is of sufficient significance to justify the costs of an appeal;

(b) the procedural consequences of an appeal (for example, loss of trial date) outweigh the significance of the case management decision;

(c) it would be more convenient to determine the issue at or after trial (PD 52, para 4.5).

'Case management decisions' are defined as decisions made under r 3.1(2) (general case management matters) and decisions about:

• disclosure;

• filing of witness statements or experts' reports;

• directions about the timetable of the claim;

- adding a party to a claim;
- security for costs (PD 52, para 4.4).

Legally aided and Legal Services Commission (LSC) funded parties

If the appellant is in receipt of services funded by the Legal Services Commission (or legally aided) and permission to appeal has been refused by the appeal court without a hearing, the appellant must send a copy of the appeal court's reasons for refusing permission to the LSC or Legal Aid Board as soon as they are received from the court. The court will require confirmation that this has been done if a hearing is requested to reconsider the question of permission (PD 52, para 4.17).

PROCEDURE FOR APPEALING

A party should make an oral application for permission to appeal to the lower court at the end of the hearing at which the decision to be appealed against is made (r 52.3(2); PD 52, para 4.6). However, if this is not done, the party wishing to appeal must make an application for permission to appeal to the appeal court in an *appeal notice* filed at court 14 days after the decision of the lower court which is to be appealed (rr 52.3(2), 52.4(2)(b); PD 52, para 4.7).

Rule 52.2 specifically provides that all parties to an appeal must comply with the relevant practice direction. Practice Direction 52 deals with the procedure that should be followed. There are additional provisions in PD 52 specified for appeals to the Court of Appeal, as well as other practice directions issued by the Court of Appeal.

The appellant's notice

An appellant's notice in Form N161 must be filed and served in all cases. Where an application for permission to appeal is made to the appeal court, it must be applied for in the appellant's notice (PD 52, para 5.1).

The appellant must file with the appellant's notice the documents specified in para 5.6 of PD 52 ('the appeal bundle') unless the appeal relates to a claim allocated to the small claims track (r 52.2; PD 52, para 5.6). Practice Direction 52, para 5.6, should be consulted for details, but the appeal bundle includes such documents as:

- copies of the appellant's notice for the court and the respondent;
- skeleton argument;
- a sealed copy of the order being appealed;
- the order giving or refusing permission to appeal with a copy of the reasons for that decision;
- any witness statement or affidavits in support of any application included in the appellant's notice; and
- any other documents which the appellant reasonably considers are necessary to enable the appeal court to reach its decision (PD 52, para 5.6(7)).

In order to accommodate the difficulties which a 14-day time limit (see below) might present in difficult cases, PD 52, para 5.7, provides that where it is not possible to file all the documents required by para 5.6, the appellant must indicate which documents have not yet been filed and the reasons why they are not currently available. Although this provision allows an appellant additional time to obtain all the relevant documents (for instance, transcripts of the judgment which might not be available yet), as the appellant has to explain why the document is not available it still puts the appellant under pressure to file all the necessary documentation as soon as reasonably practicable.

Time limits for appealing

Unless the lower court directs otherwise, the appellant must file the appellant's notice at the appeal court 14 days after the date of the decision of the lower court that the appellant wishes to appeal (r 52.4(2)(b)). This time limit of 14 days (unless the court orders otherwise) applies to all appeals made in accordance with Part 52. However, there may be different periods of time for specialised areas, and applicable statutes should be consulted. For instance, there is a 21-day time limit for appeals against a decision under s 204 of the Housing Act 1996.

The time limit for appealing a decision runs from the date the decision is given and not from the date when the order containing the decision is drawn up (*Sayers v Clarke-Walker* [2002] EWCA Civ 645).

Record of lower court's judgment

Where the judgment to be appealed has been officially recorded by the court, an official transcript of that record should accompany the appellant's notice, photocopies will not be accepted (PD 52, para 5.12). However, if an appellant is unrepresented and he can satisfy the lower court or the appeal court that he has such poor financial circumstances that the cost of obtaining an official transcript would place an excessive burden on him, the court can certify that the cost of obtaining the official transcript will be borne at public expense (PD 52, para 5.17).

Where there is no official transcript of the lower court's judgment, PD 52 sets out what will constitute a suitable record of that judgment. If there is a written judgment endorsed with the judge's signature this should be provided. Otherwise the parties should submit their notes of the judgment to the judge who made it for his approval (PD 52, para 5.12).

It should be noted that if an official transcript of the judgment is not available at the time that the appellant submits his appellant's notice, he must still file and serve his appeal notice within the specified time limits, completing it to the best of his ability on the basis of the available documents. However, the court may give permission to amend the appeal notice if need be once the transcript is available (PD 52, para 5.13).

In *Tanfern v Cameron-MacDonald*, Brooke LJ emphasised that in respect of appeals, the importance of the decision at first instance gave added weight to the need for all such decisions to be recorded accurately so that the appeal court is able to read a reliable version of the judgment it has to review. He referred to the fact that under PD 39, para 6.1, a judgment must be recorded unless the judge directs otherwise, and said that if a judge is anxious to spare a party of limited means the cost of obtaining an approved transcript, he must take steps to ensure that there is an incontrovertibly accurate record of the judgment.

In *Plender v Hyams* [2001] 1 WLR 32; [2001] 2 All ER 179, Brooke LJ stressed that it was of vital importance to take steps to obtain a note or transcript of the judge's reasons as soon as the decision is taken to seek permission to appeal, as it will often take some time to obtain. He warned that unless the appeal court is able to consider the judge's reasons for making the order under challenge, it will not be able to grant the appellant any relief at all, whether by stay of the order appealed against or otherwise.

Appeals from small claims decisions

Where the appeal is of a judgment or order made in a claim allocated to the small claims track, the appellant need only file the following documents:

(a) a sealed copy of the order being appealed;

(b) any order giving or refusing permission to appeal with a copy of the reasons for that decision; and

(c) (if so ordered by the appeal court) a suitable record of the reasons for the judgment of the lower court (PD 52, paras 5.8A, 5.8C, 5.8D).

However, if an appellant so wishes, he may also file any other document listed in PD 52, para 5.6 (PD 52, para 5.8B).

For appeals relating to small claims matters, the appellant is obliged to file a suitable record of the reasons for the judgment of the lower court only if so ordered by the appeal court in order to enable it to decide if permission should be granted, or in order to decide the appeal (PD 52, para 5.8D).

Application for an extension of time for filing an appeal notice

A party applying for permission to appeal after the hearing of the decision he wishes to appeal may ask the lower court to extend the time within which he is to file the appellant's notice at court (r 52.4(2)(a)). If the court refuses to extend time, or if no order is made regarding time limits for filing the appellant's notice, the provisions in r 52.4(2)(b) apply.

An application for a variation of time to file the appeal notice must be made to the appeal court (r 52.6(1)). The parties have no power to agree to extend the deadline for filing the appeal notice, whether made by the lower court or applied by the CPR (r 52.6(2)). The application for an extension of time must be made in the appellant's notice. The notice should state the reason for the delay and the steps taken prior to the application being made (PD 52, para 5.2).

Where permission to appeal is given, or the appellant does not need permission, and the appellant's notice of appeal includes an application for an extension of time for filing the appeal notice, the respondent has a right to be heard on that application and a copy of the appeal bundle must be served upon him. However, respondents are expressly warned that if they unreasonably refuse the appellant's application for an extension of time, they run the risk of being ordered to pay the appellant's costs of that application (PD 52, para 5.3).

The appeal court has a general power under r 3.1(2)(a) to extend the time for filing the appeal notice, even if the application for an extension is made after the time for compliance has expired. In deciding how to exercise that power the court must take into account the overriding objective.

In *Sayers v Clarke-Walker* [2002] EWCA Civ 645, Brooke LJ was of the opinion that in many cases a judge will be able to decide whether to extend or shorten the period of time for filing the appellant's notice without undue difficulty after considering the reasons for the delay and the steps taken prior to the application being made. However, he stated that in more complex cases, a more sophisticated approach is required. In cases of any complexity it is therefore appropriate for the court to have regard to the checklist in r 3.9 when considering an application for an extension of time. Brooke LJ explained that the reason for this was that the appellant has not complied with r 52.4(2), and if the court is unwilling to grant him relief from his failure to comply through the extension of time he is seeking, the consequence will be that the order of the lower court will stand and he cannot appeal it. The effect of this would be exactly the same as if this was a sanction expressly imposed by r 52.4(2).

Where a court decides, in the exercise of its discretion, to grant or refuse an extension of time for filing the appeal notice, that order can be appealed in the same way as any other decision by a judge (*Foenander v Bond Lewis & Co* [2001] EWCA Civ 759). In *Foenander*, the Court of Appeal commented that when the appeal court has the choice of disposing of a belated and unmeritorious appeal either by refusing to extend time for appealing or by refusing permission to appeal, it should bear in mind that taking the latter course will bring the appellate proceedings to an end. On the other hand, the adoption of the former course may entail further expense and delay while a challenge is launched at a higher appeal court against the decision not to extend time for appealing (at [19]).

Service of appellant's notice on the respondent

Unless the appeal court orders otherwise, the appellant's notice must be served on each respondent as soon as practicable, and in any event not later than seven days after it is filed (r 52.4(3)).

Where the appellant is applying for permission to appeal in the appellant's notice, there is no requirement at that stage for the appellant to serve the appeal bundle on the respondent. However, if permission has already been given by the lower court, or if permission is not required, the appeal bundle must be served on the respondent with the appellant's notice (PD 52, para 5.24).

The respondent's notice

Unless the court orders otherwise, the respondent need not take any action when served with an appellant's notice until such time as notification is given to him that permission to appeal has been granted (PD 52, para 5.22).

If notice of the hearing for permission to appeal is to be given to the respondent, the appellant must supply the respondent with a copy of the appeal bundle within seven days of being notified, or such other period as the court may direct. The costs of providing that bundle are borne by the appellant initially, but will form part of the costs of the permission application (PD 52, para 4.16).

A respondent who wishes to ask the appeal court to vary the order of the lower court in any way must appeal, and permission will be required on the same basis as for an appellant (PD 52, para 7.1). A respondent who is himself seeking permission to appeal from the appeal court, or who wishes to ask the appeal court to uphold the order of the lower court for reasons different from, or additional to, those given by the lower court, *must* file a respondent's notice (r 52.5(2); PD 52, para 7.3). The respondent's notice should be in Form N162.

If the respondent seeks permission to appeal from the appeal court, this must be requested in the respondent's notice (r 52.5(3)). Otherwise, a respondent has the choice whether or not to file a respondent's notice (r 52.5(1)). A respondent who simply wishes the decision of the lower court to be upheld for the reasons given by the lower court is not obliged to file a respondent's notice, but may do so if he wishes.

However, a respondent who simply wishes to request that the appeal court upholds the judgment or order of the lower court, whether for the reasons given by the lower court or otherwise, is not treated as making an appeal and does not therefore require permission to appeal (PD 52, para 7.2).

Filing and service of the respondent's notice

Where the appellant is given permission to appeal by the lower court, or does not require permission to appeal, the respondent's notice must be filed at court 14 days after the date the respondent is served with the appellant's notice (r 52.5(4), (5)). However, if the appellant has applied to the appeal court for permission to appeal, the respondent must file a respondent's notice 14 days after he is served with notification that the appeal court has given the appellant permission to appeal, or within 14 days after he is served with notification that the application for permission to appeal and the appeal itself are to be heard together (r 52.5(4), (5)). In all cases the above time limits apply unless the court orders otherwise (r 52.5(4)).

Unless the appeal court orders otherwise, the respondent's notice must be served on the appellant as soon as is practicable, and in any event not later than seven days after it is filed at court (r 52.5(6)).

Skeleton arguments

Where an appellant is represented, he must file and serve a skeleton argument in advance of the appeal hearing (PD 52, para 5.9). A respondent who is represented and wishes to address arguments to the court is also obliged to file and serve a skeleton argument (PD 52, para 7.6). However, a respondent to a claim allocated to the small claims track is not obliged to provide a skeleton argument, although he may do so if he wishes (PD 52, para 7.7A).

A litigant in person is not obliged to file a skeleton argument, but is encouraged to do so on the grounds that it would be helpful to the court (PD 52, para 5.9(3)). As there is no requirement to file a skeleton argument, if a litigant in person does not do so this cannot give grounds for dismissing the appeal for non-compliance with Part 52, even if the litigant in person has indicated in his appeal notice that he intends to provide a skeleton argument (*Plender v Hyams* [2001] 1 WLR 32; [2001] 2 All ER 179).

Skeleton arguments may be included within a party's appeal notice, or form a separate document (PD 52, paras 5.9(1), 7.6).

The appellant's skeleton argument should consist of a numbered list of points, stated in not more than a few sentences, which should both define and confine the area of controversy. Each point should be followed by references to any documentation on which the appellant proposes to rely (PD 52, para 5.10). The appellant should also consider what other information should be included to assist the appeal court, such as a chronology or glossary of technical terms. Where an authority is relied upon, the particular pages where the principle concerned is set out should be referred to (PD 52, para 5.11).

The respondent's skeleton argument should be drafted in accordance with the requirements for an appellant's skeleton argument, with any necessary modifications. It should also answer the arguments set out in the appellant's skeleton argument (PD 52, para 7.8).

The appellant's skeleton argument must be filed at the same time as the appeal notice, or, if that is not possible, it must be filed (and served on the respondent) within 14 days of filing the appeal notice (PD 52, para 5.9).

Where the respondent's skeleton argument is not included within his appeal notice, it must be filed and served on the appellant no later than 21 days after the respondent receives the appellant's skeleton argument (PD 52, para 7.7).

Striking out appeal notices and setting aside or imposing conditions on permission to appeal

Where there is a compelling reason to do so, the appeal court may:

(a) strike out the whole or part of an appeal notice;

(b) set aside permission to appeal in whole or in part;

(c) impose or vary conditions upon which an appeal may be brought (r 52.9(1), (2)).

However, where a party was present at a hearing at which permission was given, he may not subsequently apply for an order that the court set aside that permission, or impose or vary any conditions it may have made upon which the appeal may be brought (r 52.9(3)).

Striking out appeal notices/setting aside permission to appeal

Once permission to appeal has been granted, it will only be in rare circumstances that the court will exercise its jurisdiction to strike out an appeal notice or to set aside permission to appeal. Examples where the court may make such an order are if the appeal court has been misled into granting permission to appeal, or some decisive authority or decisive statutory provision has been overlooked by the court granting permission to appeal (see *Nathan v Smilovitch* [2002] EWCA Civ 759; *Barings Bank plc (In Liquidation) v Coopers & Lybrand* [2002] EWCA Civ 1155).

Imposing conditions upon which an appeal may be brought

In *Aoun v Bahri* [2002] EWCA Civ 1141, Brooke LJ said that the strong wording of r 52.9 ('only where there is a compelling reason') reflected the strict tests the Court of Appeal used to apply under the former rules when applications were made of this type. In that case, the lower court made an order that the claimant's claim would be stayed unless he provided security for the defendants' costs of the proceedings within a specified period. The claimant failed to provide the security and the claim was stayed. In the meantime the claimant was granted permission to appeal against the order that he provide security. The defendants made an application under r 52.9 for the claimant's appeal to be stayed until such time as he complied with the lower court's order to provide security for costs.

The Court of Appeal held that there were no special features of the case that would constitute a compelling reason for placing onerous conditions on permitting the progress of the claimant's appeal which he had been granted permission to bring. The claimant had already agreed to provide security for the defendants' costs of the appeal. It would also be odd to order that the claimant must comply with the order to provide security for costs of the lower proceedings, because if his appeal against that order succeeded the order was likely to be set aside or reduced in amount. The court emphasised that the stay of proceedings imposed by the lower court did not stay the proceedings in the Court of Appeal. The claimant's failure to comply with the order of the lower court could not be described as a wholesale disregard of the rules; in fact it had the negative effect that his claim would be stayed if he did not comply. Further, the claimant was entitled to seek permission to appeal, and this had been granted.

In *Hammond Suddard Solicitors v Agrichem International Holdings Ltd* [2001] EWCA Civ 1915, the Court of Appeal held that there were compelling reasons to order that the appellant pay the judgment debt as a condition of permitting it to appeal, and that it was just and in accordance with the overriding objective to make such an order. The court was satisfied that the order would not stifle the appeal, but there was a real risk that if the appeal failed the respondent would be unable to recover the judgment debt and costs from the appellant. The appellant was a company registered in the British Virgin Islands and had no assets in the UK; it would therefore be difficult for the respondent to exercise the normal mechanisms of enforcement against it. The court also took into account that the appellant had failed to provide adequate disclosure of its financial means when making the application.

The Court of Appeal held, in *Bell Electric Ltd v Aweco Appliance Systems GmbH & Co* [2002] EWCA Civ 1501, that the appeal court's discretion to impose or vary conditions upon which an appeal may be brought is unfettered by any provisions specifying the nature of the condition that may be imposed or varied. The only requirement is that the court should be satisfied that there is a 'compelling reason' why it should, for the purpose of doing justice between the parties, intervene in the ordinary progress of the appeal between leave being granted and the date for the hearing of the appeal. It was recognised that as such intervention involves placing a fetter upon the appellant's right to appeal, after permission to appeal has been granted, it will usually be undesirable, as a misuse of court's resources and a waste of costs, for the court to revisit the merits of the grounds of the appeal before the date fixed for their determination. This is why r 52.9(3) provides that a party who was present at the hearing granting permission cannot subsequently apply for an order under r 52.9(1). However, the power to impose or vary conditions upon which an appeal may be brought may be relied upon where the condition sought to be imposed does not involve consideration of the merits of the appeal. This will be the case where the application is based on some aspect of the conduct of the appellant or some other circumstance which had not occurred, or could not be advanced by the respondent, at the time of the grant of permission.

In *Bell Electric Ltd v Aweco Appliance Systems GmbH & Co*, the Court of Appeal ordered that the appellant's appeal would be stayed unless the appellant paid £135,000 into court within 14 days to abide the outcome of the appeal. The court imposed this condition on the grounds of the appellant's deliberate breach of the order to pay the judgment sum. The court also took into account that the appellant had applied for and been refused a stay of execution, and the fact that the appellant's failure to pay the judgment sum was not due to financial difficulty but was cynically based on the practical difficulties for the respondent in seeking to enforce a judgment against the appellant, whose assets were in a foreign jurisdiction.

Procedure after permission to appeal is obtained

Where the appeal court gives permission to appeal, copies of all the relevant documents specified at PD 52, para 5.6 must be served on the respondent within seven days of receiving the order giving permission to appeal (PD 52, para 6.2).

The appeal court will send the parties notification of the date of the hearing or the period of time (the 'listing window') during which the appeal is likely to be heard. In the Court of Appeal, the court will send the parties the date by which the appeal will be heard (the 'hear by date') (PD 52, para 6.3(1)).

Where permission to appeal was granted by the appeal court, it will also send the parties a copy of the order giving permission to appeal and any other directions given by the court (PD 52, para 6.3(2), (3)).

Stay of proceedings of the lower court

An appellant should apply for a stay of the order or judgment of the lower court if necessary, because the making of an appeal will not operate as an automatic stay of the judgment or order of the lower court which can therefore be enforced (r 52.7).

In *Hammond Suddard Solicitors v Agrichem International Holdings Ltd* [2001] EWCA Civ 1915, the court held that it had a discretion whether or not to grant a stay. Also, whether the court should exercise its discretion to grant a stay depends upon all the circumstances of the case, but the essential question is whether there is a risk of injustice to one or other or both parties if it grants or refuses a stay. The Court of Appeal said that the court should consider whether if it refuses a stay the appeal will be stifled because the appellant is unable to pay the judgment sum. On the other hand, if the stay is granted and the appeal fails, the court should consider what risks there are that the respondent will be unable to enforce the judgment. The court should also consider, if a stay is refused and the appeal succeeds but the judgment is enforced in the meantime, what risks there are that the appellant will be unable to recover the moneys paid from the respondent.

In any event, the evidence provided by the appellant in support of an application for a stay needs to be full, frank and clear (*Hammond Suddard Solicitors v Agrichem International Holdings Ltd*).

THE APPEAL HEARING

As a general rule, every appeal is limited to a review of the decision of the lower court, that is, not a *de novo* hearing. However, if a practice direction provides otherwise for a different category of appeal, or if the court considers that in the circumstances of the particular case it would be in the interests of justice to do so, the appeal court may hold a rehearing of the decision (r 52.11(1)).

Appeal court's discretion to hold a rehearing

The Court of Appeal emphasised, in *Audergon v La Baguette Ltd* [2002] EWCA Civ 10, the general rule that appeals at all levels are to be by way of review of the decision of the lower court. A decision to hold a rehearing will be justified only where the appeal court considers that in the circumstances of the individual appeal it is in the interests of justice to do so. The Court of Appeal held that it was undesirable to formulate criteria to be applied by the appeal court when deciding to hold a rehearing. This is because the decision to do so depends on the circumstances of the particular appeal and formulating criteria would in effect re-write the rule in more specific terms, thus restricting the flexibility inherent in the general terms within which the rule is framed.

However, it is clear that the appeal court must have good reason not to follow the general rule and conduct a rehearing rather than a review. A classic example is where there has been a procedural or other irregularity in the lower court. In *Audergon v La Baguette Ltd* (a second tier appeal), the Court of Appeal found that the judge hearing the appeal had no good reason to do so as the Master in the lower court had considered all the relevant evidence. The Court of Appeal held that the judge hearing the appeal had erred in deciding to hold a rehearing, and in the interests of justice the Court of Appeal would therefore conduct a review of the lower court's decision. In reviewing the lower court's decision the Court of Appeal found that there were no grounds on which to set it aside and it was restored.

In *Ansari v Puffin Investment Co Ltd* [2002] EWHC 234, QB, Burton J held that where the lower court has not set out its reasons for its decision at all, or at any length, then it is very difficult to review them. In that case, which was an appeal against an order for summary judgment, Burton J decided that, in the absence of proper reasons, the only way he could decide whether the Master had reached the correct conclusion was to look again at the evidence and therefore hold a rehearing rather than a review. However, this case should be considered in the light of the guidance provided by the Court of Appeal in *English v Emery Reimbold & Strick Ltd* [2002] EWCA Civ 605, as to the course of action a party should take if he wishes to apply for permission to appeal on the grounds that the lower court has failed to give reasons for its decision.

In *Dyson Ltd v Registrar of Trademarks* [2003] EWHC 1062, Ch D, the court said that an appeal from an *ex parte* (without notice) decision is a proper appeal. A review of the original decision is normally sufficient and a rehearing is appropriate only in exceptional circumstances when justice so requires. Article 6 of the European Convention on Human Rights does not require that appeals from *ex parte* decisions are to be conducted as rehearings.

Evidence at the appeal hearing

The appeal court hearing will be based on written evidence (for example, witness statements), not oral evidence, unless the court orders otherwise (r 52.11(2)(a)).

Fresh evidence

Unless the court orders otherwise, the appeal court will not admit evidence that was not before the lower court (r 52.11(2)(b)).

In *Gillingham v Gillingham* [2001] EWCA Civ 906, the Court of Appeal held that the court will exercise its discretion whether to admit new evidence in accordance with the overriding objective. The court will consider all the circumstances of the case, but there is no requirement to show 'special grounds' (the test under the former rules).

The court held that the principles in *Ladd v Marshall* [1954] 1 WLR 1489 remained relevant, not as rules but as matters which must necessarily be considered in an exercise of the discretion whether or not to permit an appellant to rely on evidence not before the court below. The principles in *Ladd v Marshall* that must be taken into account are:

(a) whether the evidence could not have been obtained with reasonable diligence for use at the trial;

(b) whether the further evidence was such that, if adduced, it would probably have an important influence on the result of the case, though it need not be decisive; and

(c) whether the evidence is apparently credible, though it need not be incontrovertible.

In *Gillingham v Gillingham*, the appellant applied for permission to rely upon further evidence which consisted of a letter that the appellant had previously forgotten existed and which was not disclosed by the other party in the proceedings in the lower court. Although the Court of Appeal could not say that the new evidence could not have been obtained with reasonable diligence for use at the trial, it found that the claim could not have been fairly or satisfactorily resolved in the absence of it. Although the court recognised the general principle that finality in litigation is of great importance, in the circumstances and the interests of justice it allowed the appeal, set aside the judge's findings and ordered a new trial. In *Meco Pak AB v Electropaint Ltd* [2001] EWCA Civ 1537, it was held that an appellant cannot succeed on a matter that was not pleaded or argued *inter partes* at first instance, even though it had been addressed in a limited way in a written argument submitted after the close of the oral hearing.

Grounds for appeal

An appeal will be allowed only where:

(a) the decision of the lower court was *wrong*; or

(b) the decision was *unjust* because of a *serious procedural or other irregularity* in the proceedings in the lower court (r 52.11(3)).

Wrong decision

The epithet 'wrong' is to be applied to the substance of the decision made by the lower court. If the appeal is against the exercise of a discretion then the appellate court should interfere only when it considers that the judge in the lower court 'has not merely preferred an imperfect solution which is different from an alternative imperfect solution which the Court of Appeal might or would have adopted, but has exceeded the generous ambit within which a reasonable disagreement is possible' (*Tanfern v Cameron-MacDonald, per* Brooke LJ, quoting with approval Lord Fraser in the House of Lords decision of *G v G* [1985] 1 WLR 647).

Serious procedural or other irregularity

It should be emphasised that the procedural or other irregularity must be a *serious* one that has caused an *unjust* decision (*Tanfern v Cameron-MacDonald*).

Appeals on findings of fact

An appeal court will be reluctant to interfere with a trial judge's findings of primary fact based on the credibility or reliability of oral evidence. However, in *Todd v Adam* [2002] EWCA Civ 509, the Court of Appeal held that the reference in r 52.11(3), (4) to the power of the appellate court to allow an appeal where the decision below was 'wrong' and to 'draw any inference of fact which it considers justified on the evidence', indicated that there are circumstances in which the appeal court must make up its own mind as to the correctness of a decision made by the lower court on matters of fact.

Accordingly, once the appellant has shown a real prospect that a finding or inference is wrong, the role of an appellate court is to determine whether or not this is so, giving full weight to the advantages enjoyed by any judge of first instance who heard oral evidence. This view was endorsed in *Assicurazioni Generali Spa v Arab Insurance Group (BSC)* [2002] EWCA Civ 1642, where the Court of Appeal considered the various ways in which a trial judge may reach conclusions of primary fact. The court distinguished between those situations where the trial judge reached findings of primary fact based almost entirely upon the view which he formed of the oral evidence of the witnesses, and the position in most cases, which was more complex.

In many cases the judge will have analysed documents as well as heard oral evidence. In some cases the findings of primary fact will be based entirely, or almost entirely, on documents. In other cases the findings will be based on direct evidence, whereas in others they will depend upon inferences drawn from the direct evidence. The court therefore concluded that in appeals against conclusions of primary fact, the approach of the appellate court will depend upon the weight to be attached to the findings of the judge, and that weight will depend upon the extent to which, as the trial judge, the judge had an advantage over the appellate court – the greater the advantage, the more reluctant the appellate court to interfere.

Reasoned decision

In accordance with Art 6 of the European Convention on Human Rights, a litigant is entitled to a reasoned decision on an application for permission to appeal and on the hearing of the appeal. On an application for permission to appeal, a judge can be brief in explaining his conclusions. However, it would not be enough merely to say that the application for permission to appeal was dismissed because PD 52 had not been complied with, without specifying in what respects it had not been complied with (*Plender v Hyams*).

In *English v Emery Reimbold & Strick Ltd* [2002] EWCA Civ 605, the Court of Appeal said that it was vital for a judge in the lower court to give reasons for his judgment. If the judgment does not make it clear why a judge has reached his decision, it may well be impossible, within the summary procedure of an application for permission to appeal, to form any view as to whether the judge was right or wrong. This may lead to permission to appeal being given simply because justice requires that the decision be subjected to the full scrutiny of an appeal. However, the court did draw a distinction between a decision that determines the substantive rights between the parties, which fairness (and Art 6) demands should be reasoned, and interim decisions such as case management decisions which do not need to be reasoned, or decisions where the reason for the decision will be implicit from the decision itself, such as a costs order in favour of a successful litigant at the end of a trial.

The court also recommended a course of action to be followed if an application for permission to appeal is made on the grounds that the judge failed to give adequate reasons for his decision, in order to avoid expensive appellate proceedings. Accordingly, if a party makes an application to the trial judge for permission to appeal on the ground of lack of reasons, the trial judge should consider whether his judgment is defective for lack of reasons. If he concludes that it is, he should attempt to remedy the defect by the provision of additional reasons, and refuse to give permission to appeal on the grounds that he has adopted that course.

If the judge concludes that he has given adequate reasons, no doubt he will refuse to give permission to appeal. If an application for permission is made to the appellate court on the grounds of lack of reasons, which seems well founded, the appellate court should consider adjourning the application and remitting the case to the trial judge with an invitation to provide additional reasons for his decision.

Where permission is granted on the grounds that the judgment does not contain adequate reasons, the appellate court should first review the judgment, in the context of the material evidence and submissions at the trial, in order to determine whether it is apparent why the judge reached the decision that he did. If satisfied that the reason is apparent and that it is a valid basis for the judgment, the appeal will be dismissed. However, if despite this exercise the reason for the decision is not apparent then the appeal court will have to decide whether to proceed to a rehearing, or to direct a new trial.

Powers of the appeal court

Every judge hearing an appeal, whether a circuit judge, a High Court judge or the Court of Appeal, has the same powers in relation to appeals. Every appeal court has all the powers of the lower court (r 52.10). The appeal court also has power to:

(a) affirm, set aside or vary any order or judgment made or given by the lower court;

(b) refer any claim or issue for determination by the lower court;

(c) order a new trial or hearing;

(d) make orders for the payment of interest; and

(e) make a costs order (r 52.10(2)).

The appeal court may exercise its powers in relation to the whole or part of an order of the lower court (r 52.10(4)).

Appeal from claim tried with a jury

Where the appeal is from a trial with a jury, for example, false imprisonment or defamation, the appellate court may, instead of ordering a retrial, award damages or vary an order for damages (r 52.10(3)).

Disposing of appeals by consent

The appellate court can dispose of an appeal, that is, dismiss it, by consent unless the appellant is a child or patient (PD 52, paras 12.1–12.4). Similarly, the appellate court can allow an appeal on the basis that the lower court was wrong and that both parties agree that the lower court was wrong, but not where one of the parties is a child or patient (PD 52, para 13.1).

Second tier appeals

Part 52 introduced a major reform to the procedure for appeals by restricting the scope of second tier appeals. As a general rule the decision of the appeal court on the first appeal will be the final decision. A second tier appeal will be allowed only where:

(a) the appeal raises an important point of principle or practice; or

(b) there is some other compelling reason for the Court of Appeal to hear it (s 55 of the Access to Justice Act 1999).

The reason for this reform was that in the interests of certainty, reasonable expense and proportionality, it was felt that there must be special circumstances before there could be more than one level of appeal. It was also felt that judges of the quality of the Lords Justices of Appeal were a scarce and valuable resource. It was therefore important that they were used effectively by being freed to devote more of their time and energy to hearing first appeals in more substantive matters which either their court, or a lower court, had assessed as having a realistic prospect of success (see *Review of the Court of Appeal (Civil Division)* (available at www.dca.gov.uk/civil/bowman/bowfr.htm)).

In *Tanfern v Cameron-MacDonald*, Brooke LJ commented that all courts are familiar with the litigant, often unrepresented, who will never take 'no' for an answer, however unpromising his cause. He said that now, under Part 52, if such litigants wish to pursue the matter further and incur the often quite heavy costs involved in paying the court fee and preparing the appeal papers, the Court of Appeal may dismiss their application quite shortly, saying that the appeal raises no important point of principle or practice, and that there is no other compelling reason for the court to hear the appeal.

Reopening an appeal

It is a general principle that where judgment has been given, either in a court of first instance or on appeal, the successful party ought, save in the most exceptional circumstances, to be able to assume that the judgment is a valid and effective one (*In Re Barrell Enterprises* [1973] 1 WLR 19 at 23H–24A, *per* Russell LJ). However, the Court of Appeal, as an appellate court, has the implicit power to do whatever is necessary to achieve the dual objectives for which it was established. The first of these is the private objective of correcting wrong decisions so as to ensure justice between the litigants involved. The second is the public objective to ensure public confidence in the administration of justice not only by remedying wrong decisions, but also by clarifying and developing the law and setting precedents. This inherent power allows the Court of Appeal to reopen proceedings after they have been heard and determined where there are exceptional circumstances in order to avoid real injustice (see judgment of Lord Woolf CJ in *Taylor v Lawrence* [2002] EWCA Civ 90 at [26]).

In *Taylor v Lawrence*, Lord Woolf recognised that there is a tension between a court having a residual jurisdiction to reopen judgments and appeals and the need to have finality in litigation. However, this tension is resolved by ensuring that proceedings are reopened only when there is a real requirement for this to happen. An example of where this might occur is where the court that made the decision was biased. If bias is established there would be a breach of natural justice. In order to maintain confidence in the administration of justice it is imperative that there should be a remedy. Another example is where judgment has been obtained by fraud.

Lord Woolf held that before the Court of Appeal is justified in taking the exceptional course of re-opening proceedings, it should be clearly established that significant injustice has probably occurred and that there is no alternative effective remedy. Further, where the alternative remedy would be an appeal to the House of Lords, the Court of Appeal will give permission to reopen an appeal only if it is satisfied that the House of Lords would not give leave for an appeal from the Court of Appeal (at [55]).

Lord Woolf set out the procedure that a party should follow who is seeking to re-open an appeal. A party seeking to reopen a decision of the Court of Appeal, whether refusing permission to appeal or dismissing a substantive appeal, must apply in writing for permission to do so. The application will be considered on paper and allowed to proceed only if the Court of Appeal so directs after considering the paper application. Further, there will be no right to an oral hearing of the application unless the Court of Appeal so directs. Lastly, Lord Woolf exhorted the Court of Appeal to exercise strong control over any such application so as to protect those who are entitled to believe that the litigation is at an end (at [56]). Lord Woolf commented that 'in due course the Civil Procedure Rules Committee may wish to consider whether rules or a practice direction setting out the procedure should be introduced', which has now been brought into effect by the introduction of Part III to Part 52, r 52.17.

The High Court similarly possesses an inherent jurisdiction to reopen its decisions if it is clearly established that a significant injustice has occurred and there is no alternative effective remedy (*Seray-Wurie v Hackney LBC* [2002] EWCA Civ 909).

There is currently no decision as to whether the county courts have similar powers to reopen their decisions. In *Seray-Wurie v Hackney LBC*, the Court of Appeal expressly stated that nothing in its judgment should be interpreted as having any effect in relation to reopening decisions made by circuit judges sitting as an appeal court in the county court. Indeed, in *Gregory v Turner* [2003] EWCA Civ 183, the Court of Appeal commented that given the tendency of a significant number of unsuccessful litigants in person to refuse to take 'no' for an answer, the work of circuit judges in the county courts would be very badly disrupted if any such jurisdiction existed. The court in that case also referred to information showing that over the course of a 12-month period, more than 200 applications were made to the Court of Appeal seeking to invoke the exceptional *Taylor v Lawrence* jurisdiction, but none of these applications had been granted (at [28]).

Judicial review of county court decisions

Section 54(4) of the Access to Justice Act 1999 (which prevents any further right of appeal from a refusal of permission to appeal if made after an oral hearing) does not oust the jurisdiction of the High Court to judicially review decisions made by circuit judges in the county courts to grant or refuse permission to appeal (*R (Sivasubramaniam) v Wandsworth County Court* [2002] EWCA Civ 1738). However, in *Sivasubramaniam*, Lord Phillips made it clear that the jurisdiction would be exercised only in those rare cases where the jurisdiction of the circuit judge could be challenged on the ground of a procedural irregularity of such a kind as to constitute a denial of the applicant's right to a fair trial (at [56]). This is because s 54(4) provides a litigant with fair, adequate and proportionate protection against the risk that a district judge may have acted without jurisdiction or fallen into error (at [54]).

In *Gregory v Turner* [2003] EWCA Civ 183; [2003] 1 WLR 1149; [2003] 2 All ER 114, the claimants were refused permission by the circuit judge to appeal the district judge's findings in a trial heard on the small claims track. The Court of Appeal strongly criticised the district judge for the way she dealt with the proceedings. It found that the district judge's case management decisions, including her inappropriate allocation of the case to the small claims track and her refusal to allow any oral evidence or cross-examination of witnesses, meant that there was in effect no proper hearing of the claimants' evidence. Under s 54(4) of the 1999 Act there was no right of appeal against the circuit judge's refusal to grant permission to appeal. Although the Court of Appeal had doubts about the circuit judge's reasoning, it found that this was as a result of the way the appeal had been presented to him. Further, there was no basis on which it could be said that there had been a fundamental departure from the correct procedure so as to justify judicial review of the circuit judge's decision.

On behalf of the other judges in the Court of Appeal, Brooke LJ accepted that the claimants 'may well be concerned to learn that we consider that this is the end of the road, despite our serious concern that something may have gone wrong in connection with the district judge's handling of the case', but found that this was the effect of the circuit judge's decision and 'of Parliament's decision not to permit any appeal against that decision'. The Court of Appeal also referred to Lord Woolf's views in his Interim Report, where he recognised the tensions that exist between a desire to achieve perfection and a desire to achieve a system of justice which is not inaccessible to most people on grounds of the time and cost involved (at [46]).

Part 36 offers and payments

A party to appeal proceedings can make a Part 36 offer or payment to protect his position in respect of the costs of the appeal proceedings (r 36.2(4)). Where a Part 36 offer or payment is made, the same principles apply as in respect of the first instance proceedings, including the fact that the Part 36 offer or payment must not be disclosed to any judge of the appeal court who is to hear and finally determine an appeal until all questions (other than to do with the costs of the appeal) have been determined (r 52.12(1)). However, if the Part 36 offer or payment is relevant to the appeal proceedings then the rule about non-disclosure to the appeal court will not apply (r 52.12(2), (3)).

If a claimant makes a Part 36 offer in respect of first instance proceedings which the defendant seeks to appeal, the claimant must make a separate Part 36 offer in respect of the appeal proceedings in order to obtain the benefits of Part 36 for the appeal proceedings. A party cannot make a 'portmanteau' offer which would provide him with protection both at first instance and on a subsequent appeal (*P & O Nedlloyd BV v Utaniko Ltd* [2003] EWCA Civ 174).

COSTS OF APPEAL

Costs are likely to be assessed by way of summary assessment at the following hearings:

- contested directions hearings;
- applications for permission to appeal at which the respondent is present;
- dismissal list hearings in the Court of Appeal at which the respondent is present;
- appeals from case management decisions; and
- appeals listed for one day or less (PD 52, para 14.1).

Thus, parties attending an appeal in any of the above circumstances must be prepared for a summary assessment. Where summary assessment does not take place, it is to be presumed that the court will order a detailed assessment.

APPEALS TO THE HOUSE OF LORDS

The procedure for making an appeal to the House of Lords when sitting in its judicial capacity is governed by Standing Orders of the House of Lords regulating judicial business (made under s 11 of the Appellate Jurisdiction Act 1876) and by practice directions.

An appeal lies to the House of Lords from any order or judgment made or given by the Court of Appeal only with the leave of the Court of Appeal or the House of Lords (s 1(1) of the Administration of Justice (Appeals) Act 1934). An application for leave to appeal to the House of Lords must first be made to the Court of Appeal at the end of the hearing before the Court of Appeal. If an application is not made at that time it must be made by written application to the Registrar of Civil Appeals. If the Court of Appeal refuses leave to appeal, an application may be made to the House of Lords by way of petition for leave to appeal (para 1.2, Practice Directions and Standing Orders applicable to Civil Appeals, November 2002).

For details of the time limits and other aspects of the procedure relating to appeals to the House of Lords reference must be made to the Practice Directions and Standing Orders applicable to Civil Appeals, November 2002. See also p 581 above, 'Leap-frog appeals', for provisions relating to appeals from the High Court directly to the House of Lords.

CHAPTER 38

JUDICIAL REVIEW

INTRODUCTION

Part 54, containing the rules applicable to judicial review, came into force on the same date as the commencement of the Human Rights Act 1998 – 2 October 2000. This is no coincidence, and although applications to challenge the actions of public authorities will continue to be by way of judicial review, they will now have the extra consideration of compatibility with the European Convention on Human Rights (ECHR). Judicial review is used to challenge the lawfulness of an enactment or a decision, action or omission by a public authority and, therefore, is fertile ground for 'vertical' challenges under the Human Rights Act 1998. Part 54 claims are dealt with by the Administrative Court instead of the Divisional Court in the Crown Office List, as under the former rules. The claimant should comply with the Pre-Action Protocol for Judicial Review before bringing proceedings for judicial review.

THE NATURE OF JUDICIAL REVIEW

A full account of the principles of judicial review is outside the scope of this book and readers are referred to Hilaire Barnett's *Constitutional and Administrative Law*, 4th edn, 2002, London: Cavendish Publishing (5th edn due 2004). In broad terms, a claim for judicial review lies against an inferior court or tribunal (that is, a court below a court of the Supreme Court), or any person or body performing public duties or functions (for example, local authorities). A claim for judicial review is a claim to review the lawfulness of an enactment or a decision, action or failure to act in relation to the exercise of a public function (r 54.1(2)).

The duty or function performed must be one of a public nature and must relate to an issue of public law rather than private law rights (*R v East Berkshire HA ex p Walsh* [1985] QB 152).

Judicial review does not involve a review of the merits of the decision made or the exercise of discretion, it being concerned instead with the lawfulness of the decision-making process itself. The grounds for judicial review are that in reaching, or failing to reach, a decision, the public body concerned has made an error of law, or there is procedural impropriety, or the decision is irrational or the public body has abused its power.

The remedies granted by judicial review are known as prerogative orders. Under s 31(1) of the Supreme Court Act 1981 (SCA), the prerogative orders are those of mandamus, prohibition and certiorari. Under r 54.2, the Latin terms for the prerogative orders are replaced with the terms 'mandatory order' (mandamus), 'prohibiting order' (prohibition) and 'quashing order' (certiorari). The court also has the power to grant a declaration or an injunction instead of or in addition to one of the other remedies in a claim for judicial review (r 54.3; s 31(2) of the SCA).

A claimant may also claim damages in addition to a claim for one of the prerogative remedies or a claim for an injunction or declaration. However, a claimant cannot bring a claim just for damages in a claim for judicial review. Further, a claim for damages will lie only if it could have been brought in ordinary proceedings, or in order to afford just satisfaction under Art 41 of the ECHR where there has been a breach of a Convention right. In *R v Enfield LBC ex p Bernard* [2002] EWHC 2282, the court made a mandatory order compelling the local authority to provide properly adapted accommodation for a severely disabled woman and her family. The court also upheld the claimants' contention that the defendant's conduct had been in breach of Art 8 of the ECHR (right to respect for private and family life) and awarded the claimants £10,000 in just satisfaction under Art 41 of the ECHR for the defendant's breach of the claimants' Convention rights.

As the duty or function challenged is of a public nature, there are often other interested parties who must be served with a copy of the claim form. For example, in a decision by a county council under the Commons Registration Act 1965 to register land as a town or village green, if the landowner brings judicial review proceedings against the county council, the community which benefits from the registration of the land as a town or village green would be an interested party, and any body representing it should therefore be served with a copy of the claim form.

The procedure for judicial review is designed to protect public authorities by means of a short time limit for bringing claims and by the imposition of a requirement for permission before a claim can be brought.

Circumstances in which judicial review is the appropriate remedy

It was established in the House of Lords, in *O'Reilly v Mackman* [1983] 2 AC 237, that as a general rule it was contrary to public policy, and as such an abuse of process of the court, to permit a person to bring an action against a public authority in respect of public law rights by way of an ordinary action, and thereby evade the rules of court for judicial review proceedings which are designed to protect public authorities. However, there are exceptions to this general rule, for example, where a case based in contract raises a collateral public law issue.

In *Clark v University of Lincolnshire and Humberside* [2000] 3 WLR 752; [2000] 3 All ER 752, Sedley LJ said that the single most important difference between judicial review and a civil claim is the differing time limits. Accordingly, he was of the opinion that to permit what is in substance a public law challenge to be brought as of right up to six years later, if the relationship also happens to be contractual, would circumvent the valuable rules of court for judicial review proceedings. These rules stipulate that applications for leave must be made promptly, and in any event within three months of when the grounds arose, unless time is extended by the court. However, the courts today will be flexible in their approach. Where the defendant is a public body and the decision challenged is one of a public law nature, the claimant should normally bring proceedings for judicial review under Part 54, unless there is an alternative remedy (*R v Home Secretary ex p Swati* [1986] 1 WLR 477, CA; *R v Birmingham CC ex p Ferrero Ltd* [1993] 1 All ER 530, CA; *R v Home Secretary ex p Capti-Mehmet* [1997] COD 61). If the proceedings are based on the contract between the claimant and the public body, they do not have to be brought by way of judicial review (*Clark v University of Lincolnshire and Humberside, per* Lord Woolf).

If proceedings of a type that would normally be brought by judicial review are instead brought by bringing an ordinary claim, the court, in deciding whether the commencement of the proceedings is an abuse of process, can take into account whether there has been unjustified delay in initiating the proceedings. Where a claimant has a claim in contract, the court will not strike out a claim that could more appropriately be made under Part 54 solely because of the procedure that has been adopted. It may do so, however, if it comes to the conclusion that in all the circumstances, including the delay in initiating the proceedings, there has been an abuse of the process of the court (*Clark v University of Lincolnshire and Humberside, per* Lord Woolf).

In the case of *R v Bedfordshire CC ex p Henlow Grange Health Farm Ltd* [2001] EWCA Admin 179, Bedfordshire County Council passed a resolution to grant planning permission to developers who owned a site adjacent to the claimant's property. However, the resolution was ineffective because the Secretary of State called in the application for his determination pursuant to s 77 of the Town and Country Planning Act 1990. In the meantime, the claimant had made an application for permission to seek judicial review of the council's resolution. Following the exercise by the Secretary of State of his powers to determine the application, the claimant amended its claim to seek a declaration that certain matters, which the council had considered relevant to its decision, were irrelevant matters and should not be considered by the Secretary of State when he made his decision. The court held that this was an inappropriate use of judicial review and was effectively a pre-emptive application for an advisory declaration as to the matters that the Secretary of State, who was not even a party to the proceedings, might or might not take into consideration in reaching a future decision on the planning application. The court also took into account that there was in place a comprehensive statutory code governing the decision making process in planning applications that should be followed, and this was also a reason for its refusing to entertain an application for judicial review.

The courts have made it clear that they should not permit (except for good reason) proceedings for judicial review to go ahead if a significant part of the issues between the parties can be resolved outside the litigation process. In *Frank Cowl and Others v Plymouth CC* [2001] EWCA Civ 1935, which involved an application for judicial review of a council's decision to close a residential care home for the elderly, Lord Woolf criticised the claimants for failing to take up an offer from the council to settle their dispute through a statutory complaints panel. Lord Woolf said, 'Today sufficient should be known about alternative dispute resolution to make the failure to adopt it, in particular when public money is involved, indefensible' (see also Chapter 6, 'Judicial Case Management: The Overriding Objective', for further cases about alternative dispute resolution).

Homelessness appeals

Challenges to the performance by a local authority of its obligations to house the homeless under the Housing Act 1996 used to be dealt with by way of judicial review. Now, any challenge is by way of an appeal to a circuit judge at the county court under s 204 or s 204A of the 1996 Act, not least because of the large number of cases.

PROCEDURE FOR APPLYING FOR PERMISSION TO BRING A CLAIM FOR JUDICIAL REVIEW

Pre-Action Protocol for Judicial Review

The claimant should comply with the requirements of the Pre-Action Protocol for Judicial Review before making an application for permission to bring a claim for judicial review (see Chapter 5, 'Pre-Action Protocols', for details of the Protocol). However, compliance with the Pre-Action Protocol is not a reason for failing to comply with the three-month time limit for bringing a claim for judicial review. Therefore, if the time limit is close to expiry, the claimant should issue an application for permission rather than comply with the Pre-Action Protocol. However, the claimant should be prepared to explain to the court why the Pre-Action Protocol was not complied with.

Requirement for permission

A claim for judicial review is a two-stage process. The claimant must first obtain permission from the court to bring a claim for judicial review. The requirement for permission applies even if the claim was not originally started in accordance with Part 54 (r 54.4).

The requirement for permission allows the court to filter out unmeritorious, frivolous and vexatious claims, and is designed to protect public bodies from having their proper functions interrupted by misconceived proceedings for judicial review (*R v Inland Revenue Commissioners ex p National Federation of Self-Employed and Small Businesses Ltd* [1982] AC 617, *per* Lord Diplock).

The court has a discretion to refuse to grant permission to bring a claim for judicial review. The court may, for instance, refuse to grant permission if there has been undue delay in bringing the claim, or if the claimant has an alternative adequate remedy (see p 604 above, 'Circumstances in which judicial review is the appropriate remedy').

The Administrative Court

A claim for judicial review must be brought in the Administrative Court at the Royal Courts of Justice in London or Wales (PD 54, para 2.1). Most claims will be brought in the Administrative Court at the Royal Courts of Justice. However, where the claim or any remedy sought involves a devolution issue, or an issue concerning the National Assembly for Wales, the Welsh executive or any Welsh public body, it may be brought in the Administrative Court in Wales. Such a claim may also be brought in the Royal Courts of Justice (PD 54, para 3.1).

Where the claim is being brought in the Royal Courts of Justice, the claim form and relevant documents must be filed at the Administrative Court Office, the Royal Courts of Justice, Strand, London WC2A 2LL. Where the claim is proceeding in the Administrative Court in Wales the address is the Law Courts, Cathays Park, Cardiff, CF10 3PG (PD 54, paras 2.2, 2.3).

Time limit for filing a claim form

In order to protect public bodies from the uncertainty of having a potential claim for judicial review hanging over them and interfering with the discharge of their public functions, the claim form must be filed promptly, and in any event not later than three months after the grounds to make the claim first arose (r 54.5(1)). In ascertaining when the claim first arose, the court will look at the substance, rather than the form, of what is being challenged (*R v Secretary of State for Trade and Industry ex p Greenpeace* [1998] Env LR 415). Where the claim is for a quashing order in respect of a judgment, order or conviction, the time limit runs from the date of that judgment, order or conviction (PD 54, para 4.1).

The time limit may not be extended by agreement between the parties (r 54.5(2)). However, the court has a discretion under r 3.1(2)(a) to extend the time for compliance with the time limit, which it will exercise in accordance with the overriding objective.

Under s 31(6) of the SCA, where there has been undue delay in making an application for judicial review, the court may refuse to grant leave for making the application, or refuse the relief sought, if it considers that the granting of relief would be likely to cause substantial hardship to, or substantially prejudice the rights of, any person, or would be detrimental to good administration.

If another enactment specifies a shorter time limit for making a claim for judicial review, that shorter time limit must be complied with instead (r 54.5(3)).

Contents of the claim form

The claim form must contain the same information as is required for Part 8 claims, but must also contain the additional information required by r 54.6 (r 54.6(1)). Although not expressly referred to in PD 54, Form N461 is the claim form specified for claims for judicial review by PD 4, para 3.1. Form N461 identifies all the matters that should be included in the claim form along with guidance notes on completing the claim form.

The additional requirements under r 54.6 are that the claimant must also state in the claim form:

(a) the name and address of any person he considers to be an interested party;

(b) that he is requesting permission to proceed with a claim for judicial review; and

(c) any remedy, including any interim remedy, he is claiming.

The claim form must include, or be accompanied by:

(a) a detailed statement of the claimant's grounds for bringing the claim for judicial review;

(b) a statement of the facts relied on;

(c) any application to extend the time limit for filing the claim form; and

(d) any application for directions (r 54.6(2); PD 54, para 5.6).

In addition, the claim form must be accompanied by:

(a) any written evidence in support of the claim or application to extend time;

(b) a copy of any order that the claimant seeks to have quashed;

(c) where the claim for judicial review relates to a decision of a court or tribunal, an approved copy of the reasons for reaching that decision;

(d) copies of any documents on which the claimant proposes to rely;

(e) copies of any relevant statutory material;

(f) a list of essential documents for advance reading by the court (with page references to the passages relied on) (r 54.6(2); PD 54, para 5.7).

Where it is not possible to file all the above documents, the claimant must indicate which documents have not been filed and the reasons why they are not currently available (PD 54, para 5.8). The claimant must file two copies of a paginated and indexed bundle containing all the documents referred to in paras 5.6 and 5.7 of PD 54 (PD 54, para 5.9).

Where the claimant is seeking to raise any issue, or seeks any remedy available under the Human Rights Act 1998, the claim form must include the information required by para 16 of PD 16 (PD 54, para 5.3).

There are a number of practice directions which specify further requirements for judicial review applications, for instance, *Practice Direction: The Administrative Court* [2001] 1 WLR 1654.

Interim remedies

The court has the power, under Part 25, to grant an interim remedy on an application for judicial review. If an interim remedy is required this must be set out in the claim form (r 54.6(c)).

Service of the claim form

The court does not involve itself in service of the claim form at all. The claim form must be served by the claimant on the defendant and any interested party within seven days after the date of issue (r 54.7; PD 54, para 6.1).

Acknowledgment of service

The defendant, and any other person served with the claim form who wishes to take part in the proceedings, must file an acknowledgment of service not more than 21 days after service of the claim form, and serve a copy on the claimant and any other named party within seven days of filing it (r 54.8(1), (2)). Again, these time limits may not be extended by agreement between the parties (r 54.8(3)).

Form N462 should be used (PD 4, para 3.1). In the acknowledgment of service, the person filing it must set out a summary of his grounds for contesting the claim and details of any other party he feels ought to be added to proceedings (r 54.8(4)). There is therefore a positive requirement for the acknowledgment of service to include a summary of the grounds for contesting the claim. The purpose of the acknowledgment is to draw to the judge's attention (who will usually be considering the matter without a hearing) any grounds to show that the claim should not proceed that may not be apparent from the claimant's application (*R v Local Administration Commissioner ex p Leach* [2001] EWHC Admin 455).

At this stage, the defendant, and any other person served with the claim form, does not need to provide detailed grounds for contesting the claim for judicial review, or to file any written evidence with his acknowledgment of service (r 54.14(2)(a)). However, such further information and documents will be required if permission is granted and the other parties wish to contest that decision or support it on additional grounds (r 54.14(1)).

It is good practice for a defendant seeking its costs, if the application for permission is refused, to include an application for costs in the body of the acknowledgment of service and to give an indication of the amount of costs being requested (*R v Local Administration Commissioner ex p Leach*).

Failure to file an acknowledgment of service

If a party served with the claim form fails to file an acknowledgment of service, he cannot take part in any hearing to decide whether permission should be given, unless the court allows him to do so (r 54.9(1)(a)). However, this will not prevent him from taking part in the hearing of the judicial review itself, provided he complies with directions of the court as to the filing of a response (r 54.9(1)(b)).

A party's failure to file an acknowledgment of service may be taken into account by the court when deciding what order to make as to costs (r 54.9(2)). The purpose of this provision would appear to be that where points which showed that the claim lacked merit were not made at the permission stage, but were raised at the hearing, the court might take the view that it was not fair that the applicant should pay the extra costs which could have been avoided if only the points had been made at the earlier stage (*R v Local Administration Commissioner ex p Leach*).

The permission hearing

The court will generally, in the first instance, consider the question of permission without a hearing (PD 54, para 8.4). However, the court may hold a hearing to decide whether to grant permission. There is no requirement for the defendant or any other interested party to attend the hearing, unless the court directs otherwise (PD 54, para 8.5). Moreover, where the defendant or other interested party attends the hearing, the court will not generally make an order for costs against the claimant (PD 54, para 8.6).

Where the court refuses permission without a hearing, or gives permission subject to certain conditions or on certain grounds only, the court will serve its reasons for making that decision with the order giving or refusing permission (r 54.12(2); PD 54, para 9.1). The claimant cannot appeal against a refusal to grant permission made without a hearing, or permission granted subject to conditions or on certain grounds only, but he may request that the decision is reconsidered at a hearing (r 54.12(3)). The request for the decision to be reconsidered must be filed within seven days after service of the reasons for the decision (r 54.12(4)).

Appeal against refusal to grant permission following a hearing

Where permission to apply for judicial review is refused at a hearing, the claimant may apply to the Court of Appeal for permission to appeal against that refusal (r 52.15(1)). The application must be made within seven days of the decision refusing permission (r 52.15(2)).

The Court of Appeal may, instead of giving permission to appeal, give permission to apply for judicial review instead (r 52.15(3)). Where the Court of Appeal gives such permission, the matter will be remitted back to the High Court for the judicial review hearing (r 52.15(4)).

Restriction on defendant's right to apply to set aside order for permission

Where a defendant, or any other person, is served with a claim form, and therefore has the opportunity to file an acknowledgment of service setting out his grounds of resistance to judicial review, he may not apply to set aside any order giving the claimant permission to make a claim for judicial review (r 54.13).

Costs of permission hearing

Practice Direction 54, para 8.6, states that the defendant, or any other interested party who attends a permission hearing, will not generally be able to recover its costs from the claimant. However, it was held in *R v Local Administration Commissioner ex p Leach*, that in principle, if a defendant incurs costs in submitting an acknowledgment of service, as required by the rules, then he ought to be able, if he succeeds, to recover the costs of so doing. Such costs should be limited to the costs incurred in actually producing the acknowledgment.

The defendant's costs in drafting the acknowledgment are likely to be greater if the application for judicial review is made without prior warning than if there is advance warning with properly reasoned grounds so that the defendant can reconsider its decision. This is because the court held in *R v Local Administration Commissioner ex p Leach* that the costs allowed for drafting the acknowledgment should not include the costs incurred in dealing with threatened, as opposed to actual, proceedings.

The court's power to award costs under s 51 of the SCA is discretionary and gives the court scope to make costs orders in appropriate cases at hearings to determine whether permission is granted.

PROCEDURE ONCE PERMISSION IS GRANTED

On granting permission the court may also give directions (r 54.10(1)). Such directions may include a stay of the underlying proceedings to which the claim relates (r 54.10(2)).

The court will serve the order giving or refusing permission, and any directions, on the claimant, defendant and any other person who filed an acknowledgment of service (r 54.11). Where a claim is made under the Human Rights Act 1998, a direction may be made for giving notice to the Crown or joining the Crown as a party (PD 54, para 8.2).

The claimant, defendant and any other person who has filed an acknowledgment of service will be given at least two days' notice of the hearing date (r 54.12(5)). The court may decide the claim for judicial review without a hearing where all the parties agree (r 54.18).

Defendant's response where permission is granted

If permission is granted, the defendant, and any other person served with the claim form who wishes to contest the claim, or support it on additional grounds, must file and serve:

(a) detailed grounds for contesting the claim or supporting it on additional grounds; and

(b) any written evidence on which he intends to rely;

within 35 days after service of the order giving permission (r 54.14). There is no prescribed court form for this response.

Where the party filing a response intends to rely on documents not already filed, he must file a paginated bundle of those documents when he files the detailed grounds (PD 54, para 10.1).

Evidence

No written evidence may be relied upon unless it has been served in accordance with directions or any order of the court, or the court gives permission (r 54.16). Disclosure is not required unless the court orders otherwise (PD 54, para 12.1).

It should be remembered that in a claim for judicial review the court is concerned with the decision-making processes of the public body, rather than with the decision itself. There will therefore, in most cases, be no need for oral evidence to be adduced. However, the court has the power, in an appropriate case, to direct oral evidence and cross-examination in judicial review proceedings. Indeed, in some judicial review cases the court will not be able to meet its obligations under Art 6 of the ECHR (right to a fair trial) unless it is able to order cross-examination (*R v Ealing LBC ex p PG* [2002] EWHC 250). In *R v Ealing LBC ex p PG*, orders for cross-examination of witnesses were upheld where the essential dispute between the claimant and the council was whether the claimant's nearest relative, her mother, did or did not object to the defendant's application for the claimant's detention under s 3 of the Mental Health Act 1983.

Where the issue of whether the claimant has acted promptly in bringing a claim for judicial review has been fully considered at the leave stage, the respondent will be permitted to recanvass the issue of undue delay at the substantive hearing only if:

(a) the judge at the initial hearing has expressly so indicated;

(b) new and relevant material is introduced at the substantive hearing;

(c) in an exceptional case, the issues as they developed at the full hearing put a different aspect on the issue of promptness; or

(d) the first judge has plainly overlooked a relevant matter or has otherwise reached a decision *per incuriam* (*R v Lichfield DC and Williams ex p Lichfield Securities Ltd* [2001] EWCA Civ 304).

Skeleton arguments

The claimant must file a skeleton argument not less than 21 days before the date of the judicial review hearing (PD 54, para 15.1). The defendant, and any other party wishing to make representations at the hearing, must file and serve a skeleton argument not less than 14 working days before the date of the hearing (PD 54, para 15.2).

Practice Direction 54, para 15.3, sets out the requirements for skeleton arguments. This includes:

- a time estimate for the complete hearing, including delivery of judgment;
- a list of issues;
- a list of the legal points to be taken;
- a chronology of events;
- a list of essential documents for the advance reading of the court with a time estimate for that reading; and
- a list of persons referred to.

Bundle of documents

The claimant must file a paginated and indexed bundle of all relevant documents required for the judicial review hearing when he files his skeleton argument. This bundle must include those documents required by the defendant and any other party who is to make representations at the hearing (PD 54, paras 16.1, 16.2).

Court's power to hear any person

Any person (not being a party) may apply for permission to file evidence or to make representations at the judicial review hearing (r 54.17). This would particularly apply to special interest groups, such as Amnesty International, Greenpeace or Friends of the Earth, who may have an interest in the proceedings. This is in stark contrast to claims under the ECHR, where the only participants can be the 'victim' and the alleged wrongdoer.

An application for permission to intervene should be made by letter to the Administrative Court Office, identifying the claim, explaining who the applicant is, and indicating why and in what form the applicant wants to participate in the hearing (PD 54, para 13.3). If the court gives permission for a person to file evidence or make representations at the hearing, it may impose conditions and make case management directions (PD 54, para 13.2).

Any application to intervene must be made at the earliest possible opportunity since it will usually be essential not to delay the hearing (r 54.17(2); PD 54, para 13.5).

Agreed final order

If the parties agree terms to dispose of the claim for judicial review, the claimant may file at the court a document (with two copies), signed by all the parties, setting out the terms of the proposed order, together with a short statement of the matters relied on to justify the agreed order, and copies of any authorities or statutory provisions relied upon (PD 54, para 17.1). The court will consider the documents filed and make the order if satisfied that it should be made (PD 54, para 17.2). If the court is not so satisfied, a hearing date will be set (PD 54, para 17.3).

Where the parties reach an agreement that relates to costs only, the parties only need to file a document signed by all the parties setting out the terms of the proposed order (PD 54, para 17.4).

APPEALS IN JUDICIAL REVIEW PROCEEDINGS

An unsuccessful party may apply to the Court of Appeal for permission to appeal against the decision in judicial review proceedings in accordance with Part 52. If the Court of Appeal refuses permission, no further appeal lies to the House of Lords (s 54 of the Administration of Justice Act 1999; *R v Secretary of State for Trade and Industry ex p Eastaway* [2000] 1 WLR 2222, HL).

See pp 609–10 above, 'Appeal against refusal to grant permission following a hearing', for the procedure under r 52.15 relating to permission to appeal against a refusal to grant permission to apply for judicial review following a hearing. See also Chapter 37, 'Appeals', for the circumstances in which the High Court has jurisdiction to judicially review decisions made by circuit judges in the county courts to grant or refuse permission to appeal.

CHAPTER 39

THE HUMAN RIGHTS ACT 1998

INTRODUCTION

The Human Rights Act (HRA) 1998 came into force on 2 October 2000. It incorporates the rights set out in the European Convention on Human Rights ('the Convention') into English domestic law (s 1 of the HRA 1998). The Act affects every area of law in England, Wales, Northern Ireland and Scotland. It requires the courts to construe legislation 'so far as it is possible to do' in a way which is compatible with those rights (s 3 of the HRA 1998). It places public authorities under a duty not to act in a manner inconsistent with those rights (s 6 of the HRA 1998) and enables litigants to allege breaches of those rights by public authorities in proceedings before the English courts or tribunals, whether as a cause of action, or as a defence or counterclaim (s 7 of the HRA 1998). All levels of the judiciary undertook intensive training to prepare them for the implementation of the 1998 Act.

The Department for Constitutional Affairs has a Human Rights Unit with the responsibility to ensure the successful implementation of the HRA 1998 by building a culture of rights and responsibilities, and by maintaining and developing the UK's position relating to human rights issues (for details see www.dca.gov.uk/hract/unit.htm).

As well as being able to bring claims for breaches of Convention rights in our domestic courts, the right also remains for litigants to seek redress from the European Court of Human Rights (ECtHR) in Strasbourg if breaches of human rights are not remedied by the domestic courts under the HRA 1998. The decisions of the ECtHR are binding on the UK Government, but ECtHR cases are not necessarily binding on UK courts (see p 616 below, 'European Court of Human Rights cases').

The Act is not retrospective. Subject to one exception, there is no right to challenge the acts of a public authority committed before 2 October 2000. The exception relates to proceedings brought by a public authority. The defendant in such proceedings can raise any violation of his Convention rights by the authority, regardless of when it took place (s 22(4) of the HRA 1998).

CONVENTION RIGHTS

The HRA 1998 incorporates only part of the Convention into domestic law. However, the Act does incorporate all the substantive rights, such as:

- the right to life (Art 2);
- freedom from torture (Art 3);
- freedom from slavery (Art 4);
- freedom from arbitrary arrest and detention (Art 5);
- the right to a fair trial (Art 6);
- the right to respect for private and family life (Art 8);

- freedom of thought, conscience and religion (Art 9);
- right to free speech (Art 10); and
- freedom from discrimination (Art 14).

Although the HRA 1998 will affect all areas of law, civil procedure is most likely to be affected by Arts 6 and 8.

The rights are drafted in very wide terms. Some rights are absolute, such as freedom from torture, but other rights, such as the right to respect for private and family life, are subject to limitations and qualifications. The policy behind the Convention is to seek to balance the rights of individuals against competing public interests.

EUROPEAN COURT OF HUMAN RIGHTS CASES

Cases decided by the ECtHR are relevant when interpreting Convention rights (s 2 of the HRA 1998), but the decisions are not binding and, in the words of the then Lord Chancellor, the courts may 'depart from existing Strasbourg decisions and, upon occasion, it might well be appropriate to do so. However, where it is relevant, we would of course expect our courts to apply Convention jurisprudence and its principles in the cases before them' (see parliamentary discussion during the passage of the Bill).

COMPATIBILITY

A litigant can argue that the Act under which he is being prosecuted violates his Convention rights. Section 3 of the HRA 1998 requires the court to construe primary and secondary legislation in a way that is compatible with Convention rights, 'so far as it is possible to do so'. This applies to all legislation, whenever enacted, and whether the legislation concerns the conduct of public authorities or private bodies (*Wilson v First County Trust Ltd (No 2)* [2002] QB 74).

A number of successful challenges have been made. For instance, in *Antonio Mendoza v Ahmad Raja Ghaidan* [2002] EWCA Civ 1533, the Court of Appeal held that the Rent Act 1977 must be interpreted to give effect to the freedom from discrimination provisions of Art 14 of the Convention, so that a same sex partner is entitled to a statutory tenancy on the death of his/her partner in the same way as a husband and wife or unmarried heterosexual couple.

The HRA 1998 also requires the courts to interpret the common law and to exercise its discretion in a way that is compatible with Convention rights (s 6(1) of the HRA 1998). There have been a number of cases in which celebrities have sought to rely on their Art 8 right to respect for private life to bolster claims for breach of confidence against the media, and in return the media have sought to rely on the freedom of expression right in Art 10 (see, for example, *A v B and Another sub nom Garry Flitcroft v Mirror Group Newspapers Ltd* [2002] EWCA Civ 337; *Douglas and Zeta-Jones and Others v Hello!* [2001] QB 967; and *Campbell v Mirror Group Newspapers* [2002] EWCA Civ 1373).

The High Court, Court of Appeal or House of Lords may make a 'declaration of incompatibility' (s 4 of the HRA 1998). This will not affect the validity of the legislation, but s 10 of the Act provides machinery whereby a minister may correct the incompatibility by order if he or she considers that there are 'compelling reasons' for proceeding under this section. The Crown is entitled to be joined as a party if the court is being asked to make a declaration of incompatibility (s 5 of the HRA 1998).

Note also s 19 of the HRA 1998: before a second reading in either House, the minister in charge of a Bill must state in writing that:

- in his view the Bill is compatible with Convention rights; or

- although he cannot make such a statement, the Government nevertheless wishes the House to proceed with the Bill.

This procedure also applies to subordinate legislation if the court is satisfied that, disregarding any possibility of revocation, the primary legislation precludes the removal of the incompatibility.

PUBLIC AUTHORITIES

Section 6(1) of the HRA 1998 makes it unlawful for a public authority to act in a way that is incompatible with a Convention right, and those rights can be enforced directly against a public authority (the so called 'vertical' effect). There is no exhaustive definition of a public authority, but the term clearly includes central and local government, prisons, NHS hospitals, the police, immigration officers, the BBC (but not ITV or the press) and 'any person certain of whose functions are functions of a public nature' (s 6(3)(b) of the HRA 1998). The case law on the direct enforceability of EU Directives against 'emanations of the State' is clearly relevant here, so that, for example, the term 'public authority' can include privatised utilities that still have public functions to perform. This subsection will apply to such 'quasi-public bodies' only where the act in question is a public act (s 6(5) of the HRA 1998).

The court as a public authority

This is the so called 'horizontal' (or indirect) effect of the Act. Having stated in s 6(1) that a 'public authority' must respect Convention rights, s 6(3) of the HRA 1998 provides that 'In this section "public authority" includes ... a court or tribunal'. The State is bound to protect Convention rights and it may be in breach if, acting through the courts, it fails to do so. Thus, litigants may expect the courts to act in a Convention-compliant manner when dealing with litigation, even where a public authority is *not* one of the parties (see below, 'Claims against private bodies').

DIRECT AND INDIRECT EFFECT

Claims against private bodies

The Convention and the HRA 1998 have direct effect only against public authorities. A litigant will *not* therefore be able to bring a claim against a private body for breach of a Convention right, for example, breach of the Art 8 right to respect for private and family life. However, s 6(1) of the HRA 1998 makes it unlawful for a public authority to act in a way that is incompatible with a Convention right. As the courts are a public authority, they have an obligation to interpret the law so that it is in accordance with the Convention, and this will apply where the court is deciding the meaning of legislation or the common law as it applies to the rights and obligations between private individuals.

The court can do this by developing existing causes of action in a Convention-compatible way. Thus in *Halford v UK* [1997] IRLR 471, the Strasbourg Court found that the UK Government was in breach of Art 8 when a public-sector employer had unlawfully tapped the applicant's private telephone calls. Now such a claim may be brought in the English courts or tribunals under the HRA 1998. If the employer had been a private employer, the applicant might have asked the court to protect her Convention rights by reference to the implied duty of trust and confidence. Similarly, in a number of cases the court is being asked to develop the law of breach of confidence by reference to a person's Art 8 rights in order to curb the unwanted activities of the media (see, for example, *A v B and Another sub nom Garry Flitcroft v Mirror Group Newspapers Ltd*; *Douglas and Zeta-Jones and Others v Hello!* [2001] QB 967; and *Campbell v Mirror Group Newspapers*).

Access to justice

There may be liability if rules of court, or orders of the court, violate the applicant's Convention rights. For example, court fees or the legal aid/Community Legal Service contracting scheme may be said unlawfully to hinder access to justice, and it could be argued that very short time periods (for example, in fast track litigation) can undermine the right to a fair trial under Art 6 (for further comment see 'Human rights and the Woolf reforms' (2000) 97/23 Gazette 51). So far there have been virtually no successful challenges as to the HRA-compatibility of the Civil Procedure Rules (CPR) which were intended to be HRA compliant.

Legal aid/Community Legal Service funding

The issue of whether litigants should be provided with legal aid to bring or defend civil proceedings has previously been decided by the ECtHR. In *Airey v Ireland* (1979) 2 EHRR 305, the Court held that in certain circumstances Art 6 may compel a State to provide a litigant to civil proceedings with free assistance from a lawyer where such assistance would be indispensable for effective access to the court. In *Airey*, the petitioner was involved in divorce proceedings that were highly emotional and legally complex, and which included issues relating to the custody of her children. The Court held that in such circumstances, in order for Mrs Airey to have real and effective access to the court, it would be necessary for the State to provide her with free legal representation.

Limitation periods

In the case of *Stubbings v UK* (1996) 23 EHRR 213, Ms Stubbings was unsuccessful in arguing before the ECtHR that the differential limitation periods for personal injury claims and intentional trespass to the person claims constituted a denial of access to justice contrary to Art 6.

Ms Stubbings was sexually assaulted as a child, but became aware that this caused her mental health problems only when she was in her 30s. She was unable to bring a claim against her abusers because the limitation period for an intentional trespass claim expired six years after her 18th birthday. She argued before the ECtHR that the inflexible six-year time limit for intentional trespass claims unfairly prevented her from bringing a claim, contrary to Art 6. If her claim had been for personal injury caused by negligence, the limitation period would not start to run until three years after the date of her knowledge that her injuries were caused by the abusers.

The ECtHR decided that the limitation period applied to Ms Stubb's cause of action was not contrary to Art 6: the six-year time limit was not unduly short; it was proportionate to the aims sought to be achieved; and Contracting States are entitled to exercise a discretion to impose differential limitation periods for different causes of action.

Cachia v Faluyi [2001] 1 WLR 1966; [2002] 1 All ER 192 provides a good example of judicial ingenuity in reaching a Convention-compatible (and obviously fair) result. Section 2(3) of the Fatal Accidents Act 1976 provides that 'not more than one action shall lie for and in respect of the same subject matter of complaint ...'. The Court of Appeal construed the word 'action' as equivalent to 'served process', with the result that a writ that had died for lack of service could be ignored. It followed that a second writ, issued while three of the dependants were still minors, was validly issued for their benefit and gave effect to their Convention rights.

In *Goode v Martin* [2001] EWCA Civ 1899, the Court of Appeal interpreted s 35 of the Limitation Act 1980 and r 17.4 in a way that was compatible with Convention rights in order to allow a claimant to amend her statement of case, after the limitation period had expired, so as to rely on facts pleaded by the defendant in his statement of case (for a summary of the facts of this case; see Chapter 3, 'Limitation Periods').

Court fees

Further increases to the level of court fees were brought into effect on 1 April 2003. The Government believes that by including provisions allowing those with limited means to claim an exemption or remission from payment of the fee it will avoid Art 6 challenges to the level of fee based on denial of access to justice (see the Consultation Paper, *Fee Changes*, published in September 2002 by the Court Service, available on www.courtservice.gov.uk).

Court's exercise of discretion

When the court is exercising a discretion it should, as a public authority, do so in a Convention-compatible way (s 6(1) of the HRA 1998). It is in the exercise of its discretion, in accordance with the overriding objective, that this aspect of the Act will have most relevance to the CPR.

The overriding objective and the HRA 1998

In *Jones v University of Warwick* [2003] 1 WLR 954; [2003] 3 All ER 760, Lord Woolf re-asserted his opinion that when making case management orders, the court will not contravene the HRA 1998 as long as it properly exercises its discretion in accordance with the overriding objective of the CPR to deal with cases justly.

Prior to this case, in *Daniels v Walker* [2000] 1 WLR 1382, Lord Woolf decided an appeal in which HRA arguments were relied upon to challenge the fairness of the court's case management decision in the case. *Daniels v Walker* was an appeal against a case management decision decided before the HRA 1998 came into force. Notwithstanding this, the appellant relied in argument, before Lord Woolf in the Court of Appeal, on the HRA 1998 and Art 6 of the Convention (the right to a fair trial).

In *Daniels v Walker*, the parties had agreed jointly to instruct an expert to give an opinion on the care requirements of the injured claimant. The defendant did not accept the findings of the single joint expert and wished to instruct its own separate expert. At first instance the court refused to grant the defendant permission to obtain another expert report. In appealing to the Court of Appeal, the defendant argued (amongst other things) that the court's order conflicted with Art 6 because it had the effect either of barring the whole of the defendant's defence, or of barring an essential or fundamental part of it.

Although in that case Lord Woolf decided that the court below was wrong, and gave permission for the defendant to obtain its own expert evidence, he was highly critical of the defendant's attempts to use arguments based on Convention rights to support his arguments. He said it would be 'unfortunate if case management decisions in this jurisdiction involved the need to refer to the learning of the European Court of Human Rights in order for them to be resolved'. Lord Woolf felt that Art 6 did not have anything to add to the issue on appeal because the overriding objective of the CPR already made it clear that the obligation on the court is to deal with cases justly. Accordingly, if in the light of the overriding objective it would be unjust not to allow the defendant to call further evidence, the defendant must be allowed to call it.

In *Jones v University of Warwick*, Mrs Jones suffered a personal injury to her right hand and brought a claim against her employer, the defendant, which included a substantial claim for damages based on a continuing disability with her hand. The defendant's insurers employed an inquiry agent, who gained access to Mrs Jones's home by posing as a market researcher and secretly filmed her carrying out activities inconsistent with her alleged injuries. The defendant's medical expert, after watching the video evidence, concluded that Mrs Jones had regained full function in her right hand.

It was not in dispute that by gaining access to Mrs Jones's home using false pretences and secretly filming her there, the defendant had trespassed and infringed Mrs Jones's Art 8 right to respect for private life. Mrs Jones had no direct cause of action against the defendant's insurers for breach of her Art 8 right because it was not a public authority. However, Mrs Jones applied for the video evidence to be excluded on the grounds that the court, as a public authority, must exercise its discretion whether to admit the evidence in a way that was compatible with her Art 8 right.

Lord Woolf found it difficult to reconcile the two conflicting public interests he identified in this case: on the one hand, that in civil litigation the truth should be revealed; and, on the other hand, that the courts should not admit evidence that has been obtained by unlawful means. He said that under the CPR and the HRA 1998, a judge's responsibility in the course of properly managing litigation and exercising his discretion in accordance with the overriding objective is to consider the effect of his decision not just on the individual case before him but on litigation generally.

After weighing up the conduct of the defendant's insurers and the reality of the situation, namely, that the defendant's case would not be struck out, Lord Woolf held that it would not be just, or in accordance with the overriding objective, for the video evidence to be excluded. However, he did go on to order costs sanctions against the defendant in order to punish its behaviour and to deter other litigants from adopting similar tactics to obtain evidence.

RAISING CONVENTION VIOLATIONS

A person alleging violation of Convention rights by a public authority may bring a private law claim against it for breach of statutory duty, or a public law claim for judicial review, or rely on the alleged violation (for example, by way of defence) in any legal proceedings (s 7(1) of the HRA 1998). The person alleging the violation must prove that he is (or would be) a 'victim' of the unlawful act (s 7(1) of the HRA 1998). The applicant must be a 'victim' under Art 34 (formerly Art 25) of the Convention.

From the large body of Strasbourg case law, the following points emerge:

(a) Individual complainants do not have to show that their rights have been violated; they need only show that they run the risk of being directly affected by the measure in question (see, for example, *Norris v Ireland* (1988) 13 EHRR 186 – Irish law prohibiting homosexual acts between consenting males; the applicant was a 'victim' even though he had not been prosecuted and the risk of prosecution was minimal). In another case from Ireland, a woman of child-bearing age successfully challenged a law prohibiting information about abortion facilities abroad (*Open Door Counselling and Dublin Well Woman v Ireland* (1992) 125 EHRR 244).

(b) An applicant may be an indirect 'victim', for example, a close relative.

(c) A trade union can be a 'victim' in its own right, but not merely as representing its members.

(d) A company can be a 'victim' in appropriate cases.

(e) The 'victim' test is narrower than the right to bring proceedings for judicial review (so that representative bodies or pressure groups such as Amnesty International or Families Need Fathers will not qualify).

TIME LIMITS FOR CLAIMS

Claims against public authorities *for breach of a Convention right* must be brought within one year, beginning with the date on which the act complained of was done, or such longer time as the court thinks equitable having regard to all the circumstances. This is subject to any rule imposing a shorter time limit under domestic law, for example, the three-month time limit to bring a claim for judicial review in the UK (s 7(5) of the HRA 1998).

RAISING A CONVENTION POINT

A party, whether claimant or defendant, who wishes to rely on any provision of or right arising under the HRA 1998, or who seeks a remedy available under the HRA 1998, must include certain particulars in his statement of case (PD 16, para 15). Claim forms and forms for defending claims include a box that must be ticked indicating whether the party's claim or defence includes any issues under the HRA 1998.

The party must also give precise details of the Convention right that is alleged to have been infringed and details of the alleged infringement. The remedy sought must be specified, including, with relevant details, whether a declaration of incompatibility under s 4 of the HRA 1998 is sought, or damages in respect of a judicial act under s 9(3) of the HRA 1998 (PD 16, para 15).

Notwithstanding Lord Woolf's repeated contention that the CPR are Convention-compliant, there may be cases where a human rights challenge is both necessary and appropriate (and where solicitors could face a negligence claim for failing to mount a challenge). Hearings in public, court fees, and fast track timetables are just three areas that may be vulnerable. It is a difficult area calling for the exercise of sound professional judgment.

Human Rights Act authorities

Where a party raises the issue whether a Convention right has been violated, he must give the court and his opponent notice and send copies of relevant authorities prior to any hearing at which the point is to be determined. Under s 2 of the HRA 1998, the court determining the question must take account of any relevant judgment, decision, declaration or advisory opinion of the ECtHR, opinion or decision of the Commission, or decision of the Committee of Ministers in which the question to be determined has arisen. The court is not entitled to decide questions relating to Convention rights in accordance only with domestic precedent or its own discretion.

REMEDIES FOR BREACH OF CONVENTION RIGHTS

A court or tribunal may grant such remedies within its jurisdiction as it considers just and appropriate (s 8(1) of the HRA 1998). However, the power to award damages is subject to a number of limitations, for example:

(a) damages may be awarded only by a civil court (s 8(2));

(b) damages may be awarded only if the court considers that they are necessary to afford just satisfaction to the applicant (s 8(3)).

The principles adopted by the ECtHR under Art 41 of the Convention must be applied; damages are discretionary and modest. Claims often fail on the issue of causation and a finding of liability is often regarded as 'just satisfaction' without the need for compensation (see Chapter 38, 'Judicial Review', for an example of a case, *R v Enfield LBC ex p Bernard* [2002] EWHC 2282, where damages were awarded against a public authority under Art 41 of the Convention).

The remedy for judicial acts (for example, failure to give horizontal effect to the Convention) is appeal or judicial review, that is, no damages. There are no damages for judicial acts done in good faith except compensation under Art 5(5), which relates to the victims of unlawful arrest or detention. Note that 'court' in this context includes a tribunal. The potential impact of the HRA 1998 is likely to be far greater in cases of tribunals than for courts, and likely to be much greater in criminal as opposed to civil cases.

CHAPTER 40

ENFORCEMENT OF JUDGMENTS AND ORDERS

INTRODUCTION

Once an order is made or judgment is entered for a claimant, if the defendant fails or refuses to comply with that order or judgment, the claimant may then take further steps to enforce it. There are a variety of different methods of enforcing orders and judgments, and a choice can usually be made as to which method to employ. However, there are some restrictions on the methods that may be employed, depending on the nature and size of the judgment and the capacity of the defendant.

WHICH COURT?

Usually, if a judgment or order is obtained in the High Court and it is necessary to enforce it, the judgment creditor will enforce it in the High Court, and similarly judgments or orders obtained in a county court will be enforced in that court. However, the judgment creditor may wish to enforce a county court judgment or order in the High Court to take advantage of the apparently more effective methods employed by the sheriffs than county court bailiffs in execution against goods, or a High Court judgment or order in a county court in order to obtain an attachment of earnings order.

An important consideration in deciding whether to enforce a county court judgment in the High Court is that interest is payable on all judgments enforced in the High Court, but only on county court judgments over £5,000 (s 17 of the Judgments Act 1838; s 74 of the County Courts Act 1984 (CCA)). In most cases, it is possible to enforce a judgment or order in a different court from that in which it was obtained, but there are some limitations and restrictions.

Enforcement of High Court judgment in the county court

A judgment creditor who wishes to enforce a High Court judgment or order in a county court must apply to the High Court for an order transferring the proceedings to that county court (r 70.3). The application should be made under s 40 of the CCA for a transfer of the proceedings from the High Court to a county court for the purposes of enforcement.

When applying to a county court with his request for enforcement of the High Court judgment the judgment creditor must file the following documents:

- a copy of the judgment or order;
- a certificate verifying the amount due under the judgment or order;
- if a writ of execution has previously been issued in the High Court to enforce the judgment or order, a copy of the sheriff's return to the writ; and
- a copy of the order transferring the proceedings to the county court (PD 70, para 3).

Enforcement of county court judgment in the High Court

Section 85 of the CCA provides that as a general rule, a county court judgment may always be enforced in the High Court (subject to Art 8 of the High Court and County Courts Jurisdiction Order 1991 (SI 1991/724); see below, 'County court judgments that cannot be enforced in the High Court').

In order to enforce a county court judgment in the High Court, a judgment creditor obtains a *certificate of judgment* from the county court and delivers it to the High Court (Civil Procedure Rules (CPR) Sched 2 CCR Ord 25, r 13). A certificate of judgment is obtained by making a request in writing to the county court, stating that it is required for the purposes of enforcing the judgment in the High Court (CPR Sched 2 CCR Ord 22, r 8).

County court judgments that cannot be enforced in the High Court

It is not possible to enforce a county court judgment for less than £1,000 by means of execution against goods in the High Court. On the other hand, a judgment for £5,000 can be enforced only by means of execution against goods in the High Court (see Art 8 of the High Court and County Courts Jurisdiction Order 1991 (SI 1991/724, as amended by High Court and County Courts Jurisdiction (Amendment) Order 1996 (SI 1996/3141), Art 3).

Agreements regulated by the Consumer Credit Act 1974

A judgment or order of the county court for the payment of a sum of money arising out of an agreement regulated by the Consumer Credit Act 1974 can be enforced only in the county court (Art 8(1A) of the High Court and County Courts Jurisdiction Order 1991). Consumer credit agreements regulated by the Consumer Credit Act 1974 are those in which the amount involved is less than the consumer credit limit of £25,000 for agreements entered into on or after 1 May 1998 (Consumer Credit (Increase of Monetary Limits) (Amendment) Order 1998).

LIMITATION

An action to enforce a judgment must be brought within six years from the date on which the judgment became enforceable, subject to an extension for part payment or otherwise under Part II of the Act (s 24(1) of the Limitation Act 1980). However, the word 'action' does not include processes of execution that are procedural matters (*Lowsley v Forbes (t/a Le Design Services)* [1998] 3 All ER 897, HL). Nevertheless, leave is often required to issue such processes of execution where more than six years have elapsed since the judgment was obtained.

A judgment creditor must obtain the court's permission to issue a warrant of execution where more than six years have elapsed between obtaining judgment and attempting to enforce it (CPR Sched 1 RSC Ord 46, r 2; CPR Sched 2 CCR Ord 26, r 5). Indeed, in *Patel v Singh* [2002] All ER (D) 227, CA, it was held that the judgment creditor must show that there are extraordinary circumstances to justify the granting of permission to issue a warrant where more than six years have elapsed. In that case the claimant applied for a writ of execution seven and a half years after default judgment. Permission was refused as there were no exceptional circumstances justifying the delay.

However, although procedural steps to execute a judgment may be taken more than six years after the judgment was obtained, arrears of interest accruing in respect of any judgment debt are not recoverable more than six years after the date on which the interest became due (s 24(2) of the Limitation Act 1980).

ENFORCEMENT OF JUDGMENT FOR THE PAYMENT OF MONEY

A judgment for the payment of money may be enforced by the following methods in the High Court or county court:

- execution against goods (writ of *fieri facias* in the High Court, warrant of execution in the county court);
- a third party debt order;
- a charging order, stop order or stop notice;
- appointment of a receiver; and
- in the case of a judgment or order for an injunction (or an undertaking) by an order of committal for contempt and in the High Court only, by writ of sequestration.

The following additional method is available only in the county court:

- attachment of earnings order (PD 70, para 1).

Enforcement methods applied simultaneously

A judgment creditor may use any method of enforcement available and may use more than one method of enforcement, either at the same time or one after another, unless an enactment, rule or practice direction provides otherwise (r 70.2(2)). Under s 8(2)(b) of the Attachment of Earnings Act 1971, no other method of enforcement of a judgment debt can be used, without the leave of the court, whilst an attachment of earnings order is in force.

Other remedies include service of a statutory demand followed by a bankruptcy/winding-up petition.

The Debtors Acts 1869 and 1878

As a general rule, a person cannot be imprisoned for non-payment of a sum of money, even if there is a court order or judgment specifying payment within a particular time. However, there are still powers in existence to imprison a person under the Debtors Acts 1869 and 1878 in limited circumstances for making default in payment of a sum of money. Those circumstances include non-payment of maintenance orders in family proceedings in the High Court, non-payment of certain taxes, and default by any 'attorney or solicitor in payment of costs when ordered to pay costs for misconduct'. The maximum term of imprisonment is one year, and imprisonment does not release the person from the obligation to pay what is due (ss 4 and 5 of the Debtors Act 1869).

In *Mubarak v Mubarak* [2001] 1 FLR 698, the procedure under s 5 of the Debtors Act 1869 was held to be incompatible with Art 6 of the European Convention on Human Rights (right to a fair trial) and was consequently amended by the Civil Procedure (Modification of Enactments) Order 2002 (SI 2002/439). In any event, the exercise of such a power by the court is rare and other methods to enforce compliance are used before it is resorted to, it being common, for instance, to make an attachment of earnings order against a party defaulting on payment of a maintenance order instead.

Orders to obtain information from judgment debtors

Where an order or judgment for the payment of money has been obtained, the judgment creditor may apply for an order compelling the judgment debtor to attend court to provide information about his means or any other matter about which information is needed to enforce a judgment or order. If the judgment debtor is a company, or other corporation, an order may be obtained for an officer of that body to attend court (r 71.2(1)).

In most cases, the questioning will be carried out by a court officer rather than by a judge, but there is provision for a judge to conduct the questioning if there is good reason to do so (r 71.6). For example, the debtor may have several business interests and/or assets that require investigation; or the creditors may feel that the debtor is likely to be more forthcoming as to his financial position before a judge than an officer of the court.

Such an order allows the judgment creditor to obtain information to assist him to decide the most effective method of enforcement to employ against the judgment debtor and is available in respect of both High Court and county court proceedings.

Procedure

The judgment creditor can apply for an order without notice to the judgment debtor (r 71.2(2)(a)). The application notice must be in Form N316, if the debtor to be questioned is an individual, or in Form N316A if the debtor to be questioned is an officer of a company or other corporation (r 71.2(3); PD 71, para 1.1).

The application must be issued in the court that made the judgment or order which is to be enforced, or (if applicable) to the court to which proceedings have been transferred (r 71.2(2)(b)).

If the application notice is in the correct form and contains the relevant information (as identified in the form and in PD 71), the court will issue an order for the debtor to attend the county court for the district in which he resides or carries on business, at the time and place specified in the order, to answer questions on oath and to produce documents at court described in the order (r 71.2(5), (6); PD 71, para 2.1).

The order will contain a *penal notice* in the following terms: 'You must obey this order. If you do not, you may be sent to prison for contempt of court' (r 71.2(7)).

The application may be dealt with by a court officer without a hearing (r 71.2(4)). However, if the judgment creditor states on Form N316 or Form N316A that he wishes the judgment debtor to be questioned by a judge, the court officer will refer the application notice to a judge for consideration (PD 71, para 1.3).

Service of the order

An order to attend court must, unless the court orders otherwise, be served personally on the person ordered to attend the court not less than 14 days before the hearing (r 71.3(1)). In most cases, therefore, after the order is made it will be returned to the judgment creditor to effect personal service on the judgment debtor. However, if the judgment creditor is an individual litigant in person the order will be served by the court bailiff, such litigants being the only category of litigant to whom this service is available (PD 71, para 3). If the judgment creditor is unable to serve the order he must inform the court of this not less than seven days before the date of the hearing (r 71.3(2)).

There is a discretion for the court to dispense with personal service, but this will depend on the circumstances of the case and, given the requirement for a penal notice to be endorsed on the order, is likely to be granted only in exceptional circumstances, and presumably when personal service cannot be effected.

Travelling expenses

The judgment debtor ordered to attend may, within seven days of being served with the order, ask the judgment creditor to pay him a sum reasonably sufficient to cover his travelling expenses to and from the court, and the judgment creditor must pay this sum if so requested (r 71.4).

Affidavit of service/payment of travelling expenses

The judgment creditor must file an affidavit, not less than two days before the hearing, or produce it at the hearing, sworn by the person who served the order, giving details of how and when it was served and stating either that the person ordered to attend court has not requested payment of his travelling expenses, or that the judgment creditor has paid a sum in accordance with such a request, whichever is applicable (r 71.5).

It should be noted that an affidavit (rather than a witness statement) is required but that the onus is upon the judgment debtor to make a claim for travelling expenses on being served with the order.

The oral examination

The usual procedure will be for the court officer to ask the judgment debtor a standard series of questions as set out in Form EX140 or Form EX141 in Appendices A and B of PD 71. Form EX140 applies to an individual judgment debtor; Form EX141 applies to an officer of a company or other corporation (r 71.6(2); PD 71, para 4.1). The judgment debtor will be questioned on oath (r 71.6(1)). The judgment creditor may either attend court and ask questions himself, or request the court officer to ask additional questions by attaching a list of proposed additional questions to the application notice (r 71.6(3)(a); PD 71, para 4.2).

The court officer will make a written record of the evidence given (unless the proceedings are tape recorded) and, at the end of the questioning, read the record of the evidence to the judgment debtor and ask him to sign it. If the judgment debtor refuses to sign, the court officer will note that refusal on the record of evidence (PD 71, para 4.3).

If the court has ordered that the hearing is to be before a judge, the judgment creditor must attend and carry out the questioning, and the standard questions in Forms EX140 and EX141 will not be used. The proceedings will be tape recorded and the judge will not make a written record of the evidence (r 71.6(3)(b); PD 71, para 5).

If the hearing is adjourned, the court will give directions as to the manner in which notice of the new hearing must be served on the judgment debtor (r 71.7).

Failure to comply with order

If the judgment debtor fails to attend court, refuses to take the oath or answer any question at the hearing, or otherwise fails to comply with the order, the court officer or judge will certify in writing the respect in which the judgment debtor failed to comply with the order and will refer the matter to a High Court judge or circuit judge to consider whether to make a committal order (r 71.8(1), (2); PD 71, para 6).

Committal for contempt

The judge has a discretion whether to make a committal order. The judge has no power to make a committal order for failure to attend court unless the judgment creditor has complied with the requirement to pay travelling expenses to the judgment debtor if he so requests, and to file an affidavit confirming service and payment of travelling expenses (if applicable) (r 71.8(3)).

If a committal order is made, the judge will direct that the committal order is suspended provided that the judgment debtor attends court at a time and place specified in the order and complies with all the terms of that order and the original order (r 71.8(4)(a)). The appointment specified will be before a judge if the original order was before a judge; otherwise, if the court so directs, it will be before a court officer (PD 71, para 7.1).

The judgment creditor is required personally to serve the suspended committal order and file an affidavit of service in the same way as for the original order (PD 71, para 7.2). There is no further requirement to make payment of travelling expenses.

If the judgment debtor fails to attend court at the time and place specified in the suspended committal order, or fails to comply with any term of the suspended committal order, and it appears to the judge or court officer that the judgment debtor was properly served with the order, the judge or court officer will issue a certificate specifying the judgment debtor's failure to attend, or other failure to comply with the terms of the suspended committal order (r 71.8(4)(b); PD 71, paras 8.1, 8.2). A warrant to bring the judgment debtor before a judge (which includes a Master or district judge) may be issued on the basis of such a certificate (PD 71, paras 8.3, 8.4).

At the hearing the judge will consider whether the committal order should be discharged. The committal order will be discharged unless the judge is satisfied beyond reasonable doubt that the judgment debtor has failed to comply with the original order to attend court and the terms on which the committal order was suspended, and both orders have been properly served on the judgment debtor (r 71.8(4)(b); PD 71, para 8.5). If the judge decides that the committal order should not be discharged, a warrant of committal will be issued immediately (PD 71, para 8.6).

Costs of examination

Fixed costs are specified where the judgment creditor attends the questioning of the judgment debtor before a court officer. However, where the questioning takes place before the judge, the costs will be in the discretion of the judge who may summarily assess them (r 45.6). If the examination does not produce any useful information (for example, the debtor is unemployed and has no other income or assets), it is unlikely that any costs will be allowed.

EXECUTION AGAINST GOODS, WRIT OF *FIERI FACIAS* AND WARRANT OF EXECUTION

Execution against goods – either by a writ of *fieri facias* (often abbreviated to *fi fa*) in the High Court, or warrant of execution in the county court – is the most common method of enforcing a judgment debt. Note that the expression *fieri facias* persists, in spite of the intention of the Woolf reforms to use plain English in the rules.

In executing the writ or warrant, the sheriff (High Court) or bailiff (county court) can seize the judgment debtor's goods and arrange for them to be sold, usually at public auction; but another method of selling the goods may be ordered instead. Certain goods of the judgment debtor are protected from seizure, such as tools and equipment necessary to carry out his employment, and clothes and bedding necessary for satisfying his and his family's basic domestic needs.

The proceeds of the sale are sent to the judgment creditor in the amount necessary to satisfy the judgment debt, court fees and costs, with any balance being returned to the judgment debtor (CPR Sched 1 RSC Ord 47, r 6; CPR Sched 2 CCR Ord 26, r 15).

Jurisdiction of High Court and county court

Article 8(1) of the High Court and County Courts Jurisdiction Order 1991 (SI 1991/724) (as amended by the High Court and County Courts Jurisdiction (Amendment) Order 1996 (SI 1996/3141)) provides that a judgment or an order obtained in a county court for the payment of money which is for a sum of £5,000 or more can be enforced only by means of execution against goods in the High Court. Therefore, if this method of enforcement is required, the judgment must be enforced in the High Court by writ of *fi fa*.

On the other hand, if a county court judgment is for a sum of less than £1,000, it can be enforced only by means of execution against goods in a county court. However, a High Court judgment for less than £1,000 can be enforced in the High Court. For amounts between £1,000 and £5,000, the judgment creditor can choose whether to enforce by means of execution against goods in the High Court or the county court.

Permission to issue writ of *fieri facias*/warrant of execution

In most cases, the judgment creditor does not need permission to issue a writ of *fi fa* or warrant of execution, but there are exceptions. These include where six years or more have elapsed since the date of the judgment or order (*Patel v Singh* [2002] All ER (D) 227, CA), or where there is any change in the parties, by death or otherwise. For other exceptions, see CPR Sched 1 RSC Ord 46, r 2 and CPR Sched 2 CCR Ord 26, r 5.

The application for permission is made in accordance with Part 23 and supported by evidence, in the form of a witness statement or affidavit, which includes an explanation for the reason why permission is necessary; for instance, the reason for the delay or how the parties have changed (CPR Sched 1 RSC Ord 46, r 4; CPR Sched 2 CCR Ord 26, r 5(2)). The application need not be made on notice unless this is required by the district judge, or it is an application concerning the assets of a deceased person when notice must be given (*Re Shepherd* (1890) 43 Ch D 131, CA).

Procedure for issuing writ of *fieri facias*

The judgment creditor must file a *praecipe* (request) for the issue of the writ of *fi fa*, signed by or on behalf of the solicitor of the judgment creditor, or by the judgment creditor personally. The writ of *fi fa* will not be issued unless the judgment or order, or an office copy of it and, if necessary, the order granting permission to issue, is also produced to the court at the same time. The court officer authorised to issue the writ must also be satisfied that the time period, if any, specified in the judgment or order for the payment of the money has expired. The writ of *fi fa* is issued when it is sealed by the court (CPR Sched 1 RSC Ord 46, r 6).

Procedure for issuing a warrant of execution

In the county court, the judgment creditor files Form N323 requesting the issue of a warrant of execution, on which he must certify the amount remaining due under the judgment or order and, where the judgment or order is for payment by instalments, certifying that the whole or part of any instalment due remains unpaid and the amount for which the warrant is to be issued (CPR Sched 2 CCR Ord 26, r 1(1)).

If the judgment creditor has obtained a judgment or order for payment by instalments and the judgment debtor has defaulted in payment of the whole or part of at least one of those instalments, the judgment creditor can request either that a warrant of execution is issued for the whole of the outstanding sum of money and costs remaining unpaid, or for a part of that amount as long as that is not less than £50, or the amount of one monthly instalment, or, as the case may be, four weekly instalments, whichever is the greater (CPR Sched 2 CCR Ord 26, r 1(2) and (3)).

If the court issues the warrant, this will be in Form N42, and a court officer will send a notice, in Form N326, to the judgment debtor warning that a warrant has been issued, unless a district judge directs otherwise. The warrant will not then be levied against the judgment debtor until seven days after the warning notice has been sent to him (CPR Sched 2 CCR Ord 26, r 1(4)).

Duration of a writ of *fieri facias*/warrant of execution

A writ of *fi fa* or warrant of execution is valid for execution for a period of 12 months from the date of issue (CPR Sched 1 RSC Ord 46, r 8(1); CPR Sched 2 CCR Ord 26, r 6(1)).

Renewal of the writ of *fieri facias*/warrant of execution

If the writ or warrant is not wholly executed it may be renewed for further periods of up to 12 months by application to the court. An application to renew the writ or warrant should be made before the expiration of the original 12-month period of validity or any renewed period (if a further extension is required). However, the court does have the power to grant an extension of its validity even outside that period (CPR Sched 1 RSC Ord 46, r 8(2); CPR Sched 2 CCR Ord 26, r 6(1)).

Therefore, if, since the issue of the writ of *fi fa* or warrant of execution, the judgment debtor has agreed to repay the judgment debt in instalments over a period of time that exceeds the original 12 months' validity of the writ or warrant, the judgment creditor may apply for it to be renewed so that the balance of the debt can be enforced if the judgment debtor defaults on repayment of the instalments.

Concurrent writs of *fieri facias*/warrants of execution

Two or more warrants of execution may be issued concurrently for execution in different districts as long as no more is levied under all the warrants together than is authorised under one of them, and the costs of only one of the warrants can be recovered from the judgment debtor (CPR Sched 1 RSC Ord 47, r 2; CPR Sched 2 CCR Ord 26, r 4).

Stay of execution of writ of *fieri facias*

The judgment debtor may apply for a stay of execution of the writ of *fi fa* if he can establish special circumstances making it inexpedient to enforce the judgment or order, or on the grounds that he is unable, from any cause, to pay the money. The court has the power to stay the execution of the writ of *fi fa* either absolutely, or for such period and subject to such conditions as it thinks fit (CPR Sched 1 RSC Ord 47, r 1(1)). The judgment debtor can apply for a stay of execution at the time the judgment or order is made, or subsequently by an application made under Part 23 (CPR Sched 1 RSC Ord 47, r 1(2)).

When making an application for a stay of execution of the writ of *fi fa* under Part 23, the judgment debtor must set out the grounds for making the application in the application notice, and a witness statement or affidavit must be filed substantiating those grounds. If the application is made on the grounds that the judgment debtor cannot pay, he must disclose his income, the nature and value of any property he owns, and the amount of his liabilities. The application notice and witness statement or affidavit must be filed at court and served on the judgment creditor not less than four clear days before the hearing (CPR Sched 1 RSC Ord 47, r 1(3) and (4)).

The court has a wide discretion when dealing with applications to stay. There would have to be a good reason to deprive the creditor of an opportunity of satisfying his judgment (*Winchester Cigarette Machinery Ltd v Payne (No 2)* (1993) *The Times*, 15 December, CA).

Stay of execution of warrant of execution

If a judgment creditor has applied for the judgment debt to be enforced by means of a warrant of execution, a similar procedure applies as where a defendant admits payment of a claim and asks for time to pay, thereby enabling the judgment debtor to offer terms of payment and thus suspend execution of the warrant (see Chapter 9, 'Responding to a Claim').

The judgment debtor can apply to the county court in Form N245 for a stay of execution of a warrant of execution. When making the application, the judgment debtor should propose terms as to repayment of the judgment debt and include a signed statement of his means. The court will then send a copy of the application and the signed statement of means to the judgment creditor, who must notify the court on Form N246A within 14 days of service on him whether he accepts the judgment debtor's proposals as to payment (CPR Sched 2 CCR Ord 25, r 8(1), (2) and (3)).

If no such response is received from the judgment creditor, a court officer may make an order in Form N41 suspending the warrant on terms of payment. Alternatively, if the judgment creditor objects only to the terms offered, the court officer may determine the time and rate of payment and make an order suspending the warrant on terms of payment (CPR Sched 2 CCR Ord 25, r 8(4) and (5)).

Both parties then have 14 days of service of the order within which to apply for the order suspending the warrant on terms of payment to be reconsidered by means of a hearing before the district judge. The district judge can confirm the order, or set it aside and make such new order as he sees fit (CPR Sched 2 CCR Ord 25, r 8(6)).

If the judgment debtor fails to abide by the terms of payment made when a warrant is suspended, the judgment creditor can re-issue the warrant by filing a request certifying the amount of money remaining due under the judgment and showing that the terms have not been complied with (CPR Sched 2 CCR Ord 25, r 8(9)).

Costs of the execution

In most cases, the costs and fees incurred in enforcing a judgment can be added to the judgment debt to be enforced by writ of *fi fa* or warrant of execution (for warrants of execution see s 85(2) of the CCA). However, in the High Court, if the judgment debt is for less than £600 and does not entitle the claimant to costs against the defendant, the writ may not authorise the sheriff to levy any fees, poundage or other costs of execution (CPR Sched 1 RSC Ord 47, r 4).

Seizure and sale of goods

Warrants are handed to the bailiff, an officer of the county court, for execution. When the bailiff levies execution, he hands to the debtor, or leaves at the place of execution, a notice of levy in Form N42(C) (CPR Sched 2 CCR Ord 26, r 7). A bailiff may not force his way into a judgment debtor's house in order to gain entry to levy execution, such as by pushing a front door against the resistance of the debtor (*Vaughan v McKenzie* [1968] 1 All ER 1154), but once the goods have been levied upon, forcible entry may be effected.

If the goods are saleable, the bailiff usually takes 'walking possession', the judgment debtor signing an agreement on Form N42(C) to this effect. The form need not be signed by the judgment debtor personally, but it is preferable that he should do so (*National Commercial Bank of Scotland Ltd v Arcam Demolition and Construction Ltd* [1966] 3 All ER 113). For a description of 'walking possession', see *Lloyds and Scottish Finance Ltd v Modern Cars and Caravans (Kingston) Ltd* [1964] 2 All ER 732. For the effect of 'walking possession' as regards third persons, see *Abingdon RDC v O'Gorman* [1968] 3 All ER 79. Where the bailiffs already have walking possession of goods, they can break into premises to retrieve those goods even if the premises have not been deliberately locked against them (*McLeod v Butterwick* [1996] 1 WLR 995, Ch D). There is no possession fee payable in the case of 'walking possession'. Appraisement is usually made after removal by the auctioneer who acts as broker for the court.

When the goods are removed, the bailiff gives or posts to the debtor an inventory (CPR Sched 2 CCR Ord 26, r 12(1)). Notice of sale must be given to the debtor not less than four days before the time fixed for the sale.

Items exempt from levy

Basically, 'necessary items' are exempt. These will include such tools, books, vehicles and other items of equipment as are necessary to the debtor for use personally in his or her job or business, and such clothing, bedding, furniture, household equipment and provisions as are necessary for satisfying the basic domestic needs of the debtor and his or her family (s 89 of the CCA). The definition is worded in broad terms without any monetary limit, and allows bailiffs to exercise their discretion in ensuring a proper balance between the interests of the debtor and his family, and those of the claimant. Guidance has been given to bailiffs to help with this process.

If furniture, motor vehicles or any other goods are alleged to be subject to a hire-purchase (HP) agreement, the bailiff asks for such evidence as there may be, for example, the HP agreement. If a claim is made to the goods by some other person, such as a wife, a claim in writing must be given to the bailiff, unless it is obvious that the goods do not in fact belong to the debtor. As to caravans and houseboats, there appears to be no authoritative decision to say whether they may be seized under a warrant of execution while used as a dwelling or intermittently as a dwelling, or when they are fixed to the land.

In the event of a dispute between the defendant and the bailiff in applying these definitions, the matter will be referred in the first instance to the bailiff manager. A levy should be made if at all possible. If the bailiff manager is unable to resolve the dispute, he consults with the court manager, who decides whether the district judge's directions should be sought. If a district judge or bailiff loses the opportunity of levying the execution by reason of neglect, connivance or omission, a complaint might be made by way of summons (N366) to the circuit judge under s 124 of the CCA and CPR Sched 2 CCR Ord 34, r 1, when an order might be made for the trial of the issue.

If payment is likely to be made, the bailiff may allow a reasonable time for payment and no further fees are payable.

Separate writ of *fieri facias*/warrant of execution to enforce payment of costs

Where a judgment or order is made for the payment of money only, along with an order for the detailed assessment of costs, if at the time when the money becomes payable under the judgment or order the costs have not yet been assessed, the judgment creditor can issue a writ of *fi fa* or warrant of execution (as appropriate) to enforce payment of the judgment debt alone. Once the costs have been assessed, the judgment creditor can then issue a separate writ of *fi fa* or warrant of execution to enforce payment of the sum ordered on detailed assessment (CPR Sched 1 RSC Ord 47, r 3; CPR Sched 2 CCR Ord 26, r 1(5)).

In the case of a High Court judgment or order, the subsequent writ issued to enforce payment of costs must be issued not less than eight days after the issue of the writ to enforce payment of the judgment debt (CPR Sched 1 RSC Ord 47, r 3).

APPLICATION FOR VARIATION OF PAYMENT OF JUDGMENT DEBT

In the county court, where a judgment or an order has been made for the payment of money, the judgment debtor or judgment creditor may apply for a variation of the date or rate of payment (CPR Sched 2 CCR Ord 22, r 10(1)).

Application by judgment creditor for payment at a later date or by instalments

The judgment creditor may apply without notice to the judgment debtor for an order that the money, if payable in one sum, be paid at a later date than that by which it is due, or that it be paid by instalments instead; or, if it is already payable by instalments, that it be payable by smaller instalments. A court officer has jurisdiction to make such a variation in the order unless no payment has been made under the judgment or order for six years before the date of the application, in which case it will be referred to the district judge (CPR Sched 2 CCR Ord 22, r 10(2)). The application does not operate as a stay on enforcement unless a stay is specifically requested and granted.

A judgment creditor, having originally requested payment of the judgment or order in one sum, may wish it to be payable by instalments so that an attachment of earnings order may be obtained if the judgment debtor defaults in payment of any instalments.

Application by judgment creditor for payment at an earlier date, in one sum or by larger instalments

The judgment creditor may also make an application to the district judge, on notice to the judgment debtor, for an order that the money, if payable in one sum, be paid at an earlier date than that by which it is due, or, if the money is payable by instalments, that it is paid in one sum or by larger instalments. The judgment creditor must set out the proposed terms and the grounds on which the application is made (CPR Sched 2 CCR Ord 22, r 10(3)). Such an application would be appropriate if the judgment creditor has evidence that the judgment debtor's financial circumstances have improved since the judgment or order was made.

Application by judgment debtor for payment at a later date, by instalments or by smaller instalments

If money payable under a judgment or order is payable in one sum, the judgment debtor can apply for an order that the money be payable at a later date than that by which it is due, or by instalments instead, or, if it is already payable in instalments, that it be paid by smaller instalments (CPR Sched 2 CCR Ord 22, r 10(5)). The same procedure applies as where a judgment debtor applies for a warrant of execution to be suspended (see CPR Sched 2 CCR Ord 25, r 8).

THIRD PARTY DEBT ORDERS

Where a judgment or order for the payment of money of at least £50 is obtained, the judgment creditor can apply for an order, known as a third party debt order, which is an order compelling a third party, who owes money to the judgment debtor, to pay the money owed to the judgment creditor rather than to the judgment debtor (Part 72). This method of enforcement was formerly known as 'garnishee proceedings'.

The court has a discretion to make the order, which will compel the third party to pay so much of the debt owed as will satisfy the judgment debt, as well as the costs of the enforcement proceedings, to the judgment creditor. The procedure is not available against the Crown, for which s 27 of the Crown Proceedings Act 1847 and CPR Sched 1 RSC Ord 77, r 16 and CPR Sched 2 CCR Ord 42, r 14 must be used.

Procedure for obtaining a third party debt order

A third party debt order is obtained in two stages. In the first instance, the judgment creditor makes an application for such an order by filing Practice Form N349 at the court that made the judgment or order which is to be enforced, or (if applicable) at the court to which proceedings have been transferred (r 72.3; PD 72, para 1.1).

The application in Form N349 must contain the information requested by that form and be verified by a statement of truth (r 72.3; PD 72, para 1). Practice Direction 72 expressly states that the court will not grant speculative applications for third party debt orders, and so Form N349 must contain evidence to substantiate the judgment creditor's belief that the judgment debtor has an account with the bank or building society identified by the judgment creditor (PD 72, para 1.3).

The application may be made without notice to the judgment debtor (r 72.3). This safeguards against the judgment debtor being alerted to the impending application and removing the funds that are the intended subject of the third party debt order before the order can be made.

Third party debt orders are commonly made against banks or building societies that may hold funds for the judgment debtor in an account. However, they are not restricted to such bodies and could be made, for instance, against a person who owes a trade debt to the judgment debtor, such information being obtained as a result of an order to obtain information from a judgment debtor (under Part 71). However, trying to make third party debt order against a solicitor's client account may be problematical, because the order has the effect of freezing the whole account (see below) and it may not be possible to identify funds in relation to a particular client unless that client has a separate designated account. If the application is granted, the court will initially make an interim third party debt order in Form N84 (r 72.4).

Interim third party debt orders

The application for a third party debt order will initially be dealt with by a judge without a hearing (r 72.4(1)). If the judge makes an interim third party debt order he will fix a hearing, not more than 28 days after the order is made, to consider whether to make a final third party debt order. The judge will also make an order directing that until that hearing the third party must not make any payment that reduces the amount he owes the judgment debtor to less than the amount specified in the order (r 72.4(2), (5)). The interim third party debt order will become binding on the third party when it is served on him (r 72.4(4)). The effect of the third party debt order is therefore to 'freeze' the amount specified until the date of the hearing. The amount specified in the order will include the amount remaining due to the judgment creditor under the judgment or order and an amount for the judgment creditor's fixed costs (r 72.4(3); PD 72, para 2).

The retaining of moneys may cause a problem where the account sought to be attached is a solicitor's general client account where funds of several clients are held in one account. It looks on the face of it as though the whole of the account must be 'retained', which could cause hardship to 'innocent' clients. However, it is to be presumed (although there is no rule that says so) that the bank, etc will retain only such part of the account as is sufficient to meet the debt. Even that may cause difficulties where there are insufficient funds attributable to the debtor in the general client account.

Service of the interim third party debt order

A copy of the interim third party debt order, the application notice and any documents filed in support must be served on the third party not less than 21 days before the date fixed for the hearing, and on the judgment debtor not less than seven days after a copy has been served on the third party and not less than seven days before the date fixed for the hearing (r 72.5(1)). Service is effected on the third party before the judgment debtor to avoid the risk that the judgment debtor will remove the funds before the order is served on the third party.

Service must be in accordance with Part 6. Service can therefore be effected by the court or, if the judgment creditor so requests, by the judgment creditor using the methods specified in Part 6 (r 6.3). If the judgment creditor serves the order, he must either file a certificate of service not less than two days before the hearing or produce a certificate of service at the hearing (r 72.5(2)).

The interim third party debt order gives details as to how the judgment debtor can apply for a hardship payment order (see Form N84 and below, 'Hardship payment orders').

Obligations of banks and building societies

A bank or building society served with an interim third party debt order must carry out a search to identify all accounts held with it by the judgment debtor (r 72.6(1)). The bank or building society must disclose to the court, and the creditor, within seven days of being served with the order, in respect of each account held by the judgment debtor:

(a) the number of the judgment debtor's account;

(b) whether the account is in credit;

(c) if the account is in credit, whether the balance of the account is sufficient to cover the amount of the order;

(d) if the balance is less than the amount specified in the order, the amount of the balance at the date it was served with the order; and

(e) whether the bank or building society asserts any right to the money in the account and, if so, giving details of that assertion (r 72.6(2)).

Unless the order states otherwise, a bank or building society served with an interim third party debt order is only required to search for and disclose information about and retain money in accounts held solely by the judgment debtor, or, if there are joint judgment debtors, accounts held jointly by them or solely by either of them (PD 72, para 3.2). Accordingly, the bank or building society is not required to retain money in or disclose information about accounts in the joint names of the judgment debtor and another person or, if the judgment debtor is a firm, accounts in the names of individual members of that firm (PD 72, para 3.2).

If the judgment debtor does not hold an account with the bank or building society, or if the bank or building society is unable to comply with the order, the bank or building society must inform the court and the judgment creditor of that fact within seven days of being served with the order (r 72.6(3)). Of course, if the account is in debit, or no moneys are owed to the debtor, there is nothing for the order to attach to and the application will fail. In that instance the court will discharge the interim order.

Obligations of other third parties

Any third party other than a bank or building society served with an interim debt order must notify the court and the judgment debtor in writing within seven days of being served with the order if he claims not to owe any money to the judgment debtor, or if he claims to owe less than the amount specified in the order (r 72.6(4)).

Hardship payment orders

If the judgment debtor is an individual and he, or his family, is suffering hardship in meeting ordinary living expenses by being prevented from withdrawing money from his accounts with a bank or building society as a result of an interim third party debt order, he may apply to the court for a hardship payment order which permits the bank or building society to make payments out of the account (r 72.7(1)). The judgment debtor can make the application to any court (r 72.7(2)).

The judgment debtor's application must include detailed evidence explaining why he needs a payment of the amount requested, and be verified by a statement of truth (r 72.7(4)). The application should be made in accordance with Part 23 and the evidence in support should include documentary evidence, such as bank statements, wage slips and mortgage statements, to prove the judgment debtor's financial position and the need for the payment (PD 72, para 5.6).

Unless the court orders otherwise, the application notice must be served on the judgment creditor at least two days before the hearing. However, it does not need to be served on the third party (r 72.7(5)). The court may order otherwise if there is exceptional urgency for the court to consider making a hardship payment order (PD 72, para 5.4). In those circumstances, if there is not enough time to serve the application on the judgment creditor, the judge will normally direct that the judgment creditor is informed of the application and given an opportunity to make representations at the hearing by telephone, fax or other appropriate method of communication (PD 72, para 5.5). The judgment debtor should explain in his application notice why the circumstances are exceptionally urgent.

If the court exercises its discretion to make a hardship payment order, the order may permit the third party to make one or more payments out of the account and specify to whom the payment is to be made (r 72.7(6)).

Final third party debt orders

If there are no objections to the interim third party debt order, the court is likely to make a final third party debt order at the final hearing (r 72.8).

The final third party debt order will require the third party to pay the amount he owes the judgment debtor directly to the judgment creditor. However, if the third party owes a sum greater than the judgment debt to the judgment debtor, the order will direct him to pay the judgment creditor so much of that debt as is sufficient to satisfy the judgment debt and the judgment creditor's costs of the application (r 72.2(1)).

Objecting to final third party debt orders

If the judgment debtor or third party objects to the court making a final third party debt order, he must file and serve written evidence stating his grounds for objection (r 72.8(1)). For instance, the third party may dispute that he owes the judgment debtor any money. If the third party has given notice under r 72.6 disputing that he owes money to the judgment debtor, or asserting that the amount he owes is less than the amount specified in the order, and the judgment creditor wishes to dispute this, the judgment creditor must file and serve written evidence setting out the grounds on which he disputes the third party's contentions (r 72.8(3)).

If the judgment debtor or the third party knows or believes that a person other than the judgment debtor has any claim to the money specified in the interim order, he must file and serve written evidence stating his knowledge of that matter (r 72.8(2)). The court will then serve notice of the hearing on that person (r 72.8(5)). Where written evidence is to be served, it must be served as soon as possible, and in any event not less than three days before the hearing (r 72.8(4)).

At the hearing of the application the court has the power to do the following:

(a) make a final third party debt order;

(b) discharge the interim third party debt order and dismiss the application;

(c) decide any issues in dispute between the parties, or between the parties and a party who claims to be entitled to the money specified in the interim third party debt order; or

(d) direct a trial of any disputed issues and if necessary give directions for that trial (r 72.8(6)).

Effect of final third party order

If the third party pays money to the judgment creditor in compliance with a third party debt order, he will be discharged from his debt to the judgment debtor in the amount of the payment (r 72.9(2)).

Further, if the third party refuses to pay the judgment creditor in compliance with the third party debt order, the judgment creditor can enforce the order against the third party as if it were a judgment debt (r 72.9(1)).

Money in court

If money is paid into court to the credit of the judgment debtor, the judgment creditor can make an application under Part 23 for the sum in court, or so much of it as is necessary to satisfy the judgment debt and the costs of the application, to be paid to the judgment creditor. If such an order is obtained, it is not a third party debt order but it has a similar effect (r 72.10(1)). The application notice must be served on the judgment debtor and the Accountant General at the Court Funds Office (r 72.10(2)).

If such an application is made, the money in court will not be paid out until the application has been disposed of (r 72.10(3)).

Costs of judgment creditor

The judgment creditor is entitled to add his costs of the application to his judgment debt, and deduct the costs from the sums recovered under the final third party order (r 72.11). The costs of a final third party debt order are fixed costs under r 45.6.

CHARGING ORDERS

Where a judgment creditor obtains a judgment or an order for the payment of money, the court has the power to make an order under s 1 of the Charging Orders Act 1979 imposing a charge on certain types of property of the judgment debtor to secure payment of the money due. Such an order is known as a charging order (Part 73). The types of property against which a charging order may be made are land, stocks and shares, unit trusts, and funds in court. A charging order does not result in payment of the debt but secures it against the property; an order for the sale of the property can then be made in a separate application.

The court has a discretion whether to make such an order and will consider all the circumstances of the case and, in particular, evidence of the personal circumstances of the judgment debtor and whether any other creditor of the judgment debtor will be unduly prejudiced by the making of the order (s 1(5) of the Charging Orders Act 1979). The court will also consider whether the size of the debt is so small as to make the granting of a charging order disproportionate, especially where there are other forms of enforcement available.

Jurisdiction to make charging orders

The county court has almost unlimited jurisdiction to make charging orders. For county court judgments, or funds lodged in the county court, the county court has exclusive jurisdiction to make charging orders. Also, county courts have concurrent jurisdiction with the High Court to make charging orders in respect of High Court judgments. The only situation in which the High Court makes a charging order is where it is in respect of a fund lodged in the High Court (s 1(2) of the Charging Orders Act 1979). However, the jurisdiction of county courts to enforce charging orders by sale is limited by s 23(c) of the CCA to judgment debts below £30,000.

Procedure for applying for a charging order

An application for a charging order is made in two stages. In the first instance, if the court exercises its discretion to make an order it will make an interim charging order. The application is dealt with by a judge without a hearing (r 73.4(1)). If an interim charging order is made there will then be a hearing at which the court may either make a final charging order, or discharge the interim charging order.

An application for an interim charging order may be made without notice (r 73.3(1)). This safeguards against the judgment debtor being alerted to the impending application and disposing of the property that is the intended subject of the charging order before the order can be made. The application must be in Form N379 for applications in respect of land, and in Form N380 for applications in respect of securities. The practice forms indicate the relevant information that must be provided and must be verified by a statement of truth (r 73.3(4); PD 73, paras 1.1, 1.2).

A judgment creditor can apply for a single charging order in respect of more than one judgment or order against the same judgment debtor (r 73.3(3)). Further, a judgment creditor may apply in a single application notice for a charging order over more than one asset, but if the court makes interim charging orders over more than one asset, it will draw up a separate order relating to each asset (PD 73, para 1.3).

Interim charging order

If the application is granted, the court will make an charging order imposing a charge over the judgment debtor's interest in the asset to which the application relates, and fix a hearing to consider whether to make a final charging order (r 73.4(2)).

Registration of an interim charging order

The interim charging order can be registered against the judgment debtor's property (s 3 of the Charging Orders Act 1979). In the absence of registration under either the Land Charges Act 1972 (unregistered land) or the Land Registration Act 1925, the judgment debtor would be able to make a binding sale of the land to a *bona fide* purchaser for value without notice. To obtain the full value of the interim charging order procedure, the judgment creditor should therefore take such additional steps before the debtor learns of the interim charging order as will ensure that the debtor is not able, on so learning, to deal with the property that is the subject of the provisional charge. Thus, as an example, it will be for the judgment creditor promptly to register the interim charging order under the Land Registration Act 1925 or the Land Charges Act 1972. The creditor for such purposes should therefore arrange with the court officer to collect a copy of the interim charging order as soon as it has been drawn up.

Service of an interim charging order

Copies of the interim charging order, the application notice and any documents filed in support must, not less than 21 days before the hearing, be filed on the judgment creditor and any other creditors as the court directs (r 73.5(1)).

If the order relates to an interest under a trust, the court will make an order for service on trustees of the trust. If it relates to securities, the court will direct service on relevant bodies including the Bank of England. If it relates to funds held in court, the court will direct service on the Accountant General at the Court Funds Office (r 73.5(1)).

The usual rules as to service under Part 6 apply to service of the interim charging order. If the judgment creditor serves the interim charging order he must either file a certificate of service not less than two days before the hearing, or produce a certificate of service at the hearing (r 73.5(2)).

Objecting to a charging order

If any person objects to the court making a final charging order, he must file and serve on the judgment creditor written evidence stating his grounds of objection not less than seven days before the hearing (r 73.8(1)).

Final charging orders

At the hearing the court may:

(a) make a final charging order, confirming that the charge imposed by the interim charging order shall continue, with or without modification;

(b) discharge the interim charging order and dismiss the application;

(c) decide any issues in dispute between the parties, or between any of the parties and any other person who objects to the court making a final charging order; or

(d) direct a trial of any issues in dispute between the parties and if necessary make directions for trial (r 73.8(2)).

The court must consider the debtor's personal circumstances and also other creditors (s 1(5) of the 1979 Act). Conditions may be imposed (s 3(1)), including an instalment order. Where there is dispute over the beneficial ownership of any property subject to the interim charging order, the court has the power to order that the dispute be tried first and to adjourn the application for the final order until it has been decided.

Any order made at the hearing must be served on all the persons on whom the interim charging order was required to be served (r 73.8(4)).

It should be noted that some courts have dispensed with the requirement for the creditor to attend the hearing of the final charging order unless the debtor has given notice of his/her intention to attend.

Effect of a charging order

If a charging order is granted, it will provide the judgment creditor with security for his judgment debt, and therefore the court will consider the position of other known judgment creditors of the judgment debtor before making such an order (*Roberts Petroleum Ltd v Bernard Kenny Ltd* [1982] 1 WLR 301, CA). The judgment creditor consequently has an obligation to notify the court of any other judgment creditors known to him.

Discharge of a charging order

On the application of the judgment debtor, or any other person interested in the property, the court may vary or discharge the charging order, either before or after it is made final (s 3(5) of the Charging Orders Act 1979; r 73.9(1)). The court may direct that any interested party should be joined as a party to such an application, or that the application should be served on any such person (r 73.9(2)). An application to discharge or vary the charging order is likely to be made where the judgment debtor has satisfied the judgment debt.

An order discharging or varying a charging order must be served on all the persons on whom the charging order was required to be served (r 73.9(3)).

Costs

Fixed costs are allowed on the making of a final charging order under r 45.6, along with reasonable disbursements in respect of search fees and the registration of the order. Judgment creditors should bring the details of costs claimed with them to court for scrutiny by the district judge. At the time of this edition, together with the said fixed costs, they can total almost £200.

Enforcing a charging order by sale

Once a final charging order has been made, the judgment creditor may apply for an order for sale of the property charged in order to enforce payment of the judgment debt (r 73.10). An application for sale of the charged property must be made using a Part 8 claim form (r 73.10(3)). In the High Court, it must be issued out of Chancery Chambers (Royal Court of Justice) or one of the Chancery District Registries (PD 73, para 4.2). In the county court, it should be issued out of the county court that made the charging order (r 73.10(2)).

A copy of the charging order must be filed with the Part 8 claim form and the application must be supported by written evidence:

(a) identifying the charging order and the property sought to be sold;

(b) specifying the amount for which the charge was imposed and the outstanding balance;

(c) verifying the debtor's title to the property;

(d) identifying prior incumbrances and the amounts due to them;

(e) giving an estimate of the sale price (PD 73, para 4.3).

In the case of land, circumstances may favour either a sale by auction, or a sale by private treaty. Time will be a factor, as will be the clearing of the charge and prior incumbrances, with, if possible, a credit balance in hand for the debtor. The court will be inclined to give the debtor one more opportunity to pay the debt, for example, by instalments with an effective order for sale in default.

Sample forms of orders for sale are set out in Appendix A to PD 73. These are not prescribed forms of order and they may be adapted or varied by the court to meet the requirements of the individual case (PD 73, para 4.4). The venue for the sale proceedings is the court that made the charging order, unless that court does not have jurisdiction to make an order for sale (r 73.10(2)). The county court has jurisdiction only where the amount owing in respect of the charging order does not exceed £30,000 (s 23(d) of the CCA).

In the case of a charging order on land, the creditor is not thereby entitled to possession; a charging order has the effect of an equitable charge created by writing under hand (s 3(4) of the Charging Orders Act 1979; *Tennant v Trenchard* [1869] 4 Ch 537). When the debtor has an interest in a property of which he is joint owner with a non-debtor, judicial sale is not appropriate and an application under s 14 the Trusts of Land and Appointment of Trustees Act 1996 (replacing s 30 of the Law of Property Act 1925) is the alternative (see below). However, the question whether an equitable chargee, for example a bank having a charging order over the interest of one only of two or more co-owners of land, can ask the court to sell the whole of the land to realise the share over which he has the charge, has been determined in *Midland Bank plc v Pike and Pike* [1988] 2 All ER 434; [1986] 2 FLR 143. The chargee is entitled to apply under s 14 of the Trusts of Land and Appointment of Trustees Act 1996 for an order for the sale of all the land as 'a person interested' within the meaning of that section; the chargee's rights are also to apply for an order for the sale of the co-owners' beneficial interest only, or for the appointment of a receiver of that interest, though obviously this would not enable the chargee to obtain as much as he could by sale of the property itself.

If a sale proceeds, a contract for sale is required, title must be proved, the costs of the proceedings and costs on sale must be provided for, a final account taken, and the proceeds distributed. Any net proceeds received on sale must be paid into court for this purpose.

ATTACHMENT OF EARNINGS

General

The Attachment of Earnings Act (AEA) 1971 and CPR Sched 2 CCR Ord 27 apply to applications for attachment of earnings orders. The effect of an attachment of earnings order is that the judgment debtor's employer is directed to make periodical deductions from the judgment debtor's earnings and pay them to the court, which then sends them to the judgment creditor in satisfaction of the judgment debt. An attachment of earnings order can be made only once the judgment debtor is in default in making payment under the judgment debt (s 3(3) of the AEA 1971).

As part of the increased computerisation of the courts, a Centralised Attachment of Earnings Payment System (CAPS) has been introduced into the county court. Where this system is in force, the relevant forms will indicate accordingly by using the prefix 'CAPS'.

Jurisdiction

A county court may make an attachment of earnings order to secure payment of a judgment debt of not less than £50, or for the balance under a judgment for a sum of not less than £50, or payments under a county court administration order (s 1(2) of the AEA 1971; CPR Sched 2 CCR Ord 27, r 7(9)).

Application for an attachment of earnings order

An application for an attachment of earnings order is made to the court for the district in which the debtor resides (CPR Sched 2 CCR Ord 27, r 3(1)). If the debtor does not reside within England or Wales, or if the creditor does not know where he resides, the application may be made to the court in which the judgment or order was obtained (CPR Sched 2 CCR Ord 27, r 3(2)). Where the creditor applies for attachment of earnings orders in respect of two or more debtors jointly liable, the application is made to the court for the district in which any of the debtors resides; but if the judgment or order was given or made by any such court, the application must be made to that court (CPR Sched 2 CCR Ord 27, r 3(3)).

Where the judgment or order was obtained in a court that is not in the district in which the debtor resides, the judgment creditor must apply for the transfer of the proceedings to the appropriate court under CPR Sched 2 CCR Ord 25, r 2(1)(c). The judgment creditor should send a letter applying for transfer and stating the defendant's address. No fee is payable. On receipt of such a request the court officer makes an order transferring the proceedings to the other court and sends a certificate of judgment or order to the court to which the proceedings are transferred (CPR Sched 2 CCR Ord 25, r 2(2)).

The judgment creditor must file an application in Form 337 certifying the amount of money remaining due under the judgment or order and that the whole or part of any instalment due remains unpaid (CPR Sched 2 CCR Ord 27, r 4(1)).

Service of the order

The court prepares a notice to the debtor and makes a copy. The form informs the debtor that unless he pays the total sum due into court, he must complete and send a reply to the court office to reach it within eight days after service. Notice of the application (Form N55) and a form of reply (Form N56) are served on the debtor in accordance with r 6.2 (CPR Sched 2 CCR Ord 27, r 5(1)). If the application is not served, notice of non-service, Form N216, is sent to the creditor.

Information about earnings

Unless the debtor pays the balance owing (CPR Sched 2 CCR Ord 27, r 5(2A)) he must, within eight days after service, file in the court office the form of reply setting out particulars of his expenditure and income, and the name and address of his employer, if any. The court sends a copy of the reply to the creditor (CPR Sched 2 CCR Ord 27, r 5(3)). If the debtor does not reply in time and the judgment creditor knows the employer, the court (court officer) should be asked by letter to request the employer (Form N338) to give details of earnings (CPR Sched 2 CCR Ord 27, r 6).

Where a reply is filed by a debtor in compliance with CPR Sched 2 CCR Ord 27, r 5(2), within eight days, and he gives the name and address of his employer, the court officer may still send notice (Form N338) to the employer requesting him to file a statement of earnings (CPR Sched 2 CCR Ord 27, r 6). Such a notice may be sent to an employer if the debtor gives information as to his earnings but the court doubts the debtor's statement.

If an employer does not send a statement of earnings in compliance with the request, the court may compel him to do so (ss 14(1)(b), 23(2)(c) of the AEA 1971; CPR Sched 2 CCR Ord 27, r 15, as to enforcement).

The attachment of earnings order

Applications for an attachment of earnings order will not have an initial hearing and the defendant will be required either to pay the amount due to the claimant, or to complete and return the form of reply, which includes a statement of means (see Form N56). If he has sufficient information to do so, the court officer will make an order on receipt of the form, sending a copy to the parties and to the employer (CPR Sched 2 CCR Ord 27, r 7(1)). Employers can obtain from the Publications Unit, Court Service Agency (tel: 020 7210 1700), a copy of the *Employer's Handbook* explaining how they should comply with any attachment of earnings order.

If the debtor fails to pay or to return the form, the court officer may (and probably will) order him to file a statement of means in Form N61. Failure to reply will then result in the issue of a notice to show cause, which will be listed before the district judge (CPR Sched 2 CCR Ord 27, r 7(A)).

The judgment creditor or the debtor may, within 14 days of service of the order on him and giving his reasons, apply on notice for the order to be reconsidered, and the court officer must fix a day for the hearing of the application and give to the judgment creditor and the debtor not less than two days' notice of the day so fixed

(CPR Sched 2 CCR Ord 27, r 7(2)). The district judge may confirm the order, or set it aside and make such new order as he thinks fit, or a day may be fixed for hearing by the district judge (CPR Sched 2 CCR Ord 27, r 7(5)).

Order 27, r 19(4), of the CCR enables a court officer to make a consolidated attachment of earnings order where a further attachment of earnings order is applied for.

No reply filed by debtor; non-attendance

If a reply has not been filed, various courses are open. If it is desired to obtain from the debtor a statement of earnings:

(a) he must be proved to have been served personally with Form N55, the form of reply and N337, or the court must be satisfied that they came to his notice in time for him to have complied with the instructions in Form N55 (CPR Sched 2 CCR Ord 27, r 5(2) proviso); and

(b) he must be personally served with N61 (CPR Sched 2 CCR Ord 27, r 15), which warns him of the consequences of failing to obey the order, to which he must reply within eight days with his statement of means. In default, he commits an offence under ss 14(1) and 23(2)(c) of the AEA 1971 and may be personally served with notice to show cause (Form N63) why he should not be imprisoned, and a date is fixed for him to be brought before the circuit or district judge to be dealt with for that offence (CPR Sched 2 CCR Ord 27, r 7A(2)).

At any stage, an N338 can be sent to the debtor's employers if they are known (CPR Sched 2 CCR Ord 27, r 6).

If the debtor does not attend, the circuit judge or district judge may commit him to prison (Form N59) under s 23(3) of the AEA 1971 for a period not exceeding 14 days, or fine him a sum up to £250 or commit him to prison for contempt under CPR Sched 2 CCR Ord 29, r 1 (Form N79/80) (CPR Sched 2 CCR Ord 27, r 7A(3)). If the debtor attends, however, and satisfactorily completes an N56, a court officer can make an appropriate order.

If the debtor has failed to supply sufficient information for the court officer to make an order, the papers are referred to the district judge (CPR Sched 2 CCR Ord 27, r 7(4)), who may either make an order (Form N60) if he feels that there is sufficient information, or direct a hearing, in which case the parties are given at least eight days' notice (CPR Sched 2 CCR Ord 27, r 7(5)). If the debtor attends the hearing and gives sufficient information, the district judge can make an appropriate order (Form N60). If, however, the debtor does not attend, the district judge may adjourn the hearing under s 23(1) of the AEA 1971.

The court officer serves notice of the adjourned hearing (Form N63) (or, if asked, delivers to the creditors for service) not less than five days before the hearing. If the debtor fails to attend or is unco-operative, the district judge may either order him to be imprisoned for not more than 14 days (Form N59) (s 23(1) of the AEA 1971), or order the bailiff to arrest him and bring him to court either forthwith or on a date to be fixed (Form N112A). If, however, the debtor does attend the hearing or is arrested in response to Form N112A, and satisfactorily completes Form N56, a court officer can make an appropriate order (Form N60) as above. If, on arrest under Form

N112A, the debtor does not satisfactorily complete Form N56, the district judge may commit him (Form N59) for up to 14 days (s 23(1) of the AEA 1971).

Form of order

An attachment of earnings order is in Form N60. This must specify the normal deduction rate and a protected earnings rate. 'Normal deduction rate' is defined in s 6(5)(a) of the AEA 1971 and is the rate at which the court thinks it reasonable for the debtor's earnings to be applied to meeting his liability. 'Protected earnings rate' is defined in s 6(5)(b) of the AEA 1971 and is the rate below which, having regard to the debtor's resources and needs, the court thinks it reasonable that the earnings actually paid to him should not be reduced. Protected earnings are normally calculated by reference to the rates (as amended from time to time) of supplementary benefits under the National Insurance Acts and to rent or mortgage payments.

An attachment of earnings order is sent by post to the debtor (or his solicitor) and to the employer unless personal service is asked for (CPR Sched 2 CCR Ord 27, r 10(2). If the debtor is employed by a corporation that has so requested, the order may be sent to the address given by it. If the order is to enforce a judgment or order of the High Court or a magistrates' court, a copy of the order is sent to the court officer of those courts (CPR Sched 2 CCR Ord 27, r 10(3)). The order to the debtor states that he must inform the court of any change in employment.

An order may be made but suspended while the debtor himself pays (Form N64). This is a common practice when the debtor is anxious for his employer not to know of the judgment. Should the debtor get into arrears with his payments, the creditors can apply without notice to remove the suspension.

Deductions by the employer from the debtor's earnings are made in accordance with Sched 3 to the AEA 1971. Priority as between orders is set out in this schedule. The employer is allowed on each deduction to deduct from the debtor's earnings, in addition, £1 towards his administrative costs. The employer is under no liability for non-compliance with the order until seven days have elapsed since the service (s 7(1) of the AEA 1971). If he does not have the debtor in his employment, or if the debtor ceases to be in his employment, he must give notice of the fact to the court within 10 days of service of the order or cesser (s 7(2) of the AEA 1971). If an employer ceases to have the debtor in his employment the order lapses, but the court may direct it to another employer (s 9(4) of the AEA 1971). There appears to be no provision that the court should notify the judgment creditor if a debtor leaves his employment.

The employer pays the sums deducted from the debtor's earnings to the court, and the sums in court are paid out to the creditor under normal procedures. There are no rules that prescribe that the court should notify a creditor when an employer makes no payment into court. The court does not act on its own initiative to inquire from the employer any reason for payments not being received. In such cases, the creditor should write to the court requiring an inquiry to be made, and should request the court to take action where an employer refuses or neglects to give the information required. In such circumstances, the court may consider serving notice to the employer (Form N449), making an order to the employer for production of a statement of earnings (Form N61A), or issuing a summons against the employer for an offence under AEA 1971 (Form N62) for which a payment of a fine not exceeding £250 or committal to prison for a period up to 14 days may be ordered.

Consolidated attachment orders

These orders are made to secure the payment of a number of judgment debts (s 17 of the AEA 1971). CPR Sched 2 CCR Ord 27, rr 18–22 apply. Consolidated attachment orders may be made by the court officer where:

(a) two or more attachment of earnings orders are in force to secure the payment of judgment debts by the same debtor; or

(b) on an application for an attachment of earnings order to secure a judgment debt or for a consolidated attachment order, it appears that an attachment of earnings order is already in force (CPR Sched 2 CCR Ord 27, r 18).

Such orders (Form N66) may be made:

(a) on an application by the judgment debtor;

(b) on an application by a judgment creditor who has obtained or is entitled to apply for an attachment of earnings order;

(c) on the request of an employer; or

(d) by the court of its own motion (CPR Sched 2 CCR Ord 27, rr 19(1)(a), (b), 19(4) and 20).

The judgment debtor may apply:

(a) in the proceedings in which any attachment of earnings order is in force; or

(b) on the hearing of an application for an attachment of earnings order (CPR Sched 2 CCR Ord 27, r 19(2)).

The requirements are:

(a) application (Form N244) and copies for service;

(b) copies of the application are to be served by post on the judgment creditor in the proceedings, and also on any other judgment creditor who has obtained an attachment of earnings order which is still in force, giving not less than two clear days' notice (CPR Sched 2 CCR Ord 27, r 19(2); CPR Sched 2 CCR Ord 13, r 1(2); CPR Sched 2 CCR Ord 27, rr 3, 4 and 5 do not apply).

Fees are deducted from payments into court.

A judgment creditor's application must:

(a) if the judgment which he seeks to enforce was given 'by the court to which the application is made', be made in accordance with Ord 13, r 1, in the proceedings in which the judgment was obtained (CPR Sched 2 CCR Ord 27, rr 3, 4 and 5 do not apply);

(b) in any other case, the judgment is automatically transferred to the court that made the attachment of earnings order (CPR Sched 2 CCR Ord 27, r 19(3)).

The application must certify the amount of money due under the judgment or order and that the whole or part of any instalment due remains unpaid (CPR Sched 2 CCR Ord 27, r 19(3A)). The court officer notifies any party who may be affected by the application and requires them, within 14 days of receipt of notification, to raise any objections (CPR Sched 2 CCR Ord 27, r 19(3B)). If no objections are received within that time period, the court officer makes the consolidated order (CPR Sched 2 CCR Ord 27, r 19(3C)). If there are any objections, the matter is referred to the district judge for his consideration (CPR Sched 2 CCR Ord 27, r 19(3D)).

An employer to whom two or more attachment of earnings orders are directed to secure the payment of judgment debts by the same debtor may himself, by a request in writing, ask the court to make a consolidated attachment order. On receipt of such a request, the court must fix a hearing at which the request will be considered and give notice thereof to the debtor and the judgment creditors (CPR Sched 2 CCR Ord 27, r 19(4)).

Where an application is made for an attachment of earnings order and there is another order already in force, the court may of its own motion make a consolidated attachment order after giving all persons concerned an opportunity of being heard (CPR Sched 2 CCR Ord 27, r 20).

Where a consolidated attachment order is already in force, any creditor to whom another judgment debt is owed may apply to the court by which the order was made for the consolidated attachment order to be extended to secure the payment of his judgment debt. Such an application is to be treated as an application for a consolidated attachment order (CPR Sched 2 CCR Ord 27, r 21, applying rr 19 and 20). It would appear that the debtor need not be in arrears for the creditor to be entitled to apply.

Cesser, discharge and variation

In the case of a judgment debt where the whole amount has been paid, the court gives notice to the employer that no further compliance is required (s 12(2) of the AEA 1971). When an attachment of earnings order ceases to have effect on the making of an order of commitment or the issue of a warrant of commitment for the enforcement of the debt, the court gives notice of the cesser to the employer (CPR Sched 2 CCR Ord 27, r 12).

The court may make an order discharging Form N339 or varying an attachment of earnings order (s 9(1) of the AEA 1971), and any party may apply on notice. An attachment of earnings order may be discharged (Form N339) by the court of its own motion:

(a) where it appears that the employer or person to whom the order is directed does not have the debtor in his employment (but the court may redirect the order to another employer if known) (CPR Sched 2 CCR Ord 27, r 13(2) and (3));

(b) where the court makes, or is notified of, another such order which is not to secure a judgment debt or payments under an administration order (CPR Sched 2 CCR Ord 27, r 13(4));

(c) where an administration order is made or an order made for the debtor to produce a list of his creditors with a view to the making of an administration order (CPR Sched 2 CCR Ord 27, r 13(5)) (but the court may vary the order to secure payment under the administration order);

(d) where the court makes a consolidated attachment of earnings order (CPR Sched 2 CCR Ord 27, r 13(6));

(e) where the defendant has been made a bankrupt (CPR Sched 2 CCR Ord 27, r 13(7));

(f) where the court grants leave to issue execution (CPR Sched 2 CCR Ord 27, r 13(8));

(g) where the maintenance order being enforced has ceased to have effect (CPR Sched 2 CCR Ord 27, r 17(10)).

Notice is to be given by the court to the debtor and judgment creditor of the time and place at which the question of any discharge or variation will be considered, unless the court considers it unnecessary in the circumstances to do so (CPR Sched 2 CCR Ord 27, r 13(1)–(9)). If the debtor, at any time, satisfies the court that he is unemployed or self-employed, the court may, accordingly, stay or dismiss the application for an attachment of earnings order or, where one has already been made, dismiss it.

Administration orders

A person with multiple debts totalling not more than £5,000 can put all of the debts in the hands of the court, which collects a regular payment from him and distributes it proportionally to creditors. A debtor can apply for an order provided at least one judgment has been obtained against him. The debtor completes a request form which includes details of his debts (Form N92 or N93) (attachment of earnings) and a return date is fixed by the court. The request also contains provision for the debtor to ask the court to make a 'composition order' (so much in the pound).

The application form (Form N92) requires information about the applicant's income and outgoings, and notes for guidance (Form N270) provide information and examples to help the debtor complete the application form. Council tax arrears should not be included, nor any other debts that are enforceable in the magistrates' court.

Not less than 14 days' notice of the hearing is given to the debtor and creditors (CPR Sched 2 CCR Ord 39, r 5), and the latter must raise any objections at least seven days before the return date (CPR Sched 2 CCR Ord 39, r 6(1)).

At the hearing, the district judge decides what order should be made. Creditors have the right to attend and, if necessary, raise objections (CPR Sched 2 CCR Ord 39, r 7(a)). A 'reasonable period' for repayment of the debt should be calculated, usually not more than about three years, if the court is inclined to make an administration order.

The order is subject to review at any time on debtors and creditors being given seven days' notice (CPR Sched 2 CCR Ord 39, r 8), including on a subsequent objection by a creditor who was not on the original list (CPR Sched 2 CCR Ord 39, r 10). Such a creditor may also ask to be included in the order (CPR Sched 2 CCR Ord 39, r 11). A 'court officer' can decide whether or not an administration order should be made or revoked and the rate of payment thereunder.

Any composition orders, reviews or objections to any part of the procedure are dealt with by the district judge. Thus, where there is default by the debtor, the court officer may require the debtor to bring payments up to date or to give an explanation as to why payments are not being made (CPR Sched 2 CCR Ord 39, r 13A(1)). If the debtor does not respond, the court officer may revoke the order (CPR Sched 2 CCR Ord 39, r 13A(2)). If the debtor gives reasons for default in payment, this will be referred to the district judge to decide whether or not to revoke or suspend the order or fix a review (CPR Sched 2 CCR Ord 39, r 13A(3)). On the review of an administration order, the court may suspend the order on terms, vary any provision of it, revoke it or make an attachment of earnings order (CPR Sched 2 CCR Ord 39, r 14(1)).

An attachment of earnings order should automatically be made to secure payments under an administration order unless there are good reasons for not doing so. Administration orders are registered at the Registry of County Court Judgments.

APPOINTMENT OF A RECEIVER

Where the judgment debtor has a business operating as a going concern, the judgment creditor may apply for the appointment of a receiver, in order to effect a sale of the business to provide payment of the judgment debt. When deciding whether to appoint a receiver, the court will determine whether it is just or convenient that the appointment should be made having regard to the amount claimed by the judgment creditor, the likely amount to be obtained by the receiver and the probable costs of his appointment (CPR Sched 1 RSC Ord 51, r 1).

COMMITTAL FOR CONTEMPT

Contempt of court includes disobedience to a court judgment or order restraining an act or requiring an act to be done within a time specified in the judgment or order. The ultimate sanction is committal of a person to prison for contempt of court for a period of up to two years, but a fine of up to £2,500 can also be imposed (s 14 of the Contempt of Court Act 1981). The usual purpose of an application for committal is to enforce compliance with the order.

Enforcement of injunctions and undertakings

The remedy a claimant seeks may be an order requiring the defendant to do or abstain from doing an act, for example, to refrain from infringing copyright in property owned by the claimant, or to shore up a party wall. Such a remedy is known as an injunction and can be obtained as an interim measure before trial and/or as a final remedy.

If a court order, requiring a person to do or abstain from doing a specified act within a specified period of time, is disobeyed, this is a contempt of court and as such may be enforced by an order for committal to prison, by the imposition of a fine, or, with the permission of the court, by a writ of sequestration against the person's property, or, where the person is a body corporate, against the property of a director or officer of the body corporate (CPR Sched 1 RSC Ord 45, r 5(1); CPR Sched 2 CCR Ord 29, r 1(1)).

Service of injunction

Order requiring an act to be done

As the methods of enforcement for breach of an injunction are potentially very serious, in order to be able to enforce an injunction requiring a person to do a particular act through committal proceedings or sequestration of assets, a copy of the injunction must be served personally on the person required to do or refrain from doing the act in question, unless the court orders otherwise (CPR Sched 1 RSC Ord 45, r 7(2), (7); CPR Sched 2 CCR Ord 29, r 1(2)).

In the case of a body corporate, such an injunction must be served personally on the officer against whose property permission is sought to issue a writ of sequestration, or against whom an order for committal is sought, unless the court orders otherwise (CPR Sched 1 RSC Ord 45, r 7(3) and (7); CPR Sched 2 CCR Ord 29, r 1(2)).

Order specifying time within which act is to be done

If the original judgment or order for an injunction does not specify a time within which the act is to be done, the court has the power to make an order requiring the act to be done within a specified time (CPR Sched 1 RSC Ord 45, r 6(2)). The party seeking such an order should make an application in accordance with Part 23 (CPR Sched 1 RSC Ord 45, r 6(3)).

Order requiring a person to abstain from doing an act

An order requiring a person to abstain from doing an act may be enforced through committal proceedings or sequestration of assets even if the injunction has not been personally served on that person, as long as the court is satisfied that pending such service that person had notice of the order because he was present when the order was made, or was notified of the terms of the order by another method such as telephone or telegram (CPR Sched 1 RSC Ord 45, r 7(6); CPR Sched 2 CCR Ord 29, r 1(6)). Again, in any event, the court can dispense with service of a copy of the order (CPR Sched 1 RSC Ord 45, r 7(7); CPR Sched 2 CCR Ord 29, r 1(7)).

Penal notice

The injunction must also carry a penal notice prominently displayed on the front of the copy of the order. A penal notice is a warning to the person on whom the copy is served that disobedience to the order is a contempt of court punishable by imprisonment. In the case of a body corporate, the warning is in terms that the assets of the body corporate may be subject to sequestration and any individual director responsible may be imprisoned (CPR Sched 1 RSC Ord 45, r 7(4)).

Undertakings

If a person agrees to provide an undertaking to the court rather than have an injunction ordered against him, if the undertaking is breached this will be enforceable in the same way as if an injunction had been ordered (CPR Sched 1 RSC Ord 52; CPR Sched 2 CCR Ord 29, r 1A). Moreover, as an undertaking is voluntarily provided, in the High Court it will be enforceable even though an order in the terms of the undertaking has not been served with a penal notice as long as the court is satisfied that the party gave the undertaking and understood its effect. However, it is good practice personally to serve a copy of the terms of the undertaking with a penal notice on the person who gave it. In the county court, the undertaking will not be enforceable unless it is recorded in a document and served on the party who provided it (CPR Sched 2 CCR Ord 29, r 1A).

Committal applications

Where the alleged contempt is contempt of a county court order, the application for committal must be made to the county court in question. Where it is contempt of a

High Court order, it must be made to the High Court (CPR Sched 1 RSC Ord 52 PD, paras 1(1)–11(3).

Procedure for committal applications

Where the application is made in existing proceedings, that is, to enforce an interim injunction, it should be made in accordance with Part 23 (CPR Sched 1 RSC Ord 52, r 2(2); CPR Sched 2 CCR Ord 29, r 1(4)). If the application is made to enforce a final injunction, it must be commenced by issue of a Part 8 claim form (CPR Sched 1 RSC Ord 52, r 2(1); CPR Sched 2 CCR Ord 29, r 1(4)). The application form or Part 8 claim form must set out in full the grounds on which the application is made, identify separately and numerically each alleged act of contempt, and be served personally on the respondent (CPR Sched 1 RSC Ord 52 PD, paras 2.5, 2.6; CPR Sched 2 CCR Ord 29, r 1(4A)).

Evidence in support

Written evidence in support of or in opposition to a committal application must be by way of affidavit and, therefore, cannot be by way of witness statement (CPR Sched 1 RSC Ord 52 PD, para 3.1). The affidavit must be filed and served personally on the other party (CPR Sched 1 RSC Ord 52 PD, para 3.2).

In the light of the seriousness of the allegation, the breach must be proved to the criminal standard 'beyond reasonable doubt'. What must be proved is deliberate failure to comply with a court order rather than a negligent omission to comply.

Committal hearing

The applicant for the committal order must, when lodging the claim form for issue or application notice for filing, obtain a date from the court for the hearing of the committal application. Unless the court directs otherwise, the date for the hearing shall be not less than 14 clear days after service of the claim form or application notice on the respondent. On the hearing day, the court can either give case management directions for the hearing of the application at a future date, or, if the committal application is ready to be heard, proceed to hear the application (CPR Sched 1 RSC Ord 52 PD, paras 4.1–4.4).

The committal hearing should normally be heard in public in accordance with the general rule. However, if it is heard in private and the court finds the respondent guilty of contempt, the judge must state in public the name of the respondent, the nature of the contempt and any penalty imposed (CPR Sched 1 RSC Ord 52 PD, para 9).

Jurisdiction to hear a committal application

A committal application can, in most cases, be heard only by a circuit judge for proceedings in the county court, or by a High Court judge for proceedings in the High Court. However, there are exceptions where the Master or district judge will have jurisdiction. For example, the district judge will have jurisdiction in respect of assaults on court officers (s 14 of the CCA) or disruption of court proceedings (s 118 of the CCA; CPR Sched 1 RSC Ord 52 PD, para 11).

Orders on committal

The court has various options open to it. It may:

(a) imprison the respondent for up to two years (s 14(1) of the Contempt of Court Act 1981);

(b) make a suspended order for committal for a specified period including on terms;

(c) order an unlimited fine;

(d) take security for good behaviour;

(e) grant an injunction;

(f) adjourn sentencing to a specified date;

(g) make no order.

Specific performance of a contract

If the court makes a judgment or order directing a party to execute any conveyance, contract or other document, or to endorse a negotiable instrument, and that party refuses or fails to do so, the court can use its powers to punish the disobedient party for contempt (CPR Sched 1 RSC Ord 45, r 5). Alternatively, in such circumstances, or if the party who should execute the document or endorse the negotiable instrument cannot be found, the court can nominate another person for that purpose (s 39 of the Supreme Court Act 1981). The court can also order that the cost of obtaining such execution or endorsement be borne by the disobedient party (CPR Sched 1 RSC Ord 45, r 8).

Enforcement of judgment for possession of land

In the High Court, except in the case of mortgage proceedings, a party must seek the permission of the court to issue a writ of possession in order to enforce a judgment or order for the giving of possession of land (CPR Sched 1 RSC Ord 45, r 3(2)). The court will grant such permission only if it is satisfied that every person in actual possession of the whole or any part of the land has received sufficient notice of the proceedings to enable them to apply to the court for any relief to which they may be entitled. In the case of an order for possession against long leaseholders, the court must additionally be satisfied that no application for relief has been made by the tenant under s 16 of the Landlord and Tenant Act 1954 (CPR Sched 1 RSC Ord 45, r 3(3)).

In the county court, if an order for the recovery of land is made by the court, this may be enforced by warrant of possession, which is issued following the filing of a request in Form N325 which certifies that the land has not been vacated in accordance with the judgment or order granting possession (CPR Sched 2 CCR Ord 26, r 17(1) and (2)).

In the High Court, if permission is granted to issue the writ of possession it will be executed by the sheriff; while in the county court the warrant of possession will be executed by the bailiff. In both courts, the writ or warrant may include provision to enforce payment of any money that is also ordered to be paid by the judgment or order (CPR Sched 1 RSC Ord 45, r 3(4); CPR Sched 2 CCR Ord 26, r 17(3)).

Enforcement of judgment for delivery of goods

Writ/warrant of specific delivery

If a claimant obtains a judgment or order for the delivery of specific goods that does not give the defendant the option of paying the assessed value of the goods instead, the judgment or order may be enforced in the High Court by a writ of specific delivery (CPR Sched 1 RSC Ord 45, r 4(1)(a)), the equivalent in the county court being a warrant of specific delivery (CPR Sched 2 CCR Ord 26, r 16(2)).

Writ/warrant of delivery to recover goods or their assessed value

If the judgment or order is for the delivery of specific goods or payment of their assessed value, the judgment or order may be enforced by a writ of delivery (or warrant of delivery in the county court) to recover the goods or their assessed value.

In the High Court, if the judgment or order is for delivery of specific goods or payment of their assessed value, the claimant cannot issue a writ of specific delivery of the goods without first obtaining the permission of the court (CPR Sched 1 RSC Ord 45, r 4(2)). Such an application should be made in accordance with Part 23 and served on the defendant against whom such an order is sought (CPR Sched 1 RSC Ord 45, r 4(2)).

In the High Court, a judgment or order for the payment of the assessed value of any goods may be enforced by the same means as any other judgment or order for the payment of money (CPR Sched 1 RSC Ord 45, r 4(4)). A writ of specific delivery or a writ of delivery to recover any goods or their assessed value may also include provision for enforcing the payment of any money that is also ordered to be paid (CPR Sched 1 RSC Ord 45, r 4(3)).

In the county court, a warrant of delivery entitles the judgment creditor to execution against the judgment debtor's goods for any money payable under the judgment or order which is to be enforced by the warrant of delivery (CPR Sched 2 CCR Ord 26, r 16(4)).

ENFORCEMENTS OF JUDGMENTS IN DIFFERENT JURISDICTIONS

Under various conventions and treaties, reciprocal enforcement is available both for a foreign judgment to be enforced in this jurisdiction and for a judgment obtained in our jurisdiction to be enforced in a foreign court. For details of the procedure to be followed, see Part 74.

CHAPTER 41

TRANSITIONAL ARRANGEMENTS

INTRODUCTION

The Civil Procedure Rules (CPR) came into force on 26 April 1999 (SI 1998/3132). The CPR apply in full to all proceedings issued after that date. The rules in existence before the CPR came into force were the Rules of the Supreme Court 1965 (RSC), which applied to proceedings in the Supreme Court, and the County Court Rules 1981 (CCR), which applied to proceedings in the county courts.

Part 51 makes provisions as to how the CPR will apply to cases commenced under the former rules. The CPR have now been in existence for a number of years and so transitional provisions have progressively diminishing applicability.

Proceedings issued before commencement of CPR

Practice Direction 51 contains general principles as well as detailed provision for the application of the CPR to proceedings issued before the CPR came into force (Part 51; and PD 51, para 1(1)).

General principles relating to the transitional arrangements

When a new step is to be taken in any existing proceedings after 26 April 1999, it is to be taken in accordance with the CPR (PD 51, para 11). However, the general scheme is to apply the previous rules to undefended cases commenced before 26 April 1999, allowing them to progress to their disposal, but to apply the CPR to defended cases as far as possible (PD 51, para 2).

The overriding objective applies to all existing proceedings from 26 April 1999, whether or not steps are taken under the CPR or under the previous rules (PD 51, para 12).

APPLICATION OF THE FORMER CIVIL PROCEDURE RULES

Initiating steps under the old rules

Where an initiating step, such as the issue of proceedings or the making of an application, has been taken in a case before 26 April 1999, in particular if it involves the use of forms and documents required by the previous rules, the case will proceed in the first instance under the previous rules. If a step is required in response to something done by the other party in accordance with the previous rules, it must also be taken in accordance with those rules (PD 51, para 3).

If a party is served with an old type of originating process, such as a writ or summons, on or after 26 April 1999, the other party must respond in accordance with the previous rules following the instructions served with the originating process (PD 51, para 4).

Where a case has been begun by an old type of originating process, whether served before or after 26 April 1999, filing and service of pleadings (equivalent to statements of case) should be carried out in accordance with the previous rules (PD 51, para 5).

Extending the validity of a writ

If a party commences proceedings before 26 April 1999, and applies for an order to extend the validity of the originating process (for example, writ or summons) on or after that date, he must make the application in accordance with CPR, Part 23, but the court will decide whether to allow the application in accordance with the principles under the previous law (PD 51, para 13(3)).

Automatic directions/discovery

Where the timetable for automatic directions under RSC Ord 25, r 8, or CCR Ord 17, r 11, had already begun to apply, or a notice of directions under CCR Ord 17, r 11, had been sent out (even if the timetable did not start until after 26 April 1999) or automatic discovery under RSC Ord 24 had already begun to apply to proceedings before 26 April 1999, those directions will continue to have effect on or after 26 April 1999 (PD 51, para 6(1) and (2)).

No automatic strike out

Although automatic directions under CCR Ord 17, r 11, given before 26 April 1999 may continue to apply after that date, the automatic direction under that order, providing for automatic strike out of proceedings for failure to request a hearing to be fixed within 15 months of the deemed date of close of pleadings, no longer applies (PD 51, para 6(3)).

This rule providing for automatic strike out of pleadings generated much case law, and was generally thought to have failed in achieving its objective to encourage the fast and efficient disposal of proceedings.

Judgment in default/on admission

If a party to proceedings started under the old rules wishes to enter judgment in default or on admissions, he must do so in accordance with the previous rules (PD 51, paras 7(1) and 8(1)). Entry of judgment in such circumstances is an administrative act that can be carried out by a court officer.

However, where there are outstanding issues to be decided, such as the assessment of damages, the court officer may refer the case to a judge for case management decisions to be carried out. The judge will apply the principles set out in PD 51, para 15, which gives him a discretion as to whether to disapply any provisions of the CPR, but with the general presumption that the CPR will apply to the proceedings from then on (PD 51, paras 7(2), 8(2) and 15).

If permission is needed to enter judgment in default or on admissions, in proceedings started under the old rules, the application for permission must be made in accordance with the procedure set out in Part 23 (PD 51, paras 7(3) and 8(3)).

In the case of judgment in default, the provisions under the CPR about applying to set aside or vary such judgment (Part 13), and about proceedings being stayed if not defended or admitted within a specified period of time (r 15.11), apply to these proceedings (PD 51, paras 7(4) and 7(5)).

Obligation to comply with court orders made under the old rules

Where a court order has been made in proceedings before 26 April 1999, that order must still be complied with after 26 April 1999 (PD 51, para 9). However, if the proceedings come before a judge for the first time after that date, he has the power to make a different order under the CPR (PD 51, para 15).

Validity of steps previously taken in proceedings before 26 April 1999

If a party has taken a step in proceedings under the old rules, that step will remain valid under the CPR. Also, a party will not normally be required to carry out effectively the same step under the CPR that has already been complied with under the old rules. So, for instance, if discovery has been provided under the old rules, it will not be necessary for a party to provide disclosure under the CPR (PD 51, para 10).

APPLICATION OF THE CPR

Commencing proceedings after 26 April 1999

Only CPR claim forms will be issued after 26 April 1999. If a request to issue an old type of originating application, such as a writ or summons, is received at the court office on or after 26 April 1999, it will be returned unissued (PD 51, para 13(1), (2)).

Case coming before the court for the first time after 26 April 1999

When a case started under the old rules comes before a judge (whether at a hearing or on paper) for the first time on or after 26 April 1999, the judge in the exercise of his discretion can direct how the CPR are to apply to the proceedings, and disapply certain provisions of the CPR. The judge may also give case management directions for the case, including allocating it to one of the case management tracks (PD 51, para 15(1)). However, the general presumption is that the CPR will apply to the proceedings from then on (PD 51, para 15(2)).

If an application is issued before 26 April 1999 with a hearing date after that date, or the first occasion a case started under the old rules comes before a judge after that date is for trial, the presumption is that the application or trial will be heard in accordance with the CPR (PD 51, para 15(3), (4)).

Applications to the court after 26 April 1999

In general, all applications made to the court after 26 April 1999 must be made in accordance with Part 23 and in accordance with the rules under the CPR relating to the application in question (for example, application for summary judgment under CPR, Part 24), unless PD 51 provides otherwise (for instance, in the case of an application to extend the validity of originating process and costs). The other relevant rules under the CPR will also apply if appropriate, such as rules about court forms in CPR, Part 4, and rules about service of documents under CPR, Part 6 (PD 51, para 14).

Note that since 26 April 1999, there have been many decisions of the Court of Appeal that have confirmed that case law which pre-dates the introduction of the CPR is now not usually of any relevance to cases dealt with after that date because the CPR is a new procedural code governed by the overriding objective (see *Biguzzi v Rank Leisure plc* [1999] 1 WLR 1926; [1999] 4 All ER 934).

By the same token, the Court of Appeal will not interfere with a pre-CPR decision merely on the basis that the CPR have provided for a different approach (*McPhilemy v The Times* [1999] 3 All ER 775, CA). In *McPhilemy*, the plaintiff, a journalist and managing director of a television production company, sued the defendants for the alleged defamatory publication in an article in the *Sunday Times* about a programme produced by the company and broadcast by Channel 4. An issue arose as to how case management had changed since the coming into force of the CPR, and the extent to which this affected decisions of the court in this matter reached before 26 April 1999. Lord Woolf stated at 792:

> In reviewing a decision made prior to 26 April 1999, the Court of Appeal would not interfere after that date, if it would not have done so if the appeal had been heard prior to that date, as the Court of Appeal would only interfere with a decision of a court below if that decision was wrong. However, if the decision was one with which the Court of Appeal would have interfered prior to 26 April 1999, in deciding what order should be made for the future, the court would take into account, in particular, CPR Part 1 (the overriding objective).

Close of pleadings after 26 April 1999

Under the old rules, in the High Court, pleadings (equivalent to statements of case) were deemed to be closed 14 days after service of any reply, or, if none, 14 days after service of the defence to counterclaim, or, if none, 14 days after service of the defence. In the county court, pleadings were deemed to be closed 14 days after delivery of the defence, or, where a counterclaim was served with the defence, 28 days after delivery of the defence (PD 51, para 16(6)).

Where pleadings are deemed to be closed on or after 26 April 1999, the case management provisions in CPR Part 26 will apply to those proceedings (PD 51, para 16(2)). Therefore, if a defence is filed at court on or after 26 April 1999, unless it dispenses with the need for one, the court will serve an allocation questionnaire on the parties in order to allocate the proceedings to one of the case management tracks (PD 51, para 16(3)).

Agreement to apply the CPR

The parties to proceedings may agree in writing that the CPR will apply to the proceedings from the date of the agreement. All the parties must agree, the CPR must apply in their entirety, the agreement is irrevocable, and the claimant must file a copy of the agreement at court (PD 51, para 17).

Costs

The court's decision as to whether to allow costs for work undertaken on or after 26 April 1999 will generally be in accordance with the CPR costs rules (Parts 43–48). Any assessment of costs that takes place on or after 26 April 1999 will also be in accordance with Parts 43–48. However, there is a general presumption that no costs for work undertaken before 26 April 1999 will be disallowed if they would have been allowed under a costs taxation under the old rules (PD 51, para 18).

When preparing a bill of costs for a period which consists of work done both before and after 26 April 1999, it is advisable to split the bill between pre- and post-26 April 1999 work, as the court can apply the principle of proportionality to the latter but not to the former.

Existing proceedings after one year

If any existing proceedings (those other than for which final judgment has been given) have not come before a judge, at a hearing or on paper, between 26 April 1999 and 25 April 2000, those proceedings shall be stayed. Any party to those proceedings may then apply for the stay to be lifted (PD 51, para 19(1), (2) and (4)). The Court of Appeal held in *Reliance National Insurance Co (Europe) Ltd and Another v Ropner Insurance Services Ltd* (2001) *The Times*, 31 January, that the writing of a letter to the court, even if that letter was brought to the attention of the judge and he responded to it, did not mean that the proceedings had 'come before a judge ... on paper' for the purposes of PD 51, para 19. The phrase was intended to denote an occasion on which the judge considered exercising his powers in accordance with the rules, whether that was in response to a CPR Part 23 application or of the court's own initiative under CPR, r 3.3.

This provision does not apply:

(a) to proceedings that have been given a fixed trial date after 25 April 2000;

(b) to personal injury cases where liability is not in issue but the court has adjourned proceedings to determine the prognosis;

(c) where the court is dealing with the continuing administration of an estate or a receivership; or

(d) in respect of applications relating to funds in court (PD 51, para 19(3)).

As a result of PD 51, para 19(4) – which says that 'For the purposes of this paragraph proceedings will not be "existing proceedings" once final judgment has been given' – the rule will also not apply to enforcement of a pre-CPR judgment. However, it will probably catch mortgage possession proceedings adjourned generally before 26 April 1999 and the assessment of damages following a pre-CPR judgment with damages to be assessed. In *Duggan v Wood* [2001] EWCA 1942, the claimant to a personal injury claim obtained judgment for damages to be assessed in 1992. In the absence of any further steps being taken in the proceedings, the claimant's claim was subsequently stayed under PD 51, para 19(1). An application was made under PD 51, para 19(2) for the stay to be lifted. The judge lifted the stay in respect of the claimant's claim for general damages, but refused to lift the stay in respect of the claimant's claim for special damages due to prejudice to the defendant and the absence of a proper explanation for the delay by the claimant. The judge's order striking out the claimant's claim for special damages was upheld by the Court of Appeal.

Applications to lift the automatic stay

The automatic stay under PD 51, para 19(1) is treated as a sanction imposed for failure to comply with a rule, practice direction or court order in accordance with r 3.9. The court must therefore apply the provisions of r 3.9(1) when considering whether to grant relief from this sanction by lifting the stay (*Audergon v La Baguette Ltd* [2002] EWCA Civ 10; *Woodhouse v Consignia plc* [2002] EWCA Civ 275). The court may also have to consider whether maintaining the stay would deprive a party of access to the court in the light of the European Convention on Human Rights.

Stayed proceedings should not be struck out unless it can be shown that a fair trial is not possible (*Taylor v Anderson and Others* [2002] EWCA Civ 1680). *Taylor* concerned a road traffic accident that occurred in the early hours of 18 January 1990, when Taylor was 20 years old, as a result of which he suffered serious injuries. There were considerable delays in dealing with the claim, as a result of which it fell foul of CPR PD 51. The district judge held that it was *doubtful* that the matter could proceed to a fair trial as a result of the delay and struck the claim out. The Court of Appeal held that proceedings should not be struck out unless an unequivocal affirmative answer could be given to the question of whether there was a substantial risk that a fair trial was impossible. 'Doubtful' was not strong enough, and the appellate court overturned the district judge's decision.

INDEX